# Humphry Repton

1  Frontispiece to Memoir (*c*.1814). Private Collection.

# Humphry Repton

*Landscape Gardening and the Geography of Georgian England*

## Stephen Daniels

*Published for The Paul Mellon Centre For Studies in British Art*
Yale University Press New Haven and London

Copyright © 1999 by Stephen Daniels

Second printing, 2000

All rights reserved.
This book may not be reproduced, in whole or in part,
in any form (beyond that copying permitted by
Sections 107 and 108 of the U.S. Copyright Law
and except by reviewers for the public press),
without written permission from the publishers.

Designed by Abby Waldman

Printed in Hong Kong

**Library of Congress Cataloging-in-Publication Data**
Daniels. Stephen.
Humphry Repton: landscape gardening and the geography of
Georgian England / Stephen Daniels.
p. cm.
Includes bibliographical references (p. ) and index.
ISBN 0-300-07964-8 (cloth: alk. paper)
1. Repton, Humphrey. 1752–1818.  2. Landscape architects—England—Biography.
3. Landscape architecture—England—History.
I. Title.
SB470.R4D35  1999
712'.092—dc21
[B]  98-52787
CIP

A catalogue record for this book is available from
The British Library

*preceding page*  After Humphry Repton, vignette,
from *Fragments on the Theory and Practice of Landscape Gardening* (1803).
Yale Center for British Art, Paul Mellon Collection.

# Contents

| | | |
|---|---|---|
| | Preface and Acknowledgements | viii |
| | Introduction | 1 |
| 1 | On the Road | 27 |
| 2 | The Prophet's Own Country | 67 |
| 3 | The Picturesque Landscape | 103 |
| 4 | Dukedoms and Royal Domains | 149 |
| 5 | In the Neighbourhood of Cities | 207 |
| | Gazetteer | 255 |
| | Notes | 271 |
| | Bibliography | 299 |
| | Index | 312 |

To Chrissie

*facing page* 'Gardens are Works of Art...'
from *Designs for the Pavillon at Brighton* (1808).
Yale Center for British Art, Paul Mellon Collection.

# Preface and Acknowledgements

This book has been many years in the making and I owe much to many people. Some have become good friends. Hugh Prince's writings, notably his pioneering studies of parks and gardens, inspired my own interest in the historical geography of eighteenth- and nineteenth-century landscape. Since supervising my doctoral thesis in the mid-1970s on industrial landscapes of Yorkshire – in which Repton had a small but significant role – he has continued to encourage my subsequent researches and offer helpful readings of my work, including chapters of this book. When I began researching Repton, John Barrell was leading a radical revision of eighteenth-century landscape study. At that time and in the years since, he has given much incisive and supportive criticism, including advice on the substance and structure of this book.

My first studies of Repton were published during preparations for the landmark exhibition on Repton in 1982–3. The organizers, George Carter, Patrick Goode and Kedrun Laurie, invited me to contribute to the catalogue and gave me access to their researches. My copy of the catalogue, well worn with use, has proved an indispensable companion, as it is to everyone working on Repton. Around this time garden history emerged as a field of interdisciplinary research. Many researchers have kindly offered observations and information, including Mavis Batey, Michael Charlesworth, Carol Colson, Fiona Cowell, Hazel Fryer, Stewart Harding, John Dixon Hunt, Peter Goodchild, Keith Goodway, John Harris, David Jacques, Mark Laird, David Lambert, Todd Longstaffe-Gowan, Kay Sanecki, Dorothy Stroud, Michael Symes, Nigel Temple and David Whitehead. I should single out two researchers with whom I have conducted keen exchanges on Repton and garden history. I have benefited greatly from Tom Williamson's guidance in East Anglian archival and field research, as well as from his challenging interpretations. John Phibbs has generously shared with me a wealth of documentary and field evidence as well as his own conclusions and speculations. The gazetteer at the end of this book is compiled jointly with him.

My interpretations of landscape owe a good deal to collaborations and conversations with colleagues. Denis Cosgrove's research on landscape design in sixteenth-century Italy influenced my own on eighteenth-century England, and the cross-fertilization of ideas in our collaborative work helped frame the cultural geographical perspective I have developed since. Teaching and researching with David Matless, Susanne Seymour and Charles Watkins has opened up the complex relations between parks, estates and the rural landscape at large, as well as connections with the theory and practice of design in the twentieth century. Louise Crewe has impressed upon me the importance of fashion in landscape research. I have learnt a great deal from the research on landscape by postgraduates I have supervised, including Ben Cowell, Zena Forster, Denis Linehan, Mandy Morris, Catherine Nash, Simon Rycroft and Setsu Tachibana. A number of scholars from a variety of disciplines have provided helpful comments on my various writings on Repton, including John Beckett, Ann Bermingham, Stephen Copley, Felix Driver, Robin Evans, Charlotte Klonk, Miles Ogborn, Roy Porter and Gareth Williams. For many years Michael Rosenthal has generously shared his expertise in eighteenth-century British art; he read the whole manuscript and made many helpful suggestions.

This book would not have been possible without the assistance of many archivists, curators and librarians including Robert Beauman, Belinda Cousens, Timothy McCann, Morag Norris, Christine North, Bret Payne, Jane Roberts, Sheena Stoddard, Tim Warner, Lavinia Wellicome and Clive Wilkins-Jones. I wish particularly to thank the staff at the following archives and manuscript departments: the Architectural Association, London; Avery Architectural Library, Columbia University, New York; the Bedford Estate, Woburn Abbey; Bedfordshire Record Office; Beineke Library, Yale University, New Haven; Bristol Record Office; Bristol University; British Architectural Library, London; British Library, London; Cornwall Record Office; Devon Record Office; Dumbarton Oaks Research Library, Washington DC; English Heritage, London; Essex, Herefordshire and Hertfordshire Record Offices; Henry E. Huntington Library, San Marino, California; Leeds District Archives; Longleat House; John Rylands Library, University of Manchester; Magdalen College, Oxford; National Library of Wales; National Trust at Attingham, Tatton Park and Polsden Lacey; Newberry Library, Chicago; Norfolk, Northamptonshire and Nottinghamshire Record Offices; Oak Spring Garden Library, Upperville, Virginia; Pierpont Morgan Library, New York; Royal Academy, London; Royal Horticultural Library, London; Royal Library, Windsor; Shakespeare Birthplace Trust; Shropshire Record Office; Sir John Soane's Museum, London; Staffordshire Record Office; Sotheby's, London; Suffolk, East and West Sussex Record Offices; Welbeck Estate, Nottingham University and West Yorkshire Record Office.

Most owners or custodians of properties where Repton was commissioned have welcomed my research visits, and some have taken a keen interest, including Mr and Mrs Robert Burton; Mr J.G. Coltman-Rogers, Paul Grinke, Lady Hastings, Sir Richard Carew Pole, the late Thomas Upcher and John and Judy Wilks. Some who have kindly given permission to quote from and reproduce Repton material in their possession wish to remain anonymous.

The Leverhulme Trust funded a year's study leave in 1995–6 which allowed me to complete the research, travelling extensively to Repton sites and archives. It is a period I recall now as one of pure pleasure. The Paul Mellon Centre contributed generously towards the cost of illustrations for this book. For help with pictures and photography, I am grateful to Sue Berry, Michael Brandon-Jones, Ed Gibbons, Haydn Hansell, Jane F. Haxby, Marilyn Hunt, Emma Leuze, Penelope Browne and Nigel Temple. Chris Lewis drew the maps from a variety of sources and with a keen appreciation of their context. Amanda Rowley steered the text through a series of word-processing systems. Laura Church and Delia Gaze edited the text with great care. Gillian Malpass has proved a highly supportive editor. Abby Waldman saw the manuscript safely through proof and skillfully designed the book.

My wife Chrissie has lived with Repton's effects as long as I have. One discovery of this research is that Repton designed the room in which we held our wedding reception and refashioned the lake where we posed for the photographer. The book is dedicated to her with my love.

# Introduction

Humphry Repton (1752–1818) set out to be the leading landscape gardener of his time. He embarked on his career in 1788, aged thirty-six, after a series of unsuccessful ventures: as a textile merchant, a country squire, and briefly as a private secretary, art critic, essayist and transport entrepreneur. Repton refashioned landscape gardening as a profession from a range of paid skills and amateur accomplishments concerned with the portrayal and improvement of landed property. The business of what was variously called placemaking, ornamental gardening or laying out grounds had lacked a national figurehead since the death in 1783 of Lancelot 'Capability' Brown. To succeed Brown, Repton hived off the contracting side of the business and supplemented the consulting side. If Brown and his provincial imitators drew up large-scale plans for their clients, Repton provided watercolour drawings and detailed written instructions, often bound in morocco in the form of so-called Red Books. The texts of the Red Books were theoretical as well as practical, making observations on landscape aesthetics as well as the actual landscape on site. Repton sought to raise the status of landscape gardening further as a polite art in published treatises on its theory and practice. Landscape gardening for Repton was never merely a business about the grounds, or a vocation concerned with portraying and improving the countryside. It was a profession that gave him an entrée to the company of the best circles, and the opportunity to frame their cultural concerns in terms of his art.[1]

Repton quickly established his name. In a career spanning nearly thirty years he carried out more than four hundred commissions, many of which involved more than one consultation, some lasting for years. He worked for a range of clients: aristocrats, country squires, merchants and professionals. While careful to respect the precise social character of a client's property, he saw his profession as a way of fashioning the consensus of polite society. He worked in a variety of places throughout England and a few in Wales. While attentive to the local circumstances of a site, its topography, land use, settlement pattern and so on, Repton was intent on incorporating properties of all kinds within a general framework of landscape gardening to place them within a national style. Like promoters of other landscape arts in this period, Repton regarded landscape gardening as a patriotic pursuit.

Repton dominated the profession he set out to redefine, but, given the scale of his ambition, it is not surprising that his career was troubled by controversy and disappointment. After two or three years of precocious success, in which he established a promising network of clients, extended his practice beyond the eastern counties of England, and prepared his first published treatise, Repton had to work hard to sustain his career in a world that appeared increasingly fractious and hostile. He

*facing page* Detail of fig. 84.

himself put the blame on a number of developments: the effects of the war with France, especially state taxation and financial speculation; the attacks on his work by connoisseurs and professional rivals; a carriage accident that disabled him; the malice of stewards and the incompetence of workmen charged with implementing his designs; and the delinquency of clients who wantonly altered his plans, took credit for his designs or failed to settle their accounts. Some of Repton's complaints were specific to him and his work, but many were of a kind that affected anyone trying to forge a career in a highly competitive field. As the sheer quantity of professionals concerned with the depiction, design and management of landscape increased so rapidly, and as landscape artists inflated their cultural pretensions, so instances of commercial failure and social anxiety multiplied.[2]

Landscape, as a material terrain and mode of representation, was central to the sensibility of polite society in later Georgian England; it was a cultural arena for its most pressing concerns, a field of inquiry, debate and conflict. During Repton's career the country underwent a series of sometimes striking transformations: parliamentary enclosure of commons, advances in agriculture, improvements in road transportation, rapid expansion of resort towns and commercial cities, innovations in manufacture, extensions of state surveillance and the growth of London in to a world metropolis. These transformations were of course not narrowly topographical; they were in a full sense geographical, involving new regional formations, networks of exchange, systems of circulation, spaces of identity and exclusion, concrete, physical places as well as more abstract spheres of influence.[3] These transformations opened up a series of opportunities for the landscape arts: new sites and subject matter to depict and design, arenas to display and exhibit, places to publish, wider circles of patrons and clients, new markets for pictures, a reformed public sphere of reading and criticism. These transformations also raised searching questions about landscape as a field of vision, notably its capacity to comprehend a range of new information and to address the relation between commercial progress and social order. Britain was not everywhere a progressively modern world: as many landscape artists showed, the power of the old regime, of monarchy, nobility and Church, persisted, indeed was reasserted in reaction to threats of invasion and insurrection.[4]

It is the purpose of this book to chart Repton's career in terms of the changing geography of his time, to show how his landscape gardening combined and competed with the various forces and interests that transformed later Georgian England. This involves examining how Repton's art engaged with other modes of representation and design, such as painting and architecture, as well as how his practice engaged with forms of production and exchange, from deciduous forestry to the mail-coach system. Repton had to reckon with the stubborn realities of physiography, the distribution of highland and lowland, the course of rivers, the configuration of coasts, to turn them in to a resource for his art. This was not a matter of working on the raw material of nature; the natural world was fully incorporated in the cultural consciousness of polite society, its ideas of landscape, regional and national identity, and it was this that made Repton's commissions in unfamiliar country, perhaps appropriated by rival improvers, all the more challenging. The book plots the course of Repton's career through various sites in the polite world of the time, not just in parks and pleasure grounds but on the road in his carriage, scrambling up mountainsides, strolling through the polite precincts of towns and cities, and later being pushed in a Bath chair, attending concerts and exhibitions, court levees and the law courts, at home in Essex, working in his garden, writing at his desk. It was an uneasy career, held together by Repton's anxiety wherever he found himself.

The book frames Repton's life and work in terms of five domains: the road, the county, the picturesque landscape, the aristocratic estate, the urban periphery. It focuses on how Repton's career was shaped in these five domains, by their physical and social regimes, and how he, in turn, attempted to shape them.

Chapter one takes as its theme the road, as the infrastructure of Repton's profession, taking him from place to place, and as a site and symbol of his art and outlook. It examines how the expanding and quickening communication system shaped Repton's career and sensibility. Roads, in the form of approaches and drives, were a significant feature of Repton's landscaping, shaping its social and scenic character. The junction of private and public circulation systems was, for Repton, a key site of his art, at the lodges of great parks, by the fence of his own garden.

Chapter two concentrates on the county as a social formation. It examines how the land and life of Norfolk, where Repton grew up and made his first career as a merchant, influenced his landscape tastes, and how Repton, in turn, represented Norfolk in his topographical writings and designs. In Norfolk, Repton felt (through his family connections) socially at home, but, despite a high concentration of commissions, saw himself professionally in exile, a prophet unheeded in his own country.

Chapter three explores the picturesque landscape as a physical region and discursive terrain centred on the county of Herefordshire, the home of Repton's antagonists Uvedale Price and Richard Payne Knight. As Repton's career took off and his field of work expanded, so Price and Knight attempted to repel his advance. At issue was the polity of landscape improvement, as expressed in issues of commerce and connoisseurship, local knowledge and professional expertise, cultivation and wildness, English and British identity.

Chapter four examines Repton's search for aristocratic patronage and the place of his landscaping on great estates. Commissions for the dukes of Portland and Bedford offered opportunities to make plans for their properties throughout England and to generate subsidiary networks of patronage, either locally or through London. Large, comprehensive schemes of estate improvement also placed limits on Repton's personal authority. Not only might the modest scale of his designs be diminished by vast parks and plantations, but he had to reckon with powerful estate staff and rival consultants. While Repton secured some noble grandees as clients, he desperately sought royal patronage.

Chapter five finds Repton on the urban periphery, on properties around London, Bristol and Leeds. It examines how Repton designed prospects to frame commercial cities, on expensive, sometimes restricted sites that were subject to various urban pressures, such as speculative housing and public recreation. While Repton resented many commissions for suburban villas, for newly enriched tradesmen who employed him to refashion a field or two, some commissions around cities for more established clients on more commanding properties offered the prospect of creating a new civic vision for landscape gardening.

Each chapter charts the full span of Repton's career through these five domains. They are distinct but not discrete; they overlap and intersect, with each other and with the regimes of other worlds, from river valleys to financial networks. It is a measure of Repton's ambition, and the polite society that commissioned him, that so extensive and complex a geography is implicated in his work.

* * *

## The Art of Landscape Gardening

Many of the primary sources for this study, especially Repton's many writings, are already conditioned by views of the landscape gardener's career. Through landscape gardening Repton sought to fashion his life as well as the properties of his clients, to shape his sense of self and social identity as he forged his profession. In this light I want to review some of the main types of text by Repton, their writing and illustrations, to draw attention to the shifting status and meaning of landscape gardening and its relation to the other landscape arts.[5]

When Repton took up landscape gardening, his accomplishment at drawing proved his most marketable asset. The portrait (fig. 2) forming the frontispiece to his treatise *Observations on the Theory and Practice of Landscape Gardening* (1803) shows him sketching some trees

2   H.B. Hall after S. Shelley, *Humphry Repton*, from *Observations on the Theory and Practice of Landscape Gardening* (1803). Yale Center for British Art, Paul Mellon Collection.

in a small pad, and Repton sometimes included himself in the foreground of watercolours of client's properties, sketching on sheets from larger portfolios. In the first years of his career Repton worked hard on his technique, drawing in various styles, after Gilpin, Rowlandson and Gainsborough. On a few commissions Repton was indebted to other professional artists. On his first commission at Welbeck for the duke of Portland he employed George Samuel to work up his sketches of the mansion (fig. 153); Thomas Daniell loaned Repton his sketches for the first volume of *Oriental Scenery* to convert in to designs for the Royal Pavilion, Brighton; Thomas Girtin did the (lost) sketches for Repton's report for Harewood House, although this may have been less Repton's recommendation than that of Edwin Lascelles, Lord Harewood's son and Girtin's patron.[6] From around 1800, after he formed a partnership with his eldest son, John Adey (*b*.1775), a trained architectural draughtsman, his compositions (many of which are joint efforts with John Adey) are more architectonic and filled with surface detail. In later career, in designs focused on small gardens and interiors, Repton drew highly coloured, emblematic compositions and some pastiches of Old Masters, notably Watteau.[7] As well as John Adey, Repton's eldest daughter Mary (*b*.1786) appears to have assisted, in plant drawing but also (after his carriage accident in 1811 when he became severely disabled) in broader landscape compositions.

Repton's watercolours had a specific function in the Red Books. They were meant to elucidate, rather than merely ornament, the proposals, and they did so by a device, a hinged overlay or slide that when removed would reveal the improvements (fig. 5). A smart sales technique, this exploited the dramatic way of viewing or depicting scenery promoted by William Gilpin, improving the dull scene you saw with the delightful one you envisaged. The actual changes proposed might be relatively minor – say removing a fence (fig. 6) or trimming some trees – but the scenic transformations were often spectacular. The device made Repton's art suspect to his more prosaic rivals in landscape improvement. John Claudius Loudon declared that it displayed Repton's 'tinsel kind of talent'.[8] William Marshall reckoned it turned 'rural improvement' in to 'rural pantomime'.[9] Sympathetically, Sir Walter Scott described Repton's designs as 'a raree show omitting only the magnifying glass & substituting his red book for the box and strings'.[10]

3 *Pantomime from Memory* (n.d.). Colman Collection, Norwich Library. Courtesy Norfolk Libraries and Information Service.

Repton was a lifelong lover of theatre of all kinds: Drury Lane plays, pantomimes (fig. 3), private theatricals, masquerades; his own play of 1783, *Odd Whims; Or, Two at a Time* (fig. 4), was staged by a touring company in East Anglian playhouses. On the way to one commission, Repton was observed at Biggleswade Fair, watching a puppet show.[11] Conscious of his critics, Repton was high-minded about his illusionism. In the Red Book for Tatton Park he deployed Edmund Burke's dictum from

4 J. Stadler after Humphry Repton, *Lady Jane and Lord Blazon*, from *Odd Whims; or, Two at a Time* (1804). Yale Center for British Art, Paul Mellon Collection.

5   Site for house and pleasure grounds, with and without overlay, from the Red Book for Northrepps (*c*.1792). Private collection.

6   View from the pleasure grounds, with and without overlay, from the Red Book for Brandsbury (1789). Dumbarton Oaks Research Library, Washington DC.

*A Philosophical Enquiry into the Origin of Our Ideas of the Sublime and Beautiful* (1757) that 'a true artist should put a generous deceit on spectators'. It was through its 'deceptions' that landscape gardening could be classed with 'the polite arts':

> We plant a hill, to make it appear higher than it is; we open the banks of a brook to give it the appearance of a river . . . Nor is the imagination so fastidious as to take offence at any well supported deception, even after the want of reality is discovered. When we are interested at a tragedy, we do not enquire whence the characters are copied: on the contrary, we forget that when we see a Garrick or a Siddons, and join in the sorrows of a Belvidere or a Beverley.[12]

For most of his career Repton supplied miniature drawings for the *Polite Repository*, an almanac-cum-diary published annually by William Peacock, to illustrate the frontispiece and each month of the year (fig. 7).[13] A few illustrations are views of established tourist sites such as Matlock High-Tor (fig. 8) and Kensington Palace, which Repton seems only to have visited, but the majority of the views are of places where he was commissioned, named with the property, county and client (figs 9 and 10). The early issues acknowledged that Repton had 'voluntarily offered to supply this work with designs of those places, where any alterations were made under his direction – by which the *Polite Repository* becomes a pleasing record of the most recent ornaments and

7 J. Peltro after Humphry Repton, *The Banks of the Frome, Oldbury Court, near Bristol*, title page and frontispiece to *Peacock's Polite Repository* (1803). Victoria and Albert Museum.

tions: 'During the last 18 years I have given 13 designs to an annual work, making 234 views, from each of which I am informed 7,000 impressions have been made'. The *Polite Repository*, he calculated, accounted for 26,250 of the '1,638,000 impressions [of his sketches] in circulation'.[14]

Repton's venture as an art critic – compiling a guide under the *nom de plume* of The Bee for Boydell's Shakespeare Gallery in Pall Mall – overlapped with the beginning of his career as a landscape gardener. Opened in 1789, the Shakespeare Gallery was a highly commercial enterprise, marketing engravings of scenes from Shakespeare, and it quickly became a venue of London literary and artistic life. In a proudly 'English School of Painting', Repton identified an expanded genre of 'Historical Picture' including scenes such as those by Sir Joshua Reynolds, in which figures were prominent, and others

8  J. Peltro after Humphry Repton, *The High Tor at Matlock*, frontispiece to *Peacock's Polite Repository* (1807). Bodleian Library, Oxford.

9  After Humphry Repton, *Scene at Oldbury Court, Glocestershire* [sic.] *– Seat of T. Graeme Esq.*, from *Peacock's Polite Repository* (1802). Private collection.

10  After Humphry Repton, *St John's in the Isle of Wight – Seat of Edward Simeon Esq.*, from *Peacock's Polite Repository* (1798). Private collection.

improvements to the country'. Repton and Peacock collaborated each with an eye on their competitors. The *Polite Repository* was a typical artefact of polite society. A slim, pocket-sized volume, it had a print run of seven thousand and was published in various bindings, mostly plain, coloured wraps in card slipcases, but some in silk, and a few in full morocco, tooled in gilt. Properties of various sizes and styles – palaces, mansions, villas, rectories – were depicted, and various scenes within their pleasure grounds, in standard vignettes (fig. 11). When Richard Payne Knight renewed his attack on professional landscape gardening in 1805, claiming that not one pleasing landscape could 'be found in any of the numerous, and many of them beautiful and picturesque spots, which it has visited in different parts of the island', Repton replied by enumerating the views in his various publica-

11 *Proof Impressions of Plates Engraved from Drawings of H. Repton of Scenery Improving under His Directions*, arranged on a decorative watercolour mount (after 1808). Mrs Paul Mellon, Oak Spring Garden Library, Upperville, Virginia.

by Wheatley, Hodges and Wright of Derby, in which 'Landscape is principal'.[15] Thereafter, in his writings on landscape gardening, Repton delivered his views on art. During his dispute around 1794 with Price and Knight, Repton began to distance landscape gardening from landscape painting, from what he saw as its disengagement from the civilizing influence of history painting. Like other conservative critics in this period, he questioned styles that seemed to shirk the responsibility of documenting a cultivated countryside centred on country houses. Repton cleaved to a Burkean view that landscape should be lived in, not just looked at. Given his brief, it is not surprising that the genres of landscape in which he worked tended to be conventional, even old fashioned: the country-house portrait, the conversation piece, the prospect. In his Red Book of 1814 for Endsleigh, Devon, for the duke of Bedford, he concurred with the criticism of Turner's naturalistic painting of a country house and park, *Somer-Hill, Kent* (fig. 12), exhibited at the Royal Academy in 1811:

> One of our most eminent Landscape Painters was desired to make a portrait of a Gentleman's Seat: he saw the place during a land-flood, and when the whole valley was covered in vapour he made a beautiful picture of a fog, after the manner of Vernet; and thus he painted an atmosphere, when he should have painted a landscape.[16]

The Red Books functioned in various ways: as plans, often as a base for working drawings and itemized

12  J.M.W. Turner, *Somer-Hill, the Seat of W.F. Woodgate, Esq.* (1811). National Gallery of Scotland, Edinburgh.

13  Thomas Medland after Humphry Repton, Trade card of Humphry Repton (1788). Private collection.

directions; as a record of work in progress which Repton had already recommended on site or by letter; as an album of views, sometimes for clients who never intended to carry out the proposals; as an advertisement for Repton's work, in the drawing-rooms of clients, passed around potential patrons, and, in the case of the Red Book for Tatton, put in the shop window of a Pall Mall bookseller to solicit subscriptions for Repton's first published treatise. There is a standard format to the early Red Books: a slim, oblong quarto. Later in Repton's career there are marked variations, and towards the end a clear separation between prestigious commissions, commemorated in large, sometimes luxurious folio volumes, and more trifling commissions, often for villas, committed to an unbound report, or merely a letter.[17]

In the front of each Red Book Repton pasted his trade card (fig. 13); occasionally in the luxury volumes it is incorporated in an elaborate frontispiece (fig. 14). Engraved to Repton's design, it shows him striking the figure of a surveyor, at his theodolite, taking a bearing. Next to him is a figure with a ranging rod who looks less like an assistant than one of Gainsborough's lounging young landowners. Behind them labourers dig and shovel earth by a lakeside. Beyond is a wooded hillside with a tower. The scene is poetic as well as practical. It alludes to some lines from Milton's poem *L'Allegro*:

> Straight mine eye hath caught new pleasures,
> Whilst the landscape around it measures; ...
> Towers and battlements it sees
> Bosom'd high in tufted trees.

Repton sometimes quoted these lines in the Red Books but quickly abandoned instrumental measurement for sketch maps or plans based on existing surveys (figs 15 and 16).

If the allure of Red Books was their pictures, Repton regarded them primarily as explanatory texts. While he described himself as 'gifted with the peculiar faculty of seeing almost immediately the way in which [a place] might be improved', he sought to make this intelligible by 'delivering my reports in writing, accompanied with maps and . . . sketches'.[18] The pages of text in the Red Books were penned in a fine copperplate (fig. 17). They follow a fairly standard form, a dedication, followed by sections under 'Character', 'Situation', 'Approaches', 'Views from the House', 'Pleasure-ground' and 'Walks', with sections specific to a site, 'Water', 'Plantations', and so on. There is cross-referencing with commissions elsewhere to exemplify certain principles, and sometimes separate theoretical sections, say, on 'The Picturesque' or 'Gothic Architecture'. The pages occasionally break in to verse, Repton's own and passages from his favourite works, notably William Mason's *The English Garden* (1777).

The writing of the Red Books was strongly influenced by relations with clients. Some clients dictated improvements, others left them entirely to Repton's discretion. Repton's preferred discourse in the Red Books was one that echoed congenial conversations as he and his client walked about the grounds, as much a record of Repton's visit as a plan of estate improvements. In its text and images the Red Book for Babworth, Nottinghamshire, exemplifies such a commission. An illustration shows the young client's family under an oak in their park, Mrs Simpson singing accompanied by Mr Simpson on guitar and another figure, presumably Repton himself, on the flute (fig. 18). This conversation piece is a scene to be conserved; it is contrasted with a bleak scene that a

14 *below* Frontispiece to the Red Book for Woburn Abbey (1805). By kind permission of the Marquess of Tavistock and the Trustees of the Bedford Estate.

15 *right* Map of the estate, from the Red Book for Brandsbury (1789). Dumbarton Oaks Research Library, Washington DC.

16 *below right* Plan of the Park, from the Red Book for Glemham Hall (1791). Dumbarton Oaks Research Library, Washington DC.

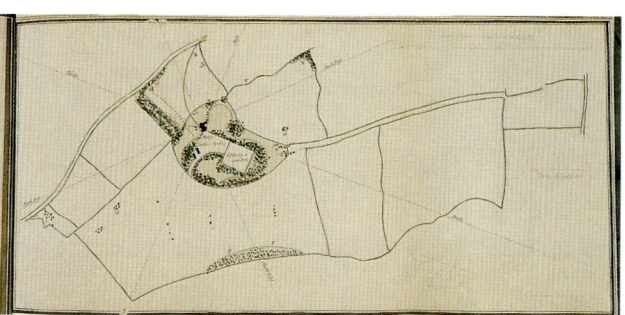

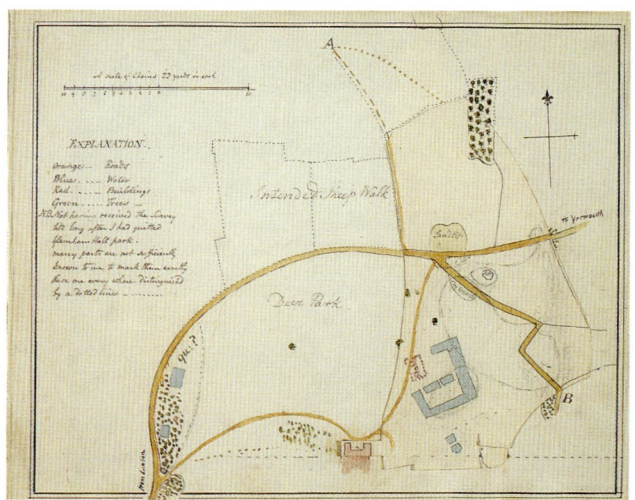

17 *left* 'Situation', from the Red Book for Claybury (1791). Reproduced courtesy of the Essex Record Office.

18 *below* View from the house, in its present 'character' and altered according to 'Despotic FASHION', from the Red Book for Babworth (1792). Private collection.

vulgar improver would suggest, felling the trees and floating a lake. The verse explaining this, the threat of 'Despotic FASHION . . . with misguided step/stalks o'er the land', echoes that of a mutual friend, Anna Seward, the leader of a literary circle in Lichfield.[19] Too few clients, Repton complained, were prepared to engage in such cultural conversation in what many, after all, must have regarded as a formally commercial transaction.[20] If Capability Brown's submitted plans took the form of large-scale, plain-style maps and allowed a good deal of scope for clients and stewards to revise and adapt his proposals, Repton's Red Books were meticulously detailed, sometimes overweeningly so. 'Stuff', scribbled one client, James Duberley, over sentences in the Red Book for Gaines Hall, Huntingdonshire, adding his own 'Advice to Posterity' on planting to the title page (fig. 19).[21]

Repton's first published book on his art, *Sketches and Hints on Landscape Gardening* (1795), is, as the title suggests, a highly pictorial volume. It was issued by Boydell's, the leading publisher of engravings and illustrated books, in an oblong quarto, like the Red Books of the period, in an edition of two hundred and fifty, selling to subscribers at £2 10s 6d. Several artists at Boydell's Shakespeare Gallery, under the supervision of J.C. Stadler, were employed on the illustrations; indeed *Sketches and Hints* was delayed months until the plates, closely replicating Repton's Red Book watercolours, overlays included, and 'finished as highly as tinted drawings', reached the required standard (fig. 20).[22] In the introduction Repton explains that he adopted the term landscape gardening 'because the art can only be advanced and perfected by the united powers of the *landscape painter* and the *practical gardener*'.

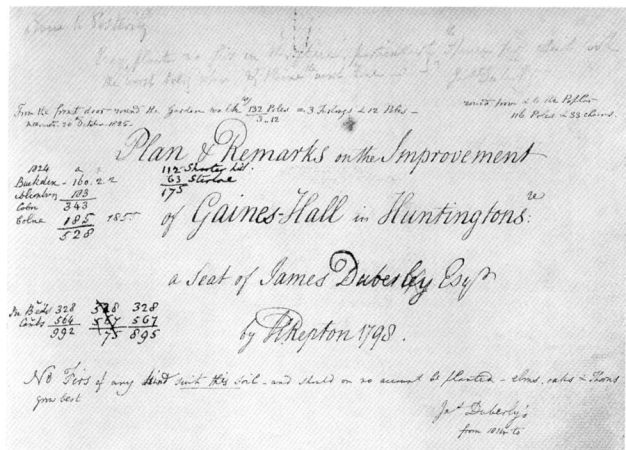

19  Title page, from the Red Book for Gaines Hall (1798). Private collection. Photograph Sothebys. The client James Duberley's 'Advice to Posterity' at the top of the title page reads 'Pray plant no firs in this place, particularly spruce which look the worst everywhere and thrice worst here.'

> The former must conceive a plan, which the latter may be able to execute; for though a painter may represent a beautiful landscape on his canvass, and even surpass Nature by the combination of her choicest materials, yet the luxuriant imagination of the *painter* must be subjected to the *gardener's* practical knowledge in planting, digging and moving earth.[23]

Moreover, the landscape gardener 'must possess a competent knowledge of *surveying, mechanics, hydraulics, agriculture, botany*, and the general principles of *architecture*'.[24] Repton delayed publication further to add a long supplement replying to the attack on him and his profession in Knight's *The Landscape: A Didactic Poem* and Price's *Essay on the Picturesque* (both 1794). Repton concluded his remarks on their 'new theory of Landscape Gardening (though in fact it ought rather to be called *Picture Gardening*)' with an endorsement by his patron William Windham: 'Places are not be laid out with a view to their appearance in a picture, but to their uses, and the enjoyment of them in real life'.[25]

Repton's second book, *Observations on the Theory and Practice of Landscape Gardening* (1803), was

> printed under a different form and title, because I am less ambitious of publishing a book of beautiful prints, than a book of precepts: I must therefore entreat that the plates be considered as necessary than ornamental; they are introduced to illustrate the arguments, rather than to attract the attention. I wish to make my appeal less to the eye than to the understanding.[26]

There are some fine coloured aquatints of sketches in the Red Books, but many of the plates are monochrome diagrams, plans and elevations (figs 21 and 22). Published in a vertical quarto format by Taylor's Architectural Library, at four guineas to subscribers and five thereafter, *Observations* reflected the increasing alignment of architecture and landscape gardening in Repton's work. After working on an occasional, and not too successful, basis with William Wilkins and James Wyatt, from around 1796 Repton entered a formal partnership with John Nash, optimistic about integrating improvements in landscape and architecture. After a bitter break with Nash around 1800, Repton took his son John Adey (who had trained with Wilkins and worked for Nash) in to partnership and introduced him in the advertizement for *Observations*:

> His name has hitherto been little known as an architect, because it was suppressed in many works begun in that of another person, to whom I freely, unreservedly, and confidentially gave my advice and assistance . . . amongst the melancholy evils to which human life is subject, the most excruciating to a man of sensibility, is the remembrance of disappointed hope from misplaced confidence.[27]

After fifteen years in his career Repton was also dismayed by the way so many circumstances had conspired to compromise his designs on the ground. Writing would redeem him.

> The death of the proprietors, the change of property, the difference of opinions . . . the frequent opposition I have experienced from gardeners, bailiffs and land stewards, who either wilfully mar my plans, or ignorantly mistake my instructions . . . It is rather through my opinions in writing, than on the partial and imperfect manner in which my plans have been executed, that I wish my fame to be established.[28]

Three years after its publication, Repton's bookseller requested a new edition of *Observations*, which he directed to be reprinted without alteration or addition. He was also asked for a new edition of *Sketches and Hints*, which had originally cost Repton more than one hundred pounds because many subscribers failed to pay for their volumes, but had 'become so scarce, that above four times the original price has been paid for some copies'.

20 *Rivenhall Place*, with and without overlay, from *Sketches and Hints on the Theory and Practice of Landscape Gardening* (1795). Yale Center for British Art, Paul Mellon Collection.

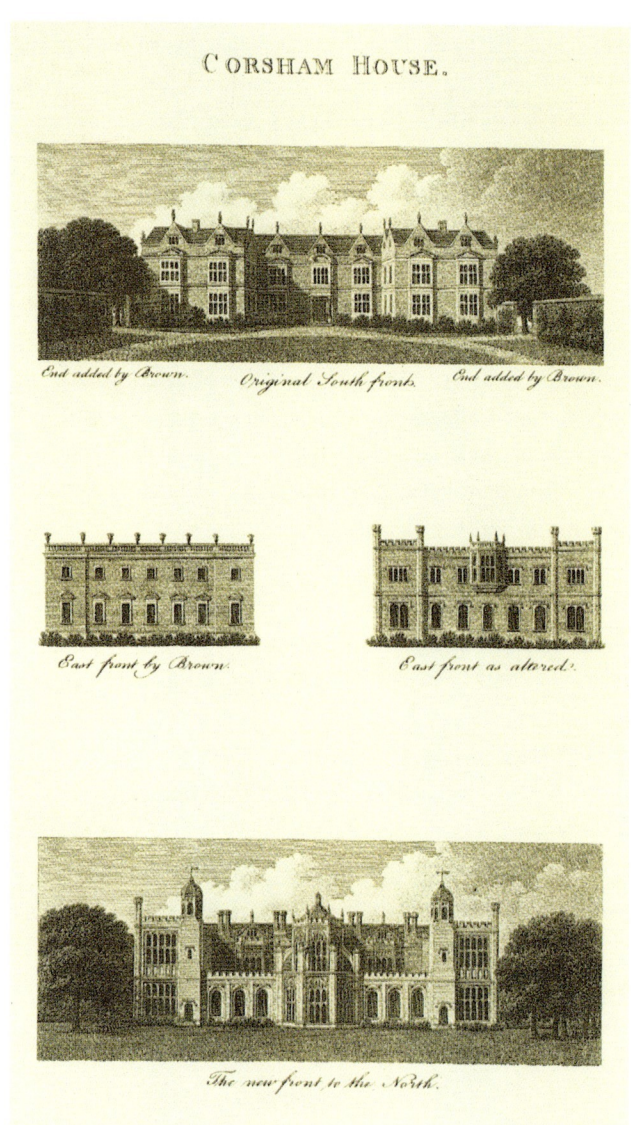

'In compliment to the present possessors of that work', Repton decided not to publish another costly edition with plates, but to extract some passages from it, add a brief 'History of Landscape Gardening', originally commissioned for a new edition of *The Gardener's and Botanist's Dictionary* (1807) and a reply to a recent attack by Knight, and issue them in a small, unillustrated octavo volume selling at five shillings, under the title *An Enquiry into the Changes of Taste in Landscape Gardening*. 'The enormous expense of engraving has hitherto so confined my opinions to a certain class of purchasers, that they have been either not generally known, or they have been repeated by some without acknowledgment, and misrepresented by others without sufficient quotation.'[29]

In his 'History of Landscape Gardening', Repton spells out his succession from William Kent and Capability Brown, taking care to dismiss the 'numerous herd of [Brown's] foremen and gardeners' who continued his practice and ignoring any other professional rivals. In charting the present development of his art, he emphasizes a convergence of landscape gardening and

21 *left* Corsham House, from *Observations on the Theory and Practice of Landscape Gardening* (1803). Yale Center for British Art, Paul Mellon Collection.

22 *below* Diagram of Reflections, from *Observations on the Theory and Practice of Landscape Gardening* (1803). Yale Center for British Art, Paul Mellon Collection.

23 *facing page* An Inquiry into the Changes in Architecture, from *Designs for the Pavillon at Brighton* (1808). Yale Center for British Art, Paul Mellon Collection.

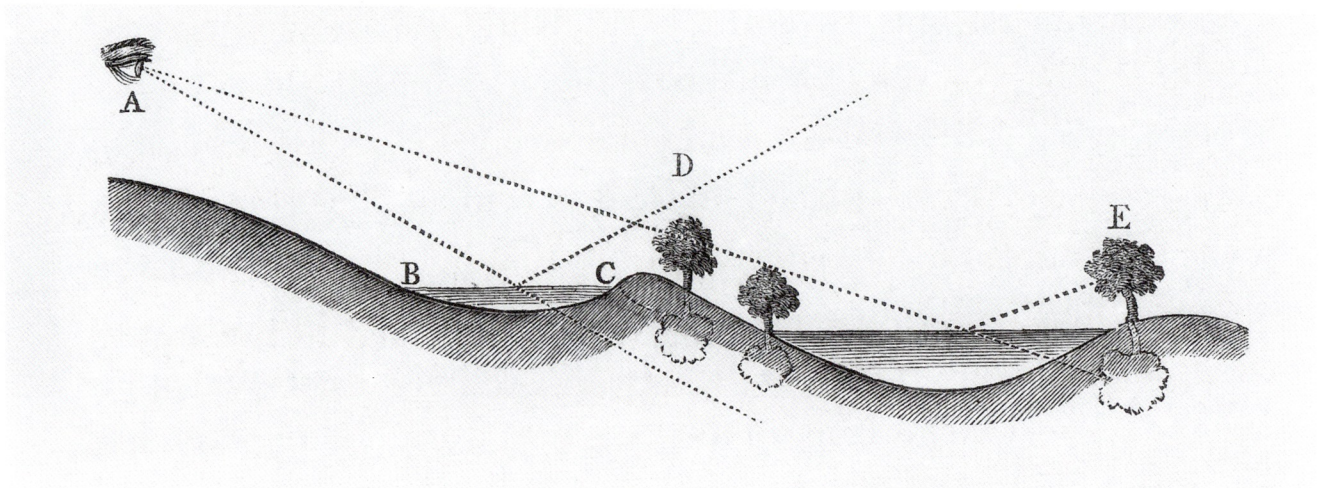

horticulture. Small gardens of various kinds – useful, ornamental, scientific, indoor, outdoor – are made a focus of his art, and he looks forward to new developments:

> After tracing the various changes in Taste in Gardening and Architecture, I cannot suppress my opinion that we are on the eve of some great future change in both these arts, in consequence of our having lately become acquainted with Scenery and Buildings in the interior provinces of India. The beautiful designs published by Daniell, Hodges, and other artists, have produced a new source of beauty, of elegance, and grace, which may justly vie with the specimens of Grecian and Gothic architecture... It is therefore with peculiar satisfaction that my opinion has lately been required in some great works of this style, which are in too early a stage of progress to be referred to in this volume.[30]

The 'great works' in the Indian style were Repton's designs for the Royal Pavilion in Brighton. This commission for the Prince of Wales, undertaken at 'the highest point of my ambition', turned out to be a deep disappointment, the work eventually being given to Nash, but Repton tried to salvage something by publishing the plans.[31] *Designs for the Pavillon at Brighton* was published in 1808 through J.C. Stadler in a sumptuous folio at six guineas (figs 23 and 24); Stadler engraved the plates himself and took the financial risk, promising Repton an equal share of profits.[32] *Designs for the Pavillon* sold its print run and was reprinted after Repton's death around 1822, presumably to coincide with the completion of Nash's rebuilding of the Pavilion, but Repton himself carried out no further work in an Indian style and soon abandoned his confidence in renewing landscape gardening.[33]

Compiled from 1814 to 1815 when Repton was largely confined to his house, without commissions and crippled with angina, Repton's last treatise, *Fragments on the Theory and Practice of Landscape Gardening* (1816), describes the break up of his profession:

24  J.C. Stadler after Humphry Repton, *West Front of the Pavillon*, from *Designs for the Pavillon at Brighton* (1808). Yale Center for British Art, Paul Mellon Collection.

During the last ten years, the Art of Landscape Gardening, in common with all other Arts which depend on Peace and Patronage, has felt the influence of War and War Taxes... Whether in the influence of returning Peace may revive its energies, or whether it is hereafter to be classed among the '*Arts perditae*', the Author hopes its memory may be preserved a little longer in the following pages.[34]

The selection of extracts from the Red Books and reports, and the attendant commentary, show the recession of Repton's landscape gardening. It endured only in a few, long-term, aristocratic commissions, such as those at Cobham, Longleat and Woburn, and a few promising new commissions, such as Ashridge and Sheringham. Decline was evident elsewhere. Clients felled plantations or ploughed up parks to make quick money; some abandoned ancestral homes for an idle round in resorts, others sold them to men with neither pedigree nor taste:

> In approaching the close of my active life, it is natural that I should look back on the various subjects which have claimed my attention, and called forth my exertions: some of these I can view with delight, and record my exultation; but alas! in how many have my time, my labour, and my contrivance been employed without producing fame or profit... I have lived to see many of my plans beautifully realized, but many more cruelly marred.[35]

Writing 'the last Fragment of my Labours', Repton described the improvements to his own small garden at Hare Street, and the contraction of his field of vision: 'I have lived to reach that period, when the improvement

25 *Sunshine after Rain,* from *Fragments on the Theory and Practice of Landscape Gardening* (1816). Yale Center for British Art, Paul Mellon Collection.

of Houses and Gardens is more delightful to me, than that of Parks or Forests, Landscapes, or distant prospects'.

> When no longer able to undertake the more extensive plans of *Landscape*, I was glad to contract my views within the narrow circle of the *Garden*. . . . While I have acceded to the combination of two words, Landscape and Gardening, yet they are distinct objects . . . one is to please the eye, the other is more the comfort and occupation of man . . . although Painters may despise Gardens as subjects for the pencil, yet Poets, Philosophers and Statesmen, have always enjoyed and described the pure delights of Garden Scenery.[36]

Repton displayed the delights of garden scenery with a 'gaudy sketch' (fig. 25) to show the effects of light after a summer shower on the shape, texture and tints of a range of plants and flowers, in beds, baskets, urns and on trellises. He relates the time that he pointed out to William Pitt 'the delight we experience on a sunny day, from an open trellis of vines overhead, or the foliage in the roof of a conservatory' and how the prime minister 'made several experiments with leaves of different shapes and tints . . . new objects of delight to a mind like his, capable of resorting to the beauties of Nature, as a relief from the severe duties of his arduous situation'. The delights of garden scenery relieved Repton's own suffering:

> Here Nature's Contrasts – Art attempts in vain;
> Who can describe the joy that follows pain?
> Or paint th'effect of sunshine after rain?[37]

Repton used other forms of writing to explain or comment on his work as a landscape gardener, principally letters and a Memoir. He constantly corresponded about his work, much of it with clients to arrange visits, suggest improvements and bill for consultations. In letters to friends and family he confided his broader concerns about landscape gardening. In one of his many letters late in life to Sir Harry Fetherstonehaugh, a client who became a close friend, Repton smiled over a passage in James Northcote's *Memoirs of Reynolds* (1813–15): 'Familiar Letters by Sir Joshua are very scarce: he was busy & too wise to spend his time in an occupation wh[ich] is more congenial to the idle and the vain, who are common[ly] very voluminous in their production of this Article'. 'In the busyest days of my life I have found relief from professional pursuits, in the employment of my pen & shall leave a large Mass to my executors to prove that Leisure was irksome to me at all times.'[38]

When he embarked on his profession, Repton was already one of Anna Seward's many pen-friends, probably through a family connection in Lichfield. She encouraged him to use his skills as an essayist and versifier as well as a watercolourist in landscape gardening. 'I rejoice in the success of your new profession', she wrote in 1790,

> that your talents have, at length, struck into a track which calls forth all their strong and brilliant powers. In this track the wealthy and the vain will seek them out, employ and reward them; – because it is there that such beings can gild themselves with lustres reflected from the poet's fancy and the painter's eye, which, in the coy bowers of abstract literature, had administered little to their cravings.[39]

Thereafter, for a few years, they exchanged views on landscape gardening, occasionally in the form of verses. Seward's last letter, in 1798, expresses the hope that 'the number of votaries' seeking 'the Muse of Landscape' and 'you, her high-priest, does not abate at the grin of those monsters of finance, the assessed taxes'.[40]

When Repton wanted to improve his knowledge of botany, around the turn of the century, he renewed his youthful correspondence with James Edward Smith, now president of the Linnean Society: 'You have reached the summit of the Science you delight in whilst I more humble have been content to climb to the top of my Art . . . I often regret that I have dedicated my life to the canvas on which Nature stretches her wonders – rather than on the individual wonders separately'.[41] In 1815 Repton presented a paper to the Linnean Society about his observations on ivy and asked to be commemorated by having his name 'affix[ed] to some plant of the Ivy tribe, or any climbing genus, which, like myself wants to be supported'.

> My great predecessor *Adam* would never have been able to find names for an hundredth part of your vocabulary; but he lived in a garden with one friend, and one enemy, who, like Buonaparte in our days was the enemy of peace. What wonders have we lived to witness! kingdoms raised and kicked down like a child's house of cards.[42]

Repton's surviving letters to his third son, William, date from 1806, when William Repton, aged twenty-three, was working as a lawyer in Aylsham, Norfolk. They are addressed from many places in Repton's field of work: the houses of clients, staging posts on the road, his villa at Hare Street, Essex. While filled with family news, they raise professional enquiries on matters that Repton considered his son would be qualified to advise: on tax demands and assessments, news of land sales, enclosures, bank failures and defaulting clients. In the epistolary style of polite society (it reminded Repton's sister Dorothy of Anna Seward's) the letters to William shift between personal, professional and political matters.[43] The prevailing tone is pessimistic, sometimes elegiac about old times and old patrons, often bitter about speculators, bureaucrats, embezzlers and ministers and their corruption of the country. 'We are now so wise', Repton reported in 1811,

> that we can only be kept in order by the bayonet – as if the people are to be shot & trampled under horses feet in the streets of London – it matters very little whether by French of English Soldiers – while we look at Lord Camden &c &c &c receiving thousands from our Taxes – There is something Rotten in the State.[44]

Compiled in 1814 and 1815 around the same time as *Fragments*, the surviving second part of Repton's manuscript memoir covers his career as a landscape gardener. Memoirs, published and unpublished, were, as John Brewer has shown, central to the culture of politeness in Repton's time. The stories they told were

> of someone seeking to understand culture and trying to develop his own taste ... not catalogues of events ... but stories of struggles for refinement, of efforts to live a richer, better life ... The writing of such works was neither fully public nor completely private. They recorded both a public cultural repertoire and a cultured private self, and the conversation between these two was what mattered.[45]

Repton deploys a number of standard tropes to shape the story of his career, his struggle for professional and social recognition.[46] His life is a voyage, enthusiastically undertaken, stoically endured. 'Now at the age 36 years – I commence a new career', Part two opens, 'And after a temporary rest and half seclusion from the world; I boldly venture forth once more, and with renewed energy and hope push off my little bark into a sea unknown'. 'Circumstances had produced such a change in men and things, that I might have been classed with the numerous hosts of disappointed men, but for the consideration that as Landscape gardener I have never been superseded by a more successful rival', so the Memoir closes; 'My own profession like myself was becoming extinct. The ship was sinking, and it was time to quit it. These pages will shew how actively I have performed the voyage – How I have glided through Life's calms – and struggled with its tempests'. The turbulence of the times is framed as a distinction between old and new worlds, dated by Repton at the turn of the eighteenth century, with the threat of invasion, and the deepening financial effects of the war. 'We now begin a new century', opens chapter fifteen, 'the first years of which excited such alarm through all ranks of people that I felt as if my profession was becoming extinct ... the whole Nation was roused to self defence ... and everyone trembled for the safety of old England'.[47]

If the Memoir presents Repton's life as a journey, during which 'I have taken my readers from the furrows ploughed by Robert Newman to the foot of the Prince's throne', it is one in which people are depicted more fully than the places they own or occupy. Much of the Memoir is written in terms of another trope of the time, the portrait gallery, and, like other biographical sketches, it is more concerned with the polite virtues of kindness, hard work and domestic worth than the heroic virtues embodied in the statesman or connoisseur.[48] In contrast to many noble clients, Lord Uxbridge was a proper gentleman, his promise of a concert ticket for Repton's daughter, 'said with so sweet a smile, that when I lately saw that smile represented by Sir Joshua Reynolds in a portrait at Beaudesert it recalled [his words] to my memory'.[49] 'As I write more to amuse myself than others',

> my portraits like those in a painter's room are not less diversified in the character or rank of the individuals represented – than in the style, size and progress of each, from the slight chalk sketch to the finished pictures, or from the whole length as it appears to the world, to the little miniature which I can take to my bosom and *wear next [to] my heart* (How few alas are these!) ... I have occasionally regretted as one of the necessary evils of an occupation such as mine; the constant succession of new, and general acquaintances

forbade the cultivation of more intimate friendships, and often my connexion, which for a time went on improving as the scenery improved, finished with the man, when I had finished with the improvements of his place.⁵⁰

The frontispiece of the Memoir (fig. 1, *frontispiece*) takes the form of a triple self-portrait. The main portrait, in a decorative frame, possibly drawn after a portrait by Samuel Shelley, shows Repton aged forty-five at the height of his profession. Below it is one in the style of a caricature, showing him a man of fashion at the time of his marriage, and another, aged sixty-three, after a silhouette, showing him broken with age and illness.

Vain flatt'ring youth which forty years hath made
The vain but drooping shadow of a shade.

The tailpiece (fig. 27), drawn 'for this last page of my life', is a vignette showing emblems of its gains and losses:

Some Weeds, some Flowers, Sunshine & Showers
Whips, Windmills, Beads and Crosses.

In his various texts Repton portrayed the 'character and situation' of both figures and landscapes, patrons and their properties, people and places he visited, and charted the progress of landscape gardening as an art of scenic

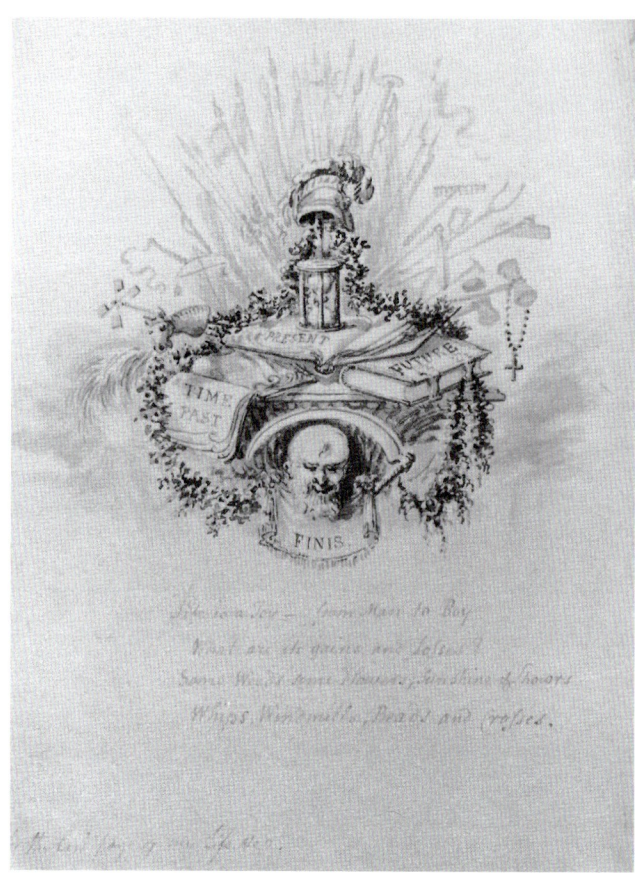

27  Tailpiece to Memoir (*c.*1814). British Library, Manuscripts Department.

26  *The Hand on the Tiller Steers the Nation from the Arts of War to the Arts of Peace* (n.d.). Colman Collection, Norwich Library. Courtesy of Norfolk Libraries and Information Service. Probably drawn to illustrate *Fragments on the Theory and Practice of Landscape Gardening* (1816) but not used there.

and social improvement.⁵¹ If Repton's writings seek to enclose landscape gardening within his own life and to correlate the rise and fall of his career with the moral condition of the country (fig. 26), they also indicate that, far from declining, landscape gardening, by whatever name, as practised and theorized by others, actually continued to flourish. Repton's early success prompted others, both professional and amateur, to promote different, sometimes rival versions, both in writing and on the ground. The riposte to Repton in the writings of Uvedale Price and Richard Payne Knight set up a strain of criticism among gentlemen amateurs which entwined Repton's profession with the vagaries of feminine fashion. Addressing Lord Byron from Trinity College, Cambridge, in 1808, John Cam Hobhouse advised his friend not to take 'an ever fond, or ever angry wife':

Shall [Newstead] no more confess a manly sway,
But changeful woman's changing whims obey?
Who may, perhaps, as varying humour calls,

28   Thomas Hornor, *Night* (with overlay) and *Daybreak* (without overlay), introducing section on Rheola in *Illustrations of the Vale of Neath, Glamorganshire* (1871). © The British Museum, London.

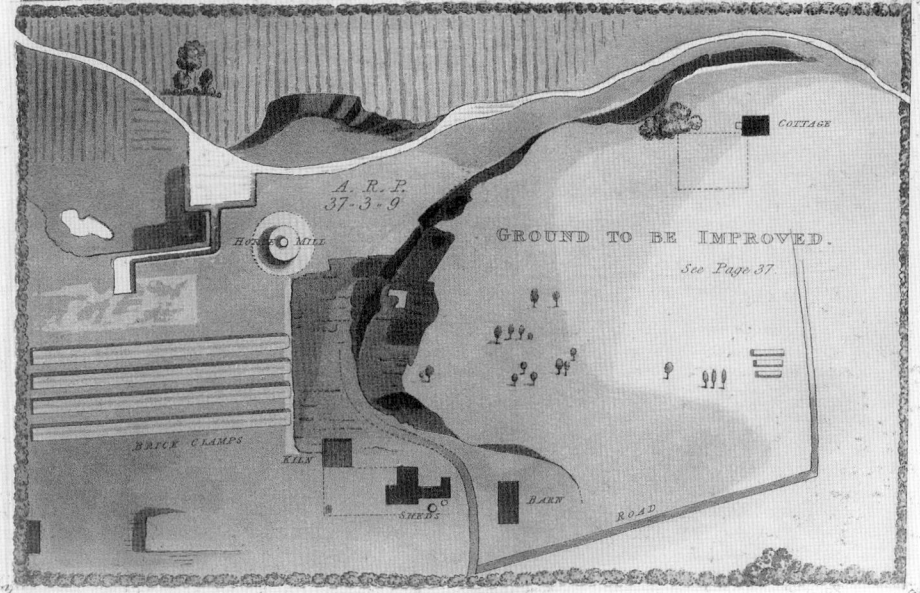

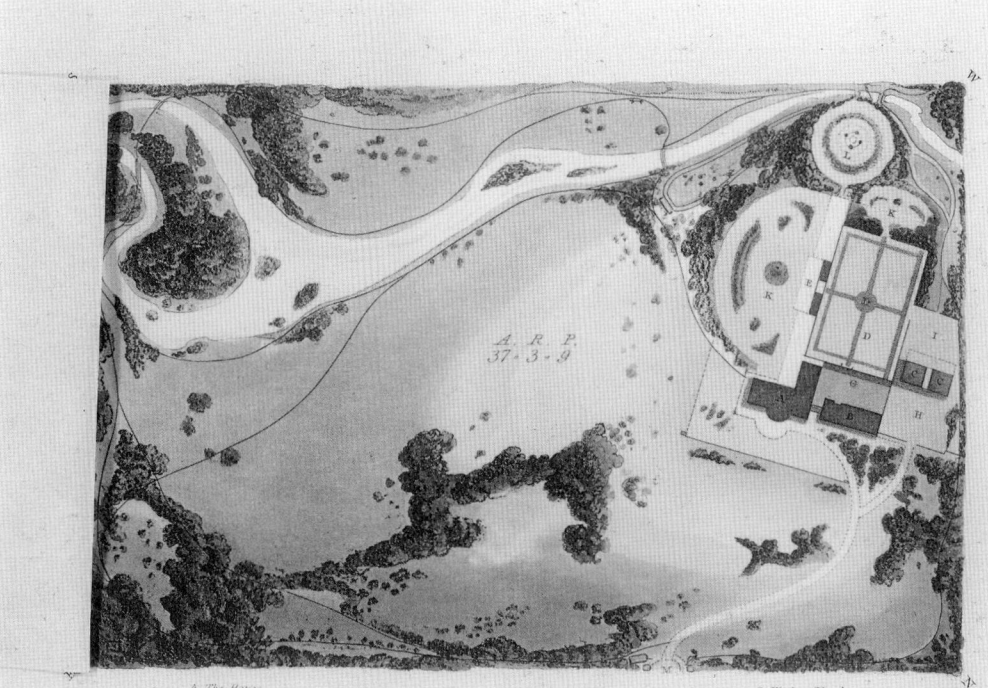

A. The House.
B. Offices.
C. Stables.
D. Kitchen Garden.
E. Conservatory.
G. Kitchen Yard.
H. Stable Yard.
I. Melon Ground.
K. Flower Garden.
L. Rookery.
M. Entrance Gate.

A GENERAL PLAN.

Contract your cloisters and o'erthrow your walls;
Let Repton loose o'er all the ancient ground,
Change round to square, and square convert to round;
Root up the elms' and yews' too solemn gloom,
And fill with shrubberies gay and green their room;
Roll down the terrace to a gay parterre,
Where gravel'd walks and flowers alternate glare;
And quite transform, in every point complete,
Your Gothic abbey to a country seat.[52]

Professional men who promoted broad programmes of estate improvement were keen to contain the charms of landscape gardening within a more virile vision of country life. William Marshall's *Planting and Rural Ornament* (1796) recognized that improvements seen from the drawing-room 'should be feminine – elegant – beautiful such as attunes the mind to politeness and lively conversation' but urged attention to be paid to the breakfasting-room which 'should have more masculine objects in view: wood, water, and an extended country for the eye to roam over; such as allures us, imperceptibly, to the ride or chace'.[53] Other professional men realized the power of Repton's appeal to the consumer culture of polite society and developed some of his marketing techniques. Thomas Hornor, for example, adapted Repton's device of overlays to display his new art of 'pictural surveying' (fig. 28). Addressing anyone with the money, Hornor announced in 1813 a new era in 'the progress of landscape gardening' and made a small fortune from big-spending patrons.[54] Elements of Repton's style were repackaged as designs in manuals and fashionable magazines (fig. 29), for any reader to admire or implement for their own grounds.[55] Manufacturers of exterior paints and wire fencing exploited Repton's name to advertise their wares.[56] While Repton was attempting to chart his alienation from commercial society, rewriting his career as a confidante of cultured, benevolent gentlemen, Jane Austen identified him in *Mansfield Park* as a brand name for money-minded delinquents: 'Mr Repton . . . His terms are five guineas a day . . . Repton, or any body of that sort . . . any Mr Repton who would . . . give me as much beauty as he could for my money'.[57]

The intention of this book is to examine Repton's enclosure of landscape gardening in relation to the wider world of landscape improvement, both in the writings of contemporaries around the country and as practised in a variety of sites on the ground.

29 *facing page* A General Plan, with and without overlay, from John Buonarti Papworth, *Hints on Ornamental Gardening* (1823). Yale Center for British Art, Paul Mellon Collection. (The overlay has at some point been inverted and therefore the top illustration is reproduced upside down.)

Chapter 1

# ON THE ROAD

REPTON SPENT much of his career on the road. Road travel helped to define his profession of landscape gardening: networks of commissions, working practices, theoretical principles, parkland designs. Moreover roads and travel largely shaped Repton's sensibility: in addressing a range of moral and emotional issues through his works, in commissions for clients and his many other published and unpublished writings, Repton expressed his concern with social order, financial probity and domestic stability in and through a career of high mobility. It was not an easy ride. Periods of almost perpetual motion had a pathological effect, as did the period after a carriage accident in 1811 when Repton's career ground to a halt.

In this chapter I examine the significance of roads and travel for Repton's career, and in doing so set out an infrastructure for the other geographies discussed in this book. First I chart some of the main developments in road transportation during Repton's career, considering their implications for the spatial organization of society, the use of land and the perception of landscape. Then I consider the importance of travel, and the culture of travel, for Repton's life and work before he took up landscape gardening. There follows an analysis of the implications of road travel for many facets of Repton's practice and theory, from the costing of commissions to the composition of designs to the formulation of principles. The next section deals with the importance of routeways of all kinds for the configuration of Repton's parkland designs, both inside the property of his clients and at the junction with public highways. The last section focuses on Repton's roadside residence at Hare Street, Essex, and how it provided a vantage point for his social and professional outlook. Each section provides a frame on the acceleration and deceleration of Repton's career, the expansion and contraction of his field of work and vision, including Repton's own narrative of the changing pace and scope of his work.[1]

## Codes of Conduct

The period of Repton's life saw striking advances in systems of road travel, in the construction and maintenance of roads, in vehicle technology and in the organization of transport. Between 1750 and 1811 journey times by the fastest coaches between London and major cities were cut by up to two-thirds. A journey of three-and-a-half days to Leeds was reduced to one, a thirty-six hour journey to Norwich cut to twelve hours. People, goods and information were on the move, at faster speeds, over increasing distances.[2] Those travelling professionally, say to purchase shipments, survey estates, sit at assizes or assess excise duties, were joined on the road by those travelling for pleasure, visiting friends, country houses, county towns, spas, seaside resorts, race meetings and beauty spots. Mobility was a defining feature of polite society.[3] In a period of rising income among the middle and upper classes, travel became move affordable and was

*facing page* Detail of fig. 67.

fully incorporated in the consumer culture of the time. Fashionable magazines carried illustrations of 'carriage dress' to wear for the journey and portable paints to take with you, as well as a range of elegant vehicles in which to make the trip.[4]

Plebeian as well as polite society was on the move. The material transformation of Georgian England was articulated by a variety of population movements, permanent and seasonal, long and short distance, regular and occasional. Harvesters, navvies, gypsies, tramps, beggars, the various 'comers and goers', filled the roads and bridleways. Some four hundred thousand men, about one eighth of the male work-force, were mobilized for the military during the Napoleonic Wars. Barracks, camps, ports and Martello towers were linked by frequent troop movements. The mass demobilization after the wars, during a severe economic depression, swelled the roads with sometimes wounded men desperately seeking employment, sharpening polite fears of vagrancy.[5]

A reformed postal system, with greater speed and security for small packages, accelerated the circulation of information: newspapers, magazines, bills, bank notes, prices, samples, patterns, correspondence of all kinds. By 1791 all major cities were connected; by 1815 most small towns. The mail-coach system symbolized the acceleration of social and commercial life and the formation of a new kind of national space, controlled by a highly centralized, increasingly bureaucratic state and articulated through a network of post towns.[6] It challenged old-fashioned county interests. When a letter to the picturesque theorist and Herefordshire squire Uvedale Price had been delayed after his correspondent had put the county instead of the post town on his address, Price replied:

> Postmasters are neither geographers, nor Topographers, but only Poligraphers (if I may use such a word) of a very confined kind; their business is with post towns only, & when you put a county they are quite disoriented... what a number of oaths the little addition of *shire* has probably occasioned! beginning in the general post office & going on through every post-town in the direct road, & then through every one in the county![7]

London was the hub of the transportation network. With improved gradients, hard, rolled-stone surfaces and abundant inns for changing horses, the road system fanning into south-east England attracted fast traffic. By the end of the eighteenth century, 'an energetic young man, driving himself in a racing phaeton, could make weekend visits within a hundred-mile radius of London'.[8] By the 1820s, forty stage-coaches a day were leaving Brighton for London, and William Cobbett reckoned that stock-brokers were commuting daily for an afternoon's speculation.[9] Escalating land values along the main roads made for a highly cultivated, prosperous looking scenery of manicured fields, ornamented farms, new or refashioned parks and grounds, a moving panorama that seldom failed to amaze visitors from the Continent.[10] The pattern was replicated down the urban hierarchy. Along main roads into provincial cities, smart, metropolitan styles of architecture and landscaping displaced the more vernacular looking work of local builders and gardeners.

Transport improvements were integral to wider transformations of the countryside. Reorganizing the road network was often the first step in parliamentary enclosure. Internal networks of roads, lanes and pathways gave way to a new system of straightened and properly hedged roads that pointed out of the parish, unfolding it to wider networks of market exchange. As John Barrell has pointed out, the reporters of the Board of Agriculture

> almost all show themselves anxious to open out the countryside, by making it more accessible to the traveller, and by making individual villages more obviously part of a national economy. They are all much concerned with mobility, so that one of the most frequent criteria they apply in forming their opinion of an area is the facility with which it can be approached and crossed.

Their field of vision and knowledge, and with it their judgement of what was a pleasing landscape in terms of structure as well as content, was predicated almost entirely on thinking about places in a linear way, as points in a network of roads.[11]

New and improved roads were integral to emparking and landscaping throughout the country. In their capacity as magistrates, landowners were given increased legal powers to control public rights of way. Hundreds, probably thousands, of roads, bridle-ways and footpaths crossing parkland were terminated or diverted.[12] Some landowners took upon themselves the expense of building new sections of turnpike away from their mansions as the first stage in a programme of emparking.[13] It was not necessary to build new roads in order to put more space between the gentry and commonality. Main

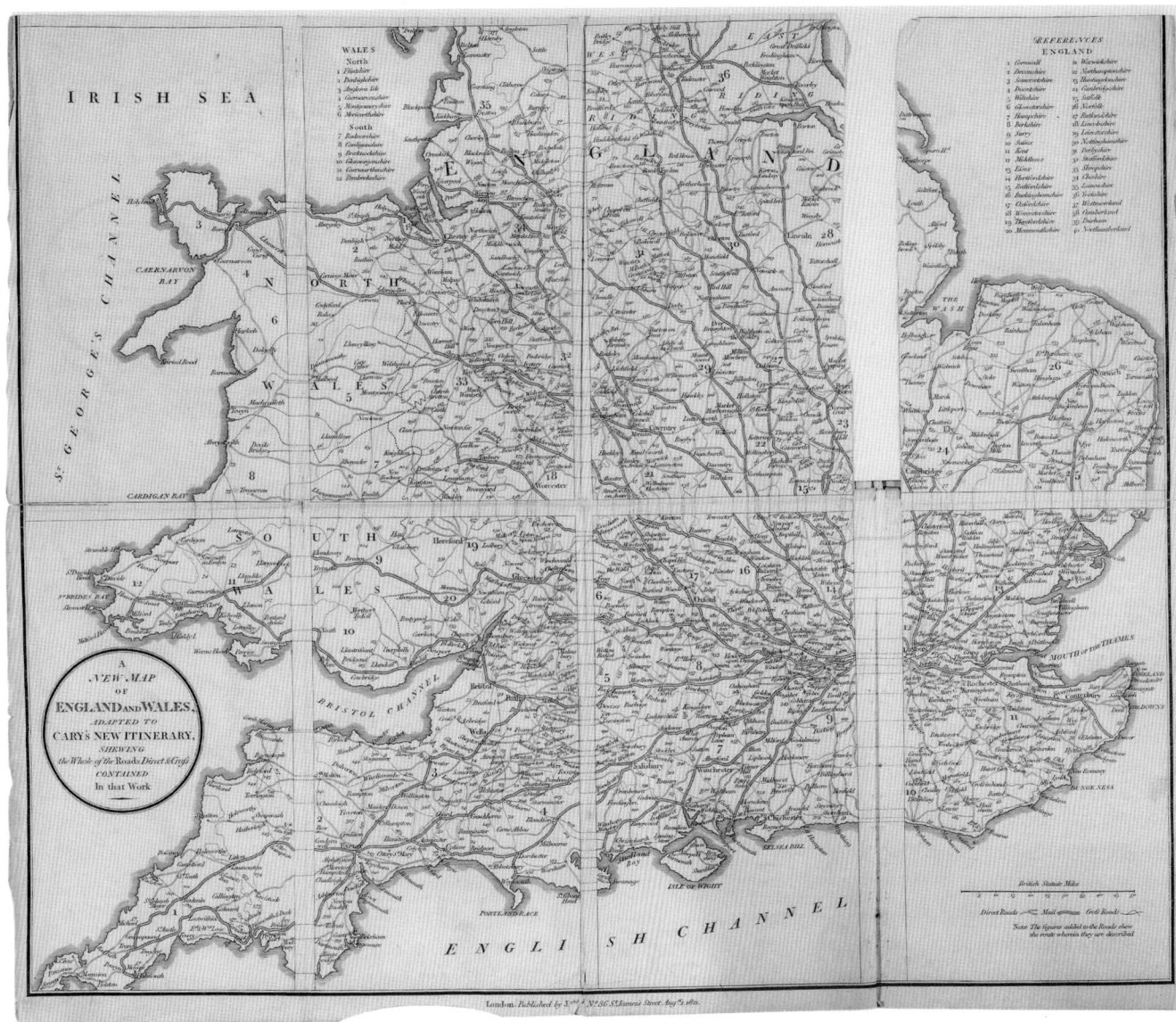

30 *A New Map of England and Wales adapted to Cary's New Itinerary* (1821). University of Nottingham Library.

approaches were resited half a mile or more from estate villages. Grand lodges marked the new approach; the former gates and forecourts from the village were reduced to tradesmen's entrances.[14] New parkland systems of approaches, drives and backroads were constructed; in some landowners redeployed former public thoroughfares, in others they went to enormous trouble to erase them. The smoothly surfaced, private circulation system of the park was connected at the lodge with the nationwide network of polite society.[15]

Landscape tastes reflected the refinement of road travel. As regions such as the Lake District and North Wales were opened up to polite tourism by improved transportation, amateur sketchers and watercolourists with their portable materials and drawing manuals joined professional artists in pursuit of picturesque scenery.[16] The experience, as well as the facility of accelerated travel, influenced landscape tastes. Reviewing the summer watercolour exhibitions of 1810, the *Repository of Arts* was struck by the overwhelming proportion of landscapes: 'In pacing around the rooms the spectator experiences something similar to those of an outside passenger on a mail coach making a picturesque and picturizing journey to the north'.[17]

An extensive travel literature was produced to cater for polite society, not just guidebooks to beauty spots, but publications such as *Cary's New Itinerary [of England and Wales]* (fig. 30), partly sponsored by the Post Office, which gave comprehensive, tabulated information on post roads and rates, stage-coach stops and timetables, and, by its ninth edition in 1821, and with the assistance of the 'intelligent Traveller' and 'Gentlemen of local information', no less than ten thousand gentlemen's seats to be seen near the main roads.[18]

The acceleration of travel, and the availability of an increasing range of options in conveyance, speed and price, provoked comment on the respective virtues of different modes of travel and their attendant experiences. The penetration of metropolitan mores along fast roads was a recurrent issue.[19] Riding on horseback through Surrey, Cobbett claimed that 'Those who travel on turnpike roads know nothing of England – From Hanscombe to Thursley almost the whole way is across fields or commons, or along narrow lanes. Here we see people without disguize or affectation. Against a *great road* things are made for *show*.'[20] This recovery of an earthier, more authentic England is integral to Uvedale Price's discourse of the Picturesque, with its contempt for professional landscaping and affection for local attachment. Price upheld the 'old neglected bye roads and hollow ways' of Herefordshire (a byword for bad roads among roving agricultural reporters) as a paradigm of improvement because they were the product of long-term, piecemeal changes, rutted by carts going to market, bearing the tread of local labourers and livestock. Such densely layered signs of locality were, he noted, erased by the 'smoothing and levelling' he had seen in two lanes bordering pleasure grounds 'within thirty miles of London and in a district full of expensive embellishments'.[21] Walking along country lanes and by-roads acquired a serious moral purpose among those intent on observing the details of God's handiwork or the lives of the poor, which speeding carriage-folk overlooked.[22] Promoters of improved travel such as John Macadam were quick to counter that better surfaced roads created new horizons and strong foundations for a progressive polity; through constant use travellers of all kinds consolidated well constructed roads.[23] How one moved through the landscape, literally 'conducted' oneself, was an important cultural concern. For polite society, landscape was characterized by a number of differing, sometimes conflicting, codes of conduct.[24]

## From Norfolk to Essex

Before taking up landscape gardening as a profession in his mid-thirties, Repton was familiar with the culture of travel, sufficiently so to appreciate its advantages in conditioning his new career. His father's profession as an excise officer took the form of regular circuits around Suffolk and Norfolk with careful observation of the topography and land use of his divisions.[25] He was, in the course of things, alert to changes in parks and gardens. 'I perfectly remember, when I was about ten years old, that my father (a man of such general observation, that no innovation or novelty escaped him) remarked to me the change which was then [about 1760] taking place in ornamental planting', the thinning of avenues to open views into the country.[26] Improvements at the time made Norfolk roads among the best in England, and sharply reduced journey times to London.[27] Upon moving to Norwich, John Repton exploited the opportunity by going in to the travel business as a 'proprietor of stage-coaches and waggons', in which he made his fortune.[28]

'Having determined to make me a rich rather than a learned man', Repton's father sent him to school in The Netherlands to learn a commercially useful language and prepare for a career in 'the exportation of Norwich manufactures'. Repton did a good deal of travelling, noting how 'a Dutch merchant's accounts and his garden were kept with the same degree of accuracy', and how the gardens bordering canals 'were always studied in their effect to the passengers'. He ventured further, to the spas of Belgium, and to the German ports.[29] A later story describes a journey to Hamburg across 'the comfortless and dreary sands of Westphalia' with a package of English prejudices: 'the roads were villainous; the horses rascally; the carriages infamous... the drivers and inn keepers infernal and diabolical'. The travellers sustain their spirits by imagining the opposite: 'the sandy roads became turnpikes; the horses, English hunters; the post waggon, a landau; and the dreary plains a fertile country'.[30]

Upon returning to Norwich, Repton was apprenticed as a textile merchant and set up in business, but severe losses made him decide to retire from trade to a small hamlet in north Norfolk to live on his remaining capital and inheritance as a gentleman amateur, doing a little farming, some sketching and writing. The financial demands of a growing family forced him to go in search

31 *Design for the Frontispiece for the Views in Wales* (c.1783). Colman Collection, Norwich Library. Courtesy Norfolk Libraries and Information Service.

32 *Conway – Drawn in 1783 on My Way from Ireland.* Colman Collection, Norwich Library. Courtesy Norfolk Libraries and Information Service.

33  *The Pump Room, Bath, in the Year 1784 with the Characters of that Day.* Victoria Art Gallery. Bath City Council. Photograph Bridgeman Art Library.

of a new career, initially as a private secretary in Dublin Castle, working for his landlord, William Windham, upon Windham's appointment in 1783 as Secretary to the Lord Lieutenant of Ireland. Windham's abrupt resignation made Repton's 'Irish expedition' a brief one, but he made the best of it in a letter home to his wife: 'I have formed some connexions with the great; I have seen a fine country in passing through Wales, and have made some sketches; I have lost very little money'.[31] The Holyhead–London road through North Wales was a main route for picturesque tourists, and among Repton's sketches is a vignette titled 'Design for the Frontispiece for the Views in Wales' (fig. 31). Nothing came of this venture, but a view from the road of Conway Castle (fig. 32), a shepherd and his flock in the foreground, the mountains of Snowdonia behind, shows a new command of the picturesque style cultivated in views of this region, a fashionable advance on the topographical character of Repton's drawings in Norfolk.[32]

Repton next headed for Bath. Here he did some drolls, whimsical or satirical drawings of the *beau monde* – *The Pump Room, Bath* (fig. 33) echoes Rowlandson's celebrated *Vauxhall Gardens* (1784) – but his main purpose was an ambitious business venture.[33] In 1784 Repton invested most of his remaining capital, and a good deal of thought and energy, in a scheme with the Bath impresario John Palmer to reform the mail-coach system. Palmer had organized special coaches to shuttle his company between theatres in Bath and Bristol; he and Repton developed the principle for the Post Office, with

34 *The Norwich Mail: Sketch for a Transparency* (c.1785). Colman Collection, Norwich Library. Courtesy Norfolk Libraries and Information Service.

toll-free passage, armed guards and cheaper rates for small packages. The trial run from London to Bristol proved so successful that the government immediately put the service in to operation and authorized other routes. Mail coaches were first established on roads to Norfolk and Suffolk in the spring of 1785 and to other major cities by the end of the year.[34] Repton's sketch for a transparency of the Norwich Mail (fig. 34), showing a guard shooting a highwayman who has held up a post-chaise, a scene surmounted by a cameo of George III, probably dates from this period. Palmer was given the credit for the mail-coach scheme, a lucrative appointment as Surveyor and Comptroller General of the Mails and a large lump sum and pension, but Repton received no recompense for his services or the losses he sustained, nor any public recognition.[35] After Repton's death in 1818, Francis Freeling, Secretary of the Post Office, was anxious to obtain from the family his original plans for mail carrying, 'considering them most valuable, as laying the foundation for the future success of that now astonishing source of revenue'.[36]

'Baffled in an enterprise which had promised as much of personal advantage as of public utility', around 1786 Repton moved nearer London to market his talents.[37] Despite his misfortunes he acquired a taste for the high life. Some lines addressed to the actress Sarah Siddons (with whom he had shared a house in Dublin) just before he departed from Sustead lament that winter snows have blocked the roads to London and caused villagers to come to his door with petty

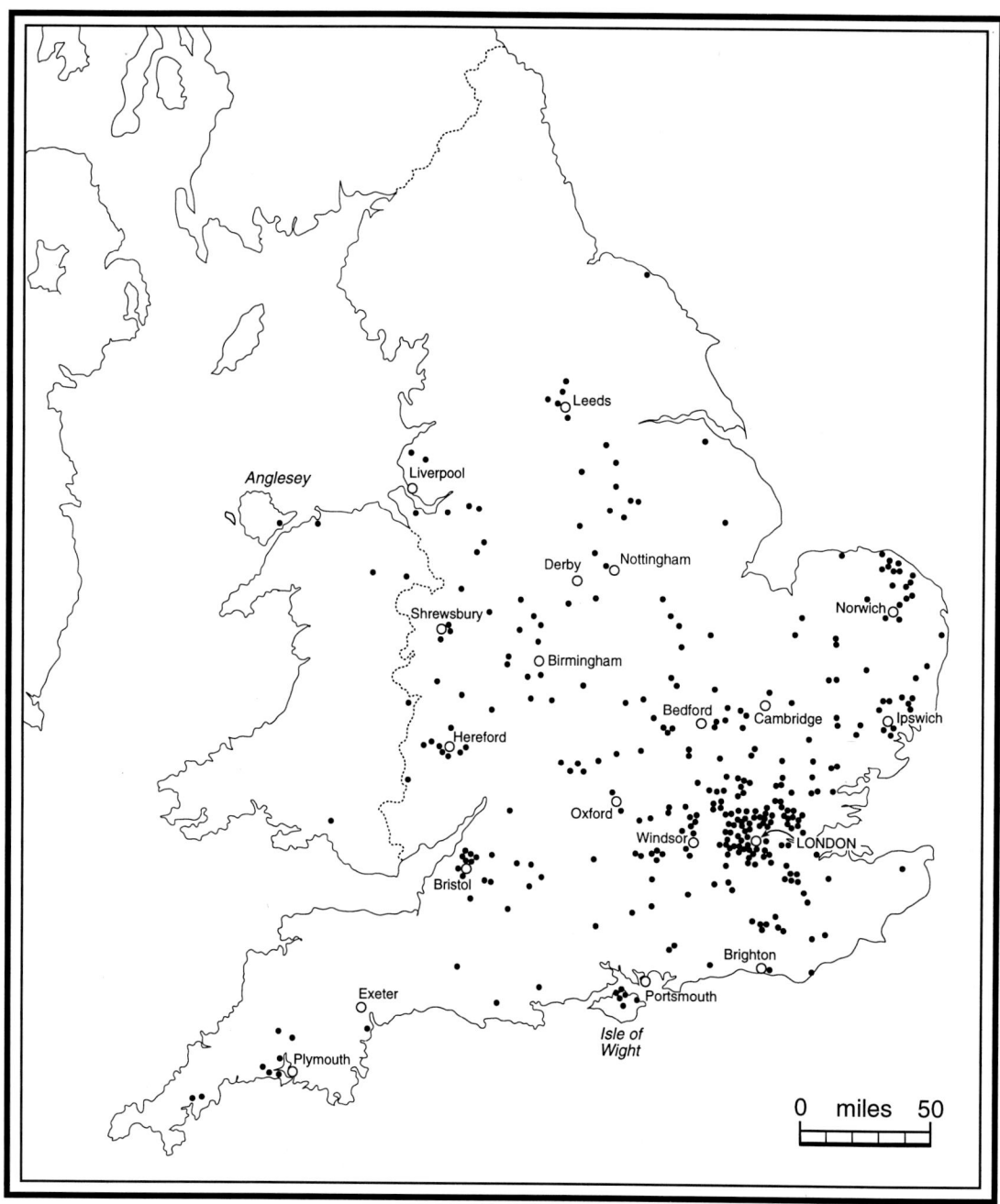

35  Humphry Repton Consultations in England and Wales. From the Gazetteer at the end of this book.

complaints.[38] Repton rented a house in Hare Street, Essex, thirteen miles from London and facing one of the busy highways into Suffolk and Norfolk. First he attempted to make a career writing and drawing for publication. He published a collection of essays, *Variety* (1787), on comical and moral topics drawn from many of the places in which he had sojourned. The anonymous author was an 'ideal character' who attributed to travel his pursuit of variety:

He divides his time betwixt the town and country, seeking Variety in the court and the cottage; yet often finding sameness of bustle in the masquerade or the village fair, and sameness of solitude in the retired coverts of a forest, or the snug corner of booth in a public coffee room.[39]

Repton tried his hand at play writing, a comedy entitled *Odd Whims; Or Two at a Time* in the style of Sheridan, which opens with a scene of highway robbery in Epping Forest and whose plot pivots on a picture left in a carriage. 'Read with pleasure by Burke', Repton recalled, and 'commended by Sir Joshua Reynolds', the play had only a minor, provincial run, staged in Romford, Yarmouth and Aylsham before another, unnamed London celebrity lost the manuscript.[40] Baffled in all these enterprises, and with money fast running out, in 1788 Repton decided to mobilize his 'natural taste for improving the beauties of scenery' and become a professional landscape gardener.[41] In little more than a year, his 'dread of poverty' receded and he found himself 'in a state of ease and comparative affluence'.[42]

*Getting to Work*

Transportation was integral to Repton's working practice; for the movement of the man himself, from job to job, and for the dispatch of papers, plans and correspondence relating to commissions. Apart from the occasional use of a coastal packet, Repton kept to the roads, travelling by stage-coach, post-chaise and hackney carriage, occasionally in the private carriages of clients.[43] Repton can be counted among the artists, surveyors, architects and land agents travelling increasing distances to depict the country and its improvements.[44] The very number of commissions confirms that he was frequently on the move. I have documented three hundred in forty-six counties, and many of these required return visits (fig. 35).[45]

Through his very mobility, Repton refashioned landscape gardening as a profession. His main task on a first visit was to go over the grounds with a client, stake out designs (often using his carriage as a marker), take notes and make sketches on his proposals. He travelled light. His own equipment was highly portable: a sketch pad and pens, a pocket telescope, and sometimes a roll of ribbon for marking out lakes. While a theodolite was one of his earliest purchases, and appeared on his trade card as a totem of his expertise, he soon abandoned precise surveying, and with it the necessity of lugging around this piece of equipment. 'The *eye* to observe and the *hand* to delineate, are always necessary, and will often supersede the use of every instrument.'[46]

Hare Street was a convenient point of departure for Repton's commissions in East Anglia, many within a day's ride of his home. In the first year of his career, when he was undertaking political campaigning for the Whig interest in Norfolk, Repton rarely ventured far from the eastern counties. This changed with the patronage, secured through his political work, of the duke of Portland. From 1789 he made an annual, week-long visit to Portland's estate at Welbeck in Nottinghamshire, receiving a salary of one hundred guineas. As well as breaking into the charmed circle of aristocratic society, this established a base for commissions in the East Midlands and Yorkshire. Still more important was Repton's entrée to Portland's grand town house, Burlington House in Piccadilly, and his out-of-town estate at Bulstrode, Buckinghamshire, in the prestigious zone around Windsor.[47] Repton extended his practice by targeting the seats of other political grandees and using them as a base for commissions locally as well as securing clients among allies from further afield. In September 1790 he was consulted at Wentworth Woodhouse, Yorkshire, the seat of Earl Fitzwilliam and the base of the Rockingham Whigs. In 1791 he planted his practice in Cheshire by securing the patronage of the Whig hostess Franceis Ann Crewe. The *rapprochement* between the conservative Portland Whigs and William Pitt's Tory administration worked to Repton's advantage. Pitt's patronage helped to extend his field of work the length of England. Shortly after a commission at Pitt's seat at Holwood in Kent in 1791, Repton travelled to Lord Mulgrave's seat near Whitby and a cluster of Tory commissions in Cornwall, notably one for Pitt's political agent, Reginald Pole Carew.[48]

Repton's own distaste for party factionalism, and his attempt to fashion an art to promote the more private virtues of polite society, such as domesticity, benevolence, professionalism and political consensus, gave him an entrée, he assumed, into the houses and the company of the élite. This took him to various social venues in London: assemblies, theatres, concerts, levees and the law courts. Repton frequented other urban centres where the alliances of polite society were brokered, and new professional opportunities arose: commercial cities, county towns, resort towns. From 1795 Repton took a winter residence in Bath, ostensibly to relax from the pressures of work, but also to make new contacts and establish a bridgehead to the west of England.[49]

The road system functioned not just to get Repton to and from the many places where polite society gathered but to establish a framework and foundation for his art. Once the various sites, in various regions, had been secured, Repton could plan his travels to consolidate his clientele, shuttling between properties of various sizes and situations, patrons of various interests and occupations. He would pay due regard to local conditions, the lay of the land, the demands of his clients, but co-ordinate them within a systematic, theoretical framework. His publications, drawing on commissions from throughout the country, were intended to establish the principles of his practice.

Repton soon realized the limitations of such a vision, not least because powerful interests of polite society entertained different ideas of social progress and cohesion. He failed to secure the full set of grand patrons that he needed, and, in any case, political factionalism increased with the prosecution of the war. While Repton attempted to work for neighbouring landowners, he often found them rivals, and his designs for adjacent properties are rarely complementary. There were large towns and cities around which Repton had little or no work, and extensive regions, notably in the north of England.

36   Extract from a letter from Humphry Repton to George John Legh, 26 September 1797. John Rylands Library. University of Manchester.

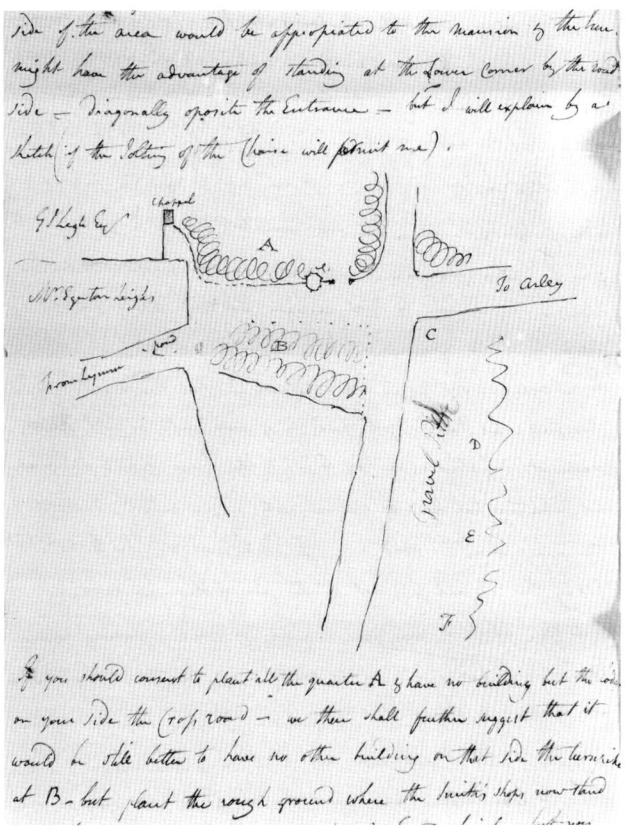

It would, of course, have been impossible for Repton, on his own, to extend his practice the length and breadth of the country; the travel costs alone were prohibitive. He searched for more efficient, and prestigious, ways of diffusing his influence, with publications, partnerships and royal patronage. Repton's initial success and foray in to publication provoked the rivalry of both connoisseurs and professionals, who attempted to mobilize resistance to his practice in some regions as well as in the pages of books and reviews. Repton's collaborations with professional architects promoted his career only occasionally, and his partnership with John Nash ended, at least on Repton's part, in bitter recriminations. In 1800 Repton took on his own architect son John Adey, but while this partnership changed the style of Repton's landscape gardening, it did not sustain its success. Repton landed the slipperiest of royal patrons, the Prince of Wales, as a client, and lost the commission at the Royal Pavilion in Brighton to Nash. Never, to his lasting regret, did Repton secure the patronage of the king. With the commercial and social changes of the war years, including the accelerated movement of people and capital, Repton's networks of custom began to unravel. He was forced with advancing age and infirmity to keep travelling to sustain his career, or rather to pick up work where he could to remain solvent, and in doing so he ran in to as many problems as he overcame.

In the earlier years of his career Repton covered great distances. Take the summer of 1792: in May he was in Bedfordshire, June in Herefordshire, August and September in Yorkshire, September near Birmingham, early October in Essex, later that month in Cornwall.[50] From September to October alone he crossed the country from Mulgrave Castle on the North Yorkshire coast to Mount Edgcumbe on Plymouth Sound. In a letter to William Windham of 1790 written in his post-chaise, 'my usual desk,' on his way to a commission in Highgate, Repton declared he had not travelled less than five or six hundred miles a month during the whole of that year.[51] By 1794 Repton was travelling much of the year, leaving little time to prepare finished plans at home: 'it is only in the winter that I can ever hope to enjoy that part of my profession which is by far the most pleasant to me – tho not the most useful to myself or others – viz – making drawings by my own fireside'.[52] He was away for weeks at a time, returning home for just a day or two to deal with correspondence. 'Your letter just shot me flying', he told a Herefordshire client, John Geers Cotterell, in 1791, 'I came from Cheshire only yesterday

& am going tomorrow into Hertfordshire – but in consequence of your letter I shall pass thru Town – that I may call on Mr [James] Wyatt [the architect] and you'.[53] 'My misfortune is to spend half my life in my post chaise', he told an old friend, 'therefore the Postmark is the only criterion of the place near which my letters are written'.[54]

Repton worked while travelling, drafting plans as well as writing letters. 'On the road northwards' for five weeks in 1793, he took the manuscript of *Sketches and Hints*, his first publication on landscape gardening, and the Red Books to be finished for two Cornish commissions.[55] His open *Letter to Uvedale Price* of 1794 'was written, at various opportunities, during my journey into Derbyshire' and finished at Matlock Bath.[56] A long letter of 1797 to a client, George John Legh, who had suddenly left his seat in Cheshire to join his regiment near Newcastle upon Tyne, was started on leaving Legh's house and finished near Daventry, in Northamptonshire, almost one hundred miles further on. Describing one feature, Repton decided to 'explain by a sketch (if the Jolting of the chaise will permit it)' (fig. 36).[57] His son John Adey may have been too meticulous a draughtsman to make sketches in transit. Repton told a client in 1809 that they had 'laid bye on the road' to do some drawings.[58]

Repton rarely travelled purely for pleasure. Riding through Kent in July 1810, Joseph Farington noted 'Repton's indifference abt. seeing places where he was not employed. At Summer Hill it was proposed to him to walk abt. the grounds, which he declined, saying "He had seen fine places enough, & after all was best contented with his own situation which was by the road side" (fig. 37).'[59] On social visits Repton exploited the professional opportunity. Uvedale Price (always hostile to Repton's commercial ways) reported the experience of a Mr Palmer: 'having some music at his house in the evening, & Repton being in the neighbourhood, he invited him: the next morning as they walked about the place he made a few remarks, for which he sent him a charge of five guineas'.[60] The farthest Repton ventured 'to see any object to which I was not called by my profession' was a week's excursion in August 1800 with two of his sons to the Lake District, a trip undertaken from a professional engagement at Harewood House in Yorkshire. Repton's Lakes excursion is notable for its disappointment. He felt 'much less pleasure . . . than do the thousands who annually seek [the Lakes] in the same track'. The place overwhelmed him, not just the scenery, 'the

37 After Humphry Repton, *The Entrance of Somerhill, Kent – Seat of W. Woodgate Esq.*, *Peacock's Polite Repository* (1811). Private collection.

vast Lakes and their mountainous accompaniments of Nature had the effect of making me feel how little were the humble attempts of my art – which had so often been extolled – and I felt regret that Nature and art were at such an immeasurable distance'. 'Sublimity was a little mixt with terror' that dry summer: a 'sullen and morose' gardener rowing them to the island on Windermere told them that his two children had been drowned the previous day, venturing out of their driedout bathing places along the shore of Lake Windermere; a maddened bull killed one man at Ambleside, another charged Repton on the shores of Ullswater, forcing Repton to scramble up a rock face to safety and reappearing to pursue him in his dreams.[61]

Repton's standard charge of five guineas a day and expenses was revised according to the distance he travelled. Letters from 1807 record rates of ten guineas for a first visit to within one stage of London, fifty guineas for up to 100 miles, seventy up to 140 miles and so on in proportion.[62] (This was broadly consistent with terms for travel charged by the architects he worked with, such as James Wyatt and William Wilkins.[63]) Repton charged return visits at half these rates, although he would make a return visit only if he were going to a new commission *en route*.[64] Norfolk clients also enjoyed a fifty per cent discount (twenty-five rather than fifty guineas), for that was his home county to which he travelled frequently to visit family and friends.[65] Repton gave discounts to some personal friends but, writing to one in 1808, when commissions were hard to come by, he was concerned about the 'consistency of my terms to others in your neighbourhood'.[66] The inflation and taxation of the war years put enormous pressure on Repton's costing and on his gentlemanly practice of rounding down, or occasionally charging as the crow flies rather than by actual road mileage.[67]

Travel may have become easier from the later eighteenth century, but landscape artists of all sorts found it a high, sometimes crippling expense.[68] When commissions were buoyant in his early years, when he was covering 500–600 miles a month, Repton was still desperate to claim outstanding travel expenses to find ready money for more.[69] In later years, when his dread of poverty returned, Repton thought carefully about long trips. Writing from Woburn in April 1809, he told his son

> whether I go farther North or not is of little consequence if I can't get more than for a concern near home – tis not worth going 150 miles. Poor Dargue my hackney man (for whose Chaise I am now waiting) – thought he had a profitable black job to take a dead Lord to Ireland to be buried – but on his way home, he tumbled over a pail on board ship – broke his shin – and got no advice & became a corpse himself when he landed in England – so much for long jobs.[70]

As Repton's clientele among the middling gentry and professions declined, so aristocratic commissions stood out more prominently as nodal centres of his network. In November 1812 Repton returned from a thirty-two day journey in the West Country, travelling 466 miles, spending seventy pounds but earning three times that, much of it from his week-long visit to Longleat.[71] In June 1814 he went west again, for a plum job of two hundred guineas for the duke of Bedford at Endsleigh, Devon, also '30 guineas for a day near Bristol en passant'; this for an outlay of sixty guineas.[72] There were risks in overextending his trips. On one to the West Country in 1809 he lost a commission from Lord Ducie in Gloucestershire by deciding at Exeter to press on to west Cornwall for another for Lord Falmouth at Tregothnan, 'such is the danger of deviation from a route once fixed'.[73] On the other hand, Repton could be too inflexible. Rather than proceed straight to Brighton when summoned by the Prince of Wales in 1805, Repton conscientiously kept to his itinerary, and risked losing the commission.[74]

The mail-coach system that Repton himself designed was central to his practice. He found it a swift, secure way of sending letters, circulars and plans.[75] It also proved an increasingly expensive one, as the government increased prices sharply to raise revenue for the war. Like other professional men, Repton took advantage of the franking privileges of his many clients who were public servants or Members of Parliament.[76] In 1801 Repton wrote to Francis Freeling, Secretary of the Post Office, begging a favour considering his service, of sending out between two hundred and three hundred circular letters free of charge; Freeling agreed to send ten or twelve a day.[77] Much of Repton's work was conducted by correspondence, setting up site visits with clients or meetings with collaborators such as architects or clerks of works, sometimes at short notice. When Repton was compiling his memoirs he noted that half the contents of clients' pigeon-holes in his office consisted of letters making appointments, 'for it is almost incredible how much of my time has been occupied in fixing the routes of my visits!'[78] Repton used the mail to solicit new patrons, even among those renowned for their own improvements. 'It is impossible not to be flattered with an offer to contribute the Ornament of my place from an Artist of your Eminence and Celebrity', replied William Beckford to Repton's letter of 1799, 'but Nature has been liberal to Fonthill, and some Embellishment it has received from Art, has fortunately gained so much the Approbation of my friends that my Partiality to it in its present state will not perhaps be thought altogether inexcusable'.[79]

Repton's surviving correspondence with one client, George Freke Evans of Laxton, Northamptonshire, fifty letters over two years, reveals how commissions could involve complex networks of information. Repton informed Freke Evans about timber prices at King's Lynn during the blockade, the price of fencing wire in Chelsea, a cheap machine in Cambridge invented by a student for turning mouldings, and the news that it was cheaper to employ exiled French artists to decorate walls than to hang paper.[80] 'I stop my chaise while I write this answer to put in the post on my way thru London to Chiswick', Repton replied to yet another demand for information.[81] In the case of this commission, Repton must have wondered whether the mail created more difficulties than it resolved. He and his son were, he said, 'frequently at a distance from home & cannot carry the detail of every different concern sufficiently in our memory to answer every question immediately'.[82] The correspondence became increasingly acrimonious and, in the end, Repton was never paid for his work.

Through Repton's correspondence we can discern the family nature of his business and the role of travel in defining Repton's domestic arrangements. Repton's wife, Mary, provided the 'hidden investment' characteristic of

38 Mary Dorothy Repton, *Floral Arrangement* (n.d.). Colman Collection, Norwich Library. Courtesy Norfolk Libraries and Information Service.

small businesses of the time, the bearing and raising of future partners, the provision of physical and moral support systems, as well as various secretarial tasks.[83] One of her main jobs was to forward letters to clients' houses or to post offices *en route*.[84] There were duties when her husband was home in the winter months. 'My dear H. has been at home this last fortnight, hard at work drawing and making Books and we are kept in constant employment of reading to him', runs a letter to her son William.[85] Visits to relations in Norfolk, and the winter residence in Bath, seem to have been the limit of Mary Repton's travels. As far as I know, she never accompanied her husband on his professional engagements, even the week-long, half-social visits to aristocratic mansions, and Repton's holiday excursion to the Lake District was undertaken with his sons. From 1797 Repton took his second son, Humphry, out of school at Eton to travel with him, 'in the expectation of forming him for my own profession'.[86] The boy preferred a sedentary, clerical job in Whitehall (courtesy of Pitt), and Repton turned to his first son, the architect John Adey. After the partnership was formalized in 1800, father and son made most subsequent journeys together. In his later infirm years, Repton's daughter Mary, an accomplished watercolourist (figs 38 and 39), both assisted her father in his designs and accompanied him on his travels as a nurse.[87]

### The Pathology of Travel

Repton reckoned that for twenty years he seldom travelled less than four thousand miles a year.[88] From about 1808 his career contracted dramatically (fig. 40). Now in his fifties, he was still striking out fair distances but in pursuit of fewer commissions, moreover in wintry conditions, which had once not much bothered him. Going into Gloucestershire in January 1809, he endured 'the

*Penshurst in Kent — drawn by Mary Repton 1800*

39 *above* Mary Dorothy Repton, *Penshurst* (1800). Colman Collection, Norwich Library. Courtesy Norfolk Libraries and Information Service.

40 *right* Humphry Repton, New Consultations 1788–1818. These figures are based on exactly datable first visits. The loss of Account Books from 1791 on means that some consultations for later years are missing, but the graph does accurately plot the course of Repton's career.

41 *facing page* Uppark from the south, from the Red Book for Uppark (1810). Private collection. National Trust Photographic Library / John Hammond.

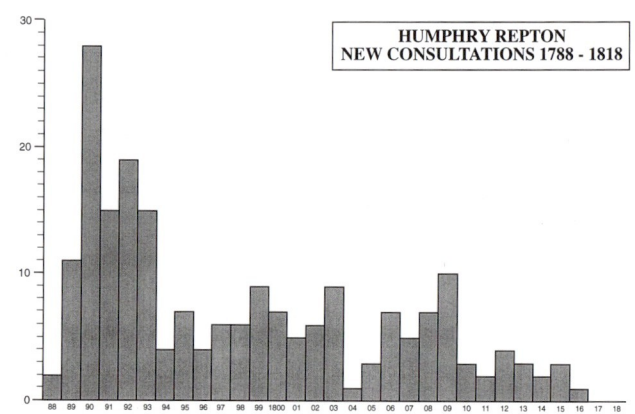

HUMPHRY REPTON
NEW CONSULTATIONS 1788 - 1818

coldest and worst journey I have ever performed'.[89] The coach almost capsized, and Repton was deposited that night in 'the coldest and dirtiest inn in Gloucestershire'.[90] In January 1811 Repton suffered a serious carriage accident, not on a distant commission but returning home with his daughters from a ball six miles away. The vehicle overturned on icy roads, and Repton suffered a spinal injury from which he never fully recovered. His heart was affected and he suffered increasingly frequent and painful attacks of angina pectoris.[91] By 1814 he was in a wheelchair. 'I can bear a journey & look at a landscape from a chaise window – but I can neither stand 5 minutes nor walk 5 yards uphill.'[92] The duke of Bedford's auditor arranged for Repton to be carried around steeply sloping Endsleigh in Devon, and he was pushed around London and Bath, but suffered the indignity: 'I that used to travel 5 thousand miles in a year', he told Sir Harry Fetherstonehaugh, 'now cannot move fifty without prudence telling me I should be satisfied with former journeys – so I will stay at home and write when tired of reading'. Repton could no longer reach Fetherstonehaugh's seat at Uppark on the Sussex Downs (fig. 41) 'as my Locomotive joys seem to be stop'd for a while if not for ever... would that I could be transported in a balloon – or by a Wishing Cap – to the summit of the hills of Uppark sans fear – sans torture & sans post horses or post chaises'.[93]

In later years Repton looked back on the first busy decade of his career as a period when he formed strong attachments through his travels, doing the rounds, monitoring improvements that all too often fell in to decline after the turn of the century, when commissions were fewer and less frequent:

After visiting a place for several years in succession and becoming greatly attached to its inhabitants by witnessing domestic happiness which promised to be lasting – I have sometimes not returned to the same spot till the lapse of 10, 15 or 20 years – Alas! too fatally marked by painful changes. The former scenes of happiness too often were flown... The house pulled down or its inhabitants removed or little children grown up – and the fond wife and mother replaced by a new mistress...

The 'slow progress of events' was imperceptible, 'no vast nor sudden change', but with the destruction of life's 'binding links' (and Repton saw himself as such a link), 'Then we at once the work of Time survey,/And in an instant see a life's decay'. 'The larger my circle of acquaintance, the more was I exposed to this common calamity'.[94]

From the outbreak of war with France in 1793, Repton was anxious for his profession. 'Though war makes the scenery of Antony more lively', he told a client whose park overlooked the fleet in Plymouth Sound, 'yet it is almost as bad for me as fogs and snows.'[95] In the first years of the nineteenth century, Repton 'trembled for the safety of old England', not just because of the threat of invasion but because the combined forces of taxation and speculation threatened to destabilize the country from within.[96] 'In France they're all beggars, marauders and robbers,/In England Directors, Contractors, Stock-Jobbers'.[97] In 1804 Repton published an allegory, an addendum to an old essay 'On Happiness', which takes the form of a journey in a dream. A figure, a version of Bunyan's pilgrim, is shown a 'View of Life' (fig. 42) by his guide, 'my conductor'. Before him lies 'a vast extensive plain . . . intersected by many roads, but all seemed to tend towards an object . . . the *Mountain of Calamity*'. Around it are a gaudy modern villa, a coastal city half obscured by a plume of smoke, perhaps, Repton thinks, the smoke of battle.[98] Repton saw wartime conditions, 'the late frequency of living in camps, or at watering places', as creating a taste for temporary-looking buildings and short-term, speculative improvements.[99] He pronounced the kind of patriotic touring in which he had situated his profession to be in terminal decline:

> It was, formerly, one of the pleasures of life to make tours of picturesque inquiry; and to visit the improvements in different parts of the kingdom: this is now changed to the residence at a watering place, where the dissipation of town life is cultivated in a continual round of idle, heartless society; without that home which formerly endeared the life of a family in the country.[100]

The lure of property, or its improvement, had not diminished, but estates were, he reckoned, now regarded as purely private resources and financial investments.

> It has frequently been observed, 'that England would, in time, become the garden of Europe, by the continual increase in number and extent if its improved places': but the improvement of individual places has rather injured than benefited the traveller, because all view is totally excluded from the highways by the lofty fences and thick belts with which the improver shuts himself up in his own improvement.[101]

Commissions were becoming brief and mercenary, often for just the day at sites around the capital to stake out a field for a villa and grounds. 'I return to my hotel in London . . . sit over my solitary dinner and compare the society I have left with that I used to keep.'[102]

Even at his busiest, Repton never managed to secure a stable network of clients. 'The Judge has his Circuit and the Physician his circle of patients,' he noted, but

> I flew from Cornwall to Cumberland – or to Kent – and from Hampshire to Derbyshire – and found no rest for the soles of my feet – I had an appointment to meet [client] No 22 at his place in Suffolk! and when wither a mile of his house where I had engaged to spend 4 days, I met him in his carriage posting to London for advice about his health! . . . *My* advice was no longer required about his place! . . . his name bears a place in my memory as one of the passing dreams, that left but a few moments of regret on waking.[103]

Rushing from place to place, chasing work, Repton began to suffer stress, a sort of travel sickness, 'alarming symptoms of nervous giddiness'. Faced with patients suffering from 'too much attention to business', Repton's physician said he usually prescribed 'a journey and visiting new scenes to amuse the mind, but yours proceeds from having already taken *too much* of that remedy . . . you require rest and some total change of habits'; this included winter walks in which 'you must not think about the surrounding scenery' and summer fishing in which he had to 'patiently watch the motion of the cork . . . on the surface of the water'.[104]

Repton never secured the two thresholds that would have raised his professional status sufficiently to make his travels easier, esteem for his architecture (in partnership with his son) and the king's patronage.[105] It is worth comparing Repton's conduct with that of someone who did secure them, James Wyatt. Wyatt was notoriously dilatory in his dealings with clients, failing to show up for appointments, as when working with Repton at Corsham and Culford.[106] Repton half envied Wyatt's relaxed ways, his casual attitude to forwarded correspondence: 'my time is agreeably spent here', Repton recalled him saying, 'and these letters would call me to other places'. Without the pressure of rushing from place to place, Wyatt relished travel. After Wyatt's death in a

42  *A View of Life and the Mountain of Calamity*, from 'Thoughts on Happiness' in *Odd Whims and Miscellanies* (1804). Private collection.

carriage accident in 1813, one of his nephews told Repton that he had 'often expressed a wish, so to make an exit from the world'.[107]

### Travel and Texts

Travel shaped Repton's books on landscape gardening, particularly his attempt to convert his practice in to principles. *Sketches and Hints on Landscape Gardening* (1795) sought to 'establish fixed principles in the art of laying out ground':

> a complete system...classed under *general rules*...but, though daily experience convinces me that such rules do actually exist, yet I have found so much variety in their application, and so much difficulty in selecting proper examples without greatly increasing the number of expensive plates, that I have preferred this mode of publishing a volume of HINTS and SKETCHES.[108]

Repton spent many hours over many months checking proofs of the engravings at the Gallery, which not only delayed publication but, as he complained to Boydell, kept him from more profitable employment on the road.[109] We learn as much from Farington, whose own drawings, many of country seats, were being engraved by the same engraver, J.C. Stadler, for Boydell's volume of views of Thameside scenery.[110] William Combe, who wrote the text for Farington's book, edited Repton's for publication.[111] Repton envisaged *Sketches and Hints* as a work, partly in the same genre as Farington's, a tour of sites, but with a finish to the sixteen plates, and a shape to the volume (an oblong quarto) that made it resemble a Red Book. Twenty-five commissions in forty counties are cited, but only a few parks are shown, and more than a quarter of the plates (fig. 43) are from the Red Books for Welbeck, 'the ground-work of the present volume'.[112] Even without the pre-emptive attack by Knight and Price, which prompted Repton to add substantially to the volume to reply, *Sketches and Hints* might have proved

43 *View of the Lake and some of the Oaks at Welbeck*, without overlay, from *Sketches and Hints on the Theory and Practice of Landscape Gardening* (1795). Yale Center for British Art, Paul Mellon Collection.

44  *Design for a Conduit Proposed at Ashridge, with a Distant View of the Rosary and Monks Garden*, from *Fragments on the Theory and Practice of Landscape Gardening* (1816). Yale Center for British Art, Paul Mellon Collection.

a commercial failure. Many subscribers were clients who already had their Red Books and probably had no wish to look at examples of others; a number failed to collect their copies, and Repton was left to settle the bill with Boydell.[113]

Repton's second book, *Observations on the Theory and Practice of Landscape Gardening* (1803), was 'printed under a different form and title . . . because I am less ambitious of publishing a book of beautiful prints than a book of precepts'. *Observations* was to yield 'general knowledge' by 'an extensive range of observation'.[114] Readers expecting a treatise such as Thomas Whately's influential *Observations on Modern Gardening* (1770), a highly general theorization of the Brown style, with a few choice examples, were dismayed. The *Monthly Review* noted 'the defect of fundamental rules of order': 'many excellent examples, selected from [Repton's] extensive practice: but unfortunately they lose much of their value under the miscellaneous form in which they are presented'.[115] Much of the text consists of extracts from the Red Books. The Red Books themselves were now organized more in terms of general principles, but the overall impression was still of a gazetteer, observations in the itinerant style of Gilpin's guidebooks.[116] In the advertizement Repton anticipated criticism:

> the author can plead in excuse, that the whole has been written in a carriage during his professional journeys from one place to another, and being seldom more than three days in the same place, the difficulty of producing this Volume, such as it is, can hardly be conceived by those who enjoy the blessings of stationary retirement, or a permanent home.[117]

On the other hand, the very point of *Observations*, announced by the list of sites and clients at the beginning, is to demonstrate to readers, among them potential clients, the range of the author's work: 'My opinion has been diffused over the kingdom in nearly two hundred volumes'. The text draws on more than one hundred commissions scattered in forty counties and includes observations on improvements by others, from well-known gardens such as the Leosowes to the dry docks at Liverpool and Hull.[118]

The commissions quoted from in *Observations* display the geographical scope of Repton's work, from North Wales to Scotland, from Plas Newyd on Anglesea to Valleyfield in Fife. Fife was actually well beyond Repton's field of operations, and Repton acknowledged that he had never seen Valleyfield himself, but had sent two sons to survey the site and based his designs on their drawings

45  *A Ferry Boat of Novel Construction*, from *Observations on the Theory and Practice of Landscape Gardening* (1803). Yale Center for British Art, Paul Mellon Collection.

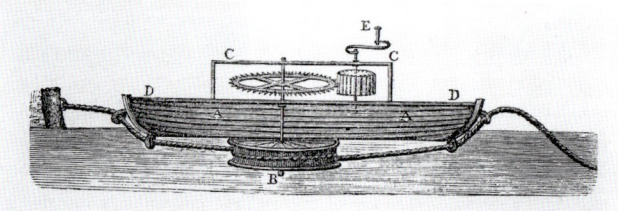

46  Approach, with and without overlay, from the Red Book for Thoresby (1791). Private collection.

and report (fig. 143). Scotland needed improvement: landscaping was poorly developed, 'introduced only by those imitators of Mr. Brown's manner, who had travelled to the north'.[119] Predictably this passage outraged the young Scot, John Claudius Loudon, who was compiling his own treatise of *Observations* and a consciously British, rather than English, vision of improvement. Loudon accused Repton of wrecking a 'dell of the most exquisite kind' at Valleyfield and called on his countrymen to 'never again admit such a formidable foe'.[120] Repton's own travels into the Marches and North Wales along the Holyhead road were highly strategic, intended to challenge the authority of his adversaries Price and Knight in the Welsh border country.[121]

Repton's last treatise, *Fragments on the Theory and Practice of Landscape Gardening* (1816), was conditioned by his immobility, by his consciousness of confinement at Hare Street while even the hereditary gentleman abandoned 'the venerable home of his ancestors' for 'a continual round of idle, heartless society' in 'camps, lodgings or watering places'.[122] The text focuses on less than forty of more than four hundred reports, from his career-long involvement at Cobham to brief consultations at 'villas daily springing up', and uses them to frame general pronouncements on the condition of the country as a whole.[123] *Fragments* is, as the Gothic title suggests, both a tale of cultural disintegration, combining a foreboding about inheritance with an oppressive sense of enclosure, and a treatise on cultural revival, showing how landscape gardening might be reconstructed through an antiquarian focus on buildings and pleasure grounds.[124] Thus the design for a lodge at Aspley on the Woburn estate (fig. 175) is a period-piece 'from the reign of Henry VI to that of Henry VIII', assembled from 'the most perfect fragments of the kind [timber-frame buildings], some of which have been destroyed'.[125] The research, including field observation, for such buildings could be extensive – that undertaken by John Adey Repton for Aspley lodge gathered details from fifteen, mainly East Anglian, sites – but it represented a journey into the past.[126]

*Landscapes of Transit*

Movement, by foot, horseback or carriage, and with it a shifting field of vision, was already a defining feature of English parks and pleasure grounds, whether in highly programmed circuits, or in freer range walks and rides. What distinguishes Repton's designs is the prominence he gave to routeways, to their exact traffic, direction, position, size, shape, construction and management, to their precise role in articulating the landscape, both in views from roads or pathways and views that incorporate them. Repton was impatient with drives or paths that ran around the grounds with no apparent purpose, but he never took a severely utilitarian view of routeways or vehicles. Loudon ridiculed the design of a ferry boat at Holkham (fig. 45), fitted with a cemented gravel deck and two handrails, to 'become a moveable part of the gravel walk': 'It is of a piece with the rest of Mr.

47  Plan of approach and drives, from the Red Book for Blaise Castle (1796). Bristol Museum and Art Gallery.

48  View of the approach, from the Red Book for Blaise Castle (1796). Bristol Museum and Art Gallery.

Repton's improvements. They tend to prettyness, which like *puns* in conversation, may produce momentary amusement'.[127]

Repton had not 'the same horror of seeing a road thro' a park which is so generally expressed'.[128] He set his designs against such examples of concealment as sinking roads in hedge-lined ditches or covering them with moss or verdure. In the one case there was a need for signposts within yards of the house at places 'where several roads are brought together (like the streets at Seven Dials)'; in the other:

> in a dusky evening, after wandering about the park in search of a road, we suddenly find ourselves upon

grass, at the door of the mansion, without any appearance of mortals having before approached its solitary entrance ... A gravel road when it gracefully follows the natural shapes of the ground is one of the most pleasing circumstances in a good landscape, indeed many pictures which are not enriched by buildings of some kind or other would be very defective in their composition and colouring if a road could not be introduced ... nothing is more beautiful than the distant glimpse of a road winding up a hill, and nothing more disgusting than the same degree of curvature undulating without reason across a plain.[129]

At Thoresby he encountered 'this strange fashion which prevails in Nottinghamshire of leaving a Mansion on Grass without any road to the door', and proposed a gravelled approach to correct it (fig. 46).[130] At nearby Babworth he advised abandoning a plan to create a 'grass road thirty feet wide' on which 'the wheels of carriages will make a zigzag track' and replacing it with 'a line of gravel of proper breadth and justifiable curvature'.[131] Well-made, well-positioned roads were guides to the landscape.

> Some few men of taste, or inquisitive travellers, hunt for beauties in every direction, but the many are heedless observers, and to such everything is lost that is not too obviously presented to be overlooked; it is for this reason that peculiar care is requisite in giving the direction of every road or walk, that we may compel the most careless to observe those parts of a design, which have a claim upon their admiration.[132]

Repton designed parkland drives to enhance a shifting field of vision. Temples terminating avenues and obelisks in glades, he said, 'artificially obtruded' on the traveller's gaze; Repton wished to give the eye 'the supposed liberty of making its own choice', composing and re-composing landscapes as it moved along.[133] In most of Repton's drives there were halts, often sheltered ones, for set piece vistas; and some long circuits, like those at Bulstrode and Shardeloes, incorporated many and various views, from farmyards to towns, to form guided tours of the estate.[134] In other places, the experience of travel conditioned scenic perceptions. At Blaise Castle, outside Bristol, Repton designed an approach and drive with switchback bends across a deep ravine (fig. 47):

> It may perhaps be urged that I have made a road where nature never intended the foot of man to tread, much

49   *General View of Sheringham Bower*, detail, without overlay, from *Fragments on the Theory and Practice of Landscape Gardening* (1816). Yale Center for British Art, Paul Mellon Collection.

less that he should be conveyed in vehicles of modern luxury, but where Man resides, Nature must be conquered by Art . . . I cannot describe those numberless beauties which may be brought before the eye in succession by the windings of a road, or the contrast of ascending and descending thro' a deep ravine of rich hanging woods.

One of the halts on the drive at Blaise took in a view of fellow tourists (fig. 48), 'a winding valley of wood and rock terminated by a smooth hill, and this enlivened by frequent groups of carriages and company who visit the spot'.[135] Many drives are designed to create sudden bursts of scenery, upon emerging from tunnels or bends. Repton's approaches follow a standard formula, passing a variety of scenes before a sharp bend suddenly reveals the first view of the house (fig. 49).[136]

Repton's routeways were not just for carriages. He paid as much attention to the design and management of walks. Those in the woods at Ferney Hall were 'neat and trim as a lady's satin shoes may require'.[137] In his later, infirm years, he designed routeways for invalids (fig. 50).

> The loss of locomotion may be supplied by the Bath chair with wheels; but, if these are to grind along a gravel walk, the shaking and rattling become intolerable to an invalid, and therefore, glades of fine mown turf, or broad verges of grass, should be provided . . . and such grass communication should be made, as to increase the interest of the scenery by varying its features . . . flowing among shrubs, sometimes under trees . . . and sometimes in one ample green mall, or terrace, commanding a distant prospect.[138]

In later life Repton reacted against his earlier enthusiasm for speed and freedom by seeking to reintroduce a degree of stately progress into his designs. In the Red Book for Stoneleigh Abbey, he waxes nostalgic about the surrounding courts, gates and flights of stairs. 'Of late fashion which always marches to the verge of absurdity had introduced not only *porte cochère* to drive under cover at the door but it has even admitted coaches into the Hall of the Mansion to set down the Noble owner at his own fireside.'[139] At Ashridge Repton designed an enclosure of antiquarian gardens for meditative walks (fig. 51) and joined the duke and duchess of Bridgwater a little way in perambulating the parish with their tenants and labourers, stopping to share cakes and ale.[140] The designs for Beaudesert include a Tudor-style gatehouse and

50  *Luxury of Gardens*, from *Fragments on the Theory and Practice of Landscape Gardening* (1816). Yale Center for British Art, Paul Mellon Collection.

51  *Arrangement Proposed for the Gardens at Ashridge, Herts*, from *Fragments on the Theory and Practice of Landscape Gardening* (1816). Yale Center for British Art, Paul Mellon Collection.

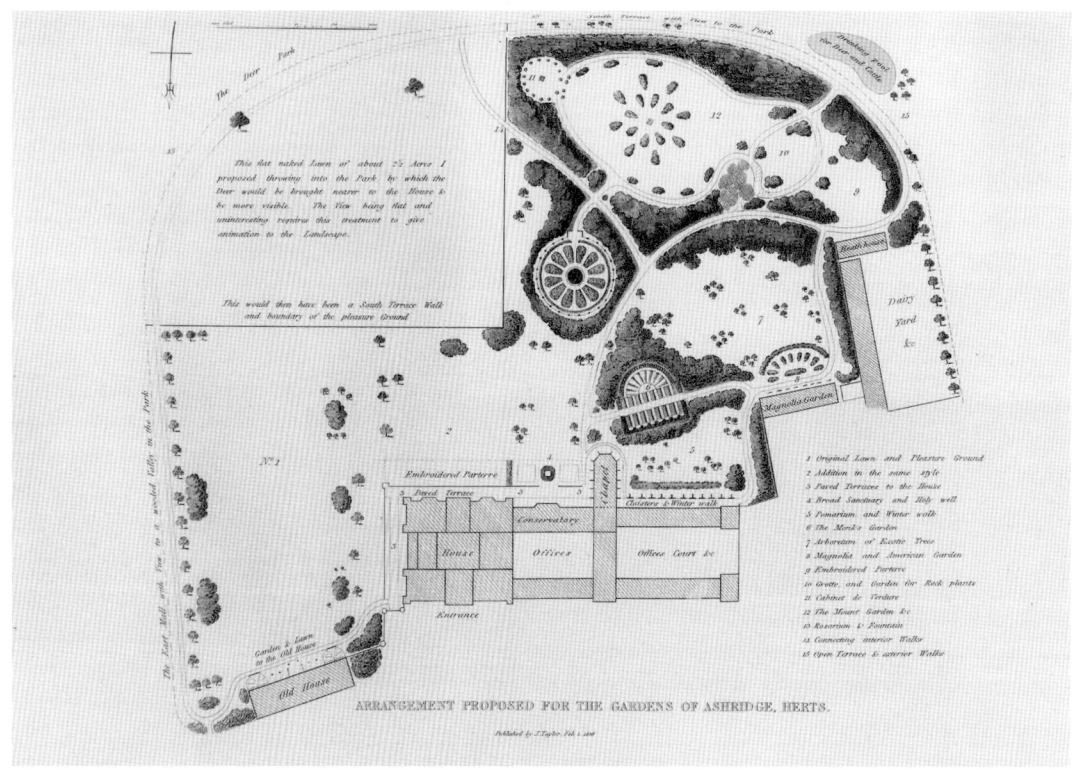

52  Gatehouse at the entrance to the park, from the Red Book for Beaudesert (1814). Princeton University, Taylor Collection.

bowing figures flanking Lord and Lady Uxbridge as they parade down the path (fig. 52).[141]

The 'lines of communication', as Repton called them, were carefully managed to control a variety of movements, from dung carts travelling from the stables to the gardens, to carriages taking guests on a tour of the park.[142] Some designs map complex regimes. That for Sheringham, Norfolk, is carefully programmed to supervise the access and movement of the poor (to the woods to gather sticks once a month, to the back door for food scraps), the polite (tourists to a temple to take in the prospect) and the rich and poor (to the beach for coursing), as well as the networks for family and guests and estate workers. No less important are connections beyond. Repton's illustration of the entrance lodge (fig. 53), which doubles as a gamekeeper's cottage, complete with look-out tower, shows a signpost. The text explains the advantages of the estate's situation: within an hour's ride of three post towns and two seaside resorts; close by three major estates on the tour of Norfolk; and within a morning's ride of Norwich.[143]

The relation between the private circulation of the park and the public one beyond was an issue that Repton addressed throughout his career. One of the texts that he claimed as his breviary when preparing for his career, Gérardin's *De la composition des paysages* (1777; translated as *An Essay on Landscape*, 1783) declares: 'public roads which may happen to go through your property; so far from being an inconvenience, rest assured that they will, on the contrary, serve to animate the picture. The nearer they are to your house, the more it will appear inhabited, and the moving scene will be an amusement to you'.[144] The phrase 'moving scene' recurs throughout Repton's designs, but the mere proximity of a public road was not the principle way of creating it. Repton conceived the relation between private and public roads in various ways, according to the kind of residence, the size, site and situation of the estate, the demands of clients and his own changing views on the social function of landscaping. He deployed a number of features to define it: lodges, fences, palings, plantations and new stretches of highway.

Some parks had stretches of public highway running through them. In places this was a condition of their celebrity. In the Red Book for Shardeloes, Buckinghamshire, Repton bows to the authority of Burke, who called the mansion (improved by Robert Adam) 'the most perfect specimen of elegant English Residence . . . And if we consider it only from the high road which is the point of view from which strangers form their judgment it appears perfectly beautiful and free from defect'. But the road formed 'a line of separation between the two parts of the park', so Repton opened 'a communication under the turnpike road' as part of a circuit drive.[145] Travellers taking the Warrington–Knutsford turnpike past the park at High Legh were unfortunately flanked by 'the exceeding heavy & uncouth Cheshire park paling . . . the poles are immense blocks of twisted and misshapen oak'. Repton recommended what he had seen at Shardeloes, a light fence of well-planed wood, which gave the impression of travelling through one park and not by the side of two (fig. 54).[146]

53  Proposed entrance, from the Red Book for Sheringham (1812). National Trust. On loan to the British Architectural Library, London.

54  Approach from the south, with and without overlay, from the Red Book for High Legh (1791). Private collection.

In places the public road was too close for comfort. The turnpike passing Stoke Edith in Herefordshire separated the house from the park, 'and both are seen from that road in the most unfavourable points of view . . . to divert, the course of this road, therefore, becomes the first object of improvement'.[147] After this had been done, at considerable expense, Repton noted 'the improvement to the place is equally felt by the proprietor, and conspicuous to every stranger who travels from Ledbury to Hereford'.[148] The tolls on turnpikes encouraged a better class of stranger, but many highroads, especially in populous districts, signified a threat to security. The Red Book for Tewin Water, Hertfordshire, condemns 'the local attachment' of the former owner who thought

> a public road no less appropriate than cheerful immediately in front of the house; or a footpath . . . cutting up the lawn in another direction . . . passing close to the windows, leaving the house on a kind of peninsula

surrounded by carts, waggons, gypsies, poachers, &c &c who feel they have a right of intrusion. Yet when the place with all its defects shall pass under the correcting hand of good taste, the view from the house will be changed.[149]

Where roads could not be moved they might be screened. A raised bank with trees transformed the impression of Hatchlands in Surrey 'from a large red house by the side of a high road, to a Gentleman-like residence in the midst of a Park'.[150] Repton could design secure palings with precision, as in a proposal for Kenwood near London: 'The most effective fence against Man – is a park pale of 5 or 6 feet not placed perpendicularly but leaning a little outwards the top over – hanging the foot about 10 inches – this is almost insurmountable by the most expert climber'.[151]

Later in his career, Repton voiced increasing concern about landowners sealing off their parks from public access. He observed the condition of the roadside to distinguish the estate management of hereditary, paternal landowners from that of parvenus. In older places he found 'the public road has a broad margin of herbage, enriched with thorn and spreading timber, under whose twisted branches the rough and knotty pale admits a view into the park'. In newer ones brick walls or high palings were built close to the road 'as to leave no margin of waste land'.[152] 'It is now a melancholy truth', he wrote in 1816, 'that every proprietor possess'd of land near a high road begins his improvement by excluding the world'.[153]

Repton devoted a chapter in *Fragments* to the issue of exclusion. In a parody of his own technique, he contrasted a recent roadside scene of 'improvements' 'in a distant county' with an unimproved view from the same spot drawn when he was passing ten years earlier (fig. 55). During this time the estate had been sold by an 'ancient proprietor' to a 'very rich man', who had proceeded to transform its organization and appearance. The changes signify the cultural decline of the country as a whole.[154]

In the unimproved view, we look from the road into the park, indeed a ladder-stile by the old beech tree invites us in, over the sunk fence that keeps in the deer. On the other side of the road, we learn, there is a common. By the roadside is a thoughtfully placed bench on which an old couple rests. It is a relaxed scene but impressed with the marks of benevolence. The common, for example, is not an ugly expanse (as Repton depicted commons he, or his clients, wished enclosed[155]); rather it has been planted in the style he approved for commons

55  *Improvements*, from *Fragments on the Theory and Practice of Landscape Gardening* (1816). Yale Center for British Art, Paul Mellon Collection.

that an owner could not or would not enclose, with deciduous trees, blending with the parkland trees on the other side of the road to form a bower.[156] The changes made by the new owner, for whom 'money supersedes every consideration', transform the scene:

> By cutting down the timber and getting an act to enclose the common, he had doubled all the rents. The old mossy and ivy-covered pale was replaced by a new and lofty close paling; not to confine the deer, but to exclude mankind, and to protect a miserable narrow belt of firs and Lombardy poplars: the bench was gone, the ladder-stile was changed to a caution about man-traps and spring-guns, and notice that the footpath was stopped by order of the commissioners. As I read the board, the old man said, 'It is very true, and I am forced to walk a mile further round every night, after a hard day's work.'[157]

The improved scene shows the labourer walking past the notice board and in the distance a figure on horseback, a farmer or landlord, pointing to, perhaps directing, a ploughman in the newly enclosed field.

Repton's narrative and illustrations are framed by a number of conservative discourses on improvement, notably by Burke and Price, and sharpened by his own sense of exile from landed society.[158] A number of features, the toiling ploughman, the precocious conifers, the forbidding notice board, were conventional signs of patrician delinquency in the early years of the nineteenth century. It is not just the presence of these features that signifies a destructive regime, but their role in the compositional structure of the scene. In the improved scene, distinctions between the park, road and common are not clearly delineated, and are softened by the dappled light through the trees. The effect for the viewer is to be taken into the estate, into an arena of landed benevolence. In the improved view, the straightened road, new palings and ploughed field form a pyramid of linear perspective. The streamlined vista conducts the eye abruptly to the horizon. Where once the viewer's gaze was invited into the landscape, now it is driven rapidly through it.[159]

'There is no subject on which I have so seldom satisfied my own judgment, as in that of an entrance to a park', Repton confessed in 1803.[160] He offered a variety of designs, in the style of the mansion or some characteristic of the park, to attract the traveller and advertize his work. He was dismayed to find two designs of which he was especially proud, the Classical entrance to Harewood (fig. 56) and the Gothic entrance to Blaise Castle (fig. 227),

56 Entrance arch, Harewood, from *Observations on the Theory and Practice of Landscape Gardening* (1803). Yale Center for British Art, Paul Mellon Collection.

57 Houses flanking entrance arch, Harewood, from *Observations on the Theory and Practice of Landscape Gardening* (1803). Yale Center for British Art, Paul Mellon Collection.

botched by local masons.[161] Repton regarded the park entrance as not only a gateway to a private world, but also a nucleus around which social relations might be improved or reconstructed. Entrances were too often symbols of social breakdown and insecurity, sited away from villages, or on the site of deserted villages and built with small lodges, 'the habitation of a single labourer, or perhaps, of a solitary old woman, to open the gate ... and very often the most squalid misery is found in the person thus banished from society, who inhabits a dirty room of a few square feet'.[162] Landowners could 'truly enrich the scenery of a country, by creating a village at the entrance of every park' (fig. 57).[163]

Repton was keen to conserve existing conjunctions of village and mansion near the highway and redefine them in paternal terms. Thus approaching the mansion at Babworth (fig. 58) from Retford along the Great North Road, it was 'hardly possible to avoid the village' nor would a traveller of sensibility wish to do so, for,

Never was a village so exactly like one described by Goldsmith, it agrees in every feature – in every charm!
>    The shelter'd cote, the cultivated farm
>    The never ailing brook, the busy mill
>    The decent church that tops the neighbouring hill

Repton conveniently revised Goldsmith's poem, *The Deserted Village*, by putting his lines in the present tense and including, as a condition of its pastoral joy, the very ingredient it conspicuously lacked in the poem, a landowner's mansion and management. Perhaps mindful of depopulation and poverty nearby, Mr and Mrs Simpson, the owners of Babworth, had already embarked on a programme of village improvements, which had Repton stooping to new depths of ingratiation:

> I was never more satisfied with my own judgement than when I perceived, that my proposal for decorating the village & then making the principal approach thro' it, was accepted with such heartfelt marks of approbation – the idea of repairing instead of removing and rebuilding these little habitations of industry & dependence was in perfect harmony with Mrs Simpson's soul – I now see her in my imagination leading the honey suckle round the cottage door & covering the humble thatch with mantling ivy ... amidst the cheerful smiles of gratitude and love; the old rising from the Benches which her indulgent care has planted at their doors to greet her as she passes – while the children of the village drop their awkward artless curtseys to welcome their patrons and benefactors.[164]

58 The approach, with and without overlay, from the Red Book for Babworth (1790). Private collection.

59 Approach through Knutsford to Tatton Park, with and without overlay, from the Red Book for Tatton Park (1792). National Trust, Tatton Park.

The industrial town of Knutsford, Cheshire, adjoining the entrance to Tatton Park presented a more obtrusive sight. In Repton's drawing of the unimproved view (fig. 59), the approach through the town is blocked. 'By taking down a few miserable cottages, and rebuilding them as tenements, in a plain uniform manner, the end of the street will be opened, to shew the entrance of the park through a simple, handsome arch.'[165] The improvement in circulation extends to the very vehicles; the small cart in the unimproved view gives way to a grand coach in the improved view, more in keeping with the new entrance. It was these proposals that provoked a fierce attack by Richard Payne Knight in *The Landscape: A Didactic Poem*:

> But in your grand approach (the critic cries),
> Magnificence requires some sacrifice; –
> As you advance unto the palace gate,
> Each object should announce its owner's state.[166]

At High Legh, Repton and John Nash collaborated in creating a village around an entrance from a new stretch of turnpike. Rejecting Repton's 'almshouse idea' of a straight row of cottages, Nash took the initiative in a more commercial, less feudal looking plan with some spectacular scenic effects. Cottages were to be 'scattered and intercepted by plantations . . . as the traveller passes along as he loses one Cottage others will unfold themselves'. This would also 'prevent the nuisances of cottagers entering into a view of the Village'. The main features were commercial premises:

> The Inn we placed at the corner that it might take advantage of all the roads – the blacksmith's shop as the next most picturesque object and requiring to be near the road we placed at the corner & we turned the smith's shop to look up the road so that the fire may illuminate the whole length of road and give a chearfulness at night to the whole village.[167]

Repton's most notable roadside development for the poor was a design for a new workhouse at Crayford, Kent (fig. 60). This was in response to a request on behalf of parishioners from Crayford's curate, his own son Edward. Edward Repton had left a curacy at Ardingly, East Grinstead, 'tired of Sussex dirt [and] unpolished clowns', in search of 'a situation where there is more politeness and less misery among the poorer sort – whose poverty I can't relieve'.[168] Conditions seemed little better at Crayford, but the potential for improvement was greater. Upon visiting his son, Repton found the existing poorhouse a 'wretched building . . . unhealthily placed in the low and wet marshes'. He proposed 'a more wholesome spot, on a dry soil' around an old gravel pit

60   *The Work-House*, from *Fragments on the Theory and Practice of Landscape Gardening* (1816). Yale Center for British Art, Paul Mellon Collection.

THE WORK HOUSE

on the edge of a heath about to be enclosed, and near the side of a high road from London to Dover. The backyard facing north was a place of 'cold darksome gloom', to be 'considered as a sort of punishment for misbehaviour and refractory conduct, where shut up between four buildings nothing can be seen to enliven the prospect'. In contrast, 'from the South Terrace, cheered by the Sun, the View of the Country will be delightful; since the immediate foreground consists of a Garden, and the perpetually varying and moving scene which is presented by the great road to Canterbury, and the Coast'.[169]

The inmates were objects of the traveller's gaze, but were granted scenic pleasures. In Repton's sketch on the south terrace it is the old 'who may enjoy their few remaining days of sunshine'; the young fill each shining hour with work, but 'more wholesome labour than spinning and other manufactures': girls learn how to sow, boys are trained to garden or drilled by a peg-legged old soldier 'to become the future defenders of their Country'. 'Fruit and flowers may be exposed to sale on the public road, and the profits of the commodities might be the reward of extraordinary industry or good behaviour.' Two ladies of Crayford make their purchases. A boy with a passing tramp points out the appeal of the place. The attractions of the site were not lost on polite residents. 'This Plan was at first highly approved by the leading persons in the Parish,' Repton reported, 'till it was discovered that the Situation proposed was so desirable, that the Site occupied in private houses would produce more profit, and therefore the Poor for the present continue in their former unwholesome abode'.[170]

Through travel, Repton considered himself well placed to observe the social condition of the country, not just in the view from the road, but in the characters he encountered on the way. In the preface to his play, *Odd Whims* (1804), Repton commented that, whereas thirty to forty years before it took three days to travel one hundred miles,

> The 'journey to London' presents now no terrors to the country squire... the manners of the capital become familiar to all ranks in the country; and the rustic booby is now confined to the very lowest orders of life, and is only applicable to farce. In the endeavour to copy the manners of the capital, all discrimination of character is done away, and even the costume and fashion of dress has tended to destroy that distinction which formally enlivened our English comedies.[171]

On the other hand, Repton recognized that travel brought a more modern virtue than distinction: 'I have met with a more original character in a stage coach, or a ferry boat, than in the presence chamber of St James, where Lace and embroidery level, as well as cover the persons who wear them'.[172]

The issue of character and travel is brought out in an episode that Repton relates in his Memoir. On a journey through the Derbyshire Dales, changing horses at Eyam, he came across a 'village pedagogue' studying the inscription on a gravestone. The man was intending to walk to Sheffield, and Repton offered him a seat in his post-chaise. Talking on various subjects, Repton soon found him 'marvellously ignorant of the world' and was glad to stop him prattling on about English pronunciation by pointing out the beauties of the surrounding scenery. Reaching the top of a hill, they saw in the distance

> a long cavalcade glittering in the sunshine... the Postboy informed us that it was Lord Fitzwilliam going to spend some time at Buxton, and as the procession approached us, we distinguished a number of carriages of different kinds with 20 outriders and a train of led horses, the whole preceded by an open Sociable drawn by four horses richly comparisoned... draped with large bouquets of flowers... in which were Lord and Lady Fitzwilliam.

Clients of Repton, the Fitzwilliams stopped their train to greet him, which had the village pedagogue 'incessantly bowing with the most ludicrous gestures... In vain I begged him to sit down'. Amid the movement of polite society, Lord Fitzwilliam retained his dignity. 'When the Noble Peer removes from one residence to another he does not drive off in a solitary curricle, nor travel by the mail coach – but with all the proper pomp of an Old English Baron, improved by the appliances of modern refinement.'[173] It was a time when, as Repton put it, 'gentlemen are learning to become stagecoachmen'. William Wilberforce asked Repton, himself no expert, how to drive a carriage in the park at Harewood and promptly crashed into some large blocks of stone where the entrance arch was being built.[174] In turn coachmen might recklessly aspire to gentility. At Hare Street, a woman 'fat, fair and forty' had inherited a fortune from an uncle '& now she gives it all to her coachman & takes his surname in return having dropped the Christian name with the reins – but he drives on like Jehu the Son of Nimshi who driveth furiously'.[175]

\* \* \*

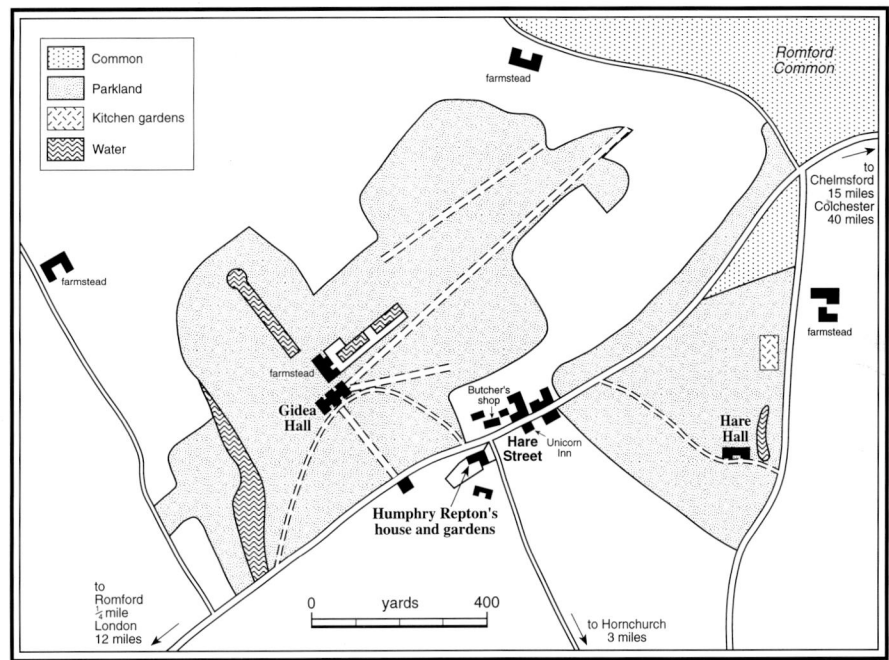

61 Hare Street during Humphry Repton's residency. After *Plan of Gidea Park & Farms Adjoining* (1807). Essex Record Office; Ordnance Survey Essex (1805), University of Nottingham, Department of Geography.

## Hare Street

Situated thirteen miles on the high road from the city of London, a mile beyond the coaching and barrack town of Romford, Repton's home village of Hare Street (fig. 61) was busy with traffic. Stage-coaches to London from throughout East Anglia passed Repton's front door, chaises and carriages too. Harvest waggons rolled into Romford market, carts carried articles of every description into the country. Drovers drove their herds and flocks towards the capital. Itinerants tramped out to the fields for work.[176] One early summer day, Repton was petitioned at his front door to save the life of one Irishman, a drover called Joseph Onions, condemned for stealing a bullock, while another, also called Joseph Onions, called at the back door looking for work hay harvesting or potato planting.[177]

This area of Essex had long been subject to a high turnover of land ownership. London merchants prized property as an attractive investment and a convenient place to live. The modest-sized estates often had relatively little farmland because their owners enjoyed the bulk of their income from other sources and could afford to create relatively large pleasure grounds. To make the claylands pay, farmers operated 'off-hand', putting together agricultural holdings from a number of estates, some farming more acres than were owned by any one owner and enjoying substantial wealth and standing. The constant movement in the land market opened up opportunities for a range of rural professionals: land agents, surveyors and solicitors.[178] The demand and purchasing power of the region allowed professionals of every kind, from surgeons to clergymen, to establish themselves in the towns and villages and declare as much by modernizing their houses with brick roofs and sash windows and laying out gardens with lawns and flower beds.[179]

The parish of Hare Street was divided between two estates: Hare Hall to the south of the turnpike, and to the north Gidea Hall, which owned most of the village, including Repton's house. Less than four hundred acres, Hare Hall was purchased around 1768 by John Wallinger, a merchant of cork and stone. Wallinger commissioned Richard Woods, whose practice was concentrated in Essex, to landscape the grounds of a new villa, and made a feature of his business with a cork tree and petrified tree of Portland limestone.[180] Twice the size of Hare Hall, Gidea Hall was the residence of Richard Benyon, son of an East India Company nabob, whose family were connected through marriage with prominent county families.[181] Woods probably had a hand in landscaping the grounds, for he leased as his residence one of the Benyon properties nearby at North Ockenden. Woods was in his seventies by the time of Repton's arrival;

62 J. Walker after Humphry Repton, *Gidea Hall in Essex, the Seat of Richard Benyon Esq.* (1794). Reproduced by courtesy of Essex Record Office.

he had largely retired from business and moved to a cottage at Ingrave.[182] Repton must have sensed an opportunity.[183]

Repton struck up good relations with each estate in Hare Street. 'My cottage could not be supposed to rival the magnificence of Gidea Hall, nor the elegance of Hare Hall and yet the inhabitants of each shewed us every kindly attention in our new home.'[184] He made a drawing of the approach to Gidea Hall from the turnpike (fig. 62), displaying its new plantations and curving drive which was published in 1794. Repton was on more intimate terms with Wallinger of Hare Hall. Their families socialized frequently. On one occasion, Repton ordered Portland stone from Richard Wallinger for a client and acted on some gossip picked up in Colchester by Wallinger's mother, 'The Walking, Talking, Essex Gazette' he called her, to pursue a commission in Norfolk.[185] Repton's drawing of Hare Hall was engraved for the 1790 issue of the *Polite Repository* (fig. 63).

Repton assumed a significant role in improving the society of Hare Street. Upon his arrival, the families of the two estates were not on friendly terms. 'Two *Halls* or great houses, like two suns, cannot well exist on the same spot – a cloud of jealousy engendered by rival wealth or adjoining property, is apt to darken the sunshine of social intercourse.' Repton took credit for reconciling the families. Indeed he saw his home as a keystone of the local community. Residing on the roadside, between the estates, opposite the coaching inn, the Unicorn, he felt ideally positioned to play the role of social mediator, master of ceremonies in a local assembly:

Many friendly people met at our house who had not before known each other and this gradually led to a more extended degree of sociability, which was greatly increased by my proposal that about half a dozen families should join in a monthly meeting at the village Inn in a room that was large enough to contain 20 couple of dancers and two card tables for those who did not dance . . . Happy days and happy nights![186]

The house at Hare Street 'was fixed upon as a temporary residence', noted Repton's early biographer, but 'subsequently became so endeared to him, as the scene of some trials and many blessings, that he never afterwards sought any other home'.[187]

Repton refashioned his house to reflect his status and publicize his profession. An engraving from his own drawing for the *Polite Repository* of 1800 (fig. 64) shows the view from the road, from the level of a passing coach or carriage. The façade of the early eighteenth-century house is fashionably modernized, with a veranda of trellis work and striped canvas awnings, and a domed central canopy over the front door.[188] Repton claimed to have started the craze for trellis work, although Uvedale Price

63 After Humphry Repton, *Hare Hall, Essex,* from *Peacock's Polite Repository* (1790). Bodleian Library, Oxford.

64 After Humphry Repton, *The Cottage of H. Repton Esq.,* from *Peacock's Polite Repository* (1800). Private collection.

had already promoted its reintroduction as part of the Picturesque. In contrast to Price's rustic vernacular, Repton incorporated 'treillage' as a part of smartly metropolitan, Parisian style.[189] A group of four fashionably dressed female figures, doubtless representing Repton's wife and daughters, are shown taking a walk in the front garden.

Repton's house originally faced the road directly, separated only by five yards of gravel path, a fence and two lime trees. The illustration in the *Polite Repository* may be a proposal, for it was not until 1802, after years of petitioning, that Repton obtained permission from the Court Leet to create a garden by enclosing a piece of grassy land beside the road in front of his house, customarily used for grazing cattle, pigs and geese. As Benyon and Wallinger were on the bench, and themselves wished to fence off roadside verges, it is not surprising that Repton was successful.[190] Repton extended his grounds by twenty yards and, as an engraving of 1816 shows, created an elaborate garden: a lawn is inset with raised beds and decorated with baskets of flowers and a pyramid of roses, the lime trees are garlanded with climbers, the hedge entwined with roses and sweet briars.[191] Writing over twenty years later, when the house and garden had been much altered, J.C. Loudon recalled the impression it made in Repton's time: 'The passing traveller has often admired, with a lingering eye, its pretty exterior, and those who were admitted to its happy fireside, could not but acknowledge, that comfort, worth a certain degree of elegance, may be contained within a very limited space'.[192]

After the turn of the century, Repton witnessed changes in Hare Street, and his position in it, which epitomized alarming developments in the country at large. The world around his house (which he took credit for integrating and improving) began, from his vantage point in the village, to break down.

Richard Benyon left Gidea Hall, after inheriting Englefield House, Berkshire, a noble mansion in a more fashionable region. The estate was let for some years; 'now uninhabited', a guidebook noted, 'the grounds together with the house, are now suffering from neglect'.[193] Gidea Hall was sold in 1802 to Alexander Black, a government contractor for military tents and bedding, one of the wartime profiteers Repton reviled.[194] Black told Repton 'some men had more pleasure in making money than others in spending it – & that was his turn'.[195] Black did not occupy the house for a few years, and when he did took just one small room in a mansion that Repton said 'Benyon had fitted up with such care and cost'.[196] Having paid a high price for Gidea Hall, thirty-four thousand pounds (more than forty pounds an acre) in inflationary times, Black was intent on making a rapid return.[197] He immediately doubled the rents of his farms and cottages. Rack-renting was a standard practice in the region at this time, as wheat prices were soaring – Benyon was doing so on his remaining estates – but it did not go unchallenged. Repton's friend, the land agent Nathaniel Kent, warned his local clients of the shortsightedness of making inordinate rent increases when rising poor rates and taxes were depleting farmers' profits.[198] Most landowners ignored such advice and suffered the consequences.[199] In a few years all Black's farms were empty, as was much of his property in Hare Street.

An eviction that particularly incensed Repton was that of 'my worthy neighbour Will Woodlands, the Wheelwright'. 'An industrious, honest fellow, always sawing and chopping and hammering ... this useful mechanic kept all the wheels going in the parish ... his cheerful ruddy face nodding to every passer by.' Woodlands was useful to Repton in other ways, letting him use part of his premises as an office, helping the Repton household 'in all the little handy offices of domestic life'.[200] In September 1812 Repton told his son that Woodlands was packing up to leave and repeated what he told Black, 'that Woodlands would be a loss to the neighbourhood'. Black 'call'd him a thief – & said he stole his Chestnuts – on enquiring I found that one day Woodlands after a high wind pick'd up 3 Chestnuts under a tree in the Park when Black gallop'd up to him & caught him in the act of taking the husk of one of them & abus'd him for a thief'.[201] 'From his going to a distance I have lost sight of him now', Repton reported in his Memoir, 'and his shop and yard are empty'.[202]

Others felt Black's malevolence, including a widow whose sow strayed into Gidea Park: Black sent it to market and pocketed the money.[203] Some locals resisted Black's harassment. One night a small farmer called Peachey and two accomplices stole into the park, shot Black's prize bullock he was fattening to exhibit, and carved up the carcass. Caught and convicted, Peachey was transported to Tasmania.[204] Others chalked abuse on Black's walls and palings, 'curses not loud', noted Repton, 'but deep from a once happy neighbourhood'.[205]

Black threatened to evict Repton too, over the details of his lease, which prompted anxious visits and letters from Repton to his attorney son, William, in Aylsham, Norfolk. Black 'came to look at my house and garden to see what he could make of it – he stood for half an hour and made it stink so, that we could not live in it for some hours... his name will stink as well as his body... this Wretch is to have the Trees I planted!'[206] The issue of the lease dragged on for several years, and for a time in 1815 Repton left Hare Street to stay with his sister and son in Aylsham. After securing his tenancy, and for what he considered a reasonable rent of thirty pounds, Repton described to William the havoc elsewhere:

> all the premises – empty – untenanted & dilapidated – no chaises or stage coaches which used to enliven our scene – now all a blank such are the changes growing out of Property. Poor Woodlands house is let on Lease 21 years for £20 per annum after long standing empty & refusing that poor industrious wheelwright's offer of £30 – requiring 40 & not taking half so it will be with the Unicorn which nobody can live [in] these hard times.[207]

Changes in the ownership and management of Hare Hall troubled Repton too. After John Wallinger's death in 1792, the landed and business interests of the family were divided between his first and second sons, a likely cause of the difficulties that beset the estate. Without transfusions of trading capital, John Wallinger the Younger mortgaged Hare Hall a number of times to support other estates in the home counties, and to increase the efficiency of farming in Hare Street.[208] Upon his death in 1805, the estate was put in trust and subject to a long legal wrangle, which Repton tried to sort out with the help of William and his contacts at the highest level in the law, including the Attorney General, Sir Samuel Romilly, and the Lord Chancellor, Thomas Erskine. In 1807 Wallinger's widow was staying with the Reptons, 'the poor thing in great trouble'.[209] The family was forced to sell, and in 1810 Hare Hall was purchased by John Coape, the head of a syndicate intent on reselling in six months.[210] Coape refused to let Wallinger's widow remain in the house as a tenant. In September 1812 Repton told his son William that she had moved away to Hornchurch, 'by order of removal of Mr Cope [*sic*.] as bad a brute to cope with as the Black Gent'n'.[211] It was another eighteen months before the syndicate was offered an acceptable price, by one Joseph Severn, to Repton another example in Hare Street of 'Wealth in Strange Hands'. 'A great Sugar baker doubles his Capital in a day', he told Sir Harry Fetherstonehaugh, 'buys Hare Hall and begins by stocking the 200 acres with 2 doz live Hares and half a dozen Squirrels – these he shuts up in the Walled Kitchen Garden from where the latter hop off – and the former crop all the Cauliflowers etc.'[212]

In the last infirm years of his life, Repton spent many months at home in Hare Street. 'I am told to do no business – & luckily I have none to do – we are to have more income tax – but I have no income.'[213] The 'solitude and seclusion' depressed him, especially when recalling 'domestic joys & splendour of high life both in Town and Country'.[214] To maintain his spirits he read, wrote letters, composed illustrated verses to family and friends (fig. 65), designed and perhaps made ornamental ware, a combined birdcage and goldfish bowl (fig. 66), and elaborate baskets of flowers.[215] Such tasks were designed to mark 'the contrast betwixt grave and gay', but offered limited amusement. 'I am tired of admiring my flowers & my kittens & my pigeons & my young canaries', he told his son William,

> When I reflect on the thousands of miles I have traveld – the hundreds of sketches – & rheams of paper I have blotted – how every hour of a long life has been filled up – & now view myself crawling from one chair to another in the garden... the sight of hopes disappointed is like the blossoms on our apple trees – the Canker has destroyed them all – and a grub nips every rose bud – while cold winds nip me.[216]

Repton took some consolation going through correspondence to write his memoirs and collecting material for *Fragments*, the volume intended to preserve the memory of landscape gardening. Repton concluded, 'these Fragments with the most interesting subject I have ever known; it is the view from the humble Cottage to which for more than thirty years I have anxiously retreated from the pomp of palaces, the elegancies of fashion, or the allurements of dissipation' (fig. 67).[217]

The scene before improvement shows the view from Repton's garden before he had enclosed the patch of grassy common. Hare Street, its very life as a turnpike village, presses in on the spectator, stage-coaches departing the inn in both directions, a cart and horseback rider travelling towards Chelmsford, a chaise calling at a house, pedestrians shopping, geese thronging the common, and, prominently, a beggar leaning on Repton's garden fence looking in. The view after improvement, after the appropriation of the common for a garden, allows Repton to obtain 'a frame to my Landscape... composed of flowering shrubs and evergreens'. It enables Repton to control the appearance of the village, to make it 'my Landscape'. The beggar and geese are gone, carcasses in the butcher's shop are concealed by climbing roses, the hedge hides the study from the prying eyes of coach passengers, the dust no longer flies through the fence. Here, carefully edited, is 'the cheerful village, the high road, and that constant moving scene, which I would not exchange for any of the lonely parks, that I have improved for others'.[218]

Two features concentrate Repton's concerns. The butcher's shop recalls Uvedale Price's discussion of paintings of butcher's shops by Teniers and Rembrandt in his later essays on the Picturesque.[219] Repton criticized Price's advocacy of Flemish or Dutch-style art for framing improvements to cottages and villages, for making tasteful subject matter that Repton found low and disgusting: 'the pig sties of Moreland . . . the filthy hostels of Teniers'.[220] Repton's climbing roses, their perfume as well as appearance, are another metropolitan refinement of village life.[221] The selling as well as preparation of meat disturbed Repton. In a letter of October 1815 to

65  *The Lady and the Looking Glass* (n.d.). Avery Architectural Library, Columbia University, New York. The illustration is of Repton's daughter Mary Dorothy at Hare Street.

66  Design for a goldfish bowl and birdcage (n.d.). Colman Collection, Norwich Library. Courtesy Norfolk Libraries and Information Service. The drawing was used as a headpiece to Repton's poem 'Birds and Fishes' (n.d.). Avery Architectural Library, Columbia University, New York.

Sir Harry Fetherstonehaugh, Repton complains about the gross appetites of 'modern *Butcher Gentry*' who prefer the stench of the farmyard to the fragrance of flower gardens.[222] The figure of the Butcher Gentleman, a corrupted John Bull, slathering over fattening livestock, bears a striking resemblance to Repton's stinking landlord, and the shop's owner, Alexander Black.[223]

Beggars were a more frequent spectre in the scenic imagination of polite society than butcher's shops. There were beggars such as those that Wordsworth described around the turn of the century in the Lakes, long-standing members of the local community who should not be 'cast out of view', who were indeed 'beautiful to see'.[224] Others, in other places, were best shut out, like those John Constable's brother Abram was pleased to avoid a few years later, 'callers or idlers', when he moved from the house on the main road at East Bergholt to live at Flatford Mill.[225] With an amputated arm and leg, and a patch over one eye, the beggar in Hare Street is evidently a war veteran, a battle-stricken soldier or sailor. The mass demobilization during the post-war depression swelled the roads with desperate men, filling the minds of polite society with fears of vagrancy, and also reminding them of Christian duties for the poor man at the gate.[226]

In the Red Book for Sheringham of 1812, Repton complains of places where 'I see lame and blind beggars driven from the door'.[227] The implication of Repton's views from his cottage may be that the beggar in Hare Street has been relieved, not sent packing to the

workhouse. Repton not only depicts the beggar in the unimproved view, he receives his gaze. The figure functions somewhat like the 'blind beggar . . . propped against a wall' in Wordsworth's account of residence in London in *The Prelude* (written in 1805), confronting the poet 'as if admonished from another world'.[228] Like the butcher's shop, whose joints of meat cruelly confront his hunger, even grotesquely mirror his amputation, the beggar is a sign of an economy of profit and hunger, smugness and suffering, which Repton regarded with disgust.[229] Like the old labourer shut out of the park in the Fragment on 'Improvements', the beggar in the Fragment on Hare Street is a pitiable figure who bears the burden of a wider sacrifice. In a letter to Fetherstonehaugh, Repton reported the shooting and amputation of a client, Lord Uxbridge, the cavalry commander at Waterloo: 'how many men do I now reflect on, who lately enjoyed Life & Limbs . . . What miserable Glory – & glorious Misery . . . how different from the garden scenes in which my Life has been consumed, yet here am I as much disabled as if I had fought my Country's battles, instead of improving its beauties'.[230] The beggar then may reflect Repton's disabilities too. 'What agony can equal that of an industrious man, who by his failure dreads the utter ruin of the fortune of his family?', Repton had once observed in an essay, 'On Happiness', 'Imagination paints his children beggars, and himself in advanced years, no longer able to support them'.[231] By 1816 Repton made his agony plain for anyone who cared to hear. He told his son William that he hoped his published works 'may perpetuate my name & perhaps contribute to my support & remove the dreadful – most dreadful of all Calamities – becoming a burthen to my children'.[232]

However it is read, the unimproved view from Repton's house represents a lack, or loss, of control with signs of economies that threaten the very existence of landscape gardening. The improved view, covering up much of the road, the commercial arena of Hare Street, establishes a fragile, temporary control. A few steps across the lawn would reveal the butcher's shop, a few more much else.[233] The view succeeds only from a stationary, sedentary vantagepoint, in the drawing-room, or from the chair on the lawn. Then, and only then, is the backdrop correct, the props in place. To leave one's seat is to break the illusion, as Repton did one day in October 1816, finding 'my breathing somewhat easier'. He tried 'a long walk by myself' to enjoy 'the warmth and beauty of the day'. 'I have been sauntering half way to the bridge – sitting and sunning against Black's pales – then walking into the Unicorn Yard & viewing all the premises – empty – untenanted & dilapidated – no chaises which used to enliven our scene – now all a blank'.[234]

67 *facing page* View from my Cottage, with and without overlay, from *Fragments on the Theory and Practice of Landscape Gardening* (1816). Yale Center for British Art, Paul Mellon Collection.

## Chapter 2

# THE PROPHET'S OWN COUNTRY

Repton was born in Suffolk and lived in Essex for most of his professional career, but regarded Norfolk as his home county. His family moved to Norwich when he was a boy; after three years' schooling in The Netherlands he lived in the city for ten years until he was twenty-six and in Sustead, a hamlet in north Norfolk, until his mid-thirties. He kept in frequent contact with the county during his career, corresponding and visiting, especially with his sister Dorothy and son William in the town of Aylsham. Repton's parents were buried in the churchyard at Aylsham, and he chose it as his burial place. The landscape and culture of Norfolk had a formative effect on Repton's scenic and social views, but Repton did not impress his influence on the county and its countryside as strongly as he hoped. While he enjoyed early patronage in Norfolk, and by the end of his career had worked on at least eighteen sites (fig. 68), more than any other county except Essex, he felt that he should have had more, and probably more important and widespread commissions, in his home county. 'There is hardly any part of England in which I am less well known professionally than in Norfolk', he repeatedly declared, 'perhaps from its being "the Prophet's own Country"'.[1]

In this chapter I examine Repton's career in Norfolk and assess his own view of it. First I consider his life and work in Norwich and Sustead before moving to Hare Street. Then I examine the combination of political campaigning and landscape gardening he undertook in Norfolk in the first year of his new profession. Repton's first professional return to the county in 1792 is assessed, as is his subsequent return, after a fourteen-year gap, for a sequence of commissions from 1807. This period culminated in the commission in the summer of 1812 at Sheringham, a property with 'more natural beauty and local advantages . . . than any place I have ever seen', and 'such a specimen of my art as I never before had an opportunity of displaying . . . this may be considered my most favourite work'.[2] The commission at Sheringham formed a climax to Repton's career, and a complex one, positioned as it was at the junction of a number of courses of development and trains of thought, including Repton's physical decline, the promise of revived patronage, the prospect of a new home for young clients who shared the ageing landscape gardener's ideals and the recognition Repton craved in his county.

Also in the course of this chapter I chart the county context for Repton's landscape gardening, for it was a context that Repton himself consciously shaped through his life and work, in Norfolk and beyond. Many aspects of county culture that modern scholars have identified – the networks of great estates and aristocratic oligarchies, market towns and professional élites; the role of county towns in brokering a polite consensus; the development of 'countries', districts of similar economic resources and topographical character; the development of specialist commercial regions through lines of communication; the formation of county cultures within larger provincial,

*facing page* Detail of fig. 78.

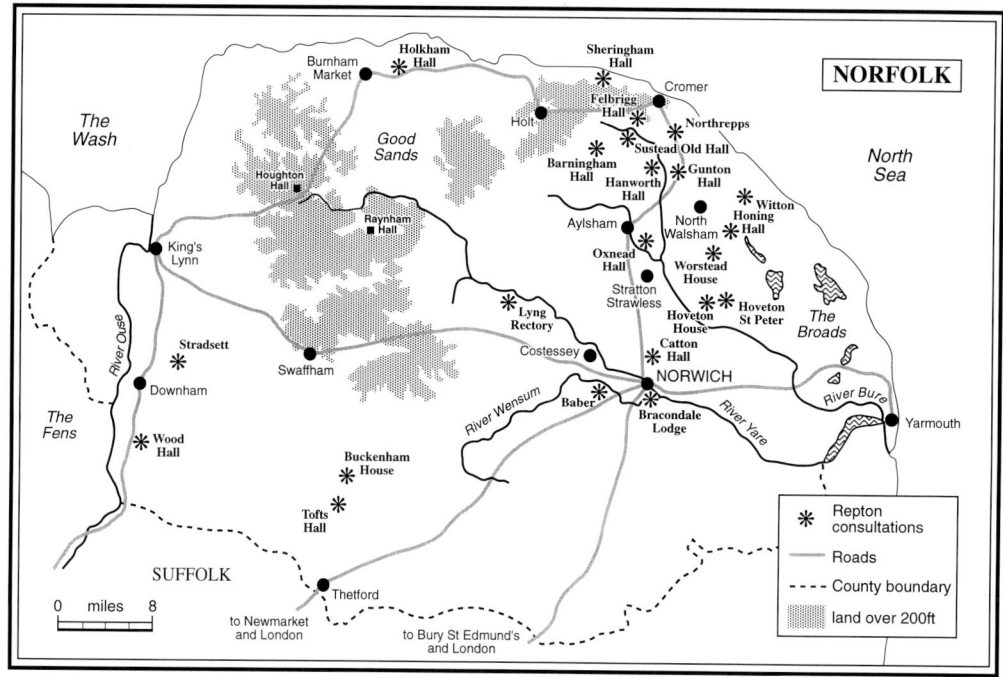

68 Humphry Repton Consultations in Norfolk.

national and international geographies; the role of London in reforming the regional geography of England and Wales; the rewriting of the county as a cultural formation through agricultural reports and antiquarian research – are represented in and through Repton's various works.³

## Norfolk and Northern Europe

Repton's parents moved to Norwich around 1762, when he was ten. Then the third most populous English city, Norwich was a long established administrative, legal and ecclesiastical centre and a major centre of textile manufacturing. At the time the Reptons moved there it was on the threshold of a boom in its export trade of fine cloths. This was marked by a reorientation of its economy and an intensification of its regional power. Hitherto most cloth was sent by waggon to London for export, and John Repton's road transport business prospered accordingly, but the new export campaign was channelled by water along the Wensum through the port of Yarmouth to the ports of Rotterdam and Hamburg; hence John Repton's eagerness to establish his son in the seaborne trade.⁴

The region that Repton first observed with a horticultural eye was across the North Sea. He was one of a number of Norwich sons sent abroad, to The Netherlands and Germany, to learn a commercially useful language. Money for Repton's education was placed with Zachary Hope, a member of the leading merchant banking family in Rotterdam and Amsterdam. After a few months as a schoolfriend of Hope's son, he was taken into the family circle and on travels around the country. Dutch fashions in gardens had long been imported and domesticated in Norfolk, along with many other aspects of Dutch landscape art and management, but in The Netherlands Repton was amazed by the display of gardens along the canals, exotic patterns of ores, china and glass to 'imitate the gardens of precious stones, described in fairy tales', or 'a parterre hanging to the water, in which the design traced on the ground was like a pattern for working muslin on embroidery':

> Nature was never consulted, they were works of art... All was neatness; the effect of incessant labour. A Dutch merchant's accounts and his garden were kept with the same degree of accuracy and attention. ... Could it be expected that the future landscape gardener of England should have studied in the parterres and clipped vistas of a Dutchman?⁵

Dutifully, Repton learnt Dutch in Rotterdam, but joining the Hope household probably encouraged his regard for spending money rather than making it. Emigré Scots and fabulously rich, the Hopes lived lavishly, patronized the arts, 'spoke French, and lived entirely *à la Française*'.[6]

The export drive in fine textiles stimulated other trades and professions in Norwich and encouraged the formation of a prosperous commercial élite. For a wide region, beyond the county, Norwich was a centre of professional services, luxury goods and polite entertainment, and a site of progressive, interdenominational, cultural developments, notably in music, natural history and medicine.[7] Repton was one of a number of young Norwich men, including the future botanist James Edward Smith and the critic William Taylor, who left the textile trade for other cultural pursuits. Looking into a (now lost) volume of the Memoir, Repton's first biographer found the apprentice

> learnedly descanting upon the nature of calimancoes, Mecklenburgs, worsted satins, and other articles [of] fashion... The records of this part of his life, however, lead us to infer, that the exercise of his talents for poetry, music and drawing, occupied more of his time than was quite consistent with the views of his affectionate, though, in this case not very discriminating, [father].

Repton's interest in fine textiles was focused on an enduring concern with his own wardrobe, 'the singular hat, or odd shaped pantaloons... the white coat, lined with blue satin and trimmed with silver fringe' in which he attended balls and concerts in the city. Here he performed with 'his fine voice and sweet-toned flute', accomplishments that later gave him the entrée to clients' households.[8]

Upon his marriage to Mary Clarke in 1771 Repton's father made over sufficient capital for his son to set up as a merchant. The reverses Repton subsequently suffered, 'ships lost at sea and failures in speculation', were not necessarily a reflection of personal failings – many Norwich firms exported so much on speculation that the markets became over stocked, and the escalation of war, which committed France, Spain and eventually Holland to the cause of the American colonists, had privateers cruising at will in the North Sea, preying on unescorted shipping.[9] When both parents died, leaving him free and provided for, Repton took the opportunity to move out of trade and out of Norwich. In 1778 Repton retired, aged twenty-six, with his wife and young son, to the hamlet of Sustead, seventeen miles north of the city, to live as a squire and gentleman amateur.

\* \* \*

*The Garden of Norfolk*

Repton did not retire in to a rural obscurity. While living at Sustead Repton wrote an account of the region for Armstrong's *History and Antiquities of the County of Norfolk* which described its enlightened character and helped to shape its reputation as a prosperous and picturesque part of the county, 'The Garden of Norfolk'.[10] Sustead was just five miles from the town of Aylsham, an outpost centre of the Norwich textile trade on a new navigation to Yarmouth, centre of a prosperous, progressive farming region, a town close to some of the county's great estates and with its own residential professional élite (figs 69 and 70).[11] 'From the beauty and richness of the country about it', wrote Repton, 'several gentlemen have been induced to build good houses and reside here'.[12] Among the élite were Repton's sister, Dorothy, married to the town's leading attorney, John Adey, a man Repton greatly admired for his 'honesty and Christian spirit'. Repton's eldest son, christened John Adey, attended the grammar school in Aylsham before his apprenticeship to the Norwich architect William Wilkins; his third son, William, trained with his uncle as an attorney before taking over the practice on his death.[13] Farming outside Aylsham, at Oxnead, was Repton's elder brother, John, a tenant on the Anson estate. John Repton was singled out for praise by Arthur Young and Nathaniel Kent in their reports on the agriculture of Norfolk for his crop rotations, seed drilling, land drainage and 'his books, kept with uncommon accuracy and care'.[14] Repton admired his brother as 'a very ingenious experimental farmer' and referred to his practice when pronouncing on progressive farming in his commissions as a landscape gardener.[15] John Repton lived in the remaining wing of the old Italianate mansion at Oxnead (fig. 73), former residence of the Paston family, who were (through the publication of their letters) the most famous Tudor gentry in Georgian England. Oxnead, wrote Repton, is 'situated on the top of three terraces, which are still in being, and command a pleasing view of the river Bure (now being made navigable)'.[16] As Tom Williamson and Anthea Taigel point out, such terraces became a defining feature of Repton's style, as a foreground to a modest-sized park (a type found throughout this region) and vistas of the countryside beyond.[17] In his later career, in partnership with John Adey (who eventually moved into Oxnead and researched its history), Repton's garden style became increasingly formal and antiquarian.[18] Throughout his career both generations of his family socialized frequently in Aylsham and Norwich and on occasion in London, especially for recitals and concerts.[19]

Humphry Repton took a tenancy on Old Hall, Sustead, a small property on the southern border of Felbrigg, the seat of the Windhams, a powerful county family (fig. 71). On rising ground, Felbrigg occupied a commanding topographical position: from here were views of the spire of Norwich cathedral in one direction and the North Sea in another. North Norfolk was a Whig stronghold, and Repton's landlord, William Windham III, was a prominent figure in the political community. Repton drew Windham making his first important political speech, in Norwich in January 1778, delivering the 'Norfolk petition' against continuation of war with the American colonies (fig. 72). After spending the year 1779 touring Italy, Windham returned to Felbrigg to be nominated as Whig candidate for Norwich in the

69  *Aylsham Market Place* (1814). Private collection. Photograph Witt Library, Courtauld Institute.

70  *Aylsham: A Celebration of the Festival of the Peace, 15 July 1814.* Private collection. Photograph Witt Library, Courtauld Institute.

71 After Humphry Repton, *Felbrigg, the Seat of William Windham, Esq. F.R.S.*, from M.J. Armstrong (ed.), *The History and Antiquities of the County of Norfolk*, vol. 3 (1787). Private collection.

72 *right* William Windham delivering the Norwich Petition, Norwich, 28 January 1778. National Trust, Felbrigg Hall. National Trust Photographic Library/John Hammond.

73 After Humphry Repton, *Oxnead Hall, Norfolk*, from *Peacock's Polite Repository* (1807). Bodleian Library, Oxford.

parliamentary election of 1780; he enlisted Repton to assist him in his campaign. Windham was not elected and spent the next two years shuttling between London and Felbrigg, where he oversaw estate improvements and cultivated a friendship with Repton. Windham's political career was revived in 1782 when he was appointed in the new ministry headed by the duke of Portland, and he was in a position to help Repton in a career at a time when retirement in Sustead had become financially untenable.[20]

During Repton's residence in Sustead, the country around acquired a reputation as a region of improvement, the new nucleus of progressive Norfolk agriculture. Pockets of good, loamy soil were interspersed with tracts of sandy heath, large estates with small farms. Riding from Costessey to Aylsham one June day in 1788, Windham found a 'dearth of objects, and poverty of ideas . . . It has been the thought of what I was going to do, or the impression of what I have left, that has protected me from the mean associations which pightels [petty enclosures] and gorse commons, Stratton and Felthorpe, naturally draw with them'.[21] The land agent Nathaniel Kent lived at Rippon Hall while implementing management plans for the surrounding Anson estates as well as for Felbrigg.[22] The agriculturalist William Marshall took up residence for two years as agent for the Gunton estate.[23] Robert Marsham, described by Kent as 'the first of all tree-planters in his district', embellished his seat at Stratton Strawless.[24] In their published writings, these men pointed out the social and scenic potential of the region, between the flat Goodsands country to the west, dominated by great estates, huge parks and farms, and the rich, loamy country of the east, with its intricate network of small owner-occupiers. Here in between was a more varied country, with a fine array of farmland and small parks, estates of various sizes and a scattering of small farms and cottages.[25]

Windham, Kent, Marshall and Marsham shaped Repton's subsequent career as a landscape gardener. Repton struck up a lifelong friendship with Kent, and the two men held each other in high professional esteem.[26] Marshall initially supported Repton in his controversy with his Picturesque critics, or rather endorsed Windham's support for Repton as a practical improver, before he recoiled from the more theatrical aspects of Repton's designs and set about establishing himself as a designer of parks and gardens.[27] Repton credited Marsham, 'my much valued friend', with one of the trade marks of his Red Books, the presentation of present and

74 After Humphry Repton, *Baconsthorpe Hall*, from M.J. Armstrong (ed.), *The History and Antiquities of the County of Norfolk*, vol. 3 (1787). Private collection.

proposed scenes of improvement.[28] Marsham's method of planting deciduous trees mixed with thorns became one of the hallmarks of Repton's technique as a landscape gardener, as did Marsham's plan of planting commons that a landowner could not or would not enclose.[29]

Repton 'passed five years of uninterrupted domestic happiness' at Sustead, raising a growing family, reading, writing, drawing, improving his farm, visiting his wealthy neighbours and poor parishioners, roaming over the surrounding countryside and sketching its scenery.[30] Repton's interest in natural history was prompted by the books that Windham had assembled at Felbrigg as well as his landlord's contacts in London. 'He has introduced me to Mr Joseph Banks and other learned men', noted Repton, 'and his library has introduced me to Buffon, De Reaumur &c; and they have brought me acquainted with all the insects in my neighbourhood'.[31] Repton's old schoolfriend James Edward Smith came out from Norwich to study plants and insects in the field. In later life, as first president of the Linnean Society, Smith recalled 'youth and Sustead, and my first botanizing days, when I hoarded up a hazel twig gathered in your grounds. There I first began to emerge from the still pool of life'.[32] The library at Felbrigg was one of the finest in Norfolk, and Repton borrowed freely from the large collection of volumes on English literature, on one occasion, poetry (Dryden and Dodley) for himself, and on another, plays (Beaumont and Fletcher) for his wife.[33] When in Norfolk, Windham sometimes came over to assist Repton in his studies, 'for he prefers my snug study at Sustead better than the old rambling library at Felbrigg'. Repton made drawings of the surrounding countryside, presenting local gentry with portraits of their estates. He submitted

75  *Sustead Old Hall* (1782). Private collection.

drawings, of country houses, parks, churches and antiquities for engraving in Armstrong's *History and Antiquities of the County of Norfolk* (1787; figs 71 and 74) and wrote the text for his district, the hundreds of North and South Erpingham.[34]

At Sustead, Repton encountered pious country virtues. In an essay he wrote there he celebrates the example of William Hewett, rector of the neighbouring parish of Baconsthorpe and Bodham, who paid for the restoration of the Gothic church, sold food from his farm at a loss to the industrious poor and gave hand-outs to the old and infirm.[35] At Repton's request, Hewett wrote a description of the parish for Armstrong's *History*, in which he praised the virtues of the small farms for promoting industriousness and keeping down the poor rates. Without the prospect of a small farm, local villagers were liable to open an alehouse 'and furnish a snug retreat for vagrants, smugglers and poachers'. If everywhere in England were like his parish, there would be no need for workhouses: 'the vallies wou'd then stand thick not only with corn but also with occupiers who would laugh and sing for joy'.[36]

Sustead was a mere hamlet with 'not even an alehouse to disturb my peace'.[37] Old Hall was a seventeenth-century house with curved Dutch gable ends. In Armstrong's *History* Repton described it as 'small but convenient, and pleasantly situated in the middle of a little farm . . . ornamented with several small plantations'. For much of the eighteenth century it had functioned as a parsonage. The previous occupants, the Revd Theophilus and Mrs Elizabeth Lowe, had exercised an improving influence that Repton sought to emulate. For the five years of her widowhood, Elizabeth Lowe continued to plant and minister. 'Those with whom she conversed or corresponded were always pleased or instructed, and those near whom she lived were always happy', he recorded. 'The grateful glow which her name awakens on the cheeks of her surviving dependents and parishioners, evinces the respect they pay to her memory.' There was a 'pleasing and picturesque' vista from the hall to the church 'pleasantly situated on a rising ground and command[ing] an engaging view to the north over an extensive lawn of rich pasture land, intersected by venerable oaks, and bounded by a full view of the south front of Felbrigg'.[38] In front of Old Hall was a cottage that Repton embellished with a new Gothic-style window.[39]

There are two surviving views by Repton of Old Hall. One, dated May 1782 (fig. 75), looks from the poultry yard towards the house backed by Elizabeth Lowe's grove of beeches. In the yard are a variety of fowl, a fashionably dressed woman and her child (perhaps Mary and John Adey Repton) who feeds the chicks and an older woman

76  Sustead Old Hall, detail, from *Map of Sustead* (c.1782). Colman Collection, Norwich Library. Courtesy Norfolk Libraries and Information Service.

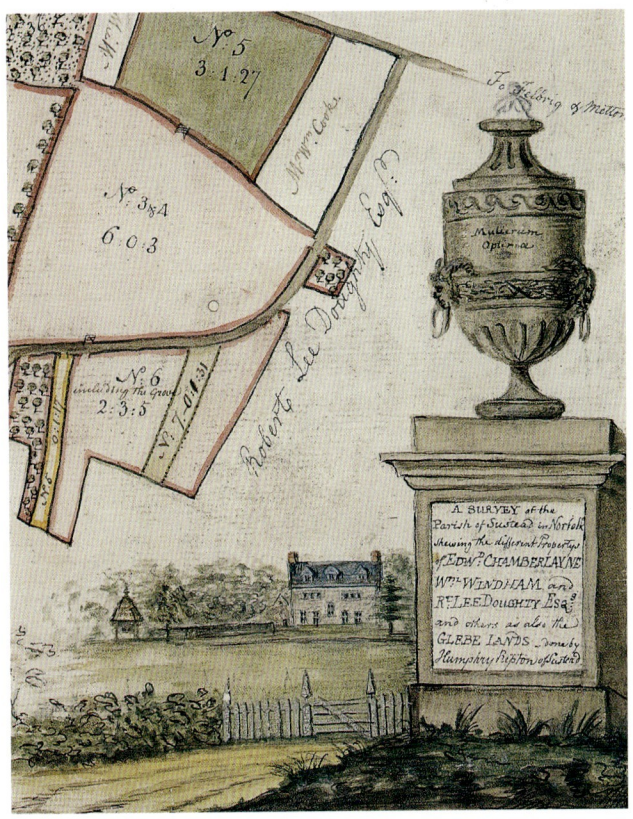

77  *Map of Sustead* (*c.*1782). Colman Collection, Norwich Library. Courtesy Norfolk Libraries and Information Service.

wearing an apron who looks like a servant. The other, an undated view (fig. 76), looks across the field at the back of the house, through a Gothic-style gate. This is a vignette inset in a map of the parish (fig. 77). Repton redrew the map from an old survey of 1732. This shows the parish lands divided in to small enclosures and commonfield strips among three owners. It is a record of a pattern that had already been reformed, for Repton's property is not listed in Windham's ownership, but that of Edward Chamberlayne, a local rector who had married in to the Windham family.[40] The map shows the grove of beeches planted by the Lowes, a recent feature superimposed on the survey. It may have been drawn for engraving in Armstrong's *History* or perhaps for Chamberlayne's son, a Fellow of the Society of Antiquaries, who was living and working in London as a clerk at the Treasury.

Sustead 'is so small a parish', Repton told the young Chamberlayne, 'that I am obliged to enact the various parts of churchwarden, overseer, surveyor of the highways and esquire of the parish'.[41] In Windham's absence, Repton intervened in estate matters, admonishing Windham's steward on his employer's behalf to build a new gate to keep cattle straying from Sustead common on to tenant's pasture, to take back two servants from Sustead he had discharged, and get a cottage built for them, or else take on another who is 'maintained out of my house notwithstanding he belongs to the parish of

Felbrigg'.[42] Repton set about improving his farm: 'I am impatient to show you the alterations in my house and lands', he told Chamberlayne, 'The wet hazy meadows, which were deemed incorrigible, have been drained and transformed to flowery meads'.[43]

In his text for Armstrong's *History*, Repton, like Kent and Marshall, presents a revisionary view of his county:

> The county of Norfolk is by no means so flat a country as it is generally described to be, and this is chiefly owing to the hasty manner in which itinerant writers view it. Every part (the fen and marsh lands excepted) is strongly marked with rising grounds, which though they ascend with almost imperceptible egravity [gradient], terminate with a prospect of twenty, some thirty miles distant.

This scenery was especially characteristic of the area Repton was to write about, the region of loamy soils and undulating topography stretching ten miles or so north from around Aylsham, rising around Felbrigg and Sustead to form a coastal ridge of sands and clays reaching more than three hundred feet. This region 'is from the superior fertility of the soil with propriety called the Garden of Norfolk'. Around Sustead, it merged with 'the picturesque part of Norfolk' along the coast. The area was now generally enclosed from common-field in small hedged fields planted with oak and ash. 'Though this in many parts impedes the view, yet from those eminences which overlook the trees, they add a prodigious softness to the landskip, that in many parts appears to be one continued grove of many miles extent.' In the parishes around Sustead, Repton found

78  J. Walker after Humphry Repton, *Felbrig Hall, Norfolk* (1793). Private collection.

FELBRIG HALL, Norfolk.

more than one thousand acres of rich pasture land, which, though many miles distant from any large town, readily lets for twenty shillings an acre. Surely much more land, which is now becoming arable, might be made more profitable by restoring it to its original state: but in farming, as in other matters, the fashion binds us to our interest.

Repton praised Felbrigg as 'by nature one of the most beautiful situations in Norfolk... nor has art been less beautiful'. Vistas cut from the woods were terminated by the sea two miles to the north, and in the other direction the spire of Norwich cathedral twenty miles away. A large tract of heathland 'has lately been enclosed and cultivated under the direction of Mr. Kent'.[44]

Nathaniel Kent's management of the heathland enclosure at Felbrigg became one of the most celebrated improvements in the county. It is described in detail by William Marshall in *The Rural Economy of Norfolk* (1787). Windham needed to take possession of a small freehold farm to effect the improvement. With Kent's mediation, Windham offered above the market value, enlarged the farm and took on the owner as a tenant.

> Having thus... got the entire parish into his possession, and having set out the least fertile part of the heath, as a common, for the poor to collect firing from, – he parcelled out the remainder to different tenants, – laid out roads and driftways, and divided the whole, whether heath or common-field, into inclosures of eight to twelve acres each; or agreeably to the desire, or conveniency, of the intended occupiers.[45]

The enclosure reflected Kent's general principles on the benefits of conserving small farmers and cottagers, which he derived from observing husbandry in Flanders during a three-year stint as an ambassadorial secretary in Brussels.[46] In his *General View of the Agriculture of Norfolk* (1796), published when he was running a highly successful London-based land agency business, Kent attributed a healthy increase in population over twenty years at Felbrigg to the enclosure, comparing it with the stagnation or depopulation of neighbouring un-enclosed parishes over the same period. Where such management was practised in the county, Kent found labourers 'who were so far from being prompt to riot that their attachment to their masters was exemplary'.[47]

Kent's principles and his practice at Felbrigg probably explain Repton's enthusiasm for enclosure at the beginning of his career as a landscape gardener. Travelling through some newly enclosed country in Cambridgeshire in May 1792, Repton got in to an argument with John Byng, who was moved to quote from Goldsmith's *The Deserted Village* at what he saw. Repton replied that enclosure 'was a fine invention and a noble thing for in Norfolk they alloted to each cottager an acre of land'.[48] Kent returned the compliment. In the *General View of the Agriculture of Norfolk*, Kent praised 'the ingenious Mr Repton, so justly famed for his taste in the embellishment of gentlemen's seats'.[49]

The landscape of Felbrigg, and its improvement under Kent's management, appears to have strongly influenced Repton's style of landscape gardening. An engraving after Repton of Felbrigg (fig. 78), first published in 1787, is revealing. The view is from the south, on the road from Sustead, a route that Repton took many times. In the foreground tree planting, using conifers as nurses, supervised by a gentlemanly figure, probably Kent, is in progress. Having turned a corner suddenly to reveal the house, brilliantly whitewashed against the woods, the road sweeps down a hill and around the lake to the park. While this was not the main entrance to Felbrigg, it was a view that Repton repeatedly used to design approaches.[50]

## Norfolk Politics

By 1783 Repton was finding it difficult to afford his life at Sustead. He had nearly exhausted his father's legacy and his 'farming experiments' had not borne fruit. The appointment of Windham as Secretary to the Lord Lieutenant of Ireland 'excited hopes of more solid advantage'. Windham agreed to take Repton to Dublin as his private secretary, 'which shall afford me the advantage and satisfaction of your company and assistance, with fair prospect of benefit to yourself'.[51] Windham resigned his position after little more than a month, saying that he found the strains of office unbearable but also because he was mindful of the forthcoming parliamentary election in Norwich.[52] Repton stayed on another six weeks until the arrival of Windham's successor. He later told Windham that his own time in Ireland was 'three months of anxiety, trouble and disappointment'; in Dublin he 'had seen enough of the path of ambition to know that it was always difficult, sometimes dangerous, and often dirty'.[53] On the return journey from Dublin to Sustead, Repton wrote to his wife:

And now my dearest Mary, what have I been doing? I have learned to love my own home; I have gained some knowledge of the world; some of public business, and some of hopeless expectations; I have made some valuable acquaintances; I have formed some connexions with the great . . . I have lost very little money.[54]

Windham stood successfully for Norwich in the election of 1784. Repton acted as his campaign manager again, but suffered from Windham's aristocratic attitude to his employment. Repton was not reimbursed for the cost of electioneering, nor for the expenses he incurred in Ireland and the trip home.[55] Repton then lost much of his remaining capital in the mail-coach scheme with John Palmer before leaving Sustead and moving to Hare Street.[56]

Throughout his struggles to fashion a career close to London, Repton kept in touch with Norfolk life: attending meetings of the Norfolk Club in the capital, reading the Norfolk newspapers and regularly visiting Aylsham and Norwich. His play, *Odd Whims; Or, Two at a Time*, was staged by the touring Norfolk and Suffolk Company at Romford, Yarmouth and Aylsham in 1786.[57] In 1787 Repton was elected honorary member, and the following year formally admitted to a new philosophical fraternity in Norwich, the College of United Friars, or Society for the Participation of Useful Knowledge. This was an expressly anti-denominational society; members wore habits to denote equality, benevolence and brotherly love. Repton described it as a 'liberal brotherhood' open to men of any rank or fortune, provided they were proficient in some branch of the liberal arts.[58] Repton was probably elected for his literary talents, for he composed a Gothic romance, *The Friar's Tale*, to recite to a meeting (fig. 79). The story is entirely appropriate to Norwich and its north European sensibilities. A cautionary tale of priestcraft, tyranny, suicide and murder set among alpine peaks and precipices, its narrator looks forward to an 'enlightened period' when a new order of friars shall 'mix with the world'.[59] In this multi-talented college of architects, artists, actors, cartographers, musicians and physicians, Repton probably saw the potential for a new, and reformed, profession of landscape gardening. 'Now at the age of 36 years – I commence a new career – and after a temporary rest and half seclusion from the world, I boldly venture forth once more.'[60]

To venture forth on his new career, Repton returned to work in Norfolk politics to establish the basis for a

79  J. Stadler after Humphry Repton, *The Friar's Tale*, from *Odd Whims and Miscellanies* (1804). Yale Center for British Art, Paul Mellon Collection.

network of clients. With the centenary celebrations of the Glorious Revolution of 1688, and a difficult election prompted by the king's insanity, the county Whigs looked to stage a show of might. A number of Repton's circle, including Windham, Marsham and his brother John, persuaded Thomas Coke of Holkham, the county's largest landowner, to stand in the election of 1788.[61] For this election, and for the next two years, in intervals between commissions on landscape gardening, Repton worked for Coke's campaigns and in general for Whig party politics. This took him to Holkham, Norwich and Aylsham, into Suffolk (to Ipswich and Melford) and to

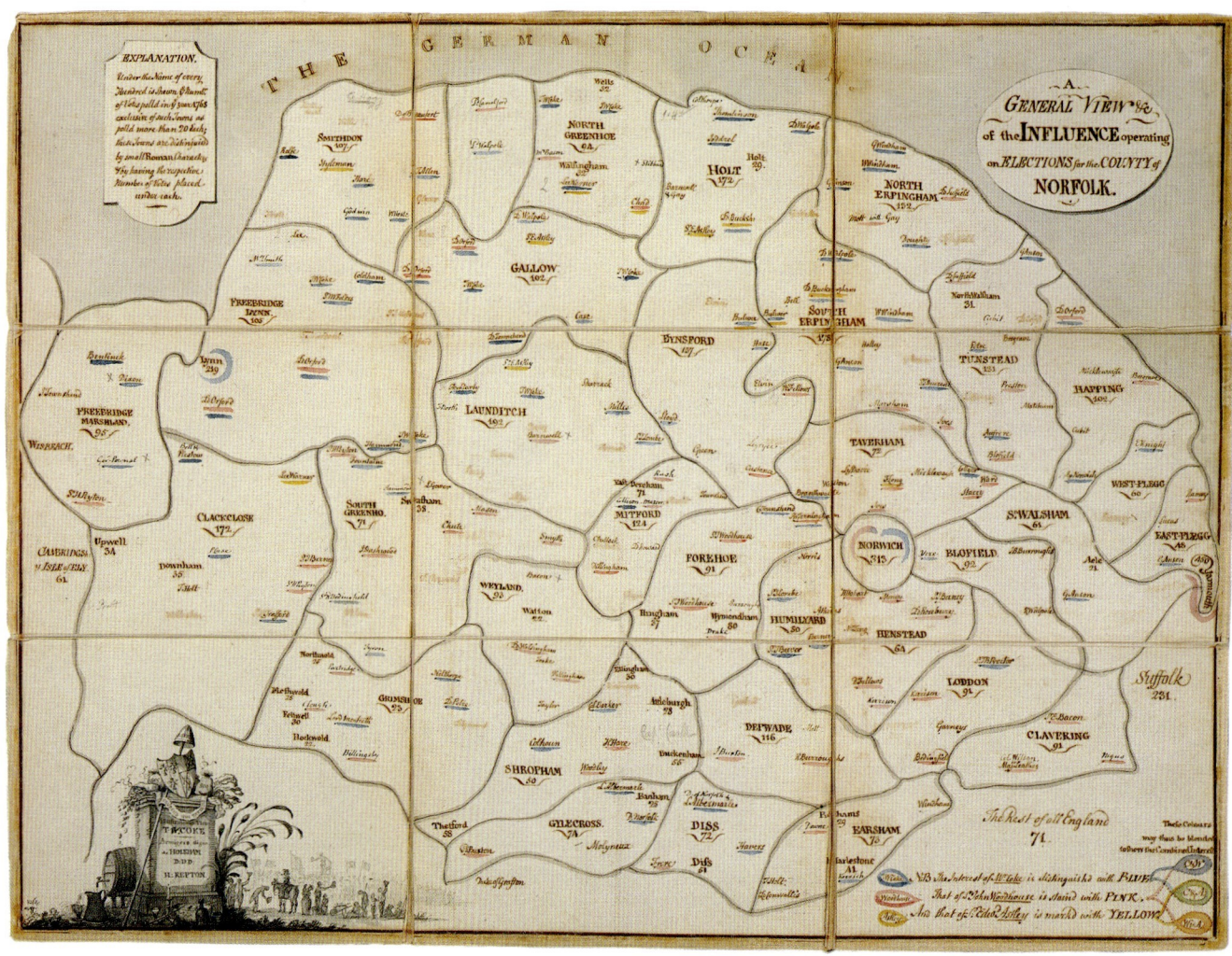

80  *A General View of Influence Operating on the Elections for the County of Norfolk* (1788). By permission of Lord Leicester.

London.[62] Repton was not the only professional man electioneering – Nathaniel Kent was enlisted too – but Repton functioned more as a political agent, working all hours, sometimes for weeks at a time.[63] The campaign of 1788 found him compiling registers of electors and drawing a political map (fig. 80). The map showed established patterns of voting, colour coded with party allegiances, and was embellished with a vignette of electioneering: a candidate speaking from the platform and a plinth piled with bags of money and flanked by barrels of beer.

In his account book Repton listed the costs of his political services for Coke at the same rate as he listed those for landscape gardening:

in my profession it is seldom necessary to give more than 5 hours attendance to the day – In this employment my time has generally been from day light till 9 o'clock at night . . . But if thro' Mr Coke's Interest I shou'd ever derive great advantage from this troublesome business – I purpose to compliment him the Amount of this acc[oun]t as a tribute of my Gratitude.

Coke eventually paid him a 'liberal present of 200£', for landscaping at Holkham as well as 'for the services I render'd him at the last Election when by my exertions he was prevented standing the contest which wou'd have cost him 10,000£ in vain'. Repton also accounted for his work for Windham 'conducted with infinite trouble & for which no other compensation is expected during my life time than the chance of advantage being reaped by me'.[64] Repton's tasks in the campaign of 1790 for Windham's election included designing a banner, organizing transport for voters and settling the account for a prodigious amount of drink. He finally wondered whether 'the advantage I derive from the honour of your friendship' was 'sufficient compensation for time sacrificed in Norwich politics'.[65]

Repton also promoted his new career in a more commercial way by sending out circulars advertizing his profession. Again he used a Norfolk network. A letter to the Revd Norton Nicholls, at Blundeston, near Yarmouth, asking him to distribute circulars, was not directed to a man of much political influence, but to a self-appointed authority on landscaping. A graduate of the Grand Tour, and a friend of the poet Thomas Gray, Nicholls was known for improving his own grounds and advising on those of some notable Norfolk landowners.[66] Repton told Nicholls how much he admired his work for Sir William Jerningham at Costessey, 'every part speaks the hand of a great master and displays the head of one deep read in all that is beautiful and lovely'.[67] But Repton noted in his Memoir: 'for 20 years [Nicholls] had been fond of talking the art of Gardening and of giving advice . . . but we seldom agreed in opinions and I felt that he looked on me with a great deal of jealousy'.[68] Repton made it clear to Nicholls that he was aiming to raise landscape gardening beyond a local rector's recrea-

82 After Humphry Repton, *Catton, Norfolk*, from *Peacock's Polite Repository* (1792). Bodleian Library, Oxford.

tion. He had improved his drawing skills, read the leading authorities on gardens – William Mason, William Gilpin, Thomas Whately and Gérardin – and had visited parks landscaped by William Kent, Mr Richmond and Capability Brown.

> I am promised very ample support from all my friends and have already been honour'd by an introduction to the Duke of York, which I am assured will be follow'd by others to the King and the Prince of Wales because my ambition leads me to hope that I may stand at the head of my profession.[69]

Repton's very first commission, beginning in September 1788, was at Catton, a farming and weaving village just to the north of Norwich (fig. 81). In this period many villages around Norwich were being gentrified with villas and pleasure grounds for the city's commercial élite. Catton was chosen by Jeremiah Ives, a prosperous silk merchant, mayor of the city, prominent Whig and, it follows, a friend of Windham. Ives managed to acquire a larger and more prominent property than most, purchasing the 112-acre manor of Catton, from the Dean and Chapter of Norwich cathedral, on a prominent site sloping down to the city.[70]

The entries for Catton in Repton's account book show how he began to organize his work. After looking over the site together, Repton and Ives were joined on one day by a professional surveyor, James North of Aylsham, and on the next by the architect William Wilkins, a fellow United Friar and another of Windham's platoon of political campaigners.[71] Repton employed North to survey the site at the going rate for the region of one guinea a day and 6d. an acre.[72] Where they collaborated elsewhere, Repton paid Wilkins for his designs, but no payments are entered, so he may have been called in

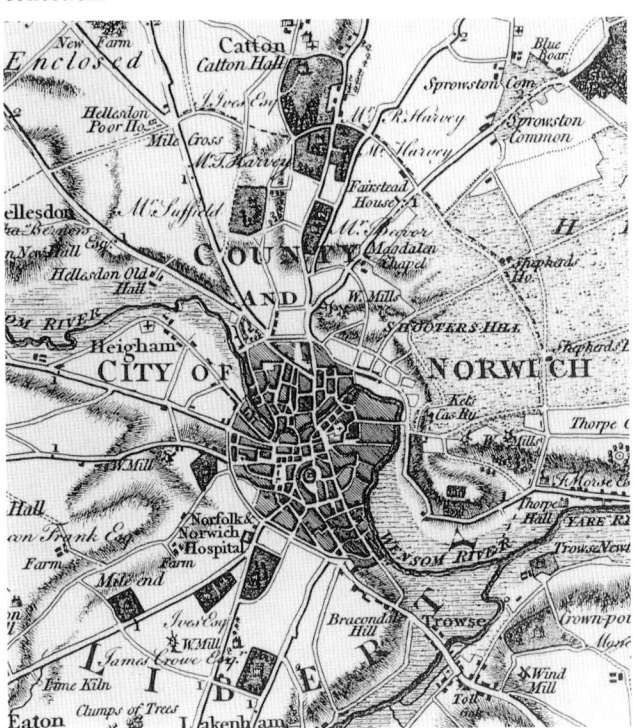

81 City of Norwich, detail, from William Faden, *A Topographical Map of the County of Norfolk* (1797). Private collection.

83  *Catton Park*, looking east (1788). Norfolk Museums Service.

informally to advise on the site of the villa (fig. 82) rather than its design. As Repton had arranged the commission to coincide with a visit to the first Norwich Festival of Music, he waived his travelling expenses. Repton returned to Catton in November to stake out the work on the ground and to redraw the survey map with Ives's requirements, taking out several small fields, and rerouting roads (including the public highway from Norwich) which Ives had successfully petitioned to be diverted. He made further visits in February, May and July 1789 to check work in progress. At three guineas a day, the bill came to £45 6s. 6d., which Ives paid promptly adding 'a compliment of 1/3 of a Lottery Ticket'. Repton listed two more visits in June 1790, perhaps not the last, for he writes that the account is carried forward to the (missing) ledger for 1791.

There is no Red Book for Catton, but two drawings (figs 83 and 84). Shortly before his visit to Catton he told Norton Nicholls: 'the habit of landscape painting I have considerably improved of late'.[73] The drawings for Catton are panoramic in scope and display a number of different vistas. In the use of wash and pen and groupings of livestock there are hints of William Gilpin; in the sepia outlines of foliage and droll-style fashionable figures there are echoes of Rowlandson.[74] One drawing, looking east, shows Repton and Ives standing on a corner looking over the projected improvements, including a line of oaks in the park (former hedgerow trees left standing when the fields were removed), a curving drive passing a rustic cottage and a thickened perimeter belt of trees, broken here and there to create views out to some ornamental plantations in surrounding fields. The other drawing looks south, with Repton seated at his sketch pad showing off his work to two stylishly dressed ladies, probably from the Ives family. This prospect commands the city, with the spire of Norwich cathedral terminating a vista.

'The basic style was that of Brown', observe Williamson and Taigel, on the basis of map and field evidence from Catton as well as Repton's drawings.[75] The positioning of the house on rising ground to command a prospect, the planting of a belt, the thinning of hedgerow trees and the sinking of a ha-ha to separate house from park were hallmarks of the Brown style. They could be found in other small parks round-about, many laid out by landowners without specialist professional advice. Repton's gloss on the Brown style, a reflection of the country around Sustead, was to create a more sociable-looking landscape, in views out across the surrounding landscape, of cottage and cathedral. Also at Catton, Repton pioneered a mode of entry from the public road, beside a group of neat cottages rather than a small entrance lodge, which he later converted in to a principle for places of all kinds, from villas to palaces.[76]

After more than a year of political service for Thomas Coke, Repton started work on a commission at Holkham in the summer of 1789. It stood in marked contrast to that for Catton. Holkham was the largest estate in

84 *Catton Park with Norwich in the Distance*, looking south (1788). Norfolk Museums Service.

Norfolk, located in a region of great estates – notably Houghton and Rainham – and large tenant farms in north-west Norfolk (fig. 85). The celebrity of the region was its highly capitalized reclamation from hitherto infertile sands. In contrast to Catton's hundred acres, from whose fields Repton fashioned a park, the park at Holkham was huge and long established, more than two thousand acres and landscaped by a succession of major figures, including Kent and Brown. Thomas Coke was continuing the efforts of his forebears to expand the park as part of a wider programme of improvements. Repton positioned his proposals within Coke's grand design.

After inheriting Holkham in 1776, Coke embarked on an extensive programme of improvements throughout the estate. He stimulated agricultural production on his tenant farms through new leases, drawn up by Nathaniel Kent, and through new buildings, including fashionable farmhouses, designed by Samuel Wyatt. He created a showpiece home farm within the newly expanded park perimeter with a massive Great Barn designed by Wyatt as a venue for agricultural shows, and conducted an extensive campaign of planting under the direction of John Sandys. Near the mansion, Coke spent lavishly on creating a new kitchen garden and improving the lake and pleasure grounds. Under the direction of William Emes, the lake (a former tidal creek) was altered, cleared of an island created by William Kent, and given a serpentine twist. The slopes around were planted with a variety of species to form a variety of views.[77] One day

85 Holkham Hall, detail, from William Faden, *A Topographical Map of the County of Norfolk* (1797). Private collection.

a week, Holkham was open to the public, and visitors singled out the pleasure grounds, especially the views to the church, as the most appealing episode on the circuit.[78]

Repton worked on the pleasure grounds at Holkham on the shores of the lake (fig. 86), an area little larger than his field of operations at Catton. The time he expended, ten days in all, was about the same too. A major difference was that half of Repton's time at Holkham was spent preparing a Red Book of designs, with a map he personally surveyed, his best artwork to date and a highly detailed text, breaking in to Italian and French verse.[79] This he presented as a gift to Coke's wife, Jane, in return for the indulgence that the family had shown to 'me and my performances [probably musical or theatrical] on so many occasions'.

> As the hints which I have now the honour to suggest relate entirely to the pleasure ground, unconnected with the great outline which Mr Coke is pursuing in the improvement of the Park at Holkham, there seem'd to me a sort of propriety in addressing my thoughts on the subject to *you*, as well as to Mr Coke, because altho' I hope he will perceive that I carefully endeavour to avoid anything that may interfere with his more extensive Plans, yet this essential part of a perfect place being peculiar to the Ladies, it requires a minute correctness of design which I trust will justify my detail.

'Magnificence', Holkham already possessed: 'a vast expanse of lawn, an immense sheet of water, & woods of such extent as to leave the parts of the Landscape too large for painting to express'. Instead Repton proposed 'convenience', a 'sheltered dry walk within those woods, or along the banks of that water'. 'Such convenience may be attained not only without interference, but may be made (tho' detached) subservient to it, as a kind of Epic ode worthy of its situation.'

Repton set out a complex series of paths through the woods, along the lake shore and across the water by means of a small ferry 'so contrived as to be navigated with the greatest ease by any Lady, without more trouble than that of turning a winch' (fig. 45). The walk took in a series of existing, improved or proposed sites – a new boathouse (designed by Wyatt), cottage and cave – with branches to the church and the projected kitchen garden. It disclosed a succession of views within and beyond the woods, including a vista along the lake to the sea, and the extensive prospect from the church on the hill. For those going on to take the grand drive around the park, a path led out to 'a seat in some lovely spot . . . to repose, or be useful until the Carriages meet us'.[80]

The scenery Repton envisioned within the pleasure grounds at Holkham, a world apart from the country beyond, was inspired by that in the west of England. Following his first survey of the grounds at Holkham,

86  The lake, from the Red Book for Holkham (1789). Holkham Hall. By permission of Lord Leicester.

87 'A cottage in the style of a fishing hut on the banks of the Severn', from the Red Book for Holkham (1789). By permission of Lord Leicester.

Repton journeyed to Shropshire, to a commission at Ferney Hall recently purchased by Samuel Phipps, a Lincoln's Inn lawyer. Repton produced the Red Book for Ferney immediately after his visit and just before that for Holkham.[81] Ferney was close to Downton, seat of the connoisseur Richard Payne Knight, and Repton asked Knight's advice on landscaping the steep rocky dells at Ferney, 'acknowledging that [he] had not been so conversant as himself in that style of scenery'.[82] On the same trip Repton met Knight's fellow connoisseur Uvedale Price, took excursions into the surrounding country and was praised for his skill in drawing.[83]

Repton proposed refashioning the pleasure grounds at Holkham in a consciously picturesque manner. A concealed gradient would conduct the stranger 'along an upper path so much above that by which he came . . . this sort of surprise tho' easily practised in hilly country, will appear a perfect wonder in Norfolk'. A projected thatched cottage (fig. 87) is 'unlike the usual cottages in Norfolk', resembling 'some Fishing Huts on the banks of the Severn'. A chalk quarry is transformed through the addition of creeper into a cavern, echoing a passage of the meditative reverie Repton quotes from Delille's poem *Les Jardins* (1782) and perhaps also the 'caves and cells' Repton observed at Knight's Downton.[84]

The pleasure ground needed to be well staffed:

The Cottage therefore must be inhabited, and however whimsically humble its outside may appear, it may afford a Comfortable residence to some Labourer within, whose employment should warrant the situation. This man should have the care of the boats and see them properly rigg'd and dress'd in their colours on public days &c, he shou'd lay out nets and liggers and be at hand to navigate the pleasure boats when any Lady may require it; he may also keep clean the paths about his own dwelling, & shou'd always work within hearing of a bell, that he may bring over the Ferry boat to the side on which it may be wanted.

How much of Repton's scheme for Holkham was carried out? Later maps show no evidence of boathouse, cottage or cave; there is no reference in the accounts to the construction of these features and no trace of them now can be found on the ground.[85] Repton's network of paths, or something resembling it, does seem to have been laid out. Repton claimed in subsequent publications that this work had been done: 'the magnificent lake has been dressed by walks on its banks, and a peculiar ferry-boat invented to unite the opposite shores'.[86]

At Catton and Holkham, in contrasting ways, Repton made his mark on the polite landscape of Norfolk. His designs for Catton enhanced the importance of the place and helped to establish it as a dominant landscape to the north of the city, a leading social venue and political headquarters. His designs for Holkham embellished an already powerful place, and by scaling down the landscape around the lake, and broadening its allusions, extended its appeal to a range of potential clients, men of middling income and wives of grandees.

In the later eighteenth century there was, as Repton witnessed, a massive increase in the number of small and medium-sized parks in Norfolk.[87] With a professional and family background in Norwich and its region, continuing connections with the county's commercial citizenry and landed aristocracy, experience as an amateur improver, familiarity with professional improvers who were redefining the cultural reputation of Norfolk, the apprenticeship of his son John Adey to William Wilkins and prime early commissions on a suburban and country estate in the county, it is hard to imagine a better basis for a career as landscape gardener to the Norfolk gentry. But Repton did not receive the rush of commissions in Norfolk that he had expected. After Catton and Holkham, there followed a few minor commissions, staking out an approach for free for a friend at Hanworth near Sustead and some work on two neighbouring estates, Buckenham and Tofts, in the far south-east of the county which probably came through the Essex property of one of the owners. But there is nothing of substance on record in Norfolk for more than two years. In his Memoir, to underline his fate as the exiled prophet, Repton lists Catton and Holkham as 'Nos 1 and 2' of his commissions and attributes his neglect to the passing of an older style of patronage, not expressly political, but a convivial form of commission, which found Repton 'enjoying the society of those who consulted me'; Ives and Coke were 'two friends who, like myself have outlived the 18th century; and have seen many changes, tho' none in the regard I have ever had for each'.[88] Repton made this complaint about changes to his career everywhere, so it is important to examine the situation in Norfolk, and Repton's relation to it, more closely.

There are a number of developments that could have frustrated Repton's ambitions. Of more than one hundred parks shown on Faden's *Topographical Map of Norfolk* (1797) just a handful are attributable to any professional designer. Repton made no greater impact than other names, such as Brown, Kent and Richmond. It was relatively cheap to fashion a small landscape park, and there were plenty of places to imitate, both observed on tours around the country and in albums of views. Like Repton himself at Sustead, many minor gentry did the work themselves, perhaps with a little assistance from nurserymen, stewards, or local advisers such as Norton Nicholls. Some local gentry may have been indifferent to, or actively resisted, new fashions. Taigel and Williamson chart the persistence and renovation of such features as walled enclosures that standard narratives of English garden history have long demolished. They quote the observations of Richard Hulton on the improvements by Richmond to the grounds of his brother-in-law Jacob Preston at Beeston St Lawrence, one of the works Repton had studied and where he was later to be commissioned:

> Mr. P. had one of the gentleman improvers here to modernize his grounds and is busy levelling his lawns, removing gardens, walls and trees, and laying down a new kitchen garden more remote from the house. It would grieve you if you were here . . . but so it must be, our ideas are more extensive than those of our ancestors . . . [we] must extend our view over improved grounds as far as the eye can see without any disagreeable object intervening.[89]

Meanwhile Repton's career had taken off elsewhere. His work for the Whig interest in Norfolk had paid off, taking him away from the county by securing the patronage of the duke of Portland and a nationwide network of clients. He used other contacts in Norfolk to open up opportunities elsewhere. An introduction to Lord Loughborough, a judge on the Norfolk circuit, led to a commission at Loughborough's seat in Yorkshire and to further meetings in London and Bath.[90] When living at Sustead, Repton knew the composer and music historian Charles Burney and sent him his circular, with specimen drawings, to give out to influential friends in London.[91]

Despite, or perhaps because of, his work for the Whig interest, Repton quickly realized that in a commercial culture too strong a political identity could be a liability. As he put it to Windham in 1804: 'In the course of my profession, I have had the honour to become acquainted with almost all the Statesmen and all the Leaders of different Parties, without sacrificing the pursuits of taste for those of politics'.[92] There was a growing professionally minded population, including Repton himself, that was repelled by the very idea of political favour. What Repton valued about the duke of Portland's patronage was being treated and paid on his merits as a professional.[93] Before he returned to Norfolk to work in 1792, Repton had begun more than forty recorded commissions elsewhere. Some were scattered widely, from North Yorkshire to Cornwall. Many were within a day's ride of Repton's residence in Hare Street, such as those in Suffolk: indeed the flourishing of commissions in Suffolk in the first two years of Repton's career contrasts with their scarcity in Norfolk.[94]

*Norfolk Fashion*

Repton was eventually commissioned in Norfolk again around 1792 at three places: Honing and Northrepps about ten miles from Aylsham, and Bracondale outside Norwich. The properties varied in character: Honing was an established farming estate with an existing house and park, Northrepps and Bracondale a few fields purchased for villa and grounds, but all the clients were drawn from the professions. Thomas Cubitt, from a long-established local family, was a Lincoln's Inn lawyer who had purchased Honing with a large cash settlement from his marriage to the daughter of a wealthy London merchant.[95] Northrepps was purchased by Bartlett Gurney, a Norwich merchant, scion of the city's leading Quaker family and a United Friar.[96] Bracondale was purchased by Philip Martineau, from the leading Unitarian family of Norwich and the most eminent provincial surgeon of the time.[97] In the Red Books for these commissions Repton takes the opportunity to show how the landscaping of Norfolk had suffered from a lack of professional attention.

'There is hardly any part of England in which I am less known professionally than in Norfolk (perhaps from it being "the Prophet's own Country") it is for this reason that I am happy to avail myself of the present instance to explain the principles on which I found my opinions', so the Red Book for Honing begins. Repton was looking forward to systematizing the opinions he had scattered 'in a hundred such volumes as this' in published form; until then he had to quote from commissions from all over the country, and his client would 'not perhaps be displeased to possess a book of scraps like the present, if it serves to elucidate my advice respecting Honing'.

The Honing Red Book is set out in categories, which by now provided Repton with a formula for his advice. Under 'Situation and Character', Repton reminds his client that Honing is not a sporting seat or a suburban retreat, but is 'to be classed with respectable country seats of gentlemen', and so 'picturesque effect' is not to be purchased at 'the price of comfort'. As the small park at Honing was surrounded by his client's farmland, it might be possible to extend the lawns, but 'however it may be the fashion of Norfolk to throw down hedges & unite Lawn with Corn Lands, I must deem this as false taste, as I hold them to be incompatible with each other'. Whereupon Repton transcribes three pages on this principle from the Red Books for Hanslope in Buckinghamshire and Wyddial in Hertfordshire, with a supporting reference from another for Ealing in Middlesex. Repton was seeking to erase local fashions to formulate a national style.

Repton had hardened his preference for pasture in to a principle. While agricultural land might be enjoyed 'in looking on a distant prospect of a richly cultivated country' or 'in a ride or a walk thro' a well dressed farm', 'we are disgusted with the nearer views of the same objects from a mansion where elegance or affluence are the prevailing characters'. Neither the 'brilliant green' of a field in spring, nor its 'golden autumnal garment', could compensate for the 'naked and comfortless appearance of its fallow state'. Moreover 'Labour and hardship attend the operations of agriculture, whether cattle are tearing up the surface of the soil, or men reaping its produce'. Only the 'permanent verdure of grass land' animated by gently grazing sheep and cattle could 'excite the pleasing idea of happiness and comfort annexed to a pastoral life'. Thus Repton proposed surrounding the park at Honing with a belt of trees, dressed in front with flowering shrubs 'as to be equally beautiful with most Norfolk views of distant objects, generally consisting of a windmill or church steeple, over hedges & flat cornfields'. Glimpses of the surrounding countryside might be admitted in

88   View towards the hill field, with and without overlay, from the Red Book for Honing Hall (1797). Private collection.

89   View from the proposed site of the house, with and without overlay, from the Red Book for Northrepps (c.1792). Private collection.

small openings through the plantations, or along a perimeter walk in summer; and the home farm would form a worthy destination if 'ornamented by sweet briar hedges and broad grass headlands'. A hill field belonging to Lord Orford in view of the house across the park (fig. 88) might be purchased and a keeper's lodge built on its summit, taking the form of Repton's trade mark, an old 'tower embosomed high in tufted trees'.[98]

The Honing accounts record just one five-guinea visit by Repton, so it failed to develop as a commission. It is moreover difficult to establish from map or field evidence how many features are an outcome of Repton's proposals, and, if so, when they were implemented. The hill field was incorporated in the landscape. One direct effect of Repton's advice was visible on the mid-eighteenth-century house and was largely cosmetic. 'The proportions of the house are not pleasing, it appears too high for its width.' Repton sought to rectify this by adding a white string-course under the first-floor windows, not 'at great expense' for it was in fact only painted on.[99]

The commissions at Northrepps and Bracondale probably came through William Wilkins, to provide settings for villas the Norwich architect designed.[100] There were extensive views at Northrepps but Repton found little in them to recommend. Ownership was so fragmented that 'we must look over a vast tract of country not in the power of any single individual to improve'. In Norfolk 'a prospect is generally described by the number of its church steeples, but it is the business of taste to shake off the fetters of local opinions'. The property was surrounded by ploughed lands and turnip fields, 'subjects not easily represented in a picture', even ones designed to represent scenes to be improved.[101] In Repton's illustration of improvements (figs 5 and 89) the ploughed land is emparked to provide a site for a house, but neither house nor park materialized.[102]

In the Red Book for Bracondale Repton calls on 'the inventive genius of my friend Mr Wilkins' to adapt his design to the site overlooking the Yare valley, notably 'to depart from all quadrangular ideas, bow windows and other hackneyed forms'. Wilkins came up with a semi-circular, bay-windowed villa for Repton's friend, the surgeon Philip Martineau, a leading figure in the cultural life of Norwich. Repton's illustrations of prospective views from the villa have a diagrammatic quality which reflects his new interest in optics and perhaps that of his client. The Red Book was presented to Martineau 'as a tribute to the eminence you have acquired in your profession'. Bracondale did not overlook Norwich; indeed Repton trusted the improvements 'may tend to soften the anxieties of your profession' by screening the industrial village of Trowse, which 'continue[s] the idea of the neighbouring city'.[103] The view he found most 'delightful' was that further along the Yare to the village of Thorpe (fig. 90). This view had both personal associations – Martineau's wife was the daughter of the rector of Thorpe – and broader cultural associations.[104] A gentrified village, with villas and summer houses, Thorpe was, according to one guidebook, the 'Richmond of Norfolk', and Repton represents it in the same way he depicts views of villas by the Thames.[105]

Bracondale was built and laid out to Repton's specifications, but it was another fourteen years before he was commissioned in Norfolk again. Repton himself may have been keen to loosen his connections with the county. If Wilkins helped to secure Repton commissions in Norfolk, outside Norfolk Repton found the architect's assistance an increasing liability. Wilkins's proposals were rejected, before and after he had drawn up plans. One of Repton's clients, John Geers Cotterell of Garnons, near Hereford, who had commissioned James Wyatt, did not bother to pay Wilkins's travelling expenses, moving the architect to protest that he was not a 'common country builder ... [nor] young inexperienced Artist from Town'. 'Oppressed by the arrears which his gout had brought upon him', as Repton put it to Cotterell,

90  View towards Thorpe, from the Red Book for Bracondale (*c.*1792). Courtesy Norfolk Libraries and Information Service.

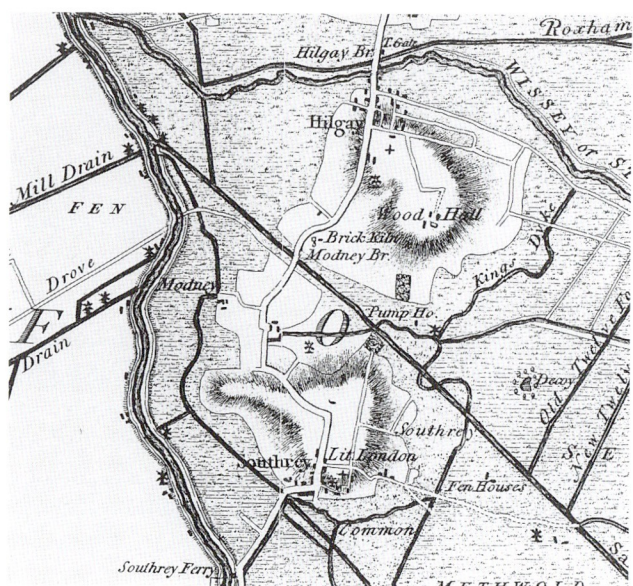

91 Wood Hall and surrounding country, detail, from William Faden, *A Topographical Map of the County of Norfolk* (1797). Private collection.

Wilkins remained in Norwich to do minor works round-about and to concentrate on running the Theatre Royal. And in 1796 Repton found a more fashionable partner in John Nash.[106]

Also, conditions in Norfolk worsened for all kinds of employment. The textile trade entered a deep depression, taking most other business with it. Building more or less stopped for the next fifteen years. The population growth of Norwich slowed virtually to a standstill, and the city may have suffered a net loss. Distress was rife throughout the city and its region. Disaffection was mobilized through Jacobin clubs and corresponding societies. Staying at Aylsham, Fanny Burney was 'truly amazed to find this country filled with little revolution societies which transmit their notions to the larger committee at Norwich which communicates the whole to the reformists in London. I am told there is scarce a village in Norfolk free from these meetings'.[107] Robert Marsham was appalled to find Jacobin clubs in Stratton Strawless.[108] The Whig alliance fractured, leaving Repton's circle divided. Standing in the election of 1796 as an anti-war candidate, Bartlett Gurney almost succeeded in ousting William Windham.[109] Norfolk was scarcely the place to market landscape gardening, let alone that of a native of Norfolk who subscribed to a consensual view of county culture.

\* \* \*

92 View towards the south, with and without overlay, from the Red Book for Wood Hall (1807). Private collection.

## Repton's Return

In the fourteen years from 1792 to 1806, before his professional return to Norfolk, Repton undertook over two hundred commissions elsewhere and published three books on landscape gardening, saw off most of his rivals and found favour with every conceivable kind of client. But latterly, as discussed in the last chapter, he suffered from the developments that had first afflicted his career in Norfolk. Repton sensed that he had passed the peak of his career but was hopeful that the partnership with his son John Adey would transform his profession. John Adey's designs were shaped by his apprenticeship with Wilkins and by his antiquarian research, much of it in Norfolk. He designed Tudor-period Norfolk-style buildings for commissions throughout the country and was preparing what his father called 'a great work on gothic architecture'.[110]

Repton's revival in Norfolk was initially as a playwright. Wilkins persuaded him to rewrite *Odd Whims* for production at the Theatre Royal, and Repton published the play for the first time with plates of important scenes (fig. 4) and a dedication to Windham.[111] Windham organized the coastal defences of Norfolk during the invasion scare of 1803 to 1805, when loyalist feeling gripped East Anglia.[112] When *Odd Whims* was performed in Ipswich in 1803, the audience stopped the show with their cheering when a character declared 'in England we fear no enemies'.[113] Repton was also revived for a Norfolk audience through the writings of Edmund Bartell, a Norwich physician and amateur artist, whose guidebooks to the north of the county and hints on cottage improvement quote extensively from Repton's published works.[114] Bartell was a leading member of the Norwich Society of Painters, and if, as Andrew Hemingway suggests, we read his writings as 'offering an aesthetic theory for Norwich painting', we can see correspondences between Repton's return to Norfolk and the cultural renaissance that focussed on the landscapes of artists such as Cotman and Crome.[115]

Repton marked his return to Norfolk with his first commission in the fen country in the far west of the county. In September 1806 the Reptons visited Wood Hall perched on a fen island at Hilgay near Downham Market. This commission may not have come through Norwich connections; indeed it was somewhat remote from the regional culture of the city. Those who knew the place only from 'The Great Map of Norfolk' (that is, Faden's celebrated map of 1797; fig. 91), wrote Repton, would reckon that it was 'incapable of being made the pleasant, the healthy & even the beautiful situation which my promises hold forth'. Through recent improvements 'the most desperate Morasses have been changed into sound Land, yielding plenteous harvests'. Such improvement alone was not sufficient to enhance the scenery, for in most directions the house was surrounded by an expanse 'taking more the appearance of the Ocean than of Landscape', and the signs of reclamation, the long drainage ditches running straight for miles, served only to disfigure it. 'It is my peculiar province to produce *beauty* in addition to *profit*, & to adorn the face of the Country, while my friend Mr Kent, and others, improve the Value.' Repton's solution was to remove a 'cabbage garden' (fig. 92) to screen much of the surrounding country and to take advantage of the view south, looking clear of a long drain and pump house, to the wooded slopes of another fen island.[116]

John Adey's contribution focused on the house, in a style he called 'Queen Elizabeth's Gothic':

> There are (proportionally) more houses of this stile, and character in the County of Norfolk than in any other part of the Kingdom yet the rage for altering has destroyed and mutilated many within the last twenty years & I was happy to find that it was proposed to restore rather than destroy the original Character of Woodhall, part of which has been taken down, leaving a gap through the Body of the House.

Repton proposed to rebuild the centre, restore the north front, replace sash-windows with bow-windows and add a chapel-like conservatory to the east side (fig. 93). The 'original Character' of the outside was to be combined with an internal arrangement adapted to 'the Comforts

93 The house, with and without overlay, from the Red Book for Wood Hall (1807). Private collection.

94 *Barningham, Norfolk*, with and without overlay, from *Fragments on the Theory and Practice of Landscape Gardening* (1816). Yale Center for British Art, Paul Mellon Collection.

of Modern Life'. The architectural aspects of the commission may have been paramount, for the Red Book was produced in February 1807 at Aylsham where John Adey was living with his aunt, Repton's sister. Moreover the London publisher Josiah Boydell (John Boydell's nephew), 'whose name', Repton noted, 'gives a peculiar sanction to every work of art', accompanied the Reptons on the site visit (he was a friend of the client, William Jones) and oversaw production of the Red Book, 'prepared under his Eye & with his full approbation'.[117] Perhaps he was considering John Adey's 'great work of gothic architecture' for publication.

Shortly after the Reptons prepared plans for another 'Queen Elizabeth's Gothic mansion' for Thomas Mott, the new owner of Barningham Hall next to Sustead, in the same modern preservationist spirit as those for Wood Hall (fig. 94).[118] John Adey was asked by Windham to design a staircase skylight at Felbrigg.[119] Humphry Repton did not think it appropriate for the 'pseudo Gothic style which neither John nor I could prevail on ourselves to imitate' and did not send it, but thought its 'pure style' could be included in his son's 'great work'.[120] At a time when Repton was finding it difficult to secure commissions anywhere in the country, he continued to petition Windham for work at Felbrigg, mentioning that while he usually charged fifty guineas to places up to one hundred miles he charged Norfolk clients only twenty-five.[121] Windham failed to pay for any of the advice, prompting Repton to complain that he 'never got a shilling' for anything he had done for his early patron, who compounded the insult by sending for Nash.[122] Despite the discount Repton offered, Norfolk landowners were proving as reluctant as others elsewhere, taxed to prosecute the war, to commission him; those who did – like clients elsewhere – ignored his advice, commissioned other consultants and were slow to settle their accounts.[123] The war, or rather a famous battle, then promised to restore Repton's reputation. Nelson's victory at Trafalgar, and the government's intention to commemorate it, held out the prospect of his most prestigious commission in Norfolk and in the nation.

## Sheringham

Following the Battle of Trafalgar, a number of monuments to Nelson were built by state patronage and public subscription. A Norfolkman, born near the coast at Burnham Thorpe, Nelson was revered in his home county; the citizenry of Yarmouth raised an impressive column to his memory.[124] Parliament voted an annual pension of five thousand pounds for a family peerage (settled on Nelson's brother, a clergyman who had never been to sea in his life) and another ninety thousand pounds for the purchase of a country seat. On a professional visit to the Speaker of the Commons, Charles Abbot, at his Sussex home in December 1808, Repton scribbled a hasty note to his son William in Aylsham:

> Before I go to bed I will tell you that the Speaker desires me to look out for a purchase for Lord Nelson, it must be in a Maritime County & ought to have a house fit for a Nobleman to be call'd Trafalgar – but if no such house exists & an addition might make it as he thinks Parl. would grant a Sum to be paid out in adding the building.

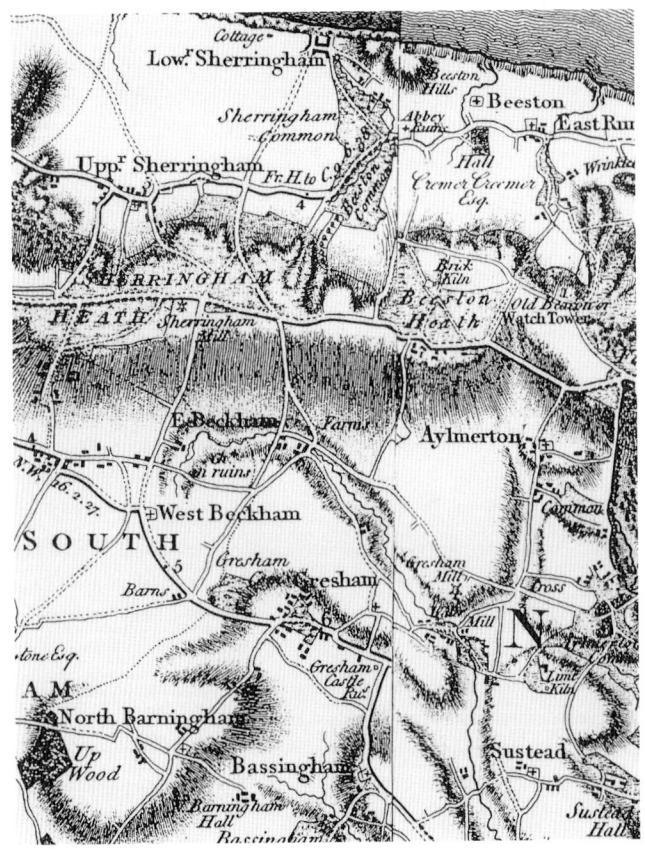

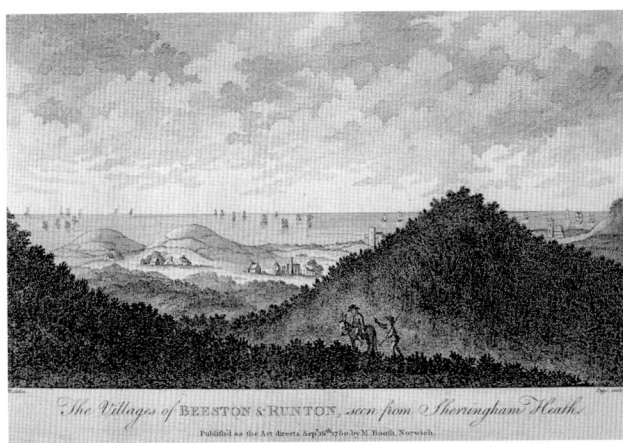

96 *above* After Humphry Repton, *The Villages of Beeston and Runton from Sheringham Heath*, from M.J. Armstrong (ed.), *The History and Antiquities of the County of Norfolk*, vol. 3 (1787). Private collection.

95 *left* North Norfolk from Sustead to Sheringham, detail, from William Faden, *A Topographical Map of the County of Norfolk* (1797). Private collection.

The Speaker preferred an elevated site overlooking the sea, which could be crowned with a commemorative flag or tower. There were surely such estates on the market on the coast of Norfolk; 'so look out sharp and write to me soon'.[125]

Repton asked his son about the estate of Sir Roger Kerrison to the west of Sustead, up for sale because its deceased owner, the Receiver General of Taxes, had embezzled more than £500,000. Kerrison had died owing William a large sum, and a commission would help ease both Reptons' financial situations. In reply William said that it was not suitable, and he suggested nearby Sheringham instead.[126] He was overseeing the impending enclosure bill for Sheringham, and his client, Cook Flower, wanted a quick sale.[127] Not only did Sheringham overlook the sea but it was a signal station in the coastal defence system, with a flag-pole and tower. The Speaker requested further particulars; 'so send me all you can – with the present & supposed improved rents – & even a sketch of the situation if you can get it map'd without expense or trouble'.[128] The Speaker was not persuaded, reckoning the value of the Sheringham estate too low and objecting to the lack of a mansion.[129]

Nearly three years later, in July 1811, Sheringham was sold through William Repton's agency to a private client, Abbot Upcher, for a little more than half the sum set aside for Lord Nelson's estate. While enchanted with the 'beautiful and romantic grounds' at Sheringham, Upcher was 'cruelly disappointed in the house, it being only a better kind of farmhouse'. So William introduced Upcher to his father to provide plans for improving the estate around a new house.[130] Repton paid his first site visit the following year in June 1812, after Upcher had taken possession, and submitted a Red Book a month later.[131]

Six miles from Sustead, Sheringham and its scenery were familiar to Repton (figs 95 and 96). Twenty-five years before, in his contribution to Armstrong's *History*, he had described 'the beauty of the country, surrounded by richly cultivated, and what in Norfolk may be called bold and lofty hills'. Sheringham was 'beautifully adorned by the extensive woods of Mr Cook Flower, the summits of the hills are planted, whilst their bottoms and the rich vallies that divide them are variegated with unenclosed arable land, which though the soil is light, produces excellent barley, wheat and turnips'. There was a 'pleasing prospect' of the 'unbounded ocean' animated with scores of fishing boats and fleets of colliers, and at low water the beach was 'enlivened by the multitude of fishermen' drying nets, hauling boats, repairing tackle and landing fish.[132] By the end of the century this coastal region had become popular with tourists. Guidebooks echoed, often transcribed, passages from Repton's description of the charming scenery of Sheringham, but their disgust at the condition of the poor could not be concealed, especially in the lower part of the village by the sea. This was 'remarkable for nothing but miserable looking huts, and by no means merry looking inhabitants – there is a large supply of little shoe and stockingless children . . . starvelings'.[133] Edmund Bartell singled out good and bad examples of dwellings and offered hints for their improvement derived from Repton's published writings on landscape gardening.[134] All polite commentators agreed that the precondition for further improvement was enclosing the remaining commons:

> tracts of rugged heath-ground, or of barren sand, gapped and encaverned by the burrowing rabbit . . . can be meliorated into cheerful pasturage, bounteous cornfields, flowery hedgerows, and future groves . . . the dreary hut can be replaced by the more comfortable cottage, and the sweet note of the linnet succeed to the plaint of the peewit.[135]

In the first decade of the nineteenth century the coastal region prospered. The decennial population increase for Sheringham was spectacular (thirty-seven per cent), which may seem deceptive for a place that grew to only 641 inhabitants, but it was sufficient to transform it in to a town where two-thirds of the inhabitants had recently arrived. Larger places along the coast, like Cromer, recorded high rates, far outstripping rates in the interior of the county (the average for Norfolk was just seven per cent).[136] Property values soared. So did wheat prices. With a rent roll of nine hundred pounds, a large labour force and the scope for improvements, William Repton reckoned that Upcher had a bargain.[137] But the social costs of inflation were soon evident.

The region's prosperity went largely into the pockets of farmers and landlords, and prices were reaching a peak. Supplies of paper money were deregulated, prompting a run on country banks. The harvest of 1812 was a failure, raising the spectre of famine. A growing labour force liberated from the dependency of farm service caused chronic concern among conservative interests; anxiety was now acute as labourers were thrown out of employment and on to the parish for relief. At the time of Repton's commission at Sheringham, in the summer of 1812, social conflicts everywhere were sharpening. The period was one of prosperity for farmers, taking advantage of the high price of wheat, and of deep distress for labourers, scarcely able to buy bread.[138] Expenditure on poor relief rose sharply in Sheringham, in line with the trend in the county.[139] Industrial relations were bitter. Handloom weavers throughout the country protested violently against the introduction of machinery and reductions in wages, and the military were deployed to control the threat of insurrection. 'The times look portentous . . . all the Country seems in Arms', Repton wrote to William at Aylsham in April. 'How do your weavers go on – have they begun to throw the Meat about the Market instead of throwing their Shuttles?'[140]

Repton told Upcher it was a distinct advantage that Sheringham was beyond the weaving region of Norfolk and the influence of its workers.

> The manufacturer is a different species of animal to the Husbandman, the Sailor, or even the Miner: not to mention their difference in Religion & Morality. The latter from being occupied in employments requiring bodily exertion, look for their Relaxations in the society of their families with whom they are shared – but the Manufacturer leads a sedentary life, always working at home & looking for Relaxation in the Society of his Club – that birthplace & cradle of discontent and of Rebellious principles.[141]

The farming and fishing settlements of Sheringham presented an easier field for the deployment of Abbot Upcher's moral stewardship, and Repton set about planning a comprehensive regime of improvements.

Despite their age difference, the 60-year-old landscape gardener and the 28-year-old squire struck up an immediate rapport. The only son of a Norfolk squire at Ormesby, near Yarmouth, Abbot Upcher had married a neighbouring clergyman's daughter. After two years' search for a suitable country seat in the county, and on the advice of Thomas Coke of Holkham, Abbot and Charlotte Upcher settled on Sheringham, purchasing it with the money from selling farms scattered around Suffolk.[142] In leasing their previous estate, the couple had already demonstrated their paternalism – relieving beggars at the door, visiting cottagers, reading the bible to servants before breakfast, distributing food and blankets, paying a poor man's debts – acts they dutifully entered in their journals.¹⁴³ Abbot Upcher entered his purchase of Sheringham in the same terms:

> How did our hearts throb with gratitude to the Father of all mercies for at last giving us a place of our own! Oh! God may we show forth our gratitude, not by mere words only, but by doing all the good which lies in our power to the poor and needy of Sheringham, and by setting a virtuous example to all around us ... What enchanting scenery for the Muses' votary ... what a region for the sportsman ... what walks with my dear wife and little ones! ... what a spot to educate them in and teach them, to the best of my humble and weak abilities, their duty towards God and their fellow creatures ... Oh! what scenes of rational yet heartfelt pleasure do we not anticipate in the lovely Sheringham.¹⁴⁴

In the dedication to Upcher in the Red Book, Repton refers to their conversations on the spot at Sheringham as 'the delightful intercourse of congenial minds', confessing that he could 'not resist the desire to cultivate a more lasting intimacy & to obtain your confidence by proving the interest I take in your future happiness: for this reason my work has been executed "con amore"'. The congeniality of his client was matched by that of the country.

> After having passed nearly half a century in the study of Natural Scenery & after having been professionally consulted in the improvement of many hundred places in different parts of England, I can with truth pronounce that Sherringham possesses more natural beauty and local advantages than any place I have ever seen ... From its being in Norfolk (which tho not classed among the picturesque counties happens to be the 'Prophet's own Country') it is with peculiar satisfaction that I leave this Record, of such a specimen of my Art, as I never before had an opportunity of displaying: and should these hints be honor'd by your approbation & adoption, this may be considered my most favorite work.¹⁴⁵

Repton assured his client that Sheringham's 'Value will increase in proportion to its Improvement, even in the opinion of those who know no standard of value but Gold or its flimsy representatives'. The place would 'be made a source of interest more interesting than the interest upon interest of the usurer'.¹⁴⁶ Upcher soon realized the importance of the commission for Repton. Calling at Barningham, the neighbouring estate, Upcher reported 'Repton hurt at seeing his oaks cut down in the park and his plans which he had given to Mott so entirely departed from'.¹⁴⁷

97 After Humphry Repton, *Scene at Osborne in the Isle of Wight*, from *Peacock's Polite Repository* (1810). Private collection.

In searching for a comparison with Sheringham, Repton alighted on the 'boasted scenery' of the Isle of Wight. Repton helped to enhance the island's current reputation as the 'Garden of England' through a number of commissions there (fig. 97), some in partnership with John Nash, who had established his home at East Cowes Castle.¹⁴⁸ While his feeling for Nash had soured, Repton continued to visit the Isle of Wight to undertake commissions and see his son George, who worked in Nash's office (and who in 1810 was preparing to submit plans for a new lunatic asylum in Norwich).¹⁴⁹ Repton took a holiday on the island with John Adey in September 1811, after securing the commission for Sheringham but before making the site visit, probably to recuperate from the effects of his carriage accident the previous winter. The Upchers were there at the same time, and Repton's comparison with the Isle of Wight in the Sheringham Red Book probably reflects their conversations.

As most people visited the Isle of Wight in the summer, observed Repton, they received a partial impression of the scenery, and a misleading one if they were thinking of establishing a permanent home. In summer 'every Cottage is deck'd with flowers, & every house is marked by that attention to Elegance, Comfort & genteel habitation; in which Sherringham is at present woefully deficient; but which it is the object of these pages to provide'. But looking into one of those cottages on the island Repton noticed 'Great Coats and Oilskin

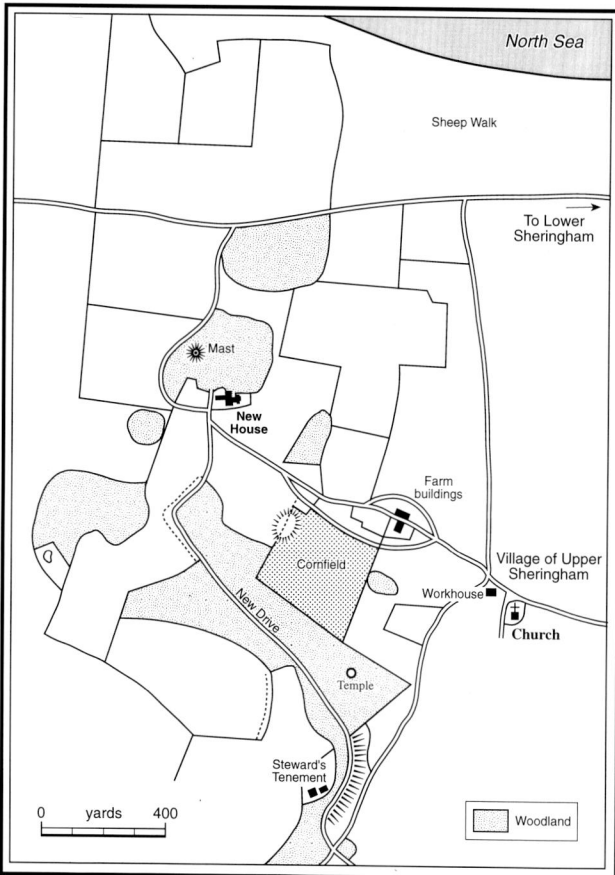

98 Plan of proposals at Sheringham, after that in the Red Book for Sheringham (1812).

Umbrellas' that indicated dismal conditions at other times of the year. Also the island's scenery was associated with 'moving from one spot to another & the cheerful animation of its Visitors and Tourists'. If you took 'any one place on that Island & can suppose it solitary and divested of its enlivening accompaniments, there is none that can be compared with the Scenery of Sherringham'. On Repton's recent visit the tourists were a nuisance. From the New Inn in Ventnor, he sent his wife Mary a poem that makes a virtue of John Adey's deafness:

> Thus when I look upon the verdant ley
> One tells me – 'it produced but little hay'
> And when th' Umrageous copse I first beheld
> Another bawl'd – 'tis time that copse was fell'd'
> But when from Steephill's height, Ocean appears
> I gaze in silent Adoration – till my ears
> Are roug'd by stories of French Privateers . . .
> . . . tis surely better
> To see – than hear – as witness Upcher's letter

'Where Nature smiles to see, by Repton's aid
A sweeter landscape than herself had made'.[150]

Once Sheringham had been made fully habitable, with a sheltered site for a family mansion, a regime that drew in every activity of the estate (farming, fishing and forestry) around the stewardship of the house, and was carefully presented to passing tourists, then, Repton maintained, it would be a model landscape. More than any other Red Book, that for Sheringham plans the social and scenic management of the entire estate. There are five main arenas: woodland, farmland, the landward village, the sea shore and the mansion (fig. 98). The soil of Sheringham, Repton noted, was ideal not just for agriculture but for road making. And he laid out a dense system of routes radiating from the mansion, which made every part of the estate quickly accessible. The woods, farm, sheepwalk, seashore and the village itself could be reached easily. Through its routeways, the landscape of Sheringham is mapped into that of Norfolk as a whole. The direction post in Repton's drawing of the new entrance lodge (fig. 53) signals Sheringham's strategic position:

> It is within a mornings drive of the city of Norwich & within an hours ride of the three Post & Market towns of Holt, Aylsham & North Walsham at each of which are Balls, Book clubs & Bowling greens, besides monthly meetings of magistrates, with annual fairs & feasts & all such society & amusements as tend to vary the sameness of a country life. It is within 5 or 6 miles of the Port of Blakeney to the West & of Cromer to the east, where those who delight in the mix'd company of a watering place may partake of its gaieties. It is within short distances of Holkham, Felbrigg & Blickling, which are the 3 great Lions in the Tour of Norfolk.

The woods at Sheringham were a valuable resource for shelter, timber, taking walks and shooting game. Repton provided the framework for a forestry campaign involving planting recently enclosed heathland and replanting existing woodland. The trees themselves symbolized a secure community: 'All planters delight in woods of their own creating, as parents are most fond of their own progeny . . . In proportion as the Trees become attached to the Soil so we become attached to them.' In making new plantations, there were hints to be had from the variety and form of oak groves on the seaward slopes. Twenty-five years before, Repton had admired their mode of planting by the previous owner, Cook Flower: 'It would at first sight appear impracticable to raise trees

99   Coursing on the beach at low tide, from the Red Book for Sheringham (1812). National Trust. On loan to the British Architectural Library, London.

100   Proposed view from the dining-room, detail showing ploughed field, from the Red Book for Sheringham. National Trust. On loan to the British Architectural Library, London.

*Scene near the Temple, with a hint of the house on the Site proposed — distant about 3/4 of a Mile.*

101 *Scene near the* [proposed] *Temple*, from the Red Book for Sheringham, (1812). National Trust. On loan to the British Architectural Library, London.

in a situation exposed to the keenest sea breezes, but by planting the young trees amongst the furze and ling, that after a few years they become able to brave the most tempestuous blasts from the north-east.'[151] Now that he witnessed them maturing they offered 'an apt lesson to the Planter as well as the Moralist', for

> While Ocean's breath may blast a single tree:
> England's combined Oaks resist the Sea.
> Emblem of Strength, increas'd by Unity.

Repton planned a new entrance lodge for the keeper, 'distinguished from a common cottage by a few rude trees & also by a small platform or spy as it is called ... convenient as a lookout for sea and land, overlooking the covers for game'. Instead of forbidding all access to the poor, as was becoming the practice, Repton recommended 'one day in the month, or oftener if necessary, to admit them into the woods, under the eye of a keeper to pick up dead sticks for firing'. Where this was done 'no wood is stolen, no trees are lop'd or disfigured'.

'With respect to the Game, that eternal source of Temptation, I forsee that at Sherringham it will be a source of happiness.'[152] While Upcher enjoyed shooting in the privacy of his woods, he was passionate about coursing, which was best practised on the public space of the beach at low tide. Repton envisaged public matches in which villagers participated 'as they do in some counties where the games of cricket or prison-bars [a tagging game] are celebrated & frequented by all ranks'. 'This promotes a mutual intercourse betwixt the landlord, the Tenant, & the Labourer which is kept up at little expense, & secures the ready and reciprocal assistance of each to the other. This is the happy medium between Licentious Equality and Opressive Tyranny.' Repton illustrated such a sociable scene on the Sheringham sands (fig. 99) and glossed it with verse:

> Smooth as the level Sand 'twixt Cliff and Sea;
> So may our middle Course of Life run free
> Twixt overwhelming Power, and mad Equality.

With wheat prices soaring, and cornfields challenging oak groves as patriotic symbols as well as commercial resources, Repton tempered his aversion to arable scenes in the view from the mansion.[153] Moreover, Upcher was an admirer of the agricultural look of Holkham: 'the fields are like gardens', he declared.[154] While Repton proposed emparking some fields immediately in front of the dining-room windows, he was careful to conserve others in the middle distance between pasture and woods (fig. 100). The ploughed field, yellow with wheat, made 'some variety in the colouring of the picture & . . . at seed time & harvest it may be enlivened by men as well as beasts – if I might be permitted to indulge my favorite propensity for *humanizing* as well as *animating* beautiful scenery'. Here he adds some lines in the style of *The Landscape: A Didactic Poem*, by his old adversary Richard Payne Knight, on the landlord who surrounds his house with the 'everlasting green' of pasture:

> Now, not one moving object must appear
> Except the owner's Bullocks, Sheep & Deer
> As if his Landscape were all made to eat
> And yet he shudders at a crop of wheat.

Faced with the prospect of such dull, depopulated pastoral scenes, it was little wonder 'at the desertion of family mansions for a residence in London in winter, & at watering places in Summer'. Repton proposed a varied, animated prospect from the mansion, which would sustain the family's interest and commitment. This included 'the motion of carriages coming to the house' down the new approach and 'the occasional glitter' of tourists coming to view the grounds from a new temple where they might take their refreshments (fig. 101).

> I do not mean to molest [Sheringham's] comfort & privacy by admitting *near the house* all the Tourists and Felicity Hunters of Cromer and the Coast: but one day in the week permission might be given at the lodge to admit all proper persons, whose names should be enterd in a book by the keeper & who might attend their walks restrained within certain limits.

While the old farmhouse was adjacent to the village, the proposed site of the new mansion was a mile away, in a new park, protected by a lodge. Repton revisioned the relation between propinquity and community. What mattered was not just the existence of space between gentry and commonality but how this was filled and controlled.

The vicinity of a village is very differently mark'd in different parks, in some I see lame and blind beggars sorrowfully driven from the house; in others I see women and children with cheerful faces, bearing away jugs of milk & broken victuals at stated periods, & I know before I enter the house which are the happiest families – In some places I hear that all the neighbouring poor are idle thieves and active poachers; in others that every man in the neighbouring villages would rise at night to serve the Liberal patron & I have been tempted to investigate this difference in its causes and effects.

Repton's investigations were vested in the conservative sensibilities of his old circle in Sustead – Kent, Windham, Marsham and Hewett – and energized by the evangelical currents represented by his young clients.[155] They focused on the Sheringham workhouse. This was prominently sited on the main road at the centre of the village, near the existing entrance to the grounds.

102  Approach, with and without overlay, from the Red Book for Sheringham (1812). National Trust. On loan to the British Architectural Library, London.

The incorporated workhouses in Norfolk were a focus of discontent, not just for the poor but for paternal landowners who saw their power over the poor transferred to wealthy tenant farmers among the guardians.[156] The workhouse at Sheringham was built in 1805, under the provision of the Gilbert Act, to replace the poorhouses of eight neighbouring parishes, and leased to the guardians for twenty-five pounds a year.[157] Such workhouses were condemned for encouraging farmers to 'throw the labourers out of employment, in order that they might afterwards contract for their labour on lower terms'.[158] Repton's comments on the Sheringham workhouse echo many other writings, from local pamphlets to the passage on the 'pauper palace' in George Crabbe's poem, *The Borough* (1810). Whereas once, Repton observed, the 'common farmer' had worked alongside his labourers, the 'gentleman farmer' now drove them hard all hours, committing them to 'prisons erected under the name of workhouses' when he reckoned they were too old or sick to work. 'And whether the poor slave be driven by the Lash of the Whip, or the dread of Confinement in a workhouse, he must feel that Men are not all equal altho' he may be taught to *read* that they are so.' There might have been little a squire such as Upcher alone could do about the existence or regime of the workhouse, but he might have at least made it look more appealing: 'The workhouse instead of being an object of disgust to the Rich & of terror to the Poor, might be made to look more like a Hospital or Asylum & less like a Prison, by removing the high wall the street might be converted into a neat *village green* with its benches & a *May pole, that* almost forgotten Emblem of rural happiness & festivity.'[159]

Repton proposed a fresh approach to the new mansion at Sheringham, more than a mile from the village (fig. 102). In a striking version of Repton's standard style, this left the main road, went through the woods, cut into a hill, and turned a corner to reveal the mansion in its park against the sea. The approach demanded the excavation of a deep cutting. In the illustration of the original view three pick- and spade-wielding labourers set to work. It is a scene that recalls other landscape paintings of the time that show the virtues of honest toil in the landscape, particularly various forms of digging.[160] It corresponds to Repton's sentiments, echoed by Malthus, that 'wealth is never so well employed, as in improvements which daily display the genius of art, and call into active employment the labourer and the artificer'.[161] This sturdy group of estate workers building the drive stands as a reproach to the corruption of labour in the workhouse. The effect of their effort is evident in the improved view. A couple, probably representing the Upchers, gesture to the park, while the figure of Repton sits opposite sketching, and a carriage careers downhill to the mansion, now revealed 'like some enchanted Palace of a fairy Tale!'.

The Upchers initially decided to call their new house 'Marina'.[162] The eventual style of the new house was a blend of seaside villa and manor house, a 'modern Italian villa' embellished with bow-windows 'to create that sort of intricacy which is so admirably conspicuous in the old houses of the date of Queen Elizabeth'.[163] The first design Repton proposed was much plainer, perhaps in response to his clients' evangelical outlook and their wish for a 'temple' dedicated to good works. Repton proposed a row of Doric columns not only to divide the view out in to 'distinct landscapes' but also to give 'a certain degree of elegance to a building which would resemble a workhouse without it' (fig. 103).[164] Subsequently Repton modified the elevation for the house at Sheringham, shortening the length and introducing Gothic bow-windows.[165]

In October 1812 Upcher moved into the old farmhouse at Sheringham to begin his campaign. Within days he 'was seized with a violent nervous fever' so severe that he was taken to London to be attended by a doctor, and remained there for three months.[166] Upcher had purchased Sheringham at the peak of the property market, and it seems his breakdown was brought on by the collapse of prices. News of Upcher's illness reached Repton through his neighbour in Hare Street who had heard about it in Colchester. Feverishly Repton wrote to William in Aylsham: 'Mr Upcher is gone mad – entirely owing to the Estate for which he gave 50 thous'd – and has offered it to sale & nobody will give more than 30 thous'd'. Repton approached Upcher's physician who diagnosed severe depression and through him offered to find a purchaser. This Upcher accepted. The purchaser that Repton had in mind was the Nelson Trust, which was still searching for a suitable estate. Repton suggested to his son William that they re-open negotiations with the Speaker.[167]

Repton knew from his own survey the potential value of the estate. He had copies made of some of the sketches he had made for the Red Book that showed to advantage the features, notably the new mansion, that the Speaker desired. Repton asked William to find out whether the estate had in fact depreciated so dramatically, and, if the Speaker objected to its modest size, whether he could persuade neighbouring landowners, the Walpoles, clients of his, to sell or exchange some of their property. The Walpoles, moreover, were related to the

*South Front with West front in perspective. an Elevation perhaps too plain.*

103 [Proposed] *South Front with West front in perspective,* from the Red Book for Sheringham (1812). National Trust Photographic Library/John Hammond. On loan to the British Architectural Library, London.

Nelsons: '*perhaps* it might *suit* your Noble client to *accommodate* a Relation to accomplish a National purpose – It is a fair stalking horse'. Repton also enquired whether there was any chance of

> letting Upcher off his bargain & upon what terms – that I may have two strings to my bow if I fail with the Speaker . . . I think it possible I may still have some benefit from building the house – & you from sale and resale etc etc etc. but I hope you will make Flower pay well for your agency & consider on the Sale of such an estate you ought to have a percentage. Your advice added 2500 Slap & the odd 500 should be yours – ha! Slap.[168]

Four days later Repton wrote again to William, saying that the Speaker wanted a 'full acc. of the Value present and improveable with price and full particulars'. He suggested that he 'set the woods and Game & improvement from Inclosure pretty high – then add so much for Situation and Beauty'.[169]

As it turned out, Upcher recovered from his breakdown, refused to sell, and in January 1813, 'gradually restored to sound and vigorous health', returned to Sheringham to pursue his campaign of improvements.[170] Repton continued his search for a seat for Lord Nelson, who was settled, without Repton's help, at Stanlych Park in Wiltshire in 1814.[171] A chastened Repton told William: 'our hopes for Lord Nelson are blown over. 'Tis all for the best'. In his parlous financial state a large commission like this would have been too risky. He had heard of an architect in the north of England who had been sued ten thousand pounds for incompetence. Repton told William to hold on to the drawings for the Nelson Trust until they met: 'the sight of hopes disappointed is like the blossoms on our apple trees – the Canker has destroyed them all'.[172]

104 W. Wallis after J.S. Cotman, *Sheringham Hall. The Seat of Abbot Upcher Esq.*, from *Excursions through Norfolk* (1818). Norfolk Libraries and Information Service.

Innocent of Repton's manoeuverings, Upcher carefully implemented many of the proposals set out in the Red Book. Upcher's journal for the next three years records an extensive programme of planting and ploughing, repairing and rebuilding cottages and farm buildings, constructing lime kilns and brick kilns, building a school and refurbishing the church. The old parish poorhouse, 'an eye-sore and disgrace to Sherringham, [is] pull'd down . . . by which means the Church now boldly opens to the street and our woods also are made more visible to the traveller'. Among many acts of moral welfare were 'to reconcile the domestic feuds and quarrels of two familys, and to persuade the son of the principal farmer in the parish to marry his mistress . . . getting several poor people to receive the Sacrament'. 'The mornings I have dedicated to external improvements in my woods and fields', he noted one November day, 'the evenings to sacred mental acquirements'. He pronounced the approach to the house 'the greatest possible Masterpiece of Repton's Art in Landscape Gardening . . . I thought it impossible at first to make this Road, but the facility with which we executed it is astonishing'.[173]

Humphry and John Adey Repton returned to Sheringham each summer to monitor work in progress and suggest further improvements. In June 1813 they supervised the setting out of the new mansion and gardens. Building work on the mansion was halted for two years. Costs were perhaps prohibitive, and Mr Harrison, master of the workhouse, seems to have proved an obstructive clerk of the works. In 1815 Upcher appointed a new clerk of the works, Thomas Bedford, to oversee the rest of the building work on the house.[174] Bedford contracted for the stonework, ironwork and leadwork through local men in Aylsham, Bodham and Cley, purchased oak wreck timber at Blakeney and 'very valuable timber' from a local granary that was being demolished. He sailed to Hull to purchase Prussian timber, deal, slate, plaster and nails. 'The various cargoes we got safely to our own shore . . . and by this means acquired our materials at a very diminished price to what we could have bought them in the county – I mean in Norfolk.' By the end of 1816 the house was largely built.[175]

After two years' suffering acutely with angina – during which he struggled to Sheringham from Aylsham, lamenting the passing of old friends as he drove past Sustead – Repton enjoyed a remission: he had, he pronounced, 'come to life again'.[176] 'Repton gave us a love-visit in June for 3 days with his son John', Upcher noted. 'They were much satisfied with Bedford's operations and the whole construction of the house. During the time they staid, they were indefatigable in their exertion to improve our grounds, views from the Bower, and a thousand other things.'[177] Repton proudly published extracts from the Red Book and subsequent revisions, in *Fragments*, for a place now called 'Sherringham Bower', elevating labourers from his original characterization as a 'species of animal' to a 'class of mankind'.[178]

Early in 1817, nearing completion, work on the house was halted, irrevocably. Upcher was again taken ill with a 'violent inflammatory fever'. Repton was dismayed to discover that

> my favorite & darling child in Norfolk has ceased to be an object of delight – its amiable Proprietor my endear'd friend Mr. Upcher is ill, very ill, both in body & mind & his delightful wife thus describes her feelings . . . 'As to Sherringham, that once happy paradise, what is it now to us? We have been married eight years tomorrow & I suppose eight years is as much as we can expect in this world'.

To compound her misery, Bedford, the clerk of the works, had died '& when I last left Sherringham during my illness poor Upcher turned to him as my chaise drove off & said Look Bedford – look at my friend Repton – we shall never see him more. Little did he then see the

Death, Disease & Coercion he was to suffer . . .'. Upcher made a brief recovery, during which Charlotte Upcher wrote to Repton with 'some few instructions, what to stop and what to finish', whereupon they left for a house in Brompton, Kent.[179]

The mansion at Sheringham remained unfinished. A drawing by John Sell Cotman was engraved for a guidebook, *Excursions in the County of Norfolk* (1818; fig. 104). This shows the south front awaiting its portico, surrounded by an abandoned site for the pleasure grounds, conservatory and flower garden. There is no accompanying text.[180] Abbot Upcher remained in Kent, separated (on medical advice) from the company of his children, before suffering a stroke from which he died in February 1819.[181]

Despite his remission, Repton did not outlive Upcher. His letter of May 1817 to Sir Harry Fetherstonehaugh at Uppark, recording Abbot Upcher's final illness and his advice to Charlotte Upcher on how to put improvements at Sheringham on hold, is the last surviving record of his own life. The letter intimates as much: 'How do you employ time, the Paston fireside was our last resource, can you recommend anything worth reading. I am tired writing & *my life* you know was finished when I was last at Uppark'.[182] Repton died, probably of a heart attack, in March 1818.

He had chosen his burial place more than three years earlier, a plot against the south wall of Aylsham parish church (fig. 105). In a letter to the vicar dated January 1815 he explained he was standing

> on the spot during a gleam of sunshine last October when I often enjoyed the thought of converting a weedy corner into a beautiful Flower Garden, and gathering a barren ear of wild barley I promised it would be a rose. After twenty years of War which abridged me of many comforts I am now happy that I shall depart in Peace to sleep near the Ashes of my Parents, and have desired that mine may be so slightly enclosed as soon to dissolve and form part of the Garden mold of my warm, snug corner where I will soon be converted into the pabulum of Roses.[183]

He composed some lines on the spot for his inscription, adapted from some on a memorial inside the church to a seventeenth-century bishop which he had transcribed forty years earlier for Armstrong's *History and Antiquities of the County of Norfolk*.

> Not like the Egyptian tyrants – consecrate,
> Unmixt with others shall my Dust remain;
> But mold'ring, blending melting into Earth,
> Mine shall give form and colour to the Rose;
> And while its vivid blossoms cheer mankind,
> Its perfumed odours shall ascend to Heaven.[184]

The first obituary of Repton in the *Gentleman's Magazine* for April 1818 offered a capsule biography: 'He was born in *Norfolk*, on the estate of the late *Mr Windham*, and bred the business of a stocking manufacturer; and his sister and daughter for many years kept a stocking-shop at Hare-Street.[185] Resigned as they were to years of misrepresentation, Repton's family rushed to correct this in the next issue, and set out some facts as a framework for their father's life.[186]

105 Attributed to John Adey Repton or George Stanley Repton, The grave of Humphry Repton, St Michael and All Angels' church, Aylsham (n.d.). Private collection.

## Chapter 3
# THE PICTURESQUE LANDSCAPE

AFTER RISING rapidly to prominence in his new profession, Repton sought to establish his reputation with the publication of a finely illustrated treatise on landscape gardening. Eventually issued in 1795, *Sketches and Hints on Landscape Gardening* sought to 'establish fixed principles in the art of laying out ground'. It did so by drawing on the Red Books for various commissions around the country, notably that for Welbeck for Repton's most powerful patron, the duke of Portland, and by positioning Repton's work as a direct, genealogical development from that of Capability Brown. Repton found that Brown's work and name had been corrupted by his many imitators and the men who had been employed to execute his plans. He knew as much because he had been commissioned by some of Brown's clients, and Brown's son had 'presented me with the maps of the greatest works in which his late father had been consulted, both in their original and improved states'.[1] Repton would refine Brown's 'place making', focus on fine detail, highlight scenic views, and express this fully in writing and drawing, raise the profession to a polite art. 'Neither Mr Brown nor his immediate followers were men of Liberal Education and therefore they have left no record in writing to explain their practice; but always having delivered my opinion in writing, I have endeavour'd from a multiplicity of different subjects, to collect & arrange some principles to assist those who may think more highly of the art.'[2] Brown did not sketch, but 'there exist many pictures of scenery, made under his instruction, which his imagination alone had painted'.[3] From the outset of his career, five years after Brown's death, Repton sought the mantle of the man he called 'my predecessor'. Meeting Repton on the road in Cambridgeshire in 1792, John Byng called him 'Capability R[epton]' – but sarcastically, in response to his professional ambition and enthusiasm for enclosure. Like many other conservative spokesmen, Byng was concerned at the anti-social effects of emparkment and quoted Goldsmith's *The Deserted Village* against Repton's work. Brown's reputation was already in question and Repton's allegiance carried a risk.[4]

Planned for publication in 1794, *Sketches and Hints* was delayed at the printers for many months. Repton experienced 'so much anxiety – expense & trouble' in getting it through the press, initially because he demanded the plates be re-engraved, 'finished as highly as tinted drawings', and then because he added extensive sections to reply to a pre-emptive, co-ordinated attack on his work that appeared in two manifestos: *The Landscape: A Didactic Poem* by Richard Payne Knight and *Essay on the Picturesque* (both 1794) by Uvedale Price.[5] This attack was the more wounding for being unexpected. Knight and Price had established a reputation as metropolitan connoisseurs and as improvers of their estates at Downton and Foxley in Herefordshire. Repton had become friendly with them at the beginning of his career, when he was commissioned at places near their own and sought

*facing page* Detail of fig. 134.

their advice in his designs. Five years on, provoked by Repton's professional success, his allegiance to Capability Brown and his implicit challenge to their own authority, Knight and Price set out to ambush Repton's career. The terrain they chose was a physical region and aesthetic discourse: the picturesque landscape.[6]

In this chapter I chart the controversy between Repton, Knight and Price and the other protagonists it drew in, such as William Marshall, William Windham and John Claudius Loudon. I examine Repton's commissions in and around Herefordshire in the light of Knight's and Price's improvements on their estates. Then I examine the discourse of the picturesque landscape in Knight's and Price's published writings and Repton's response to it in subsequent commissions in their vicinity. As a public event, the controversy was at its height in the year 1794–5, when, in the context of the wartime emergency and domestic conflict of those years, the tactics and engagements assumed a sharp, geopolitical edge. At issue was the patriotism of landscape improvement: its allegiance to various geographical identities, local and national, provincial and metropolitan, English and British. The controversy was articulated not just in the landscaping of various sites around the country but in the way it was presented in publication. London was thus a crucial site in the production of the picturesque controversy, but it reached polite audiences wherever they might be – conversing on tour or in resorts, reading at home in country towns and suburban villas. The controversy between Repton, Price and Knight dispersed after the 1790s but did not dissipate. Other protagonists, such as Loudon, took it in new directions, some of which had a bearing on Repton's career. The controversy was reproduced in regions beyond Herefordshire. The picturesque landscape, in its various permutations, in questions of perception, painting and improvement continued to frame Repton's theory and practice.

There are clear differences in the temperaments of the protagonists in the picturesque controversy, shaped by their social roles, which help to explain the force and style of their arguments. Knight was renowned for expressing his freeborn, free-thinking connoisseurship in a highly confrontational and consciously virile fashion.[7] Repton was, by all accounts, genial to a fault, inclined to shun confrontation, to turn the other cheek. In his Memoir he tells of an occasion when he attended a Royal Academy lecture by Sir John Soane, one of the architects he had tried working with, and 'heard myself abused and held up to ridicule without mercy'. On descending from the rostrum, Soane 'seemed surprised to see me' and astonished when Repton told him that he should 'not expect to make such home thrusts without a little parrying': 'I know I shall have nothing to fear', said Soane, 'for your good nature will always prevent your doing or saying an ill natured thing'.[8] Repton could vent his spleen on subordinates, such as nurserymen and stone masons, and in private on a range of social equals and superiors, but being agreeable in public was part of his professional persona and his vision of consensual polite culture. Having chosen to publish his views, Repton entered a highly competitive arena, and for the sake of his career had to strike a combative posture.[9]

## Border Country

Price and Knight reformulated picturesque aesthetics in terms of two horizons of knowledge: estate management in their home county of Herefordshire and the connoisseurship of the Grand Tour. Eighteenth-century Herefordshire was mythologized as a classic ground, the home of the English Georgic (fig. 106), a varied, garden-like country of woodlands, pasture, orchards, hopyards and cornfields, a county governed by an indigenous gentry with modest estates, overseeing small farms and snug cottages.[10] For much of the century, most Herefordshire gentry carried out their landscaping themselves in a piecemeal way, aware of current fashions but retaining relic features such as avenues and ancient trees, and incorporating agrarian land uses. The comprehensive schemes of professional landscapers such as Capability Brown and his followers made little impact.[11] Relative newcomers themselves, Price and Knight drew on the mythology of the county and used local practices as a basis for their picturesque principles. They further raised the register of landscape appreciation by demanding a high level of connoisseurship. To look at the countryside from the picturesque point of view, it was not enough to be familiar with the compositional rules gleaned from the guidebooks of William Gilpin or their many imitators; the spectator required a detailed knowledge of the art of the Old Masters. Both horizons of knowledge, county and cosmopolitan, were designed to protect picturesque landscape as a field of knowledge from commercial invasion, from middle-class tourists and professional landscapers, to make it the preserve of the sophisticated gentleman amateur.[12]

106 Cartouche, from Isaac Taylor, *New Map of the County of Hereford* (1786). Hereford Library.

'How rich, how gay, how picturesque the face of the country', enthused Horace Walpole, in support of Brown.[13] Knight and Price stripped away and appropriated for themselves features that Brown's admirers saw in his style: its naturalism, its scenic appeal and its projection of Whig liberty and prosperity. They represented the Brown style as a betrayal of Whig patriotic ideals. They likened its spread to a military invasion, levelling the landscape, erasing familiar landmarks, sterilizing the countryside, imposing a despotic form of power. Lubricated by a London-based financial system reaching into the most remote regions of the country, such landscaping represented two sides of an increasingly centralized state. As Foxite Whigs, hostile to the coalition of Portland Whigs with Pitt's ministry, Price and Knight presented themselves as provincial gentry, proud of their independence, in virtuous exile from corruption. Picturesque landscape, modelled on Old Masters, old landmarks and traditional forms of husbandry expressed the variety, freedom and vitality of country virtue and independence.[14]

An understated, latent source of picturesque power in Price's and Knight's writings is located in the history of Herefordshire as a border country between England and Wales and as an integral part of the ancient British territory of Albion which encompassed the two nations. The county continued to be a zone of transition between English and Welsh culture; the Welsh language was prominent in its harvest fields, hopyards, river barges and market places. The city of Hereford was the leading urban centre for mid-Wales; the *Hereford Journal*, or *British Chronicle* to give it its alternative name, circulated throughout this region. The Revd John Duncumb, a former editor of the *Hereford Journal* (and later the recipient of a living at Foxley), published a history of Herefordshire in 1804 that provided an ancient British context for the county (fig. 107). He located Herefordshire in the tribal kingdom of Siluria, which stretched across the modern border between England and Wales. Siluria was revived by eighteenth-century writers as a source of patriotic virtue. The Silures were revered for their martial and agrarian virtues, and their resistance to Roman invasion under the leadership of Caractacus was a potent episode in histories of British liberty activated during the Napoleonic Wars. Guidebooks were keen to locate the site of Caractacus's last stand; the two main contenders were Credenhill near Foxley and Coxwall Knoll near Downton.[15]

The relationships between Herefordshire and Siluria, England and Albion, modern and ancient Britain, were not settled; consciously English and Welsh interests

108  J.C. Stadler after John Warwick Smith, *Cascade above the Mossy Seat*, from James Edward Smith, *Tour to Hafod* (1810). Yale Center for British Art, Paul Mellon Collection.

107  Title page, from John Duncumb, *Collections Towards the History and Antiquities of the County of Hereford* (1804). Hereford Library.

framed them in various ways. Price, of Welsh ancestry, and Knight, of English, both had a stake in the estate upheld as an epitome of modern Silurian virtue: Thomas Johnes's Hafod, in the Cardiganshire hills of mid-Wales. Johnes was Knight's cousin, and Hafod was situated half-way between Foxley and Price's summer house at Aberystwyth. Price and Knight may have advised on the programme of improvements at Hafod in the 1780s and 1790s, in forestry, agriculture, housing, road building and education, which were esteemed for enhancing the appeal of the rocky peaks and foaming waterfalls, turning a dreary waste in to a picturesque landscape (fig. 108).[16] In forging an alliance with Price and Knight, in a proudly British, anti-English view of landscape improvement, the Scot John Claudius Loudon quoted 'Lines left written on a seat at Havod':

> Far hence! let REPTON, BROWN, and EAMES,
> Zig-zag their walks, and torture streams;
> But let them not my dells profane,
> Or violate my Naiad train;
> Nor let their arrogance invade
> My meanest Dryad's secret shade,
> And with fantastic knots disgrace
> The native honours of the place;[17]

Repton never breached Hafod, but he did extend his landscaping into Herefordshire (fig. 109), 'in the enemy's quarters' as he put it, and eventually into Wales.[18]

*Downton*

Richard Payne Knight's Downton estate was located in the far north of Herefordshire, near the border with Shropshire, in the valley of the River Teme. Knight's grandfather, Richard, had moved to the area from Coalbrookdale in the early eighteenth century and developed the estate with a string of forges and furnaces. Knight's father, Thomas, the second son, had no part in the business, taking a modest living as a domestic chaplain, but because his elder brother had died without an heir, the estate passed to his eldest son. Upon inheriting Downton on his coming of age in 1772, Richard Payne Knight embarked on a Grand Tour, and over the next few years spent much of his time abroad, in Switzerland, Paris, Naples and Sicily, collecting Old Masters and antiquities, recording (in the company of the painters John Robert Cozens and Jacob Philipp Hackert) the Mediterranean landscape and studying aspects of Greek philology and mythology. Knight returned to England in 1780, thence dividing his time between Downton and a London house in Soho Square. He was elected MP for Leominster in 1780, but anti-Foxite feeling there prompted him to accept another Shropshire seat at Ludlow, four miles downstream from Downton. Like many MPs, Knight's county loyalties were apportioned

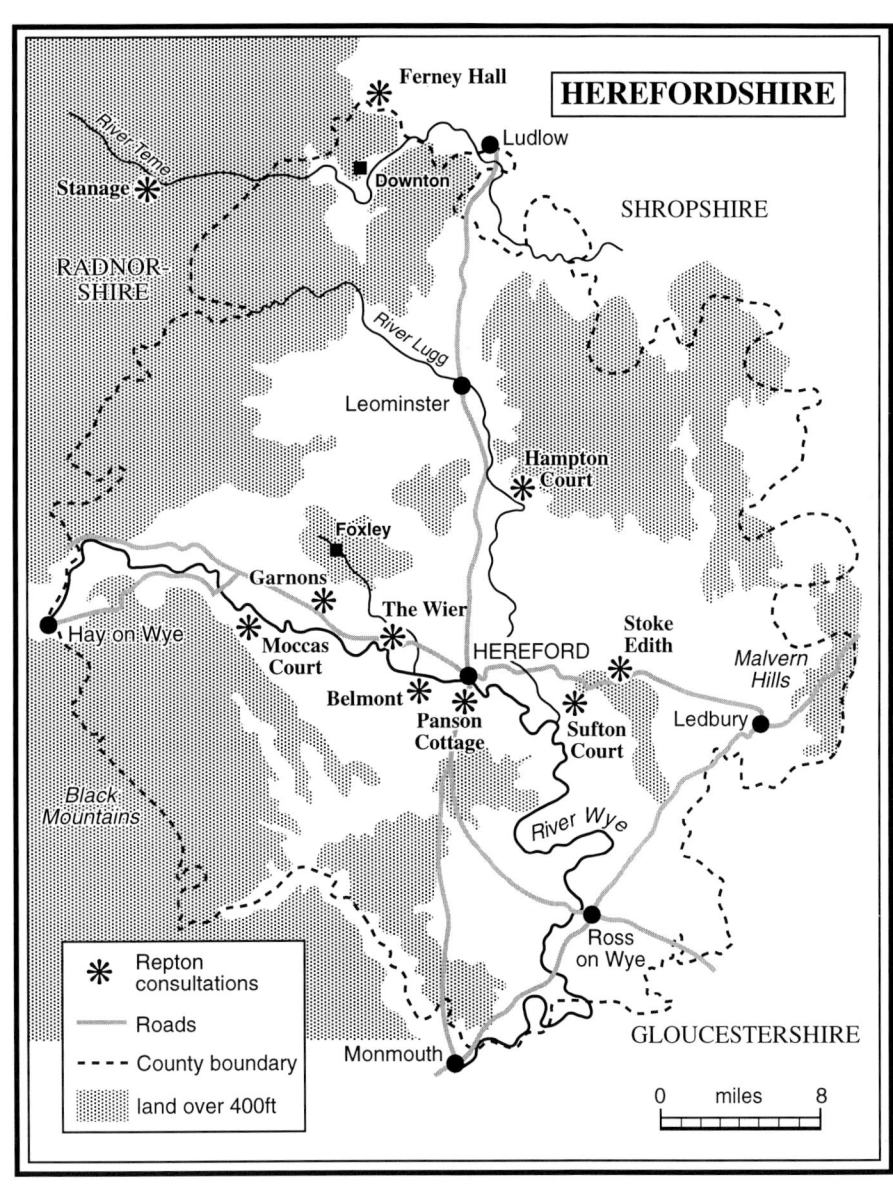

109 Humphry Repton Consultations in Herefordshire.

110 Thomas Hearne, *Downton Castle, viewed from the South Bank of the Teme*, from *Twelve Views of the River Teme at Downton* (1784–6). Private collection. Photograph National Museums and Galleries of Wales.

111 Thomas Hearne, *The Overhanging Boulder with the Bow Bridge beyond*, from *Twelve Views of the River Teme at Downton* (1784–6). Private collection. Photograph National Museums and Galleries of Wales.

between his residence and constituency, but these were close together and part of the same 'country', the rocky, mineral-rich region of the upper Severn and its tributaries.[19] Knight played comparatively little part in the civic culture of Hereford (Ludlow was his local county town), but he did play a leading role in London meetings of the Herefordshire Society.[20]

Upon taking up residence at Downton in 1780, Knight instituted a comprehensive programme of development throughout the ten-thousand-acre estate. He maintained the ironworks along the Teme, improved pasture lands and planted the hills. Knight designed his mansion at Downton, a battlemented house that echoed both the baronial mansions of the Welsh borderland and the fortified towns and palaces he saw in Italy and in pictures by Gaspard Dughet and Claude Lorrain. He then set about landscaping a one-and-a-half-mile stretch of the Teme Gorge below his mansion, which became known as Downton Vale. The landscaping of Downton Vale involved creating a walk along the river, hewing a path from the rock, planting the banks and building various structures – caverns, bridges and tunnels – to create dramatic viewpoints. Knight commissioned the landscape painter Thomas Hearne (previously employed by him to paint finished watercolours, probably for publication, of some drawings from his tour of Sicily) to depict the landscaping of Downton Vale in a series of watercolours from 1784 to 1786 (figs 110 and 111). Knight had been careful to plan painterly, Claudian, views on the ground, and Hearne faithfully transcribed them in views out to the mansion and along the wooded path.[21]

### Ferney Hall

Repton's commission at Ferney Hall near Ludlow in September 1789 took him close to Downton, in the same country of wooded glens and rocky dells. Ferney's owner, Samuel Phipps, was a barrister at Lincoln's Inn, where Repton picked up a number of commissions, but Repton's Norfolk connections may also have been influential: William Windham knew Knight through Whig politics and had visited Downton two years earlier, collecting 'many useful particulars'.[22] The Red Book for Ferney suggests that Repton had been called in to redress what a local man, one Woodward, had proposed.[23] The following account is based on what the protagonists in the picturesque controversy recalled about the commission.

Ferney was, in Knight's words, 'a small, but romantic place near my own, in the fate of which I was of course much interested, and consequently dreaded the approach of a professed improver'.[24] Repton said that he felt obliged to visit Knight, 'who has given such consummate proof of good taste in the improvement of his own place . . . one of the most beautiful and romantic valleys that the imagination can conceive'.[25] He asked Knight's advice especially with regard to plans for a rocky dell (fig. 112), acknowledging, Price recalled, that he 'had not been so conversant as himself in that style of scenery'.[26] When Knight found Repton to be 'conversant (in some degree at least) with almost every branch of polite literature and skilled in the art of design' his fears for Ferney were allayed and transformed in to 'pleasing expectations . . . when I heard him launch out in praise of picturesque scenery'.[27] But Repton felt no less obliged to his client, 'a Barrister of the highest character as a Chamber Counsel'. In his Memoir, Repton recalled Phipps's words when he presented his plans:

> Mr Repton, I have looked at these drawings with feelings which extend well beyond the subject before us – I see in you one who will have much of the landed

112 'A picturesque bridge over the narrow part of the pool', from the Red Book for Ferney Hall (1789). Pierpont Morgan Library, New York.

> property of this country under your control. I see you possess powers of fascinating with your pencil which will require great restraint in the exercize of an exuberant imagination. Now I have too often witnessed the distress and anxiety of great families from the excess of indulging their tastes and inclination for expense . . . do not on your death bed have to reproach yourself for having been necessary to the embarrassment of those who may often apply to you to gratify their vanity rather than their actual comfort.[28]

These words, recalled Repton, 'made a very deep impression on my mind . . . and have so far operated on all my schemes of improvement'.[29]

Knight was thoroughly dismayed by Repton's plans for Ferney (fig. 113). The 'only part of them which would have pleased a landscape painter', the preservation of an old fruit garden as a foreground to a distant view to the Welsh mountains, 'was the only part which did not please that gentleman [Phipps]; who, though a man of sense and information . . . only employed an improver, to be like the rest of the world, and have his grounds laid out in the newest fashion'.[30] Knight credited Repton with resisting Phipps's wish to turn the garden into a 'little lawn, surrounded by a sunk fence, a belt of low shrubs and a serpentine gravel walk', but he found little to admire elsewhere and 'communicated to him in writing my disapprobation of the greatest part of what he proposed doing'.³¹ Phipps was highly satisfied with Repton's plans, especially 'when he saw how easily they could be realized at a small cost'.³² Knight recalled that Repton 'declared himself to be convinced' by his objections, and 'furthermore, did me the honour . . . of requesting my assistance in reviewing the ground, and forming a plan more suitable to its natural character'.³³ Repton revisited Ferney a year later in October 1790, but the sudden death of Samuel Phipps soon after 'put an entire stop to the business'.³⁴

## The Landscape

Knight's *The Landscape: A Didactic Poem* was published early in 1794. Its critique of Brown and its promotion of picturesque principles of landscape improvement were developed in conversations with Uvedale Price, to whom the poem is dedicated. Price later claimed that he had already drafted some unpublished essays on the subject and there were plans to issue a joint publication, but Knight took the initiative, perhaps because he recognized philosophical differences that he later made explicit to Price, and probably because he knew his work would make more impact.³⁵ Knight already had a reputation as a free-thinking dilettante and had upset pious opinion with a treatise on ancient phallic cults.³⁶

A long poem of some fifteen hundred lines in three books, *The Landscape* continued the eighteenth-century poetic tradition of censuring fashionable landscaping.

Much of *The Landscape*, especially in earlier passages of the books, is, as Jay Appleton points out, conventionally Virgilian, with passages that directly echo Dryden's translation of the *Georgics*.³⁷ 'Retir'd from business, toil, and strife', the poet celebrates a 'bless'd land' where 'fleecy flocks . . . heedless of the wolf . . . o'er verdant pastures stray'. This 'bless'd land' has a distinctly Herefordshire character. Nowhere was 'so beautiful a stream/ As the wide-tanging Wye, or rapid Team [*sic*.]'. It is threatened from within by vain landowners commissioning Brown, 'whose innovating hand/ First dealt thy curses oe'r this fertile land'. Brown is followed by others, a 'fantastic band,/ With charts, pedometers and rules in hand'. In contrast to their mechanical ways, the responsible landowner deploys a painterly approach to improvement. If the nature of Italy and Holland was unenviable, heat and disease in one country, damp and depression in the other, the painters esteemed for painting it provided a model for native improvers: 'Where Claude extends his prospect wide . . . where great Salvator's mountains rise . . . in the iv'd cottage of Ostade,/ Waterloe's copse, or Ruysdael's low cascade'.³⁸ Much of Knight's detailed advice on picturesque improvement in *The Landscape* corresponds, as Tom Wall has discovered, to his own landscaping of Downton Vale, often in a direct way.³⁹ Both the poem and the place confirm the county's Georgic reputation.

The less lyrical, more emotive and energetic passages towards the end of the books of *The Landscape* are, as Andrew Ballantyne points out, less Virgilian, more Lucretian.⁴⁰ What gave *The Landscape* its shock value was

113 View from the front rooms, with overlay, from the Red Book for Ferney Hall (1789). Pierpont Morgan Library, New York.

114  *View from the House at Tatton*, without overlay, from *Sketches and Hints on Landscape Gardening* (1794). Yale Center for British Art, Paul Mellon Collection.

its closing passage. Here Knight proposed wrecking Brown-style parks, releasing torpid lakes in a turbulent stream that would 'sweep down the fences and tear up the soil' before spreading out to water the 'fertile meads' and 'swell the wavy corn'. Knight made a direct analogy with the French Revolution: 'from these horrors, future times may see/ Just order spring, and genuine liberty'.[41] Rather than seeing this, as Ballantyne inclines to, as evidence of the poem's release from the material landscape and its improvement, it may be seen as grounded in the spectacular country of the upper Severn and its social development: its rushing streams, flaming forges and furnaces, its commercial freedoms and radical, hermetic, currents, the cultural geography of Coalbrookdale that shocked respectable opinion.[42]

Knight singles out Repton for criticism in *The Landscape* for his designs for Tatton Park, Cheshire. Knight came across the Tatton Red Book in Nicol's bookshop in Pall Mall, London, where it was displayed to attract subscriptions for *Sketches and Hints*. Knight assumed (wrongly) that it would feature in the publication: to justify a published response to an unpublished manuscript he said that he thought the Red Book in the shop was like the pictures displayed in the Shakespeare Gallery, originals 'of which a print has not yet been delivered'.[43]

It is scarcely surprising that Knight found in the Tatton Red Book plans for improvement that were quite at odds with the views he had developed and doubtless communicated to Repton at Ferney Hall four years earlier. Since then, Repton's work had taken a different direction from the one that Knight envisaged. If Repton complained about Brown's professed followers, he had not turned against Brown himself. If pictorial composition in landscaping was important to Repton, he now saw less correspondence between landscape painting and landscape gardening. The commission for the duke of Portland at Welbeck probably had a decisive influence here; Repton claimed that he learnt more from Portland's comments walking about the grounds 'than if I had studied and copied the works of the best masters . . . he never talked of pictures in the cant language of connoisseurship'.[44] The patronage of Portland, now Secretary of State and responsible for highly repressive measures against civil liberties, would not have endeared Repton to Knight. William Windham too had impressed his ideas on Repton. In the Red Book for Hill Hall, Essex (1791), Repton confessed: 'however enthusiastically fond I am of Landscape, yet I am fully aware of the truth of an observation made by my friend Mr Windham of Felbrigg, "that as Historical painting is superior to Landscape; so the comfort and convenience of a man's home should take the lead of picturesque beauty"'.[45] In his speeches supporting state repression, Windham used the image of a comfortable country home to promote a Burkean view of the constitution under

115 Benjamin Pouncey after Thomas Hearne, An 'undressed' park; A park 'dressed in the modern style', from Richard Payne Knight, *The Landscape: A Didactic Poem* (1794). Private collection.

threat.[46] Repton was becoming an established, even establishment, figure.

A large park on the Cheshire plain, landscaped by John Webb, Tatton was, said Repton, 'too vast to be deemed picturesque... beyond the pencil's power to imitate... yet it is altogether beautiful' (fig. 114). Repton wished to amplify Tatton's character of 'greatness', to give an impression of a 'united and uninterrupted property', which was presently compromised by the approach through the industrial town of Knutsford. So he proposed a grand new entrance (fig. 59) and suggested some measures to signal the importance of Tatton's owners, the Egertons, including coats of arms on the church, market house and merestones. Within the large park, Repton planned to break the old formal avenue and create a sweeping gravel approach to Samuel Wyatt's proposed Neo-classical mansion. There is some discussion in the Red Book of manipulating linear and aerial perspective to compose views but little attempt to create picturesque scenery. The controlling design of the Red Book is the large, Brown-style map at the beginning (which Repton reduced from an existing survey) showing the disposition of wood, water and roads.[47]

Knight had sufficient material to smear Repton's reputation. He lampooned Repton's advice for the entrance to Tatton Park:

'As you advance unto the palace gate,
Each object should announce the owner's state;
His vast possessions, and his wide domain;
His waving woods, and rich unbounded plains.'
He, therefore, leads you many a tedious round,
To shew th' extent of his employer's ground;
Climbs o'er the hills, and to the vales descends;
Then mounts again, through lawn that never ends.
But why not rather, at the porter's gate,
Hang up the map all my lord's estate,
Than give his hungry visitors the pain
To wander o'er so many miles in vain?
For well we know this sacrifice is made,
Not to his taste, but to his vain parade;
And all it does, is but shew combin'd
His wealth in land, and poverty in mind[48]

Knight illustrated the arguments of *The Landscape* with engravings after drawings by Thomas Hearne (fig. 115), for which he made written instructions, parodying Repton's technique of showing improvements by contrasting scenes.[49] To 'be perfectly fair', Knight chose 'the commonest English scenery', 'and that I might not be supposed to take advantage of tricks of light and shadow of my own system, I have given mere engraver's etchings which have no pretension to effect'. The engraver, Benjamin Pouncey, 'has indeed favoured that which I condemn, by giving more breadth, in the light and shadow that there is, to the second plate rather than the first'. The first plate shows an unimproved scene, pleasingly picturesque. We look from the borders of an 'ancient forest', across a boulder-strewn, fern-covered foreground. In the middle distance is a rippling stream, crossed by a wooden bridge on which a man (of what class, it is hard to make out) pauses in his walk. In the distance, 'well mix'd and blended in the scene', is an

Elizabethan house, 'a stately mansion rising to the view'. The poem tells us, though the engraving only suggests, that there is an intricate arrangement of terraces, walls and mounds in the garden. The second plate shows the scene 'dressed in the modern style'. The whole place has been emparked. The trees have been thinned to a few clumps dotting shaven lawns. The stream has been channelled to make a placid, serpentine stretch of water, over which has been built a Chinoiserie bridge. It conducts our eye directly to the house, remodelled in Palladian style, standing in 'solitary pride' amidst 'wide blank spaces'. 'Cold and dead', it is a scene that demands revolutionary liberation to restore its former energy and grandeur.[50]

Upon publication *The Landscape* caused an immediate stir. 'It seems the town is busy in reading [it]', noted William Mason in March 1794.[51] Repton placed an advertizement in *The Times* complaining about Knight's misuse of the Tatton Red Book. He told a Norfolk acquaintance, Norton Nicholls, of his shock 'for the *false* & I may say *malicious* attack of Mr Knight with whom I have lived in some habits of intimacy and had no reason to suspect his contumelious treatment of my profession' and of how he was consoled by letters of support from Mason, Gilpin and Windham.[52] He was further supported by the first review of *The Landscape* by William Marshall in the *Monthly Review* for May. Marshall condemned 'the attack on a work which is *not yet published*, – the work, too, of a professional man; and while subscriptions for it, we understand, are still depending'. And he mocked the 'wild imagination' and 'poetic derangement' of Knight, which would transport readers into 'the dear sequestered shades of Siberia' or the 'labyrinth of a Dutchman's garden'. A well-travelled rural reporter, Marshall could not recall 'a single *improved* place which bears the smallest resemblance to Mr Knight's description'.[53] Conservative commentators regarded Knight's poem as unpatriotic, even subversive. In a letter in September to Samuel Johnson, Repton's pen-friend Anna Seward found the principles of *The Landscape* 'the Jacobinism of taste . . . Mr Knight would have nature as well as man indulged in that uncurbed and wild luxuriance, which soon would render our landscape-island rank, weedy, damp, and unwholesome as the incultivate savannas of America'.[54] William Mason complained about this 'dictator to all taste, who Jacobinically would level the purity of gardens, who would as malignantly as Tom Paine or Priestly guillotine Mr Brown'.[55]

Repton added a chapter to *Sketches and Hints* to respond to *The Landscape*. It includes extracts from the Red Book for Tatton, which he had not originally intended to publish because the designs had not been executed, but which he now felt obliged to because Knight had misrepresented them. He also added extracts from other Red Books, including those for Pitt's seat, Holwood in Kent, and Antony House in Cornwall, the seat of a leading Pittite, Reginald Pole Carew. These contradicted Knight's correspondence between landscape painting and landscape gardening. Repton presents the conservative case that *The Landscape* promoted disorder, the reduction of a civilized, well-cultivated country to wildness.

'The enthusiasm for picturesque effect' had 'completely bewildered' Knight, Repton declared. The language of *The Landscape* conjured pleasing images of places – old quarries, mouldering abbeys, ivy-choked cottages – 'in situations ill adapted for the residence of man', but it was wholly inappropriate as a model for landscape gardening. 'Are we to banish all convenience from close-mown grass, or firm gravel-walks, and bear the weeds, and briers and docks, and thistles, in compliment to the slovenly mountain nymphs?' Repton reaffirmed the distinction between 'forest' and 'park' that the duke of Portland had impressed on him at Welbeck: the one 'the romantic wildness of nature', the other 'the habitation of men', and accused Knight of 'confounding the two ideas' in making painting and gardening equivalent. If taken as principles, passages from Knight's poem threatened 'to vitiate the taste of the nation, by introducing false principles; by recommending negligence for ease, and slovenly weeds for native beauty'.[56] A vignette shows a serpent emerging from a clump of docks and thistles (fig. 116).

116 'Docks and thistles', from *Sketches and Hints on Landscape Gardening* (1795). Yale Center for British Art, Paul Mellon Collection.

Repton, as Farington noted, had 'strong fears of the consequences of Knight's enmity... which checks him in answering'.[57] This explains the conciliatory tone of some remarks and why a word was pumiced after printing from every copy of *Sketches and Hints*: 'a very severe [...] attack from Mr Knight' left readers wondering about the missing word or words – perhaps 'and malicious', the phrase Repton used in the letter to Nicholls, perhaps something worse.[58] Repton ended on a respectful note. Downton Vale was 'one of the most beautiful and romantic valleys that the imagination can conceive', a testament 'to that taste which has displayed these charms to the greatest advantage':

> A narrow, wild, and natural path sometimes creeps under the beetling rock, close by the margin of a mountain stream. It sometimes ascends to an awful precipice, from whence the foaming waters are heard roaring in the dark abyss below, or seen wildly dashing against its opposite banks; while, in other places, the course of the river Teme being impeded by natural ledges of rock, the vale presents a calm, glassy mirror, that reflects the surrounding foliage. The path, in various places, crosses the water by bridges of the most romantic and contrasted forms; and, branching in various directions, including some miles in length, is occasionally varied and enriched by caves and cells, hovels, and covered seats, or other buildings, in perfect harmony with the wild but pleasing horrors of the scene. Yet, if the same picturesque objects were introduced in the gardens of a villa near the capital, or in the more tame, yet interesting, pleasure-grounds which I am frequently called upon to decorate, they would be as absurd, incongruous, and out of character, as a Chinese temple from Vauxhall transplanted into the Vale of Downton.[59]

Knight was not placated. In 1795 he issued a second edition of *The Landscape*, with additions replying to his critics and at length to Repton. If Repton was 'ill-treated by Mr Knight in his first Edition of *The Landscape*', as one of Repton's neighbours told Pole Carew, 'the wound is made still deeper by the note in the second'.[60] Because Repton did not 'consider picturesque beauty as belonging to his profession', Knight said that he would 'have nothing more to do with him':

> All that I beg of him is, that if he takes any *professional title*, it may be one really descriptive of his profession, such as that of *walk-maker, shrub planter, turf cleaner*, or *rural perfumer*; for if *landscapes* are not what he means to produce, that of *landscape gardener* is one not only of *no mean*, but of *no true pretension*.[61]

The rancour of Knight's remarks suggests some concern at Repton's comments or the views they represented. He was particularly intent on countering the 'insinuat[ion]' that my system of improvement tended *to turn this beautiful kingdom into one huge picturesque forest*'. He added new lines to the poem to affirm his Georgic views:

> But let not the still o'erbearing pride of taste
> Turn fertile districts to a forest's waste:
> Still let utility improvement guide,
> And just congruity in all preside.
> While shaggy hills are left to rude neglect,
> Let the rich plains with wavy corn be deck'd.
> And while rough thickets shade the lonely glen,
> Let culture smile upon the haunts of men;
> And the rich meadow and the fertile field
> The annual tribute of their harvest yield.[62]

With the Terror in Paris alarming polite England, and social disaffection rife in the country, Knight protested, rather too much, that his critics had taken him too literally when he likened picturesque improvement to political revolution. 'All I entreat is, that they will not at this time, when men's minds are so full of plots and conspiracies, endeavour to find analogies between picturesque composition and political confusion; or suppose that the preservation of trees and terraces has any connection with the destruction of states and kingdoms.'[63]

Any doubts about the link Knight made between aesthetics and politics were dispelled the following year by another didactic poem, *The Progress of Civil Society*. Mason found it sufficiently seditious to suggest to Walpole that Knight's 'principles ought to be exposed before the next election, that such honest freeholders, who detest the French Jacobins, may be led to make it a point of conscience not to vote for him'.[64] Knight's notoriety put Downton off-limits to some connoisseurs. 'I might as well propose to you a journey to the moon or the new comet as to Downton', Uvedale Price told Sir George Beaumont in 1797, 'especially as the party is a little rebellious... Knight has at last cut off that last mark of loyalty & aristocracy ycleped a pigtail... I imagine some celestial democrat has been docking the new comet, who I find is called the Crop'.[65]

117  J.J. Schalch, *Foxley* (1756). Private collection.

## Foxley

Uvedale Price's vision of picturesque landscape was less libertarian than that of Knight. In contrast to Knight's invocation of 'the rays of genius that inflame/The freeborn soul', Price settled for a conservative, country-Whig view of liberty, as securely rooted in landed property and its responsibilities; freedom was, he reassured Repton, a 'steady influence, like that of a fine evening, [which] gives at once a glowing warmth, and a union to all within its sphere'.[66] Whereas for Knight 'picturesque landscape' was a way of seeing, a subjective aesthetic in the eye of the beholder which could in principle be deployed to depict and design any promising piece of landscape, for Price 'The Picturesque' was inherent in the landscape, an objective quality that could be discovered by cultivating an eye for both art and the country and manifested by a careful programme of improvement.[67] Price's picturesque vision was rooted in the historical evolution and abiding memories of localities and was strongly informed by his own patrimony, by his sense of following his father and grandfather in developing the family seat of Foxley (fig. 117) as a visually attractive estate with a strong sense of social integration.[68] Price's *Essay on the Picturesque* is more obviously a primer of estate improvement than Knight's didactic poem; indeed it was, like Foxley, 'new modelled' in three editions between 1794 and 1810.[69]

A land-owning lawyer from North Wales, nicknamed 'the Welsh patriot' for his opposition to the king's granting titles to the first duke of Portland, Uvedale Price's great-grandfather Robert Price married into a Herefordshire family and took full possession of Foxley in the early eighteenth century. A new Neo-classical brick mansion with formal, Italianate terraced gardens formed the nucleus of a property that was expanded and remodelled by successive generations in to a compact estate of some four thousand acres. The Prices were enthusiastic sketchers and improvers of landscape. Uvedale Price's grandfather Uvedale Tomkins Price befriended Gainsborough in Bath and invited him to sketch Foxley (fig. 118). In his *Essay on the Picturesque* Price recalls making sketching excursions with Gainsborough, 'the mildest and most benevolent of men' and the painter's expression of 'gentleness and complacency' when they came across 'cottage or village scenes'. Price's father, Robert, took his Grand Tour with William Windham I of Felbrigg and the naturalist Benjamin Stillingfleet. Stillingfleet moved to Foxley to assist Price in a programme of improving woods, pasture and cottages, and to take sketching tours of the Welsh countryside.[70] Price saw a correspondence between his family's love of painting and their exercise of paternalism. The 'cheerfulness of the scene' in their villages attested to their 'attentive kindnesses', and this was 'amply repaid by affectionate regard and reverence'.[71]

Uvedale Price inherited the family estate shortly after his own Grand Tour in 1767–8 and focussed his energies on improving Foxley, selling off lands in North Wales and consolidating his property in Herefordshire. It was then, in a youthful flush of enthusiasm, that Price momentarily fell for the Brown style. In a '*testament politique*', Price describes how he had impulsively destroyed the old, walled garden at Foxley:

118  Thomas Gainsborough, *Beech Trees at Foxley* (1760), Whitworth Art Gallery, University of Manchester.

I doomed it and all its embellishments, with which I had formed such an early connection, to sudden and total destruction; probably much upon the same idea, as many a man of careless, unreflecting, unfeeling good-nature, thought it his duty to vote for demolishing towns, provinces, and their inhabitants in America.[72]

In 1774 Price commissioned Nathaniel Kent, then improving Felbrigg for William Windham II, to survey Foxley with a view to reorganizing the estate. As a result of amalgamating fields and consolidating farms, the rental of Foxley rose by about one-fifth. In his plans, Kent was careful to preserve smallholders and cottagers, retaining that 'connection' between landlord, tenant and labourer that he espoused as a principle in his published works. Kent's plans also transferred a considerable amount of tenanted land and woodland to Price, establishing an extensive domain for his landscaping expeditions. Foxley provided a paradigm for the careful authority that characterizes all Price's writings, on woodland management, landscape aesthetics and civil defence.[73]

Foxley was a very different estate to Downton. Seven miles from Hereford, it was located in a tributary valley of the Wye. The wooded slopes encircling the house reached four hundred feet, but it lacked the rocks and rushing water that characterized Downton Vale. Half the size of the Downton estate, Foxley yielded less than half the income. It was less diversified, mainly agricultural and silvicultural, with no industrial resources, and so more vulnerable to recession and taxation. Price made a virtue of close, personal supervision at Foxley, often telling friends that he could not afford to leave it for London. After his youthful Grand Tour, Price never, to my knowledge, ventured abroad. Many of his excursions were made in and around the Wye Valley within reach of Foxley and his villa at Aberystwyth, the main seaside resort for the gentry of Wales and the West Midlands.[74]

While Price was remodelling Foxley, much of Herefordshire, especially in the Vale of Hereford along the Wye, was undergoing a rapid phase of modernization. The profits from corn, cattle, timber and cider were invested in a range of improvements such as river channelling, turnpiking, street widening, enclosures, the building and rebuilding of wharves, bridges, public institutions, manor houses and cottages, towpaths and riverside walks.[75] Many ancestral Herefordians welcomed modern, metropolitan-style improvements, both to the city of Hereford and to their surrounding estates along the River Wye. Local guidebooks hoped that such improvements would attract tourists who rarely ventured into the upper reaches of the Wye Valley beyond Ross because Gilpin had been so dismissive of its scenery. They promoted a 'salubrious' city in 'the Garden of England'.[76]

Foxley featured in guides to the upper Wye because of Robert Price's improvements, in particular the ride to The Ladylift, at the summit of the estate and one of the main viewpoints of the county, from which its fertile, varied countryside was best displayed, and it achieved greater celebrity after Price published his views. 'Well known in the literary world as author of *An Essay on the Picturesque*', with 'a conspicuous knowledge of the liberal arts', Uvedale Price had improved the grounds 'in a very

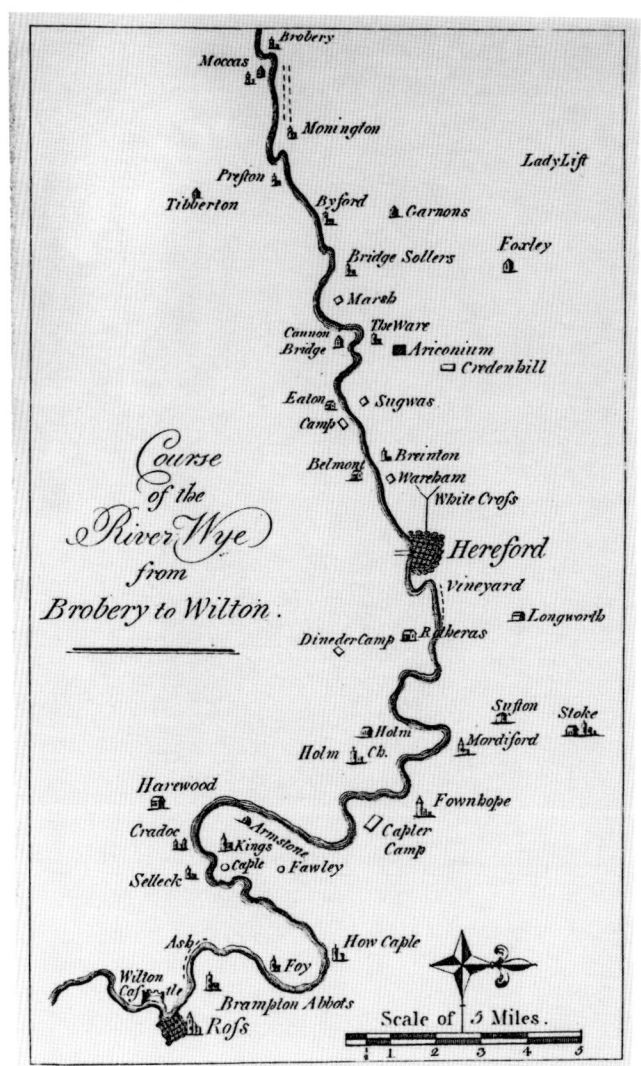

119 *Course of the River Wye from Brobery to Wilton*, from John Price, *An Historical Account of the City of Hereford* (1796). Hereford Library.

eminent manner' with a 'superior judgment in the real beauties of natural landscape', so a guide of 1796 to the Vale of Hereford was proud to declare.[77] The guide also included a variety of other improved estates and parks belonging to aristocrats and professional men, newcomers and ancestral squires along the vale (fig. 119), designed by local men or nationally known professionals. 'The ingenious Mr Repton' is singled out for his 'masterly direction' at Sufton and Stoke Edith, two of seven, probably eight, places he advised on in the Vale of Hereford – as high a concentration of commissions as anywhere.[78] It is in the nature of guidebooks, particularly progressive-style promotional guides, to present a harmonious view of different places and interests, a unity in diversity.[79] In the next section I put this image in to question by examining the dispute between Price and Repton in terms of the claims they made on the Vale of Hereford and the forms of authority to which they appealed. I do so by examining Repton's main commissions in the vale before and after the published exchange of views in 1794.

## The Vale of Hereford

When Price was shown Repton's drawings for Ferney in 1789, he discovered a talent that made him wish to get to know Repton better; moreover, to form an alliance. 'I wished to be your ally, not your opponent, I flattered myself that . . . we might have been of reciprocal use to each other.' During an excursion along the Wye he noted Repton's powers of picturesque discrimination in his remarks along the way and reckoned that, with some education in the finer points of connoisseurship, Repton might realize in his designs some of the ideas that Price had been drafting in his unpublished essays.[80]

Repton's first commission in the Vale of Hereford was at Garnons, the adjacent estate to Foxley, in February 1791. The client, John Geers Cotterell, had inherited Garnons the previous year and still more lands in the county through marriage to a local heiress. Price probably recommended Repton to Cotterell. Their two families had long exchanged lands in consolidating the respective estates, a procedure these men continued. Price's gardener, James Cranstone, executed Repton's improvements for Garnons. Nevertheless it is difficult from the surviving records to discern a strong or decisive influence from Price's direction. Neither Foxley nor Price is mentioned by name in Repton's plans for Garnons,

120  View towards the park, with and without overlay, from the Red Book for Garnons (1791). Private collection.

and while the Red Book acknowledges the 'wild and romantic . . . beautiful scenery' to the north of Garnons, Repton was reluctant to make much connection with it. A new carriage drive on to the hills was mooted but not made a priority. The focus of Repton's plans was the area to the south, immediately around a remodelled mansion overlooking Cotterell's lands near the banks of the Wye at Byford. The term 'picturesque' is an important word in the Red Book, but it owes relatively little to the highly painterly way in which Price defined it.[81]

Many of Repton's proposals for Garnons are connected with his collaboration on the commission with James Wyatt, the most renowned architect in England. Wyatt had come to Hereford to make plans to restore the cathedral after the collapse of its west front, and Cotterell persuaded him to design a new mansion. Repton had already worked with Wyatt for Lord Darnley at Cobham, Kent. Wyatt was a far more famous figure than Price and, for Repton, a more important ally. Wyatt's

121  View from the park, with and without overlay, from the Red Book for Garnons. Private collection.

notoriously dilatory dealings compromized Repton (although not his esteem for the man), and the Garnons commission was no exception.[82] When the Red Book was delivered, fully eighteen months after Repton's first visit, Wyatt had still not delivered the plans he had promised, and Repton had to envisage what the mansion would look like on the basis of their conversations (fig. 120).

In order to show Wyatt's proposed mansion to best effect, Repton suggested or endorsed moving the turnpike from its course immediately in front of the house and emparking the fields in between. Although more removed from the road, the enlarged, remodelled mansion would appear 'the seat of Hospitality, and where according to the customs of Herefordshire, not only the neighbouring Families, but even their servants may receive a welcome'. Although the house overlooked the Wye Valley and the riverside village of Byford, the Wye itself was invisible. So Repton suggested 'some reach . . . may be rendered visible from the house with proper management or at least some part of the wet moor may be made to shew an apparent continuation of the river'. And he shows just this in a drawing from the proposed new road, planting trees to suggest the banks of the river, draining a duck pond and creating a curved pool with a sham bridge to give the illusion of a Wye meander (fig. 121). Garnons would take full command of this stretch of the Wye Valley.

In his written explanation, in which he claims to deliver Wyatt's sentiments as well as his own, Repton defends the 'Picturesque stile' of his integration of architecture and landscape with a long passage from Gérardin's *De la composition des Paysages* (1777), in which the author argues that 'l'effet pittoresque' should be sought for contriving a building to present as many sides as possible at once, 'seduire et fixer les yeux', to attract and rivet the eye. Gérardin was one of the authors (along with Mason, Gilpin and Whately) that Repton claimed as 'my breviary' in 1788, as he embarked on his career.[83] Price and Knight do not cite Gérardin, although Knight derived his meaning of picturesque from the same idiom in Italian, and there are echoes of his essay (probably via Repton) in Price's writings on architecture; moreover the figure of the improving landowner theorizing about landscape had obvious parallels with the Herefordshire connoisseurs. After establishing his practice, Repton confessed to reservations about Gérardin. In a passage from the Red Book for Stoke Poges around 1792, which he reproduced when replying to Knight in *Sketches and Hints*, Repton disputes Gérardin's directive that 'no scene in nature should be attempted till it has first been painted', and finds the 'just observations' of the essay 'often mixed with whimsical conceits, and impracticable theories of gardening'.[84] It is significant that, despite his inclinations, the English translator of *De la composition des Paysages*, Daniel Malthus, supported Repton in the picturesque controversy.

> You may have perceived that I am rather *too much* inclined to the Price and Knight *party*, and yet I own to you, that I have been often so much disgusted by the affected and technical language of connoisseurship, that I have been sick of pictures for a month, and almost of Nature, when the same jargon was applied to her. I know the abilities of the two gentlemen, and am sorry they have made themselves such pupils of the Warburtonian school, as to appear more like Luther and Calvin than a couple of west country gentlemen.[85]

Wyatt failed to deliver his plans for Garnons. On Repton's recommendation the Norwich architect William Wilkins, who had already designed some cottages for Garnons, submitted plans for the mansion, but Cotterell rejected these, somewhat contemptuously.[86] Repton revisited Garnons in 1793, but work on the mansion was suspended when Cotterell left to join his regiment.[87]

Following Garnons, Repton was next commissioned in the Vale of Hereford in June 1792, at Stoke Edith, six miles to the east of the city. Stoke Edith was the main seat of the Foleys, a powerful dynasty with lands throughout the West Midlands. Repton's commission at Stoke Edith was probably arranged as early as 1790, when his client, Edward Foley (well known to Windham through Whig circles), inherited the family property and called in Repton to the Staffordshire estate of Prestwood, a centre of the iron founding, which he inherited with his second marriage. Prestwood was surrounded by canals, wire mills and a 'dirty village', and Repton found it a difficult site; he jokingly suggested flooding the factories under a lake to restore the place's 'natural beauties'. Prestwood had 'a character subordinate to the more magnificent Family Residence at Stoke'. The last page in the Prestwood Red Book is a view of Stoke Edith where Foley was planning to return after a fire and which Repton had his eye on improving.[88]

The Foleys had purchased Stoke Edith in the seventeenth century, attracted by its woods for charcoal production. On selecting it as their family residence, they had the mansion remodelled and the grounds refashioned by George London, the leading garden designer of the time.[89] The place had remained relatively unaltered until Repton was called in, while the country around had been highly cultivated as a prime area of orchards and hop gardens. In Herefordshire Foley enjoyed a reputation as a Georgical landlord. In 1791 a new edition of Phillips's poem *Cider* was dedicated to Foley, annotated with new footnotes on up-to-date methods of pro-duction and a view of a cider mill on the title page. Repton was called in to Stoke Edith in June 1792 and produced the Red Book three months later.

Although surrounded by woods and pasture, orchards and hopyards, and next to a farming village, Stoke Edith appears in the Red Book as no less difficult a site than industrial Prestwood. Repton suggested removing 'those impediments' that 'encumbered the natural beauties of Stoke'. These included the high road, village, parsonage and church.[90] Repton found the existing highroad poorly placed in relation to the mansion. It ran in a cutting close to the back of the house, offering a view from which 'all its beauties are entirely lost'. Rerouting the road away

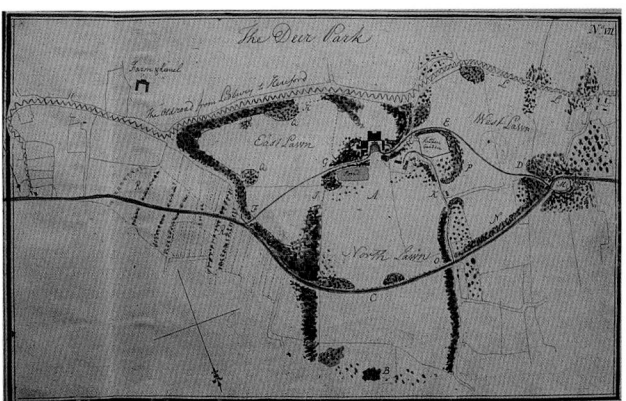

122  Map of road realignment, from the Red Book for Stoke Edith (1792). Private collection.

from the mansion, but in sight of its front across the park, was 'the first object of improvement' (fig. 122). As Foley was to bear the expense, it was reasonable that his convenience would 'have its full share' in the new alignment, but Repton reckoned that 'the convenience of the public' should not be neglected either, and any increase in distance the diversion entailed was compensated for by the fine view they would enjoy of Foley's house and grounds (fig. 123).

From the road realignment other improvements would follow. Repton proposed demolishing the village of Stoke to the west of the mansion and rebuilding it around a new entrance on the diverted road. He was quick to mention those occasions when he had 'ventured to condemn as false taste that fatal rage for depopulating a country under the idea of its being necessary to the importance of a mansion'. 'A number of labourers constitutes one of the requisites of grandeur', but it was no more necessary that their dwellings should be close to the house than 'that their inhabitants should eat at the same table'. 'If their humble dwellings should be made a subordinate part of the general scenery, they will so far from disgracing it, add all the dignity which wealth can derive from the exercize of benevolence.' The designs for the village buildings were supplied by William Wilkins (figs 124 and 125). These included seven double cottages, housing two weavers, a cooper, butcher, blacksmith, shoemaker and eight labourers, a school for boys and girls and a cider mill. The cottages, in a vernacular style, were set round a village green at the centre of which was the cider mill, embellished 'by a Colonade of twelve trees with the Bark on, giving the building an appearance of a Rude Primitive Temple'. The village was to be surrounded by

123 Proposed view from the new road, from the Red Book for Stoke Edith (1792). Private collection.

orchards and planted around with firs, laurels and flowering shrubs.[91]

Dealing with another impediment at Stoke Edith was a more delicate matter. Foley's forebears had placed the mansion near the church, 'a misfortune with respect to picturesque beauty', Repton reckoned. The 'picturesque harmony of parts to whole' was disrupted because the dominion of the mansion, which should be the 'leading feature' in the 'composition', was challenged by the spire of the church and the size of the parsonage. The church spire 'fortunately shows some symptoms of decay' and might be removed, replaced by a battlemented tower, but the parsonage was more problematic. It was 'not only a mere residence, it is a vast territory, including all its orchards, glebe, gardens, barns, cottage, coach-house, stables and offices of every description, it is in fact an Imperium in Imperio, and little less than its total removal can give adequate importance to Stoke House'. Short of removal, Repton thought its impact might be reduced by removing the servants' rooms in the garret and the ground floor, subduing the colour of the roof and planting vines and creepers up the walls and some lime trees near the windows. Here Repton anticipated some difficulty with the rector, Dr Napleton: 'the duty of my profession . . . may not entirely coincide with his own wishes'. A sketch of the improvements (fig. 123) shows the mansion across the park from the rerouted road, rising above a spire-less church and a reduced parsonage engulfed in greenery. The scene is completed by the effect of a few cottages left in the park, to be converted to 'a keepers house, a dairy or a menagerie'. 'There is hardly anything more picturesque and pleasing than smoke curling amongst the trees.'[92]

Soon after the Red Book was completed, Foley put the road improvements in to effect. He spent a considerable sum, more than one thousand pounds in two years; nearly eight hundred on the new stretch of turnpike, over two hundred on the new entrance drives and more than three times that on other alterations to the grounds in this period.[93] After this had been done, Repton reported that 'the improvement in the place is equally felt by the proprietor, and conspicuous to every stranger who travels from Ledbury to Hereford'.[94]

The actual improvements to Stoke Edith were less radical than Repton had originally proposed. While two of Wilkins's cottages were built around the new entrance by 1794 – the blacksmith's shop and the weaver's house (converted to a toll house) – the new village with its primitivist cider mill was never realized. The existing village was preserved and connected to the rerouted highway by a new road. The church and parsonage were untouched. The precise reasons for this are unclear, perhaps expense, perhaps the resistance of the rector, perhaps Foley accommodating his improvements to local sentiments. In 1799 Luke Booker, rector of Tedstone Delauncey above Stoke Edith on the Malvern Hills, dedicated a new poem in the style of *Cider*, *The Hop-Garden*, to Foley, 'your magnificent Seat . . . being surrounded by the Scenery of which the Poem professes to treat'. In Booker's poem, the hop-pickers return to their 'cottage homes', flush with the 'sparkling store of Pomona's beverage', 'By Justice guarded and Britannia's laws'. Booker praised 'princely STOKE,/That yonder lifts its heaven-directed Spire'.[95] The *Hereford Journal* also celebrated the virtues of Foley in verse, overseeing improvements to the estate all year round, creating an Elysium at Stoke of 'stately trees', 'polished lawns . . . and glades . . . the haunt of happy swains and artless maids'.[96] The entry on Stoke Edith in the guide to Hereford of 1796 credits Repton with a scene that he had originally proposed to alter:

> improvements were conducted under the inspection of the ingenious Mr. Repton, who has here displayed his taste and judgement to great advantage . . . the façade of this elegant seat, its extensive shrubberies, the spire of its parish church, the handsome parsonage and village, with the park richly cloathed with fine timber in the background . . . present to the traveller a very pleasant and lively scene.[97]

Stoke Edith proved a significant site for Repton's career. In 1793 John Nash, then engaged on building Hereford Gaol, was commissioned by Foley to remodel the parlour at Stoke and drafted in many of the workmen building the gaol.[98] Although Nash was already working for Price on his villa at Aberystwyth, it was at Stoke Edith that he first met Repton. 'Two such congenial minds were never brought together since the days of David and Jonathan', Repton recalled. He felt his income was '*certain* to increase greatly from the percentage which was agreed between us . . . I had now reached the pinnacle of my expectations'. Repton recalled Foley's reaction: 'If you two, whom I consider to be the cleverest men in England, could agree to *act together* you might carry the whole world before you.'[99]

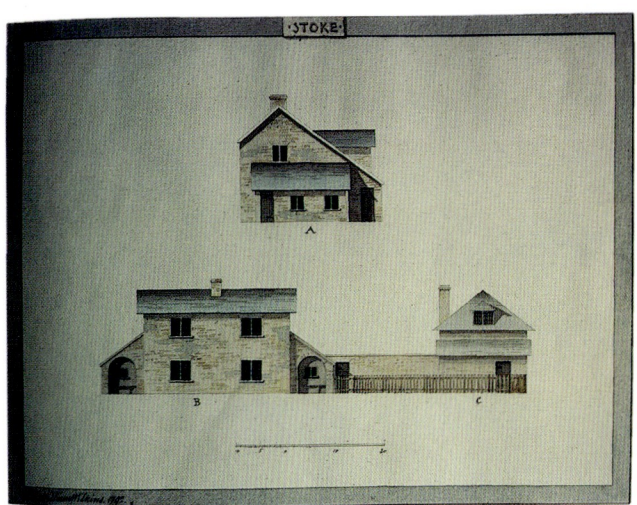

124  William Wilkins, *Double Cottage and Blacksmith's Shop*, from *Designs for the Village of Stoke* (1792). Herefordshire Record Office.

125  William Wilkins, *Cider Mill*, from *Designs for the Village of Stoke* (1792). Herefordshire Record Office.

If Repton had initially derived some benefit from Price's support in securing commissions, by 1793 he had little need of it. If Repton looked to a partnership with Nash as a way of raising the status of his profession as well as his own income, Nash realized that a partnership with Repton was more promising than the patronage of Price: it would help him regain his national reputation after exile in Carmarthenshire. Not only was Repton working the length of England, but he had begun to work extensively around London. On Windham's advice he had sent the Red Book for Wembley to Burke and earned fulsome approval for making the house 'a principal Object in all improvements... this essential Circumstance has been much overlooked in all speculations'.[100] And after hearing of approving remarks from George III on some Red Books, Repton secured permission to dedicate *Sketches and Hints* to the king.[101]

## Essay on the Picturesque

Price's *Essay on the Picturesque* was published some six months after Knight's *The Landscape*, in June 1794. Although Price referred to Repton only by name in a footnote, Repton reckoned that 'many pages are directly pointed at my opinions; although with more delicacy than your friend Mr Knight has shewn'. Moreover, Price's pronouncement that 'Mr Repton . . . is deservedly at the head of his profession' was empty praise 'since you attack the very existence of the profession'.[102]

'There is no country, I believe (if we except China) where the art of laying out grounds is so much cultivated as it now is in England', observed Price, and yet this was no reason for national rejoicing. If 'there is something of patriotism in the praises which Mr. Walpole and Mr. Mason have bestowed on English gardening', that 'zeal for the honour of their country has made them overlook defects, which they have themselves condemned'. 'My love for my country, is, I trust, not less ardent than theirs, but it has taken a different turn; and I feel anxious to free it from the disgrace of propagating a system [the landscaping of Capability Brown and his followers] which, should it become universal would disfigure the face of all Europe.' Far from expressing Whig ideals of liberty, as Walpole and Mason saw it, Brown's landscaping represented its betrayal. 'Levelling' everything around a mansion, planting 'clumps' and 'belts', signified the despotism of power. Price likened the spread of the Brown style to a military invasion, 'fearful of an enemy being in ambuscade among the bushes of a gravel pit, or hiding in some intricate group of trees' and his own 'more liberal and extended idea of improvement' as a defence against it.[103]

The problem, as Price saw it, was that the 'art of improving' in England was cultivated in isolation from 'that of painting'. 'This reflection may account for what otherwise seems quite unaccountable: namely that many enthusiastic admirers and collectors of Claude, Poussin, &c. should have suffered professed improvers to deprive the general and extended scenery of their places, of all that those painters would have most admired and copied.' Such collectors considered 'pictures merely with a reference to other pictures . . . they rarely look upon them in that point of view in which alone they can produce any real advantage – as a school in which we may learn to enlarge, refine, and correct our ideas of nature, and in return, may qualify ourselves by this liberal course of study, to be real judges of what is excellent in imitation'. A closer appreciation of Claude, in the light of exchanges with the world beyond the picture gallery, would reveal a careful, compositional structure to the human and natural world – 'connection' Price called it – a structure destroyed by the designs of Brown and his followers.[104]

There was 'something despotic in the general system of improvement . . . all that obstructs levelled to the ground; houses, orchards, gardens, all swept away',

> *Painting* on the contrary, tends to humanize the mind: where a despot thinks every person an intruder who enters his domain, and wishes to destroy cottages and pathways, and to reign alone, the lover of painting, considers the dwellings, the inhabitants, and the marks of their intercourse, as ornaments to the landscape.

Price's own family had been considerate in laying out their estate 'for the comfort and pleasures of its inhabitants':

> Such attentive kindnesses are amply repaid by affectionate regard and reverence; and were they general throughout the kingdom, they would do much more towards guarding us against democratical opinions, 'Than twenty thousand soldiers arm'd in proof'.

Connection was Price's controlling principle of picturesque improvement, 'from the most extensive prospect to the most confined wood scene'.[105]

Price's ambition was to establish the Picturesque, through the currency of landscape improvement, as a commanding aesthetic category alongside those of Burke: 'To hold a station between beauty and sublimity . . . to fill up a vacancy between the sublime and the beautiful'. If the Sublime was largely beyond the scope of improvers, the Beautiful was too confined to smoothly verdant scenes. A new category was needed to comprehend other kinds of scenery, arguably the majority of scenery in Britain, which otherwise would be overlooked, or, worse, colonized by vulgar tastes intent on transforming it. The scope of the Picturesque had the advantage of bringing many styles of landscape painting in to play, not just those of Claude and Poussin, but of Rembrandt, Rubens, Ruisdael and Titian, and more affordable artists, such as Van Ostade and Wouvermans. If the 'higher schools of painting' presented 'magnificent' views to be contemplated by 'men of princely revenue', the study of 'Dutch and Flemish masters' was appropriate to 'men of moderate fortunes', especially 'in all that relates to cottages, hamlets and villages'.[106]

Price found the Picturesque exemplified in a common feature of the Herefordshire countryside: 'old neglected bye roads and hollow ways'.[107] Rutted by carts, trodden by passengers and animals, weathered by wind and water, these lanes 'discover[ed] the different strata of earth, and shaggy roots of trees' in hollows 'overgrown with wild roses, with honeysuckles and other trailing plants'. Such lanes provided 'useful hints' for walks and drives close to a gentleman's house. Price describes in detail the destruction of two lanes by professional landscaping, a process of smoothing and levelling. These 'two specimens of dressed lanes' were 'not in a distant county, but within thirty miles of London, and in a district full of expensive embellishments'.

> the rash hand of false taste completely demolishes what time only, and a thousand lucky accidents can mature, so as to make it become the admiration and study of a Ruysdal or a Gainsborough; and reduces it to such a thing, as an Oilman in Thames-street may at any time contract for by the yard at Islington or Mile-End.[108]

New fashions were threatening extensive prospects, 'the most popular of all views'. The connectivity of the field of vision, its network of associations – what Price called 'the local geography and history of an extensive prospect' – was being disrupted by glaring, distinctive effects. Vain landowners were creating 'beacons of taste', whitewashing houses, planting larches, converting churches in to gazebos, to attract 'the curiosity and admiration of the vulgar', the 'prospect hunter (a very numerous tribe)', who assessed views on the number of such 'vouchers' they contained. At the same time, 'travellers of taste will naturally be provoked to enquire, though from another motive, to whom those hills belong'. Travellers of taste explored prospects for 'some ancient castle-like mansion', 'the mossy weather-stained tower of an old church', 'a cottage of a quiet colour half concealed among the trees, with its bit of garden, its pales and orchard'.[109]

So much of Price's picturesque vision is framed by his admiration for ancient woodland, 'the superior variety and richness of unimproved parks and forests', that the wider agrarian economy is glimpsed only through their glades: the 'flat square meadow surrounded by a neat hedge' and the 'piece of arable of excellent husbandry'. Autumn was the picturesque season, with a glowing, unifying light and colourful foliage. 'Many years ago', upon entering Herefordshire during springtime when the fruit trees were in blossom, Price rode in high expectation, 'for I had heard that at the time of the blow, the whole country from the Malvern Hills looked like a garden'; indeed 'it did look like a garden, but it made a scattered discordant landscape . . . and though the scene conveyed to my mind the chearful ideas of fruitfulness and plenty, I could not help feeling how defective it was in all those qualities and principles, on which the painter sets so high a value'.[110]

Price sent an advance copy of the *Essay* to Burke and received the statesman's endorsement:

> It gave me a few hours very seasonable relief from Books of a very different kind, which teach too clearly, the art, not of improving, but of laying waste a Country, and of defacing the Beauties both of nature and of contrivance. I have the happiness of agreeing with you in almost everything you have said about Brownism.[111]

Repton asked for an advance copy too and took it to read on a journey to Derbyshire in June 1794. During the journey he drafted his reply in the form of the open *Letter to Uvedale Price*, which, with the editorial assistance of a literary hack, William Combe, he published the following month.[112]

With Price's *Essay* as his 'companion' during the journey, Repton recalled the author's 'animated conversation on the subject', in particular 'the pleasant hours we passed together amidst the romantic scenery of the Wye'. Repton remembered acknowledging then 'that an enthusiasm for the picturesque had originally led me to fancy greater affinity betwixt *Painting* and *Gardening*, than I found to exist after more mature consideration and practical experience'. The 'health, cheerfulness, and comfort of a country residence' should not be sacrificed 'to the wild but pleasing scenery of a painter's imagination'. '*Beauty*, and not "*picturesqueness*", is the chief object of modern improvement', and although 'some nurserymen, or labourers in the kitchen garden have badly copied Mr. Brown's manner, the unprejudiced eye will discover innumerable beauties in the works of that great self-taught master'. If sometimes badly executed and managed, Brown's 'clumps' and 'belts' were not massive, impenetrable features, but ways of 'connecting and displaying the various pleasing point of view, at a distance from each other, within the limits of a park'.[113]

The love of painting, which Price regarded as a condition of careful, practical management, Repton saw as a seductive distraction:

> Your new theory of deducing *landscape gardening* from *painting* is so plausible, that, like many other philosophic theories, it may captivate and mislead... I cannot help seeing great affinity between deducing gardening from the painter's studies of wild nature, and deducing government from the uncontrolled opinions of man in a savage state... The neatness, simplicity, and elegance of English gardening, have acquired the approbation of the present century, as the happy medium betwixt the wildness of nature and the stiffness of art; in the same manner as the English constitution is the happy medium betwixt the liberty of savages, and the restraint of despotic government ... Let experiments of untried theoretical improvement be made in some other country.

In a period of war, when popular tourism in Britain was seen as patriotic, Repton made Price's criticism of 'prospect hunters' look suspicious:

> in spite of the fastidiousness of connoisseurship, we must allow something to the general voice of mankind. I am led to this remark from observing the effect of picturesque scenery on the visitors of Matlock Bath (where this part of my letter has been written). In the valley, a thousand delightful subjects present themselves to the painter, yet the visitors to this place are seldom satisfied till they have climbed the neighbouring hills, to take a bird's eye view of the whole spot, which no painting can represent.

Finishing the letter on the way home to Hare Street through eastern England, Repton reflected that Price's 'habit of admiring fine pictures' and his life 'amidst bold and picturesque scenery... may have rendered you insensible to the beauty of those milder scenes that have charms for common observers'.[114]

Thus Repton reappropriated the terrain of Whig liberty. He pushed Price's picturesque vision, so carefully constructed as a constitutional polity, beyond the borders of patriotic landscape. If Price saw himself as a responsible Georgical squire among his cottages, woods and country lanes, Repton represented him as a wild man of the western forests.

Price's reply to Repton, also in the form of an open letter, was published in December 1794, but at six times the length it was also written as a 'Supplement to my Essay... enlarging upon some points'. Price attempted to reclaim his ground. Repton's aim, he complained, was to show that 'by an attention to pictures... only wild and unpolished ideas are acquired', that an admiration for picturesque scenery 'should convert its admirers into so many Cherokees, and make them lose all relish but for what is savage and uncultivated'. Anyone reading Repton's letter would think Price beyond the borders of culture itself, 'a sort of tyger, who passes my life in a jungle, with no more idea of the softer beauties of nature than that animal'. In these times of political tension,

> he who expresses warmly his love of freedom and hatred of despotism... will be treated by zealots, as a friend of anarchy and confusion... I have been represented as a person, who, had I the power, would destroy all the comforts of a place... wet everybody in high grass – tear their clothes with brambles and briars – and send them up to their knees through dirty lanes between two cart-ruts.

To Price it was Repton who was uncivilized, degraded by his ignorance of the art on which picturesque beauty was based. He had clearly proved unwilling to take Price's advice of studying 'what the higher artists have done':

> I cannot recollect... amidst all the romantic scenes [of the Wye] we viewed together, your having made any of those allusions to the works of various masters, which might naturally have occurred to a person who had studied, or even observed them with common attention... I could not help observing at the time (and with great concern) how lightly you treated the

idea of taking any hints from any part of the natural river, towards forming an artificial one.

Repton had misrepresented his views on prospects:

> If I do despise prospects, I am constantly acting against my inclination... In my own place I have three distinct prospects – bird's eye views seen from high hills – of which I am not a little proud, and to which I carry all my guests of every description. If they like nothing else in the place, I do not converse with them on pictures, or landscape gardening; but if they have the affectation I have sometimes been witness to, that of holding all prospects in contempt as unworthy of the attention of a man of true taste, I do not feel eager to converse with them on any subject.

It was not prospects as such that disgusted him, but the way they were disfigured by glaring landmarks. The virtue of a prospect was in presenting

> the real geography of what is really spread out before us, and the many doubts, enquiries, and observations it suggest to the curious traveller, and also to the painter in his own line; who from such eminences can best remark, what districts promise the most interesting scenery.

Price found it incredible that Repton could disavow the importance of painting to improvement when the principal part of his art was to make drawings of the main views of a place as they were and as they were to be. 'In reality you make the best *pictures* you can.' Surely 'connection' was as important to Repton as it was to Price, especially in 'the present crisis':

> The mutual connection and dependence of all the different ranks and orders of men in this country; the innumerable, but voluntary ties by which they are bound and united to each other... are perhaps the firmest securities of its glory, its strength and happiness ... as [the principle of connection] so happily pervades the true spirit of our government and constitution, may it no less prevail in all our plans for embellishing the outward face of this noble kingdom, 'Till Albion smile/ One ample theatre of sylvan grace'.[115]

Through his publisher, Price asked Repton's permission to reprint his letter with his own, but Repton declined, saying that he would do so himself in an Appendix to *Sketches and Hints*, where 'I shall more fully enter into the question between Mr Knight, Mr Price, Mr Brown and myself'.[116] As the book was about to appear in February 1795, Repton informed Price in a private letter that he had 'softened some passages' of his open letter, and that the differences between them were 'by no means so great as either of us pretend in our publick controversy', if only that 'many of my sentiments and opinions have been anticipated in your publication'. He concurred with Price's views on the banks of artificial water, having introduced 'large rocks as a picturesque circumstance', 'tho in the execution the gardener is liable to do away with my intention as I fear you may find at Lord Malden's [Hampton Court] in your Neighbourhood'.[117]

Repton's retaliation in an Appendix to *Sketches and Hints* turned out to be more strongly worded than Price might have expected. Repton knew Price 'as a gentleman, long before he became an author'. Had he known of Price's forthcoming *Essay*, 'of which I had not the most distant idea... I should certainly have been more guarded in my conversations'. Not only had Price misrepresented Repton's work, but he 'has frequently robbed me of my ideas; and has, in some instances, robbed me of originality', notably some 'observations concerning the prevalence of lines in architecture' from the Red Book for Wembley admired by 'the Right Honourable Mr. Burke'. Repton offered a new defence of Brown. Far from being insensible to 'the wild scenery of nature, he frequently passed whole days in studying the sequestered haunts of Needwood forest, as I have done those in the forest of Hainault; and I trust, from these studies, we have both acquired not only picturesque ideas, but this useful lesson; *that the landscape ought to be adapted to the beings which are to inhabit it* – to men and not to beasts'.[118] Repton relegated the Picturesque to one of sixteen 'sources of pleasure in landscape gardening'. He did allow

> there is a shade of difference betwixt the opinion of Mr. *Price* and Mr. *Knight*, which seems to have arisen from the different characters of their respective places; *Foxley* is less romantic than *Downton*, and therefore Mr. Price is less extravagant in his ideas, and more willing to allow some little sacrifice of picturesque beauty to neatness near the house; but by this very concession he acknowledges that *comfort*, and his ideas of *picturesqueness*, are incompatible.

The Appendix ends with a letter from William Windham declaring his support for Repton in the conflict with 'these wild improvers':

Places are not to be laid out with a view to their appearance in a picture, but to their uses, and the enjoyment of them in real life; and their conformity to those purposes is that which constitutes their beauty ... You know of old that I am quite on your side in the question between you, and am certain that the farther you go in the controversy, the more you will have the advantage.[119]

'So our game of controversy will now be as regular as a game of whist', Price told Sir George Beaumont. 'Knight and Price partners against Repton with Brown as DUMMY, whose cards of course Repton must manage.'[120] William Marshall joined the game in a book-length review of 240 pages, which endorsed many of Repton's criticisms and expressed them in particularly virulent terms. Price was a 'blockhead' with little practical idea of estate improvement:

> Who but a man totally ignorant of all scenery, except that of a picture gallery, or the wild coppices of the Welch [*sic*.] mountains, could have imagined that woods were, in nature, raised with the same facility that they are on canvas ... By *dint of neglect* places, heretofore beautiful, have been rendered picturesk [*sic*.], and highly irritating both to the minds and bodies of those who explored them.

The point of improvement, declared Marshall, was not to copy paintings, but to produce 'LIVING LANDSCAPES'.[121] Price found Marshall's review 'as clumsy as it is coarse', but the chorus of criticism was having an effect.[122] Burke probably revised his opinion of Price in its light. 'He spoke often and with great respect of Mr. Repton & considered him as having much more comprehensive, correct and even pure views of these subjects, than his late Antagonists', recalled the Whig hostess Frances Anne Crewe. While Burke admired parts of Price's *Essay* and respected Knight's learning, 'like most system-mongers, they had pursued their Theories to a dangerous length'.[123]

## The Regions of Taste

A rapid riposte to Price and Knight came from the Vale of Hereford and from a probable client of Repton's. In 1794 John Matthews, whose seat at Belmont overlooked Hereford, published *A Sketch from the Landscape*, a lampoon of Knight's poem, to which he added a postscript addressed to Price.[124] The poem was published anonymously. Farington noted Matthews as the author two years later, but the attribution may already have been known.[125]

As David Whitehead has discovered, Matthews made a career as a physician in London at St George's Hospital and a minor reputation as a scholar-poet (notably with a parody of Pope's *Eloisa to Abelard*), before retiring to his home county of Herefordshire in 1783. After five years' residence in Hereford, during which he took on various public duties, including stewarding the committee for the new infirmary, Matthews purchased Old Hill, a small manor comprising a farmhouse and 150 acres of land, high on a bluff on the opposite bank of the Wye. Old Hill was transformed in to the modishly named Belmont. Like Cotterell at Garnons, Matthews secured the services of James Wyatt, who had just presented his survey of Hereford cathedral, to design a new house for him. On 5 November 1788, following celebrations in Hereford of the great triple anniversary of Whig supremacy (the Armada, the Gunpowder Plot and the Glorious Revolution), a party proceeded to Old Hill to lay the foundation stone for Belmont. Price was surely in the party, for Matthews ceremoniously planted an oak sapling from an acorn sown in Foxley fifteen years before.[126]

Wyatt designed a smart house for Matthews, a Neo-classical villa built of Bath stone, with a great semi-circular bay-window providing views up and down the Wye Valley. Although there is no surviving Red Book for Belmont, or reference in his published works, Repton probably designed the grounds, perhaps as his first commission in the Vale of Hereford. In February 1794 an engraved view of Belmont, from Repton's drawing, was published in the *Polite Repository* (fig. 126). It shows a view from the south-east. Wyatt's house is on one side surrounded by lawns, shrubbery and a thinned clump of trees; on the other side a vista follows the river meandering up-valley in the direction of Foxley Woods and the Radnorshire hills.[127] The guide of 1796 mentions other

126 After Humphry Repton, *Belmont, Herefordshire*, from *Peacock's Polite Repository* (1794). Private collection.

127 'Desperate amateurs' besmirch the name of Capability Brown, from title page to [John Matthews], *A Sketch for the Landscape* (1794). Private collection.

128 'A huge and terrible priapus', tailpiece to [John Matthews], *A Sketch for the Landscape* (1794). Private collection.

vistas for which Repton may have been responsible, including one of the city of Hereford terminated by Stoke Edith and the Malvern Hills.[128]

Belmont was an appropriate base for Matthews's career as a civic dignitary with twenty years in office as mayor and senior alderman, a colonel in the Militia and a Pittite MP. With a collection of 'some valuable pictures' at Belmont, and some experimental farming on new lands, Matthews enjoyed a local reputation as a promoter of both agricultural improvement and fine art.[129] Matthews had some influence in London. In August 1794 Farington invited him to visit to advise on an illustrated book he was contemplating on the scenery of the Wye and Severn, and recorded some comments on Price's and Knight's recent publications. Matthews distinguished the authors in his judgement, but was more generous in person than he was anonymously in print. 'Mr Prices book is written with information & spirit', Farington reported him saying, 'He thinks very moderately of Mr Knights'.[130]

In *A Sketch from the Landscape* Matthews defends the reputation of Brown and Repton in the 'regions of taste' against the 'unnatural extravagances' of 'these desperate amateurs' (fig. 127). Knight is described as seditious, an apostle of wildness, accused with Thomas Paine, Mary Wollstonecraft and the sansculottes of promoting the natural right of men and women to run rampant, break hedges and crop trees. Matthews's mind may have been concentrated by opposition to the enclosure of common fields to the north of Hereford in July 1794, when local

Jacobins erected a gibbet, threatening enclosers with the guillotine.[131] Knight is also described in Matthews's poem as an apostle of artifice, accused of promoting stiffly formal, French-style gardens, in a sketch of which (fig. 128) is an enormous yew statue of a god of gardens, 'a huge and terrible Priapus', its erect phallus pointing at two startled young women. The poem firmly identifies Knight's pagan classicism with the aesthetic ideology of the French Revolution.

The postscript addressed to Price is less combative, in the end conciliatory. Price's views are seen as more snobbish than subversive. While praised for invoking the 'rural graces', Matthews contends that 'the higher style of the Picturesque is not much in the power of the Improver'. Hollow lanes, and their attendant effects, may 'furnish good subjects for the pencil', but it is smooth lawns, variegated with trees and shrubs, in short 'the *Beautiful*, which is more within reach of the Improver'.

> Why are the purchasers of 'ready-made taste' to be treated so contemptuously? . . . are there no wealthy characters, who, having for the best part of their days been 'in populous cities pent' retire from their shops and counting-houses, to some newly purchased estate in the country, *stung* by the raging love of improving? May we not find here and there a fox-hunting squire, with no very accurate ideas of the picturesque and beautiful, who is at the same time *goaded* on by the desire of imitating his more tasteful neighbours? In these cases, and some others, I am inclined to think, that 'ready-made taste' is a great public benefit.

Matthews called for 'the Art then, [to] continue to be cultivated, and encouraged by the Public, *as a profession*', for that was the only means of 'diffusing wide the blessing of rural beauty'.[132]

Knight dismissed Matthews's poem as a 'doggerel ode', a 'bungling attempt' of 'blundering dullness' to ridicule him.[133] Price, in a passage in his *Letter* to Repton, made more an engagement with the postscript to Matthews's poem. There were always a sufficient number of 'rich and helpless persons, who must endeavour to purchase what they have not themselves', but 'it is not to such men (who must always be directed) that I have addressed my advice'. Price was more concerned with the broader population of country gentry. If they took only 'one part' of Price's advice, and that 'contrary to its spirit and obvious meaning', they would still cause less damage than 'the regular system of clearing and levelling'.[134]

129  View of the house, without overlay, from the Red Book for Sufton Court (1795). Private collection.

Repton enjoyed further support in the Vale of Hereford in his commission there following the publication of Price's essay and Knight's poem. At Sufton Court, 'in the near neighbourhood of my antagonists', in the spring of 1795, he seized the 'opportunity of justifying my practice, in opposition to the wild theory of improvement which has lately sprung up in Herefordshire . . .'. 'It is no small circumstance of triumph to me that I am still consulted even in the enemy's quarters', and Repton thanked his client 'for that good opinion of my professional skill, which induced you to call in my advice'.[135]

The owner of Sufton, James Hereford, was not only a prominent public figure, mayor of the city in 1795, but possessed, as his name suggests, a strong, indeed unparalleled, local pedigree. The Herefords had occupied Sufton for some six hundred years. Their estate commanded the main river and road routes into Hereford from the rest of England. In the seventeenth century Sufton was an important site in the construction of the region's Georgic reputation, the vantage point of John Beale's 'Elysium'.[136] James Hereford set about modernizing Sufton. He vacated the medieval manor house tucked into its combe and commissioned a new mansion built of Bath stone on the hill overlooking the Vale of Hereford (fig. 129). The date (1788–9), style and siting echo Belmont. Once attributed to Wyatt, the mansion is presently attributed to the Gloucester architect Anthony Keck.[137]

Sufton adjoined Stoke Edith and was the next estate on the new turnpike into Hereford; it was probably improvements at Stoke, as much as those at Belmont, that recommended Repton to Hereford. Some landscaping had

130   Panoramic view, without overlay, from the Red Book for Sufton Court (1795). Private collection.

already been carried out around the new mansion that Repton was keen to alter to open up views across grounds enlarged by the removal of the old turnpike. In so doing he directly confronted the views of Price and Knight. Their 'public controversy' had become 'indecently personal', and Repton was about to retaliate in kind.

Contrary to Price's and Knight's principles of lifelong, local knowledge in landscaping, Repton made a virtue of his flying visit.

> The whole of my observations on Sufton Court were made in two days of excessive rainy weather [with] no assistance from previous knowledge of the spot, or from any accurate survey of the premises . . . neither do I regret that the whole was the result of two days only, since I am convinced that a month's attention to the subject would not have altered my opinion.

The parkland was to be given the 'cleaning, rolling and mowing so essential to modern elegance and comfort that I would not see a blade of grass on the walk, or a daizy on the lawn'. Against Knight's views on woodland management, 'the overcautious advice of timorous experience', improvements in the park at Sufton were to be effected 'by the axe rather than the spade'. He suggested 'boldly taking away all the young trees and several of the old ones, but particularly one large oak' which 'lessens the magnitude and importance' of the park. He ridiculed his opponents' painterly vision, to the point of denying the artistry of his own drawings.

131   Picturesque view, from the Red Book for Sufton Court (1795). Private collection.

I should no more advise the Landscape Gardener in laying out a place to affect the confined field of vision, or the careless graces of a Claude or a Poussin, than I should recommend to a Landscape Painter the quincunx or formal rows of the kitchen garden . . . My sketches, if they were more finished, would be a sort of Panorama, or facsimile of the scenes they represent, in which very little effect is attempted on the principles of composition in painting, but like the shadow of a silhouette they may serve to please as portraits, while they offend the connoisseur as paintings.

The Red Book's panoramic, 180-degree drawing of the view from the house is (despite the rainy weather when Repton made his sketches) a model of clarity and legibility, labelled, like popular prospect views, with the names of various landmarks (fig. 130). It maps the vaunted variety of Herefordshire scenery, ranging from a 'snug cottage and small enclosures' tucked in to a hillside through plantations, meadows, hedged fields, hills, rivers and roads, to another Keck mansion at Longworth 'well backed by wood'. The causeway carrying the new turnpike to Hereford is displayed to advantage, as is the River Wye, from its confluence with the Lugg, conducting the eye to the city. As a contrast Repton parodied what Price might have proposed (fig. 131). A small, occluded composition, heavy with chiaroscuro, on a blue/green mount shows the view towards Hereford along an embanked road, possibly the old highway:

> First, we must suppose the station so low and so near the trees as to look under their branches instead of over their tops: this could only be effected by moving the house to the trees... Secondly we must suppose the ground broken, with a hollow way, and a bank of rugged earth or rock; which I think will hardly be preferred in this situation to the fine turf of a smooth velvet lawn. Thirdly we must suppose the naked bald banks of the river Lugg cloathed with trees, which the first flood would sweep away. And lastly the whole must be enriched by a few beggars and ragged gypsies; which would perhaps be thought to be less in character with the place than a red and white [Hereford] cow, or a group of spotted deer.

The Red Book, with its polemic, would have been satisfying enough to have in the house at Sufton for Hereford's guests to peruse, but Repton would have found more satisfaction in knowing that what he proposed was largely carried out, visible to every traveller by road or river to Hereford. The guide of 1796 reported: 'the grounds are in an improving state under the masterly direction of Mr Repton'.[138]

### Rural Economy

By 1796 Repton's career had reached a further threshold. His partnership with Nash began promisingly. 'Our homes were alternately united – whether in Town or Country', he recalled, 'our carriages – our offices (in which my sons assisted) were as the property of both'.[139]

Repton began a regular winter sojourn at Bath, a base for his commissions in the west of England. *Sketches and Hints* had begun to establish, or re-establish, Repton's reputation, but was still proving a liability. Repton reported in February 1796 that he had received requests for his book from 'half a dozen noble personages & three times as many other people who fancy it is in my power to furnish them with books because I reservd abt 40 Copies – for 58 Gentlemen who had consulted me & omitted to become subscribers'.[140] The publishers, Boydells, were demanding the two hundred pounds that Repton owed them. Five months later Repton was at a loss to understand why he still owed Boydells £148, and demanded to see the list of subscribers who had not claimed their copies.[141]

The first major review of *Sketches and Hints*, by William Marshall, which appeared in the *Monthly Review* of January 1796, proved troublesome. In reviews of works in the picturesque controversy up to this time, Marshall had supported Repton, but now blamed him for provoking and prolonging it. If Repton had not assumed 'the titles *Landscape Gardening* and *Landscape Gardener*', the dispute would never have arisen. 'The production of *landscape* is the least part of the profession under consideration. Places in general will admit of nothing which can deserve the name. We have seen very few of Mr. R's drawings which can lay a claim to it.' Marshall distrusted the illusionism of Repton's pictorial technique, noticing how the unimproved view 'is represented as a scene without spirit or animation, while to the other every master-stroke of Mr. R's pencil is given', and found his theoretical writing 'a maze of words'. The extract from the Red Book for Tatton was 'the greatest waste of argument', and the justification of visual trickery there threatened to turn 'rural improvement' in to 'rural pantomime'. Marshall reserved his approval for the published *Letter* 'from a right honourable friend of our author (WINDHAM by name, we believe)', which, 'as his arguments are *strong*, and come from *high authority*', Marshall transcribed in full.[142]

Repton recognized the stratagem. Marshall's own book *Planting and Rural Ornament* was about to be published. 'The malice & pecking of this Critique' was a way of 'puffing himself into notice'. Repton wondered whether he had any 'hope of reaping fame or profit' from *Sketches and Hints*. 'I am dunn'd by the bookseller & damnd by the reviewer' but consoled by 'the Compliments I daily receive from literary Correspondents & the more solid proof of its merit by the increase in my professional engagements'.[143]

Marshall may have been promoting his book at Repton's expense, but *Planting and Rural Ornament* represented a powerful utilitarian strain in landed sensibilities prompted by the exigencies of war. When Mediterranean ports were closed in 1795, after Spain entered the wars, the British authorities feared the spectre of famine. The House of Lords and the press praised patriotic noblemen, such as the courtier Lord Harcourt who 'ploughed up a great part of his park to raise grain'.[144] *Planting and Rural Ornament* applauded landowners who transformed temples in to cornmills, cultivated coppices, maintained sheepwalks, managed their plantations to produce timber for warships, and in general promoted agrarian landscapes. The incentive was not just patriotic, for plantations 'accumulate in value, as money at interest upon interest'.[145]

In commissions from this time, agricultural land use in and around parks was an issue that Repton felt forced to clarify (fig. 132). Thus in the Red Book for Burley of 1796:

> At a time when all ranks of society in the kingdom are laudably exerting their influence to promote the agriculture of the kingdom, it is peculiarly necessary that I should not be misunderstood when I assert that the *park* and the *farm* should be *distinct* objects. But the prevalence of fashion is in this instance likely to endanger the good taste of the country, since there is not less impropriety in pulling down fences and lawning a hundred good acres of wheat to convert farms into parks, than in ploughing up rich pastures, and intersecting old lawns with hedges to make a park into a farm.[146]

Repton emphasized that he was in favour of farming and of agricultural landscapes: the maintenance of small tenant farms, the development of model home farms, and the making of money from farms; the pleasure farmers took in surveying their fields, and the pleasure landowners took in walking or riding to look over their farms; and of limits on the size and expense of parks to allow this rural economy to flourish. What he set himself against was the blurring of scenic and social distinctions by the fashion for agriculture, the rise of rich tenant farmers and a greedy gentry, and the distress of the poor they affected to feed. 'The monopolist can only contemplate with delight his hundred acres of wheat in a single enclosure; such expanded avarice may *enrich the man*, but will impoverish and distress, and (I had almost added) will ultimately *starve mankind.*'[147]

132  *Farm and Park*, from *Observations on the Theory and Practice of Landscape Gardening* (1803). Yale Center for British Art, Paul Mellon Collection.

## The Prospect of a Country

Repton resumed the engagement with Price and Knight when he returned to their region in 1797. In July he took up his commission at Garnons and was glad 'to revisit the spot & retrace my own ideas – which from the distance of time & variety of other subjects which have occupied my mind required to be refreshed'. He saw no reason radically to change his original plans for the still unbuilt mansion, on which he would now consult with Nash.[148] Following his visit to Garnons, Repton called at Lord Berwick's Attingham in Shropshire, for a new commission that promised both to enrich him and enhance his stature in the controversy with his opponents.

Like a few other illustrious clients, including the duke of Portland, Berwick agreed to pay Repton a stipend of one hundred guineas a year for two visits.[149] Nash was commissioned to work on architectural improvements that, under their agreement, promised to net Repton more money still. What made Berwick an attractive client to Repton was not only his wealth but his connoisseurship. What made Attingham attractive was its prominence, its palatial front facing Watling Street, the main road from London to North Wales, on the approach to Shrewsbury. Moreover Price had just published the second volume of his *Essay on the Picturesque* with an essay on the treatment of water, the focus of Repton's plans for Attingham.

After inheriting Attingham, and a fortune from its industrial development for coal and iron, the second Lord Berwick promptly set off for Italy in 1792 for two years, staying mainly in Naples, to start acquiring a considerable art collection. This included purchases of seventeenth-century landscapes by Claude and Ruisdael, and of contemporary landscape paintings in a Classical style, notably by Phillip Hackert, who had accompanied Richard Payne Knight to Sicily fifteen years before.[150]

After his return from Naples in 1794, Berwick got in touch with architects about schemes to remodel the house at Attingham, a monumental Neo-classical mansion by George Steuart built for his father ten years before, far grander than any other country house in Shropshire. The park, a flat, ill-drained site, landscaped with Brown-style clumps for the old house in the 1770s by Thomas Leggett, required more urgent attention. It was no match for the mansion, as passing tourists pointed out. Restyling the parkland was part of a wider scheme of improvement. In 1796 the Shrewsbury canal, in which Berwick had a controlling interest, was opened, linking the town with the Shropshire coalfield. The canal, engineered by Telford, passed along the north side of the park at Attingham. A new settlement, Berwick Wharf, was built there, and further road, canal and house building was planned to link with the River Severn, which flowed on the south side of the park.[151]

In the introduction to the Attingham Red Book, Repton told Berwick that he would explain at length the principles on which he based his improvements, 'as a neighbouring County to your Lordship has produced two Theorists in the Art of Landscape gardening'. By the conclusion, Repton had challenged Price's and Knight's claims to the art's title. 'In spite of the wild theories of *picture-gardeners*, Attingham will be a lasting monument of Lord Berwick's taste, in having committed its improvement to the rational plans of a Landscape-gardener.' Repton reaffirmed his claim to the title by restoring the meaning of landscape to 'that original and more extended signification of the word defined by Dr. Johnson, "a region, or prospect of a country"'. A definition of landscape 'confined ... to pictures' would do nothing to enhance the stature of Attingham; indeed it would belittle it.[152]

Repton illustrated the 'futility' of Price's principles with examples from pictures from his client's collection. Near the house, on the River Terne, were the ruins of an iron forge. These 'fragments of an old mill and brick arches ... make a charming study for a painter and the composition is not unlike that beautiful picture of Ruisdale's [*sic*] at Attingham which every connoisseur must admire'. But the scene, as Repton drew it (fig. 133), showed just part of the mansion's colonnade, which made it seem 'the fragment of some Grecian temple in ruins, and not a part of the modern inhabited palace'.[153] So Repton suggested the 'ruined bridge give place to one more useful ... something beyond picturesque effect', a modern-looking structure of cast iron, across a re-channelled river framing a full view of the body of the house. Repton looked to a picture by Claude at Attingham to make another point against Price in improving the view from the breakfast-room across the park. The Claude was large, five feet long, but in order to plant the park to echo the picture, it would be necessary to 'divide the whole field of vision into separate landscapes ... like putting five or six pictures of Claude into one long frame'.[154]

If 'Mr Knight endeavours to ridicule all apparent extent of property ... I consider [it] as one of the first principles to be attended to', especially for a 'modern house by the side of a high-road'. Before Repton was consulted, there had been plans greatly to extend the park about a mile to the east, but this would do little to enhance the importance of Attingham where it mattered – in the space between the highroad and the house. There was no chance of moving the road, but a number

133  *Scene at Attingham*, from *Observations on the Theory and Practice of Landscape Gardening* (1803). Yale Center for British Art, Paul Mellon Collection.

134   View from the Terne Bridge, with and without overlay, from the Red Book for Attingham (1798). National Trust Photographic Library/John Hammond.

of manipulations might be carried out on his client's property on either side to make the place look magnificent. Building new approaches to the house and improving the River Terne that ran through the park would appropriate their respective junctions with the highroad and River Severn in the view. Repton proposed emparking some land beyond and restyling the turnpike house, 'so that we shall induce the stranger to conceive that he passes thro' the park and not on the outside of it'. Some alterations beyond, such as adding a spire to the distant church of Wroxham, would further enhance the impression of Berwick's domain.

Repton focused his objections to Price and Knight in his plans for the River Terne (fig. 134). With the abandonment of the ironworks, and attendant controls on flow, the river had braided in to a number of channels. It was liable to flood with every shower, and dry up with every drought. While 'these irriguous appearances may perhaps have charms in the eye of a Landscape-painter...in some detached part...at a happy moment when the water is neither too high, nor too low...the Landscape-gardener has a nobler object in view...to secure a constant and permanent effect of water'. Attingham did not require 'an occasional meandring brook', but 'an ample river, majestically flowing'. This meant building a new weir, embanking the river and altering its course. Repton could practise the skill he claimed to have learnt from observing celebrated civil engineers cutting canals.[155] Repton's drawing of the improved river, swinging in a smooth curve towards the mansion, recalls Hearne's illustration from *The Landscape* of a scene that Knight despised, grounds 'dressed in the modern style' (fig. 115).

Repton's main target was Price. Price's *Essay on Artificial Water* was published as Repton was compiling his plans for Attingham, 'but I confess after reading it with much attention I am totally at a loss to comprehend his meaning, and indeed he confesses that no workmen can be trusted to execute his plans'. Repton acknowledged that in some of Brown's works the edges of banks of water were too trim, but that 'the treading of cattle' (which he shows in his drawing) 'will give them all the irregularity they require'. If a workman were to attempt 'to imitate these irregularities...he must do it by notches, and scotches, and scallops, and knobs, which is all I can understand from Mr. Price's directions'. There were a few stretches of the river, around the old works, where 'many picturesque bits of broken bank exist, some of which I shall endeavour to preserve', but nothing could realize 'the rude and enthusiastic visions of Mr. Price's fancy...which he seems to confess must be the work of a half a century'. The major elements of Repton's plans in his Red Book for Attingham, the river improvement, the planting, the new approaches, were put in to immediate effect.[156] He must have seen Attingham as a triumph over his antagonists and another threshold in his career.

In a letter of 1798 Anna Seward expressed her concern for Repton's profession at the spectre of 'those monsters in finance, the assessed taxes', but Repton's sights were fixed on more secure employment.[157] Having been granted permission to dedicate *Sketches and Hints* to George III, 'the great arbiter of true taste in the country', Repton now sought a more rewarding form of royal favour.[158] The death of Thomas Sandby had left vacant the Deputy Rangership of Windsor Great Park, and Repton beseeched Portland, Pitt and Windham to use their influence to secure him the post. Here was an opportunity to establish his art in the very citadel of power. The king had read some Red Books and had taken Repton's side in his controversy with Knight and Price.[159] In 1798 the king reaffirmed the 'great fault' he found with Price's picturesque views. He pronounced Price 'an enemy to all neatness & comfort; and professed himself a most zealous admirer of Mr Brown...I should like to see all Europe like a place of Mr Brown's'.[160] Price responded to his informant, Sir George Beaumont, in verse 'On His Majesty's Improvements':

Windsor! thy injur'd towers, parks, forests groan
England! thy wealth, power, freedom, all are flown
What various ruin from his pretty tricks
Whose taste was form'd by Brown; by Bute his politicks[161]

As it turned out, Repton was not granted the Deputy Rangership at Windsor.[162] Portland and Windham confessed that they had no influence. Pitt said that he did, but by the time he opened Repton's letter the position had been filled. Repton later discovered the king had adjudicated his dispute with Price and Knight solely on the size of the protagonists' volumes: 'he took my little book in his hand and said "I suspect Repton has the best of it...for *truth* lies in a small compass"'.[163]

Pitt's income tax was yet to exercise its damaging effect, but Repton was forced to travel almost continuously to sustain his career. Having been introduced by Repton to powerful patrons, including the circles around the Prince of Wales, Nash probably saw no further use for him, and around 1800 terminated their partnership, paying him nothing of the percentage they had agreed. The *'thousands we were to share'* lamented Repton; Nash coolly explained that the board of Repton's sons 'had swallowed up anything I might consider due to me from the profits of our professional engagements'.[164]

Price was seriously affected by the new tax. He had no money for improvements, and in 1798 considered leasing or selling Foxley, 'this beautiful but expensive place', and buying a small farm near Aberystwyth.[165] Price held on to his estate, but with the threat of invasion and a landing by a French party on the Pembrokeshire coast, developed a siege mentality in his writing. In *Thoughts on the Defence of Property*, published in Hereford in 1797, he addressed local landowners on the importance of their 'local attachments' to prevent the insurrection. 'He who can scarcely buy bread will hardly buy arms unless driven to despair by long ill treatment.'[166] Upholding the example of his own troop of volunteer farmers, he demanded 'a spirit of confidence & union, & of security, from the means of resistance in every quarter; not a spirit of general enterprise and military ardour'.[167] Price focused his attentions on agriculture at Foxley but did not neglect aesthetics. A second edition of *Essay of the Picturesque* was published in Hereford in 1798.

While he confined himself to Foxley, Price's views on the picturesque were diffused widely, to the constituency of middling gentry he cultivated, everywhere in Britain, even close to Repton's home. In a letter of 1796, in between news of cattle prices and a neighbour's rheumatism, a squire in Nottinghamshire told his brother in Essex:

> I wish you would get Mr Price's Essay on the Picturesque, you will find it of use to you in your improvements – He is a friend to old Pollards and detests Belts and Clumps – you should see it before you advance too far in the improvement of your Lane – if you are not going to Town soon, you might get it from Chelmsford.[168]

By the time that Repton's second treatise, *Observations on the Theory and Practice of Landscape Gardening*, was published in 1803, the picturesque controversy had cooled as a public issue, but Repton returned to it in ways that eventually formed an accommodation with the views of Price and Knight. A short chapter in *Observations* consisting of extracts from the Red Books from Sufton and Attingham restates the differences between landscape gardening and painting but omits or tones down the sharper comments on Price and Knight. As Sufton was in Herefordshire, Attingham in Shropshire, Repton absent-mindedly assigned his adversaries to different counties, describing Uvedale Price as a Shropshire man.[169] Repton's attention seems to have been fully occupied by the exigencies of his job and new intellectual interests in the theory of perspective, colour and shadows, and in techniques of drawing, painting and reproducing landscape art. *Observations* also reveals a deeper concern with history, reflecting not only his partnership with his son John Adey, who already had a strong antiquarian interest, but also Repton's sense that the nineteenth century inaugurated a new, less venerable, social and scenic order. These new perspectives on the theory and history of landscape served to reawaken Repton's interest in picturesque aesthetics and to revise his views of the works of Price and Knight.

In the autumn of 1803, Repton applied the 'general principles' he had recently 'published to the world' in *Observations* in a commission at Stanage Park in Radnorshire, and in the text of the Red Book he revised his position on picturesque landscape.[170] The commission was firmly in Knight's sphere of influence. Six miles upstream from Downton in the Teme Valley, Stanage was formerly owned by the Knight family; Repton's client, Charles Rogers, had purchased the estate from Knight's cousin, Thomas Johnes. Descended on his father's side from an old Shropshire family, and on his mother's from an old Radnorshire family, Rogers selected Stanage Park as a seat of retirement after making a fortune as a merchant in the City of London. Here he intended to do what Johnes had done at Hafod, undertake a campaign of improvement to make the place productive.[171] Repton had 'rarely seen, and never before been consulted, in one of those cases where the honest pride of antiquity has been blended with Prudence and success of commercial Importance', and he congratulated Rogers on 'the honourable ambition of establishing your family in the neighbourhood which it has inhabited with respectability for more than six hundred years'. Repton thought it proper to consider the situation of Stanage 'with respect to the neighbouring scenery, especially as the opposite opinion of two gentlemen in this neighbourhood have produced that controversy in which I have endeavoured to become a moderator'.

> When I compare the picturesque scenery of Downton Vale with the meagre efforts of art which are attributed to the school of Brown, I cannot wonder at the enthusiastic abhorrence which the *Author of the*

135 View of the west front of the house, without overlay, from the Red Book for Stanage Park (1803). Private collection.

*Landscape* expresses for modern gardening: especially as few parts of the kingdom present more specimens of bad taste, than the road from Ludlow to Worcester (in which I am now digesting the matter of this small volume, and while I am writing in the Carriage, according to my general custom) I see, surrounded by plantations of firs and larches and Lombardy poplars, under the forms of Belts and Clumps, new houses like red brick clamps with all the fanciful apertures of Venetian and Pseudo Gothic windows, which disgust the traveller who looks in vain for the picturesque shapes and harmonious tints of former times.[172]

The park at Stanage had been badly managed, and Repton offered some advice on making it productive as well as picturesque, reducing its size (converting parts to arable), destroying fern, draining bogs, folding sheep, grubbing up firs and larches from new plantations and replacing them with birches and thorns. In planning a residence to provide accommodation for the Rogers family, local entertainment and reception for visitors 'who may come from the Capital or other distant parts' within a prudent budget and with due regard to the 'wild scenery' of Stanage, Repton followed 'the example set at Downton, where the *inside* was first consulted, and the *outside* afterwards made to conform to *that*, under the idea of a *picturesque* outline'. Repton would have been happy to mimic the 'castle character' of Downton, but that exceeded his 'prescribed limits', and so he took 'for my model the Character of the Grange or old Manor Farm' (fig. 135). He would extend the existing house at Stanage with a set of domestic apartments in the style he called Elizabethan Gothic, a style that John Adey Repton derived from East Anglian manor houses and which looked nothing like those in the Welsh border country. In so doing he endeavoured 'to restore that sort of importance, which formerly belonged to the *old Manor house*, where the lord of the soil resided among his tenants, not only to collect the rents, but to share the produce of his estate with his humble dependants, and where

136 The brook, without overlay, from the Red Book for Stanage Park (1803). Private collection.

plenteous hospitality was not sacrificed to ostentatious refinements of luxury'. His view differed in one respect from Knight's 'at least so far as I have been told he has endeavoured to reduce it to practice near the house at Downton'; he would enclose the grounds and make a contrast with the 'rude Character' beyond by laying out 'straight lines of garden walls and walks'. Repton's plans for diverting water into the dells and ravines that ran dry in summer echo Price's views on pool making in woodland scenery (fig. 136). And his remarks on the approach to the house reflect Price's views on lanes: 'The road will pass along the hollow lane [which] may furnish one of those scenes so often represented by painters, nor must the sacrilegious spade of modern improvers shave down the steep and rugged banks.'[173]

Following his visit to Stanage, Repton travelled to a commission in Shropshire at Longner, adjacent to Attingham. Repton used both commissions to fashion a position on picturesque landscape, but the Red Books, compiled five years apart, envision contrasting, indeed

137 After Humphry Repton, *Old Longner Hall & the Tomb of Edward Burton Esq.* (c.1810). Private collection.

138 View of the proposed terrace and tomb canopy, detail, from the Red Book for Longner (1804). Private collection.

scarcely compatible worlds. Attingham was designed for a cosmopolitan aristocrat, Longner for an ancestral squire.[174] At Longner Repton found 'the counterpart of the building that I had previously formed in my mind for Stanedge [*sic*.] Park'. It is 'a fragment of one of the mansions of the sixteenth century which were called "Manor Houses"' (fig. 137).[175] What made the discovery poignant was that the owner, Robert Burton, asked Repton to make plans only for the park, commissioning John Nash (who was still employed at Attingham) separately to prepare designs for a new house. Nash offered a building in any style, Grecian, Swiss, any kind of Gothic.[176] Repton took the liberty of including in his Red Book some proposals for the house. While feeling 'some degree of delicacy' on the subject, Repton frankly disagreed with the site for the new house, the style, 'or indeed in the necessity for a new house at all'.[177]

Although not authorized to provide detailed plans, Repton made sketches that 'may prevent the entire demolition of this venerable fragment of antiquity'. Not everything could be restored, not, for example, the moat, because the springs that once fed it had been cut off by the Shrewsbury canal. Rebuilding would be necessary for the 'increased comforts of modern times'. Repton's main objections to Nash's plans were to the proposed new sites, which disrupted both of Longner's assets, 'picturesque scenery and vestiges of antiquity'. At the corner of the old house was a 'sacred relick which must not be disturbed'. This was the tomb of his client's ancestor Edward Burton, who, 'having early become a protestant, died thro excess of joy on the accession of Queen Elizabeth to the throne, and was refused burial in St Chad's church, at Shrewsbury'. The epitaph, in characters of the time though scarcely legible, explained how Burton 'Truly professing Christianity/ Was like Christ Jesus in a garden laid'. Repton proposed repairing the tomb, re-inscribing the epitaph on a brass plate and covering it with a 'Gothic canopy of the same date'. The tomb was made the central feature in a terrace garden planted with flowers and weeping willows and 'commanding an extensive view of the Severn, and the distant Welsh mountains' (fig. 138). The tomb had a 'dignity . . . a modern palace elsewhere could never possess', surely a reference to Attingham and its recently ennobled family.

> I cannot quit this subject without a little reflection upon the vicissitude of human events, by observing how few ancient families have outlived the influx of wealth from Trade, and while we may see the rapid encroachments of Commerce on Nobility, and the extinction of Gentry and Yeomanry from the Kingdom, when every iron master becomes a landlord, and every shopkeeper a country squire, let me indulge in the fine hope of preserving one valuable vestige of former times and congratulate the present owner of Longner, that he lived where his Ancestors have died.[178]

As it turned out, the old house at Longner was demolished and a new house by Nash built between 1803 and

1807, at a cost of ten thousand pounds.[179] Its style was Tudor Gothic and it was positioned near the old house, but Repton deducted the cost of his architectural hints in the Red Book from the final account 'as being useless to Mr Burton'.[180] As a memento, Repton had an engraving made of his drawing of the old house and tomb (fig. 137), an impression of which he presented to Burton's wife. Repton's designs for a new Gothic lodge at Longner were implemented. This was, Repton was later pleased to report, used as a school, 'endowed and patronized by Mrs Burton'.[181]

Repton's proposals for the mansion at Stanage Park were realized, but not in the form he had originally proposed, and with revisions he found irksome. Rogers commissioned a rival set of designs from the Shrewsbury-based architect John Hiran Haycock, one heavily influenced by Nash's designs for Longner, which Haycock had been employed as builder to execute. The designs were a pastiche of Repton's parkland designs by a Shrewsbury man, William Pearson.[182] Rogers rejected these proposals and instead appointed Haycock to execute Repton's design, but Haycock still managed, against Repton's objections, to incorporate many of his own suggestions in the final design. Richard Payne Knight also advised on some aspects of construction. Repton's letters to Rogers over the next five years complain how he and his son were losing control of the building and credit for the design. In 1810 they were paid a fee of one hundred guineas for their labours, rather than the usual percentage, that Repton reckoned on a building costing eight or ten thousand pounds would have yielded four to five times as much: 'You cannot wonder my dear sir that we should feel hurt at so little value being placed on our professional exertions'.[183] Repton reclaimed authorship when he published the final design for the house (fig. 139) in *Fragments* as an example of 'castle-gothic' echoing the style of Downton.[184]

139 *Example of outline in Castle Gothic* [Design for Stanage], from *Fragments on the Theory and Practice of Landscape Gardening* (1816). Yale Center for British Art, Paul Mellon Collection.

### Changes of Taste

To meet the demand, Repton republished *Observations* in 1805, and the following year, perhaps in response to the popular success of Price's *Essay*, he issued a cheaper, un-illustrated octavo volume, *An Enquiry into the Changes of Taste in Landscape Gardening*. 'The enormous expense of engraving has hitherto so confined my opinions to a certain class of purchasers, that they have been either not generally known, or they have been repeated by some without acknowledgment, or misrepresented by others without sufficient quotation.'[185] The *Enquiry* was made up of three parts: a short history of landscape gardening (originally commissioned for a new edition of *The Gardener's Dictionary*, 1807), large extracts from *Sketches and Hints* (which had become so scarce that it was fetching four times its original price), augmented by extracts from recent Red Books such as those for Longleat and Longner, and a response to a recent book by Richard Payne Knight, *An Analytical Inquiry into the Principles of Taste*. Repton had thought the published and 'gentlemanlike' exchanges between himself and Price 'left no room for further controversy; and it might reasonably have been supposed the subject had been dropped; but I find myself again personally (though not by name) called upon to defend the Art of Landscape Gardening'.[186]

Published in 1805, *An Analytical Inquiry* proved highly successful, running rapidly in to three editions. Its pretext, and much of its shock value, was an attack on the aesthetics of Uvedale Price. Repton did not engage with the finer points of the dispute, which centred on whether beauty was inherent in beautiful things or in the mind of the beholder, but he sympathized with

Price as a fellow target of Knight's asperity. The point of Repton's reply to Knight was to find 'no real difference between us'. 'Whatever trifling differences may still exist in our theories, it is no small satisfaction to me to discover that many of my opinions have been confirmed, and many of my thoughts repeated, although new clothed, or disguised in other words.' What exercised Repton most was Knight's declaration that 'not one painter's composition' had been made by 'this art . . . called Landscape Gardening'. Even if an illustration of Repton's drawings could have been made in the book, this might not have been sufficient to make his point; so Repton calculated the number of his sketches and engravings in circulation, 1,638,000, he reckoned, to prove the worth of his compositions to 'the numerous purchasers and admirers'. Painting and gardening, Repton reaffirmed, were still distinct, and Knight had inadvertently proved this by 'an experiment made . . . near his own mansion, where large fragments of stone were irregularly thrown among briars and weeds, to imitate the foreground of a picture'.[187]

Repton's arguments about the picturesque landscape were not now driven by any hesitation about the virtues of painting or his own competence in watercolour, or by the resolutely realist, practicable view of landscape gardening it was politic to espouse in the 1790s. Repton now assumed an authority in the history, theory and criticism of painting that allowed him, according to the circumstances of a commission, to formulate the relation between the arts of painting and gardening in various ways. Moreover the naturalism of Repton's drawings was giving way to a decorative, highly coloured style with a conscious sense of artifice. In his remarks 'On the Picturesque' for the Red Book for Endsleigh (1814), attacking painters who represent 'all that is visible, without selecting what is beautiful', Repton not only attacked Moreland and Teniers for their 'pig-sties' and 'filthy hostels' but also criticized a recent piece of avant-garde naturalism, Turner's *Somer-Hill, Kent* (fig. 12): 'he painted an atmospheric effect, when he should have painted a landscape'.[188]

While Repton admitted criticizing the use of painting as a model for landscape gardening, he proposed doing just this at Stoneleigh Abbey, Warwickshire, from 1808, 'to realize a collection of Landscapes by the best Masters'. Stoneleigh presented 'circumstances very different from any other place in which I have been consulted'; it was a place 'sui generis'.[189] The grounds had remained untouched by fashion for more than 150 years and were full of venerable features, old terraces, avenues and ancient trees. Difficult to reach by road, surrounded by a meander of the river Avon, inhabited for years by the Leighs, a Jacobite family who refused to take any part in public affairs, even to worship in the parish church, Stoneleigh seemed an enclave of another world. Repton secured the commission when Stoneleigh was unexpectedly inherited by an existing client, and a very different representative of the family, the Revd Thomas Leigh of Adlestrop, Gloucestershire. One improvement for Stoneleigh, a binocular view through trees, was modelled on one 'which has succeeded so well at Adlestrop', the rest were modelled on scenes by painters.[190]

Repton proposed to widen the Avon and bring it closer to the house. In the pleasure grounds around the river he planned to imitate 'those graceful and picturesque combinations which we admire in the works of the best painters such as Gaspard Poussin and Claude Lorraine, and in the garden scenery of the graceful Watteau' (fig. 140). Repton cites a copy of the *Liber Veritas* in Devonshire House as a source for his Claudian scenes. There is no source cited for Watteau; Mavis Batey suggested that he may have had *La Perspective* in mind, which was well known in Crepy's engraving, but the source is probably more diffuse.[191] Since a surge in popularity in England in his own lifetime of prints and engravings, Watteau had infiltrated English garden design and its associated literature.[192] In Paris in 1770 Walpole admired statues, vases, flowers and rippling waters (the ingredients of Repton's scene for Stoneleigh) that 'suit the galant and idle society who realize the fantastic society of Watteau and Durfe'.[193] Repton's use of Watteau as a vehicle at Stoneleigh was a response to the reactionary, other-worldly atmosphere he encountered there but also part of his deployment of a range of French *ancien régime* motifs at this time, a style made fashionable by the Prince Regent, a recent patron.[194] Indeed the eclecticism of plans for Stoneleigh, the deployment of Watteau as well as Claude and Ruisdael, is part of the fashion that became known as the Regency style. Many of Repton's exotic scenes of this period remained on paper, but the Stoneleigh Red Book records improvements realized on the ground.[195]

In his last works Repton continued his reformulation of picturesque landscape but assumed that the picturesque controversy had faded as a public concern. He recalled it for a late commission at Hewell Grange, Worcestershire, in 1812 for the earl of Plymouth. The earl had spent much of the period since abroad, notably as Governor of Madras, and Repton thought that the con-

140 View of the pleasure ground, with and without overlay, from the Red Book for Stoneleigh Abbey (1809). Stoneleigh Abbey Ltd and the Shakespeare Birthplace Trust.

141 J. Peltro after Humphry Repton, *Scene on the Wye near Goodrich Castle*, frontispiece to *Peacock's Polite Repository* (1799). Victoria and Albert Museum.

troversy 'may not have engaged your attention'. Moreover, at Hewell 'I have nowhere seen a Spot, in which are so strongly exemplified the two great objects of our controversy; viz. The use to be made of the Art of painting, and the Errors of Mr. Brown's school & practice'. With twenty-four watercolours to revise Hewell's bleak park and a suggestion that the improver in question, who appeared to have 'never seen the Spot, but on a map', was Brown himself ('it certainly bears strong marks of his System and Practice'), Repton had shifted his former position dramatically, probably in this difficult period as much to secure favour as to demonstrate a principle. With an annotated bibliography of the main works in the picturesque controversy, unpublished letters as well as books in their various editions, the Hewell Red Book charts the dispute as a historical event.[196]

In publishing the extract from the Stanage Red Book in *Fragments*, Repton felt obliged to add a note informing his readers about the works of Price and Knight – 'so many years have now elapsed since the controversy'.[197] Their works are referenced or alluded to throughout *Fragments*, notably in the Fragment 'Concerning Improvements', which rewrites Price's parable of the improved lane.[198] In his Memoir, Repton wrote up the controversy more briefly and less bitterly than other difficult episodes in his career, notably those with Nash and the Prince of Wales. Most of the disappointments in the Memoir are associated with the secular decline that exiled Repton from the cultural world in which the picturesque controversy was conducted. He was, at least for a time, a figure to be reckoned with by leading connoisseurs. The works of Knight and Price, 'two ingenious authors', were 'likely to outlive the squibs and crackers of fugitive assailants' and 'will probably preserve my name to future ages – while they were endeavouring to keep alive their own'.[199]

Knight withdrew from the controversy. He devoted himself to Downton Vale in the summer months, vacating the mansion in 1808 for a dwelling in the grounds, where, according to Ballantyne, he achieved the philhellenic state of *ataraxia*, a state of psychological serenity, free from guilt and anxiety, as well as from physical discomfort'.[200] Price, as prone to outbursts of illness and anxiety as Repton, prolonged the controversy.

Repton had strongly impressed his influence on the Herefordshire landscape (figs 141 and 142). After his first visits in the 1790s Repton continued to be consulted by local clients, old and new.[201] In 1809 Repton told his family how he had accompanied Cotterell and Foley to the concerts and dinners of the Three Choirs Festival in Hereford '& gay days we have had'.[202] Tucked away in its tributary valley, Foxley may have appeared to be a marginal place and Price regarded with some suspicion by gentry with deeper roots in the region. Despite Price's declared commitment to local virtue, he seems to have remained an outsider in Hereford society, never holding major public office and taking little more than a routine role in city and county affairs.[203] The one appointment he held for the region came with the change of ministry on the death of Pitt. Price was brought, along with Nash, into the Office of Woods and Forests; 'technically, at least, he was the first and last Superintendent to the Deputy Surveyor of the Forest of Dean', but his exact duties are obscure.[204] He spent most of his time in his

142 After Humphry Repton, *The Wier in Herefordshire*, from *Peacock's Polite Repository* (1799). Victoria and Albert Museum.

own woods, with parties of workmen, occasionally visited by fashionable friends. Wordsworth described him 'striding up the steep side of his wood-crowned hills with his hacker... slung from his shoulder like Robin Hood's bow'.[205]

In 1810 Price issued a third, three-volume *Essays on the Picturesque*, including a lengthy reply to the 'very pointed attack by my friend Mr Knight'.[206] In his letters to friends Price continued to set out his views on landscape improvement, and in visits to their estates led parties of gentlemen and labourers to realize them on the ground. If Repton made his peace with Price, Price did not reciprocate. Even after Repton's death in 1818, he complained to correspondents about Repton's commercialism, accusing him of overcharging, even charging for unsolicited remarks on social visits.[207] Price encouraged them to use cheaper, more pliant men, such as his nurseryman James Cranston and the draughtsman William Sawrey Gilpin, nephew of the Gilpin who had first promoted the fashion for picturesque landscape. In Gilpin Price reckoned that he had at last found a professional improver willing to project his ideas.[208]

The controversy between Repton, Knight and Price was played out in fiction, famously in Thomas Love Peacock's *Headlong Hall* (1816) but also in Jane Austen's *Mansfield Park* (1814), where Fanny Price, in her occluded view of landscape, discerning even strata of soil on the trip to Sotherton, echoes Uvedale Price's sentiments in the *Essay on the Picturesque*, and Repton is a brand name for delinquents such as Mr Rushworth and Mary Crawford: 'Mr Repton... His terms are five guineas a day... Repton, or any body of that sort... any Mr Repton who would... give me as much beauty as he could for my money'.[209]

## From Picturesque to Gardenesque

In this last section I chart the representation of Repton's work by John Claudius Loudon (1783–1843), the man who assumed the mantle of the nation's landscape improver from Repton, as Repton had assumed it from Capability Brown. Loudon revived the picturesque controversy at the turn of the century to launch his career, declaring himself for Price against Repton, and a British, as opposed to English, view of landscape improvement. After Repton's death, and during his own establishment as an industrious reformer of agriculture and horticulture, Loudon made a *rapprochement* with Repton's landscape gardening, eventually editing the first publication of collected works and enlisting Repton in his genealogy of the Gardenesque.[210]

Loudon launched his career in Edinburgh and London in 1803. His first major commission, at Scone Palace, Perth, to establish the seat of the earls of Mansfield as 'the most eminent place of residence for a Nobleman in the British Empire', testifies to the ambition of the twenty-year-old, Edinburgh University educated, son of a Lothian farmer. The plans for Scone are modelled on a Repton Red Book but presented, in a consciously academic mode, as a *Treatise*, in a show of Classical and botanical erudition designed to eclipse his English predecessor and establish a threshold for his own career. Loudon would base his improvements on 'real principles – in place of being blindly led by any Landscape Gardener'.[211] With letters of introduction to Joseph Banks and Jeremy Bentham, Loudon took his campaign to London, firing off a letter to the *Literary Journal* 'On Laying out... Public Squares in London to the Utmost Picturesque Advantage' for 'the beauty of the metropolis, the health of its inhabitants... the honour of the British nation', in the process making a lightly veiled attack on Repton's work in progress, the landscaping of Russell Square.[212] While lodging in London, Loudon wrote his first published treatise, *Observations on the Formation and Management of Useful and Ornamental Plantations, on the Theory and Practice of Landscape Gardening*, which, as its title suggests, was intended as a riposte to Repton's volume of *Observations* published that year.[213]

Published in London and Edinburgh in 1804, Loudon's *Observations* declared its support for the works of Knight and Price, in particular for the more practical *Essay on the Picturesque*: 'I believe I am the first who has set out as a landscape gardener, professing to follow Mr Price's principles'. Loudon mounted an allied attack on Repton's work at Valleyfield, Fife. 'Many dells of the exquisite kind occur in Scotland and Wales... one of the finest sort was treated lately in the most barbarous manner.' The banks were shaved, rocks stripped of moss and stains, the woods cut back, larches and flowers planted in clumps, and the 'natural-like road' replaced by a 'formal, finished gravel walk' (fig. 143).[214] Repton admitted he had never seen Valleyfield himself, sending his two sons to direct the design, and pronounced that it 'remains a specimen of the powers of landscape gardening in that part of Scotland where the art had been

143 *Flower Garden at Valley-Field*, from *Observations on the Theory and Practice of Landscape Gardening* (1803). Yale Center for British Art, Paul Mellon Collection.

introduced only by those imitators of Mr. Brown's manner, who had travelled into the north'.[215]

In his next publication, the two-volume *Treatise on Forming, Improving and Managing Country Residences* (1804), Loudon had the confidence to name Repton as the destroyer of Valleyfield: 'I hope the proprietors of that lovely country will never again admit such a formidable foe. If they do, I conjure all my countrymen to unite in declaiming against their taste.' Loudon devoted whole sections in the *Treatise* to attacking Repton and endorsing Price and Knight. He rejected Repton's description of Downton Vale for omitting those features, 'steep mountains' and 'a rich canopy of old wood', that distinguish the vale 'from most others in England'; defended Price's *Essay on Artificial Water* against Repton's criticisms; and in general concluded that Repton's landscape gardening was 'puerile' and 'pretty', and thus 'dangerous and ruinous' to 'the British nation'. He coined a new term, 'Landscape Husbandry', to describe improvements, an 'awkward appellation', he admitted, but 'much better than Landscape Gardening'.[216] I have no evidence of what Price and Knight thought about Loudon's endorsement – I suspect they would have wondered why he made so little of the basis of their views, the knowledge of painting – but they would have appreciated his recognition of the pragmatic, functional and sociable aspects of their views, which most English critics failed to see, or deliberately overlooked.

Although he made a veiled response to Loudon's criticisms of his plans for Russell Square, Repton kept his council in public, probably because he did not then regard Loudon as a serious rival as a landscape gardener.[217] But Loudon then established a practice and set of principles that directly challenged Repton's career.

144 *Panoramic View of the Farm, Farm Buildings and Farm Lodge at Tew Lodge Taken from a Field Opposite the House*, from John Claudius Loudon, *Observations on Laying out Farms in the Scotch Style* (1812). Yale Center for British Art, Paul Mellon Collection.

While Repton was searching for commissions towards the end of the first decade of the nineteenth century, Loudon made his reputation and fortune as a farming consultant, transplanting a so-called Scotch style of husbandry (along with staff, 'North Britons' he called them) into English estates. Loudon took a tenancy on a small estate in Middlesex, and then took on the management of the Oxfordshire estate of Great Tew, creating what he called 'the most magnificent *ferme ornée* in England' (fig. 144).[218] Repton probably had Loudon in mind in his attacks on the very idea of the *ferme ornée* and the increasingly utilitarian, agricultural strain in landscape improvement.[219] For it was Loudon who replaced Repton as consultant at Great Tew. On a commission in 1803 Repton had proposed a new house, in alternative styles, Classical or Gothic, at the head of an old avenue near the church and village.[220] Repton's proposals were not executed, and five years later, on Arthur Young's advice, Tew's owner, General George Stratton, shifted the focus of improvement to his farms. Loudon took the tenancy of the home farm and reorganized the rest of the 3,700-acre estate, replacing sixteen English farmers with two Scottish ones, amalgamating small pastures in to large fields, and more than doubling the rental to ten thousand pounds.[221] In an open letter to the doyen of Scottish improvement, Sir John Sinclair, Stratton expressed his pleasure at the changes:

> All the trees that were in the hedge-rows are left standing, and have a more picturesque effect than they had, which is increased by that of the new roads which serpentine round the farm on the sides of the hills (that the level may be kept), and appear like rides through an arable *ferme ornée*.[222]

Loudon published his plans for Great Tew and a few other commissions, notably Hopton Court, Shropshire, and Hope End, Ledbury, in Herefordshire, whose hop and cider farms 'admit a considerable degree of picturesque beauty'.[223]

In his publications, Loudon took over Repton's territory of gardens and pleasure grounds, not just by emphasizing the importance of botanical science and horticultural technology, but by repackaging the aesthetics of garden design. *Hints on the Formation of Gardens and Pleasure Grounds* (1812) presented off-the-peg patterns for sites from one to a hundred acres, on various terrains, to be implemented by nurserymen, builders and owners themselves; among the styles were the 'Reptonian', and the 'Brownian'.[224]

After a two-year tour of the Continent, Loudon returned to his house in Bayswater in 1816 to compile material for the *Encyclopaedia of Gardening*. When this was published in 1822, Loudon reaffirmed his regard for Price and his formulation of the picturesque, but revised his opinion of Repton after reading his late work. The shortcomings of *Sketches and Hints* and *Observations* were still evident, but in *Fragments* he 'appears much more a disciple of Price than a defender of his "great predecessor [Brown]"' and displayed 'practical taste', 'dignity, refinement and appropriation to man'.[225] Loudon's regard for Repton increased when he and his correspondents for the *Gardener's Magazine* reported on the condition of eighteenth-century gardens in the 1820s. Repton's horticultural and botanical knowledge was made apparent in reports on the development of his gardens at Woburn.[226] The post-war depression had taken its toll on other Repton gardens, and many were going to ruin; Valleyfield 'is now comparatively neglected, and some of the terrace walls have actually fallen down'.[227] Elsewhere, as at Kenwood, changes in ownership, and the effects of restyling and overgrowth, not only obscured Repton's design but concealed all memory of his authorship.[228]

In 1839 Loudon restored Repton for a new audience with the first instalment – priced 2s. 6d. plain, 5s. 6d. coloured – of his published writings on landscape gardening. *The Landscape Gardening and Landscape Architecture of the Late Humphry Repton Esq.* was issued shortly after in a one-volume octavo, with a Biographical Notice expressly written 'by a member of Mr Repton's family', probably John Adey, some notes by Loudon showing where Repton's ideas had been confuted or confirmed by recent knowledge, and an introduction that positioned Repton centrally, and Price and Knight marginally, in a tradition that culminated in the style Loudon himself invented, the Gardenesque. 'Repton's School' combined 'all that was excellent in the former schools', including the 'Picturesque School', through 'the union of an artistical knowledge of the subject with good taste and good sense'. The union of Repton's style with 'the present prevailing taste for botany and horticulture' gave rise to the Gardenesque, 'the display of the beauty of trees, and other plants, individually'.[229] Loudon still had reservations about Repton's aquatints and slides, and reckoned that the crude line engravings (fig. 145) of his edition were in fact an improvement on the original aquatints (fig. 20): 'Mr Repton's ideas will be rendered more clear by our plates than his own'.[230] But Loudon, the reformer, who reckoned that gardening flourished best under vigorously commercial, mass-educated, republican democracies, found lessons in Repton's style for the conflict-ridden countryside of the 1830s. The persistence of miserable lodges and houses for gardeners working on estates showed 'the want of sympathy' of architects and landscape gardeners, 'both in Scotland and England', to 'those who they consider beneath them'; 'Mr Repton, having been born a gentleman, was under no such dread . . . and we find him continually advocating the improvement of cottages'. 'Humanity dictates this line of action, as well as prudence; for it would be easy to shew, that, if improvement did not pervade every part of society, the breach between the extreme parts would soon become so great as to end in open rupture.'[231]

145 After Humphry Repton, *Rivenhall Place* 'rendered Picturesque and Cheerful', from John Claudius Loudon, *The Landscape Gardening and Landscape Architecture of the Late Humphry Repton Esq.* (1840). Private collection.

*facing page* Detail of fig. 20.

# Chapter 4
# DUKEDOMS AND ROYAL DOMAINS

WHEN REPTON decided to become Capability Brown's successor, he set his sights on the highest ranks of society. Not only was Brown commissioned to improve the parks and gardens of the peerage and royal family, but he 'dined with dukes and shared confidences with statesmen'. So great was Brown's esteem in the powerhouses of the aristocracy, as a professional dealer and table-talker, that he played a political role, acting as an intermediary between the Whigs and Tories. Brown's world was one of large horizons: great estates, high politics, big money and, in the writings of admirers such as Thomas Whately, grand theory. With contracts of up to twenty thousand pounds, and a one thousand pound salary as Royal Gardener, Brown became a rich and favoured man. The former kitchen gardener eventually entered the ranks of the gentry, with a 13,000-acre estate and the Sheriffdom of Huntingdonshire.[1]

If Brown remained largely silent about his success, rarely wrote in detail about his designs and never published, Repton penned reams about the social significance of his work and his careful efforts to enter the best circles. Looking back at his career, against the ambition he first entertained, Repton judged it a failure. He enjoyed the patronage of some peers and followed Brown to aristocratic estates, but despite an ardent hope he was never commissioned by the king. In this chapter I examine in detail Repton's commissions for two powerful peers, the dukes of Portland and Bedford, commissions for the Prince of Wales and efforts to solicit the patronage of the king, George III. I examine the various properties of these noblemen before and after Repton's proposals, the opportunity the commissions offered for developing new styles of design and for formulating theoretical principles in published works. These commissions enhanced the scope of Repton's work, in proposals for a range of sites in different regions, from county seats to city squares, and by generating local and national networks of patronage. I also consider the limits they placed on Repton's authority and ambition. The commissions were but one part, often a minor one, of large-scale programmes of estate improvement, employing a range of permanent, salaried staff and visiting consultants.

What made the noble clients he secured so appealing to Repton, although it gave him some unease, was their willingness to spend prodigious amounts of money on pleasurable pursuits. What distinguished the dukes of Portland and Bedford as much as their estates, pedigree, talent, statesmanship and education was their massive debt, more than half a million pounds each at their deaths.[2] And there was no more infamous figure of excess than the Prince of Wales. Writing in the post-war depression, Repton offered a principled view of aristocratic consumption:

*facing page* Detail of fig. 200.

Although, during a long and active life, my efforts have contributed to the happiness of some hundred individuals, and the employment of some thousands; I trust that not a single instance can be adduced in which useless expenditure was advised, for unreasonable gratification of vanity; but wealth is never so well employed, as in improvements that display the genius of art, and call into active employment the labourer and artificer.[3]

## Gentlemen and Nouveaux Riches

As a prelude to these case studies I outline the changing configuration of landed society in later Georgian England at least as Repton saw it, in the relation between his career and the aristocratic circles to which he hoped it would provide access.

In one respect Repton's entrée, from the world of commerce, might have been easier than Brown's, from the offices of the kitchen garden. As Linda Colley has pointed out, the 'governing style' of aristocratic society in the later Georgian era was less patrician, more polite; it emphasized the virtues of hard work, professionalism, consensus politics and domestic virtue, the patriotism of the private sphere.[4] Repton's commissions for aristocratic clients were designed to reinforce this style, notably in their focus on home and garden. He liked nothing better than to stay with the family of an aristocratic client who cultivated the same polite accomplishments as his own, music-making, drawing, reading, perambulating, conversing. Sometimes this seems the summit of Repton's ambition. Hence his discomfort at Lord Colchester discouraging his friends from visiting while Repton was working at his estate in Surrey so as not to disturb the landscape gardener: 'If such things were known to me to have occurd I would forswear my profession – since the chief benefit I have derived from it – has been the society of those to whose notice I could not otherwise have aspired'.[5]

Repton was less business-like than Brown, less wealthy and less independent. He rarely, and reluctantly, took on contracting, not least for its financial risks, nor did he have Brown's acumen in dealing with the range of estate staff, tradesmen and consultants required to implement designs. The governing style of aristocratic society may have changed, but its mansions and grounds were still at the centre of a complex estate economy and society, which Repton knew much less well than his predecessor and cared for less. On great estates especially Repton had to deal with a series of intermediaries. He complained about 'the opposition of stewards, the presumption or ignorance of gardeners, and the jealousy of architects and builders'; he desired direct access to 'the first characters in the kingdom'.[6] An entrée to the family circle was no guarantee of professional success. At Harewood Repton was delighted to join in the nightly music-making, in 'a palace of peace and love and a magnificent receptacle of domestic harmony', and so mortified later to discover his designs ignored or botched by local workmen.[7] Stewards on great estates were powerful men, especially when overseeing a general programme of improvements, and Repton needed to secure their support. The marquess of Bath's steward, Thomas Davis, was an expert on forestry, a reporter for the Board of Agriculture, and possessed his own estate as well as residing at Longleat. In his working plan of Repton's Red Book, Davis endorsed many of the recommendations, and ventured some theoretical points in Repton's favour on the picturesque controversy; but he objected to felling some old limes, planes and elms near the house to make way for maples, thorns and alders as a 'Stage Trick' and reckoned that the steepness of the approach reflected Repton's taste for effect and his inexperience as a horseman.[8] While Repton thanked the marquess personally for his fee, a basket of game and the loan of a coat, payment for the Red Book was entered in Davis's accounts under 'Miscellaneous Articles', between bread, cheese and beer for the volunteer infantry and the cost of covering a chestnut mare.[9]

Repton's focus on homes and gardens, on polite accomplishments and domestic virtue generally, earned him some direct dealings with aristocratic women. Throughout the eighteenth century, women in polite society took a close and often personal role in the design and management of gardens.[10] Repton affected a tutorial authority with aristocratic women by demonstrating the importance of principles of design. Thus he published a *Letter to Lady* \*\*\*\*\* explaining a design for a garden after finding that 'those who perfectly understand a drawing in perspective, have, sometimes, no idea of a plan, or map' (fig. 146). 'Suppose the embroidery in the corner is a plan for a flower garden', Repton begins, before explaining the mysteries of colour coding compass bearings and key numbering. Repton added a footnote that highlights the delicacy of his dealings, and the vulnerability of his authority compared to that of other men. He had foolishly shown a pencil sketch of the plan to a clerk of the works who had put it in to execution without Repton's knowledge. Not only did the design yield

Repton neither 'emolument nor fame', but the proprietor of the house claimed it as his own.[11]

Repton's Memoir lists a series of examples of ungentlemanly conduct among aristocratic clients. After scores of letters 'with the most trifling queries about the line of a fence or a gravel walk', Lord Essex 'boasts that *every thing* that was done at his place *was his own taste and design*' and 'referred [to] me as a common tradesman'. Noble mansions that he had visited early in his career, witnessing 'domestic happiness which promised to be lasting', he returned to find vacant, or demolished, or with a 'wife and mother replaced by a new mistress of the family'. 'The King can make a Lord', Repton pronounced, 'but he cannot make a gentleman'. Repton looked to his village wheelwright, Will Woodlands, a good Christian but 'no Methodist', for a definition of a gentleman, 'one as delights in seeing people happy – and will give up caring for himself to make them so'.[12] Repton attributed patrician delinquency, along with his professional decline, to the 'influence of war, and war taxes':

> The sudden acquirement of riches, by individuals, has diverted *wealth* into new channels; men are solicitous to *increase* property rather than to *enjoy* it . . . The country gentleman, in the last century, took more delight in the sports of the field, than in the profits of the farm; his pleasure was, to enjoy in peace the venerable home of his ancestors; but the necessity of living in camps, and the habit of living in lodgings, has, of late, totally changed his character and pursuits; and, at the same time, perhaps, tended to alienate half the landed property of the country.[13]

'I have had perhaps more than most men, opportunities of observing the gradual changes by which the barriers have been removed betwixt the two classes of the landed and the monied interests.'[14] Repton had a particular view of the monied interest. He was happy to have big bankers such as Francis Baring and Charles Hoare as clients; these men were an accepted part of aristocratic society, financing aristocratic expenditure and investing themselves in estates to establish landed dynasties. Wholesale merchants, at least from established houses, Repton also welcomed as honourable clients.[15] Many landed families made good profits during the Napoleonic Wars, and cherished clients such as Lord Darnley at Cobham made spectacular returns from agricultural rents.[16] To be sure, some established families felt the burden of tax for the first time, some sold up, or sold out to the spirit of speculation. Most enjoyed a good income

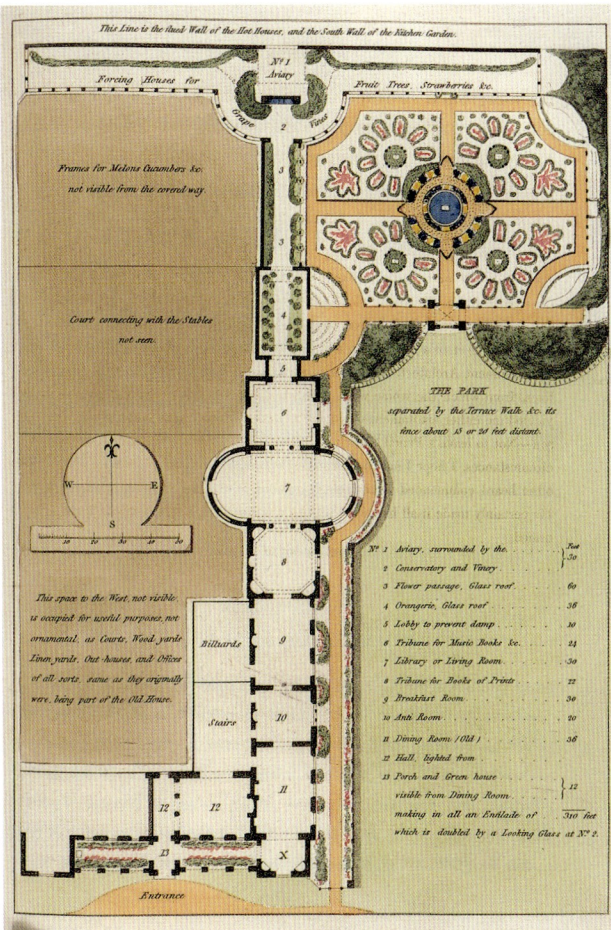

146 *A Plan Explained*, from *Fragments on the Theory and Practice of Landscape Gardening* (1816). Yale Center for British Art, Paul Mellon Collection.

from a variety of sources; some still spent handsomely on embellishing their estates. They just failed to spend as much as Repton thought they ought on the art of landscape gardening, or rather his practice. Repton saw their place in his circle of clients taken by wartime profiteers on the look-out for a place in the country, men with neither pedigree, talent nor taste.

Repton lists in his Memoir 'the nameless nouveaux riches with whom I have had transactions'. A 'person of very low origin who had lately purchased the estate of a Duke boasted to me "that he had been obliged to double the size of the Cellars"'; a man 'who boasted that "money could do everything"' purchased a library of valuable books 'in a lump with the house, for he was told that books were the fashion . . . "but for my part I never look into them"'; a man 'who had made his fortune as mere shopkeeper' desecrated a temple dedicated to Pope,

Addison and Swift; a 'worthy cockney' took possession of three hundred acres 'just as the haymaking had begun [and] was so charmed with the novelty of the scene... that he ordered no more hay should be cut until he came again into the country'; a man who 'acquired great wealth by contracts, loans and fortunate speculations' pulled down every house and cottage he could see from his mansion to 'command a view over 2,000 acres where no *human being had a right to set his foot!*'; a 'very rich man' purchased a villa and wanted to improve the grounds, 'but how could I hope to *suggest an idea* to this man, who shewed me what he called "The *largest acorn* he had ever seen!" at the same time producing the *cone* of a *stone pine* that grew near an oak and had fallen among the acorns (fit emblem of him I thought who had fallen among gentlemen but could not often be mistaken for one)':

> A man of no education, but of much adventure contracts for something to carry on the war – no matter what – perhaps bread – or cannon – or gun powder, or it may be hats, caps, coats, or saddles, swords, belts, bullets – or in short anything by which money can be got – In two or three years the same person who lived in a hired workshop must inhabit a house of his own in the country so a field is bought – and a villa is to be built and Mr. Repton must come to fix the spot. I can look back on many such concerns, and one day is much like another – A letter arrives... 'Sir, I have bought an estate xxx – and I trouble you to name an early day to meet my Surveyor... and myself'... we meet at '12 precisely' – I walk the length and breadth, and from corner to corner of a flat field... put down four stakes for the four corners of the house... mark the situation for the offices, gardens &c... go into a shed to take a sandwich and a glass of wine... We talk of the pleasures of the country and I take my leave, and my fee... I return to my hotel... and as I sit over my solitary dinner I compare the society I have left with that I used to keep – instead of wit, science, elegance and courtly conversation, I can picture these calculators thus talking – 'Landscape Gardening is a good line, no risk of capital! – all profit, no loss! – a very pretty morning's work!'.[17]

In his last years Repton confided to patrician clients his fears of cultural decline. A memorial exhibition to Sir Joshua Reynolds at the British Institution in 1815 included many portraits: 'It was like an admission into Heaven', he told Sir Harry Fetherstonehaugh, where I not[ed] all the illustrious dead with whom I had been in habits of intimacy in the last Century. I knew most of them – & those whom I did know call'd me back to the Noblest Mansions in which I had spent the busyest & of course happyest days of my life... Days before Wars and Taxes – Pains & Penalties...[18]

On hearing that Fetherstonehaugh was keen to get to Paris after the cessation of hostilities, Repton told him:

> I have conversed with many who have been to Paris & returned dissatisfied – nay almost disgusted – everything is changed & from what I can gather – the Great Nation conquer'd is like a great family reduced by misfortune. The Pride, the Gloriose Magnificence is ostentatiously display'd in the splendour of Spectacle & old Finery, while Poverty & Filth & sour discontent rancle in the heart & they can neither resume the former Society of their Equals – nor condescend to mix with those who have risen from being their inferiors – & whose success like that of all Nouveaux Gens in all countries – is their only merit or object of thought.[19]

Repton's vision of gentlemanly refinement had both a strain of pious evangelism and of raffish pleasure seeking. This is exemplified in his Memoir by an account of two commissions around the turn of the century; one for a grandee, Lord Harewood, the other for a merchant, Richard Walker. Repton esteemed Harewood House as a harmonious domestic household, defined by its nightly music-making, but it was still set in a large park landscaped by Capability Brown and heavily funded by income from Caribbean sugar plantations. Repton rode about the grounds with William Wilberforce, newly elected (with Harewood's son Edward Lascelles) as MP for York. Taking from his pocket a volume of Cowper's poems (a popular antidote to aristocratic excess), Wilberforce asked Repton to read to him, and both men were so absorbed that they entirely 'forgot the beauties of the park'. Moving to the hothouses, they came across a plant of 'the most beautiful tender green'. When the gardener told them it was a young sugar-cane plant, 'we could read in [Wilberforce's] glistening eye all the complicated train of thought which had called forth his extraordinary energy and engaged his deep attention ... in the abolition of the slave trade'.[20]

Repton also relished the metropolitan world of fashion and respected the way that it dissolved social distinctions to form the consensus of polite society. Here was a medium for integrating commercial and hereditary wealth, channelling new money and ambition, renovating ancestral pride. This is exemplified in the Memoir by an account of Richard Walker, 'a very rich merchant and his wife from a distant seaport [in fact a major shipper from Liverpool in the West Indian sugar and rum trade] [who] wished to become known in the fashionable circles of London'.[21] Walker, we are told, paid one hundred thousand pounds unseen for a 'large picturesque old mansion' and estate at Michel Grove in the Sussex Downs close to Brighton, badly run down and partly occupied by a farmer.[22] When Repton accompanied them to the house, they discovered 'some large rolls of vellum – old maps of the premises, and a curious pedigree of the ancient family who had been owners of the estate ever since the time of Edward IV'. They planned improvements both to modernize the estate – a new road system, a prefabricated pavilion, 'a work of enchantment', sent by water from London for viewing the sea – and to enhance its sense of history – restoring the mansion and repairing the village church with its decayed family tombs. Walker also commissioned Repton to fit up his London house for a masquerade, strengthening the floor and festooning the scaffolding with 'flowery garlands and coloured lamps'. The Princes of Wales and Orange were there, exercising their prerogative to be unmasked, but otherwise it was 'a mixed mob of every character ... from the King to the Cobbler, from the Sultan to the Slave'. Repton sallied forth in 'the dress of a Dutch Burgomaster', which he considered decorating with a toy windmill 'to put on my cap'. The Prince of Orange was surprised to see the burgomaster approach talking in Dutch, until Repton removed his mask to tell him that he had been presented to him in The Hague thirty years before. Only 'when day begins to dawn and by the aid of two *real* watchmen we make our escape thro' the mob collected in the streets' does Repton 'wish for rest ... after this night of fashionable dissipation', but without too much regret: the Walkers 'burst upon the World of Fashion like meteors that cross the sky', and Repton passed 'many happy days' with them 'during my frequent visits to them both in Sussex and in London'.[23]

These modes of moral and fashionable reform framed Repton's sensibility and that of polite society.[24] He veered between the playful and the pious. In 1814 he published a sermon addressed 'to the Fashionable World at the West End of the Town' on the providential effects of winter snow on Napoleon's campaign and the

147 Design for a stained-glass window for the dining-room at Uppark (1813). Private collection. National Trust Photographic Library.

folly of flirting with radical politics, a sermon 'to excite attention during the interval of *ennui* on Sunday morning, when shops, and auctions, and exhibitions are shut up, and nothing open but churches and chapels [when] something must be done betwixt breakfast and the park'.[25] The previous year Repton told a highly fashion-conscious client, Sir Harry Fetherstonehaugh, how much he enjoyed wandering around the show-rooms of the West End choosing wallpaper, drapes, mirrors, stained glass (fig. 147) and argand lamps for the mansion at Uppark: 'the effect will be magic'. 'You will wonder at the interest I take in such triffles [sic.] on the verge of eternity... but the best recipe for happiness here is to make the most of triffles and I find more amusement in drawing a lamp or inventing a paper-hanging than in designing a Palace or planning a Church.'[26]

## The Duke of Portland

The third duke of Portland (1738–1809), one of the most powerful political figures of his time, proved Repton's most influential client: 'a Nobleman to whom I am more deeply indebted than to any in the list of my professional patrons'.[27] Portland's patronage helped to transform Repton's practice from a regional to a national one. For twenty years, from 1789, Portland paid Repton an annuity of one hundred guineas for advice on his parks at Welbeck, Nottinghamshire, and Bulstrode, Buckinghamshire. These commissions helped to secure many others, both nearby and among Portland's many visitors and guests. Repton's annual week-long, half social, visits to the duke's country houses, and frequent visits to his London residence of Burlington House, gave him an entrée into a nationwide network of aristocratic patronage. Repton acknowledged the formative influence of Portland's ideas on landscaping and Portland's parks as a testing ground for his own theory and practice. He was proud to acknowledge the Red Books for Welbeck, of 1790 and 1793, as 'the ground-work' of his first treatise, *Sketches and Hints on Landscape Gardening*.[28]

Repton was brought to Portland's notice through his landscaping and electioneering for the duke's Whig allies in Norfolk, especially William Windham. Repton professed himself a 'sincere friend of the Portland interest' but wondered whether it was 'sufficient compensation for time sacrificed in Norwich politics'.[29] If Portland's patronage initially entangled Repton in Norfolk culture and politics, it eventually helped to release him by allowing him to pursue a purely professional career throughout the country. The growing rapprochement between the conservative Portland Whigs and Pitt's Tory administration, culminating in Portland's office as Home Secretary, worked to Repton's advantage. 'In the course of my profession', he told Windham in 1804, 'I have had the honour to become acquainted with almost all the statesmen and Leaders of different Parties, without sacrificing the pursuits of taste for those of politics'.[30]

When he compiled his Memoir, Repton looked back on Portland's patronage as an escape from factional political interests and an entrée into a world of private virtue. Repton avoided 'all mention of him in his public capacity – the public have portrayed him in different lights according to the point of view from whence his portrait was taken: for myself I only knew him in his private and domestic character'. Repton could always discern a 'genuine politeness', and 'natural spirit of benevolence' 'even at times when it might be partly obscured by the artificial pomp that surrounded him'. In their 'frequent tête-à-tête conversations', Repton found 'the most solid judgment of men and things... interspersed with cheerful or interesting anecdotes unmixd with satire or asperity'. 'When at the head of his party, he was free from party prejudice, and when he was Prime Minister I never heard him express resentment or indignation at undeserved abuse from the public.'

> He would sometimes ask me to bring my papers and sit with him in the same room while he was occupied with official business, our two tables stood on opposite sides of the fire, and occasionally he would hand me over some curious or ridiculous projects – or threats, or abuse, to which all are subject who hold high stations – and these again would lead to the relation of some amusing or singular events.

Repton appreciated Portland's regard for his professionalism. On their first meeting Repton 'begged him to inform me to whom I was indebted for the honour of this introduction'. Portland refused to name anyone in particular; he made enquiries 'whenever I consult any professional gentleman in whom I wish to place implicit confidence both in his skill and integrity', so 'it is to *yourself* alone that you are indebted'. Rather than summon him at short notice, Portland invited Repton on the understanding that he did not have business elsewhere, 'and it is always flattering to a professional man to suppose his time fully occupied'.[31] Not that Repton passed up any opportunity of Portland's favour. 'I should never let any engagement whatever prevent me from attending first to his Grace's wishes', he said the last time he saw Portland in 1806, 'I should always consider his notice and early patronage as the source of all the fame I had acquired in my profession'.[32]

\* \* \*

## Welbeck Abbey

The Portland title was impeccably Whig. Of Dutch mercantile origins, the Bentinck family accompanied William of Orange to England; George I conferred the dukedom in 1716 in recognition of the family's service to the House of Hanover. Through the eighteenth century the Portlands built up one of the most extensive aristocratic estates, with land in nine counties. The first family seat, at Bulstrode in south Buckinghamshire, stood in the region around Windsor Castle settled by the Hanoverian court and their followers. The second seat, at Welbeck Abbey, in north Nottinghamshire, came in to the Portland's possession through the marriage of the second duke into the Cavendish family, the dukes of Devonshire.[33] On the death of his father in 1761, the third duke, aged twenty-four, inherited many of the Welbeck lands. While he did not inherit the core estate of Welbeck Abbey until the death of his mother in 1785, he resided there and ran the estate from the time of his marriage in 1766 to the daughter of the fourth duke of Devonshire.[34] Through this marriage, Portland not only cemented the alliance between Welbeck and Chatsworth, but also acquired from the Devonshires the loan of Burlington House, according to Portland 'the most comfortable Habitation in all London'.[35]

Welbeck Abbey was one of four massive ducal estates that dominated north Nottinghamshire, in a region dubbed 'the Dukeries' by Horace Walpole in 1777 (fig. 148).[36] The dukes of Portland, Newcastle, Norfolk and Kingston vied with each other in improving extensive tracts of a largely denuded Sherwood Forest, enclosing long neglected Crown lands that had been colonized by customary usage and rights. Old hunting parks were landscaped, new mansions were built.[37] Towards the end of the century the parks were incorporated in comprehensive programmes of estate improvement, and systematically managed for game, livestock, timber, hay, vegetables and fruit, as well as for amenity. New tenant farms were built, new villages and roads laid out.[38] The remnants of ancient woodland in Sherwood Forest were incorporated in the improved landscape of the Dukeries. 'It is with pleasure we see that efforts are making to adorn this ancient Forest in a manner truly patriotic and worthy of imitation', noted the local antiquarian Hayman Rooke in 1799, 'the many respectable Persons, whose Mansions and Parks border on the Forest, have made, and continue to make, large Plantations in honour of the splendid Victories gained by our gallant Admirals'.[39]

The 900-acre park at Welbeck was restyled in the 1740s by Francis Richardson, with lawns and formal clumps of trees, and a mile-long lake as its centrepiece. Portland instituted a large-scale, long-term programme of improvements, especially in planting and horticulture, directed by William Speechly, his resident gardener from 1767 to 1804. Portland's political career kept him for long

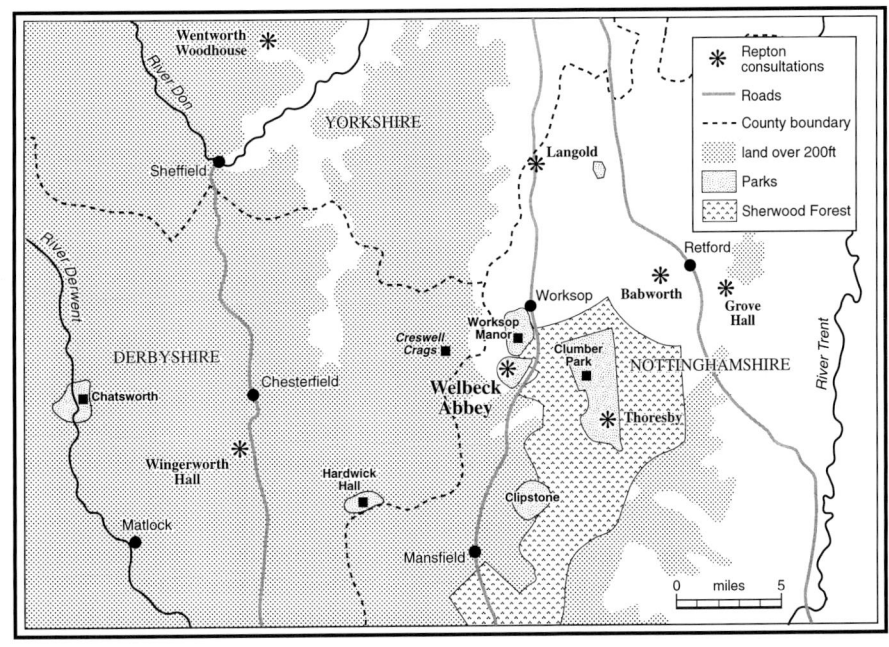

148 Welbeck Abbey and surrounding country.

149 W. Ellis after Hayman Rooke, *The Oak and Ash* and *A Venerable Tree near the Seven Sisters*, from Hayman Rooke, *Descriptive Sketches of Some Remarkable Oaks in the Park at Welbeck* (1790). University of Nottingham Library.

periods in London but he maintained regular contact with Speechly by letter, making suggestions, vetting proposals and ordering hampers of produce and plants for the grounds at Burlington House. Portland sent Speechly to Holland, to some notable gardens, including those of the Bentinck family. Suitably impressed by the investment in these places, Speechly observed: 'There is enough of the English Nobility that are afraid of their thousands at Newmarket & which would Grumble to lay out small sums on their own Estates, particularly their Gardens'.[40] In cultivating the grounds of Welbeck, growing tender fruits and vegetables, nursing trees from seed, planting huge stands on hillsides, co-ordinating the parkland cropping of turnips, potatoes and hay, and mobilizing a large labour force to do so, Speechly became nationally renowned. He wrote on horticulture, agriculture and forestry, notably an account of planting at Welbeck for Hunter's edition of Evelyn's *Silva* (1775), republished in 1798 in the *General View of the Agriculture of Nottinghamshire*.[41] Visitors to the Dukeries sought out Speechly, his gardens, nurseries and plantations and copies of his publications as souvenirs.[42]

The pride of Welbeck was its trees. These included a number of ancient oaks, including curiosities such as the Greendale Oak (through which a horseman could ride) and Seven Sisters (with seven stems growing from one trunk), which frequently appeared in prints (fig. 149).[43] Their acorns were carefully conserved as gifts for Portland's close friends.[44] By the later eighteenth century some of the older oaks were in terminal decline. Their felling was a sensitive issue in correspondence between Speechly and Portland:

> Your Grace has it continually in Your Power (and I hope will do it) to lay a Beauty open to the House [although] this scheme will I fear be disagreeable to Your Grace, as I know the great Aversion that your Grace has to cutting down Timber ... I am in a manner charmed with your Grace's Picturesque and Beautiful Idea of the Noble and Venerable Oaks, I did not mean to rob the water of the wood adjoining it in the manner Your Grace supposes, I think I said 'single Trees should be left and here and there a clump for variety'.[45]

By the end of the century descriptions of Welbeck praised the sensitivity of felling of some of the older trees; indeed lauded it as a patriotic act when the timber was used for shipbuilding.[46] The forestry campaign involved planting on a vast scale, more than two thousand acres over twenty-five years, not just oak saplings but beech, birch, larch and Spanish chestnuts, Weymouth pine, firs of many varieties, imports such as American oak and Virginian tulip tree, all, in Speechly's phrase, 'part of a one great design'.[47] Placing a Cedar of Lebanon on the highest hill, Speechly promised Portland that it would 'top the rest of the planting, and have a Noble and Beautiful appearance all round the County'.[48]

The campaign of improvement at Welbeck was affected by Portland's overall financial troubles. An aristocratic custom of indebtedness, which began in his youth on a three-year Grand Tour, was exacerbated by the price of political life, including a costly fight for land

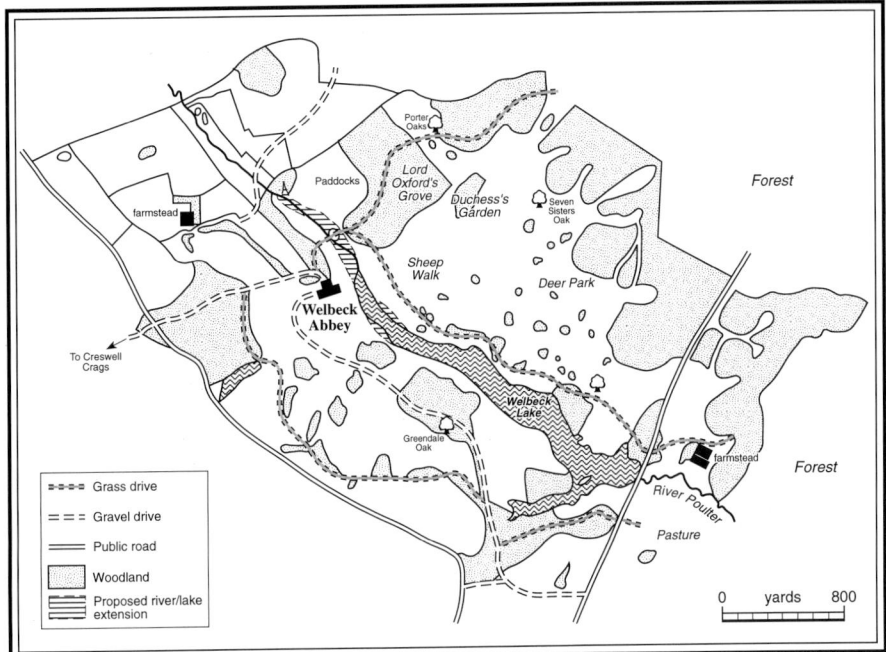

150 Map of the park at Welbeck Abbey after plans in the Red Book for Welbeck (1790; 1793). Private collection.

and influence in Cumberland with the Tory Sir James Lowther. To remain solvent in the later 1770s Portland sold off estates in Hampshire and Northumberland, mortgaged his property in London, and cut back drastically on expenditure at Welbeck, spending nothing, according to the accounts, on the pleasure grounds and gardens (although Speechly's letters indicate continuing activity), making over his home farm to his steward, even giving away his pack of hounds. By the end of 1780 servants' wages were unpaid and domestic bills outstanding. Portland was rescued by the inheritance on the death of his mother in 1785. He remained solvent for ten years until there was another financial crisis in 1795, when he considered selling Bulstrode and his Soho property. It was in this period that Portland commissioned Repton to prepare Red Books for Welbeck and spent large sums on the landscaping that Repton proposed (fig. 150).[49]

Repton's anxiety at his first interview with Portland in 1789 at Burlington House was allayed by the duke explaining 'his wishes concerning the improvements at Welbeck in a manner so clear and decided, that all diffidence of my own skill was removed'.[50] Repton paid his first visit to Welbeck for nine days in December 1789. At home at Hare Street after Christmas, Repton immediately set to work for another ten days, preparing a Red Book. Hesitant about his skill as a draughtsman, he employed George Samuel, a London-based drawing master known for country house portraits, to execute the finished watercolours showing the mansion.[51] Portland was pleased with the plans: 'All I proposed doing there met with his entire approbation'.[52]

Repton made much of Portland's pictorial sensibilities, and of their superiority to those of connoisseurs:

> His pictures were all good and he knew well their excellence, if not their value (for his notions of *value* were seldom narrowed by the common standard of *price*) yet with a correct knowledge of works of art, he never talked of Pictures in the cant language of connoisseurship. For pictures in Nature, he looked with a more inquisitive eye than man professed Artists, and he would discover effects of light and shade and combinations of forms and colouring in a landscape as if he were selecting subjects for his pencil (tho' I believe he never made a sketch).[53]

Like a huntsman, Portland stalked his pictorial subjects:

> Walking with him at Welbeck, he would often delight in following the tracks of deer or sheep, into the most sequestered haunts of the forest, and pause when any fresh scene of beauty or interest claimed particular attention, directing my eye to prototypes of a Salvater [*sic*] or a Redinger – Sometimes during the hours of repose from labour he would cautiously approach the spot where a group of men and children were resting or taking their noon day's meal, and pointing out some beautiful contrast in their attitude, or cheerful smile or countenance, he would stop in fear of destroying the magic of the picture by our intrusion. From his

admirable comments on such picturesque scenes I learnt more as a painter than if I had studied and copied the works of the best masters.

On one excursion Portland said: 'It will make an odd coincidence in the history of your life Mr. Repton that you should have first learnt gardening amongst the Dutch in Holland', to which Repton dutifully replied that his 'ablest teacher was descendant from a Nobleman long ago transplanted from that Country and naturalized in England'.[54]

Repton's first Red Book for Welbeck defers almost entirely to Portland's views. 'The great stile of improvement which Your Grace has with so much good taste & on so bold a scale adopted all round Welbeck leaves me with no other opportunity of displaying my skill than that of entering into the more minute detail of carrying your Grace's own ideas into execution.' While detailing Portland's ideas, Repton also ventured 'to hint (in my usual manner of doing business) all that occurred to me in my walk through the grounds'. The Red Book focuses on the vicinity of the mansion, on moving earth to enhance the eminence of the main façade, enlarging the lake and making a new circuit of paths around it (figs 151 and 152).

Through his design and the walks with Portland that informed it, Repton staked a claim to an area that overlapped with parkland improvements by William Speechly and architectural improvements to the mansion by the York architect John Carr. Repton reported that Carr agreed to his suggestions to alter the façade of the mansion to conform to plans for earth moving. He is more accommodating to Speechly's work,

> The *Cat Hills* are beginning to be planted, & will be continued of course to the water's edge in places. I have also secur'd and enlarg'd the SMALL WOOD your Grace mentioned by letter, giving it a concave line not only as a contrast to the plantation opposite which is convex, but to show a small esplanade of grass where the light will catch in the general view down the lake.

Repton suggested a ferry across the lake to connect with a path 'made under your Grace's direction thro' the Grove by Mr Speechly'.[55]

Repton's path crosses the lake, passes through a grove and sheepwalk, into the deer park past plantations of young beeches, along an avenue of sweet chestnuts to the 'Dutchesses [*sic*.] Garden'. He suggested a dressed walk with a grass verge, 'sometimes accompanied by flowering shrubs & sometimes opening to the most interesting views of the water, lawns and woods, all of which views may be infinitely varied by the management of the foregrounds'. The Duchess's Garden had decayed, and Repton proposed to restore it by replanting and some thinning to create 'a cabinet of delightful landscapes', including views of some of the ancient oaks in the park (figs 153 and 154). 'It includes a distant view of two of the *vegetable wonders* of Welbeck, viz: the seven sisters, and the small hollow tree which is sometimes used by the keepers as a covering from whence he shoots at the deer.'

151 View of the mansion, with and without overlay, from the Red Book for Welbeck (1790). Private collection. Photograph Nottinghamshire County Libraries.

152   The lakeside, from the Red Book for Welbeck (1790). Private collection. Photograph Nottinghamshire County Libraries.

153   Design for a Gothic seat and proposed planting in the Duchess's Garden, from the Red Book for Welbeck (1790). Private collection.

154   Proposed view of the Seven Sisters oak tree from the Duchess's Garden, from the Red Book for Welbeck (1790). Private collection.

While many of Repton's 'plans, hints and views' are a model of tact, he miscalculated badly by the economy of his suggestions. At the end of the Red Book Repton included 'Estimates of Expense':

> Contrary to the general assertion that Expense ought not to enter in any consideration where objects of beauty, and not of necessity are suggested, I have ever been of the opinion that where I can suggest great improvements with least expense I am most effectively doing the duty of my profession, for this reason I hope your Grace will not think the following page the least worthy perusal in this little volume.

On this page are priced various items from earth moving (at 4d. per cubic yard), plantation rail (between twelve

159

and eighteen shillings a rod), to the cost (between twenty and forty pounds) of a 'gothic pavilion of canvas' for the Duchess's Garden, bringing the total to less than a thousand pounds, a sum 'very inconsiderable in proportion to the improvement expected'. Other costs were hinted at in the text, principally that of a new crossing for the lake. Upon inheriting Welbeck, twenty-five years earlier, Portland had commissioned an ambitious three-arch bridge, with a total span of 240 feet, which, as some guidebooks unkindly pointed out, was 'a very costly undertaking [which] removed many fine oaks from the park' and collapsed as soon as it was completed.[56] Doubtless aware of Portland's folly, Repton rejected 'a handsome bridge' as 'an enormous expense', favouring the expedient of an island joined by two smaller bridges at half the cost (fig. 155). Repton recalled Portland's reaction with a shudder:

> When I presented my plan and drawing to the Duke I saw his countenance change and he returned me the papers with these words. 'I thank you, Mr Repton, but when I receive a hint from you, I do not expect to find any *second best expedient*' – I was much hurt and withdrew – to my room.

Fortunately for Repton, and his career, the duchess, who had been present at the interview, interceded and persuaded the duke to adopt Repton's plan. 'Thus did I save him a very considerable sum of money at the hazard of giving offence by my economy: a word which he detested, when applied to his own concerns.'[57]

Notwithstanding the list of estimates and savings on the lake crossing (Repton's bridges cost sixty-eight pounds) Portland still spent a prodigious sum on improvements around the house. Earth moving around the mansion alone in 1790 came to £541, vastly exceeding Repton's estimate of thirty-eight pounds, and continued for another six years at a cost of nearly three thousand pounds. This amounted to three-quarters of the total listed expenditure on alterations to the pleasure grounds; most of the rest went on alterations to the façade of the mansion. Portland raised the ground not only near the west front as Repton advised but all around, and insisted that Carr raise battlements on the upper storey. Repton credited Portland with 'the prophetic eye of taste'.

> Few could comprehend the seeming paradox of burying part of the house as the means of elevating the whole structure, or as it was very wittily expressed, moulding up the roots of the venerable pile, that it might shoot up fresh towers from its top.[58]

The accounts suggest that Portland spent much less on the dressed walks than Repton estimated, just £27 7s. on shrubs and gravel compared with £180 (which included railings and verges). Not all the materials for the walk may have been accounted for – Welbeck produced much of its own timber, stone and plants.[59]

After submitting the Red Book in 1790, Repton paid further visits to Welbeck in April, August and September. With the work at Bulstrode, Repton's expenses for journeys and plans came to more than £184, well in excess of the hundred guinea annuity agreed with Portland. 'For the first year or two I must expect to be a loser by this agreement', Repton noted in his account book.[60] The disappearance of all his subsequent account books makes it difficult to establish whether Repton covered his losses. He may not have minded much. His debt to Portland was not in 'the paltry consideration of pecuniary emolument but in the importance his kindness and partiality gave my professional career'.[61] Every year Repton enjoyed an annual engagement around Easter, passing 'at least ten days every year in the delightful society of his Grace's family where I always found a welcome reception'.[62]

In 1791 Repton was commissioned at Thoresby, adjacent to Welbeck, for Charles Pierrepont, MP for Nottinghamshire and a political ally of Portland. After a naval career, Pierrepont had inherited Thoresby in 1789 in his fifties, without succeeding from his uncle, the duke of Kingston. He switched his allegiance to Portland from the Tory duke of Newcastle at neighbouring Clumber and was rewarded with three successive titles: Baron

155 The island between the two bridges, with overlay, from the Red Book for Welbeck (1793). Private collection.

156   Canal and cascade, with and without overlay, from the Red Book for Thoresby (1791). Private collection.

Pierrepont, Viscount Newark and finally the first Earl Manvers. In contrast to Portland, Pierrepont was a consciously county man, resident for long periods at Thoresby or in Nottingham, and a figurehead in local associations, for example in agriculture and defence. The 1,800-acre park at Thoresby had already been extensively improved by the dukes of Kingston, with a mansion designed by Carr and landscaping by Richardson and Brown. By an upward revision of rents, Pierrepont funded a range of further improvements, notably planting, including Bentinck Border and Portland Grove in honour of his patron, and Howe Plantation and St Vincent's Grove in honour of victorious admirals in the Napoleonic Wars. He spent twenty-two thousand pounds on improving the mansion and building new offices and seventeen hundred on executing Repton's improvements to the pleasure grounds and cascade.[63]

Going through his files to compile his Memoir, Repton passed over several clients before arriving at Pierrepont, 'a name ever dear to me – altho' its owner has by accession of titles changed it three times, since I knew it as belonging to *that title which the King's power cannot confer – The Gentleman*'.

> His manners ... were gracious and princely – His mansion was an example of elegant hospitality – There are few places where I have found such uniform ease and comfort blended with all the graces of higher nobility. Here I have enjoyed in perfection, good music, cheerful conversation, amusing literature, and above all that sort of domestic love and harmony of mind which prevailed in this family more than in any other I have known with the exception of my own.

The Pierrepont's domestic harmony was not merely a matter of residence. Repton once called at Thoresby to see Charles Pierrepont when 'the ladies were left in Town', but 'every day's post brought from them the most animated accounts of all that was doing at Court and in the capital'.[64]

Repton's improvements at Thoresby were concerned mainly with the watercourses surrounding the mansion (fig. 156). The existing arrangement of formal canal and stepped cascade appeared a poor imitation of that at Chatsworth, itself a feature that now seemed tamely old fashioned: 'That forced and formal cascade', Anna Seward told Repton, 'in which the sullen waters take their measured leaps ... surely they might yet be allowed to strike the eye with transient sublimity, and roar down the mountain over craggy fragments, and flash through intercepting bushes'.[65] Repton proposed a naturalistic scheme for the cascade at Thoresby, linking the lake with a rocky, overgrown cascade spilling into a winding riverine channel. He was pleased to hear that Brown had proposed something similar, despite his tendency (as at Chatsworth) to check running water. The cascade could only be 'divested of the disgusting formality of Art ... by an equally violent interference of Art'. This involved adding huge masses of rock, conducting the water by concealed lead pipes and inserting a substratum over which the rising water would spill, 'wearing itself a channel among the craggy fragments'. The rock was brought from Creswell Crags eight miles away in Derbyshire, 'one of those aweful and picturesque vales in which that County abounds'.[66]

Creswell Crags was part of the Welbeck estate, located just beyond the park (fig. 157).[67] It was not very accessible to the touring public. There was no public road, and it

157 Samuel Hieronymous Grimm, *The Cresswell Crags* (1790). Tate Gallery, London.

158 J. Peltro after Humphry Repton, *The Cascade at Thoresby*, frontispiece to *Peacock's Polite Repository* (1801). Private collection.

could be reached only by calling at Welbeck and requesting one of the attendants to act as guide on a difficult rocky track.[68] So with Portland's permission, and perhaps with the help of his workmen, 'we transported the rocky bed of a mountain stream, and some large masses of stone together with the bushes that were growing in their fissures, these were artfully placed with a large flat slab called Nature's Bridge around which the water foamed and roar'd'.[69]

Repton considered the cascade 'one of the most successful efforts of my art'.[70] He illustrated it for the *Polite Repository* (fig. 158) but not to accompany publication of extracts from the Red Book: 'the best reference is to the spot itself, which will, I trust, long continue to prove my art above the pencil's power to imitate'.[71] Pierrepont was well pleased too: 'The Cascade is perfect – scarce a day passes that I do not cross the "Nature's Bridge" to see and hear the roaring flood. The very rocks appear to shake'.[72]

159 Welbeck Park, 'with the Roads, Drives & Walks either finished in 1793 & 4, proposed to be made', from the Red Book for Welbeck (1793). Private collection.

The cascade was the centrepiece of Repton's plans for the pleasure grounds, which included walks and a new bridge carrying a gravelled approach to the front door (fig. 46).[73] The cascade cost five hundred pounds (although Repton reckoned he saved much expense on earth removal by adapting the existing basin rather than building a new one) and the other improvements another twelve hundred.[74] Pierrepont was happier than Portland with Repton's prudence. He declared Repton 'a Person who to great taste unites great economy. This I will proclaim on the housetop'.[75]

Portland's patronage established a base for Repton in the Midlands and a higher threshold of influence than that offered by his pen-friend Anna Seward and her literary circle. Writing to Repton from Mansfield Woodhouse near Welbeck in 1791, Seward said: 'I seem to be in a domain of yours, since everywhere I go you are mentioned'. Seward was keen to gain the duke and duchess of Portland's influence, through Repton, on behalf of an 'accomplished youth', one William Otter, 'at present wholly unprovided for': 'You are benevolent, and have the Duke's ear. I wish you would try to animate his attention and friendship towards a rising genius . . . you, who have been long one of the most ingenious, and who are now the busiest of human beings'.[76]

The range of Portland's influence enabled Repton to establish bases in many counties. Repton recalled Cobham Hall in Kent, seat of the Whig nobleman Lord Darnley, as 'one of the first places of great importance to which I was introduced by the Duchess of Portland'. In return, Repton was asked to supply some intelligence: 'the Duke said he should be anxious to know my opinion of the place, and still more anxious to hear my opinion of its young Lord'. After his first visit in July 1790, Repton was glad to compile a report to the Portlands on the character and prospects of Darnley and Cobham. Darnley was spoilt and vain, but

> naturally affectionate and benevolent, and I think I may predict that this will be the source of his future happiness if he should become a husband and father . . . his ideas are very magnificent, and they have already been realized by very costly specimens of architecture from designs by James Wyatt [the mausoleum and the interior of the music room]. But while such great works are nearly completed, little or nothing at present seems done for the comfort of the place . . . The Park is extensive, the trees large and the verdure beautiful, but there are no walks, no shrubberies, no agremens, nor any object of interest to ladies. We must give it time.

Repton used the Red Book for Cobham to initiate a twenty-five-year programme of improvements, which culminated in surrounding the mansion with gardens and dressed walks and seeing 'the fulfillment of my predictions of domestic happiness'.[77]

160 'Design for a Cottage in the wood'; 'Design for altering a Cottage', from the Red Book for Welbeck (1793). Private collection.

In May 1793 Portland commissioned a second Red Book for Welbeck.

> Three years have since elapsed, in which the experience derived from the constant practice of my profession, the more intimate knowledge of scenery at Welbeck, and above all the encouragement I have received from your Grace's patronage and approbation of my former designs, induce me to submit some further remarks on the same subject for your Grace's perusal.

The scope of this Red Book is much broader than the first. It covers a far greater area, to the borders of the park, and includes such features as cottages, lodges, gates and roads that form connections with the estate at large. A number of differences in the presentation of the respective Red Books declare Repton's ambition. The sketch map of walks around the house is supplanted by a finely drawn map by the duke's surveyor of the park as a whole, showing work in progress and that proposed (fig. 159). Whereas the first Red Book was organized in terms of specific sites at Welbeck, 'The West Front', 'The Dress'd Walk', 'The Sheep Walk' and so on, the second is organized according to the generic categories that came to characterize all the Red Books, such as 'Situation', 'Character' and 'View from the House'. Each section contains essays making general observations, for example on ground-shaping and architecture. Indeed, the occasion of the Red Book was a more crucial stage in Repton's career than the improvements at Welbeck. He was preparing *Sketches and Hints* for publication, and the Red Book gave him 'an opportunity of explaining and elucidating some general principles by referring to the scenery of Welbeck'.[78]

The second Welbeck Red Book demonstrates the increasingly architectural definition of Repton's style, his deployment of various built structures (some designed by William Wilkins) including lodges, cottages, bridges, boathouses, fences and roadways to accentuate the social character of scenery (fig. 160). The section on views from the house provides a key axiom for *Sketches and Hints*. The setting for a palatial mansion like Welbeck, Repton declared, should not be just extensive but 'magnificent'. While forests and parks share the ingredients of trees, grass, water, oaks and deer, park scenery was distinguished by its artefacts:

> A park has a character distinct from a forest, for while we admire and even imitate the romantic wildness of Nature, we ought never to forget that a park is a habitation of men, and not solely devoted to beasts of the forest. I am convinced that some enthusiastic admirers of uncultivated Nature are too apt to overlook this distinction. Park scenery compared with forest scenery, is like a historical picture compared

161 'General view of the South and East fronts, taken from the mouth of one of the Valleys in the Park', from the Red Book for Welbeck (1803). Private collection. Photograph Nottinghamshire County Libraries.

162 Gothic gate, from the Red Book for Welbeck (1793). Private collection.

with a landscape; nature must prevail in both, but that which relates to man should have a higher place in the scale of arts... Woods enriched by buildings, water enlivened by a number of pleasure boats, alike contribute to mark a visible difference betwixt the magnificent scenery of a park, and that of a sequestered forest: the trees, the water, the lawns, and the deer are common to both.[79]

Repton proposed repeating the trademark Gothic of the Welbeck mansion throughout the artefacts of the park, from the boathouse to the gates at the lodges (fig. 162). By designing these buildings and structures, Repton wished to extend 'English Gardening' beyond its 'more confined sense of *Horticulture*' evident in 'the well known labours of Mr. Speechly ... and from many other books produced by kitchen gardeners'.[80]

While the second Welbeck Red Book formed part of the 'ground-work' of *Sketches and Hints*, little was implemented at Welbeck.[81] Portland experienced a deepening

165

financial crisis in the mid-1790s, and after his wife died in 1794 he made over Welbeck to his newly wedded son, the marquess of Tichfield. Tichfield wished to relieve his father of 'a deadweight' that could be 'of no possible comfort during his continuance in administration'. Retaining only a room at Welbeck for occasional use, Portland resided at Burlington House and Bulstrode.[82] He commissioned Repton again to design a font as a gift for his son's first child, which Repton proudly claimed as an example of his virtuosity: 'one of the most sumptuous presents of gold plate which was ever executed in this country: it consisted of a basin, in the form of a broad flat vase, and pedestal, around which were the figures of Faith, Hope, and Charity'.[83]

When Tichfield took over Welbeck, he undertook a new programme of estate improvements, incorporating some of Repton's proposals for the grounds.[84] He commissioned Repton for a third Red Book for Welbeck in 1803. This is an un-executed scheme, largely the work of John Adey Repton, for a new Classical-style house on a knoll in the deer park (fig. 161):

> The Abbey and the surrounding Trees coeval with the building itself have alike suffered by the lapse of ages. Those venerable oaks which no axe had dared approach, have gradually fallen under the Scythe of Time, while the Mansion from the changes, the additions & repairs of various Generations, has lost almost every advantage of its original Situation. However the mind may be gratified with contemplating the rude and decayed trunks of trees which have outlived the common period of vegetation, they excite a degree of Melancholy incompatible with the cheerful enjoyment of modern life. For these reasons it is now become advisable to remove the site of the mansion to some other part of Welbeck Park, where different generations of the same Family, may live among generations of Trees that the Family has judiciously provided to succeed those whose existence can no further be prolonged.[85]

## Bulstrode

At two thousand acres, the Portland seat at Bulstrode in Buckinghamshire was a fraction the size of Welbeck but a valuable property in an expensive area in which many jostled for land and influence (fig. 163). Bulstrode occupied a strategic location. Less than twenty miles, a morning's ride, from Westminster on the Oxford road, it was part of a densely emparked zone around the Thames Valley settled by the Hanoverian Court, a region styled and restyled by successive waves of professional landscaping.[86] A park of more than six-hundred acres occupied nearly one third of the Bulstrode estate.[87] It was extensively fashioned, initially in a formal layout, perhaps by Henry Wise, later de-formalized in the style of Capability Brown.[88] This was an area with a high concentration of commissions by Brown and his imitators.[89] A hill-top site, Bulstrode commanded extensive views, one to the south terminated by Windsor Castle five miles away.[90] Under the second duke, Bulstrode was a cultural as well as a political centre. The duchess was a celebrated patron of natural philosophy, especially botany, and her garden of rare plants and museum of shells and minerals attracted many discerning visitors, including the king and queen.[91]

The third duke took possession of Bulstrode after his mother's death in 1785. He sold the contents of the natural history museum but redeveloped the flower and kitchen gardens and extensively replanted and landscaped the park (figs 164 and 165).[92] The park and home farm supplied the households at Bulstrode and Burlington House with produce; it was not a model agricultural estate, rather an amenity one.[93] Portland preferred Bulstrode to Welbeck as a family residence, and it was obviously convenient for his political career.[94] He

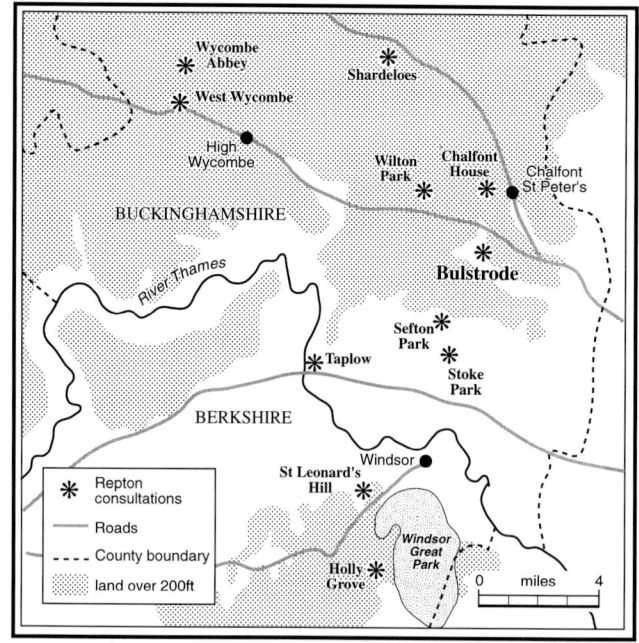

163 Bulstrode and the surrounding country.

counted allies among his neighbours, including Burke three miles along the Oxford road at Gregorys.[95] As a county seat, Bulstrode was a bulwark against rival political interests, notably the dukes of Buckingham.[96] During Portland's financial crisis of 1795, when Bulstrode was costing more than four thousand pounds a year to run, and when a valuation of more than eighty-five thousand attracted an eager buyer, Portland was willing to give up 'my garden, my flowers, my plants, my trees' for a smaller place half the distance from London, but not at the price of abandoning the family's parliamentary seat.[97] Nor did he. With his son installed at Welbeck, Portland continued to develop the house, park, gardens and pleasure grounds, spending up to seven thousand pounds a year.[98] Portland maintained Bulstrode's function as a cultural rendezvous. During one visit in 1800 Repton's fellow guest was the botanist bishop of Carlisle, Samuel Goodenough; on another in 1808 the music historian and old Norfolk friend Charles Burney.[99] Repton first visited Bulstrode in 1790 and made regular calls thereafter. The visits helped to secure commissions both nearby and on the estates of visitors and passers by.[100] On the look-out for landscapers for his park at Kenwood, Lord Stormont admired the improvements at Bulstrode in July 1791 and made a memorandum in his Account Book:

> Mr Ruffort who calls himself (I have probably mistaken the name as Lanolon spells it Repton) a Landscape Gardener and whose Residence is at Hare Street near Rumford is a very ingenious man has an admirable eye and lays out ground remarkably well. He is imployed by the D of Portland . . . He has succeeded full well at Bulstrode. I saw his Improvts there July 1791.[101]

Until the mid-1790s, and possibly before Repton's involvement, the contract for executing the landscaping was in the hands of Samuel Lapidge who had taken over Capability Brown's business, and day-to-day supervision was directed by Brown's former foreman William Ireland.[102] While Repton described the groundwork at Bulstrode as correcting the distortions of 'the geometric taste in gardening', he may also have been mindful of correcting the customary practice of the contractors:[103]

> One of the greatest difficulties I have experienced in practice proceeds from that fondness for levelling, so prevalent in all Brown's workmen: every hillock by them is lowered, and every hollow filled to produce a level surface . . . Such operations must, of course, be

164  J. Peltro after Humphry Repton, *Bulstrode in Buckinghamshire, a Seat of His Grace the Duke of Portland*, frontispiece to *Peacock's Polite Repository* (1805). Victoria and Albert Museum.

165  J. Peltro after Humphry Repton, *Flower Garden at Bulstrode*, from *Peacock's Polite Repository* (1802). Victoria and Albert Museum. V&A Picture Library.

> confined to subjects of small extent, and it is in these that they produce great beauty and variety . . . I may refer to examples of this mode of levelling ground at Bulstrode, where two small dells in the flower-garden are united into one valley.[104]

The duke directed the work. In *Observations*, Repton describes operations at Bulstrode as

> Among the greatest examples of moving ground . . . under the direction of his Grace the Duke of Portland himself; whose good taste will not suffer any part of that beautiful park to be disguised by the misjudging taste of former times, and who, by opening the valleys and taking away a great depth of earth from the stems of the largest trees, which had formally been

buried, is, by degrees, restoring the surface of the ground to its original and natural shape.[105]

In his Memoir, Repton reported that Portland employed

> more than fifty children who were furnished with little spades and wheelbarrows in proportion to their strength – and he had mild beer brewed on purpose for them – sometimes he would order their dinner bell to ring half an hour before the usual time, for the sake of witnessing the joy such an unexpected event produced on their happy faces.[106]

Repton's account of the landscaping of Bulstrode in *Observations*, in which he doubles the young labour force, suggests more strongly that they are paupers:

> In this great work are occasionally employed, among the more efficient labourers, a hundred children, from ten to fifteen years old, who are thus early trained to habits of wholesome industry, far different from the foul air and confinement of spinning in a cotton-mill; to the benevolent observer no object can be more delightful than park scenery thus animated.[107]

Part of the park was in the parish of Iver, where Sir Thomas Bernard, the founder of the Society for Bettering the Condition of the Poor, lived and was locally active in promoting his principles of getting children out of the workhouse or the factory into the fields for work or into schools for instruction.[108]

Repton's main brief at Bulstrode was to design a drive system and fashion a series of specialist gardens, including an 'ancient garden' and an 'American garden'.[109] In 1800 he sent to his old schoolfriend James Edward Smith, founder of the Linnean Society, a letter from Bulstrode that reveals his concerns about 'my ignorance in botany', for he saw it as an impediment to aristocratic patronage.[110]

The main published account of Repton's contribution to Bulstrode is his detailed description of the drive being constructed accompanied by a map of its route (fig. 166).[111] The map is one of the few that Repton published and by far the most comprehensive and elaborate, displaying not just the park but virtually the whole of the estate. The main elements of relief are hachured and different kinds of land use shaded and the main features labelled or keyed. Finely drawn and engraved, with a compass rose and scale, it includes an elegantly scripted dedication to Portland. The map also appears to be a homage to Capability Brown, whose son had presented Repton with the maps of his 'greatest works', in a region where Brown had established a strong reputation.[112]

One of Repton's complaints about the corruption of Brown's style by 'the numerous herd of his foremen and working gardeners' was the tedium of their circuits: 'we look at [their parks] without interest, and fly from them to farms and fields, even preferring a common or a heath, to the dull round of a walk or drive, without objects and without variety'.[113] At Bulstrode the existing drive went through the woods with 'a total absence of interest or variety of objects'. The drive Repton designed touched almost every part of the estate and took in many kinds of scenery. Repton asks his readers to trace its course on the map through no less than forty-four stations. Going over knolls and dells and taking some sharp curves, the drive passes cottages, copses, various gardens, plantations, paddocks, sheep pasture, meadows, fields, rough ground, lawns, open groves, farmhouses, farmyards, drinking pools, green ways, common land, two villages, ancient trees and a Roman camp.

Repton published the Bulstrode map and description not just for its specific features but 'as an archetype or example, from whence certain principles are reduced to practice'. Repton derived many of these principles, he acknowledged, from Thomas Whately's *Observations on Modern Gardening* (1770).[114] Whately advocated Brown's style, and his description of Brown's approach at Caversham, with its rapidly changing views, within and without the park, is reflected in Repton's design for Bulstrode. Moreover, Whately was a useful authority in Repton's dispute with connoisseurs of the picturesque and their contempt for a cartographic vision of landscaping, 'the map of all my lord's estate' as Knight put it.[115] Whately's treatise begins:

> Gardening is superior to landskip painting, as a reality to a representation: it is an exertion of fancy, a subject for taste . . . it is no longer confined to the spots from which it borrows its name, but regulates also the disposition and embellishments of a park, a farm, or a riding.[116]

Bulstrode, Repton declared, 'must be acknowledged one of the most beautiful [parks] in England, yet I doubt whether Claude himself could find, in its whole extent, a single station from whence a picture could be formed. I mention this as a proof of the little affinity between pictures and scenes in nature'.[117]

Repton's description and map of Bulstrode made the park accessible to the reading public; they are effectively a guided tour. Three entrances from main roads, from London, Windsor and Oxford, form approaches to the

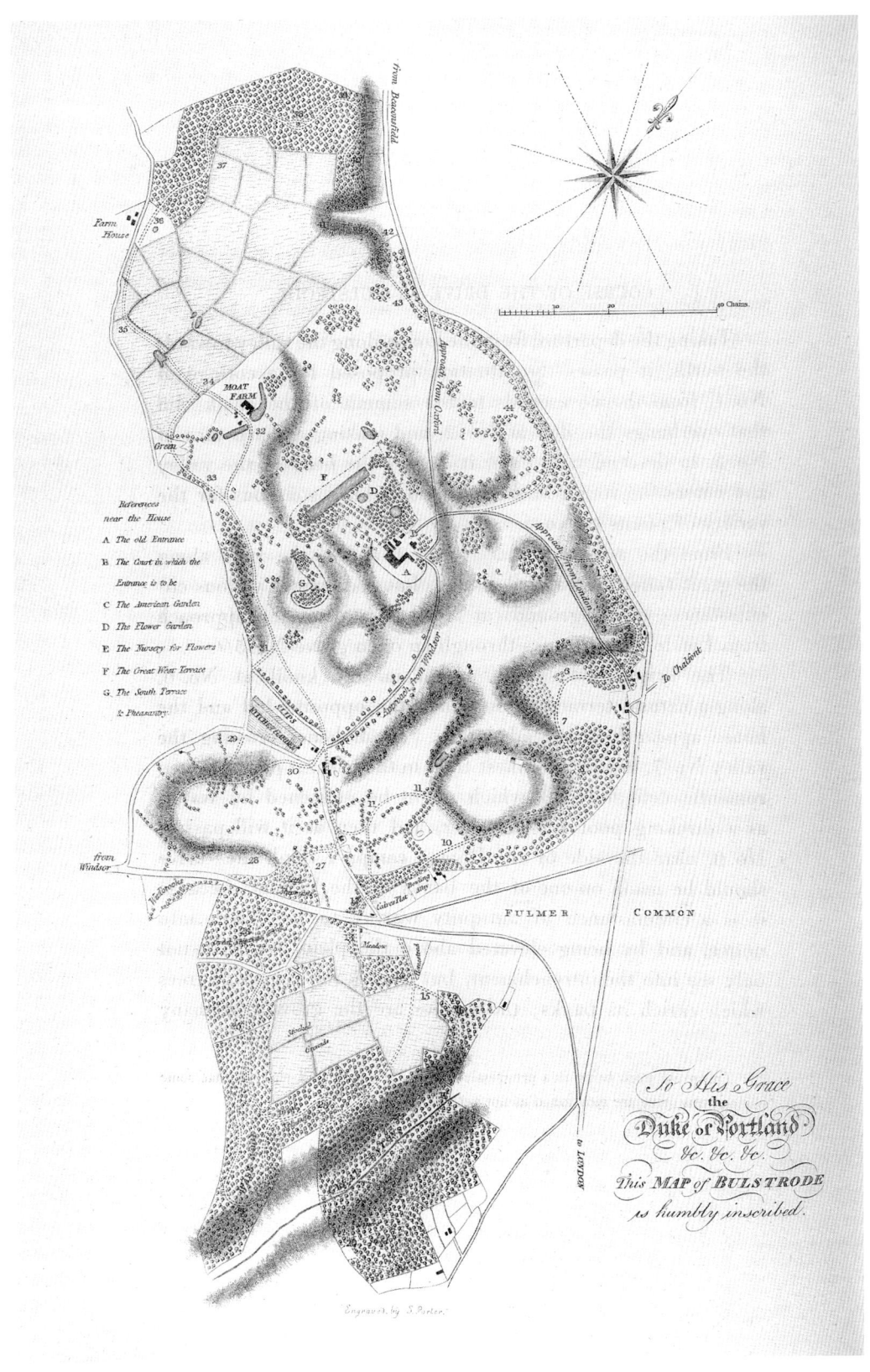

166 *Map of Bulstrode*, from *Observations on the Theory and Practice of Landscape Gardening* (1803). Yale Center for British Art, Paul Mellon Collection.

mansion and connecting routes to the drive system. Writing after Portland's death, Repton reported that the duke

> gave leave to all persons to pass through the park at Bulstrode, and even encouraged the neighbouring inhabitants to play at cricket on the lawn. How different is this from the too common orders given at the gates and lodges of new places, recently purchased by strangers, and only visible to themselves and their own inmates! For the honour of the country, let the parks and pleasure-grounds of England be ever open to cheer the hearts and delight the minds of all.[118]

## The Duke of Bedford

The sixth duke of Bedford (1766–1839) was Repton's most important patron during the last decade of his career. Bedford commissioned designs for his family seat at Woburn, Bedfordshire, residential squares in Bloomsbury, London, a holiday home at Endsleigh and a hotel in Tavistock on his Devon estate. Bedford introduced Repton to the Prince of Wales, paving the way for the commission at the Royal Pavilion, Brighton. For a brief period, while the duke of Portland was still alive, Repton was well connected to both political wings of high society. The year 1805, which began with the Red Book for Woburn and ended with that for the Royal Pavilion, Repton recalled as the 'pinnacle of my ambition'.[119] In subsequent years the income from Bedford's patronage alone helped to cushion Repton's professional and physical decline.[120]

Politically reformist, artistically avant-garde, Bedford cut a contrasting figure to the duke of Portland. He is mentioned only in passing (as a contact for the Prince of Wales) among clients in Repton's Memoir. While Bedford does not appear among the moral worthies in this portfolio of character sketches, neither does he appear, even anonymously, among the rogues. Repton did not know Bedford well, or familiarly, enough. The duke was abroad for significant periods, from 1806 to 1809 and in 1814 and '15, during Repton's commissions for him. Repton's main dealings were with Bedford's senior staff, two of whom, the inventor Robert Salmon and attorney William Adam, famous men in their own right and with whom he seems to have cultivated the kind of intimacy he enjoyed with favourite clients, do appear in the Memoir.[121] In Repton's letters to Adam, the duke appears a remote but not unsympathetic figure. There was much about Bedford's aristocratic style that appealed to Repton's later sensibilities. He displayed a modern, cosmopolitan taste for art and fashion and an enthusiasm for English antiquarianism, focussed on the period of his own family's aristocratic origins in the reign of Henry VIII. If the Bedford dukedom was conferred by a Hanoverian monarch, it succeeded a Tudor earldom and recognized the family's role in preserving the Protestant succession. In respect to Repton's employment Bedford and Portland were similar figures. Both promoted progressive estate improvements, took a keen interest in horticulture and lavished enormous sums on restyling their grounds and houses.

The Bedford estate was one of the largest and most lucrative in Britain. The three main country estates, at Woburn, Tavistock and Thorney, Cambridgeshire, together with a scattering of smaller properties in Dorset and Buckinghamshire, totalled more than eighty thousand acres. The 119-acre London estate was immensely valuable. From the seventeenth century, the dukes of Bedford had earned a reputation for advanced estate development, from the large-scale reclamation of fenland in Cambridgeshire, to improvement of agriculture at Woburn, to the building of Bloomsbury as an upper-class residential precinct, to the exploitation of mining consols in Devon. By the early nineteenth century, management was highly bureaucratic, each local estate organized in to 'departments' overseen by agents of professional standing. The entire Bedford estate was presided over from its London office by an 'auditor', an agent-in-chief, William Adam, the leading Whig lawyer and a Scottish MP. Adam strove to control expenditure on innovative projects that engaged a large and skilled permanent staff, relatively well-paid labourers and the best professional expertise money could buy.[122]

## Woburn Abbey

From the later 1780s, under the fifth duke, the family seat of Woburn Abbey was extensively redeveloped. After the demolition of Bedford House, Bloomsbury, in 1800, Woburn Abbey became the family mansion (fig. 167). Readily accessible to London along Watling Street, Woburn was developed as a large-scale showpiece of the Bedford's advanced tastes and opinions. While the redeveloped 30,000-acre estate and its 3,000-acre park dominated Bedfordshire, it was part of a broader influx of money into the county that gave it a smartly metropolitan air. The Bedfords settled in the county from London along with scores of successful merchants and businessmen, notably their political ally, the brewer Samuel Whitbread, who purchased the 10,000-acre estate of Southill from the Torrington family and refashioned it in the style of his ducal neighbours.[123]

The fifth duke employed Henry Holland, the Prince of Wales's architect at Carlton House, to remodel Woburn Abbey. Holland designed a new range of rooms on the south, including a magnificent new library. He opened a new entrance to the east, and here extended the courtyard in to a large square flanked by new buildings: a riding-house, a tennis court and a greenhouse, which was transformed in 1800 in to a sculpture gallery, with a miniature Temple of Liberty displaying busts of Bedford's political friends. He laid out pleasure grounds adjacent to the mansion to provide a setting for a Chinese Dairy with fine porcelain for ladies to make butter.[124] Holland took on landscaping around his architectural improvements, arguing that if he failed to do so the duke would have to employ 'some such person as Repton or Eames or Haverfield or Malcolm'.[125]

Robert Salmon, Holland's former assistant at Carlton House, was employed permanently at Woburn as clerk of the works and, as well as designing a model farm within the park, turned his hand to a series of award-winning inventions, including machines for ploughing, sowing, reaping, pruning and haymaking, canal equipment, surgical instruments and a 'humane man trap'.[126] Bedford instituted week-long agricultural shows known as 'sheep shearings', held at the model farm, with exhibitions of state-of-the-art machinery and livestock. He employed a succession of progressive figures at Woburn, such as the geologist John Farey and the planter William Pontey, noted for their theoretical as well as practical views on estate improvement.[127] For a period in the mid-1790s, the duke's patronage of both political radicalism and agricultural experiment alarmed conservative spokesmen.[128] Burke's pamphlet, *A Letter to a Noble Lord* (1796), warned Bedford that his landed possessions were 'a downright insult upon the rights of man'. They were more extensive than the territory of many states in Europe and more fertile than most. The 'geographers and geometricians' of revolutionary France 'want new lands for new trials', and while they 'have an eye on his grace's lands, their chemists are not less taken with his buildings'.[129]

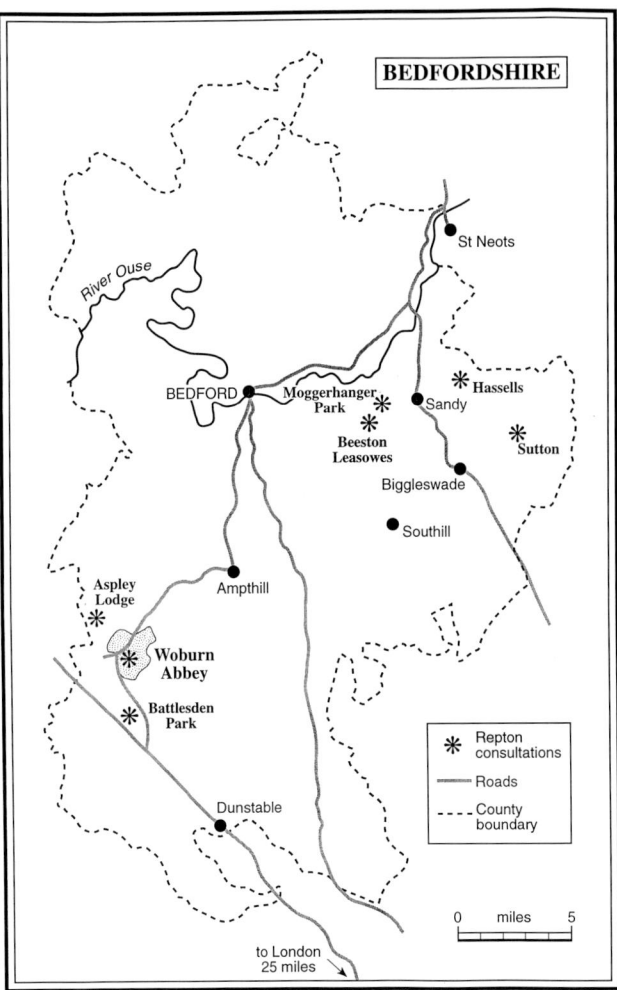

167  Humphry Repton Consultations in Bedfordshire.

Inheriting the estate in 1803, upon the death of his elder brother in a tennis accident, the sixth duke extended the experimental regime at Woburn. Salmon's responsibilities were extended first to forestry, in which he undertook a campaign of close pruning, and then, as steward, to directing the entire operation of the estate.[130] The model farm was augmented with workshops, a steam engine and a timber yard, 'resembling...the regular arrangements of a dockyard', and machines made there were advertized for sale.[131] The annual sheep shearings were expanded. Portrayed with the specimens of livestock in George Garrard's engraving of the shearing of 1811 (fig. 168) are two hundred leading men in the world of agricultural improvement: the duke on horseback inspecting a piece of merino cloth, various friends, staff and consultants, Thomas Coke, Arthur Young, Joseph Banks, Henry Holland, Robert Salmon, William Adam and

168 After George Garrard, *Wobourn Sheepshearing* (1811). Institute of Agricultural History and Museum of Rural Life, University of Reading.

Humphry Davy, and Garrard himself at a table with his agricultural models and medallions.¹³²

The sixth duke instituted a new focus of innovation in horticultural science in gardens adjacent to the mansion. Among the duke's new appointments were George Sinclair, Edmund Cartwright and James Forbes, each charged with investigating a variety of plants, from kale to heather, conducting trials in glasshouses and experimental plots, writing articles in learned journals and in lavish, limited edition volumes. Humphry Repton was one of a number of hired consultants including the chemist Humphry Davy, the botanist James Edward Smith, the seedsman Thomas Gibbs, the glasshouse technologist William Atkinson and the architect Jeffry Wyatville.¹³³

By the time the sixth duke took over Woburn, scientific innovation had lost its revolutionary reputation. In his lectures, to a select audience, in a combined laboratory and lecture theatre at the Royal Institution, Humphrey Davey reformulated agricultural chemistry in paternalist terms.¹³⁴ Under the influence of Joseph Banks, botany, the most popular, even democratic, of sciences, practised in the public house and country lane, became a luxury science based on lavish funds and aristocratic patronage.¹³⁵ Woburn was an important centre in a network of aristocratic estates, including Bulstrode, Whiteknights, Syon Park, Sandwell, Wimpole and Harewood, where horticultural science was established, and it became a leading research institution to rival the Royal Gardens at Kew.¹³⁶

Horticulture was more congenial than agriculture to the duke. He was a great collector, of artworks as well as inventions, books and sculpture as well as plants and shrubs. Attending Woburn Abbey one Sunday in 1804, reluctantly leaving his Suffolk farm on the Sabbath to dine with the duke and his friends, an evangelized Arthur Young noted

> several apartments newly furnished, and many very expensive articles, clocks, &c from Paris to the amount of 2,000l. Much done to the greenhouse, and everywhere a profusion of expense... An extravagant duchess, Paris toys, a great farm, little economy and great debts, will prove a canker in all the rosebuds of his garden of life... What has a Christian to do with such scenes?.[137]

Soon after, in September 1804, Repton paid his first professional call.

The Red Book for Woburn Abbey, submitted in January 1805, is one of the longest and most lavish.[138] A large folio, it runs to ninety indexed pages and has forty-seven drawings, maps and diagrams, including some of Repton's most elaborate watercolours and dramatic scenic transformations. The Red Book was to be worthy of 'the magnificent library in which this volume aspires to hold a place'. The significant word of the Woburn Red Book is 'greatness'. The park was renowned as one of the largest in England, computed in terms of its twelve miles of walling, but the Red Book represents the place's greatness as a quality distinct from its dimensions. It charts the cultural depth and resonance of Woburn, bringing to bear on a number of sites allusions to forms of observational knowledge, botanical, antiquarian, geological, the stock-in-trade of learned societies patronized by the aristocracy; it envisages Woburn reflecting the speculative outlook of the duke. Thus in the section on water, Repton ponders the erosion of valleys of different soils over thousands of years; on bridges and viaducts he suggests a design based on 'those wonderful excavations... which have been lately made known to us by the drawings of Hodges, Daniell and other artists'; the section on drives traces the progress of fashion in planting since Pliny; a design for a gamekeeper's house is assembled from antiquarian engravings of various timber-framed buildings and for its garden from flowers and furniture shown in Tudor portraits.[139]

While the Red Book surveys a variety of sites – entrances, drives, plantations, lakes, bridges and cottages – its focus is the pleasure grounds (fig. 169). The duchess of Bedford exercised a strong influence on the grounds, and it is she who appears fashionably dressed on the balustrade overlooking one of Repton's improved scenes (fig. 170), but Repton's dealings were largely with the duke.[140] One reason that Bedford commissioned Repton was his dissatisfaction with Henry Holland's landscaping. He told Repton: 'Much has been done here, but much remains to be done, and something, I think to *undo*'. He was 'not partial to destroying works recently executed' but wanted Repton 'to freely give me your opinion, as to what alterations or improvements suggest themselves to your judgment, leaving the execution of them to my own discretion or leisure'. While praising Holland's work as an architect, and finding it difficult 'from my delicacy as a professional man how to express disappropriation with the works of another', Repton nevertheless opens the Red Book by declaring 'I must condemn what Mr. Holland has done at Woburn, as a Landscape Gardener'.

169 Repton's Plan for the park at Woburn Abbey, after the plan in the Red Book for Woburn Abbey (1805).

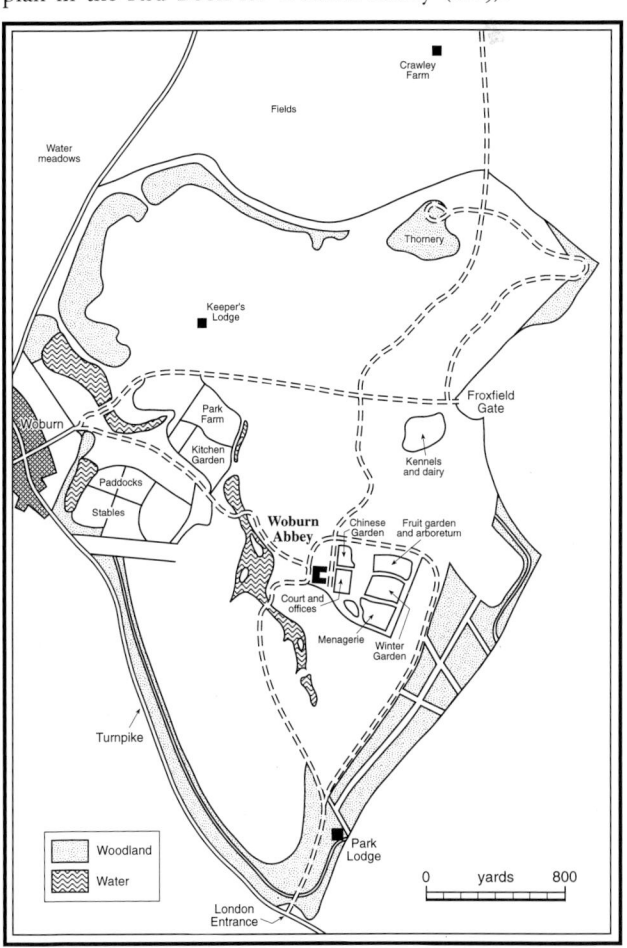

*The present View to the Westward as seen from the windows of the Salon above*

*The same View as proposed to be altered, with the addition of the Portico.*

170 View from the Salon, with and without overlay, from the Red Book for Woburn Abbey (1805). By kind permission of the Marquess of Tavistock and the Trustees of the Bedford Estate.

In burying the lower storey of the south front, Repton claimed that Holland had made a ham-fisted copy of Repton's design for Welbeck, although Holland's work was in fact nearing completion before Repton's first visit to Welbeck.[141] The accounts make it clear that while Repton took charge of landscaping, he collaborated with Holland.[142] Repton's ambition made it politic to do so. Holland not only enjoyed royal patronage but was Capability Brown's son-in-law and sometime collaborator. As part of his attempt to redeem Brown's reputation, Repton published in 1803 a list of Brown's architectural works compiled from papers in Holland's possession.[143]

For the pleasure grounds, Repton designed a co-ordinated series of specialist gardens, extending the grounds and integrating them more closely with Holland's architecture (fig. 171). Repton's vision for this area is highly architectural:

> The gardens or pleasure-grounds near a house may be considered as so many different apartments belonging to its state, its comfort, and its pleasure. The magnificence of the house depends on the number, as well as the size of its rooms; and the similitude between the house and the garden may be justly extended to the mode of decoration . . . If in its unfurnished state there chance to be a looking-glass without a frame, it can only reflect the bare walls; and in like manner a pool of water, without surrounding plantations or other features, reflects only the nakedness of the scene. This similitude might be extended to all articles of furniture for use or ornament required in an apartment, comparing them with the seats and buildings and sculpture appropriate to a garden. Thus the Pleasure Ground at Woburn requires to be enriched and furnished like its Palace, where good taste is everywhere conspicuous.

The covered passage designed by Holland 'enriched with flowers and creeping plants', which connected the stables, riding-house, tennis court and Chinese Dairy, Repton proposed extending to a forcing garden. With hothouses, flue walls and a series of terraced winter gardens, this was to form the centre of a series of specialist gardens, including an American garden, an arboretum, a Chinese garden surrounding the Dairy, a rosary, a taxonomic botanic garden and a menagerie. In the pool-side garden for the Chinese Dairy (fig. 172), Repton suggested planting some recent arrivals that had been 'naturalized in England': *hydrangea macrophylla*, *aucuba japonica* and the repeat-

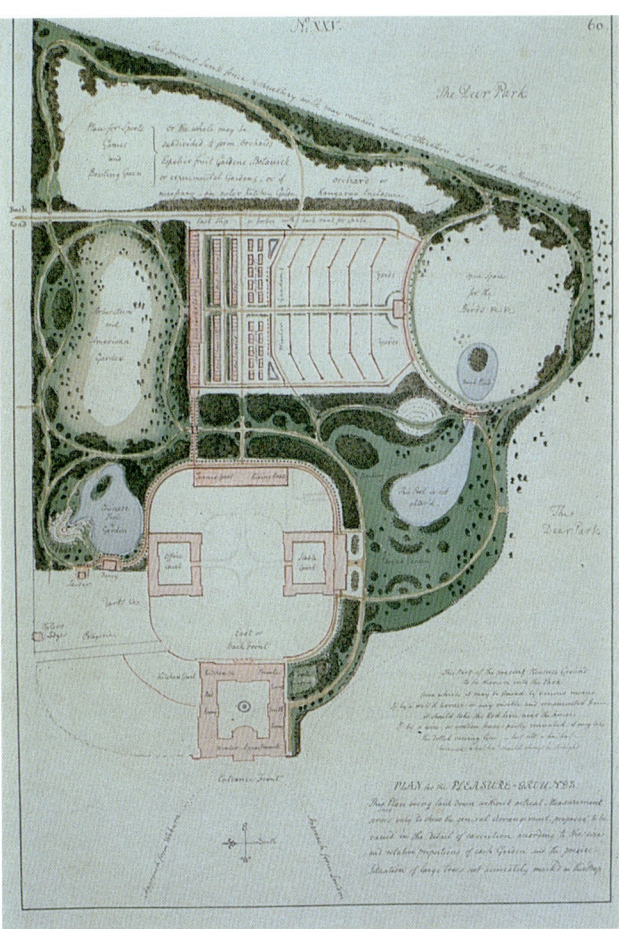

171 Plan for the pleasure grounds, from the Red Book for Woburn Abbey (1805). By kind permission of the Marquess of Tavistock and the Trustees of the Bedford Estate.

flowering China Rose. Repton was careful to avoid the cheap Chinoiserie found 'in the neighbourhood of Islington and Clapham', but the China Rose carried the salacious associations of many luxuriants.[144] In his Memoir he confessed that he had 'of late viewed with a jealous eye the irruption recently made by the new China Rose, which however valuable in winter from its dark glossy foliage and hardy flower is but like a rouged beauty – and must not attempt to vie with the genuine English scented Rose'.[145] A decently 'English garden' took the form of 'a shrubbery walk, connecting the whole', sometimes commanding views into each of the various specialist gardens, into the park and country beyond. The 'Nucleus, that combines the several parts into one magnificent whole' was the forcing garden. Repton illustrates this illuminated on a frosty night, with gardeners working and family and guests promenading (fig. 173).

172 The lakeside by the Dairy and the Chinese Garden, with and without overlay, from the Red Book for Woburn Abbey (1805). By kind permission of the Marquess of Tavistock and the Trustees of the Bedford Estate.

173 The Forcing Garden, from the Red Book for Woburn Abbey (1805). By kind permission of the Marquess of Tavistock and the Trustees of the Bedford Estate.

In the summer of 1805, Robert Salmon prepared a plan to implement Repton's design, and Repton was contracted to direct some of the operations.[146] Groundwork was begun in the late autumn and carried on until the spring of 1806.[147] In his yearly audit of June 1806, William Adam included a progress report. With earth moving, turfing and ditching still underway, the operation was proving costly, the site looked chaotic and nobody seemed fully in control. 'It seems to me that there is more levelling of ground proposed at the Aviary than is necessary – But as Repton did not keep his appointment I had no means of discussing it with anybody who knows the plan, as I doubted from Dowdale's [the site foreman's] description whether he was master of it.' The new gardens were not securely enclosed, and deer were plundering tender plants. Adam had two 'ringleaders' shot because 'many hundred pounds worth of plants might have been destroyed', ordered fencing and proposed a new ditch to be excavated.[148] The following year Adam reported that the pleasure ground was in better shape. Dowdale's labour force had been increased and paths were being completed, bare earth now neatly turfed, planting progressing and glasshouses in good order. Repton had sent some working drawings but there was little sign of the man himself. 'Mr Repton has never been here since the Duke went to Ireland but once and it is thought he should not be asked to come until the Duke has time to see and consider things.'[149]

If Repton neglected his plan for Woburn on the ground during the duke's absence, he developed it for publication. Large extracts from the Red Book form the centrepiece of *An Enquiry into the Changes of Taste in Landscape Gardening*, published in 1806. This was an inexpensive, un-illustrated volume, targeted at a different 'class of purchasers' than his previous ones, but pursuing the speculative line of the lavish Woburn Red Book.[150]

174 After Humphry Repton, *The Thornery at Woburn Abbey*, from *Peacock's Polite Repository* (1810). Private collection.

The *Enquiry* elaborates a preface commissioned by Thomas Martyn, professor of botany at Cambridge, for the new edition of *The Gardener's Dictionary* (1807), in which Repton proposed to 'take up the History of Landscape Gardening from the period when Mr. Walpole left off, and trace it from Kent, through Brown, to the present time'. For Repton the motor of change was 'fashion', 'the love of *change* or *novelty* in a few, and of *sameness* or *imitation* in the many'. 'If persons only of superior sense were the leaders, or if mankind always examined what they followed, fashion might, perhaps, be more reasonable.' There was currently a taste for the exotic, in particular for forms of Indian scenery and architecture: 'When a partiality for such forms is patronized and supported by the highest rank, and the acknowledged taste, it becomes a duty of the professor to raise the importance, by increasing the variety of his art'. Repton had to contend with rival 'professors of the fine arts', such as Price and Knight, who, as self-conscious connoisseurs, were proud to formulate their views independently; 'yet my *practice* has been supported by the first characters in the kingdom'. Designed for a middle-class readership, the *Enquiry* affirms the virtue of hereditary landed culture. Along with material from the Woburn Red Book is a report of Repton's work for the Bedfords in Bloomsbury, as well as extracts from a recent commission at Longleat for the marquess of Bath. The other main extracts are from Stanage and Longner, for ancient, if not titled, families. The *Enquiry* presents a cautionary tale. Fashion was fortunately 'a source of wealth and commerce', but 'we daily see wealth, acquired by industry, or by fortunate speculations, succeeding to the hereditary estates of the most ancient families; and we see the descendants of these families reduced by the vain attempt to vie with the successful sons of commerce'.[151]

After the duke of Bedford's return from Ireland in 1806, Repton resumed his regular visits to Woburn, staying every spring for up to ten days at a time. Finding other work increasingly hard to come by, Repton came to rely heavily on Bedford's patronage. He worked hard on various sites around the park, notably a Thornery (fig. 174), in which 'are to be found every species of thorns which will bear the climate' and a drive flanked by evergreens, 'a circumstance of grandeur, of variety, of novelty, and, I may add, of winter comfort'.[152] He paid frequent visits to Robert Salmon, 'the most ingenious man I have ever known', enquiring about making an artificial hand and a building material, pise, with which Salmon had constructed his house at Woburn, as well as consulting him on the woods and plantations.[153] 'It is bitter cold weather here but I potter about after the different workmen & come in to drop at 6', Repton told his wife in April 1809; the following year he told his son William that he had 'been on foot from 11 – till 6 – & am tired and hungry'.[154]

Repton used his visits to Woburn to advance his botanical reputation. From information gathered in the winter of 1808–9 he presented a paper on ivy to the Linnean Society in April 1810. This was dedicated to his former schoolfriend and the Society's founding president, James Edward Smith, now strongly patronized by the duke of Bedford. Repton supported Linnaeus against the opinion expressed by most other authorities (including John Evelyn and Joseph Banks) that ivy was a destroyer of trees. The manuscript was written at Woburn, an important site in Repton's survey:

At Woburn Abbey the timber has so generally been denuded of Ivy, that I despaired of finding any example . . . I afterwards discovered in the park a remarkable specimen, which is the outermost tree of a grove, and the most exposed to the south-west. The tree nearest to it has some dead branches, and seems evidently to have yielded to its neighbour's superior vigour. As this is an example obvious to all the agriculturalists who attend the Woburn sheep shearing, I have, with the Duke's permission, marked a drive very near this specimen, which may serve to call the attention of the curious to this subject. I should further add the result of some experiments made by Mr. Salmon,

175  *The Cottage at Aspley Wood*, from *Fragments on the Theory and Practice of Landscape Gardening* (1816). Yale Center for British Art, Paul Mellon Collection.

In 1810 Repton made an addition to the Red Book, displaying his antiquarian interests. The duke

> one day observed, that out of the numerous cottages called Gothic, which everywhere present themselves near the high roads, he had never seen one which did not betray its modern character and recent date. At the same time, his Grace expresses a desire to have a cottage of the style and date of buildings prior to the reign of Henry VIII, of which only some imperfect fragments now remain.[156]

The cottage that Repton proposed was a keeper's house on the estate at Aspley Wood, about three miles from Woburn Abbey (fig. 175). John Adey Repton was largely responsible for the design, made up of 'some curious specimens of timber buildings', printed in *Archaeologia*, the journal of the Society of Antiquaries. Among the sources were fragments of fifteen buildings from various sites in the eastern counties. The ornaments painted on posts and rails were taken from a portrait of Henry VIII

176  English School, *Edward Lord Russell, Son of Francis, Earl of Bedford* (1573), detail. By kind permission of the Marquess of Tavistock and the Trustees of the Bedford Estate.

who is well known for his mechanic ingenuity, and who has the superintendence of His Grace's woods at Woburn. He tried the comparative substance and strength of several kinds of timber with the same kinds *Ivy-bound* as he calls it; but he could not find any difference, and is of the opinion 'that in old trees it does not harm . . .' but he is still convinced that he has seen young trees killed by the Ivy . . . But experience has discovered that the destruction of turnips and other plants while young, and the thinning of green fruit from trees, is a part of the economy of nature.

Repton demanded 'a less rigorous persecution of the plant' (he told Smith that Banks called it a *'vegetable beast of prey'*), for the leaves and berries of ivy provided food in winter for livestock and game, and it did much to 'improve the beauty of our winter scenery'.[155]

and his family at the Society of Antiquaries. The Reptons attempted to 'assimilate a garden to the same character', taking hints from various Tudor paintings and engravings.[157] The design of the garden and the selection of flowers were taken from details in portraits in the picture gallery at Woburn (fig. 176).[158]

Perhaps in recognition of his various works at Woburn, George Garrard exhibited a bust of Repton at the Royal Academy in the summer of 1810, but it failed to find a place with his earlier bust of Holland in the sculpture gallery at Woburn.[159] Publishing much of the Red Book for Woburn in *Fragments*, Repton reported that his plans at Woburn 'have no where been so fully realized'.[160] Bedford was keen to establish his personal role in the work. 'It was *I*', he told his son, 'who carried the approach from the London entrance to the west front assisted by Repton . . . Repton was a coxcomb, but he had infinitely more genius than one half of his critics and detractors'.[161]

Repton's designs for Woburn helped to establish his horticultural reputation. In *Fragments* Repton indicates that, while the 'disposition' of the gardens had been completed, a number, including the forcing garden, and the American garden, had yet to be constructed and a new one, a botanic garden for grasses, had been included.[162] This was the responsibility of George Sinclair, appointed 'botanist gardener' at Woburn.[163] Sinclair undertook a programme of investigating which grasses were profitable for different kinds of pasture, conducting field trials and writing up his findings in *Hortus Gramineus Woburniensis* (1816), illustrated by actual specimens, dried and coloured, with examples of seed.[164] Sinclair later reported for the first number of Loudon's *Gardener's Magazine* on the pleasures of cultivating botanical arrangements of grasses in pleasure grounds and flower gardens.[165] By the time Woburn's gardener James Forbes described the pleasure grounds in *Hortus Woburniensis* (1833), Repton's design had been further adapted to the duke's botanical demands, with a heathery, pinery, holly garden, willow garden and camellia house.[166] The space that had been the 'nucleus' of Repton's design, the walled enclave of the forcing garden, was now turfed and planted, but the framework of Repton's plan of thirty years earlier had been retained. Forbes was keen to give Repton credit for the design of the pleasure grounds and so was the main guidebook to Woburn Abbey.[167]

\* \* \*

## Bloomsbury

The earliest of the Bedfords' London estates, Covent Garden, was granted by the Crown in the sixteenth century and developed in the seventeenth in a regular layout of square and terrace, the template for fashionable urban development in the capital. The family acquired Bloomsbury, the adjacent estate to the north, from the earls of Southampton through marriage in the late seventeenth century, and proceeded to develop it along a similar pattern but with much tighter controls on building and leasing to preclude some of the piecemeal and commercial developments at Covent Garden. The central feature was the ducal mansion, Bedford House, which formed the north side of what became known as Bloomsbury Square and enjoyed an uninterrupted vista to the hills of Hampstead and Highgate. From the 1770s the pasture lands beyond its pleasure grounds were developed with more comprehensive planning and design controls to create a highly uniform suburb of squares and terraces. Initially the fifth duke intended Bedford House and its pleasure grounds to form an integral part of the northward development, and in 1795 he commissioned a plan, probably from Henry Holland, to show this. But meaner streets were encroaching from the Foundling Estate to the east, and the potential value of so large an area of building land could not be ignored, so another plan was drawn up in 1800 that proposed demolishing Bedford House and gardens and covering the site with a succession of streets and squares. If some commentators lamented the demolition, and were critical of so speculative a development, others applauded an initiative that was employing so many in a period of the war that had largely checked building elsewhere in London (fig. 177).[168]

The landscaping of London squares with trees, shrubs, lawns, statuary, seats, gravel paths and railings had been in progress throughout the eighteenth century. Improvement acts were used to raise a local rate for construction, planting and maintenance. Some landowners commissioned leading professional landscapers and began planting well before building to enable gardens to mature, but many left the design in the hands of speculative builders who opted for cheap designs.[169]

By the early nineteenth century, the landscaping of London squares and its implications for a civic vision for the world's fastest growing city were matters of public debate. In 1803, on his first stay in London from Scotland, the 21-year-old John Claudius Loudon opened his campaign for professional recognition in the *Literary Journal* by attacking the way squares had been laid out and planted and offering some proposals of his own to enhance 'the beauty of the metropolis, the health of its inhabitants; and even in some degree to the honour of the British nation'. 'Nothing can be more ridiculous than the formal clumps and patches that disfigure and distort our squares at present; they are totally destitute of connection or harmony, with each other, or with the surrounding scenery.' The laying out of London squares 'has ever been committed to what are called *ground-workers* – illiterate men, ignorant of the principles of taste, they have no idea of design in gardening'. Loudon had little more time for 'the arrangement of trees, shrubs and flowers, as everywhere practised by *landscape gardeners* [which] I hold to be totally in opposition to the principles of taste, or utility'. Loudon proposed planting on the 'same principles of natural scenery', choosing as his example 'natural Forests' with their particular associations of tree, shrub and flower.[170]

Loudon headed his article with his address in Bedford Row on the edge of Bloomsbury, and probably directed his comments at Repton's landscaping of Russell Square, after Lincoln's Inn Fields the largest square in London. The starting date of Repton's commission is not clear. The building contractor, James Burton, offered to enclose and plant Russell Square along with Bedford Square for the fifth duke of Bedford, 'either according to his own plan or according to the more elaborate plan of James Gubbins, the Duke's surveyor'.[171] Soon after his brother's death in 1802, the sixth duke seems to have commissioned Repton to create a garden focussing on a commemorative statue. While the duke was keen to oversee landscaping of squares in Bloomsbury, the committee of rate-paying residents (who represented such powerful figures as Sir Samuel Romilly and Sir Thomas Lawrence) had a decisive role in the design process.[172] There is no surviving manuscript design. Repton published the details of work in progress in *Enquiry*, partly in answer to the kind of proposals Loudon advocated.[173]

The work already done in Russell Square was not to Repton's liking. 'The ground of this area had all been brought to one level plain at too great an expense to admit of its being altered; and the great size of the square is, in a manner, lost by this insipid shape.'[174] The committee raising subscriptions for Richard Westmacott's statue of the fifth duke thus placed it not in the centre of the square, where it would lose distinction, but on one side, 'facing Bloomsbury, and forming an appropriate perspective, as seen through the vista of the streets crossing the two squares'. The statue, subscribed to by men of all political persuasions, commemorates the duke as a heroic agriculturalist. The figure is robed, grasping a sheaf in one hand and a ploughshare in the other, and placed on a high pedestal with reliefs of harvesters and herdsmen.[175] Repton advised that all trees and shrubs should be pruned so that not only the figure of the duke

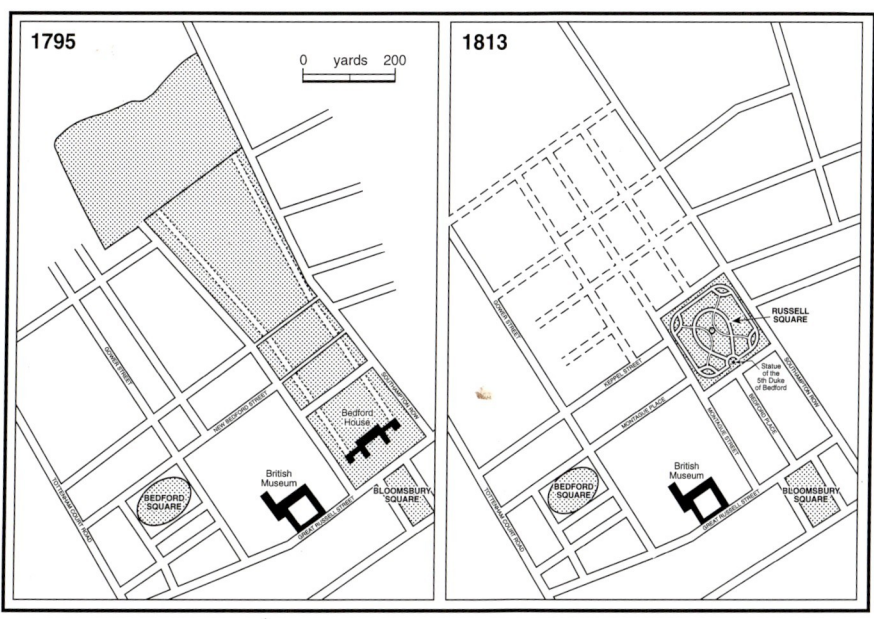

177 Bloomsbury in 1795, before the demolition of Bloomsbury House, and in 1813, after the building of Russell Square. After the Bloomsbury estate survey of 1795, Bedford Estate Office; *Map of the Cities of London and Westminster* (1813). British Library.

178   C. Mottram after Thomas H. Shepherd, *Russell Square and the Statue of the Duke of Bedford*, from Thomas H. Shepherd, *London and Its Environs in the Nineteenth Century* (1829). Crace Collection © The British Museum.

but the figures surrounding the pedestal could be seen against the sky (fig. 178). A walk under an avenue of lime trees (intended eventually to form a closed arch like the covered walk at Woburn) converged on the statue in two straight lines.

It is possible that some fanciful advocates of natural gardening will object to this disposition of trees as too formal; and they will be further shocked at my expressing a wish that the arch formed by these trees over the walk should be cut and trimmed so as to become a perfect artificial shade . . . In the due attention to the training and trimming of such trees by art, consists the difference between a garden and a park, or forest; and no one will, I trust, contend that a public square should affect to imitate the latter.

Near the statue were to be a small grove of trees and some small plots enriched with flowers and shrubs, 'each disposed in a different manner to indulge the various tastes for regular or irregular gardens'. The private, domestic function of Russell Square was not to be sacrificed to civic grandeur. A six-foot hedge of hornbeam and privet, hardy enough to survive the London atmosphere, screened a gravel walk from the street. Within the walk was a circular lawn 'on which the children may be kept always in sight from the windows of the houses immediately opposite; and, for this reason (founded on the particular wishes of some mothers), the lawn is less clothed with plantation than it might have been on the principle of beauty only'. Repton went in to some detail about how the square would look because the statue was not yet built, and 'for the first years of its growth [the planting] will be liable to some criticism'.

> A few years hence, when the present patches of shrubs shall have become thickets, – when the present meagre rows of trees shall have become an umbrageous avenue, – and the children now in their nurses' arms shall have become the guardians or grandsires of future generations, this square may serve to record, that the Art of Landscape Gardening in the beginning of the nineteenth century was not directed by whim or caprice, but founded on a due consideration of utility as well as beauty, without a bigoted adherence to forms and lines, whether straight, or crooked, or serpentine.[176]

Shortly after publishing this, Repton was consulted on the landscaping of Bloomsbury Square. Repton repeated elements of his plan for Russell Square: a space for children, a pleasure garden for inhabitants and a shaded walk of lime trees. He was concerned to keep open the view from Holborn through Bedford Place – 'forming a fine enfilade thro' the two squares' – for he observed that just such a view from Cavendish to Hanover Square had recently been blocked off. The co-ordination of Russell and Bloomsbury Squares would have created not just an impressive piece of townscape but a showpiece of Repton's talent. Walking a potential client into Bloomsbury Square, Repton could reveal a vista through Russell Square to his landscaping on the hills of Hampstead and Highgate at Kenwood and Fitzroy Farm. This helps to explain his despondency when his plan for Bloomsbury Square was rejected. There was a difference of opinion on the committee, which agreed only to adopt a part of Repton's plan, a path and belt of shrubs. In a letter of March 1807 to William Adam, Repton asked to submit a supplementary report justifying his plan in its entirety, and to meet the committee, expressing

> the satisfaction I feel as a Professional Man being consulted on a Public concern, & a sort of Pride in contributing to the Embellishment of the Capital... If my plan be so partially adapted to make me ashamed of its effect I must regret the mortification, instead of acknowledging the satisfaction of having been consulted on the subject.[177]

Perhaps to respect his professional integrity, Repton's plan was rejected in its entirety. Another by an Islington nurseryman, Thomas Barr – four oval clumps surrounded by a gravel path – was submitted in August and approved two months later.[178]

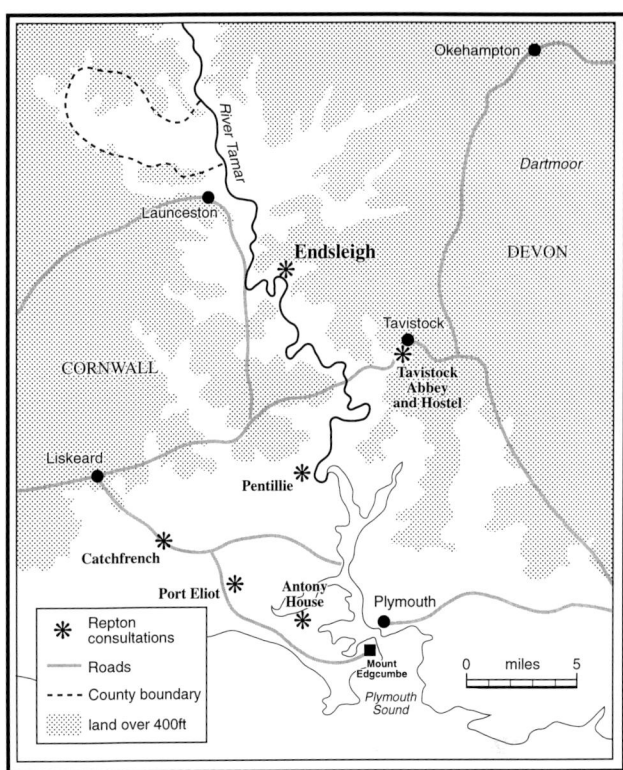

179   Endsleigh and the Tamar valley.

## Tavistock

The Bedfords' 15,000-acre Devon estate, originally owned by the abbots of Tavistock, was granted, along with Woburn Abbey, to the first earl in 1540. In a county of small gentry, the Bedfords were a powerful but for generations a remote force. The family had no residence there, and showed little interest in developing it until the fifth duke commissioned Nathaniel Kent to assess 'the Great Property in the West', and upon his succession he and his younger brother instituted a new regime.[179]

The redevelopment of Plymouth during the Napoleonic Wars, its demand for wood, stone, minerals and foodstuffs, helped to stimulate development on the Tavistock estate, incorporating the upper reaches of the Rivers Tamar and Tavy in a larger economic region and bringing it to national attention (fig. 179). The Bedfords began a programme of improvement on their farms, especially in convertible husbandry (continuous tillage under an alternation of grain and grass crops), built new roads and buildings and undertook a campaign of tree planting and woodland management. They developed the town of Tavistock as a regional capital, with large and frequent markets for corn and cattle, and as a nucleus of a rich mining region, in copper, iron, manganese and tin.[180] The sixth duke brought in John Taylor, a noted geologist and friend of Humboldt, to manage his copper mines, as well as to develop the Tavistock canal, of which the duke was the main shareholder, which stimulated development throughout the navigable reaches of the Tamar. Taylor's efforts did not stop there; he founded a library in Tavistock and compiled a survey of the region which celebrated its variety and prosperity: 'in point of picturesque scenery, few districts exceed it'.[181] With the support of his steward, Edward Bray, the sixth duke rebuilt Tavistock as an attractive town with amenities for both residents and a growing number of tourists. Already drawn by the mild, restorative climate of Devon, visitors ventured inland along the meandering rivers to discover a prosperous and picturesque region of lush pastures, thick woods, quarries, lime kilns, barge traffic, docks and farmhouses perched on the bluffs. In 1809 the duke decided to build the first Bedford residence in Devon, a winter sporting lodge at Endsleigh on the banks of the Tamar.[182]

Repton was first commissioned on the Tavistock estate in 1809 to provide a plan for the centre of the town around the abbey and the Bedford estate office, and to draw up designs for the sporting lodge at Endsleigh. He was familiar with the southern coast of Devon and the lower Tamar around Plymouth. In 1792 he had prepared plans for two established estates on the tidal waters, Antony and Port Eliot, and was shown over the most spectacular, Mount Edgcumbe, overlooking Plymouth Sound.[183] In 1799 he had collaborated with John Nash on designs for Luscombe near Dawlish, a marine villa to accommodate the invalid wife of the banker Charles Hoare.[184] Writing from Woburn to his son William in the spring of 1809, Repton said that the costs of travel now made him cautious about undertaking long journeys.[185] The trip to Tavistock was combined with and probably prompted by another commission for Charles Coryton at Pentillie, overlooking the Tamar a few miles above Plymouth and a landmark for boat trips (fig. 180). According to Antony's owner, Pole Carew, Pentillie was 'the admiration of all who explore the banks of the Tamar . . . you will therefore have the Eyes of all upon you in what you do'.[186]

Many of the remains of Tavistock abbey had been taken down on the orders of the fifth duke's steward, a Mr Saunders, who also set about modernizing his own house in the grounds, removing mullion windows to make way for sash windows and plastering over the others. The sixth duke's steward, a solicitor, Edward Bray, in alliance with his son Edward, a parson who occupied the neighbouring vicarage, sought to restore the abbey, excavating remains (perhaps during the cutting of the Tavistock canal which ran close by), stripping away his predecessor's alterations and laying out gardens. The Brays regarded this as part of an overall programme of estate improvements; the younger Bray sketched and composed verses to the various developments, from the cottage ornée to the copper mines, which his father managed.[187]

Repton visited Tavistock in August 1809 and, with his sons John Adey and George, produced a plan for preserving the remains of Tavistock abbey, landscaping the grounds and building a public hall and hostel for visitors in a Gothic style (fig. 181).[188] This was supplanted by a design by John Taylor.[189] Repton complained that he was wrongly briefed, and after a second visit in December 1810 submitted counter proposals. These were partially

180 After Humphry Repton, *Scene on the Tamer above Pentille*, from *Peacock's Polite Repository* (1809). Private collection.

executed, for a letter from Repton to William Adam in 1814, concerning a subsequent visit, states that 'our Hostel at Tavistock must be my headquarters, as I could not intrude myself & nurse on Mr Bray'.[190] Repton stayed with the younger Bray. 'My friend Bray . . . In him, let it record, tho all must know it/ The Man of Taste, the Painter, and the Poet.'[191] Bray's wife, Elizabeth, told Robert Southey that 'so highly did the late Mr Repton, the celebrated landscape gardener, estimate Mr Bray's taste in the art, that he more than once consulted him; and used, good-humouredly to say, that if all trades failed Mr Bray might succeed him in his profession'.[192]

181 Humphry Repton with John Adey Repton and George Stanley Repton, *The Interior View of Tavistock Abbey* (c.1809). By kind permission of the Marquess of Tavistock and the Trustees of the Bedford Estate.

182 Humphry Repton with John Adey Repton and George Stanley Repton, *Endsleigh Cottage* (1809). By kind permission of the Marquess of Tavistock and the Trustees of the Bedford Estate.

## Endsleigh

In 1809 the Bedfords decided to demolish a farmhouse on the banks of the Tamar at Endsleigh to make way for a sporting lodge for shooting and fishing. The location was superb, above a deeply incised meander of the river, looking across extensive woodland. Following the current vogue, especially prevalent in the resorts of south Devon, the Bedfords wanted a cottage ornée, a dwelling small enough and so blended with its surroundings to evoke rustic felicity, but large enough (much larger than the irregular-looking farmhouse it was to replace) to accommodate a retinue of servants and sufficiently appointed to cater for expensive tastes.[193]

In 1809 Repton submitted a plan for the cottage (fig. 182), revealing the strong hand of his son George who was designing a number of cottages ornées in Nash's office.[194] The Reptons prepared a flexible plan of thatched buildings (echoing the farmhouse) that could be combined in various ways on two possible sites. Their plan was rejected soon after for a larger and more lavish scheme on the same articulated principle by Jeffrey Wyatville on another site chosen by the duchess. Built of granite, with gabled slate roofs, it looked a little raw to Repton when he was brought in later to landscape the grounds, but he appreciated the way its horseshoe shape exploited the picturesque possibilities of the great meander in the Tamar, with apartments angled to various views up and down the river. Wyatville's design has distinctly Reptonian features. Its integration of architecture and scenery echoes the design for Luscombe, and its exploitation of views of the river reflects that for Pentillie.[195]

The foundation stone of Endsleigh cottage was laid in September 1810 by the Bedfords' four elder sons, and the building was largely completed over the next four years. Wyatville was commissioned to design the grounds, to lay out gardens on the terraced site and to shape the ground falling away to the river. Robert Salmon was responsible for constructing drives, for planting and for establishing a nursery with a quarter of a million plants. By late 1813 the duke was dissatisfied with the state of the grounds. As Wyatville and Repton had just collaborated at Ashridge, it was reasonable to call in Repton again.[196]

After his carriage accident, and the onset of angina, Repton was unwilling to undergo a long trip with winter approaching. 'You will smile at my difficulty about a hundred miles', Repton wrote to Bedford as the duke was about to embark on another continental tour, 'but I fear I must look forward every year to more reluctance on undertaking long journeys'.[197] Repton proposed making the trip the following May, combining the visit to Endsleigh with one he had already arranged to Longleat, and asked Adam to authorize it if a reply from the duke in Paris did not arrive in time.[198] Adam's authorization did not arrive until after Repton had returned from Longleat, but he decided to make a special trip in August 1814. He told Adam he would not travel down in a hackney chaise with him and Wyatville (on the grounds that the architect's corpulence would discomfort them both) but in his own carriage with his daughter Mary as nurse. The cost was considerable, sixty guineas, but he looked forward to a fee of two-hundred pounds for the visit and picking up a commission outside Bristol on the way.[199] Adam arranged for Repton's visit to Endsleigh to be made as comfortable as possible, including having him carried from place to place in an invalid chair. Repton stayed for four days. In Tavistock, Repton scribbled his report in pencil, intending to make a fair copy in ink, but 'severe spasmodic pains in my limbs – the effect of a little too much exertion' – prevented him, and he left them to be transcribed in Bray's estate office. The report is addressed to Adam – 'I doubt that this ought to be for his Grace's eye in so slovenly a form' – on the understanding that the auditor would discuss it with Repton in London and perhaps submit a report 'in your own words which the Duke may like better'.[200]

After returning from Devon, £370 better off, Repton repaired to his sister's house at Aylsham, Norfolk, for two months. He told Adam that he had been 'full engaged in marshalling and bringing before the Duke's eyes – Endsleigh & my mind has been happy – my body miserable'.[201] As well as preparing the Red Book for Endsleigh, Repton was also compiling *Fragments*, his valedictory work, and planning the garden for his own grave in Aylsham churchyard. As his physician had just 'bid me leave off the loco-motive part of my profession', Repton seems to have realized that the Red Book for Endsleigh would be his last, but preparing it sustained him through a difficult period. In November he returned to Hare Street, where he informed Adam that the Red Book was ready for delivery. He was concerned that Adam should see it first: 'I should be mortified to send it to the Duke without passing thro' your hands'.

> I hope you would be pleased with it – I will confess I never so well pleased myself – but we are apt to make a favourite of the youngest child – especially after a difficult Labour & being L-Enfant de la Viellesse & you saw me on my last legs in Devonshire.[202]

Repton's site report for Endsleigh is largely concerned with the alterations he discussed with the gardener Mr Forrester as they made their way around the immediate vicinity of the house: the removal of a bastion wall, a gravel walk along the terrace, and, at great length and technical detail, the construction of winter gardens.[203] The Red Book, produced in Aylsham, is a very different document, of much greater scope and more general register. It omits much of the information in the Report and includes other proposals along with extensive theoretical sections on such matters as river channels and the Picturesque. The extra proposals committed to the Red Book look beyond the immediate environs of the house.[204]

In the dedication of the Red Book addressed to the duke in Spain during a Continental tour, Repton appealed to the homely feelings that he considered came naturally with hereditary wealth:

183  Endsleigh cottage from across the river Tamar, without overlay, from the Red Book for Endsleigh (1814). By kind permission of the Marquess of Tavistock and the Trustees of the Bedford Estate.

the misery and humble poverty of a cottage may disgust the unfeeling possessor of newly aquired wealth; but the benevolent mind will ever associate with a cottage – its content – its snugness – and above all its domestic enjoyment enlivened by the happy smiles and lively prattle of cheerful innocence.

The duke and duchess of Bedford were not known as paragons of domesticity. Despite bearing and nursing ten children, the duchess was frequently on the move in pursuit of pleasure, trailing salacious rumours, to Brighton, her own villa in Kensington and abroad. At Woburn she was renowned for hosting boisterous parties.[205] Despite, or perhaps because of this, Repton looked upon Endsleigh (fig. 183) as a nursery of family feelings. He found Wyatville's childrens' garden (fig. 184) especially appealing. Children were:

playthings for every benevolent Heart often more grateful than the laboured controversy of Philosophers and Statesmen . . . They are the best weapon of defence against the gloom of solitude & happy the Cottager that has his quiver full of them.

Nature echoed culture. Repton

looked down on the infant River, struggling through its rock channel, and hurrying onwards with all the impetuosity of ungoverned youth, till it becomes useful to mankind . . . but even in this apparently useless state it is busy collecting 'the little streams which run among the mountains' and on tracing its progress we find that it soon becomes more and more useful to man, till at length it is acknowledged as the great source of the Harbour of Plymouth, to which England owes much of its Glory and Commerce.

184 The Children's Cottage and Garden, from the Red Book for Endsleigh (1814). By kind permission of the Marquess of Tavistock and the Trustees of the Bedford Estate.

In an illustration (fig. 185) of a proposed change to Wyatville's garden, Repton shows two girls playing with dolls, one boy playing with model ships in a miniature harbour, the other whipping a top.

> The mimic Doll to girls; the whip to boys
> Are but the Emblem of their future Toys
> Soft tender cares, the tender Sex delight
> 'Fleets, Colonies & Trade' the Man of Might

'At this enchanting Retreat the most pleasing attention has been paid to the Comforts and Infancy of Youth', observed Repton. 'Let the same attention be extended to solace the infirmities of age.' He saw his improvements

> furnishing employment and amusement to its Noble possessors for many years to come; and having in a manner provided against the rigours of Winter, I will not be unmindful of that Winter of Life which must alike assail the Cottage and the Palace. With this in view I venture to advise, that all the walks be made sufficiently wide to admit a carriage; and having myself lost the power of gathering a flower or picking up a fossil from the ground, I have found great comfort in banks raised to the height of three or four feet . . . to bring nearer to the eye those lesser rock plants or delicate blossoms which are too minute to be seen from the ground.

Repton envisioned Endsleigh not merely as a holiday home but as the nucleus of an improved estate (fig. 186):

> Everything that can contribute to the enjoyment of its scenery, I know must also contribute to the enjoyment of the neighbouring Country in its Agriculture, its Mineralogy, its Civilization, and the general happiness of all who dwell within the influence of this Cottage on the Banks of the Tamar.

Many signs of progress are included in the designs. The terrace walk terminates in a quarry that 'might be converted into a grotto-like receptacle for specimens of the fossils and ores abounding in the neighbouring mountains'. The pasture sloping to the river is stocked with sleek looking Devon cattle. The land recently acquired on the opposite side of the river is lushly wooded and developed with a cottage and corn mill: 'the occasional traffic and busy motion of persons crossing the Tamar, would add to the picturesque effect'. John Rennie had been consulted about building a bridge some way from the house, but Repton proposed to cross the river here with a weir paved with stones to make a crossing for carriages. Weirs had recently been publicized in the improvement literature on Devon as ways of harnessing the volatile rivers of the county.[206] Repton had closely observed the fluctuating flow, shifting channel and bed of the Tamar and had come to the same solution. His weir provided salmon leaps and controlled irrigation of the cattle pasture. Repton was confident that 'By the regular & systematic completion of what I had to suggest for Woburn; your Grace has insured me the certainty, that my plans for Endsleigh, will not (as I have too often experienced) be a waste of Time, Thought and Contrivance'.[207]

Bedford expressed a wish to meet Repton at Endsleigh the following August.[208] Repton spent the intervening nine months in a parlous state, largely confined to Hare Street, deeply depressed about his own condition and that of the country, and uninterested in anything except revising his manuscripts for publication. In August 1815 he set out for Endsleigh to meet Bedford. He stayed in Devon for about three weeks, taking a seaside holiday in Sidmouth and returning feeling much better for it.[209] A two-hundred-guinea fee for his August visit also greatly eased his debts.[210] Repton secured permission to publish a long extract from the Endsleigh Red Book in *Fragments*. Some important features from his proposals that he published – the grotto, the mill and cottage, viaduct, conservatory – were not in fact executed, and some that he omitted from the publication – such as the dairy dell to the west of the house – were.[211] As at Ashridge, it was Wyatville who imprinted his influence most strongly on the site, adapting and modifying Repton's proposals over the next thirty years and extending his own.[212]

Endsleigh proved an expensive amenity, especially as it was used for such a short time each year. The whole ongoing scheme proved a costly undertaking that William Adam strove from a distance to control. Spending on buildings, woods and plantations, gardens and pleasure grounds escalated, with comparatively little return on timber, rents or farm produce and little regard for commercial conditions at large.[213] The Tavistock estate was meant to provide a sinking fund for the rest of the Bedford estate, but Endsleigh threatened to exhaust it.[214] William Adam constantly reminded Bedford of the burden:

> Suppose Endsleigh had never been built your Grace would in 1824 have received £3090 more from Devonshire than you did ... I have always thought that your Grace never did a wiser thing than to build a residence in Devonshire, tho' of course the Expenditure there was necessarily increased by it. The only question is whether that Expenditure is greater than it need or ought to be ... All this expenditure however

185 *Play-Things*, from the Red Book for Endsleigh (1814). By kind permission of the Marquess of Tavistock and the Trustees of the Bedford Estate.

186  *General View from the South and East Fronts of Endsleigh Cottage*, with and without overlay, from *Fragments on the Theory and Practice of Landscape Gardening* (1816). Yale Center for British Art, Paul Mellon Collection.

carries no advantage except the amusement it affords your Grace. Which I admit is a sufficient exception. Only it is fit that you should know the price it costs you.[215]

\* \* \*

### George III

From the outset of his career Repton sought royal patronage. In the letter to Norton Nicholls announcing his new profession, he reported that 'I have already been honour'd by an introduction to the Duke of York, which will I am assured be follow'd by others to the King and Prince of Wales'.[216] With the loosing of purse strings to fund improvements to the various royal palaces, financial conditions were right for Repton to follow Capability Brown as Royal Gardener. The king and queen were figureheads of horticultural and agricultural improvement and had a reputation for domestic respectability that helped to transform the image of Windsor Castle from a courtly palace in to a country house. Repton was drawn irresistibly to the royal household. The duke of Portland told him a number of anecdotes that confirmed its homely reputation and made him privy to 'the little negotiations between a King and Queen, who are well known to have lived more like an affectionate husband and wife than any Sovereigns in Europe'.[217]

After receiving permission to dedicate *Sketches and Hints* to the king, Repton had the privilege of presenting a copy at a levee: 'The King said "Mr Repton I have been very patient to see this book, I have seen several of your manuscript books, and *have read them*" . . . pay[ing] me a compliment which many of his Majesty's liege subjects . . . apt to look at the pictures without reading the book . . . had never thought of'. The king took Repton's side in the picturesque controversy, if his judgement depended more on the size of the contending volumes.[218] Reading Repton's books apparently failed to impress him; Farington reported that he 'seems to think them rather coxcomical works'.[219]

Repton secured commissions close to, and in view of, royal parks and forests around London, and a number around Windsor Castle, notably Bulstrode, St Leonard's Hill, for General Hon. William Harcourt, later Third Earl Harcourt, an intimate of the royal family with responsibilities for managing Windsor Great Park and, on the borders of the Park itself, Holly Grove for Lady Jennings Clerke.[220] Repton was working at Holly Grove at the same time as the king was enclosing neighbouring forest land to extend Windsor Great Park. The stakes diverting a road towards Holly Grove were removed, and Repton heard that the king accused him of doing it. He protested his innocence to Harcourt who was pleased 'to vindicate an ingenious, eminent and worthy man'. The king read Repton's letter and 'was pleased with it', claiming that he had never attributed the removal to him. Repton depicted the queen's own lodge and gardens at Frogmore as the frontispiece to the 1796 edition of the *Polite Repository* (fig. 187). This may indicate that he had already offered advice or was angling to do so.

When the watercolourist Thomas Sandby died in 1798, Repton sought his position of Deputy Ranger of Windsor Great Park. Officially the position was largely concerned with land agency, but during his long tenure Sandby had defined his job as one of landscaping and architectural design. As his friend Nathaniel Kent was employed as agricultural consultant at Windsor Great Park, and as he was by now working for leading members of the government, Repton reckoned he was well placed. He wrote to Windham, Pitt and the duke of Portland to petition the king; Windham and Portland said that they lacked sufficient influence, Pitt said he had but received Repton's letter too late to exercise it.[222] Already fulfilling the land agency aspects of Deputy Rangership, Lord Harcourt was formally appointed to the post.[223] Despite 'the *most ardent hope*', Repton was never commissioned by the king; he occasionally paid his respects at court, 'where I was always graciously recognized by my Sovereign, but I have never received his command to attend him professionally'.[224]

187   J. Peltro after Humphry Repton, *View of Her Majesty's Lodge at Frogmore, near Windsor*, frontispiece to *Peacock's Polite Repository* (1798).

## The Prince of Wales

While failing to secure a commission from the king, Repton was consulted a number of times by the Prince of Wales, notably to prepare designs for the Royal Pavilion, Brighton. The prince and his pavilion stood, at least in the public imagination, at the opposite pole of high society to the king and his castle. Repton found the prince's fashionable world alluring; indeed he attempted to reform his vision of landscape gardening to accommodate it.

Brighton was already established as a stylish seaside resort when the Prince of Wales made his first visit in

1783. It was not just the sea air, but the presence of a military barracks, the prosperity of east Sussex (fig. 188) and the accessibility of London (in 1784 the prince drove his phaeton there in a fast four-and-a-half hours) that attracted the *beau monde*. Brighton's growth was prodigious. It was a magnet for investment, initially from the region and then from further afield. It was sufficiently close to London to attract flows of visitors and money, and sufficiently far to sustain its own infrastructure of manufacture and trade, much of it catering to its high-spending population. Brighton fast became the racy alternative to respectable Bath.[225]

After renting a house for three years, the prince decided to have a permanent residence, and because of his debts his steward Louis Weltje personally took a lease on the property with an option to buy. The house was in a prominent location just north of the commercial centre, beside the main road to London and facing the fashionable promenade, the Steine (fig. 189). Upon purchasing the property in 1787, Weltje paid for Henry Holland to remodel the house in the style of a 'pavillon', a Parisian villa, with a domed roof and bow fronts (fig. 190), and set about buying or leasing land around it to create space for extensions and pleasure grounds. This proved a difficult and protracted process. Property ownership was highly fragmented, and the prince's residence had begun to attract other developments, notably a neighbouring terrace of lodging houses fronting the Steine, and thus inflating already soaring land prices. A view of the pavilion soon became more prestigious than a view of the sea. The prince was able to exercise increasing control over both the pavilion and its surroundings after his marriage in 1795 to Princess Caroline of Brunswick settled his debts, and Parliament in 1803 granted a substantial increase in his allowance. He had the pavilion renovated and extended, and his agents bid highly for land to erect more buildings and lay out pleasure grounds. Holland added a Chinese suite of rooms in the years 1801–3. A road diversion and land purchases totalling five acres to the west of the pavilion made space for new pleasure grounds and a large oriental-style riding-house and stables designed by William Porden. As well as accommodating the prince's horses, Porden designed a new house on the Steine for the prince's mistress, Mrs Fitzherbert. In 1805, as the frame of the riding-house began to dwarf the pavilion, Porden submitted designs for enlarging it. He chose a Chinese style, patterned, it seems, on some of William Alexander's drawings of the emperor's summer palace made during Lord Macartney's embassy to the Chinese Court. The drawings were exhibited at the Royal Academy in 1805, but in the autumn of that year Repton persuaded the prince to commission a fresh set in an Indian style.[226] The pavilion was now the nucleus of the fastest growing town in the country: 'what was only a small fishing town', noted Repton, 'is now become equal to some cities in extent and population' (figs 191 and 192).[227] The spectacular growth and style of Brighton was epitomized by the enlargement and reconstruction of the Royal Pavilion.

Repton was first consulted at the pavilion in the years 1797–1802, to advise on groundwork around some additions to Holland's building.[228] Then followed a more

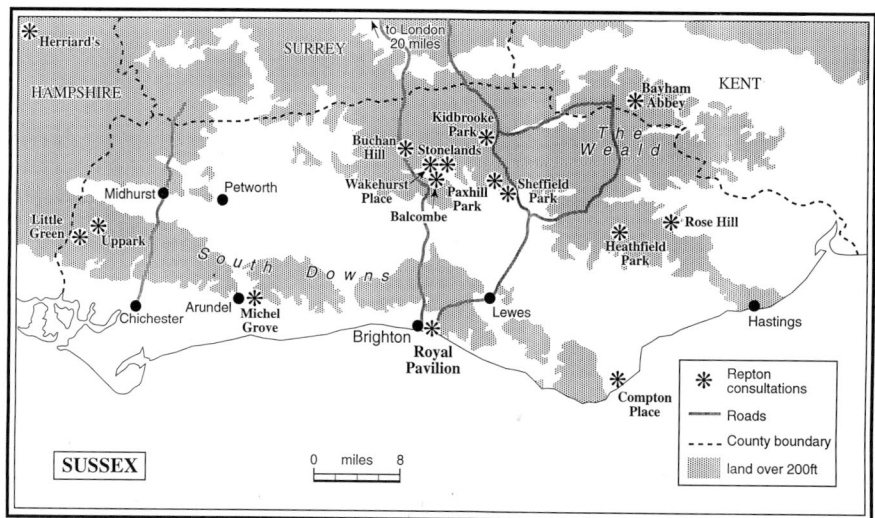

188 Humphry Repton Consultations in Sussex.

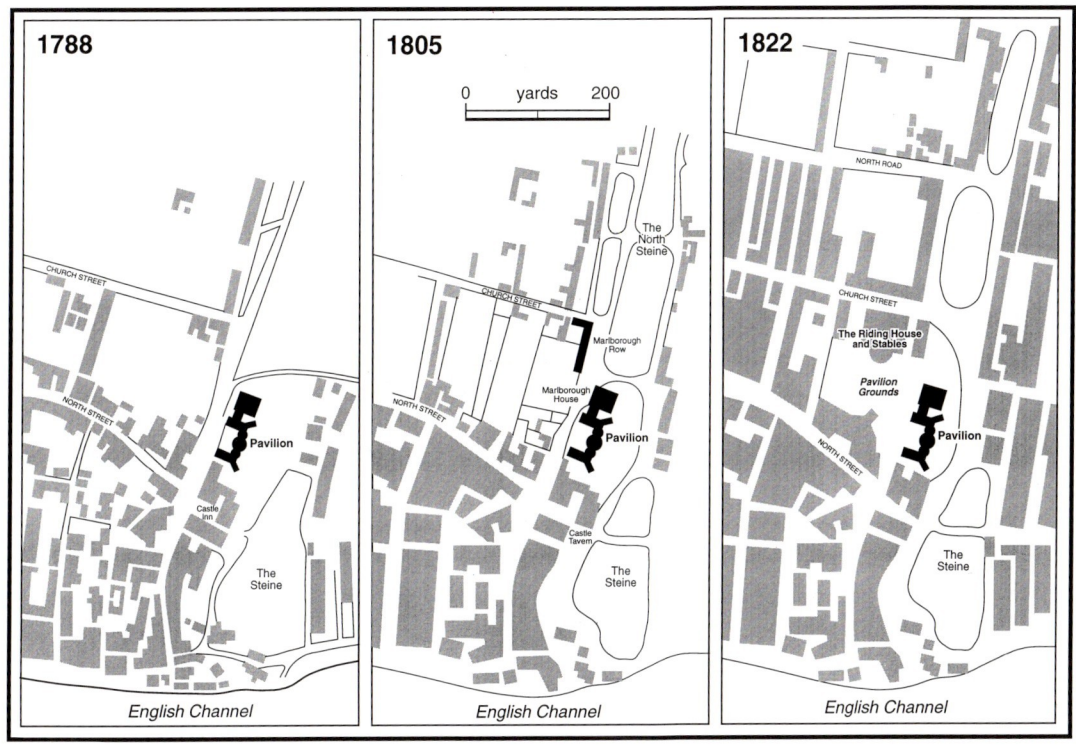

189   Brighton and the Royal Pavilion in 1788, 1805 and 1822. After Sue Farrant, 'The Physical Development of the Royal Pavilion Estate and Its Influence on Brighton (East Sussex) 1785–1823', *Sussex Archaeological Collections*, 120 (1982).

190   *The Pavilion, Brighton*, from T. Attree, *Topography of Brighton* (1809). Private collection.

prestigious commission to prepare a design for remodelling the prince's London residence, Carlton House (fig. 193). This focussed on the view from the principal floor of Holland's building, over the entrance front and gardens. Repton planned to shut out views in from the mall and open up a vista over St James's Park to Westminster abbey, a Gothic eye-catcher matching proposed restyling elsewhere in the building.[229] The lawn and shrubberies look unremarkable in Repton's drawing, but they were to provide a setting for the prince's elaborate fêtes.[230]

When Repton asked the prince why he was commissioned again in 1805 to design grounds at the pavilion, he 'mentioned several concerns of mine with which he had been much pleased, and particularly one "in which" he said "you *dared* to make a perfectly strait [*sic.*] gravel walk. The moment I saw it I was determined to see you before I proceeded . . ."'.[231] The prince was referring to the mall at Cassiobury in Hertfordshire for Lord Essex, although he may have seen in *Observations* the illustration of a similar, straight gravel walk for Valleyfield (fig. 143).[232] The recent commission at Woburn may have attracted the prince's notice too, for it was the duke of Bedford who notified Repton of the summons to the Royal Pavilion.[233]

Hearing that the prince was an admirer of Walsh Porter's Craven Cottage in Fulham – an extraordinary concoction of exotic styles – Repton paid it a visit.[234] There he saw many things 'done out of the common way with good effect and others so whimsical and absurd, that I dreaded the sort of taste I might have to encounter at Brighton'. Repton hoped to enthuse the prince with his recent, more academic interest in 'representations of Indian scenery'.[235]

'Not being aware that the etiquette when serving Royalty admitted of no excuse or delay whatever', Repton proceeded with other engagements in Sussex and Hampshire, leaving directions for letters to be forwarded, 'instead of setting out for Brighton immediately'. Arriving at Kidbrooke, the seat of Charles Abbot, Speaker of the House of Commons, a servant thrust a letter from an equerry at Repton before he alighted, saying that alterations to the grounds of the pavilion had already started, the prince thinking that Repton considered the commission too trifling. Mortified, Repton immediately sent a contrite reply, telling him of his proposals to remodel the place in an Indian style. Repton then received notice of a letter to come to Brighton: 'I turned my horse's head round and set off immediately to answer this letter in person'. The prince kept Repton waiting a week for an appointment. When they eventually met, Repton was relieved to discover that the prince shared his distaste for some of the extravagant features of Craven Cottage and his delight in a purer Indian style.[236]

Repton walked over the new grounds for an hour with the prince, discussing how the surface might be remodelled, the garden buildings designed, the trees and plants arranged. Repton returned to Brighton three weeks later with the drawings and with three of his sons, John Adey, George Stanley and Humphry, who collaborated on the designs. The prince called at Repton's lodgings, took a look at the drawings, already prepared with overlays, and declared that 'they beautifully realized all he had imagined from my conversation, but far exceeded his expectations'. Moreover, he asked Repton to give an opinion about an entirely new house in an Indian style that would harmonize with the dome of Porden's riding-house. Such was Repton's excitement, he had to take a walk on the seafront. Breathing in the sea air and breathing forth 'my gratitude to Him "Who ruleth the raging of the sea"'. Repton felt he had attained 'the highest point of my ambition': 'I found myself – in conjunction with my boys – appointed to direct the taste of the Country in its Architecture as well as in its scenery'. The prince wanted the pavilion not merely as '"a Marino, or Summer retreat"' but as '"a Residence as I may *hereafter live in*"', 'by which I understood that it was a Royal Palace for a King that I was now commanded to design'. Moreover, the prince asked Repton to take charge of the execution of his plan.[237]

Repton's interest in Oriental style reached back to 1790, when he had marvelled at a hermitage at Louth decorated with bamboo furniture, wall matting (along which snails were trained to leave glittering trails) and 'Asiatic Manuscripts', as well as polished horses' teeth, silver crucifixes and stained glass: 'the effect was magical . . . an Arabian Night's entertainment'.[238] Now he assumed a more serious, academic interest. Before the summons to Brighton, he had been consulted at Sezincote in Gloucestershire, where Sir Charles Cockerell wished to introduce styles of architecture and gardens that he had seen during his office with the East India Company. Repton assisted his client's brother, the architect Samuel Pepys Cockerell, to select 'accurate sketches and drawings made on the spot by my ingenious friend Mr T[homas] Daniell', which were published as plates from 1795 in *Oriental Scenery*, as a basis for the design.[239]

The taste for Indian architecture had provoked some ridicule. In 1798 the architect James Malton observed

191  J.C. Stadler after Humphry Repton, *North Front towards the Parade*, with overlay, from *Designs for the Pavillon at Brighton* (1808). Yale Center for British Art, Paul Mellon Collection.

192  J.C. Stadler after Humphry Repton, *View from the Proposed Private Apartment*, with overlay, from *Designs for the Pavillon at Brighton* (1808). Yale Center for British Art, Paul Mellon Collection.

EXPLANATION. The large trees near the Wall are become so naked & open below, that not only the Wall is seen, but the garden is exposed to the Mall; therefore, as no shrubs will grow under them it is proposed to take down a few of the Limes opposite to the House, then to raise earth towards the Wall & plant it with shrubs, over which a view of the Park and canal may be obtained without exposing the Gardens to the Publick.

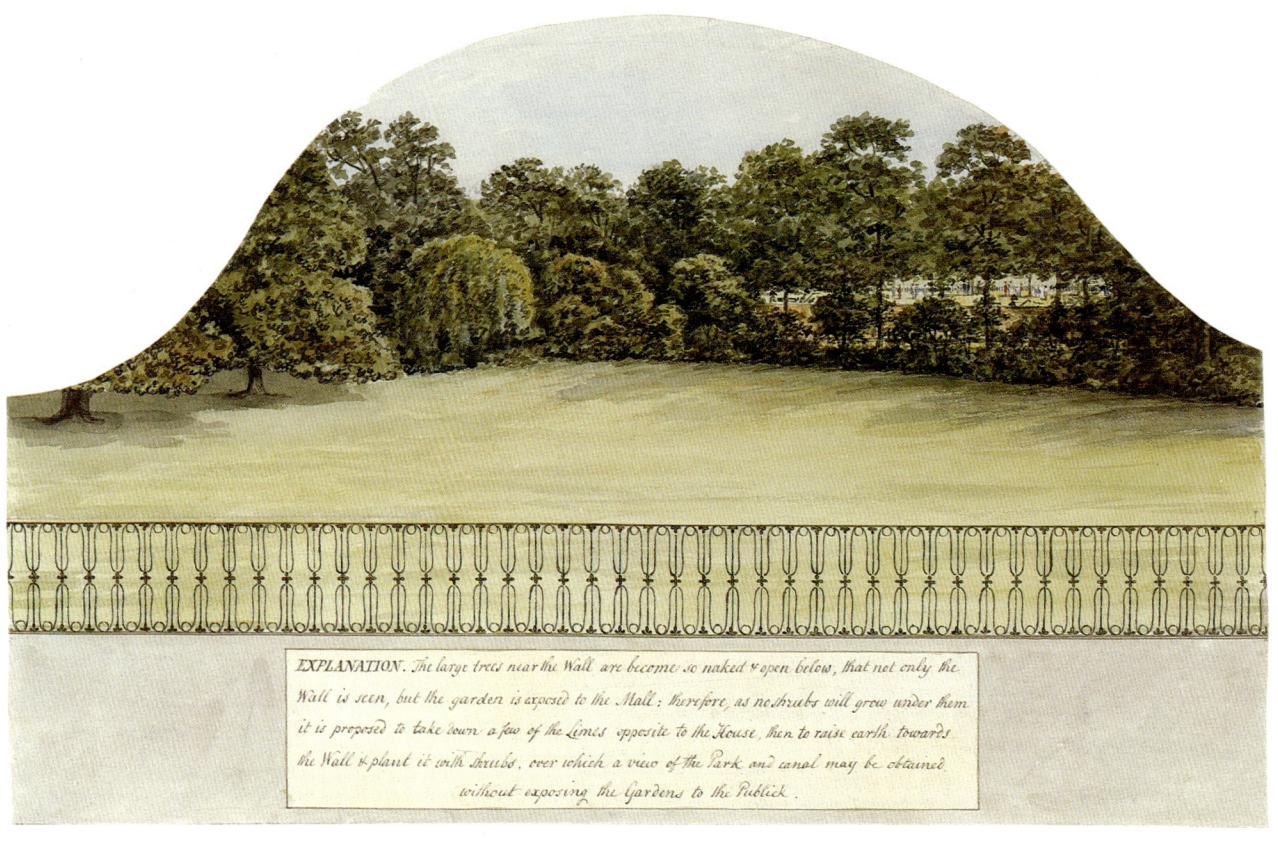

VIEW FROM THE PRINCIPAL FLOOR OF CARLETON-HOUSE the foreground supposed a balcony in the style of the House whether GOTHIC or GRECIAN

how 'The rude ornaments of Indostan supersede those of Greece; and the returned Nabob, heated in the pursuit of wealth, imagines he imports the *châleur* of the East with its riches'.[240] But there was a powerful lobby for its cultural seriousness. Sir Joshua Reynolds, no less, in his *Thirteenth Discourse* had recommended architects to imitate the buildings being published by William Hodges in his *Select Views in India* (1786–8). Hodges himself positioned India as one of the great ancient cultures.[241] The East India Company, whose officers had to study Indian languages, history and law as part of their training, displayed an academic interest in Indian culture in the exhibits in its museum at their London headquarters.[242] While more sophisticated than the taste for Chinese scenery, that for Indian scenery shuttled between the spectacular and the scholarly, the pedantic and the picturesque. From whatever perspective, Indian scenery was a trophy of British imperialism, rivalling the French appropriation of Egyptian culture. With the occupation of Delhi in 1803, the remains of the Mughal empire were firmly in British hands. Francis Blagdon's *History of Ancient and Modern India* (1805) announced that 'The British have aquired an ascendancy in India of which nothing but an extraordinary want of policy can ever deprive them'.[243]

Repton worked on the Red Book for the Royal Pavilion (which he insisted on spelling 'pavillon') during most of January 1806 and delivered it to Carlton House the following month. It includes not only specific recommendations for the pavilion but also 'an inquiry into changes in architecture', which heralds 'the introduction of Indian architecture' as an advance on Grecian and Gothic styles. In Daniell's drawings of Hindu and Muslim architecture, Repton and his sons saw both foundational, load-bearing power and ornamental delicacy. Indian architecture appeared deeply ancient, notably in 'specimens discovered in the Indian excavations', and highly modern, 'cast iron . . . is peculiarly adapted to some light parts of the Indian style'.[244] Repton reckoned 'we are on the eve of some great future change in . . . gardening and architecture'.[245]

As Patrick Conner has shown, virtually all the details of Repton's architectural design are transcribed from Daniell's drawings for the first volume of *Oriental Scenery*

*193 facing page View from the principal floor of Carleton-House*, overlay (top) and main picture (1803). The Royal Collection © Her Majesty the Queen.

(1797). As Porden's stable block was based on Daniell's drawing of the gateway to the Jummah Musjed, the principal mosque of Delhi, so Repton's design for the pavilion (fig. 194) is based on the drawing of the mosque itself (fig. 195). A gateway from the town framing the riding-house draws on *An Ancient Hindoo Temple in the Fort of Rotas*, the upper part of a pheasantry (fig. 197) on a kiosk shown in *Part of a Palace in the Fort of Allahabad* (fig. 196). Some adaptions show a little wit. The design for an aviary (fig. 198) is based on a drawing of the Hindu temples at Bindrabund (fig. 199). The octagon that terminates the private apartments of the pavilion (fig. 200) is drawn from one on the upper storey of the eastern bastions of Shahjahanabad, as depicted in Daniell's *View of the Cotsea Bhaug* (fig. 201). The text to *Oriental Scenery* reports that the roof of the octagon commands a fine view of Delhi and the river Juma, and Repton echoes this in his design for the Pavilion, mounting a telescope on the octagon roof. It is pointed towards the sea but could be swivelled to survey the Steine.[246]

Daniell had shown Mughal palaces surrounded by gardens full of flowers. Repton went further to sketch a theory proposing that forms of Indian architecture correspond to forms of flowers, as Gothic forms corresponded to buds and Grecian to leaves (fig. 202). The plans for the pavilion gardens were more varied. They owed much to an observation that Repton quotes from Lord Bacon: 'that in the royal ordering of gardens, there should be a garden for every month of the year'. He wanted to create 'a garden which should not be affected by any variations of season, or soil, or weather, or situation; and thus form a perpetual garden, enriched with the production of every climate'. Thus a substantial proportion of the grounds was taken up with hothouses and greenhouses for bedding out and filling great wicker baskets of flowers on the lawns. The lawns in front of Holland's suite of Chinese rooms next to the private apartments are designated a 'Chinese Garden'. The artifice of the gardens extended to the decor of the pavilion, in some suggestions for stained glass.

> There is a curious effect from purple glass, of which little advantage has yet been taken; viz. All green objects seen through purple glass appear white and thus a beautified landscape illuminated by the midday sun of Summer will appear a perfect Winter scene covered with snow; the strange effect of contrast may perhaps be worth considering, in a room exposed to the Western sun.[247]

194  West front of the Pavilion, without overlay, from the Red Book for the Royal Pavilion, Brighton (1806). The Royal Collection © Her Majesty the Queen.

195  Thomas Daniell, *The Jummah Musjed, Delhi*, from *Oriental Scenery* Part 1 (1795). Yale Center for British Art, Paul Mellon Collection.

196  Thomas Daniell, *Part of the Palace in the Fort of Allahabad*, from *Oriental Scenery* Part 1 (1795). Yale Center for British Art, Paul Mellon Collection.

THE PHEASANTRY.

THE GENERAL VIEW FROM THE PAVILLON

197 *preceding page* The Pheasantry, from the Red Book for the Royal Pavilion, Brighton (1806). The Royal Collection © Her Majesty the Queen.

*facing page* Detail of fig. 198.

198 *above* General view from the Royal Pavillon, from the Red Book for the Royal Pavilion, Brighton (1806). The Royal Collection © Her Majesty the Queen.

199 *left* Thomas Daniell, *Hindoo Temples at Bindrabund on the River Jumna*, from *Oriental Scenery* Part 1 (1795). Yale Center for British Art, Paul Mellon Collection.

200  The north front towards the Parade, without overlay, from the Red Book for the Royal Pavilion, Brighton (1806). The Royal Collection © Her Majesty the Queen.

In Brighton Repton was asked to submit his plans to the scrutiny of Mrs Fitzherbert.

> The room into which I was ushered was sumptuously furnished – but almost darkened by the quantity of muslin and silk draperies drawn across the windows – Here – half reclining on a Sofa – surrounded by cushions and footstools – was the favourite friend (and *Wife* as she thought herself) of the future King of England – Her person was large, and loaded with lace and drapery.

The prince showed her Repton's plans, taking out his pencil to 'point out in the minutest detail' everything in the drawings

> which I saw were not very clearly understood by the Lady – and as to the maps, they were totally incomprehensible to eyes which shone to be admired, rather [than] admire any thing... All the remark she made was 'And pray what is all this to cost'.

The Prince proceeded regardless. '"Mr Repton I consider the whole of this book as perfect", "I will have every part of it carried into immediate execution".' Repton asked to whom he should apply for instructions while he supervised the work. '*Me only*', replied the prince, asking to see Repton in Brighton during the ensuing Race Week.[248]

The prince proved elusive. When Repton left his name at the pavilion no appointment was made, and he 'never saw him except on horseback when surrounded by a crowd when he one day bow'd to me'. After a solitary

201  Thomas Daniell, *North East View of the Cotsea Bhaug on the River Jumna, Delhi*, from *Oriental Scenery* Part I (1795). Yale Center for British Art, Paul Mellon Collection.

stroll on Brighton beach, Repton went to the theatre, there to be summoned in mid-performance by one of the prince's servants to a soirée at the pavilion. Here the prince arranged to see him, but Repton was again made to wait for some days. The day before the prince left for Yorkshire, Repton was summoned again. William Porden was there 'in the open air and sitting down on the grass, and I was told it was the best way to catch the Prince's attention'. Repton preferred to wait under cover, and after three hours the prince rushed towards the waiting carriages with the working plans for the pavilion, pointing out a few minor alterations and waving away

Repton's enquiry about money for beginning the work of earth-moving. The building of Porden's riding-house and stables was absorbing much more money than anticipated, with its complex cupola roof and the steep rise in timber prices following the blockade of Prussian ports. Repton was finally told that the Treasury would not advance any more money for the pavilion before other arrears were paid. 'So ended my Royal hopes.'[249]

At the time Repton still lived in hope. The following year, 1807, the prince attended a regimental review near Hare Street. At the breakfast, Repton was seated opposite the prince, who immediately asked to see him at Carlton House the following week. Repton was kept waiting for two days before being ushered into the garden for his advice for a great conservatory.[250] After having his plans accepted, Repton 'was superseded without the least ceremony or consideration' by James Wyatt, as Surveyor of the Board of Works. Repton comforted himself with the thought that the Nation was at least saved from wasteful expense, until he learned that, after Wyatt's sudden death, 'twice as much as my estimate had been lavished at Carlton House under the direction of Mr. Walsh Porter'.[251]

In 1808, when lucrative commissions were hard to come by, Repton tried to salvage something from the Pavilion scheme by publishing the plans for which he had yet to be paid. The engraver J.C. Stadler agreed to undertake the financial risk on the understanding that he shared half the profits.[252] *Designs for the Pavillon at Brighton* comprises a transcription of most of the Red Book with the addition of some drawings of Hindu columns. It is prefaced by an essay promoting the 'great future change' in gardening and architecture Repton had predicted and 'anticipating some of the objections that I suppose will be urged against this novel application of the most ancient style of ornamented architecture in the world'. After all, Repton had declared his opposition 'to that inordinate thirst after novelty, the characteristic of uncultivated minds', as he put it in the dedication to the king in *Sketches and Hints*.[253] If Indian architecture appeared complex and costly, he assured his readers it was actually simple and cheap, for example, in Hindustan columns were not carved but '*turned by a lathe*'.[254] If the style looked too exotic, there was in fact less contrast between the climate of England and Hindustan than that of Greece or Italy. Indian architecture dignified England as more familiar styles were everywhere degraded. High-minded claims for Grecian and Gothic styles were made 'with all the zeal of party bigotry'. At the other extreme, vulgar mixtures of these styles were evident on villas 'in the vicinity of every wealthy town, where large rooms,

202 'General forms of enrichment', from the Red Book for the Royal Pavilion, Brighton (1806). The Royal Collection © Her Majesty the Queen.

203 R. Alford, *View of the Pavilion taken from Wright's Circulating Library* (1818). Private collection.

with sumptuous furniture, are "BOXED UP" under the direction of carpenters, builders and surveyors, who may be ingenious artisans, but who have no science as architects'. Most recent public buildings were severely utilitarian.

> While, therefore, the security of public property is the chief motive for the only public buildings now erecting in the country, which are prisons and workhouses, we cannot wonder that our royal mansions should have more the appearance of workhouses and prisons, than of palaces worthy the residence of royalty!'[255]

As the Prince of Wales embarked on another spate of land purchase in Brighton from 1808 to 1812 to extend the pavilion, Repton may have held out some faint hopes of seeing his designs realized.[256] In 1815 he was 'surprised and mortified' to discover that the publisher still had the Red Book, the prince not having bothered to reclaim it.[257] Repton called at the pavilion around this time, only to be refused admittance. His vain hopes were 'like a brilliant bubble burst and vanished into the air'. Repton recalled the 118th Psalm: 'It is better to trust in the Lord than to put any confidence in Princes'.[258] Despite his predictions for Indian scenery, Repton never essayed any further designs in the style, nor promoted it in *Fragments*.[259]

The final indignity was the commissioning of John Nash to remodel the Royal Pavilion after the prince had formally assumed the title of Regent; this after everything he had told Repton about Nash 'suggesting plans of such enormous expense that they can hardly ever be realized'.[260] Nash now enjoyed an official appointment in the Department of Woods and Forests, and his schemes for developing Crown lands in London and restyling royal palaces were to express the prince's ambition to 'quite eclipse Napoleon'.[261] Money was made available from the privy purse for the pavilion because Nash quoted costs for each year, rather than for the full project. Nash copied Repton's Indian style but patterned the building much more loosely on drawings from Daniell's *Oriental Scenery*. As Nash put it, his main purpose was scenic effect, 'not pedantic but picturesque'. Work proceeded

204　*The East Front of the Royal Pavilion* [as built] from John Nash, *The Royal Pavilion at Brighton* (1826). Private collection.

slowly. Until 1818, the year of Repton's death, visitors to Brighton would doubt whether it would be completed, but over the next five years it was (figs. 203 and 204).[262] 'The Palace *has been built*', notes the editor to Repton's Memoir next to Repton's prediction that it never would be. 'How injurious to the beautiful designs of Mr Repton may be seen by the Vol published on "The Pavillon Brighton" but which is now a very scarce work.'[263]

Repton dedicated *Fragments* to the Prince Regent, 'our pseudo Sovereign' as he called him in private.[264] The book makes no mention of any commission for the prince; indeed its tenor is a reproach to his manners and morals. *Fragments* focusses on a number of aristocratic landscapes: Cobham, Woburn, Endsleigh, Ashridge, Longleat, and on small commissions, such as Ealing Park and White Lodge, which took in views of royal parks. They commemorate a historically minded, public spirited nobility. Other Fragments on commissions for a range of clients, from Norfolk squires to Essex merchants, establish a polite consensus around highly detailed plans for gardens. The final Fragment on Hare Street incorporates the outlook of 'venerable noblemen' such as the duke of Portland and Viscount Torrington in the view from Repton's own garden:

> To demonstrate the little consequence of Quantity or Value, when speaking of Beauty of scenery, many places have been mentioned, which may perhaps appear too inconsiderable in a work that treats of Dukedoms and Royal Domains: but I wish to evince, that in many cases great effect may be produced by a very contracted quantity of land... nothing more is necessary than a terrace, or a few shrubs and flowers to form a frame to the picture.[265]

Chapter 5

# IN THE NEIGHBOURHOOD OF CITIES

THE DISTRIBUTION of Repton's commissions shows pronounced clusters around cities, prominently London but some provincial cities as well (fig. 35). This provincial urban clustering distinguishes the pattern of Repton's commissions from that of Capability Brown. Norwich, Bristol, Hereford and Leeds feature strongly in the network of Repton's career but not comparable places such as Nottingham, Liverpool, Exeter and Manchester. So while all towns and cities expanded during Repton's career, some prodigiously, and most were social and economic centres for polite society, it was not the increasing growth and power of cities *per se* that accounts for the urban concentration; but the pattern is striking, and, if all Repton's commissions were on record, would probably be more pronounced. Later in his career Repton made an increasing number of proposals for villas, few of which were commemorated in a Red Book, and many of which he preferred to forget. 'These have, of late, had the greatest claim on my attention', Repton wrote in *Fragments* (1816): 'in the neighbourhood of every city or manufacturing town, new places, as villas, are daily springing up; and these, with a few acres, require all the conveniences, comforts and appendages, of larger and more sumptuous, if not more expensive places'.[1]

Urban commissions did not necessarily mean purely commercial clients or *nouveaux riches*. The aristocracy not only socialized in towns and cities, they owned large areas in or near them and could exercise strong control on urban development. A few might be said to have inhibited urbanization, at least as it was expressed in some forms of land use and building, but most sought to manage it in carefully commercial ways, such as developing leasehold housing for polite society or releasing parcels of land for pasture, paddocks or villas. In turn, successful commercial, professional or industrial men purchased fields or small parks on the edges of cities and sought to expand and improve them as country-style residences, not just as a social amenity but, when land values were rising sharply, as a substantial capital gain and secure asset. Some commercial men, or more usually their sons, eventually moved further into the country, away from day-to-day business commitments, to live permanently as squires, but in Repton's time many purchased estates on the urban periphery to maintain their position in civic society.[2]

From the outset of his career, as previous chapters have shown, Repton was commissioned to improve estates in and around towns and cities. Some towns were part of the estate itself, adjacent to the park, and Repton designed grand entrances to redefine patrician control. This was particularly evident at Tatton Park, where the cotton and silk mills of Knutsford flanked the approach to the main drive. Repton's designs for garden squares on the Bedford and Cadogan estates in London were an integral part of the expanding frontier of residential development. At Brighton Repton was involved in the

*facing page* Detail of fig. 218.

most spectacular example of aristocratic urban design in the form of the Royal Pavilion, in a town with a highly fragmented property ownership which was experiencing the highest rate of population increase of any town in the most dramatic decade of national urban growth between 1811 and 1821. Repton was commissioned on estates at the edge of cities to incorporate cities, or parts of them, in views from the park. The main vista of his first commission, at Catton in 1788, focussed on Norwich (fig. 84); then in 1795 Repton designed a broad prospect from Sufton to centre on Hereford (fig. 130). The commissions contrasted in some ways: Catton was a new estate for a Norwich silk merchant and Sufton the hereditary domain of a local squire, but both were for clients who were mayors of the cities they overlooked, and the main feature in view from their parks was a traditionally civic one, the cathedral. Moreover, in each commission Repton himself had a strong stake in positioning his authority over the city; his home city of Norwich, where he had professed one career and wished to initiate another one, and Hereford, the county town of his great adversaries in the picturesque controversy.[3] More impersonal commissions adjacent to populous parts of explicitly commercial or industrial cities presented more difficulties. In 1791 Repton found Mosely Hall, the villa of a Birmingham banker, John Taylor,

> in so populous a neighbourhood, scarce a branch can be lopped off that will not let into view some red house or scarlet tiled roof. The Town of Birmingham tho' in some parts of view may be a beautiful object, must be introduced only in part, and instead of removing that ridge of hill, and the trees to the Northwest, I should rather advise that a few more be placed upon the lawn, so as to hide more of the gaudy red houses.

Repton managed to find another spot from which Birmingham 'looks so picturesque . . . so low down the hill, as to not see much of that flaming red part of the town, but merely St Philip's Church, and the neighbouring houses dimly thro' the intermediate smoke, which gives that misty tone of colour, so much the object of Landscape-painters' (fig. 205).[4]

In this chapter I discuss in detail Repton's commissions around three cities of different kinds: London, the premier centre for every form of business, a metropolis, as contemporaries called it, whose population rose to more than a million; Bristol, the commercial capital of the West Country, still at more than sixty thousand inhabitants in the top tier of provincial cities but losing its primacy as a port city to Liverpool; and Leeds, a city with a population of more than fifty thousand, overtaking Norwich as the centre of the wool textile industry and establishing itself as the major commercial and cultural city of the north. I examine how Repton envisaged the relation between a client's property and its urban situation at various sites around these cities at different stages of his career. This involves charting Repton's role in a number of developments in the environs of cities with different economies in periods of boom and slump: the transformation of farms in to villas, and of villas in to permanent residences; the intensification of land use on estates, by cultivating pasture or gardens or by building factories and canals; the development and dereliction of housing estates; the conversion of public space, or recreational space claimed by the urban excursionists, in to private property; and the selling of landscape parks for new forms of suburban development. I assess Repton's urban sensibility, as an emissary from the fashionable world of London, in terms of both his work around the capital and the conditions he encountered in commissions around provincial cities. To explore these issues is to position Repton's landscapes, on paper and on the ground, in terms of the many ways that cities and their surroundings were designed, described and depicted during his time and the various ideological interests these representations served.[5]

## London

The capital was the centre of Repton's professional ambition. London was not only the place of established power and patronage, where the aristocracy spent half the year and much of their money, but a centre of commercial and cultural innovation and diversification, where newly defined trades and professions catered for an expanding market in polite society. The power of London was national, indeed imperial, in scope. By the end of the eighteenth century, the capital was expanding at a spectacular rate, fast approaching a population of one million, the largest city in Europe and ten times the size of any other in Britain. London interests exercised a formative influence on the nation's culture and society, recycling rents from rural estates, diffusing fashions to provincial towns, transferring resources from one region to another.[6]

205 View towards Birmingham, without overlay, from the Red Book for Mosely Hall (1792). Harvard University, Frances Loeb Library.

Repton moved close to London at Hare Street to forge a metropolitan career, initially writing essays, a play and house criticism for that most commercial of artistic institutions, Boydell's Shakespeare Gallery. When he decided to become a landscape gardener, he took full advantage of the metropolitan economy to transform a pursuit he had developed in Norfolk as a gentleman amateur in to a modern profession, and to market it nation-wide. Repton was not the first London-based, nationally known park and garden consultant, but there was no other obvious candidate to succeed him since the death of Capability Brown, five years earlier. The practices of Brown's followers were provincial in scope, their designs not as fashionable or as innovative as other contemporary arts. Repton refined landscape gardening as a polite art and specialist profession, by incorporating fashionable developments in watercolour, engraving and book publishing. As Repton paid more attention to architectural interiors, so he took stock of the skills of a wide range of London craftsmen, including stained-glass makers and theatrical lamp makers.[7]

Repton could on occasion repeat the conventional criticisms of London, of its giddy pleasures and their corruption of country manners and morals.[8] The capital's very extent and nodality could create problems; 'that dreadful Metropolis [which] divides Essex from Sussex', he once referred to it. Still, London was the hub of Repton's world, for both business and pleasure.[9] He frequented the venues of polite society: Westminster, Whitehall, Lincoln's Inn, and the various entertainments of the West End, plays, concerts, museums, assemblies and exhibitions. He entertained designs on the scenery of the capital. He was keen to have the lofty balustrade of Westminster Bridge rebuilt to frame 'one of the finest rivers in Europe' for both pedestrians and carriage passengers.[10] And in an echo of 'the gilded domes of Constantinople . . . I have often considered gilding the dome of St Paul's as a subject worthy of this nation's wealth and glory'.[11]

Repton's influence on the landscape in London proved to be limited. His plans for exclusive residential areas in London, those developed on aristocratic estates, were confined to garden layouts for Russell, Bloomsbury and Cadogan Squares, the front of Carlton House, and the interior of a merchant's house one night for a masquerade.[12] The field was left to John Nash, Repton's former partner and successful rival for royal patronage, to make the most impressive impact on London since Wren; deploying elements of Repton's style, Nash transformed large areas of the West End in to spectacular scenery.[13]

Repton's influence on London was less civic than suburban. Following Capability Brown's example, and sometimes in his footsteps, Repton was commissioned at a number of sites in the environs of London in those parts of surrounding counties regarded as part of the metropolis, places within ten miles of the central city along the Thames (fig. 206). These included a few long-established estates with mansions and parks, as well as many new sites for villas and grounds. Clients with smaller properties ranged widely in status – aristocrats and statesmen with convenient retreats from Whitehall or Westminster, merchants and bankers commuting to the City. The issue of money, culture and pedigree was pronounced in metropolitan commissions. Repton esteemed clients from older, wholesale merchant families for hosting cultured households, men such as William Salte, whose father had entertained Sterne and Samuel Johnson, who himself welcomed 'the Lord Mayor, other City celebrities [and] some of the Royal Dukes' to soirées at his villa in Tottenham. In contrast were the 'nameless *nouveaux riches*' who increasingly constituted Repton's clientele, the 'worthy cockneys' and 'shopkeepers' who purchased a field and hired Repton for the afternoon to stake out the grounds and site for a villa: 'I can look back on many such concerns, and one day is much like another'.[14]

Repton was careful to adjust his designs to the distance of property from London and variations in land value. 'In the neighbourhood of London where the soil is rich and produces valuable herbage, there is unpardonable extravagance in making large plantations', so Repton declared in the Red Book for Claybury in Essex.[15] He advised the earl of Coventry that the forty-acre grounds

206  Humphry Repton Consultations in and around London. Base map after 'The Environs of London', from *Cary's New Itinerary [of England and Wales]*, ninth edition (1821).

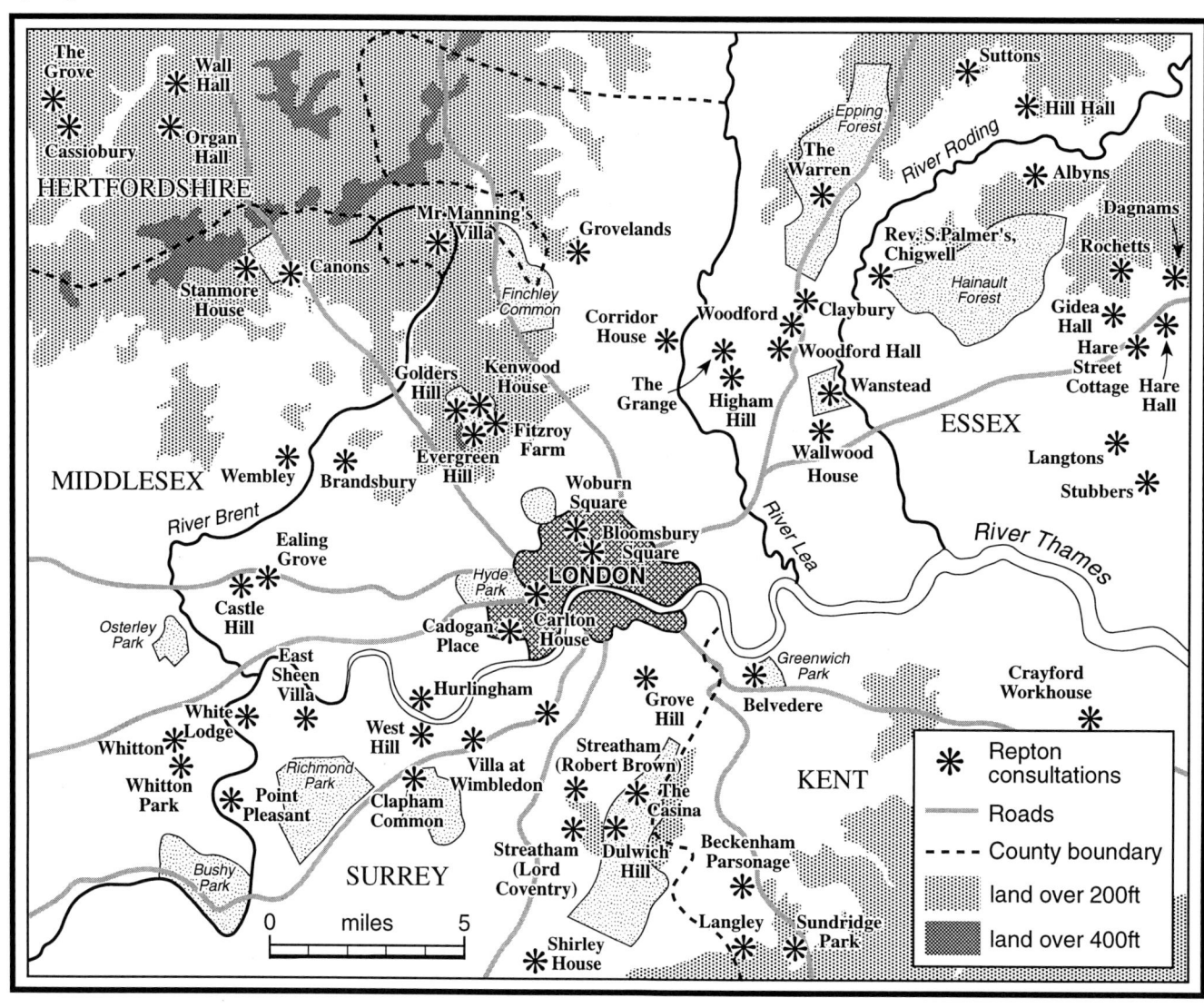

207 View along the River Thames, without overlay, from the Red Book for Point Pleasant (1796). Mrs Paul Mellon, Oak Spring Garden Library, Upperville VA.

of his villa at Streatham were undervalued as pasture: it 'may be worth five pounds [an acre] for cattle; but... may be worth twenty pounds as a garden' supplying 'the daily consumption of a town house' as well as the pleasures of summer and winter walks.[16]

Repton fashioned designs to deal with the various ecologies of the metropolis: river, forest, claylands and sandstone hills. Unlike Brown, Royal Gardener at Hampton Court, Repton had relatively few commissions in the corridor of the élite in the Thames Valley upriver from Westminster. In 1795, in partnership with John Nash, he was commissioned to stake a claim in the region for General The Hon. Frederick St John, to transform Bank Farm, on the river between Richmond and Kingston, in to Point Pleasant. The front entrance of Nash's villa commanded a view of Richmond Hill, and different rooms were positioned to take advantage of two reaches of the river (fig. 207). Repton adopted a highly naturalistic view of this royal region, one that would grant to his client and the public who took the road along the bank the right of any subject to admire the Thames and its associations:

It is not the glitter, or the colour, or the pleasure boats on its surface; it is the vast body of moving element that distinguishes this magnificent object from the tame pieces of artificial water with which parks and gardens are frequently ornamented... its *motion* is beyond the power of Art, in *that* alone consists the sublimity and majesty of this river, for that awakens all the aforesaid associated ideas of its uses to the community. Thus (if I may be allowed the

208  *Epping Forest, with Mr Knight Cutting out Joint Names – and my Low Forest Car and Captain* (c.1789). Colman Collection, Norwich Library. Courtesy Norfolk Libraries and Information Service.

comparison) it is not the crown, the sceptre, the throne, or the outward trappings of Royalty, but the consciousness of kingly power that excites the ideas of happiness, of security, and all the blessings of a well ordered government.[17]

Repton had more commissions in a more commercial, less fashionable, region to the east of the city in Essex, in the vicinity of the forests of Epping and Hainault. This was near Repton's own roadside villa at Hare Street and in a region long favoured by city merchants and financiers for residence and for recreation by a range of excursionists. At the outset of his career, Repton had invited Anna Seward to join him in an excursion to the Essex forests, in a conscious echo of Capability Brown, who 'frequently passed whole days in studying the sequestered haunts of Needwood Forest'.[18] Seward declined, and Repton went with a friend and early client, Samuel Knight, commemorating the event with a sketch (fig. 208) of the two cutting their names in an ancient oak tree.[19]

The Essex forests were regarded by improving interests as a nuisance for harbouring deer, who destroyed crops on adjacent fields, and criminals, who poached the deer and preyed on villas and villages nearby.[20] The Epping Forest authorities strongly resisted enclosures, pulling down palings erected for illegal encroachments and reopening ridings and footpaths. There were plans in 1793 by the Crown Commissioners to disforest Hainault and manage the remaining timber for the nearby shipyards, but they met sufficient local opposition for the bill not to reach the Commons.[21] At Highams, the banker John Harman commissioned Repton to landscape an enclosure from Epping Forest. The forest authorities allowed Repton's plans for a pleasure ground as long as the deer were allowed free passage to drink at the lake.[22] In the Red Book for Claybury, for the merchant James Hatch, Repton recalled Hainault Forest as 'the school from whence I have drawn those lessons of beauty which I am now called upon to teach others', and suggested a woodland walk from the villa to ancient trees (fig. 209), but with a 'rude picturesque cottage' near the gate, where 'a labourer's family might be so disposed as to give security to a place, which from its vicinity to the Capital may not otherwise be safe for women, at a late hour, if the charms of the forest should invite them beyond the boundary of this wood'.[23] Improvements were intended to reclaim the forests from excursionists as well as from deer and poachers. Repton was commissioned to turn a dilapidated, former public house, the Reindeer Tavern in the middle of Epping Forest, in to a smart private residence. The tavern was

> in a sequestered part of the forest, with summer access by green lanes, or broad grass glades; and appropriated to the Sunday visits of those who made holiday, fancying they enjoyed solitude in a forest, amidst the

209  Woodland walk, from the Red Book for Claybury (1791). Reproduced courtesy of the Essex Record Office.

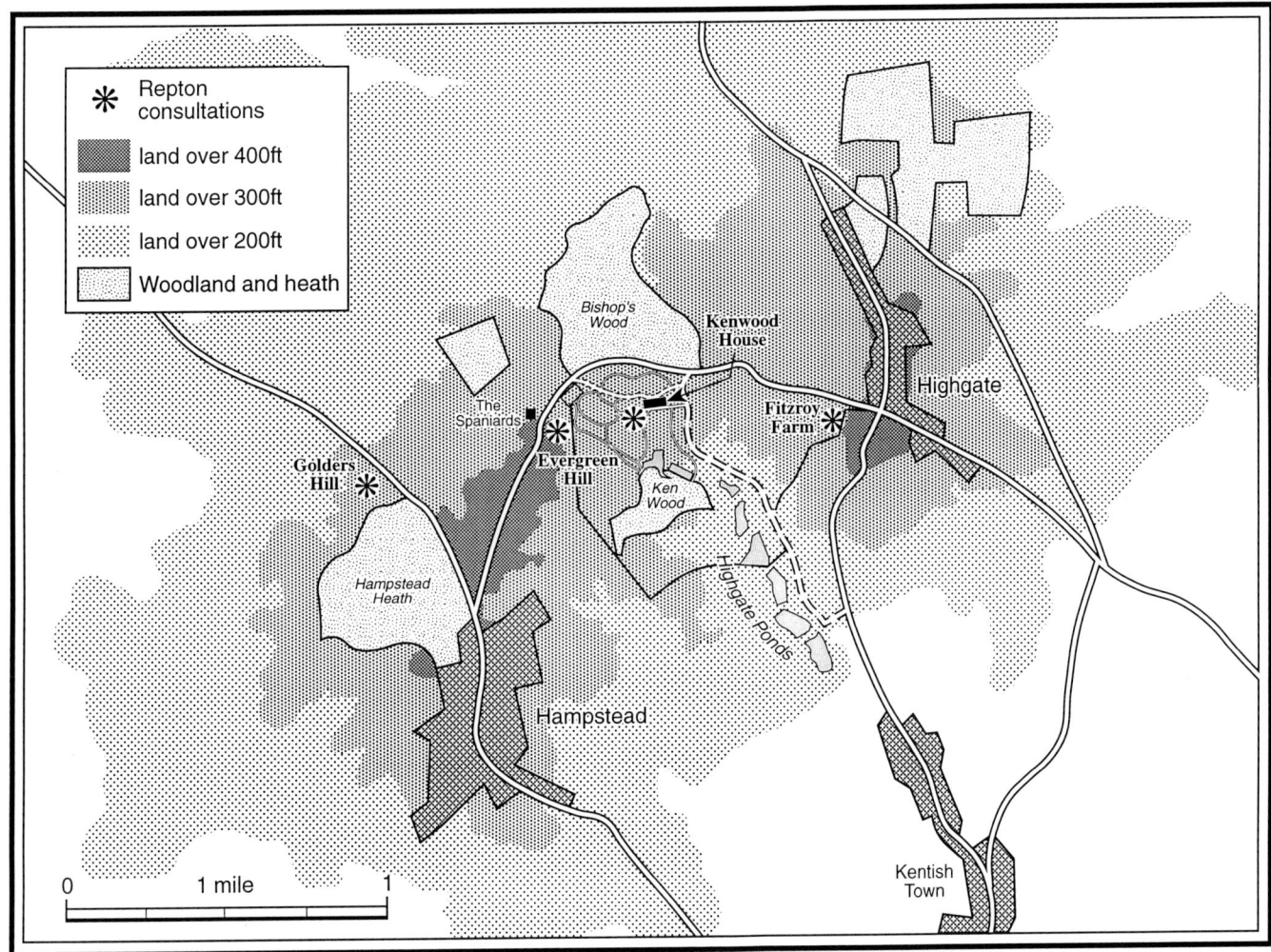

210 Humphry Repton Consultations on the Northern Heights, Middlesex. After maps in the Red Book for Kenwood House (1793); J. Thompson, *Map of the Parish of St Pancras* (1804). British Library.

crowd of *'felicity hunters'*, who came here to forget the cares of London. It was not uncommon to see fifty horses in the yards and stables, and twice as many guests filling the large rooms . . . it is not only a spot of four or five acres enclosed from the forest, but is surrounded by a rabbit warren, which the late occupier made an object of profit . . . the place altogether is a scene of slovenliness.[24]

The rest of this section on the London area is devoted to a discussion of Repton's commissions five to six miles north-west of the city, on a ridge of land reaching four hundred feet, running from Willesden through Hampstead and Highgate (fig. 210). In the eighteenth century the demands of the growing metropolitan market transformed these northern heights.[25] Farms on the claylands concentrated on the production of hay, and sandy ridges were quarried for building material. The demand for fresh air and fine prospects transformed hamlets near main roads in to weekend resorts and commuter villages, farms and heathland in to villas and grounds. It was not all prosperity and polish. The very presence of the capital and the sensitivity of the region to sudden shifts in demand resulted in pockets of blight. Those who applauded the plush hay farms and pleasant villas also complained about the seediness of roadside resorts, mismanagement of estates, neglect of woods and pilfering from fields.[26]

The northern heights offered new opportunities for polite society, a domain and vantage point to define a new élite. The Thames Valley was largely occupied by established interests, colonized by courtly society below

Richmond Hill and by colonial merchants and naval men below Greenwich Park. The main axes for the northern heights were the roads running into the City and Westminster travelled by businessmen and professionals. Many of this group had already taken up town houses just to the north of the city in Bloomsbury and, as the urban frontier advanced around them, they looked to the heights of Hampstead and Highgate for more spacious accommodation. The northern heights lacked a resident nobility or hereditary landed gentry, neither did they yet possess an established landscape iconography, a package of painterly and literary associations. The cultural character that this region acquired owed much to its colonization by a profession that Repton greatly esteemed, the law.[27]

The law had long been an entrée into landed society; at the end of the eighteenth century landed families looked upon the law as a source of income for their sons. With its relative openness in its various ranks to men (such as Repton's son William) from less prestigious families and a reforming wing in London that raised its profile as an independent profession, the law was valued as a powerful force for social cohesion.[28] With huge sums to invest and the right connections, members of the legal profession fashioned themselves as a resident gentry on the northern heights and sought to expand their estates. Law lords and judges bought substantial properties, barristers and attorneys smaller ones between. They not only enjoyed swift access to the Inns of Court, but looked down on a metropolis whose expansion and complexity enhanced their own influence.

In this section I consider three of Repton's commissions on the northern heights at various stages in his career. First I examine the commission of 1789 at Brandsbury for Lady Salusbury, widow of a High Court judge, then that of 1793 for Lord Stormont, heir to Chief Justice Mansfield's estate at Kenwood, and finally the commission in 1808 at Evergreen Hill for the most celebrated barrister of the day, Thomas Erskine.

## Brandsbury

The commission at Brandsbury, beginning in March 1789, was Repton's third, and the first for which he prepared a Red Book. In the dedication he explains that he will be 'minute and particular in delivering my sentiments; because this is the first place of any consequence in which I have been consulted so near London, and I consider that in proportion to the proximity of the Spot to the Capital, my reputation may be advanced or retarded'.[29] Brandsbury was located about five miles north of Hyde Park Corner near the village of Willesden, just off Watling Street, one of the main roads from London. His client Lady Salusbury, a seventy-year-old widow of a judge of the High Court of the Admiralty, already owned a small estate at Offley in Hertfordshire as well as a town house in the West End.[30] Lady Salusbury makes a dramatic appearance in the opening pages of Repton's Memoir, 'presiding in a magnificent mansion in upper Harley Street'.

> I was conducted to a room on the second floor. No sooner was the door opened than I was saluted by the barking of half a dozen pet dogs, pugs, lap dogs, and spaniels all joined in chorus with not less than 20 birds of various kinds exercizing their lungs to the utmost pitch – thus surrounded I found one of the most dignified but pleasing old ladies I ever beheld, her age was about 70 and she was dressed in the richest brocade – with treble ruffles of costly lace. She received me with all the kind and gracious manners of *le vieille coeur* and she explained to me that she had lately purchased a little land in Middlesex, with a small house and requested my opinion on paper how the place could be improved by planting – for that it was naked and wanted shade.[31]

The property was modest – 'some hundred acres', 'little more than sixty acres', Repton variously recalled – although the sale deed to Lady Salusbury describes it as 160 acres, an area to which Repton's map in the Red Book approximates (fig. 15).[32] But for Repton the scale of his undertaking was considerable. Brandsbury had suffered neglect after passing through the hands of a swift succession of owners: a London distiller, a Southwark brewer, a professional gambler and a Long Acre coach-maker. After the last man died, it was three years before Lady Salusbury purchased the property, in the long term as an investment settled in trust for her heir (her husband's nephew), in the short term as a summer retreat for herself.[33]

In his Memoir Repton describes his dismay when he first visited the site, finding the house 'without a tree near it, except 2 Elms and a few old apple trees', and he 'trembled' at this presumption to create shady walks given the time that trees took to grow and the years left

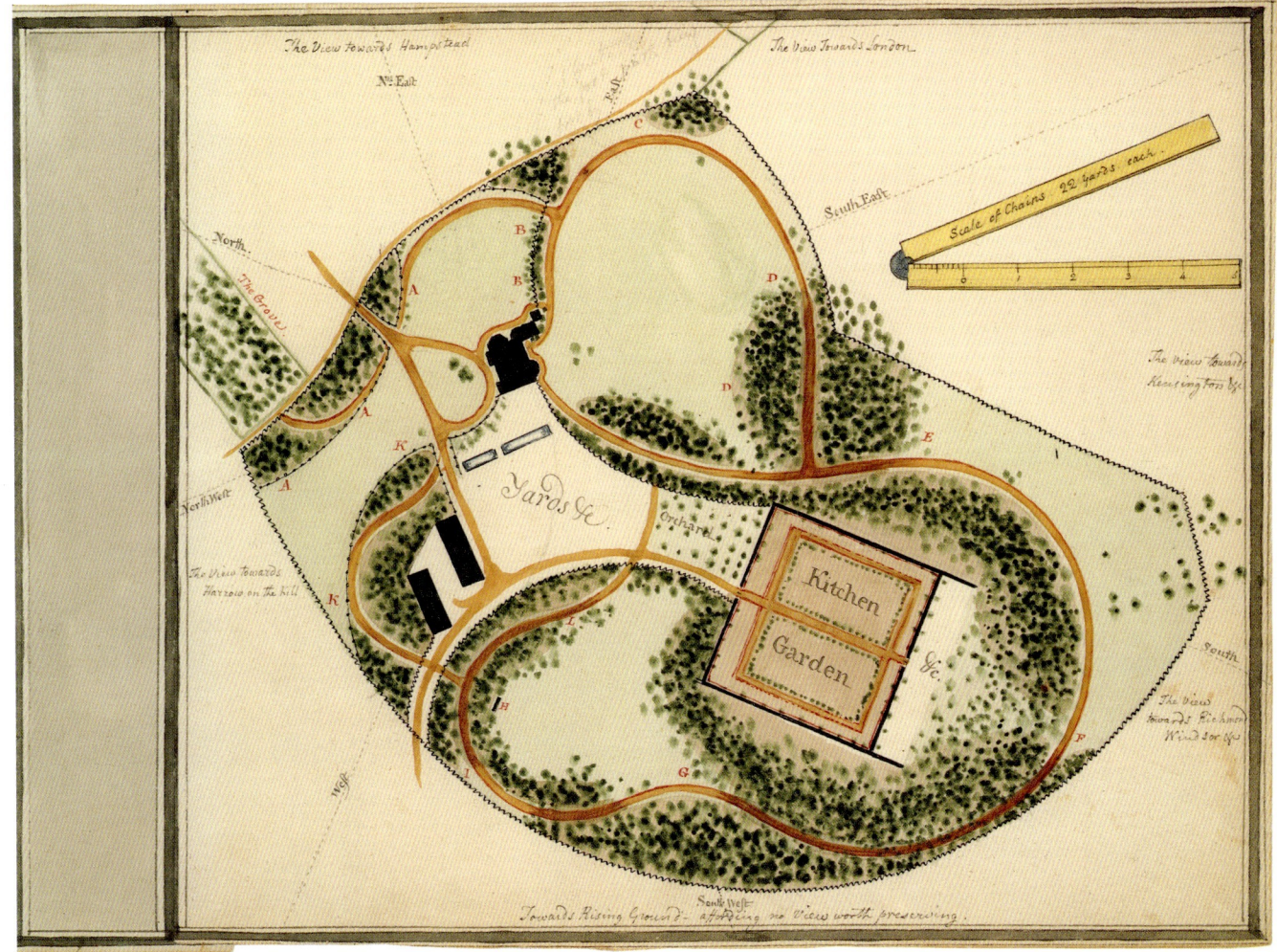

211 Plan of the pleasure grounds, from the Red Book for Brandsbury (1789). Dumbarton Oaks Research Library, Washington DC.

to his client.[34] The Red Book records a little more cover than Repton remembered, a narrow strip of plantation to the north and a few oaks and elms, 'old inhabitants of the spot', in hedgerows, relics of a wooded landscape laid to grass. Local hills grubbed up and 'appropriated to the scythe' were reckoned to increase their value tenfold in ten years and Repton appreciated this in his design. 'All the surrounding Country is already the most beautiful grassland imaginable . . . the surface uniformly covered with the most beautiful verdure yielding hay & pasture so valuable that the land lets from 40s to 60s per Acre.' Thus Repton advised enclosing just ten to twelve acres 'for private use, and so much more will remain to be lett off, consequently my plan has the united recommendation of *Pleasure* and *Profit*'. The private grounds would include hay barns and stables, a newly planted orchard, a kitchen garden and shrub- and tree-lined walks winding nearly a mile (fig. 211). A little planting in the surrounding meadows was intended to improve the views from the home enclosure, hiding 'an ugly red house near the road', screening some ponds and clothing the horizon.[35]

Repton felt obliged to repair the efforts of a part-time landscaper whom Lady Salusbury had previously consulted, 'a person incompetent to the subject'. The offending man had slavishly copied Capability Brown's design for nearby Stanmore, without taking account of the contrasting topography of the properties, surrounding Brandsbury with a paling, screening out views that 'an eminence should command' (fig. 4). When Repton saw what 'had so expensively been done,' he tried vainly to 'accommodate my plan of improvement' to it, but as the new paling had collapsed in several places into drainage

212  Proposed view north-east towards Hampstead, from the Red Book for Brandsbury (1789). Dumbarton Oaks Research Library, Washington DC.

ditches in the last high wind, he decided to remove it and begin again.[36]

In his surviving account book for 1789 to 1790, Repton lists no less than thirty site visits to Brandsbury, for a total of seventy-nine days, far more than for any other commission at the time. As well as using his post-chaise from Hare Street or from other commissions, he took the stage-coach each day from Oxford Street, where he stayed overnight in a hotel. Repton's visits were concentrated in the first year of his career, as he was building up his practice. Indeed the commission largely funded his early career. By May 1790 it had realized £413, more than twice as much as any other commission, and almost exactly the surplus that placed him 'in a state of ease and comparative affluence'. It subsidised commissions such as those at Holkham and Welbeck, where Repton reckoned his financial losses were compensated by the influence of his clients. At Brandsbury, Repton was granted 'uncontrolled command of men and money'. Moreover his style was not cramped by the presence of his client, who 'never would consent to visit the villas with me, she said she was perfectly satisfied to leave it all under my direction'.[37] Brandsbury was a proving ground for Repton's technical expertise. The commission helped the landscape gardener formulate exactly how he would define his profession, which skills to develop, which tasks to take on and which not.

During the commission Repton purchased the various tools of his trade, theodolite, level, chain, telescope, scale, protractor, T-square and rulers.[38] The plans in the Red Book reflect the use of these instruments. Serpentine walks and straight vistas are measured with mathematical precision. Indeed the pleasure grounds are designed like an observatory, each view plotted with a compass bearing (fig. 211). Repton's ruler appears in a vignette to show the scale of the plans. After Brandsbury, Repton seldom undertook such precise surveying, even if his trade card always showed him with his hand at the theodolite.[39]

213 Proposed view south-east towards London, from the Red Book for Brandsbury. Dumbarton Oaks Research Library, Washington DC.

Repton took on contractual duties at Brandsbury, such as dealing with the Justices to move the course of a path and paying the nurseryman for plants, that he rarely assumed thereafter. Perhaps the most important skill he developed was in groundwork. 'To this early concern I am indebted for more lasting benefits, as it made me practically acquainted with draining and planting and moving of ground.'[40] Repton devoted most of March and April 1789 to groundwork. He likened it to preparations for painting: 'I am now straining the canvas', he wrote to Norton Nicholls, 'or rather (the fence being nearly completed) the canvas is strain'd and I am making a few charcoal dashes to my picture – to be finish'd hereafter'.[41] Planting could not begin until autumn, but when it did it was a large operation which was finished by the end of 1790. 'By employing a number of labourers to plant a great many trees and shrubs – of the largest size it was possible to move, by the second year the character of the place was quite altered.'[42]

Repton planted both to provide shelter and to create vistas in every direction, from the house and from the walks. Northwards the neighbouring hills were brought into the picture; Hampstead and surrounding villas seen through some of the old elms (fig. 212), Harrow framed by new flanking plantations. To the south views were made over London, views of the City and Westminster from the garden through new shrubberies and small plantations massed with old elms (fig. 213). Views of Kensington, Richmond and Windsor were made from perimeter walks. In a supplement to the Red Book dated December 1790, detailing deviations from the original plans, Repton acknowledges 'the general prevalence of fashion to have an extensive prospect, made it dangerous in me to advise that much of it should be shut out by plantations', but that Lady Salusbury demanded 'more shade and less prospect' in the view of London. So the garden was planted with large young trees, and installed with Gothic garden seats designed by William Wilkins,

214  Designs for Reposoir and Gothic Seat, from the Red Book for Brandsbury. Dumbarton Oaks Research Library, Washington DC.

one inscribed to Lady Salusbury, one to her companion Miss Maud (fig. 214). But the trees and garden furniture were placed so that it was still possible to see 'those objects which heighten the value of this peaceful situation by the charm of contrast; a view of the distant cupola of St Paul's and the towers of Westminster Abbey are still preserved'. Moreover, by grubbing up some old, cankered apple trees further to the east, Repton opened up the view towards Kew and Richmond, now with 'handsome groupes of large Elms and Oaks... enrich[ing] the foreground to the distant scenery'. Repton glossed his design with a passage from William Mason's *The English Garden* (1777). Mason's lines on a winding garden path with glimpses out between the flowers and shrubs, 'each step/Shall awaken fresh beauties; each short point present/ A different picture', highlight the daintiness of Repton's design.[43]

Repton reported Lady Salusbury happy with his work at Brandsbury, so 'delighted with everything I had done' that she paid him '50£ above the balance of my account' and gave him 'a small rouleau in red morocco sealed and directed "To Mrs Repton tho' unknown", containing '19 new guineas and one new shilling, all fresh from the Mint'! His client, he was happy to report, 'lived nearly twenty years... in good health and spirits... to enjoy [her pleasure grounds]'. Repton had made sure his plans would not interfere 'with any future views of more extensive improvements' should his client 'hereafter wish to increase the property by purchasing the neighbouring *prospect-hills*, to which a delightful *drive* might be conducted'. As Lady Salusbury 'never used other exercize than to come down to dinner', it is not surprising that she declined Repton's overtures, but she continued to expand her property.[44] Five years on, Repton reported that Brandsbury 'has since been augmented, by several purchases, to so great an amount, that my plan, and indeed the house itself, are on too small a scale for the present size of the estate; which extends two miles in length from the toll-gate of Kilburn turnpike, and is therefore one of the largest landed properties within so short a distance of London'.[45]

215 Benedetto Pastorini and Giovanni Vitalba after Robert Adam, *View of the South Front of the Villa at Kenwood*, from *The Works in Architecture of Robert and James Adam* (1774). Photograph English Heritage.

### Kenwood

Sited on the summit of the steep ridge between Hampstead and Highgate, Kenwood House commanded the northern heights. It was the climax of the carriage excursion from London, a fine house, designed by Robert Adam, by the main road looking over pleasure grounds, possibly landscaped by Capability Brown, and framing a spectacular view of the city. In 1793, a year after Adam's death, Repton was called in to remodel the house and grounds. It was his most prestigious and challenging commission on the northern heights, and probably, at that time, anywhere.[46]

Kenwood owed much of its charisma to its former owner, Attorney General William Murray, later Chief Justice Lord Mansfield. Murray had purchased Kenwood from his political master and fellow Scot, Lord Bute, in 1754, as a convenient retreat from his work in the Inns of Court and town house in Bloomsbury Square and as a place to entertain. He expanded the estate from ninety to 230 acres, refashioned the fifty-acre pleasure grounds immediately below the house and, in 1764, on Bute's introduction, commissioned Robert Adam to remodel the house.[47] Adam designed a parade of reception rooms that culminated in what he called 'the great room' on the south front, a library, drawing-room and long gallery looking over the grounds to London. The parade was continued on to the terrace outside. In his published works, Adam dilated on the view:

Over the vale, through which the water flows, there is a noble view let into the house and terrace, of the city of London, Greenwich Hospital, the River Thames, the ships passing up and down, with an extensive prospect, but clear and distinct, on both sides of the river. To the north-east and west of the house and terrace, the mountainous villages of Highgate and Hampstead form delightful objects. The whole scene is amazingly gay, magnificent, beautiful and picturesque.

A new façade for the south front, decorated with linear patterns that echo those of the great room, was made 'suitable to such a scene' (fig. 215).[48]

Lord Mansfield's reputation as a reforming judge, in mercantile law, religious discrimination and court procedure, made him a hero in commercial and professional circles, not least in the profession of the law, whose moral and cultural reputation he greatly enhanced.[49] Mansfield was mindful of this. Adam's great room featured a full-length portrait showing Mansfield accompanied by a bust of Homer pointing to a page of Cicero. Flanking mirrors reflected the prospect of London. The ceiling was decorated with allegorical lunettes showing Justice embracing Peace, Commerce, Navigation and Agriculture. There was a flourishing souvenir industry in casts, cameos and engravings of Mansfield. Visitors flocked to Kenwood as to a shrine, to look over the house and grounds, hoping to catch a glimpse of the great man himself.[50]

When Mansfield's nephew David Murray, the seventh Lord Stormont, succeeded to the title and estate in 1793, he was anxious to remodel Kenwood, both the house and grounds. Aged sixty-six, he was also in a hurry. He decided to use Kenwood not as a summer or weekend villa but as his main country house, in preference to his family seat of Scone Palace, Perthshire. The second Lord Mansfield promoted the cult of his uncle and was himself a patron of Robert Adam (who designed his town house in Portland Place) and a pallbearer at Adam's funeral. So he would have wished to maintain some continuity at Kenwood; indeed if Adam had not died suddenly, he might well have been re-commissioned. The second Lord Mansfield was more a connoisseur than his uncle. During a long career on the Continent as a diplomat, he had amassed a large collection of paintings and furniture which he wished to install at Kenwood.[51] On his return to England he took a close interest in landscape gardening, noting in 1789 the 'fair character and good taste' of William Emes and Samuel Lapidge, and in 1791, after a visit to the duke of Portland's estate at Bulstrode, that Humphry Repton 'as a very ingenious man, has an admirable eye and lays out grounds remarkably well'. He misspelt Repton's name – 'Ruffort' – but he correctly noted his address, terms and conditions.[52] Stormont's remarks suggest that he knew of other examples of Repton's work. Repton had been employed at the adjacent estate east of Kenwood, Fitzroy Farm. This was for two brief site visits in 1790, to advise on landscaping grounds for a new villa by Henry Holland.[53]

On 8 May 1793, less than two months after Stormont came in to possession of Kenwood, Repton paid his first visit. He completed the Red Book in just twelve days. A supplement was added on 1 July detailing further improvements now that Repton had the advantage of a new survey of the grounds.[54] He submitted an account, totalling £78 15s., the following month, saying 'I was so much interested in the subject as to make every other give place to it until I had completed my general outline'.[55] Repton was given responsibility to remodel the house in collaboration with the relatively unknown Robert Nasmith, whom Stormont had already employed elsewhere. Hitherto Repton had not been commissioned to landscape the grounds of a house by Adam, let alone alter the architecture. But given Adam's integration of landscape and architecture, indeed the primacy he placed on picturesque scenery, Repton was an appropriate choice.[56]

Repton outlined his objectives at the outset of the Red Book:

> Kenwood has hitherto been considered only as a Villa, but notwithstanding its proximity to the Capital, yet the command of property by which it is surrounded entitles it to a much higher degree of importance . . . I shall therefore beg leave to consider the subject not merely as a Villa, but as a superb and elegant Mansion, surrounded by a sufficient extent of landed property, to give all the importance, convenience, and even privacy, of many situations in more distant parts of the Kingdom.

So long as Kenwood remained a villa, 'it was no reflection on the taste of my late ingenious friend Mr. Robert Adam, that he had provided only *one room* for almost every purpose, especially as that room is confessedly one of the most elegant that was ever built in England'. Adam's library was 'perfectly calculated for every purpose of living with elegance in a place of occasional retreat: but when the house is considered as the residence of a family, it is very deficient in other apartments'. Repton did not want to disturb 'the grand façade to the south' and proposed adding two wings to the north. As well as providing for a new suite of rooms, these would open up new views, once the space to the northern side of the house had been transformed. The main road was to be moved two hundred yards to the north, beyond the Bishop's Wood, creating space for a new entrance drive. The clutter of buildings and walls – of the service section, kitchen garden, farmyard and menagerie, which, 'with no accurate plan of the premises', made it difficult enough for Repton even to envisage what he proposed in a drawing – was to be cleared away. A new dining-room in the east wing would look north over Bishop's Wood. A new library in the west wing would look west over a new winter garden and beyond towards a new farm and a large portion of grazing land that Mansfield had taken in. The various components of Repton's improvements, in each quarter of Kenwood, were linked by a series of new walks. There was no need to pass through Adam's house in the ordained way to see the landscape aright; you could now walk around the house to gain access to the grounds.

If Adam's interior no longer exercised a commanding influence, Repton enhanced the role of his south front

216  The approach, with and without overlay, from the Red Book for Kenwood (1793). Private collection.

217 View of the south front and terrace, with and without overlay, from the Red Book for Kenwood (1793). Private collection.

and terrace in defining the landscape. Repton wished to make more of the south front of Kenwood as a feature, both as a scene in itself and as a vantage point for viewing London. The proximity of Fitzroy Farm, less than a hundred yards from the eastern edge of the house, presented problems. Repton pencilled in on his sketch map the possibility of an exchange of land but went ahead assuming that this would not be forthcoming. Fitzroy Farm presented a challenge to Kenwood. It was the northernmost portion of the large and lucrative Southampton estate that stretched down through the resort of Kentish Town to the prestigious Fitzroy Square, designed by Adam.[57] Southampton not only enjoyed a more extensive prospect of London than Stormont, but incorporated the grounds of Kenwood in the view. Repton's proposals for Kenwood make little concession to Fitzroy Farm; indeed they seek to overpower it.[58]

Repton proposed a new, better graded and more direct approach to Kenwood from London, bypassing Highgate and Fitzroy Farm. This was to branch off from Kentish Town and run up the valley, past the string of ponds leased as reservoirs to the Hampstead Water Company (fig. 216). Repton was pleased to reflect that they 'contribute to the existence and happiness of so many thousand human beings', for 'the mind is ever ready to admit Utility as a great source of beauty'. For the same reason he suggested demolishing the sham bridge, 'which however beautiful from some parts of the terrace, yet as it is a deception is so frequently liable to be detected, I think it is an object beneath the dignity of Kenwood'. The approach would display the 'wonderful elegance' of the south façade of Kenwood House, 'at present no where to be seen with the advantage it deserves'.[59] A distant view of the façade would have proved superior to the close, oblique view in Adam's published work which revealed the fine decorative details, for the new stucco that the Adam brothers had patented had proved a disaster, deteriorating and demanding continual and none too

successful repair.[60] Repton later reported that 'the great Lord Mansfield often declared that had the front of Kenwood been originally covered with Parian marble, he should have found it less expensive than stucco'.[61]

Repton proposed extending 'that magnificent terrace which is doubtless one of the first ornaments of Kenwood' eastwards across the valley. This involved removing a walled fruit garden sunk into the valley, infilling and bridging with an 'ornamented front of masonry' (fig. 217). The celebrated vista over London had been obscured by the growth of trees on the lawns. 'By extending the terrace as proposed across the deep valley, we shall acquire a view totally unlike any other at Kenwood, and indeed superior in splendour to most others in the kingdom.'

Repton's illustrations show the improvements required to create the grand view (fig. 218). On the left Fitzroy Farm and the public footpath between the estates are screened by a row of conifers (perhaps nurses for hardwoods). On the right deciduous trees on the lawns are cut back revealing the dome of St Paul's. In the right foreground, some felling reveals the cedars planted by the first Lord Mansfield. In the left a balustrade over the bridge with an ornamental urn make a feature of the framing tree that is included in the 'before' view but is on other evidence, including other Repton views, an invention. If 'it could be made to appear (which indeed is almost literally the fact) that the domain of Kenwood extends to the suburbs of the metropolis it would add greatly to the importance of the scene'. Kenwood actually extended nowhere near the length of the Southampton estate, so Repton recommended planting a field downvalley near the proposed private entrance, 'to exclude the red houses of Kentish town', so 'we may avail ourselves of the whole valley'. Ornamenting the ponds with trees, a Classical temple and a sailboat gave the appearance of river flowing into the distance. Thus 'the valley may be opened to display in its full force a terminating scene the

218 View from the terrace, with and without overlay, from the Red Book for Kenwood (1793). Private collection.

most magnificent that can be conceived', a 'superb *coup d'oeil*; which I consider a specimen of the sublime, or epic style in Landscape Gardening'.[62]

Repton's illustration of the improved view of London from Kenwood is modelled on prospects of Rome done in a Claudian style, notably Richard Wilson's views of the mid-1750s from above the Ponte Molle (fig. 219). From right to left in Repton's view the wooded hill, the dome of St Paul's, the landscaped ponds, the bridge at the end of the terrace and the framing tree at Kenwood appear in the place of the hill of the Villa Madama, the dome of St Peter's, River Tiber, foreground bridge and framing tree in Wilson's view.[63] It was an entirely appropriate tribute to Adam, who had been in Rome in the mid-1750s and found it

> the most glorious place in the universal world ... the hills it stands on give you everywhere elevated prospects of town and country – the town rich with domes, spires and lofty buildings, ancient and modern; the country near Rome uneven, hilly, woody and adorned with villas and churches ... for a man of taste the day is too short, as you never tire of agreeable, grand and picturesque walks.[64]

Repton had the view of London from the terrace at Kenwood engraved for the 1795 issue of the *Polite Repository* (fig. 220). Another view, of the front of the house from the south, was published in the issue for 1812. But these remained Repton's only published references to his work at Kenwood. He mentions Kenwood in his published writings only in connection with architectural details, and then does not claim direct authorship for the designs. There is no mention of Kenwood in his Memoir. Repton had reason to feel slighted, his authority put in to question. His involvement in Kenwood after submitting the Red Book seems to have been limited. He made a further visit there in July 1794, then after a two-year gap in July 1796, after Mansfield had died. He borrowed the Red Book 'because so much time had elapsed between the visits to Kenwood – that from the multiplicity of other matters – the changes which had taken place in the grounds – I could hardly distinguish what was my plan from what had been alter'd'. So Repton wrote in October 1796 to Mansfield's executors who requested the Red Book's return.[65]

Work on the foundations of the house extensions began immediately after Repton had submitted the Red Book, but within a month the architect Nasmith died. As a replacement, Repton recommended the Norwich architect William Wilkins, with whom he was collaborating elsewhere.[66] The commission was given to the London-based George Saunders. Saunders was already employed as surveyor at Kenwood and had contracted for the diversion of the high road, but he also had an academic reputation as an antiquarian and architectural theorist.[67] Whereas Repton attempted to design the wings with a decorative surface to complement the entrance of Adam's house, Saunders made them plain, in brick, and more prominent, perhaps a sign of the fashionable reaction against the impurity of Adam's classicism, perhaps a deliberate attempt not to ape the work of the master.[68] In a footnote in *Observations*, Repton claims some indirect, if marginal influence on the remodelling of Kenwood, suggesting to Saunders the idea of the octagonal kitchen based on that in the ruins of

219 Richard Wilson, *Rome from the Ponte Molte* (1754). National Museum of Wales, Cardiff.

220 After Humphry Repton, *View from the Terrace at Kenwood*, from *Peacock's Polite Repository* (1795). Bodleian Library, Oxford.

Glastonbury abbey.[69] In a long notice of *Observations* for the *Monthly Review* (July 1804), Saunders robustly rejected Repton's 'claim to the character of an architect'. He maintained that the landscape gardener had little understanding of architectural form and function, of the rational order of solid and void, even the basic principles of construction. If Repton thought Capability Brown demonstrated 'Palladian abilities' in his buildings, 'we cannot think that Mr Repton is well acquainted with Palladio's history, nor that he is aware that the most celebrated architects have been good practical builders and sound mathematicians'. Repton's designs, all ornament and surface, produced not buildings, but 'baubles', his improvements were mere 'patch-work'. It was Repton's very claim to be able to design everything 'from the sofa to the sideboard, from the tomb to the temple' that exposed his pretensions. 'And to crown it all here is a proposition for gilding the outside of the dome of St Paul's!'[70]

A plan of Kenwood prepared for the third earl of Mansfield in 1797 shows the realization of some improvements for the grounds that Repton had proposed or endorsed in the Red Book.[71] The new entrance drive from the north is marked, also the extension to the south terrace. But the main axis of Repton's proposals, the new private drive from the south, is not evident. While an approach from Kentish Town was later, in 1838, described by Loudon, he did so to indicate the opportunity that had been missed: 'This approach if widened, and properly planted, would form the noblest avenue to a gentleman's seat in the neighbourhood of London'.[72]

The plan of 1797 also shows the work of others who were commissioned in Repton's wake. The new garden was laid out in curved beds, a design that Loudon attributed to the estate gardener and described as a disfigurement.[73] The agriculturalist William Marshall designed a new, octagonal-shaped farmhouse, and probably advised on the management of the fields. Marshall had been commissioned at Scone Palace just before the third earl inherited Kenwood, and was launching his own publishing career as an expert on landscaping and estate management, with an emphasis on improved farming as the functional key to estate improvement.[74] Kenwood acquired a model farm. Milne's land utilization map of the London area (1800) shows the eight arable fields of the 200-acre farm in bright yellow in a sea of green pasture on the northern heights; guides reported them 'in a very high state of cultivation'.[75] The countess of Mansfield exercised a strong influence on Kenwood's new agrarian image. She commissioned Julius Caesar Ibbetson to paint two pedigree cows grazing the pasturelands with Kenwood House in the distance, and in the years 1794–6 to execute a set of decorative paintings for the new music room, showing 'various operations of agriculture, fancifully represented as performed by unattired children'.[76] William Emes, in semi-retirement, was consulted in July 1795, probably to advise on the lake. The figure who probably mattered most in the improvements was the long-serving estate steward, Edward Hunter. A description of Kenwood in the London and Middlesex volume of *The Beauties of England and Wales* (1816) mentions Adam, Saunders, Marshall and Ibbetson by name but not Repton. It reported that 'the leading improvements in these grounds have been effected under

221 *View at Kenwood from the Terrace Walk near the House*, from John Claudius Loudon, *The Suburban Gardener and Villa Companion* (1838). Yale Center for British Art, Paul Mellon Collection.

the guidance of Mr Hunter, who resides on the estate as land-steward to the Earl of Mansfield, and was likewise retained as steward by the Lord Chief Justice'.[77] Repton is not mentioned in Loudon's lengthy account of Kenwood of 1838 (fig. 221), or in any of the footnotes to his 1840 edition of Repton's works. By the time of Loudon's visit to Kenwood, Repton's 'superb *coup d'oeil*' of London from the terrace had been occluded by spreading trees and foliage. Moreover, 'a stranger walking around the park would never discover that he was between Hampstead and Highgate, or even suppose he was so near London'.[78]

\* \* \*

## Evergreen Hill

Repton was engaged for a number of years on a more modest and more congenial commission on the western border of Kenwood, by the main road near the Spaniards Inn. The celebrated barrister Thomas Erskine purchased a small house there around 1795 as a summer and weekend residence. The house was divided from its grounds by the high road but joined by a tunnel under the road. The 25-acre property had been enclosed from Hampstead Heath and ran up to the edge of the Kenwood estate. Erskine proceeded to plant bays and laurels in the grounds, naming the property Evergreen Hill.[79]

The youngest son of an impoverished Scottish earl, Erskine made his reputation in London as a brilliant radical barrister, notably at the Treason Trials of 1794. He became a passionate advocate of that most urbane of causes, animal welfare, taking on reactionary squires such as William Windham in the Commons, thrashing a man who was beating a horse on Hampstead Heath and keeping a pet goose in his garden. Erskine stood at the opposite end of the political spectrum to Lord Mansfield, a distant relation, but had enjoyed some support from the Chief Justice when making his career. Like Mansfield, Erskine became a legal celebrity, his speeches rushed in to print, his image struck in souvenir portraits, busts and tokens. He was a cult figure for his profession, helping to raise the fees and status of lawyers. Erskine himself made a handsome living, with earnings of up to ten thousand a year at the Bar, most of which he spent freely. His villa at Evergreen Hill never pretended to rival neighbouring Kenwood but became established as a social rendezvous for leading figures in the law, and, as Erskine had literary enthusiasms, something of a salon too.[80]

Repton first met Erskine at Buxton, the spa for the Midlands, in 1790, perhaps through Anna Seward who attended the barrister's literary soirées.[81] Thereafter Repton 'shar'd his wit and festive meals'.[82] It is probable that Repton was involved in improvements at Evergreen Hill from the time Erskine purchased the property around 1795. Repton's regard for barristers in general, and Erskine in particular, was such that he made no charge for his advice, and Erskine was pleased to follow it in every detail.[83] The relationship was perhaps too familiar to justify a Red Book; proposals were made on social visits and by correspondence. Repton published a view of the grounds of Evergreen Hill in 1808 for the *Polite Repository* (fig. 222) when Erskine was appointed Lord Chancellor. The view is through the tunnel under the road, across the garden to the grounds of Kenwood. It was a view Erskine recalled Burke commenting on during a visit shortly before the statesman's death:

> We took a turn round the grounds. Suddenly he stopped. An extensive prospect of Caen Wood broke upon him. He stopped wrapped in thought, gazing on the sky as the sun was setting. 'Ah, Erskine!' he said, pointing towards it, 'this is just the place for a reformer; all the beauties are beyond your reach – you cannot destroy them'.[84]

Erskine is granted a long entry in Repton's Memoir. Repton was attracted to Erskine's performances in court:

222  After Humphry Repton, *The Entrance to Lord Chancellor Erskine's Garden at Hampstead*, from *Peacock's Polite Repository* (1808). Victoria and Albert Museum.

'It is almost as difficult to describe the eloquence of the bar, as the acting of the stage, and those who have never heard the speeches of an Erskine or the tones of a Garrick can form little idea of either – yet those speeches of Erskine will be handed down to future ages, when the sentiments may outlive the language in which they are written'. Erskine's 'general feeling of benevolence' extended 'to the whole of the human race' and 'to all Animal nature'. Those who opposed Erskine in Parliament on issues of animal cruelty would 'only feel contempt' for the story Repton relates about Erskine ordering a live sturgeon, a present from the Lord Mayor, to be 'put back into the Thames, that he might have the pleasure of feeling it was restored to its former life of enjoyment'. Repton regarded Erskine as a fellow, fraternal professional.

> I had made it a rule to give my gratuitous opinion to all gentlemen at the Bar – And Mr. Erskine who always asked and followed my advice at his place at Hampstead, had an opportunity of repaying me in my own coin, in a case which was the only one in my own life where I was driven to consult the law. A person of considerable property whom I will not name, nor miscall a gentleman, after repeated excuses for not paying the trifling balance of 60£ and having expressed his shame at the delay of 14 years at last denied the debt, and represented me as having visited his Estate *en ami* and afterwards making unwarranted claim for a professional visit.

When Erskine threatened to go to the assize a hundred miles away to sue the man for the debt and vindicate Repton's character, 'the money was immediately paid'. Repton 'lost sight' of Erskine when he became Lord Chancellor, until walking into Lincoln's Inn one day he caught sight of him sitting on a bench. The court was about to rise, and Erskine asked Repton to go to his town house.

> He drove up in his coach, just as I had reached to the door – and after heartily welcoming me, he pulled off his Chancellor's wig, dashed it on the floor – and putting on his brown scratch said 'There – You and I must go together to Hampstead, I have two or three choice friends coming'.[85]

Erskine sold Evergreen Hill in 1810, to a Chief Justice, moving to Buchan Hill in the Sussex Weald.[86] William Howitt considered that Erskine 'committed . . . the mistake of selling this noble situation, and buying a barren estate in Sussex, which produced little but stunted birch trees and where he is said to have set up a manufactory of brooms, as the only valuable produce of the property'.[87]

## Bristol

Repton's first commission in Bristol, the first of eight in and around the city (fig. 223), came in 1795. Staying at the local spa, the Hotwells, he told a Cornish client that he hoped to secure more commissions in 'the west of England to which I am grown very partial'. He made the short journey to Bath, which he said was for the good

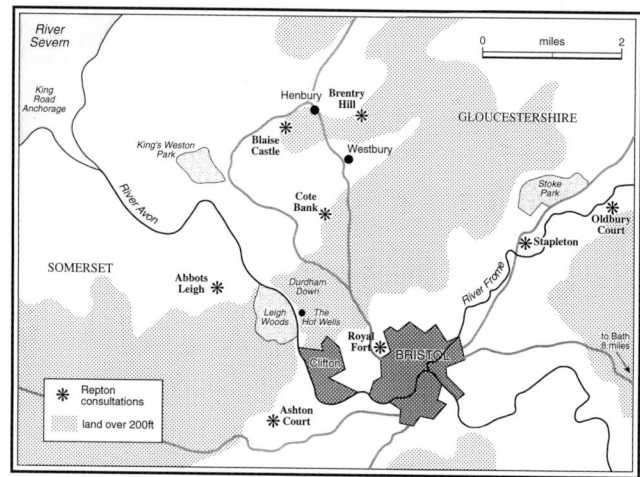

223 Humphry Repton Consultations in and around Bristol. Base map after Ordnance Survey, first edition (1830).

of his health, '[which] is not equal to the multitude of claims on my professional service', but the presence of the company in and around the resort generated still more business. The stay in Bath proved to be the first of a regular late autumn and winter sojourn and a new base for his career.[88]

Bristol was the commercial capital of the west of England, and for much of the eighteenth century the country's second largest city. Control of ocean-going trade to the West Indies and Americas, of coastal trade to South Wales and the Cornish peninsula, and of river and canal traffic in the Severn and Wye Valleys, gave the city's merchants, bankers and industrialists a commanding geographical influence. The topography of the city and its environs, a succession of steeply sloped hills, offered a series of prospects of its mercantile might, with vessels thronging the Avon and the Bristol Channel and ocean-going ships docking with the tide in the very centre of the city.[89] County gentry with long-established commercial interests, including the ownership of West Indian plantations, landscaped their broad acres to make a feature of the marine prospects. The city's powerful coterie of Quaker merchants and industrialists laid out rococo gardens around their houses in the city, commanding views of the docks, foundries and furnaces.[90] The city's corporation, dominated by the guild-like Merchant Venturers, was mindful of maintaining an influence in Westminster and the Court. Burke was elected MP between 1775 and 1780, the duke of Portland appointed Lord High Steward from 1786 until 1809. But neither man spent much time in the city nor left much

224 Samuel Hieronymous Grimm, *Blaise Castle* (1788). City of Bristol Museum and Art Gallery.

225 Nicholas Pocock. *View over Kingsweston to the Bristol Channel* (*c*.1785). City of Bristol Museum and Art Gallery.

impression on its civic culture.[91] The prospects from the hills confirmed what the guidebooks, quoting Defoe, never failed to mention, that Bristol's merchants traded 'with a more intire independency upon London than any other town in Britain'.[92]

By the end of the eighteenth century, Bristol's command was slipping. The American War of Independence, the Abolitionist Movement and the precocious growth of Liverpool and Manchester loosened the city's grip on the Atlantic trade. Inland Birmingham exercised a rival influence on the river and canal network. The waterborne basis of Bristol's power was threatened by improved road transport from London, and with it increased metropolitan influence on commercial intelligence and professional expertise. By 1800 thirty-eight coaches a day left London for Bristol, seven making the journey in a day. The outbreak of war with France provoked a financial crisis in the city. The evidence was not only a decline in shipping but the abandonment, in mid-terrace, of extensive building schemes that had been fuelled by property speculation. From 1793 until the end of the century, great swathes of the suburbs had a ruinous appearance. But the city's economy did not collapse. Sectors such as sugar refining, brass founding and especially banking were still strong, sufficiently so for their owners to spend money on improving their estates and to commission Repton to re-fashion them.[93]

Repton's commissions in and around Bristol cover a spectrum of commercial interests. To the south of the city, on the Somerset side of the Avon, he was employed to landscape two extensive estates, one at Ashton Court for an elderly member of an ancestral family with long-established interests in the West Indies, the other at Leigh Court for a young banker who had recently made a fortune in the sugar trade. To the north-west of the city, in a wealthy commuter belt, Repton was commissioned to transform a neglected villa property, Blaise Castle, in to a residential estate for a rich Quaker banker and industrialist, and to build a series of small villas for other merchants. To the north-east of the city, in the industrialized Frome Valley, Repton was employed by a new owner intent on reassembling an ancient estate, Oldbury Court. Close to the city, on the site of a Civil War fort, Repton was called in to reclaim land that had been left a ruinous building site after the collapse of the property boom.[94]

\* \* \*

## Blaise Castle

Blaise Castle lay four miles to the north-west of Bristol on a ridge of wooded ground with panoramic views across the Severn Estuary (fig. 224).[95] The countryside and the views it offered were restyled for polite society. Villages on the main roads were rebuilt with villas and summer-houses; cottages and inns were refurbished to cater for the tourist trade.[96] Blaise Castle was an important destination on the circuit, popular for day trips from Bath such as that undertaken by Catherine Morland in Jane Austen's *Northanger Abbey* (1818), which took in Clifton, the Avon Gorge, the gentrified villages of Henbury and Westbury and the neighbouring park of Kingsweston (fig. 225).

The name and popularity of Blaise Castle were established in the 1760s, when fragments of the Henbury estate around Blaise Hill were purchased by a Bristol merchant, Thomas Farr, and transformed in to a spectacular scenic landscape. Paths were cut around the caverns and precipitous gorges. Culverts were constructed in an abortive attempt to fill the dry, limestone valley with water for a cascading stream. A steam engine, intended to raise water, was installed in the sham-Gothic castle on the summit. The hill was fortified with mock bastions and cannon. Farr modelled Blaise Castle on the most famous garden in Bristol, that of the Quaker merchant Thomas Goldney, which commanded a view of the Avon and his brows docking with iron goods from Coalbrookdale.[97] Farr built a spectacular fortune on the sugar trade. A leader of the Merchant Venturers, he was elected mayor of Bristol in 1775. From the summit of Blaise Castle, Farr, his guests and an increasing number of tourists enjoyed the prospect of merchantmen returning up the Bristol Channel and assembling in the King Road anchorage, waiting to dock with the tide. As the Bristol poet H. Jones wrote,

> Here *Farr* with inbred rapture may resort,
> And see his ships glad sailing into port,
> With *Indian* treasures on the current ride,
> To crown the prospect and enrich the tide.

In position and scope, and some of the landscaping, Blaise echoed Piercefield, the renowned cliff-top estate of a fellow sugar merchant, Valentine Morris, which was visible across the Severn Estuary at the mouth of the Wye. Farr was bankrupted by the disruptions to trade during the American War of Independence. He sold Blaise Castle to a Bath lawyer, Denham Skeet. Skeet spent little time or money on Blaise and sold the estate in 1789 to raise capital for property development in Bath. The purchaser was Repton's client, John Scandrett Harford.[98]

Harford was an influential Merchant Venturer and a leading light of Bristol's Quaker community. A banker, Harford also had extensive industrial interests, especially in metallurgy: brass-making in Bristol, iron-works in South Wales and in the upper Severn Valley at Coalbrookdale. The eleven thousand pounds he paid for Blaise Castle was a fraction of a considerable fortune, assembled and managed with the care and prudence that made him a figurehead in the Society of Friends. Upon purchasing the estate, Harford set out to transform its look and management. He steadily enlarged the property, secured its boundaries, and instituted a programme of improving woodland and pastures. Under Farr's and Skeet's ownership, Blaise Castle seems to have been regarded by local people as almost public space. Harford was intent to secure greater privacy. Blaise Castle was still maintained as a beauty spot, if less whimsical in appearance and with more controlled access, but it was also made, and made to appear, more of a diversified, efficiently run, residential estate.

On taking possession of Blaise, Harford immediately set about reorganizing the estate, and in the process antagonizing his neighbours. He recalled keys to gates into the grounds formerly granted to local residents. The key holders declared that they would ignore Harford and continue to walk in the woods, which prompted an anxious Harford to check with the former owners that there were no public rights of way. 'I think myself very ungenteely treated by the Gentn of Henbury', he told Farr, 'to be thus threatened before I have even taken possession of the place'. 'I am sorry to say there is a jealousy in Country Gentlemen against those who have been brought up in Trade', Farr replied, 'that nothing but prudence and good temper is a match for & with this. I have found that one may in time get everything one wishes for. I beg you will not stand on ceremony'.[99] In 1791 a local gentleman complained of Harford's thinning the woods: 'The Depredations daily committing on your Property in Blaze Wood are beyond description bad not even a Sunday is suffered to pass without your property being destroyed'. He seized the woodman's axe, daring Harford to respond: 'Should you think proper to Prosecute, we Shall most readily attend'.[100]

Harford's designs on the house and pleasure grounds were no less radical. He rerouted villagers, who were accustomed to walking to church across the lawns in front of the house, along a new path along the main road. He demolished the old, gabled manor house and felled elms from its great avenue to clear a site for a large cubic mansion. This was designed by William Paty, one of a family firm of Bristol architects, surveyors, masons and decorators, who were responsible for many town houses in the city, including Harford's. The plain style of the new mansion represented 'qualities readily associated with a prosperous Quaker banker of the time: substance, directness, dignity and security'.[101]

Repton made his first visit in August 1795 as the new house was being built. It is not clear how the commission, his first in Bristol, came about. It may have followed one for another leading Quaker and a close friend of Harford's, Samuel Galton, at Warley outside Birmingham.[102] It could have come from civic contacts with the duke of Portland. Or Harford may have read a copy of Repton's *Sketches and Hints* and admired the prudent riposte to his critics over the picturesque controversy. By this time, Repton's reputation was established in various ways. After another visit, in October 1795, Repton presented his Red Book early the following year.[103] The proposals, which were largely carried out, if with significant departures in detail, redefine the landscape along the lines that Harford had already instituted, making Blaise Castle more modern and more respectable.

For Repton, the new mansion helped to shift the focus of the landscape from the sham castle. While the situation of the castle was 'sublime in itself as an occasional spot to be visited', it was 'wholly inapplicable to a family residence'. Repton was pleased that

> the comfort of the house was not to be sacrificed to extensive prospect, but that several spots had been judiciously proposed, each partaking of the quiet and sequestered scenery in which this place so remarkably abounds. It is a most singular circumstance that within a short distance of the largest City in England except London, and even in the neighbourhood of the most frequented watering place in the kingdom, the woods and lawns and deep romantic glens belonging to Blaise Castle are perfectly secluded from the 'busy hum of man'.

The size of the estate and mansion, and its use as a family residence, justified 'treating the subject less under the character of a Villa, than its relative situation with respect to the City of Bristol might suggest'. The style and siting

226   View of the house, with and without overlay, from the Red Book for Blaise Castle (1796). City of Bristol Museum and Art Gallery.

227   *Entrance to Blaise Castle*, with and without overlay, from *Observations on the Theory and Practice of Landscape Gardening* (1803). Yale Center for British Art, Paul Mellon Collection.

of the new house made little concession to Anglican sensibilities. Repton's views before and after its building show the transformation from an intimate ensemble of church and manor house to a plain mansion that marginalizes the church (fig. 226). Harford's new house may not have been a villa, but its style made it appear an outpost of the city's Quaker community. Repton complimented Paty the architect for the 'simplicity' of the design, but could not resist suggesting a portico for the south-east front, a proposal not executed.[104]

'The greatest improvement in the character of the place' was to move the main entrance of Blaise six hundred yards closer to Bristol on the high road, without passing through Henbury 'where a number of Villas or large country-houses seem to dispute with each other by their size and cumbrous importance'. The new entrance, marked by an arch and lodge, was to be on the site of a gate to a track through the woods that had hitherto been separated from the main grounds around the house by a steep gorge (fig. 227). By cutting away the rock face in some places, and building supporting walls in others, Repton created a winding, switchback carriage road to cross the gorge (figs 47 and 48). The gate was designed in Gothic style, in character 'with the castle to which it is the prelude' and also with the 'wildness of the scenery' along the way. Repton expected 'the stranger will be agreeably surprised to find that quitting this wood, he is not going to a mouldering castle whose ruined turrets threaten destruction and revive the horrors of feudal strife; but to a mansion of elegance, cheerfulness and hospitality'. To reach the castle, visitors had first to approach the mansion, taking in a view across the lawns, before branching off on a drive through the estate.[105]

Repton opened out views over the Severn Estuary through woodland, so that for the passenger 'the whole expanse of water, of shipping, and distant mountains will pass before the eye' (fig. 229).[106] In his published account of Blaise, Repton was pleased to report that the drive had been constructed according to plan, 'carriages pass this chasm with perfect ease and safety', but the entrance gate suffered from the 'obstinancy and bad taste of the Bristol mason who executed the design . . . I was mortified to find that Gothic entrance built of dark blue stone, with dressings of Bath stone'.[107]

Around the castle, Repton discovered the 'barbarous taste' of an earlier generation; the wooden cannon, culverts and the steam engine 'exposing the Genius of the Place to all the horrors of fire and steam, and the clangour of iron chains and forcing pumps'. This taste was still popular in Bristol, Repton realized, where a guidebook publicized Thomas Goldney's garden laid out 'in the old style'.[108] Demolishing the apparatus at Blaise, grassing over the site and planting the scarred cliffs would make the castle look more 'romantic', like the tower on Repton's trade card, with its allusion to Milton's lines 'embosom'd high in tufted trees' (fig. 228).

228 *above* The castle, from the Red Book for Blaise Castle (1796). City of Bristol Museum and Art Gallery.

229 *below* View over the Bristol Channel from the drive, without overlay, from the Red Book for Blaise Castle (1796). City of Bristol Museum and Art Gallery.

230  View from the house, without overlay, from the Red Book for Blaise Castle (1796). City of Bristol Museum and Art Gallery.

Repton counterpointed the castle with a substantial cottage, a building integral to the new regime of the estate:

> it must look like what it is, the habitation of a labourer who has care of the adjacent woods ... it must seem to belong to the proprietor of the mansion and the castle, without affecting to imitate the character of either. I think a covered seat at the gable end of a neat thatched cottage will be the best means of producing the object here required, and the idea to be excited is 'la Simplicité soignée'.

Repton provides two views; one close up, as it was passed on the drive, the other in the view from the house (fig. 230):

> This is the first instance in which I have been consulted where all the improvement must depend on the axe, and tho' fully aware of the common objection to cutting down trees, yet it is only by a bold use of that instrument that the wonders of Blaise Castle can be properly displayed.

Felling the trees in the improved view from the mansion reveals the woodman's cottage:

> This cottage will give an air of cheerfulness and inhabitancy to the scene which would without it be too sombre, because the castle tho' perfectly in character with the solemn dignity of the surrounding woods increases rather than relieves the apparent solitude.

With an annual income of seven thousand pounds, and a deep depression in the building trade, Harford could afford to have many of Repton's proposals carried out quickly.[109] The woodman's cottage was built in 1797, the drive finished at the same time. Visiting Blaise as a guest in 1797, and noting how 'the grounds are improving under the hands of Repton', Joshua Gilpin, a Quaker industrialist from Pennsylvania, reported that the views from the carriage road were 'more various and beautiful than anything I had seen. They include an immense stretch of the Bristol Channel, the coast and mountains of Wales and the interior country everywhere'.[110] Access for tourists who were not guests may have been more difficult. On tour in Wales in 1796, Repton's old friend, the botanist James Edward Smith, did not bother to see Blaise, because 'the present proprietor is not fond of visitors'.[111] The complete drive system through the woods was completed shortly after Harford moved into the new mansion. 'Friday, July 26', noted Harford in his journal for 1799, 'Drove Mr Battersby in his Phaeton, entering the new Road in the Woods opposite Mr Brooke's, to the New House and back again, returning through the Village; the first time a four-wheel Carriage was ever driven through the new road, and afterwards drove my Wife in the Phaeton through the woods and back again'.[112]

Harford's programme of improvements continued, but Repton was replaced as consultant by his former partner John Nash. Repton's partnership with Nash had been forged in the region. When Repton first visited Blaise, he went on to Corsham Court outside Bath, where he secured architectural work for Nash for the next five years, although, as he bitterly recalled, none of the financial reward that Nash had promised.[113] Soon after their partnership dissolved, Nash moved in on Blaise, initially assisting William Paty with some outbuildings, including a thatched dairy and conservatory, then in the years 1810–12 designing, with the help of Repton's son George, a picturesque group of cottages around a green, Blaise Hamlet (fig. 231). As Nigel Temple has pointed out, the idea of such a hamlet emerged during the Nash–Repton partnership in a commission of 1797 at High Legh in Cheshire, although Nash privately claimed the credit, confiding to the client that 'Mr Repton suggested putting them in a Row but I must step out of the slippers and inveigh against so alms house an idea'. The plan for High Legh was not executed, and Nash revived it for Blaise.[114] The cottages at Blaise Hamlet were not homes for old retainers but 'retreats for aged persons, who had moved in respectable walks of life, but had fallen under misfortunes', 'a comfortable Asylum for Persons advanced in years, and who had sufficient income to maintain them comfortably when relieved from the expense of House-Rent'.[115] Nash recommended that Harford build the hamlet 'in a picturesque manner & in a retired spot & not in a row', according to the architect C.R. Cockerell (who remodelled the mansion):

he says the pride which is natural to men & makes them ashamed of receiving alms is an honorable one & should not be crushed . . . he built therefore irregular cottages with all those little penthouses for beehives, ovens & c. & irregularities which he found in peasant's cottages & they are so beautiful that it is a sight visited from Clifton & I have always called it Sweet.[116]

Despite his dissatisfaction with some details of execution, and seeing his rival take on a new development, Repton had reason to be pleased that the main proposals in the Red Book for Blaise were put in to effect and with such immediacy. The commission extended the range of his work, not least in working with a new kind of topography, and helped to secure other commissions locally. In his next published treatise, *Observations* (1803), Repton cites six commissions in and around Bristol in addition to Blaise. He quotes at length from the reports for three of them, Brentry Hill, The Fort and Ashton Court, to show how, in partnership with his son John Adey, he fashioned designs to deal with various demands in the neighbourhood of a large city.

231 Francis Danby, *Blaise Hamlet* (1822). City of Bristol Museum and Art Gallery.

## Brentry Hill

Around 1802 Repton was called in at Brentry Hill, just half a mile from Blaise Castle and on the same ridge of land, but for a commission of very different character. If the scale of Blaise overcame its proximity to Bristol to distinguish its improvements sharply from those of a villa, the 'field of a few acres' at Brentry Hill left no other option. Nor was this inappropriate. Repton's client, William Payne, a merchant with a town house in Queen's Square in the centre of Bristol, had purchased a small roadside site for Repton to make plans for 'the entire plan of the house, appendages and grounds'. In contrast to schemes where Repton had to adapt the grounds to an existing, altered or newly designed house, Brentry Hill was the kind of 'creation' where he exercised control over 'the *whole*, with the assistance of my son'. In 1802 the design was exhibited at the Royal Academy in the name of John Adey Repton, and the following year a large extract from the report was published in *Observations* (fig. 232).[117]

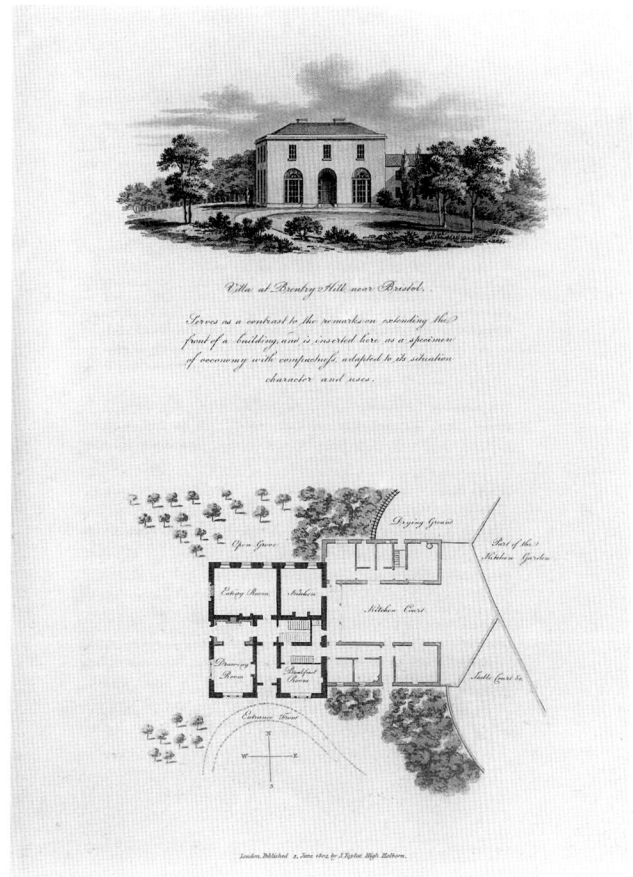

232 *Villa at Brentry Hill near Bristol*, from *Observations on the Theory and Practice of Landscape Gardening* (1803). Yale Center for British Art, Paul Mellon Collection.

Brentry Hill commanded the 'pleasing and extensive view' that attracted people to the area:

> In the foreground are the rich woods of King's Weston, and Blaize Castle, with the picturesque assemblage of gardens and villas in Henbury and Westbury; beyond which are the Severn and Bristol Channel, and the prospect is bounded by the mountains of South Wales. The view is towards the west, and I have generally observed, that the finest prospects in England are all towards this point. This . . . has been so often confirmed by repeated observations, that I have endeavoured to discover some natural cause for its general prevalence; and perhaps it may, in some degree, be accounted for from the general position of the strata in all rocky countries, which appear to dip towards the east and rise towards the west.

Yet given the prevailing wind and afternoon sun, a westward direction 'of all aspects, is the most unpleasant for a house', so while it was not 'advisable to give an extended front in this direction, yet it would have been unpardonable not to have taken advantage of so fine a prospect'. In a large, rambling mansion, with different rooms for winter and summer use, the problem was not acute, but a compact villa demanded a careful design. 'Under this restraint, perhaps, few houses have been built with more attention to the situation and circumstances of the place than the villa at Brentry.' The eating-room faced north with one window towards the prospect 'which may be opened or shut by Venetian blinds'; the drawing-room had two windows facing west, but in winter a panel at the end of the room could be removed 'when a window will be less desirable than a fireplace'. 'Thus the same room will preserve, in every season, its advantages of aspects and views.'[118]

## The Fort

The house known as The Fort took its name from a Royalist fortress on the site overlooking Bristol from the north-west. In the 1750s the banker Thomas Tyndall acquired the leases to various properties around it for sixty-eight acres of pleasure grounds. A fine Palladian house by the Bristol architect James Bridges, who designed a range of public and private buildings in the city, The Fort was completed in 1761.[119] Within twenty years a building

233   *View from the Fort near Bristol*, with and without overlay, from *Observations on the Theory and Practice of Landscape Gardening* (1803). Yale Center for British Art, Paul Mellon Collection.

boom had spread crescents and terraces for the well-to-do to the edge of its grounds. In 1791 Tyndall sold the property to a syndicate headed by a fellow banker, T.G. Vaughan, who planned a further extension of five hundred houses in crescents and squares. The depression of 1793 bankrupted the company, and their scheme collapsed, leaving the grounds a building site. Abandoned and grassed over, the site was treated as a public recreation ground. Thomas Tyndall died in 1794, and the land eventually reverted to his son Thomas, a colonel, in 1798.[120]

In February 1799 Tyndall called in Repton to advise on landscaping the property. It was another two years and eight months before Repton produced a Red Book for The Fort. This was in response to a request from his client for a record of the work now nearing completion. Repton also included some additional proposals should his client consider altering the architecture of the house. And he took the opportunity to make some general points about managing foregrounds to screen unsightly features in the neighbourhood of cities:

> Few situations command so varied, so rich, and so extensive a view as The Fort; situated on the summit of a hill which overlooks the vast city of Bristol, it formerly surveyed the river, and the beautiful country surrounding it, without being incommoded by too much view of the city itself: but the late prodigious increase in buildings has so injured the prospect from the house that its original advantages of situation were almost destroyed, and there was some reason to doubt whether it could ever be made desirable either as a villa or as a country residence; because it was not only exposed to the [backs of] unsightly rows of Houses in Park Street & Barclay Square but was liable to be overlooked by the numerous crowds of people who claimed a right of foot path thro the park immediately before the windows. It was therefore as publick as any House on any Street or Square of Bristol ... When I first visited the Fort, I found it surrounded by large chasms in the ground ... immense heaps of earth & broken rock which had been dug out to form the cellars and foundations of those additions to the City of Bristol which were afterwards relinquished.

While the obvious, if expensive, method of restoring the ground was to fill the chasms with the spoil that had been extracted, Repton decided that 'some advantage might be taken of the mischief that had been done'. He proposed leaving the spoil tips where they were, and planting them to screen the rows of houses; also digging the sides of the chasms to create gentle hollows for the lawns and a bank to hide the passage of the public beyond the boundary of the park. The view from the principal drawing-room required 'nice management to exclude what ought to be hid, without hiding what ought to be seen'.[121] The effect, as shown in the illustrations, is to exclude the suburban frontier – the terraces of houses, the crowds of citizens – while conserving a vista of the commercial city, the port of Bristol with its shipping backed by the countryside beyond (fig. 233).[122]

The building site was successfully restored to parkland stocked with cattle and sheep. This effectively enhanced the prestige of the surrounding area for the building of large detached villas. It was not until a generation later that the urban frontier once more pressed in on The Fort, the park walls came down and the land was sold for streets of houses.[123]

## Ashton Court

Ashton Court lay on the southern, Somerset side of the River Avon. It was a large ancestral estate owned by the Smyths, a family long active in the full range of the region's economy: agriculture, forestry, coal mining, slave trading and sugar planting. Repton's client, Sir Hugh Smyth, played the role of country squire, but he was also an enthusiastic theatre-goer and took a keen interest in witnessing the arrival of his cargoes of sugar and rum.[124] In designs drawn up around 1802 (fig. 234) Repton proposed reorientating the mansion towards the city, altering the entrance, adding a battlemented tower with a bow-window 'placed at the angle in such direction as to command an interesting view of Bristol, and the river Avon with its busy scene of shipping'.

> To take advantage of this view, from a house in the country, may appear objectionable to some; but I consider it among the most interesting circumstances belonging to the situation of Ashton Court. To the wealthy mechanic, or the more opulent merchant, perhaps the view of a great city may recall ideas of labour, of business, of difficulty, and dangers, which he would wish to forget in the serenity of the country; but to the country gentleman, who never visits the city but to partake of its amusements, has very different sensations from the *distant* view of a place which by its neighbourhood increases the value and the enjoyment of his estate.[125]

234 *Ashton-Court*, from *Observations on the Theory and Practice of Landscape Gardening* (1803). Yale Center for British Art, Paul Mellon Collection.

The view was not spoiled by any speculative urban development, only its own rather old-fashioned pleasure grounds running down to the river.[126] Repton suggested that Smyth use the same contractor for landscaping who had worked at The Fort. Smyth died shortly afterwards; while the planting was carried out, the architectural improvements opening a new prospect of Bristol were not.[127]

There is no record of Repton's revisiting Bristol for another twelve years, until the very end of his career. In part this reflects the general contraction in his field of work, and perhaps the recession in the fortunes of the city, but these were highly selective processes. What mattered for Repton in this period was securing one important client or a sufficient number of smaller clients to make such a long trip worthwhile. It was easier and more economic to pick up villa commissions near London, and he had no great aristocratic patron near Bristol. Perhaps more significantly, he stopped his annual sojourn in Bath. When he did visit Bath it was for specific medical reasons, after his carriage accident and the onset of angina, when his physician there 'bid me leave off the loco motive part of my profession'.[128] Repton paid his next and last visit to Bristol in 1814 *en route* to Devon, to help pay for the trip to the duke and duchess of Bedford's cottage ornée at Endsleigh.[129]

## Leigh Court

In July 1814 Repton visited Abbots Leigh, the neighbouring estate to Ashton Court on the southern bank of the Avon, recently purchased by the Bristol banker Philip John Miles. Like his neighbours the Smyths, Miles inherited a fortune from the sugar trade but had no landed pedigree.[130] The first millionaire citizen of Bristol, Miles purchased Abbots Leigh in 1811. He proceeded to pull down the Elizabethan house, replace it on another site with a Neo-classical mansion designed by Thomas Hopper, and to call it Leigh Court.[131] When the mansion was partly built, Miles called in Repton. Repton's now hostile attitude to money men, and his indulgent views of hereditary aristocrats, helps to explain the ill-tempered tone of the Report for Leigh Court.[132]

Predictably, Repton was dismayed by the situation of the house on the very summit of the estate, and much

235  View to the east, from the Report for Leigh Court (1814). Bristol University Library.

236  View to the south, from the Report for Leigh Court (1814). Bristol University Library.

237 Francis Danby, *Landscape near Clifton* (*c.*1822–3). Yale Center for British Art, Paul Mellon Collection.

of his Report is taken up with proposals to alter the fabric of the house and its immediate surroundings. The ground fell away suddenly, giving little sense that the house possessed a domain, or of views that might be appropriated for the owner. There were sites and scenery that were 'common to all elevated sites' in 'every field and lane in the neighbourhood'. In 'point blank' range of the house was a hillock which Repton proposed to crown with a building, a rotunda 'to arrest the attention & draw it off from the less appropriate objects' (fig. 235). Moreover, the building would 'command most interesting *views of the Avon* & its rocky & wooded banks. & also will be the best station for seeing the Architectural East front of the House'. The view south was potentially enchanting, towards the village church of Abbots Leigh, over 'small inclosures interspersed with farmhouses', 'but unfortunately in the point blank view is a *large staring yellow house*' (fig. 236). This 'upstart mansion', this 'obtrusive yellow mass of ugliness' as Repton called it, belonged to another Bristol banker, Edward Prothero.[133] It was 'not only an ugly object in itself, but it injures the importance of the scenery'. Repton suggested the colour might be changed 'by covering the whole front with slate or with a green trellis'. Hopper might be persuaded to move the windows of Miles's new mansion. Prothero's house virtually defeated Repton's attempts to screen it with trees, poplars on the opposite hillside or three acacias in a small garden.[134]

Apart from the terraced gardens, many of Repton's proposals around the house were implemented.[135] Repton's text ventures only briefly beyond the immediate surroundings of the house to Leigh Woods, on the steep slopes down to the Avon, where he recommended walks planted with native species that 'will yield the most romantic scenery'. Repton hoped 'some expedient may be discovered to make the place more accessible by crossing the Avon without the troublesome circuit through the crouded city of Bristol'.[136] As it turned out, the connection between Bristol and Leigh Court was strengthened and in a way that opened it up to the citizenry. When the mansion was built, Miles purchased a notable collection of Old Master paintings. These were regularly on view to the public, who collected admission tickets from his town house in Queen's Square.[137] An excursion to Leigh Woods, a popular beauty spot, could thus be extended to take in the house and grounds. The local artist and cleric John Eagles saw in the paintings by Gaspard Dughet owned by Miles a potentially democratic form of landscape that informed his idea of Leigh Woods as a suburban sketching ground. The figures in Dughet's landscapes, observed Eagles, were 'a part with and influenced by the whole of scenery – not as if they commanded it, or could command it, or would turn aside streams or cut a twig in all their land'. Eric Adams argues that Eagles' views influenced Francis Danby's paintings of the scenery. Danby's excursionists relax in Leigh Woods, reading, conversing, looking across the Avon to the terraces of Clifton (fig. 237).[138]

## Leeds

Repton undertook two commissions around Leeds (fig. 238) at the end of 1809, a year in which there was a temporary revival in his fortunes. Travel costs made him reluctant to go far north for work at this time, but the combined visit, and the clients' demands for remodelling houses as well as grounds, made it worthwhile.[139] After the visits Repton's family thought that his 'prospects [were] brightening'.[140] It was nearly ten years since Repton's last commission in the area, at the great political and artistic headquarters of Harewood House to the north of Leeds. On that occasion Repton had been rowed about the lake while he noted the improvements made by the new Tory MP for the county, Henry Lascelles, and was given the services of Thomas Girtin, the favourite painter of Henry's art-patron brother, Edward Lascelles, to draw the designs. News of how his proposals for Harewood had been counteracted 'mortified' Repton, and he never returned.[141] The new commissions near Leeds were to the west and south of the city, in a zone of industrial development along the Aire Valley, for two clients, John Blayds and Benjamin Gott, who had made their fortunes in the city. These men were not vulgar upstarts; both were leading figures in the Tory alliance in the region that cemented the connection of commercial and landed wealth.[142]

Leeds was the leading centre of the British woollen industry and, along with Manchester, Liverpool, Bristol and Birmingham, one of the leading commercial cities outside London. It was dominated by an oligarchy of 'gentleman-merchants'. Tory and Anglican, they formed a powerful alliance with the county aristocracy. Indeed Leeds, rather than Wakefield, effectively functioned as the county town of the West Riding of Yorkshire, a social centre for brokering a variety of exchanges, from marriages to mortgages. The very success of Leeds merchants as hard bargainers made for a leisurely life. Visits to the Cloth Halls, their warehouses and counting houses, even their longer journeys to shippers and customers in London and Liverpool, left time for a variety of social and cultural pursuits. Their work was more than a matter of buying and selling. Many owned their own finishing plants, and some employed workers at other stages of production, but most left manufacture to the mass of small clothiers scattered around the city. They claimed that they could make more money selling cloth than making it, but their arguments were not narrowly economic: selling cloth was gentlemanly, making it was not.[143]

The gentleman-merchants presided over Leeds' prosperity, not only its cloth trade but its role as the commercial and cultural centre of the north of England. Buildings as various as the New Cloth Hall, the Commercial Exchange, Civic Library, Theatre and Assembly Rooms were funded by their patronage. In 1808 Leeds was the first city outside London to form an artistic institution, the Northern Society for the Encouragement of the Fine Arts. Exhibitions showed the work of local as well as London painters, and Leeds became a marketing centre for modern art.[144] The power of the gentlemen-merchants did not go uncontested; after the turn of the century it faced the challenge of rival interests, Dissenter mill owners, radical gentry (such as Turner's patron, Walter Fawkes) and de-skilled artisans. The various factions in Leeds, each committed to the city during its rising prosperity, made for a vigorous civic life. There was not only a profusion of institutions but of texts and images – maps, engravings, guidebooks, directories, newspapers, histories – representing the dynamism of the city from different perspectives.[145]

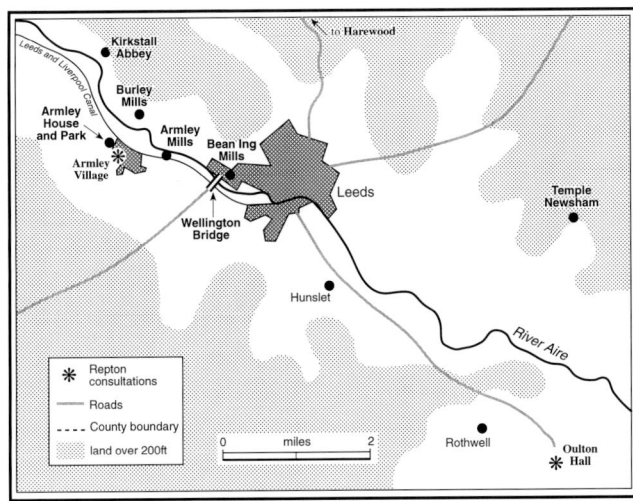

238 Armley and Leeds. Base map after *Plan of Leeds and its Environs* (1813). Brotherton Library, University of Leeds and Ordnance Survey, first edition (1822). Department of Geography, University of Nottingham.

Repton's commissions came at a significant moment in the development of Leeds, when its expansion was being physically and imaginatively shaped by new interests. Some of the old oligarchy sought to escape the city, to transfer their social and economic investment to the countryside; others tried to enlarge and transform their control of the city.

## Oulton

Repton's first commission in Leeds was in November 1809 for John Blayds at Oulton, five miles to the southeast of the city. Son of a wholesale grocer, Blayds, under his former name Calverly, became a merchant banker in the city and a leading figure in the Corporation, holding the office of mayor in 1785 and 1789. Blayds inherited Oulton and his new surname, with its coat of arms and distant aristocratic connection, in 1807 from a senior partner in the bank.[146] Oulton was, in Repton's words, 'a mere farm house on the border of a Green or Common', to which had been added 'two good rooms' – 'for the sake of that distant and richly wooded prospect which its elevated situation commands'. The enclosure of Oulton in 1809 gave Blayds the opportunity of transforming the area immediately around it and creating a 'more finished villa', with the option, in future, of 'conversion into a permanent residence'.[147] The expansion of Leeds was an incentive. Blayds had a house and grounds in Park Lane on the west side of the city, which 'was lately in the Country but is now surrounded by streets and other houses'; it was a development that Blayds himself encouraged, selling off parcels of land for workshops, packing houses and warehouses.[148]

Oulton commanded a prospect across the Aire Valley towards the mansion and grounds of Temple Newsam, which had been improved by Capability Brown and was one of the most celebrated landscape parks of its time.[149] The immediate landscape of Oulton in Blayds's possession formed a depressing contrast. Repton shows the common as an unruly place occupied by squawking geese, braying donkeys and squabbling children, crossed by a number of tracks with a horse and cart going in one direction and a wayfarer in the other. The common is ringed by the houses of the village, but this semi-industrial settlement, numbering more than a thousand inhabitants, with its combined cottages and workshops, mill and chapel, had little to redeem it in Repton's eyes: the buildings 'remind us of a busy town, rather than a rural scene of retirement'.[150] 'The change to be made in the Character of this place can hardly be classed under the name of Improvement', declared Repton, 'it is rather the creation of a new place'. The view of improvements in one view from the house covered 'so much that it is in fact another Drawing, but there was no other way of identifying the Spot'. The enclosed common is transformed in to a well-planted pleasure ground, the lawns grazed by peaceful cattle and sheep, the lake graced by swans, the gravel paths walked by the well-to-do. A double cottage on the common is demolished, the other buildings around it are screened by a raised bank with trees. With the village shut out, the grounds blend elegantly with the wood and parkland beyond. Repton gave the house a patrician polish, adding two wings, a balustrade and a colonnade.[151]

Repton published his plans for Oulton in *Fragments* (fig. 239) as an example of the kind of villa commission he detested, a 'nameless specimen of improvement in the north of England'. Repton had estimated four thousand pounds for the improvements at Oulton but 'I had the mortification to find that fifteen thousand had been expended; and the proprietor told me that he would gladly

239  *A Common Improved in Yorkshire* [Oulton], with and without overlay, from *Fragments on the Theory and Practice of Landscape Gardening* (1816). Yale Center for British Art, Paul Mellon Collection.

add five thousand more to make it as I had originally proposed'. The distasteful character of Oulton resided as much in its villagers as its landlord:

> The leading feature of the landscape was a mean row of tenements, with some of those places of worship too apt to disfigure the neighbourhood of all great manufacturing districts. These white-washed scars, in modern landscape, form a melancholy contrast to the venerable churches and remnants of edifices of former times, which are now suffered to moulder into ruins.[152]

## Armley

Repton moved on from Oulton to a commission for Benjamin Gott at Armley in December 1809, staying with his client's family in their house at Park Lane. Gott and Blayds were friends, neighbours and leading figures in the Leeds oligarchy. Their careers took contrasting directions, which is reflected in their respective choices of suburban estate and the designs that Repton made for them. Armley proved the more complex and challenging commission.

The son of a civil engineer, wealthy enough to afford the premium for an apprenticeship and partnership, Gott joined a leading woollen merchant house, and by 1790 was the senior partner. Unusually for a merchant, he moved into manufacture and with spectacular success. He captured a large share of the American market for fine cloth from West of England clothiers, and the Napoleonic Wars helped to enlarge that for other woollens in Europe; Gott was not only contracted to the British government for blankets and uniform cloth but supplied other allied armies too. By the time of Repton's visit, Gott owned or leased three large woollen mills in and around Leeds, employing almost a thousand, one of the largest firms in the country.[153]

Gott purchased a meadow to the west of his house in Park Lane and proceeded to develop Park Mills as the largest woollen factory in the West Riding. It was also the most conspicuous development to blight the west end of Leeds for its wealthy residents. Streets of cheap terrace houses were built, and the smoke and smells from the dyehouses and workshops drifted into drawing-rooms. Park Mill also threatened other interests, especially those of small independent clothiers and croppers (cloth finishers). There were periodic threats to Gott's life as well as his factory. An armed guard was put around his house in 1801, cloth workers testified bitterly against the enterprise to the Commons Select Committee on the Woollen Trade in 1806, and in the Luddite summer of 1812 an informer warned of a plot on his life: 'Be Carful of your self for a few weeks – alter your usal walks to your Busness'.[154]

Gott also developed his enterprise in a different mode to Park Mill, further to the west of the city. He jointly leased a large woollen mill three miles along the Aire Valley at Armley, and, after a damaging fire in 1805, purchased and rebuilt it. Armley Mill was incorporated in the small estate that Gott first leased and then purchased for his family; it lay directly below the villa and pleasure grounds. Unlike Park Mill, which engrossed all stages of production, Armley Mill was not seen as a threat by the local clothiers. Built for scribbling wool and fulling cloth, it dovetailed into the domestic system. Moreover, unlike Park Mill, a smoke-belching industrial complex, Armley Mill was a pleasantly proportioned, water-powered building surrounded by water meadows. This is not to say that it was in any sense archaic. Gott had Armley Mill rebuilt at considerable cost as one of the most powerful, technically advanced mills in the country: gaslit, steam heated, fire resistant and spacious. Nor was Gott's economic support of small clothiers a disinterested one. He always purchased more cloth in the Halls than he manufactured himself. Gott's entire industrial venture may be seen as an extension of two mercantile precepts: the maintenance of cloth supply and the control of its quality. In Leeds Gott lived close to his premises, and so he did at Armley. Many textile manufacturers had the setting of their mills landscaped, but it is a measure of Gott's cultural confidence that he commissioned the country's leading landscape gardener.[155]

While amassing his fortune in Leeds, Gott sustained a strong commitment to the political, social and cultural life of the city. A figurehead of the Tory Anglican establishment, he was elected to the corporation in 1791 and served as mayor in 1799. He was a founder member of the Literary and Philosophical Society, a patron of the Northern Society for the Encouragement of the Fine Arts, and a subscriber to public sculpture. He collected small-scale Flemish and Italian pictures, patronized the landscape painter J.C. Ibbetson and the sculptor Francis Chantrey.[156] Gott expected his sons, like himself, to combine a commercial, scientific and cultural education. 'In the present state of society, in the duties you will reasonably be expected to discharge', he wrote to his

240   The house, with and without overlay, from the Red Book for Armley (1810). Mrs Paul Mellon, Oak Spring Garden Library, Upperville, VA.

eighteen-year-old son Benjamin in 1811, 'every branch of learning has its full share of effect'.[157] The Gott household was a culturally accomplished one, musical, well read and well versed in the arts. Visiting in January 1810, the actress Dorothy Jordan told her lover, the duke of Clarence: 'I was obliged to give up seeing Mr Gott's exhibition . . . He and his family were at the theatre every night'.[158] In some respects, Gott and his circle would have reminded Repton of his former life in Norwich as a textile merchant. 'At home we have had Mr Repton for a week', Elizabeth Gott wrote to her son on Christmas Day 1809, 'and other company almost without interruption since'.[159]

The Gott family divided their time between their house in Leeds and the villa at Armley (which was home to Gott's sister and mother-in-law), but one of Gott's reasons for commissioning Repton was to plan for the villa's conversion in to a permanent residence and a place to house his collection of books and artworks. With its central block and two wings, Repton found the villa well proportioned, but the details made it look 'like the work of an ignorant country builder'. He advised enlarging the building (fig. 240) to accommodate more residents and transforming its interior to entertain them and their guests: 'The great world of London must be copied at a distance of two hundred miles, as well in the shape and uses of a room as in its furniture.' The drawing-room, living-room and library would open *en suite* to reveal 'organs, pianofortes and harps . . . a variety of chairs . . . profusion of cabinets and sophas and footstalls, and music stands and workboxes and flower pots and clocks and bronzes and cut glass and China and Library tables covered with books and pamphlets and reviews and newspapers; which contribute to the elegant and rational enjoyment of modern life'. The great world of Leeds was a more immediate challenge for Repton. In every direction along the Aire Valley, Armley house commanded views of its industrial power.[160]

Repton's own, published views of large-scale industrial plant were often negative, if not hostile. He found the duke of Portland's employment of children in his park in Buckinghamshire an example of 'wholesome industry, far different from the foul air and confinement of spinning in a cotton mill'.[161] Fearing insurgent workers, he was pleased that there was 'no manufactory near' Sheringham in Norfolk; 'this for the comfort of habitation is of more importance than is generally supposed'.[162] He recalled the burning of Samuel Wyatt's Albion Mill, on the south bank of the Thames in 1791, as a cautionary tale:

> He erects a large edifice – collects together men of large capital – a large monopoly is established (to grind the poor . . . under the pretence of grinding wheat for their use). The price of corn advances – the people murmur – and they finally proceed to that common remedy of a mob when there is a scarcity . . . destruction by fire.[163]

Industrial sites could be redeemed, indeed enhanced, by being firmly under a landowner's control. The summer before his visit to Armley, Repton was commissioned to frame a prospect of an iron-works at Wingerworth in Derbyshire (fig. 241), not for some urban *nouveau riche* but for an old, titled family who had exploited the mineral wealth of their estate for generations and were enjoying the income of the works at the peak of its production. While the 'smoke and flame of [the] foundry attract our notice', reported Repton, he proposed 'the eye would be more powerfully fixed' by the lake he proposed floating. This would both enlarge the field of vision and its industrial potential. The lake would be 'more profitable than the richest pasture, because it may be so managed as to admit of being occasionally drawn down two or three feet to supply canals, and other circumstances of advantage, in this populous and commercial part of the kingdom'. The improved view raises both the cultural and commercial register of the view, placing the squire and his wife on a balustraded terrace pointing over the pleasure grounds to the lake and foundry, but it was not one that Repton had engraved to accompany the published extract from the Red Book.[164]

Repton remodelled the house and grounds at Armley to frame the industrial landscape in a pictorial way in terms of the 'three distances of the painter, viz. the foreground – the landscape – and the offskip' (fig. 242). In the offskip lay Leeds, presently three miles away, 'but that distance is very precarious and will daily become less, and less, as the increasing prosperity of the two daily increases its dimensions'. Chimney smoke announced the city but obscured it too. 'The busy town of Leeds' was 'softened by its misty vapour'. Repton proposed the 'landscape' in the middle distance be subject to careful management. Many fields near Armley were scattered with clothier homesteads

> And it is a proud consideration to reflect that instead of the adjoining property being appropriated to the feeding of a few sheep or cattle, almost every acre supports hundreds of human beings, whose labour and ingenuity are usefully directed to the aggrandisement of the country; while it increases the happiness by increasing the employment of each individual. Yet even this consideration cannot compensate for that quiet and seclusion which the country is supposed to afford.

Such fields were to be screened by trees, and the park stocked with a few sheep and cattle. Repton also proposed planting to soften the visual impact of the Leeds–Liverpool canal:

> However advantageous such a canal may be in a *commercial point* of view, when its artificially stiff and

241 View from the house, without overlay, from the Red Book for Wingerworth (1809). Private collection.

> parallel lines are compared with the natural bend of the river Ayre we cannot in a *picturesque point* of view but regret Brindley's discovery 'that Nature did not intend rivers to be navigable, but that she created them to supply canals with water'.[165]

The industrial focus of the landscape, closing the vista, was to be Armley Mill. Shortly before Repton's visit, Gott installed gas-lighting apparatus from Boulton and Watt. He was one of the first Leeds factory owners to replace the older, more flammable oil lamps. Moreover, gas lighting anywhere, even in the West End of London, was still a novel spectacle.[166] Gott was entranced by the entire effect. 'A beautiful and interesting object it is', he told his son Benjamin, 'the shade of light so pure – and the quantity so great at so small a price'.[167] Repton concurred with his client's view:

242  View from the house, without overlay, from the Red Book for Armley (1810). Mrs Paul Mellon, Oak Spring Garden Library, Upperville, VA. Photograph Greg Heins.

243  View from the Kirkstall Road, without overlay, from the Red Book for Armley (1810). Mrs Paul Mellon, Oak Spring Garden Library, Upperville, VA. Photograph Greg Heins.

244 Kirkstall Abbey from the park, from the Red Book for Armley (1810). Mrs Paul Mellon, Oak Spring Garden Library, Upperville, VA. Photograph Greg Heins.

The prominent feature of this scene is that large building which at such a distance and so accompanied by trees can never fail to be an interesting object by daylight and at night presents a most splendid illumination of gas light. I must here compliment the good taste of the proprietor on the unaffected simplicity of this large building, which looks like what it is – a Mill and Manufactory; and is not disguised by Gothic windows or other architectural pretensions.

Armley Mill was more prominent still in Repton's view from the road from Leeds (fig. 243). From here the effect of the proposed planting in the park and the improvements to the villa was to consolidate, for the travelling public as well as the proprietor, the connection between Gott's residence and his mill, to establish his image as a paternalist employer. The concluding vignette (fig. 244) of the Armley Red Book proposes pruning a young plantation to reveal a local landmark that was as much of a tourist attraction as the mills: the ruins of Kirkstall Abbey alongside the meandering River Aire.[168]

In the long and complex Red Book for Armley, Repton reformulates Gott's outlook as a gentleman-merchant, with its combined commitment to commercial, cultural and industrial concerns, within a scenic framework of landed paternalism. At the same time, the very idea of paternalist landscape undergoes a transformation. The Armley Red Book does not conform to the simpler, oppositional, social vision of Repton's *Frag-*

*ments*, and no extracts are published there. Indeed, apart from the Red Book, I have found no private or public mention of the Armley commission in Repton's writings.

A surviving diary of Elizabeth Gott for 1810 shows that Repton's proposals for planting Armley Park were immediately implemented, some supervised by her husband.[169] The Gotts moved permanently to Armley in 1816. Publishing a description of Leeds that year, the county historian the Revd T.D. Whitaker, a fierce critic of the 'wild spirit of adventure' in commerce and industry that disfigured parts of the Leeds periphery, praised Gott's planting in Armley and found a new taste for landscape in the politer suburbs: 'If a merchant smitten with the charms of rural quiet and retirement erected a country house it was a gloomy habitation with a few distorted evergreens and miserable pot herbs impounded within four walls', he recalled, 'but now cheerfulness and even elegance have descended almost to the cottage and a rood of land about a country house is a little landscape'.[170] It is not certain whether the remodelling of Armley House was carried out to Repton's specifications. By 1822 a new, iron-framed, Neo-classical house designed by Robert Smirke had been built (fig. 245).[171] Smirke's design had a progressive style and functional simplicity that both complemented Armley Mill more successfully than Repton's design and provided a more appropriate setting for Gott's impressive art collection, which now included

245 A.C. Askey after J.P. Neale, *Armley House, Yorkshire*, from J.P. Neale, *Views of the Seats of Noblemen and Gentlemen*, vol. 5 (1821). Yale Center for British Art, Paul Mellon Collection.

Old Master paintings, Claudes and Poussins, as well as modern sculpture, notably two busts of Gott's friends and fellow industrial heroes John Rennie and James Watt.[172] The new house also functioned as a mausoleum. Gott's son Benjamin died in Greece in 1817, on a Grand Tour on which he gathered commercial intelligence on the cloth trade as well as collecting antique marbles. He is commemorated by a plaque on the temple of Theseus below the Acropolis, elements of which building are incorporated in Smirke's design for Armley House.[173] Gott also commissioned a commemorative picture, *A View of Athens* by H.M. Williams, to hang in the house, 'a great coloured drawing in a gold frame'.[174] Loaned to the Northern Society for the Encouragement of the Fine Arts in Leeds for its exhibition of 1823, the picture was singled out by the press as the best watercolour, superior to the seven by Turner loaned by Walter Fawkes.[175] Gott's commissioning of Repton was an early step in a cultural trajectory culminating in his commissioning of Sir Thomas Lawrence to paint his and his wife's portraits in 1827; 'they are two of the best I have ever painted', Lawrence told Gott, recalling the 'kindness and tranquil happiness of Armley House'.[176]

Gott continued to invest in the commercial and social infrastructure of Armley. He initiated the building of Wellington Bridge across the Aire in 1818–19 by John Rennie, which strengthened the connection with the city.[177] He sponsored various charitable institutions in the township too.[178] Between 1811 and 1821, the population of Armley increased by more than a third to more than 4,500, making it the largest township in Leeds.[179] Not everyone worked for Gott, although a good many walked over Wellington Bridge to Park Mills, but his estate and enterprise formed the main nucleus of Armley's growth. The development of Armley exemplifies an important point about industrial towns and cities, especially those based on textiles: they grew in a cellular fashion, around separate industrial colonies, many of which continued to have a rustic appearance and hierarchical social relations.[180]

Gott did not commission Repton to impede industrial development or to cover it up but to control it in a particular fashion. In other places on the periphery of Leeds, the structure of land ownership and form of industrial production made for a different landscape and views of it. When Turner depicted Leeds from Beeston Hill to the north of the city in 1816 (fig. 246), he chose a contrasting landscape, a different vantage point and another repertoire of cultural associations. With its range of smoking mills in the background, busy workers in the foreground, and view from the high road, it is a proudly public, energetic and democratic image.[181]

## A Place near the Capital

In conclusion to both this chapter and this book, I will give an account of a late commission near London that recapitulates many of the themes that run through my discussions of the various domains of Repton's career: the complications of county, courtly and commercial patronage; the deployment of styles to suit the social character of a place and patron; the role of roads and public access in defining designs; the relation of designs on paper to those on the ground; the issue of money and land; the critique of professional landscaping in didactic poems; the position of landscape gardening in large-scale schemes of estate improvement and aristocratic programmes of conspicuous consumption; and the role and nature of landscape gardening in a culture that Repton regarded as increasingly inhospitable to his art.

Situated eight miles to the east of London by the main road through Essex and the eastern counties, Wanstead was one of the most renowned mansions and parks in England. The estate had long held a place in the courtly and commercial power structure of London; it had been used as a royal palace and conveyed to favourites before being purchased in the later seventeenth century by Sir Josiah Child, a merchant banker and the chairman of the East India Company. Over the next eighty years or so, the Childs, ennobled as the earls Tylney, invested heavily in and around Wanstead, accumulating one of the largest estates in Essex. At its centre was a spectacular formal park, probably to a design by George London, with an extensive system of avenues and lakes and some rococo flourishes, a mock castle, grotto and an island cut in the shape of Britain (fig. 247). The park formed the setting for a new and palatial mansion, designed by Colen Cambell in the Palladian style that particularly appealed to the Whig Englishmen who wished to emulate the Venetian model of patrician culture. Its great ballroom and stock of art treasures made the mansion a centre for high society.[182]

By Repton's time, the Wanstead estates were still extensive and immensely lucrative. The yearly income (from funds as well as rents) increased from 1794 to 1812 to more than twenty-eight thousand pounds, outstripping that received by all but the greatest estates.[183] But inheritance problems resulted in relatively little spending on the park

246 J.M.W. Turner, *Leeds* (1816). Yale Center for British Art, Paul Mellon Collection.

and mansion. The estate passed in 1794 to a minor, Catharine Tylney Long, and was held in trust by the Crown. The house was used as a residence by various members of the exiled Bourbon family; the king occasionally reviewed troops in the park. Everything changed in 1812 when Catherine Tylney Long, now the richest heiress in Essex, married a nephew of the duke of Wellington, William Wellesley Pole, in the society wedding of the year. Pole took the name William Tylney Long Pole Wellesley along with his wife's fortune and set in train his ambition to restore Wanstead to its former grandeur, even to surpass the Prince of Wales's Carlton House as a lavish spectacle and social rendezvous.[184] Shortly after his wedding, in 1813, Wellesley commissioned Repton to improve the grounds.

The Wanstead commission had a compelling appeal. Not only would it bring Repton much-needed money, but also, in the wake of his disappointments with the Prince of Wales and his usual commissions around the capital for *parvenus*, it would restore his esteem and that of his art. Wellesley was newly rich but not *nouveau riche*. Wanstead was a place deeply layered with the history of high society, in its cross-currents of wealth, culture and politics, which he might reconnect, to his own advantage, with prevailing networks of patrician power. Wanstead had personal resonances too, as a house that had provided the architectural model for the mansions of some of Repton's favourite aristocratic commissions, such as Wentworth, Harewood and Holkham. Here was a famous park that he passed on every journey from Hare Street to London. In contrast to the estates in the area that he found had fallen prey to property speculators, Wanstead was, like Woburn or Longleat, a preserve of patrician luxury. Moreover, the commission offered the prospect of reviving a palatial style of landscape gardening near the capital.

Repton made his first site visit to Wanstead in April 1813 and submitted the Report in September.[185] The covering letter endorsed his client's wish to respect 'the old original Stile' of the grounds but expressed concern that Wellesley did not want the Report bound as a Red Book: 'I must confess I am a little mortified that it should be your wish not to have it seen, because it is a subject I am not a little vain of.'[186] The following year, Repton secured permission to publish part of the Report in *Fragments*. It was not mentioned by name, because 'little time had been given to the development of the plans', but this 'Place near the Capital' was easily recognizable, 'one of the magnificent places in this country which furnishes examples of the Geometric Style of Gardening'.[187]

The published extract from the Wanstead Report compares 'The Ancient Style . . . of strait lines and geometric figures . . . as introduced into this country by *Le Notre*' with 'The Modern Style . . . open to the surrounding scenery of Nature . . . as invented by *Brown*', emphasizing that both had been taken to extremes, applied to every garden everywhere, and so rightly ridiculed by their respective poet-critics, Pope and Knight. Repton justified renovating the ancient style at Wanstead because it was integral to the character of the place, deeply inscribed in the site and situation.

We can see nothing natural, except the materials which Nature has furnished, of land, trees, and water; but all these have been so forcibly brought under the control of Art, that they are no longer to be considered as natural objects, any more than the stones and masonry of the house can be considered as natural rocks . . . The great character of this place must be considered as it relates to the vicinity of the capital. Those who would treat this splendid Palace like the seat of an English country gentleman, at the distance of a hundred miles from the metropolis, would rob it of all its importance, and more than half its beauty . . . it must be classed with those royal and princely residences, which form the retreats of the great from the court or city: we do not expect near *a Metropolis* any thing like the perfect seclusion from mankind, either in the Palaces of Versailles, Potsdam, or Kensington, any more than in *the Metropolis*, as at Carlton House or St James.[188]

247  John Rocque, *Plan of Wanstead* (1735), detail. Reproduced courtesy of the Essex Record Office.

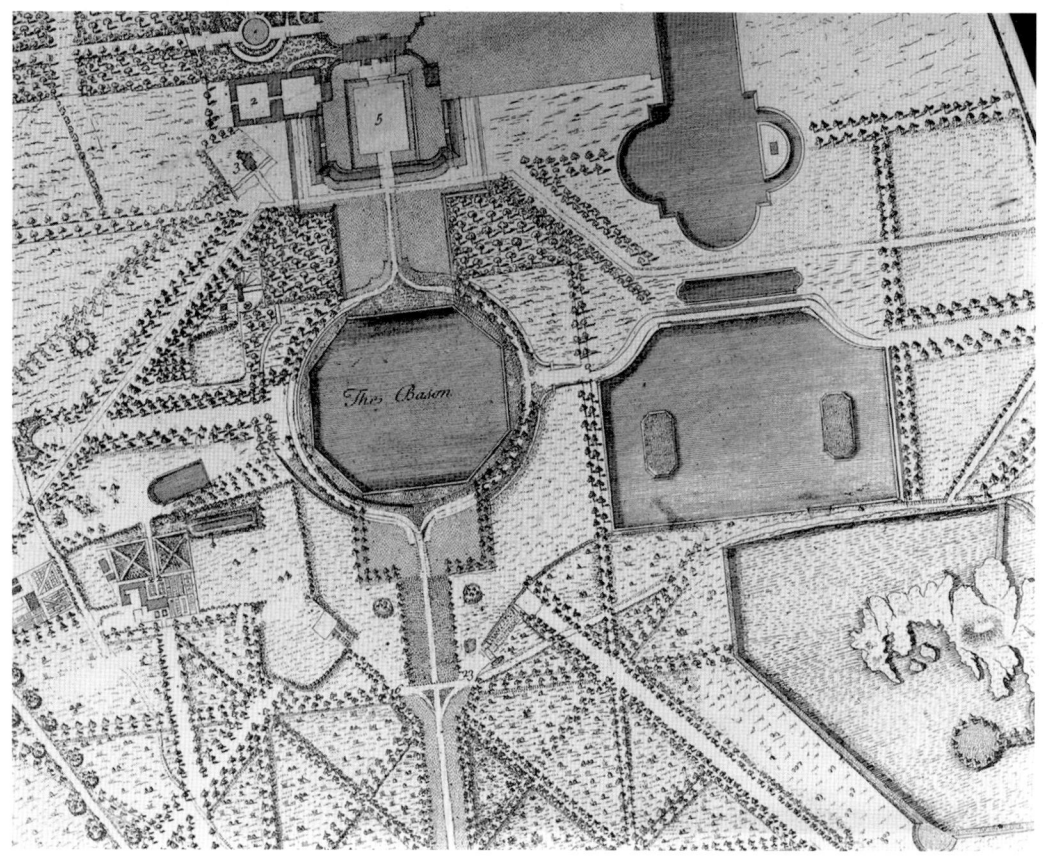

248  *View from the Portico of a Villa* [Wanstead House] *near London*, with and without overlay, from *Fragments on the Theory and Practice of Landscape Gardening* (1816). Yale Center for British Art, Paul Mellon Collection.

The plan for a metropolitan palace, in which 'the entrance front must be exposed to the public', made a civic virtue of local necessity. Upon taking over the estate, Wellesley discovered that the years of leasing had left the park open to the establishment of rights of way: 'carts with offensive loads passed under the windows'. After stopping up the offending road by padlocking the gate and opening a trench, Wellesley was indicted by a Mr Wilson of East Ham and twenty others at Essex Assizes and forced to reopen it.[189] Repton reconciled Wellesley to his loss with a vision of civic sociability: 'if it were possible to exclude from Hyde Park or Kensington Gardens the gay assemblage of company which enlivens the scene, we should only produce one dull and cheerless solitude'. Repton would preserve the dignity of Wanstead by laying out a formal parterre in front of the mansion, surrounded by a high, trellised hedge to prevent the passengers from looking in, but, as it appears in his illustration, with an arched opening to the road to let people walk in (fig. 248). The parterre, with its quartered, Union Jack pattern, would be displayed to the principal rooms above the basement storey, 'a rich carpet spread under the eye'. The vista from the portico was presently occluded by an overgrown plantation; Repton planned to cut it back to reveal the shining string of lakes leading the eye towards St Paul's and the City, 'that view of the Metropolis which, at such a distance, is a most impressive feature, and in perfect harmony with the grandeur of the scene'.[190]

Obviously pleased with Repton's proposals, Wellesley began implementing them at once but was slow to pay for the design. Calling at Hare Street on his way to Suffolk in October 1815, Wellesley promised Repton an instalment of £120 but proved no better than a series of other clients who failed to settle their accounts. 'Rub[bing] on with small concerns' around London, Repton devoted most of his time to finishing *Fragments*.[191] 'In a few years', Repton wrote of the Fragment for Wanstead, 'I trust, there will be no reason for regretting that the following Sketch and Extract from the Report have been allowed to form a part of this volume'.[192] An estate survey of 1815–16 shows that Repton's published plans for the grounds of Wanstead materialized, perhaps with other proposals from the Report, as part of a rapid and expensive programme of improvements in and around the house.[193] Still no payment was forthcoming. Repton was just one of Wellesley's many creditors. Even opinion hardened by the profligate ways of the aristocracy condemned Wellesley as a shocking rake. Squandering his wife's fortune with astonishing speed, he ruined the entire estate.[194] Pope's satire on 'the use of riches', which Repton quoted from in the Wanstead Red Book, as a way of clearing the ground for a defence of formal gardening in the grand style, turned against him. In March 1816, with 'ruin pressing', Repton told William that he counted the commission for Wanstead, with those for Brighton Pavilion and Carlton House, as a scheme that he had vainly hoped would bring him fame and fortune.[195]

Repton did not give up on a grand civic vision. Still burdened by debt, he found in the winter of 1816–17 that his health had improved sufficiently to walk two hundred yards instead of twenty. Peace in Europe had him contemplating his first professional visit abroad. 'Nobody knows what may happen', he told Sir Harry Fetherstonehaugh,

> for example – the King of Wurtemburg has announced to Lord Sidmouth that he wishes to have the gardens of Stutgard laid out by an English Landscape Gardener & desires that one be sent to him as if we swarmed like Swiss soldiers – but Lord S. has written to explain – that there is only one in all England & he is too far gone to go so far – yet it is possible that in the course of the Summer he may be tempted to make a journey with one or two of his sons, to collect materials for a plan to meet His Majestie's wishes. Now this does not look like my expected trip to lay out Walks of Paradice just yet – & if I do go – what should you say to our going together part or all of the way – My heart twinges at the thought since pain & pleasure affect its pulsations alike & the accelleration of the pulse – proves my disease not quite gone.[196]

Come the summer, Repton told Fetherstonehaugh that his condition had worsened and he could not walk unaided; the projected commission in Stuttgart was abandoned (if indeed it was actually offered), along with the prospect of any more work in England. 'I am tired writing & my life you know was finished when I was last at Uppark.'[197] There is no further record of Repton until his death, probably from a heart attack, at his home at Hare Street one morning the following March: 'He no sooner reached the breakfast-room, than he fell into the arms of his servant, and fell without a groan.'[198]

# GAZETTEER

## Compiled with John Phibbs

*Notes*

This is a list, county by county, of all Repton's recorded consultations and paid commissions, as well as a few examples of unpaid advice. It is more a catalogue of designs than a guide to Repton's work on the ground. Not all commissioned designs were executed, and of those that were some have been abandoned, built over or survive only in part. At the end of his career Repton claimed that he wrote 'more than four hundred different reports in MS'.[1] Some of these were new reports for return visits to the same place in commissions that extended over a few years, but the great majority were for initial consultations. We have listed 342 consultations, a few of which were not committed to a report, and some of which, as we indicate, are not firm attributions. So there are more Repton sites to be discovered.

This gazetteer follows the format of that in George Carter, Patrick Goode and Kedrun Laurie, *Humphry Repton: Landscape Gardener 1752–1818* (1982). It includes most of its entries, and those in Kedrun Laurie, 'Humphry Repton 1752–1818: New Discoveries', *The Garden* (September 1983), 361–5. This list collates their findings with our own and those of a number of other researchers, including Mavis Batey, Fiona Cowell, Jean Hugh Jones; David Lambert, Helen McKee, Patrick McCullough, Hugh Prince, Dorthy Stroud, Nigel Temple, David Whitehead, Liz Whittle and Tom Williamson. Some of these researchers may dissent from some of our attributions – it has been hard enough to agree on some between ourselves – but we have made clear the grounds of an attribution, and how conclusive we feel it to be.

The **county** in the first column is that in Repton's time. Where appropriate, modern counties or administrative regions are given in parenthesis.

The **site** in the second column is named as that in Repton's time. Modern spellings or new names are given in parenthesis.

**Grid references** are to Ordnance Survey maps. Where both co-ordinates end in 0, it may be only a four-figure reference.

**Clients** are named as those who initially commissioned Repton.

**Dates** are of the *first recorded visits* (some commissions involved return visits). The symbol < means *before* a certain date, > *after*.

**Sources**. Not every source is recorded for a commission, only those on which an attribution and date can be made. The sources vary in reliability and information. An asterisk in the first column indicates that the documentary evidence is inconclusive.

Red Books are listed with their dates in the Bibliography. The short titles refer to Repton's other published and unpublished works (See Bibliography for details). Gaz. 82 refers to the Gazetteer in Carter et al., *Humphry Repton*. PR followed by a date refers to an entry in *Peacock's Polite Repository*. Many of these, as the *Polite Repository* states, are views of places where Repton was consulted, but some are of sites that he visited only. A few of these, for example, *Lambeth Palace from Westminster Bridge* and *Scene on the Derwent at Matlock*, have been omitted from the list. Most others have been included, even when (as in 1790) they do not appear in Repton's Account Book. Friends, neighbours and business associates may well have been given free consultations. Nevertheless, where sites are documented only in the *Polite Repository*, no matter how strong the circumstantial evidence, the entries are marked with an asterisk. Many of these drawings, especially in later editions of the *Polite Repository*, were published some years after Repton's first visit. (See Nigel Temple, 'Humphry Repton, Illustrator, and William Peacock's *Polite Repository* 1790–1811', *Garden History*, 13 (1985), 161–73.)

---

[1] Humphry Repton, *Fragments on the Theory and Practice of Landscape Gardening* (London, 1816), vii.

| County | Site | Grid Ref. | Client | Date | Source |
|---|---|---|---|---|---|
| ENGLAND | | | | | |
| *Beds. | Battlesden Park | SP 959 292 | Sir G.O. Page Turner | <1808 | PR 1808; Gaz. 82 |
| Beds. | Beeston Leasowes | TL 140 475 | Col. William Thornton | 1798 | Report [addition to the Red Book for Mogenhanger, Beds] |
| Beds. | Hassel's (Hassells) | TL 190 501 | Francis Pym | 1791 | Red Book |
| Beds. | Mogenhanger (Moggerhanger) Park | TL 135 485 | Godfrey Thornton | 1792 | Red Book |
| Beds. | Sutton Park | TL 235 475 | Montague Burgoyne | 1792? | Correspondence, Dorthy Stroud Papers |
| Beds. | Woburn Abbey | SP 965 325 | Sixth duke of Bedford | 1804 | Red Book |
| *Berks. | Bear Hill | SU 811 791 | Harry Fonnereau | <1805 | PR 1805 |
| *Berks. | Chilton Lodge | SU 330 706 | John Pearce | <1801 | PR 1801 |
| Berks. | Coombe Lodge | SU 628 778 | Samuel Gardener | <1801 | PR 1801; Gaz. 82 |
| *Berks. | Danesfield | SU 818 843 | R. Scott | <1797 | PR 1797 |
| *Berks. | Frogmore | SU 976 760 | Queen Charlotte | <1796 | PR 1796 |
| Berks. | Holly Grove | SP 960 760 | Lady Jennings Clerke | c.1796 | Memoir |
| Berks. | Holme Park | SU 752 752 | Richard Palmer | 1793 | Red Book |
| Berks. | Maiden Erlegh (Maiden Early) | SU 753 707 | Edward Golding | <1793 | *Observations*; PR 1793 |
| Berks. | Purley | SU 646 758 | Anthony Morris Storer | 1793 | Red Book |
| Berks. | St Leonard's Hill | SU 935 750 | Gen. The Hon. William Harcourt | <1808 | *Brighton Pavillon* |
| Berks. | Sunning (Sonning) Hill | SU 755 756 | James Sibbald | 1790 | Red Book |
| Berks. | Woodley Lodge | SU 750 725 | Henry Addington | <1795 | *Observations*; PR 1795 |
| *Berks. | Worfield (Warsfield) | SU 888 705 | Sir John Hippesley | <1798 | PR 1798 |
| Bucks. | Bulstrode | SU 986 884 | Third duke of Portland | 1790 | Account Book |
| Bucks. | Chalfont House | TQ 007 897 | J. Hibbert | <1790 | Memoir; PR 1799 |
| Bucks. | Gayhurst | SP 845 462 | George Wright | <1793 | *Sketches and Hints*; PR 1793 |
| Bucks. | Hanslope House | SP 815 458 | Edward Watts | <1794 | *Sketches and Hints* |
| *Bucks. | Lamport Manor House | SP 682 375 | John Dayrel | n.d. | Memoir |
| *Bucks. | Stoke Farm (Sefton Park) | SU 980 820 | Second Baron Sefton | <1808 | PR 1808; Gaz. 82 |

| Bucks. | Shardeloes | SU 938 979 | William Drake | 1793 | Red Book |
|---|---|---|---|---|---|
| Bucks. | Stoke Park (Stoke Poges) | SU 982 840 | John Penn | c.1792 | Red Book |
| Bucks. | Taplow | SU 910 820 | J. Fryer | <1796 | *Observations*; PR 1796 |
| Bucks. | Tyringham | SP 856 469 | William Praed | <1794 | *Sketches and Hints* |
| Bucks. | West Wycombe | SU 830 942 | Sir J.D. King | <1796 | *Observations*; PR 1796 |
| Bucks. | Wilton Park | SU 960 905 | James Du Pre | <1796 | *Enquiry* |
| *Bucks. | Wycombe Abbey | SU 856 929 | First Baron Carrington | <1803 | PR 1803; Gaz. 82 |
| Cambs. | Abington Hall | TL 130 489 | John Mortlock | <1803 | *Observations*; PR 1803 |
| Cambs. | Bourn Hall | TL 332 562 | Fifth earl De La Warr | c.1815 | J.P Neal, *Views*, first series |
| Cambs. | Dullingham | TL 628 580 | Col. Christopher Jefferson | 1799 | Red Book |
| Cambs. | Milton | TL 481 628 | Samuel Knight | 1789 | Account Book |
| Cambs. | Wimpole | TL 335 520 | Third earl of Harwicke | 1801 | Red Book |
| Ches. | Aston Park | SJ 558 782 | Harvey Aston | 1793 | Red Book |
| Ches. | Crewe Hall | SJ 733 550 | John Crewe | c.1791 | *Sketches and Hints*; *Odd Whims* |
| Ches. | High Legh | SJ 697 836 | George John Legh | 1791 | Red Book |
| Ches. | Hooton | SJ 364 785 | Sir Thomas Stanley | 1802 | Red Book |
| Ches. | Rode Hall | SJ 819 573 | Wilbraham Bootle | 1790 | Red Book |
| Ches. | Tatton Park | SJ 743 815 | William Egerton | 1791 | Red Book |
| *Ches. | 'Mr Anson's in Cheshire' (perhaps Anson's seat in Shugborough, Staffs) | | Mr Anson | 1792 | Repton to John Geers Cotterell, 27 November 1792, Herefordshire RO |
| Corn. | Antony House | SX 415 563 | Reginald Pole Carew | 1792 | Red Book |
| Corn. | Catchfrench | SX 308 595 | Francis Glanville | 1792 | Red Book |
| Corn. | Pentillie | SX 410 646 | John Tillie Coryton | 1809 | Red Book |
| Corn. | Port Eliot | SX 362 578 | First Baron Eliot | 1792 | Red Book |
| Corn. | Tregothnan | SW 857 416 | Viscount Falmouth | 1809 | Red Book |
| Corn. | Trewarthenick | SW 903 442 | Francis Gregor | 1792 | Red Book |
| *Derby. | Drakelow Park | SK 235 198 | Sir Nigel Griefly | <1793 | PR 1793 |
| *Derby. | Matlock Bath | SK 295 981 | Sir Richard Arkwright? | <1806 | PR 1806 |
| Derby. | Wingerworth Hall | SK 375 675 | Sir Windsor Hunloke | 1809 | Red Book |
| Devon | Endsleigh | SX 391 786 | Sixth duke of Bedford | 1814 | Red Book |

| | | | | | |
|---|---|---|---|---|---|
| *Devon | Shute House | SY 250 960 | Sir John de la Pole | <1797 | PR 1797 |
| Devon | Luscombe | SX 796 571 | Charles Hoare | 1799 | Red Book |
| Devon | Tavistock Abbey and Hostel | SX 480 740 | Sixth duke of Bedford | 1809 | Report and Drawing |
| *Dorset | Merly | SZ 010 994 | John Willet Willet | <1797 | PR 1797; Gaz. 82 |
| Dorset | Stafford House (Frome Bilet) | SY 724 900 | Nicholas Gould | <1816 | *Fragments* |
| *Essex | Albyns | TQ 508 969 | J.R. Abdy | <1801 | PR 1801 |
| *Essex (Suffolk) | Auberies | TL 850 410 | Charles Greenwood | <1811 | PR 790 |
| *Essex | Bel-House (Belhus) | TQ 572 812 | Sir Thomas Barrett Leonard | <1807 | PR 1807 |
| *Essex | Blake Hall | TQ 538 052 | Capel Cure | <1799 | PR 1799 |
| Essex | Claybury | TQ 433 974 | James Hatch | 1791 | Red Book |
| *Essex | Chelmsford, 'Garden of Dr Baddely' [Guy Harlings] | TL 709 069 | Dr John Baddely | <1811 | PR 1811 |
| *Essex | Chigwell, 'Revd S. Palmers' (Tourners) | TQ 459 957 | Revd S. Palmer? | <1811 | PR 1811 |
| Essex | Dagnams | TQ 550 933 | Sir Richard Neave | <1802 | PR 1802; Humphry Repton to William Repton, 31 March 1813, Huntington Library |
| *Essex | Down Hall | TL 520 130 | Lady Ibbetson | <1802 | PR 1802 |
| Essex | Felix Hall | TL 845 195 | Charles Callis Western | <1795 | PR 1795; *Fragments* |
| *Essex | Gidea Hall | TQ 520 900 | Richard Benyon | 1787 | Engraving after Repton |
| *Essex | Gillwell House | TQ 386 964 | W. Chinnery | <1807 | PR 1807 |
| Essex | Gosfield Place | TL 789 300 | J.G. Sparrow | <1811 | Humphry Repton to Mary Repton, 23 Oct 1811, Huntington Library; *Excursions into Essex* (1819) |
| *Essex | Hare Hall | TQ 532 898 | John Wallinger | <1790 | PR 1790 |
| Essex | Hare Street Cottage | TQ 525 898 | Humphry Repton | 1786 | Memoir; *Fragments* |
| Essex (Greater London) | Higham Hill (Highams) | TQ 370 910 | John Harman | 1793 | Red Book |
| Essex | Hill Hall | TL 488 995 | Sir Thomas Smyth Bart | 1791 | Red Book |
| Essex | Hylands (Highlands) | TL 680 040 | Cornelius Kortright | <1803 | *Observations* |
| Essex | Langleys | TL 699 138 | W. Tufnell | <1803 | *Observations* |
| *Essex | Langtons | TQ 538 875 | J. Massu | <1805 | PR 1805 |

| County | House | Grid Ref | Client | Date | Source |
|---|---|---|---|---|---|
| Essex | Mark Hall | TL 465 111 | Montague Burgoyne | 1789 | Account Book |
| Essex | Moor Hall | TL 495 116 | John Perry | 1808 | Report |
| Essex | Riffhams Lodge | TL 772 063 | J.R. Spencer Phillips | 1815 | Plan |
| Essex | Rivenhall Place | TL 819 191 | Charles Callis Western | 1789 | Account Book |
| *Essex | Rocketts (Rochetts) | TQ 567 942 | Sir John Jervis | <1797 | PR 1797 |
| Essex | Saling Grove | TL 705 254 | John Yeldham | 1790 | Account Book |
| Essex | Spains Hall | TL 678 342 | Thomas Ruggles | 1807 | Report |
| Essex | Stansted Hall | TL 525 245 | William Heath | 1790 | Red Book |
| Essex | Stubbers | TQ 576 847 | William Russell | 1796 | Red Book |
| Essex | Suttons | TQ 512 978 | Charles Smith | <1803 | *Observations* |
| *Essex (Greater London) | The Grange, Leyton | TQ 378 874 | T. Lane | <1809 | PR 1809 |
| *Essex | The Parsonage, Stordon Massey | TL 582 005 | Revd J. Oldham | c.1800 | Archdeaconry of Essex; Return on expenditure on glebe houses; 1796–1833, Essex RO |
| *Essex | The Rookery, Woodford | TQ 404 902 | G. Smith Esq. | <1806 | PR 1806 |
| Essex (Greater London) | The Warren | TL 408 957 | H.P. Engstrom | >1816 | *Fragments* |
| Essex | Thorndon Hall | TQ 618 919 | Ninth Baron Petre | c.1790 | View, Colman Collection, Norfolk RO |
| Essex | Wallwood House | TQ 395 881 | William Cotton | c.1810 | *Fragments*; Gaz. 82 |
| Essex (Greater London) | Wanstead House | TQ 405 875 | William Tylney Long Pole Wellesley | c.1813 | *Fragments*; Repton to Wellesley, 22 September 1813, Beineke Library, Yale University. |
| Essex | Little Warley | TQ 603 905 | Sir George Allanson Wynn Bart | 1790 | Account Book; PR 1798 |
| Essex | Woodford | TQ 406 925 | Richard Puller | 1790 | Account Book |
| Essex | Woodford Hall | TQ 420 910 | John Maitland | 1801 | Red Book |
| Glos. | Adlestrop Park | SP 243 270 | James Henry Leigh | 1799 | *Observations*; Account Books, Leigh Papers, Shakespeare Birthplace Trust |
| Glos. (City of Bristol) | Blaise Castle | ST 562 784 | John Scandrett Harford | 1795 | Red Book |
| Glos. (City of Bristol) | Brentry Hill | ST 576 788 | William Payne | c.1802 | *Observations*; Drawing, RA 1802 |

| | | | | | |
|---|---|---|---|---|---|
| Glos. (City of Bristol) | Cote Bank | ST 600 880 | W. Broderup | <1803 | *Observations* |
| Glos | Dyrham Park | ST 744 757 | William Blaythwayt | 1800 | Letters on Dyrham, Gloucestershire RO |
| Glos. (City of Bristol) | Oldbury Court | ST 635 768 | T. Graeme | c.1800 | Letters on Dyrham, Gloucestershire RO |
| Glos. (City of Bristol) | The Fort (Royal Fort) | ST 584 730 | Thomas Tyndall | 1799 | Red Book |
| Glos. | Sezincote | SP 170 310 | Sir Charles Cockerell | c.1803 | Drawing, RIBA; *Brighton Pavillon* |
| Glos. (City of Bristol) | Stapleton | ST 610 750 | Dr Lovell | <1803 | *Observations* |
| Glos. | Woodchester Park | SO 809 015 | Lord Ducie | c.1809 | Humphry Repton to William Repton, 23 January 1809, Huntington Library |
| Hants | Herriards | SU 667 462 | George Purefoy Jervoise | 1793 | *Sketches and Hints*; Estate papers, Hampshire RO |
| Hants | Norman Court | SU 360 350 | Charles Wall | c.1807–10 | Plan (attrib.), Archives of Baring Brothers & Co. |
| *Hants | Stratfield Saye | SU 698 615 | Lord Rivers | <1810 | PR 1810 |
| Hants | Stratton Park | SU 580 590 | Sir Francis Baring | <1803 | *Observations* |
| *Heref. | Belmont | SO 477 338 | John Matthews | <1794 | PR 1794 |
| Heref. | Garnons | SO 396 438 | John Geers Cotterell | 1791 | Red Book |
| Heref. | Hampton Court | SO 520 525 | Viscount Malden | <1794 | PR 1794; Humphry Repton to Uvedale Price, 5 February 1795, Newberry Library, Chicago |
| Heref. | Moccas Court | SO 355 435 | Sir George Cornewall | c.1793 | *Observations*; George Cornewall's Journal, private collection. |
| Heref. | Panson Cottage | SO 500 390 | C.J. Bird | <1810 | Drawing, Dumbarton Oaks Library, Washington, DC |
| Heref. | Stoke Park (Stoke Edith) | SO 605 407 | Edward Foley | 1792 | Red Book |
| Heref. | Sufton Court | SO 575 380 | James Hereford | 1795 | Red Book |
| *Heref. | The Wier (New Weir) | SO 434 420 | Edward Parry | <1799 | PR 1799 |
| Herts. | Ashridge | SP 985 125 | Seventh earl of Bridgwater | 1813 | Red Book |

| Herts. | Bedwell Park | TL 276 077 | Sir Culling Smith | 1808 | Humphry Repton to William Repton, 25 February 1808, Huntington Library |
|---|---|---|---|---|---|
| Herts. | Brookmans | TL 250 045 | Samuel Robert Gaussen | <1794 | *Sketches and Hints* |
| Herts. | Cashiobury (Cassiobury) | TQ 093 970 | Fifth earl of Essex | c.1801 | *Observations*; Memoir |
| Herts. | Haileybury | TL 358 108 | East India College | 1808 | Report |
| Herts. | Lamer | TL 181 161 | C. Drake Garrard | 1790 | Account Book |
| Herts. | Little Court | TL 363 293 | Richard Spurrier | 1790 | Account Book |
| *Herts. | Marchmont House | TL 060 070 | J. Abbot Green | <1804 | PR 1804 |
| Herts. | New Barnes (Sopwell) | TL 155 053 | Matthew Towgood | 1802 | Red Book |
| *Herts. | Offley | TL 140 270 | Lady Salusbury | <1795 | PR 1795 |
| Herts. | Organ Hall | TQ 160 950 | William Towgood | <1803 | *Observations* |
| Herts. | Panshanger | TL 290 130 | Fifth Earl Cowper | 1799 | Red Book |
| Herts. | Tewin Water | TL 260 145 | Fifth Earl Cowper | 1799 | Red Book |
| *Herts. | The Grove | TQ 081 988 | Earl of Clarendon | <1798 | PR 1798 |
| Herts. | Wall Hall | TQ 138 944 | George Woodford Thellusson | 1802 | Red Book |
| Herts. | Wood Hill | TL 266 058 | George Stainforth | 1803 | Red Book |
| Herts. | Wyddiall Hall | TL 373 318 | John Thomas Ellis | 1790 | Account Book |
| Hunts. (Cambs.) | Gaines Hall (Gaynes) | TL 130 140 | James Duberly | 1798 | Red Book |
| Hunts. (Cambs.) | Waresley | TL 245 544 | William Needham | 1792 | Red Book |
| *IoW | Debourne Lodge, Cowes | SZ 495 965 | Mr Mackenzie | <1810 | PR 1810 |
| *IoW | East Cowes Castle | SZ 520 960 | John Nash | c.1799 | PR 1800 |
| *IoW | Norris Castle | SZ 515 963 | Lord Henry Seymour | <1805 | PR 1805 |
| *IoW | Osborne | SZ 516 948 | B.P. Blachford | <1810 | PR 1810 |
| *IoW | St John's | SZ 584 917 | Edward Simeon | c.1797 | PR 1798; Gaz. 82 |
| *IoW | Swainston | SZ 442 878 | Sir J. Barrington | <1811 | PR 1811 |
| Kent | Bayham Abbey | TQ 645 369 | Second Earl Camden | 1800 | Red Book |
| Kent | Beckenham Parsonage | TQ 373 694 | Revd William Rose | 1790 | Account Book |
| *Kent | Belvedere | TQ 495 785 | Lord Eardley | <1810 | PR 1810 |
| Kent | Blendon Hall (Blenden) | TQ 477 741 | John Smith | <1816 | *Fragments* |
| Kent | Cobham | TQ 685 689 | Fifth Baron Darnley | 1790 | Red Book; Account Book |

| | | | | | |
|---|---|---|---|---|---|
| Kent (Greater London) | Crayford Workhouse | TQ 510 740 | Revd Edward Repton | c.1812 | *Fragments* |
| *Kent | Halstead Place | TQ 480 610 | P. Cazalet | <1806 | PR 1806 |
| Kent | Holwood | TQ 422 636 | William Pitt | c.1791 | *Sketches and Hints*; Memoir |
| Kent | Kippington | TQ 521 546 | Francis Motley Austen | 1808 | Report |
| *Kent | Knole | TQ 540 542 | Duke of Dorset | <1807 | PR 1807 |
| Kent | Langley | TQ 798 517 | Peter Burrell | 1790 | Red Book |
| *Kent | Lee Priory | TR 223 568 | Sir Francis Baring | <1807 | PR 1807 |
| Kent | Montreal | TQ 513 555 | Lord Amherst | 1811 | Red Book |
| *Kent | Seven Oak | TQ 520 560 | M. Lambard | <1811 | PR 1811 |
| Kent | Sundridge Park | TQ 418 707 | E.G. Linde; Claude Scott | 1793; >1796 | Red Book; Angus, *Seats of Nobility* (1797) |
| Kent | Vinters | TQ 777 562 | James Whatman | 1797 | Red Book; Gaz. 82 |
| *Kent | Wildernesse | TQ 548 564 | Second Earl Camden | <1801 | PR 1801 |
| Lancs. | Lathom | SD 459 092 | Wilbraham Bootle | <1794 | *Sketches and Hints* |
| *Lancs. | New Hall (Garswood) Park | SJ 560 980 | Sir John Gerard | 1796 | T.C. Baker and J.R. Harris, *A Merseyside Town in the Industrial Revolution*, St Helens 1750–1900 (1959), pp. 235–6. |
| Lancs. | Scarisbrick | SD 392 127 | Thomas Scarisbrick Ecclestone | 1802 | Red Book |
| Leics. | Buckminster | SK 875 235 | Sir William Manners | 1793 | Red Book |
| Leics. | Donnington Park | SK 420 270 | Lord Loughborough | 1790 | Account Book |
| Lincs. | Brocklesby | TA 135 115 | First Baron Yarborough | <1791 | Claybury Red Book |
| Lincs. | Scrivelsby Court | TF 270 660 | Lewis Dymoke | 1790 | Account Book |
| London | Bloomsbury Square | TQ 380 820 | Sixth duke of Bedford | c.1807 | Humphry Repton to William Adam, 3 March 1807, Hardwick Correspondence, Sir John Soane's Museum |
| London | Cadogan Square (Place) | TQ 270 790 | First Baron Cadogan | <1806 | *Enquiry* |
| London | Carlton House | TQ 290 790 | Prince of Wales | 1803 | Drawings, Royal Library, Windsor |
| London | Russell Square | TQ 270 790 | Fifth/Sixth dukes of Bedford | <1806 | *Enquiry* |
| Middx. (London) | Brandsbury (Brondesbury) | TQ 240 840 | Lady Salusbury | 1789 | Red Book |

| | | | | | |
|---|---|---|---|---|---|
| Middx. (Greater London) | Canons | TQ 182 920 | Sir Thomas Plummer | 1816 | Humphry Repton to William Repton, 31 March 1816, Huntington Library |
| Middx. (Greater London) | Castle Hill | TQ 170 800 | H. Beaufoy | <1793 | PR 1793; *Sketches and Hints* |
| Middx. (Greater London) | Corridor House | TQ 330 900 | William Salte | 1806 | Drawing, British Architectural Library |
| *Middx. (Greater London) | Ealing Grove (Ealing Park) | TQ 170 180 | Mrs Ballie (owner), Lord Oxford (occupier) | <1802 | PR 1802; Gaz. 82 |
| Middx. (Greater London) | Evergreen Hill | TQ 260 860 | Thomas Erskine | c.1795 | PR 1808; Memoir |
| Middx. (Greater London) | Fitzroy Farm | TQ 280 870 | First Baron Southampton | 1790 | Account Book |
| Middx. (Greater London) | Golders Hill | TQ 240 880 | John Coore | n.d. | Memoir |
| Middx. (Greater London) | Grovelands (Southgate Grove) | TQ 302 902 | Walker Gray | 1797 | Drawing, Oscar and Peter John Ltd.; PR 1798; J.N. Brewer, *London and Middlesex*, vol. 4 (1816) |
| Middx. (Greater London) | Kenwood House | TQ 272 874 | Second Baron Mansfield | 1793 | Red Book |
| *Middx. (Greater London) | 'Mr Manning's Villa', Totteridge (The Darlands) | TQ 240 940 | Mr Manning | <1808 | PR 1808; Gaz. 82 |
| Middx. (Greater London) | Stanmore House | TQ 167 905 | Countess Aylsford | <1794 | *Sketches and Hints* |
| Middx. (Greater London) | Wembley | TQ 194 855 | Richard Page | <1793 | *Sketches and Hints*; Humphry Repton to R. Pole Carew, 6 May 1793, Antony House Muniments |
| Middx. (Greater London) | Whitton Park | TQ 150 740 | George Gosling | 1797 | PR 1799; Humphry Repton to George Gosling, 15 August 1797, private collection |
| Middx. (Greater London) | Whitton | TQ 140 730 | Samuel Prime | 1795 | Red Book |
| Norfolk | Baber (Bawburgh?) | TG 150 080 | John Patteson | 1789 | Account Book |
| Norfolk | Barningham Hall | TG 146 354 | John Thurston Mott | 1807 | Drawings |
| Norfolk | Bracondale Lodge | TG 240 070 | Philip Martineau | c.1792 | Red Book |
| Norfolk | Buckenham House | TG 078 905 | Ninth Baron Petre | 1789 | Account Book |

| | | | | | |
|---|---|---|---|---|---|
| Norfolk | Catton Hall | TG 230 122 | Jeremiah Ives | 1788 | Account Book |
| Norfolk | Felbrigg Hall | TG 195 395 | William Windham | <1795 | PR 1795; Drawing (1806), Colman Collection |
| Norfolk | Gunton Hall | TG 228 342 | Second Baron Suffield | c.1810 | Drawings, National Trust, Blickling |
| Norfolk | Hanworth Hall | TG 197 351 | Robert Lee Doughty | 1798 | Account Book |
| Norfolk | Holkham Hall | TF 883 429 | Thomas Coke | 1788 | Red Book |
| Norfolk | Honing Hall | TG 327 292 | Thomas Cubitt | 1792 | Red Book |
| Norfolk | Hoveton House | TG 305 175 | Thomas Blofeld | 1807 | Drawings |
| Norfolk | Hoveton St Peter (Hall) | TG 305 175 | Christobel Burroughs | 1809 | Drawings |
| *Norfolk | Lyng Rectory | TG 070 180 | Revd Charles Anson | <1806 | PR 1806; Gaz. 82 |
| Norfolk | Northrepps | TG 232 399 | Bartlett Gurney | c.1792 | Red Book |
| *Norfolk | Oxnead Hall | TG 227 240 | Viscount Anson | <1807 | PR 1807 |
| Norfolk | Sherringham Bower (Sheringham Hall) | TG 133 424 | Abbot Upcher | 1812 | Red Book |
| Norfolk | Stradsett | TF 660 060 | Thomas Bagge | 1808 | Stradsett Papers, Norfolk RO |
| Norfolk | Sustead Old Hall | TG 185 370 | Humphry Repton | 1778 | Letters, Ketton-Cremer, Norfolk RO; *Biographical Notice*. |
| Norfolk | Tofts Hall | TL 835 929 | Stephen Payne Galway | 1789 | Account Book |
| Norfolk | Witton | TG 330 320 | Col. N. Wodehouse | <1796 | Handlist, Norfolk RO |
| Norfolk | Wood Hall | TL 630 980 | William Jones | 1806 | Red Book |
| *Norfolk | Worstead House | TG 310 260 | Sir G.P. Brograve | <1803 | PR 1803 |
| Northants | Aynho | SP 510 330 | W.R. Cartwright | 1796 | Letter, H. Repton to W.R. Cartwright, 11 February 1798, Northamptonshire RO |
| Northants | Barton Seagrave | SP 888 773 | Charles Tibbets | 1793 | Red Book |
| Northants | Courteenhall | SP 760 530 | Sir William Wake | 1791 | Red Book |
| Northants | Finedon | SP 911 720 | John English Dolben | 1793 | Red Book |
| Northants | Harlestone Park | SP 705 645 | Robert Andrew | 1808 | *Fragments*; Humphry Repton to William Repton, 24 August 1808, Huntington Library |
| Northants | Laxton Hall | SP 940 960 | George Freke Evans | 1806 | Letters, copies in Northamptonshire RO |

| | | | | | |
|---|---|---|---|---|---|
| Northants | Milton Park | TL 140 990 | Earl Fitzwilliam | 1791 | Red Book |
| Northants | Norton Hall | SP 605 635 | B. Botfield | 1809 | Report |
| Notts. | Babworth | SK 687 810 | John Bridgman Simpson | 1790 | Red Book |
| Notts. | Grove Hall | SK 735 810 | Col. Anthony Eyre | 1790 | Account Book |
| Notts. | Thoresby Hall | SK 638 712 | Charles Pierrepont | 1791 | Red Book |
| Notts. | Wansley Park | SK 462 513 | Lord Melbourne? | <1794 | *Sketches and Hints* |
| Notts. | Welbeck Abbey | SK 560 748 | Third duke of Portland | 1789 | Red Book |
| Notts. | Wollaton Hall | SK 530 293 | Sixth Baron Middleton | <1816 | *Fragments* (inconclusive) |
| *Oxon. | Brightwell Place | SU 652 952 | W. Lowndes Stone | <1797 | PR 1797 |
| *Oxon. | Chastleton | SP 248 291 | J. Jones | <1809 | PR 1809 |
| Oxon. | Great Tew | SP 397 291 | Col. G.F. Stratton | 1803 | Red Book |
| Oxon. | Magdalen College | SP 522 063 | Magdalen College | 1800 | Red Book |
| *Oxon. | Nuneham | SU 544 985 | Gen. The Hon. William Harcourt | <1800 | PR 1800 |
| Oxon. | Sarsden | SP 290 230 | John Haughton Langstone | 1795 | Red Book |
| *Oxon. | Sherburn Castle (Shirburn) | SU 690 960 | Earl of Macclesfield | <1797 | PR 1797 |
| Rutland | Burley on the Hill | SK 883 102 | Ninth earl of Winchelsea | 1795 | Red Book |
| Rutland | Normanton Park | SK 935 065 | Sir Gilbert Heathcote | c.1797 | PR 1808; Drawing, Lincolnshire RO |
| Salop | Attingham Park | SJ 550 099 | Second Baron Berwick | 1797 | Red Book |
| *Salop | Condover Park | SJ 490 050 | Owen Smith-Owen | <1800 | PR 1800 |
| Salop | Ferne (Ferney) Hall | SO 434 776 | Samuel Phipps | 1789 | Red Book |
| Salop | Hopton Court | SO 640 760 | Thomas Botfield | 1798 | B. Botfield, *Stemmata Botvilliana* (1858) |
| Salop | Longner Hall | SJ 540 100 | Robert Burton | 1803 | Red Book |
| Salop | Shavington | SJ 637 388 | First Viscount Killmorey | 1792 | Red Book |
| Som. (City of Bristol) | Abbots Leigh (Leigh Court) | ST 543 748 | Philip John Miles | 1814 | Report |
| Som. (City of Bristol) | Ashton Court | ST 558 718 | Sir Hugh Smyth | c.1802 | *Observations*; Humphry Repton to Sir Hugh Smyth, 11 October 1802, Bristol RO |
| *Som. (Bath and N.E. Somerset) | Bailbrook House, Bath | ST 765 672 | V. Jones | <1806 | PR 1806; Gaz. 82 |

| Som. (Bath and N.E. Somerset) | Bath, The Ham (Pierrepont Street) | ST 740 640 | Viscount Newark | 1799 | Drawing, private collection |
|---|---|---|---|---|---|
| *Som. | Marston Bigott | ST 750 450 | Earl of Cork | <1805 | PR 1805 |
| Som. (Bath and N.E. Somerset) | Newton Park | ST 696 643 | William Gore-Langton | 1796 | Red Book |
| Som. | Stoneaston Park | ST 623 540 | Henry Hippesely Coxe | 1792 | Red Book |
| Som. | West Coker | ST 522 134 | unknown | <1803 | *Observations* |
| Staffs. | Aqualate Hall | SJ 770 190 | John Fletcher Boughey | 1812 | Letters, Staffordshire RO |
| Staffs. | Beaudesert | SK 030 130 | First earl of Uxbridge | 1813 | Red Book |
| Staffs. | Great Barr | SP 110 970 | Joseph Scott | <1801 | Stebbing Shaw, *History of Staffordshire*, vol. 2 |
| Staffs. | Hilton | SJ 952 053 | H. Vernon | <1796 | PR (Proof Sheet) |
| *Staffs. | Himley | SO 880 894 | Viscount Dudley & Ward | <1797 | PR 1797 |
| Staffs. | Ingestre | SJ 980 240 | Lord Talbot | <1813 | Letter, Humphry Repton to J. Boughey, 17 January 1813, Staffordshire RO |
| *Staffs. | Lichfield | SK 110 090 | Anna Seward | c.1791 | Letter, Anna Seward to Humphry Repton, 4 June 1791 (inconclusive) |
| Staffs. | Prestwood | SP 870 000 | Edward Foley | 1790 | Red Book |
| *Staffs. | Shugborough | SJ 980 240 | Anson | 1792 | see Cheshire, 'unknown' |
| *Staffs. | Wetton | SK 110 550 | J. Williamson | <1805 | PR 1805 |
| *Suffolk | Blundeston | TM 510 970 | Norton Nicholls | <1790 | PR 1790 |
| Suffolk | Culford | TL 835 705 | Earl Cornwallis | 1791 | Red Book |
| Suffolk | Glemham Hall | TM 345 591 | Dudley Long North | 1791 | Red Book |
| Suffolk | Glevering Hall | TM 298 575 | Chaloner Arcedeckne | 1793 | Red Book |
| Suffolk | Helmingham Hall | TM 180 580 | Lord Tolmache | n.d. | Drawings, private collection |
| Suffolk | Henham Hall | TM 455 775 | Sir John Rous | 1790 | Red Book |
| Suffolk | Heveningham | TM 350 730 | Lord Huntingfield? | 1790 | Account Book |
| Suffolk | Holbecks | TM 020 418 | Sir William Rowley | 1790 | Account Book |
| *Suffolk | Kentwell Hall | TL 860 470 | Richard Moore | <1797 | PR 1797 |
| Suffolk | Livermere Park | TL 875 715 | Nathaniel Lee Acton | 1790 | Red Book |

| | | | | | |
|---|---|---|---|---|---|
| Suffolk | Nacton | TM 230 400 | Philp Bowes Broke | 1791 | Red Book |
| *Suffolk | Redgrave Hall | TM 040 780 | T. Holt | <1790 | PR 1790 |
| Suffolk | Rendlesham Hall | TM 340 540 | Peter Thellusson | <1799 | *Observations*; PR 1799 |
| Suffolk | Shrubland | TM 120 520 | William Middleton | 1789 | Red Book |
| Suffolk | Tendring Hall | TL 990 360 | Sir William Rowley | 1790 | Account Book; Red Book (whereabouts unknown) |
| Suffolk | Whersted (Wherstead) | TM 157 407 | Sir Robert Harland | c.1792–4 | *Sketches and Hints* |
| *Suffolk | Wickham Market, House at | TM 300 550 | unknown | <1803 | *Observations* (inconclusive) |
| *Suffolk | Wolverston (Woolverstone) | TM 180 380 | C. Berners | <1790 | PR 1790 |
| Surrey | Betchworth | TQ 201 497 | W.H. Bouverie | 1799 | Red Book |
| *Surrey (Greater London) | Clapham | TQ 290 740 | J. Lubbock | <1790 | PR 1790 |
| Surrey (Greater London) | Clapham Common, House on | TQ 280 740 | William Holme | c.1800 | Drawings, Mallets, London, January 1997 |
| *Surrey (Greater London) | Dulwich Hill | TQ 330 730 | Philip Martineau | <1804 | PR 1804 |
| *Surrey (Greater London) | East Sheen Villa | TQ 200 750 | H. Hope | <1808 | PR 1808 |
| *Surrey | Esher Place | TQ 140 640 | John Spicer | <1811 | PR 1811 |
| *Surrey (Greater London) | Grove Hill, Camberwell | TQ 330 770 | Dr Lettsome | c.1800 | Letter, Repton to Dr Lettsome, c.1800. Bodleian Library, Oxford; J. Scratcherd, *Ambulator or Pocket Companion* (1800), 97 |
| Surrey | Haling House | TQ 323 640 | William Parket Hammond | 1790 | Account Book |
| *Surrey | Ham Common | TQ 170 270 | Viscount Torrington | <1813 | Memoir (inconclusive) |
| *Surrey | Hampton Lodge | SU 906 466 | Nathaniel Snell | <1800 | PR 1800; Gaz. 82 |
| Surrey | Hatchlands | TQ 066 520 | George Holme Sumner | 1800 | Red Book |
| Surrey (Greater London) | Hurlingham | TQ 251 758 | J. Ellis | <1799 | PR 1799; *Observations* |
| Surrey | Mickleham | TQ 170 532 | unknown | 1815 | Letters to Sir Harry Fetherstonehaugh, 3 and 8 October 1815 |
| Surrey (Greater London) | Point Pleasant | TQ 180 700 | Gen. The Hon. Frederick St John | 1795 | Red Book |
| *Surrey | Shirley House | TQ 350 660 | J. Maberley | <1808 | PR 1808 |

| | | | | | |
|---|---|---|---|---|---|
| Surrey (Greater London) | Streatham, Villa at | TQ 290 720 | Lord Coventry | <1816 | *Fragments* |
| Surrey (Greater London) | Streatham | TQ 290 720 | Robert Brown | <1803 | *Observations* |
| Surrey (Greater London) | The Casina | TQ 340 720 | Richard Shaw | c.1797 | Memoir |
| Surrey (Greater London) | West Hill | TG 247 742 | David Rucker | <1803 | PR 1803; Memoir |
| Surrey (Greater London) | White Lodge | TQ 200 730 | Lord Sidmouth | 1805 | *Fragments* |
| *Surrey (Greater London) | Wimbledon, Villa at | TQ 240 720 | J. Meyricke | <1809 | PR 1809 |
| *Sussex (W. Sussex) | Buchan Hill | TQ 250 330 | Thomas Erskine | 1812 | Humphry Repton to William Repton, 15 December 1812, Huntington Library (inconclusive) |
| *Sussex (W. Sussex) | Balcombe | TQ 300 300 | unknown | <1807 | PR 1807 |
| Sussex (E. Sussex) | Compton Place | TV 600 980 | Lord George Henry Cavendish | 1803 | Red Book |
| Sussex (E. Sussex) | Heathfield Park | TQ 590 210 | Francis Newberry | 1794 | Red Book |
| Sussex (E. Sussex) | Kidbrooke Park | TQ 415 765 | Charles Abbot, first Baron Colchester | c.1803 | Colchester MSS; *Memoir* |
| Sussex (E. Sussex) | Little Green | SU 771 158 | Thomas Peckham Phipps | 1793 | Red Book |
| Sussex (W. Sussex) | Michel Grove | TQ 030 070 | Richard Walker | c.1800 | PR 1802; *Observations*; Memoir |
| *Sussex (E. Sussex) | Paxhill Park | TQ 360 260 | Mrs Borde | <1809 | PR 1809 |
| Sussex (E. Sussex) | Rose Hill (Brightling) | TQ 683 210 | John Fuller | 1806 | Red Book |
| Sussex (E. Sussex) | Royal Pavilion, Brighton | TQ 310 050 | Prince of Wales | 1805 | Red Book |
| Sussex (E. Sussex) | Sheffield Park | TQ 413 241 | First Baron Sheffield | 1789 | PR 1790; *Sketches and Hints* |
| Sussex (E. Sussex) | Stonelands (Buckhurst) | TQ 350 330 | Lord Whitworth | 1805 | Red Book |
| Sussex (W. Sussex) | Uppark | SU 779 177 | Sir Harry Fetherstonehaugh | 1810 | Red Book |
| *Sussex (W. Sussex) | Wakehurst Place | TQ 330 310 | Captain Peyton RN | <1810 | PR 1808 |
| War. | Barrels House | SP 127 667 | Robert Knight | <1796 | PR 1796 |
| War. | Stoneleigh Abbey | SP 318 713 | Lord Leigh | 1808 | Red Book |
| Wilts. | Bowood | ST 975 700 | First marquess of Landsdowne | <1801 | PR 1801; *Observations* |

| | | | | | |
|---|---|---|---|---|---|
| Wilts. | Corsham Court | ST 874 705 | Paul Cobb Methuen | 1796 | *Observations*; Corsham Court MSS, Wiltshire RO |
| Wilts. | Longleat | ST 809 430 | Second marquess of Bath | 1803 | Red Book |
| Wilts. | New Park (Roundhay) | SU 020 630 | James Sutton | 1794 | Red Book |
| Worcs. | Hewell Grange | SP 006 690 | Fifth earl of Plymouth | 1811 | Red Book |
| Worcs. (Birmingham) | Mosely Hall | SP 080 830 | John Taylor | 1792 | Red Book |
| *Worcs. (Glos.?) | Stockwell Parsonage | SO 940 140 ? | Unknown | <1807 | PR 1807 |
| Worcs. (Birmingham) | Warley | SP 010 860 | Samuel Galton | 1794 | Red Book |
| Worcs. | Witley Court | SO 770 650 | Lord Foley | 1806 | Humphry Repton to John Geers Cotterell, 28 January 1807, Garnons Letters, Herefordshire RO |
| Yorks. (Leeds) | Armley | SE 263 344 | Benjamin Gott | 1809 | Red Book |
| Yorks. (S. Yorks.) | Bessacre Manor | SE 615 002 | B.D.W. Cooke | <1794 | *Sketches and Hints* |
| *Yorks. (W. Yorks.) | Esholt Hall | SE 180 390 | T. Crompton | <1811 | PR 1811 |
| Yorks. (W. Yorks.) | Harewood | SE 311 446 | First Baron Harewood | 1799 | Report |
| *Yorks. (Notts.) | Langold | SK 570 860 | H.K. Knight | <1807 | PR 1807 |
| Yorks. (N. Yorks.) | Mulgrave Castle | NZ 845 125 | Lord Mulgrave | 1792 | Red Book |
| Yorks. (Wakefield) | Oulton Hall | SE 358 278 | John Blayds | 1809 | Red Book |
| Yorks. (Rotherham) | Ouston (Owston) | SE 550 110 | B. Cooke | 1792 | Red Book |
| Yorks. (N. Yorks.) | Rudding Hall | SE 334 531 | Lord Loughborough | 1790 | Account Book Red Book Sold 1917, (whereabouts unknown) |
| Yorks. (Sheffield) | Wentworth Woodhouse | SK 396 977 | Earl Fitzwilliam | 1790 | Red Book |
| WALES | | | | | |
| Anglesey (Clwyd) | Plas Newydd | SH 521 797 | Lord Uxbridge | 1798 | Red Book |
| Merionith (Clwyd) | Rûg Hall | SJ 055 440 | Col. E.V.W Salusbury | 1794 | Red Book |
| *Monmouth (Gwent) | Llangaanthrick House (Llangattock) | SO 210 118? | Vice-Admiral Gell | <1799 | PR 1799 |
| Radnor (Powys) | Stanedge (Stanage) Park | SO 333 717 | Charles Rogers | 1803 | Red Book |
| *Denbigh (Clwyd) | Bodlondeb | SH 770 780 | R. Holland | <1800 | PR 1800 |
| *Denbigh (Clwyd) | Ruabon | SJ 300 440 | Unknown | <1802 | PR 1803 |
| *Glam. (W. Glam.) | The Knoll (Gnoll) | SN 830 040 | J. Hanbury Leigh | <1799 | PR 1799 |

| SCOTLAND | | | | | |
|---|---|---|---|---|---|
| Fife | Valleyfield | NO 010 850 | Sir Robert Preston | c.1801 | Red Book |
| IRELAND | | | | | |
| Limerick | Bulgadeen (Bulgaden) | | George Freke Evans | 1806 | Humphry Repton to George Freke Evans, 8 September 1806, Laxton Letters |
| PORTUGAL | Garden near Oporto | | Mr Harris | <1816 | *Fragments* |

# Notes

Works = *The Landscape Gardening and Landscape Architecture of the Late Humphry Repton Esq*, ed. J.C. Loudon (London, 1840).

## Introduction

1. Previous surveys of Repton's life and work are Dorothy Stroud, *Humphry Repton* (London, 1962); George Carter, Patrick Goode and Kedrun Laurie, *Humphry Repton: Landscape Gardener 1752–1818* (Norwich and London, 1982). I owe much to them, but my approach is different. Published by *Country Life*, Stroud's pioneering book presents a chronological account of events in Repton's life and cleaves to its publisher's style of architectural history. The book by Carter et al. is the catalogue accompanying the exhibition on Repton at the Sainsbury Centre, University of East Anglia, and the Victoria and Albert Museum, London. It is organized thematically, and includes some interpretative essays on elements of Repton's style and cultural concerns. My essay 'The Political Landscape' (110–21) explored some of the issues developed in this book. A chapter in David Jacques, *Georgian Gardens: The Reign of Nature* (London, 1983), 133–63, considers Repton in terms of the notion of picturesque landscape, and one in Tom Williamson, *Polite Landscapes: Gardens and Society in Eighteenth-Century England* (Stroud and Baltimore, 1995) positions Repton in terms of wider issues of estate management and social order. A special number of the *Journal of Garden History* (ed. John Dixon Hunt, vol. 16, 1996) is devoted to various aspects of Repton's work, including articles on horticulture, aesthetics and one by me on road transport.
2. Conal Shields, Introduction to Tate Gallery, *Landscape in Britain c.1750–1850* (London, 1973), 12–13.
3. On geography in this full sense, see R.A. Dodgshon and R.A. Butlin (eds), *An Historical Geography of England and Wales*, second edition (London, 1990).
4. There is now an extensive literature on landscape art and society in Georgian England. See especially John Barrell, *The Dark Side of the Landscape: The Rural Poor in English Painting 1730–1840* (Cambridge, 1980); David Solkin, *Richard Wilson: The Landscape of Reaction* (New Haven and London, 1982); Michael Rosenthal, *Constable: The Painter and His Landscape* (New Haven and London, 1983); Ann Bermingham, *Landscape and Ideology: The English Rustic Tradition 1740–1860* (Berkeley, 1986); Andrew Hemingway, *Landscape Imagery and Urban Culture in Early Nineteenth-Century Britain* (Cambridge, 1992); Stephen Daniels, *Fields of Vision: Landscape Imagery and National Identity in England and the United States* (Cambridge and Princeton, 1993); Katherine Baetjer (ed.) *Glorious Nature! British Landscape Painting 1750–1850* (New York, 1993); Nigel Everett, *The Tory View of Landscape* (New Haven and London, 1994); Stephen Copley and Peter Garside (eds), *The Politics of the Picturesque* (Cambridge, 1994); Michael Rosenthal, Christiana Payne and Scott Wilcox (eds), *Prospects for the Nation: Recent Essays in British Landscape 1750–1880* (New Haven and London, 1997); Kay Dian Kriz, *The Idea of the English Landscape Painter: Genius as Alibi in the Early Nineteenth Century* (New Haven and London, 1997).
5. On texts on and by Turner and Constable, see Marcia Pointon, 'Aesthetic and Commodity: An Examination of the Verbal in Turner's Artistic Practice', and Ann Bermingham, 'Reading Constable', in Simon Pugh, *Reading Landscape: Country–City–Capital* (Manchester, 1990), 81–96; 97–120.
6. On these three commissions, see Chapter four.
7. Carter et al., *Humphry Repton*, 98–105.

8  John Claudius Loudon, *A Treatise on Forming, Improving and Managing Country Residences* (London, 1804), vol. 2, 705–8, 659.
9  *Monthly Review*, January 1796, 7.
10  Quoted in A.A. Tait, *The Landscape Garden in Scotland 1735–1835* (Edinburgh, 1980), 204.
11  Humphry Repton to Reginald Pole Carew, 20 December 1794, Antony House Muniments, CE/E/66/8; Humphry Repton, *Odd Whims and Miscellanies* (London, 1804), vol. 2, 1; C. Bryn Andrews (ed.), *The Torrington Diaries* (London, 1938), vol. 4, 51.
12  Humphry Repton, Red Book for Tatton Park (1792), National Trust, Tatton Park.
13  Carter et al., *Humphry Repton*, 139–44; Nigel Temple, 'Humphry Repton, Illustrator, and William Peacock's *Polite Repository* 1790–1811', *Garden History*, 13 (1985), 161–9.
14  Humphry Repton, *An Enquiry into the Changes of Taste in Landscape Gardening* (London, 1806), 121–2 (Works, 355).
15  [Humphry Repton], *The Bee; Or, a Companion to the Shakespeare Gallery* (London, 1789), 40, 26, 31; Carter et al., *Humphry Repton*, 106.
16  Humphry Repton, *Fragments on the Theory and Practice of Landscape Gardening* (London, 1816), 217 (Works, 589). Repton identifies the painting and artist in the Red Book for Endsleigh (1814), Woburn Abbey. On Turner's picture and its controversial naturalism, see the entry in Martin Butlin and Evelyn Joll, *The Paintings of J.M.W. Turner*, revised edition (New Haven and London, 1984), 82.
17  Stephen Daniels, 'The Red Books of Humphry Repton', Introduction to *Humphry Repton: The Red Books for Brandsbury and Glemham Hall* (Washington, DC, 1994), vii–xiv; Carter et al., *Humphry Repton*, 19–22.
18  Humphry Repton, Memoir, Part two, autographed draft, British Library, Add. MS 62112, 2.
19  Humphry Repton, Red Book for Babworth (1790), private collection. Anna Seward, 'The Lake; or Modern Improvement in Landscape' (n.d.), *The Poetical Works of Anna Seaward*, ed. Walter Scott (Edinburgh, 1810), vol. 3, 34–8. On Mrs Simpson's singing voice and early death, and the monument Repton designed for her in Babworth church, see Anna Seward's letter to William Hayley, 15 May 1793, *Letters of Anna Seward Written between the Years 1784 and 1807*, ed. A. Constable (Edinburgh, 1811), vol. 3, 238.
20  Daniels, 'The Red Books', vii–viii.
21  Humphry Repton, Red Book for Gaines Hall (1798), private collection.
22  So Joseph Farington observed in his diary for 23 June 1794. Kenneth Garlick and Angus MacIntyre (eds), *The Diary of Joseph Farington*, vol. 1, July 1793–December 1794 (New Haven and London, 1978), 204.
23  Humphry Repton, *Sketches and Hints on Landscape Gardening* (London, 1794), xiii–xiv (Works, 29).
24  Ibid., xiv (Works, 30).
25  Ibid., 84 (Works, 116).
26  Humphry Repton, *Observations on the Theory and Practice of Landscape Gardening* (London, 1803), 6 (Works, 120).
27  Ibid., 7 (Works, 121).
28  Ibid., x, 2n (Works, 126, 127, 132n).
29  Repton, *Enquiry*, v (Works, 323–4).
30  Ibid., 41–2 (339–40).
31  Repton, Memoir, 224–5.
32  Humphry Repton with the assistance of John Adey Repton and George Stanley Repton, *Designs for the Pavillon at Brighton* (London, 1808); J.C. Stadler to Humphry Repton, 13 April 1808, Huntington Library, San Marino, CA, HM 40945.
33  Carter et al., *Humphry Repton*, 107, 87. For an extended discussion of the commission for the Royal Pavilion, see Chapter four.
34  Humphry Repton, *Fragments*, viii (Works, 410).
35  Ibid., 113–14, 237 (Works, 506, 605).
36  Ibid., 137, 141, 237, (Works, 525, 530, 605).
37  Repton, Fragments, 98n, 100 (Works, 494n, 495).
38  Humphry Repton to Sir Harry Fetherstonehaugh, 30 May 1815, Uppark Letters, private collection.
39  *Letters of Anna Seward*, vol. 2, 371.
40  Ibid., vol. 5, 74. All letters to Repton: vol. 1, 124–9, 192–3; vol. 2, 78–82, 309–14, 370–73; vol. 3, 62–5; vol. 5, 67–74. See Seward's poem 'To Humphry Repton Esq.', *Poetical Works*, vol. 3, 64–6.
41  Humphry Repton to James Edward Smith, 5 November 1800; 14 April 1816, Scientific Correspondence of Sir James Edward Smith, vol. 8, nos 160, 169, Linnean Society, London.
42  Humphry Repton to James Edward Smith, 9 July 1815, Ibid., vol. 8, no. 169.
43  Stephen Daniels, 'Cankerous Blossom: Troubles in the Later Career of Humphry Repton Documented in the Repton Correspondence in the Huntington Library', *Journal of Garden History*, 6 (1986), 146–61. Humphry Repton to William Repton, 22 May 1815, Huntington Library, no classmark, HM 40893?
44  Humphry Repton to William Repton, 10 May 1814, Huntington Library, HM 40874. Camden was Teller of the Exchequer for sixty years, from 1780 until his death in 1840. Emoluments to the office increased nearly tenfold from £2,500 per annum in 1782 to £23,000 in 1808. There was an unsuccessful attempt in 1812 to limit this income and, under pressure, Camden relinquished his income. Parliament thanked him formally for his patriotic conduct. *Dictionary of National Biography* (London, 1921–2), vol. 16, 290. Camden was a major client of Repton. The commission at Bayham Abbey, Kent, began in 1800.
45  John Brewer, *The Pleasures of the Imagination: English Culture in the Eighteenth Century* (London, 1997), 110–11.
46  On these tropes see Dorinda Outram, 'Life Paths: Autobiography, Science and the French Revolution', in Michael Shortland and Richard Yeo (eds), *Telling Lives in Science: Essays on Scientific Biography* (Cambridge, 1996), 85–102.
47  Repton, Memoir, 1, 167, 235.
48  Ibid., 234; on polite portraiture see Marcia Pointon, *Hanging the Head: Portraiture and Social Formation in Eighteenth-Century England* (New Haven and London, 1993), 79–104;

Nadia Tscherny, 'Reynolds' Streatham Portraits and the Art of Intimate Biography', *Burlington Magazine*, 128 (January 1986), 4–10.
49 Repton, Memoir, 121.
50 Ibid., 26–7.
51 On 'character and situation' in designs see Carter et al., *Humphry Repton*, 43–4.
52 *The Works of Lord Byron. Poetry*, vol. 1, ed. Ernest Hartley Coleridge (London, 1918), 269. My thanks to David Lambert and Jan Piggott for this reference.
53 William Marshall, *Planting and Rural Ornament*, 2 vols (London, 1796), vol. 1, 285.
54 Thomas Hornor, *Description of an Improved Method of Delineating Estates with a Sketch of the Progress of Landscape Gardening in England* (London, 1813), 58. On Hornor, see Ralph Hyde, 'Thomas Hornor: Pictural Land Surveyor', *Imago Mundi*, 29 (1977), 23–34.
55 See John Buonarti Papworth's Reptonian designs in Ackermann's *Repository of Arts* from 1816 to 1820, published in Papworth's *Rural Residences* (1818) and *Hints on Ornamental Gardening* (London, 1823).
56 Broadside for James Crease and Sons, Manufacturers of Cheap Paint (London, c.1820); Ken Spelman, *Catalogue Thirty Four* (York, 1996), 28; Broadside for James Pilton's Manufactory, Invisible Pleasure Ground Fences (London, c.1820), Ken Spelman, *Catalogue Thirty-Three* (York, 1965), 30. My thanks to Charles Watkins for these references.
57 Jane Austen, *Mansfield Park* (1814; Oxford, 1980), 47, 49, 51. On some implications of these lines see Richard Quaintance, 'Humphry Repton, "any Mr Repton", and the "Improvement" Metonym in *Mansfield Park*', *Studies in Eighteenth-Century Culture* 27 (1998), 365–84.

CHAPTER 1

1 The literature on the history and ideology of travel, even in eighteenth-century England, is now extensive. I have focussed on the issues of mobility, information, space and visuality, which are often discussed most closely in connection with more recent technologies, for example in Wolfgang Schivelbusch, *The Railway Journey: Trains and Travel in the Nineteenth Century* (Oxford, 1980), and Nigel Thrift, 'Inhuman Geographies: Landscapes of Speed, Light and Power', in Paul Cloke, Marcus Doel, David Matless, Martin Phillips and Nigel Thrift, *Writing the Rural: Five Cultural Geographies* (London, 1994), 191–248.
2 John A. Chartres and Gerard Turnbull, 'Road Transport', in Derek Aldcroft and Michael J. Freeman (eds), *Transport in the Industrial Revolution* (Manchester, 1983), 64–99; John Copeland, *Roads and Their Traffic* (New Abbot, 1968), 85–108; Eric Pawson, *Transport and Economy: The Turnpike Roads of Eighteenth-Century Britain* (London, 1977).
3 Mark Girouard, *Life in the English Country House: A Social and Architectural History* (New Haven and London, 1978), 189–240.
4 Simon Jervis, 'Rudolph Ackermann', in Celina Fox (ed.), *London – World City 1800–1840* (New Haven and London, 1992), 97–109. See also Ann Pullan, 'Conversations on the Arts: Writing a Space for the Female Viewer in the *Repository of Arts* 1809–15, *Oxford Art Journal*, 15 (1992), 12–26.
5 M.A. Crowther, 'The Tramp', in Roy Porter (ed.), *Myths of the English* (Cambridge, 1992), 91–113; Raphael Samuel, 'Comers and Goers', in H.J. Dyos and Michael Wolff (eds), *The Victorian City: Images and Realities* (London 1973), vol. 1, 123–60; K.D.M. Snell, *Annals of the Labouring Poor: Social Change and Agrarian England 1660–1900* (Cambridge, 1985), 25–6, 315; Linda Colley, 'Whose Nation? Class and National Consciousness in Britain 1750–1830', *Past and Present*, no. 113 (1986), 97–117 (102–3); J.W.M. Hichberger, *Images of the Army: The Military in British Art, 1815–1914* (Manchester, 1988), 140–41.
6 Derek Gregory, 'The Fiction of Distance? Information Circulation and the Mails in Early Nineteenth-Century England', *Journal of Historical Geography*, 13 (1987), 130–54.
7 Uvedale Price to Lady Margaret Beaumont, 13 July 1802, Pierpont Morgan Library, New York, MA 1581 (Price), 34.
8 Girouard, *Life in the English Country House*, 190.
9 Pawson, *Transport and Economy*, 332.
10 Peter Brandon, 'The Diffusion of Designed Landscapes in South-East England', in H.S.A. Fox and R.A. Butlin (eds), *Change in the Countryside* (London, 1979), 165–87.
11 John Barrell, *The Idea of Landscape and the Sense of Place 1730–1840: An Approach to the Poetry of John Clare* (Cambridge, 1972), 84–97, 100–9, quotation on p. 87.
12 Tom Williamson, *Polite Landscapes: Gardens and Society in Eighteenth-Century England* (Stroud and Baltimore, 1995), 44–6.
13 Brandon, 'Diffusion of Designed Landscapes', 174.
14 Tim Mowl and Brian Earnshaw, *Trumpet at a Distant Gate: The Lodge as Prelude to the Country House* (London, 1985).
15 Girouard, *Life in the English Country House*, 214–42.
16 Malcolm Andrews, *The Search for the Picturesque: Landscape Aesthetics and Tourism in Britain, 1760–1800* (Stanford, 1989).
17 Quoted in Michael Clarke, *The Tempting Prospect: A Social History of English Watercolour* (London, 1978), 49.
18 *Cary's New Itinerary [of England and Wales]*, ninth edition (London, 1821).
19 Pawson, *Transport and Economy*, 310.
20 Quoted in Brandon, 'Diffusion of Designed Landscapes', 174.
21 Uvedale Price, *Essay on the Picturesque* (London, 1810), vol. 1, 23–4, 32–5. Price's views are discussed in detail in Chapter three below.
22 Anne D. Wallace, *Walking, Literature and English Culture: The Origins and Uses of Peripatetic in the Nineteenth Century* (Oxford, 1994).
23 Greg Laugero, 'Infrastructures of Enlightenment: Roadmaking, the Public Sphere and the Emergence of Literature', *Eighteenth Century Studies*, 29 (1995), 45–67.
24 Many of Jane Austen's novels explore the cultural implications of different forms of travel, and more than most *Mansfield Park* (1814) maps the moral vision of polite society, including fashions of landscape gardening, in terms of 'conduct', an important word in the novel.

25 A.B., 'Biographical Notice', in Works, 3. On geography for excise men, see Ezekial Polstead, *The Excise Man* (London, 1697). For a discussion of excise geographies, see Miles Ogborn, *Spaces of Modernity: London's Geographies; 1680–1780* (New York and London, 1998), 158–200.

26 Humphry Repton, *An Enquiry into the Changes of Taste in Landscape Gardening* (London, 1806), 19 (Works, 333).

27 Trevor Fawcett, 'Argonauts and Commercial Travellers: The Foreign Marketing of Norwich Stuffs in the Later Eighteenth Century', *Textile History*, 16 (1985), 151–82.

28 Kenneth Garlick and Angus Macintyre (eds), *The Diary of Joseph Farington*, vol. 1, July 1793-December 1794 (New Haven and London, 1978), 198.

29 A.B., 'Biographical Notice', in Works, 6–7.

30 Humphry Repton, *Odd Whims and Miscellanies* (London, 1804), vol. 1, 4–5, 118.

31 A.B., 'Biographical Notice', in Works, 9–14, quotation on p. 13.

32 George Carter, Patrick Goode and Kedrun Laurie. *Humphry Repton: Landscape Gardener* (Norwich, 1982), 99.

33 Ibid., 99.

34 On Palmer's role, see Howard Robinson, *The British Post Office: A History* (Princeton, NJ, 1948), 131–50.

35 Copeland, *Roads and Their Traffic*, 114.

36 A.B., 'Biographical Notice', in Works, 14, 14n.

37 Ibid., 14.

38 Repton, *Odd Whims and Miscellanies*, vol. 2, 145–7.

39 Humphry Repton, *Variety: A Collection of Essays* (London, 1787), 5.

40 Repton, *Odd Whims and Miscellanies*. vol. 2, 1, 9, 135, 141.

41 A.B., 'Biographical Notice', in Works, 15.

42 Humphry Repton to William Windham, 8 November 1790, British Library, Add. MS. 37917, fol. 154; Repton, Memoir, Part two, autographed draft, British Library, Add. MS. 62112, 3.

43 Humphry Repton to William Repton, 30 August 1808, Huntington Library, San Marino, CA, HM 40846; Repton, Memoir, 42.

44 Clarke, *Tempting Prospect*, 31–53; Sarah Bendall, *Maps, Land and Society* (Cambridge, 1992), 84–95.

45 At the end of his career Repton counted over four hundred reports. Humphry Repton, *Fragments on the Theory and Practice of Landscape Gardening* (London, 1816), vii (Works, 409).

46 Humphry Repton, *Observations on the Theory and Practice of Landscape Gardening* (London, 1803), 3 (Works, 133n).

47 On Repton and Portland, see Chapter four below.

48 Stephen Daniels, 'The Political Landscape', in Carter et al., *Humphry Repton*, 110–21 (110–12).

49 Humphry Repton to Reginald Pole Carew, 20 October 1795, Antony House Muniments, CE/E/66/13; Humphry Repton to George John Legh, 22 January 1796, Cornwall-Legh Papers, John Rylands Library, University of Manchester; Humphry Repton to Freke Evans, 8 September 1806, Freke-Evans (Laxton) Collection.

50 John Byng, *The Torrington Diaries*, vol. 3, ed. C. Bryn Andrews (London, 1936) 9; Humphry Repton, Red Book for Stoke [Edith] Park (1792), Herefordshire Record Office, BE 37; Red Book for Owston, cited in Kedrun Laurie, 'Humphry Repton: New Discoveries', *The Garden* (September 1983), 361–6 (365); Peter Goodchild, *Humphry Repton: On the Spot at Mulgrave Castle* (n.p., n.d.); Humphry Repton, Red Book for Mosely Hall (1792), Harvard University, Frances Loeb Library; Humphry Repton to John Geers Cotterell, 6 October 1792, Herefordshire Record Office, D52 6/2; Humphry Repton, Red Book for Antony House, reproduced in Edward Malins, *The Red Books of Humphry Repton* (London, 1976).

51 Humphry Repton to William Windham, 8 November 1790, British Library, Add. MS. 37917, fol. 154.

52 Humphry Repton to George John Legh, 26 September 1797, Cornwall-Legh Papers, John Rylands Library.

53 Humphry Repton to John Geers Cotterell, 8 May 1791, Herefordshire Record Office, D52 6/1.

54 Humphry Repton to James Edward Smith, 5 November 1800, Scientific Correspondence of Sir James Edward Smith, vol. 8, no. 10, Linnean Society, London.

55 Humphry Repton to Reginald Pole Carew, 25 March 1793, Antony House Muniments, CE/E/66/4.

56 Humphry Repton, *Sketches and Hints on Landscape Gardening* (London, 1795), 73 (Works, 108n).

57 Humphry Repton to George John Legh, 4 May 1797, Cornwall-Legh Papers, John Rylands Library.

58 Humphry Repton to Edward Rogers, 4 October 1809, Stanage Letters, uncatalogued, private collection.

59 Katherine Cave (ed.) *The Diary of Joseph Farington* vol. 10, July 1809–1810, (New Haven and London, 1982), 370. Repton claimed that 'the first visit I ever felt inclined to take independent of all professional pursuit' was to Uppark in 1815, to convalesce from his crippling angina. Humphry Repton to Sir Harry Fetherstonehaugh, 21 August and 8 October 1815, Uppark Letters, private collection.

60 Uvedale Price to Lady Margaret Beaumont, 10 August 1820, Pierpont Morgan Library, Coloerton MS MA 1581 (Price) 91. Repton's host is probably Richard Palmer of Holme Park, Berkshire, where Repton was first commissioned in 1793. Holme Park is near Sunning Hill where Price had a summer residence.

61 Repton, Memoir, 100, 105.

62 Humphry Repton to William Windham, 3 July 1807, British Library, Add. MS. 37919, fol. 40; Humphry Repton to John Geers Cotterell, 28 January 1807, Herefordshire Record Office, D52 6/9.

63 James Wyatt's account for building at Endsleigh, Bedford MSS, Devon Record Office, W1258 LP 4/3; William Wilkins to John Geers Cotterell, 24 December 1794, Herefordshire Record Office, D52 5/7.

64 Humphry Repton to John Geers Cotterell, 28 January 1807, Herefordshire Record Office, D 52 6/9; Humphry Repton to J. Boughey, 17 January 1813, Staffordshire Record Office, D(W) 1788 P56 B28.

65 Humphry Repton to William Windham, 3 July 1808, British Library, Add. MS. 37919, fol. 90.

66 Humphry Repton to Charles Smith, 31 January 1808, Pierpont Morgan Library, MA 1937.
67 Carter et al., *Humphry Repton*, 18.
68 In his early years J.M.W. Turner commanded less for a drawing than for the expense of getting to the site, and even in his later affluent years budgeted travelling expenses very carefully. Thomas Girtin was indebted by his expenses. Clarke, *Tempting Prospect*, 51.
69 As he said to Windham in a letter claiming outstanding expenses, £26 4s. 6d., for travel to Norfolk from Dublin, where Repton had worked as Windham's private secretary seven years previously. Humphry Repton to William Windham, 8 November 1790, British Library, Add. MS. 37917, fol. 154.
70 Humphry Repton to William Repton, 4 April 1809, Huntington Library, HM 40859.
71 Humphry Repton to William Repton, 16 November 1812, Huntington Library, HM 40872.
72 Humphry Repton to William Repton, 3 June 1814, Huntington Library, HM 40875.
73 Humphry Repton to Reginald Pole Carew, 16 September 1809, Antony House Muniments, CE/E/66/25.
74 Repton, Memoir, 17, 219.
75 Humphry Repton to William Blaythwayt, n.d., letters on work at Dyrham, Gloucestershire Record Office, D1799 C171.
76 Humphry Repton to William Repton, 30 August 1807, Huntington Library, HM 40846.
77 Laurie, 'Humphry Repton: New Discoveries', 365.
78 Repton, Memoir, 119.
79 Louis Melville, *The Life and Letters of William Beckford* (London, 1910), 256. My thanks to John Phibbs for this reference.
80 Humphry Repton to George Freke Evans, 28 April 1806, 9 April 1808, 16 August 1807 and 8 February 1808, Freke Evans (Laxton) Collection.
81 Humphry Repton to George Freke Evans, 22 September 1808, Freke Evans (Laxton) Collection.
82 Humphry Repton to George Freke Evans, 10 June 1808, Freke Evans (Laxton) Collection.
83 Leonore Davidoff and Catherine Hall, *Family Fortunes: Men and Women of the English Middle Class 1780–1850* (London, 1987), 279–84.
84 In a letter to Lord Mulgrave written 'going into the edge of Yorkshire', Repton wrote: 'letters directed to me at Hare Street follow me to all parts of the Kingdom'. Quoted in Goodchild, *Mulgrave Castle*, 10. On another trip Repton had reached Havering before he realized that he had forgotten to send plans to Sir John Cotterell in London, and sent a note to Mary to do so. Humphry Repton to Mary Repton, 1800, Herefordshire Record Office, D 52 6/10.
85 Mary Repton to William Repton, 7 February 1810, Huntington Library, HM 40862.
86 Repton, Memoir, 60.
87 Humphry Repton to William Repton, 16 November 1812, Huntington Library, HM 40872.
88 Repton, Memoir, 100.
89 Humphry Repton to William Repton, 21 January 1809, Huntington Library, HM 40857.
90 Humphry Repton to William Repton, 22 January 1809, Huntington Library, HM 40858.
91 A.B., 'Biographical Notice', in Works, 20.
92 Humphry Repton to William Adams, 17 July 1814; 12 November 1814, Repton Papers, Bedford MSS, Devon Record Office.
93 Humphry Repton to Sir Harry Fetherstonehaugh, 9 June 1814; 25 June 1815, Uppark Letters, private collection.
94 Repton, Memoir, 64.
95 Humphry Repton to Reginald Pole Carew, 20 December 1794, Antony House Muniments, CE/E/6/66/8.
96 Repton, Memoir, 168.
97 Repton, 'The State of Europe in 1803', in *Odd Whims and Miscellanies*, vol. 2, 163. First published anonymously in *The Lady's Magazine*, vol. 34 (June 1803), 328.
98 Repton, *Odd Whims and Miscellanies*, vol. 1, 29.
99 Repton, Observations, 158n (Works, 258n).
100 Repton, Fragments, 234–5 (Works, 602). He exempted one client, the London wholesale merchant William Salte, who named his garden at Tottenham the 'Trip to Matlock' because it was funded with money saved by not going. Repton, Memoir, 174–5.
101 Humphry Repton, *Designs for the Pavillon at Brighton* (London, 1808), ii (Works, 362).
102 Repton, Memoir, 209–10.
103 Ibid., 129.
104 Ibid., 81–2.
105 Ibid., 218.
106 Ibid., 200, 202.
107 Ibid., 219.
108 Repton, Sketches and Hints, ix–x (Works, 25–6).
109 Farington, vol. 1, 204 (Entry for diary, 24 June 1794). Indeed the recorded number of Repton's new commissions dropped dramatically from 1793 to 1794, from fourteen to four.
110 Andrew Hemingway, *Landscape Imagery and Urban Culture in Early Nineteenth-Century Britain* (Cambridge, 1992), 220–21.
111 Harlan W. Hamilton, *Doctor Syntax: A Silhouette of William Combe Esq.* (London, 1969), 183–4.
112 Repton, Sketches and Hints, ix (Works, 26).
113 Humphry Repton to John Boydell, 19 July 1795. Letter tipped into Repton's copy of *Fragments*, private collection.
114 Repton, Observations, 8, 11 (Works, 121, 125).
115 *Monthly Review*, July 1804, 229.
116 Even the material on optics and aesthetics was obviously lifted from reading, which Repton did on the coach, as well as in his home and those of his clients. Humphry Repton to James Edward Smith, 5 November 1800, Scientific Correspondence of Sir James Edward Smith, vol. 8, no. 160, Linnean Society, London.
117 Repton, Observations, 7 (Works, 120).
118 Ibid., 92, 131 (207, 239).
119 Ibid., 100n (215n).
120 John Claudius Loudon, *Observations on the Formation and*

121 Repton, *Observations*, 107–20, 138 (Works 220–230; 245).
122 Repton, *Fragments*, 234–5 (Works, 602).
123 Ibid., 69 (469).
124 Ibid., 69 (469).
125 Ibid., 14 (423n).
126 Ibid., viii (410).
127 Loudon, *Treatise*, vol. 1, 713–14. Repton would have agreed. Railing against 'the contemptuous sneer of those dull dogs in society', Repton praised puns for producing surprise and laughter, in Shakespeare as well as more ephemeral works such as the *New Bath Guide*. Repton, *Variety*, 81–91. His own writing, in the Red Books as well as correspondence, puns frequently.
128 Humphry Repton, Red Book for Milton Park (1791), private collection.
129 Humphry Repton, Red Book for Tatton Park (1792), National Trust, Tatton Park.
130 Humphry Repton, Red Book for Thoresby (1791), private collection. Photographed copy, Nottingham University Manuscripts Department, 4P 21/1.
131 Humphry Repton, Red Book for Babworth (1790), private collection.
132 Repton, Red Book for Stoke [Edith] Park.
133 Humphry Repton, Red Book for Shardeloes (1794), private collection. Copy in Buckinghamshire Record Office, Aylesbury.
134 Repton, Red Book for Shardeloes; Repton, *Observations*, 66–72 (Works, 187–92).
135 Humphry Repton, Red Book for Blaise Castle (1796), Bristol Museum and Art Gallery.
136 In some parks, on dramatic sites, the scenic purpose of Repton's drives seems sacrificed to the experience of travel; they appear designed to test the speed and manoeuverability of modern carriages and the daring of their occupants, 'race tracks with trees'. The phrase and observation are by John Phibbs. He has in mind the drive at Mulgrave Castle, skirting the cliff near Whitby.
137 Humphry Repton, Red Book for Ferney Hall (1789), Pierpont Morgan Library.
138 Repton, *Fragments*, 179 (Works, 559).
139 Humphry Repton, Red Book for Stoneleigh Abbey (1809), Leigh collection, Shakespeare Birthplace Trust, Stratford-upon-Avon.
140 Humphry Repton, Red Book for Ashridge (1813), Huntington Library; Diary of William Buckingham, 11 June 1813, Hertfordshire Record Office, D/EX230Z1.
141 Humphry Repton, Red Book for Beaudesert (1814), The Taylor Collection, Princeton University.
142 Repton, *Enquiry*, 31, 16 (Works, 339, 332).
143 Humphry Repton, Red Book for Sheringham (1812), National Trust, on loan to the Royal Institute of British Architects, London.
144 R.L. Gerardin, *An Essay on Landscape*, translated by Daniel Malthus (London, 1783), 88–9.
145 Repton, Red Book for Shardeloes.
146 Humphry Repton to George John Legh, 27 January 1797; 4 May 1797. Cornwall-Legh Papers, John Rylands Library, High Legh II, Box 12.
147 Repton, Red Book for Stoke [Edith] Park.
148 Repton, *Observations*, 137 (Works, 244n). An Account of the New Buildings, Road and Alterations at Stoke Edith by John Edwards the Younger [steward], Herefordshire Record Office, E 12/III/620. David Whitehead, 'The Purchase and Building of Stoke Edith Park, Herefordshire 1670–1707', *Transactions of the Woolhope Naturalists Field Club*, 43 (1980), 181–202 (193–94); David Whitehead, 'John Nash and Humphry Repton: An Encounter in Herefordshire 1785–98', *Transactions of the Woolhope Naturalists Field Club*, 47 (1992), 210–36 (221–27).
149 Humphry Repton, Red Book for Tewin Water (1799), Hertfordshire Record Office.
150 Humphry Repton, Red Book for Hatchlands (1800), Pierpont Morgan Library.
151 Humphry Repton to Lord Mansfield, 16 August 1793, Scone Palace Archives, Kenwood Box 74, Bundle 3.
152 Repton, *Designs for the Pavillon*, ii–iii (Works, 362–3n); *Fragments*, 191–4 (Works, 567–70); Humphry Repton to Sir Harry Fetherstonehaugh, 8 October 1815, Uppark Letters, private collection.
153 Humphry Repton to Sir Harry Fetherstonehaugh, 8 October 1815, Uppark Letters, private collection.
154 Repton, *Fragments*, 191–4 (Works, 567–70).
155 Ibid., 76 (Works, 474).
156 Repton, *Observations*, 49–50 (Works, 172–4).
157 Repton, *Fragments*, 191 (Works, 567).
158 Stephen Daniels, 'The Political Iconography of Woodland in Later Georgian England', in Denis Cosgrove and Stephen Daniels (eds), *The Iconography of Landscape* (Cambridge, 1988), 43–82; Nigel Everett, *The Tory View of Landscape* (New Haven and London, 1994), 184–9.
159 Repton's critique of this compositional format, for its funnelling of vision, draws on early objections he made to 'the false taste of the last century' for formal avenues (Repton, *Sketches and Hints*, 24 (Works, 65)). But it derives its ideological currency from his later objections to the design of 'public edifices', which by sacrificing ornament to utility 'may be considered as manufactories or warehouses for carrying on a species of traffic' (Repton, *Designs for the Pavillon*, x (Works, 373)).
160 Repton, *Observations*, 142 (Works, 247).
161 A.B., 'Biographical Notice', in Works, 18–19; Repton, *Observations*, 161–2n (Works 261n).
162 Repton, *Observations*, 142 (Works 247–8).
163 Ibid., 142–3 (249).
164 Repton, Red Book for Babworth. Repton has slightly rephrased the lines he quotes from Goldsmith as well as changing their tense. M. Laird, *A Topographical Description of the County of Nottingham* (London, 1820), 314–15.
165 Repton, Red Book for Tatton Park.

166 Richard Payne Knight, *The Landscape: A Didactic Poem* (London, 1794). This dispute is fully discussed in Chapter three below.
167 John Nash to George John Legh, undated, quoted in Nigel Temple, *John Nash and the Village Picturesque* (Gloucester, 1979), 153–4. The plan was not executed.
168 Edward Repton to William Repton, 11 July 1809, Huntington Library, HM 40909.
169 Repton, *Fragments*, 227–31 (Works, 597–600).
170 Ibid., 231 (600). After this episode, Edward reported: 'nobody at Crayford worth knowing'. Edward Repton to William Repton, 2 January 1813, Huntington Library, HM 40914.
171 Repton, *Odd Whims and Miscellanies*, vol. 2, 7.
172 Repton, Memoir, 71.
173 Ibid., 154–7.
174 Ibid., 95.
175 Humphry Repton to Sir Harry Fetherstonehaugh, 28 October 1816, Uppark Letters, private collection.
176 George Terry, *Memories of Old Romford* (Romford, 1880); Victoria County History, *Essex*, vol. 7, 57–63.
177 Repton, Memoir, 147. On Irish migrant labour near London, see Arthur Redford, *Labour Migration in England 1800–850*, second edition, ed. W.H. Chaloner (Manchester, 1964), 137–8.
178 Colin Shrimpton, *The Landed Society and the Family Community of Essex in the Late Eighteenth and Early Nineteenth Centuries*, unpublished PhD thesis, University of Cambridge, 1965, 100–01, 397–401.
179 Davidoff and Hall, *Family Fortunes*, 366–8.
180 Arthur Searle and Colin Brazier, *A History of Hare Hall* (n.p., 1960), 12, 31–2.
181 I.G. Sparkes, *Gidea Hall and Gidea Park* (Romford, 1966), 36–47.
182 Fiona Cowell, 'Richard Woods (?1716–93): A Preliminary Account', part 1, '"Woods Surveyer at Chertsey in Surry and at London Stile"', *Garden History*, 14 (1986), 85–119 (87); part 2, '"Mr Wood of Essex"', *Garden History*, 15 (1987), 19–54 (27–44); part 3, 'Influences, Style and Working Methods', *Garden History*, 15 (1987), 115–35.
183 Repton does not mention Woods in his available writings, but it is hard not to discern some design influence, notably the modest scale of Woods's work and his fondness for roses. Cowell, 'Richard Woods', part 3, 'Influences', 117, 124.
184 Repton, Memoir, 107.
185 Statement of Account betwixt Sir H. Featherstone-[haugh], Bart. & H. and J.A. Repton, 1813, Uppark Letters, private collection; Humphry Repton to William Repton, 11 December 1812, Huntington Library, HM 40837.
186 Repton, Memoir, 108.
187 A.B., 'Biographical Notice', in Works, 13.
188 George Carter, 'Humphry Repton at Hare Street, Essex', *Garden History*, 12 (1984), 120–31 (121).
189 Ibid., 121; Repton, *Observations*, 157–8 (Works, 257); Price, *Essays on the Picturesque*, vol. 2, 143.
190 Minute Book of Quarter Sessions and Courts Leet for the Liberty of Havering-atte-Bower 1730–1803, Essex Record Office, Q/HMI.
191 Repton, *Fragments*, 234–6.
192 A.B., 'Biographical Notice', in Works, 14n. I have suggested that a similar style of flower garden at the Constables' house in East Bergholt, further along the high road, may have been influenced by Repton's garden. Stephen Daniels, 'Love and Death Across an English Garden: Constable's Paintings of His Family's Flower and Kitchen Gardens', *Huntington Library Quarterly*, 55 (1992), 433–538.
193 *The Beauties of England and Wales*, vol. 5, ed. E.W. Brayley and J. Britton, (London, 1803), 476.
194 Sparkes, *Gidea Hall*, 47; Shrimpton, *Landed Society*, 176–7.
195 Humphry Repton to William Repton, 27 September 1812 Huntington Library, HM 40871.
196 Ibid.
197 Alexander Black to Richard Wright Benyon, 6 June 1815, Essex Record Office, D/DBE E62.
198 Nathaniel Kent to Lady Dacre [of Belhus], 4 February 1802, quoted in Shrimpton, *Landed Society*, 245.
199 Shrimpton, *Landed Society*, 245–6.
200 Repton, Memoir, 74.
201 Humphry Repton to William Repton, 27 September 1812, Huntington Library, HM 40871.
202 Repton, Memoir, 76.
203 Ibid., 73.
204 J.B. Talbot, 'Romford As It Was and As It Is', *Essex Times* (13 February 1869). My thanks to Peter McCaul for this reference. Upon his release for good conduct, Peachey made a success of farming in Tasmania and made a return visit to Hare Street to provide for his aged parents and relations.
205 Humphry Repton to Sir Harry Fetherstonehaugh, 20 October 1816, Uppark Letters, private collection.
206 Humphry Repton to William Repton, 27 September 1812, Huntington Library, HM 40871.
207 Humphry Repton to William Repton, 23 [October?] 1816, Huntington Library HM 40879.
208 Searle and Brazier, *Hare Hall*, 13–14; Shrimpton, *Landed Society*, 103–04.
209 Humphry Repton to Mary Repton, 8 [December?] 1807, Huntington Library, HM 40932.
210 Searle and Brazier, *Hare Hall*, 15–16.
211 Humphry Repton to William Repton, 27 September 1812, Huntington Library, HM 40871.
212 Humphry Repton to Sir Harry Fetherstonehaugh, 20 October 1816, Uppark Letters, private collection. From the admiring description of his cattle management in J.P. Neale's *Seats of Nobleman and Gentlemen*, vol. II (1819), Severn may have been a better farmer than Repton suggests.
213 Humphry Repton to William Repton, 22 May 1815, Huntington Library no classmark, HM 40893?
214 Humphry Repton to Sir Harry Fetherstonehaugh, 1 May 1817, Uppark Letters, private collection.
215 Dorothy Adey to William Repton, 29 April 1813, Huntington Library, HM 40892.

216 Humphry Repton to William Repton; 22 May 1815, Huntington Library, no classmark, HM 40893?
217 Repton, *Fragments*, 237.
218 Ibid. Repton expressed similar sentiments earlier in his career. In the Red Book for Barton Seagrave, Northamptonshire of 1794, he compares the alignment of a public road from the house to the view from his house at Hare Street. It was more 'wholesome' than 'agreeable'. 'I would not exchange the lively scene of moving objects for a more parkish landscape.' Red-Book for Barton Seagrave, The Holden Arboretum, Kirtland, OH. Microfilm in Exported Manuscripts, British Library.
219 Price, *Essays on the Picturesque*, vol. 2, 335–6; vol. 3, 315–16.
220 Repton, *Fragments*, 217 (Works, 589).
221 Repton reported that Viscount Torrington had them in his garden at Ham Common, and asked Repton about bulk supplies (Repton, Memoir, 25).
222 Humphry Repton to Sir Harry Fetherstonehaugh, 8 October 1815, Uppark Letters, private collection.
223 There is an interesting parallel with disgust at slaughtered prize livestock referred to by Harriet Ritvo in *The Animal Estate: The English and Other Creatures in Victorian England* (Cambridge, MA, 1987), 73–4.
224 Everett, *The Tory View*, 164–5.
225 John Barrell, *The Dark Side of the Landscape: The Rural Poor in English Painting 1730–1840* (Cambridge, 1980), 135–6. We might speculate that a regional sensibility is operating, for it was the Essex squire Thomas Ruggles, author of tracts on picturesque management and a client of Repton's, who found that the pleasure of benevolent feelings, formed by the sight of comfortable cottages, was inverted by 'the hideous appearance of misery and distress . . . and we turn with anguish from those objects, which reveal to the mind, scenes of misery we are not able to relieve'. Thomas Ruggles, *The History of the Poor* (London, 1793–4), vol. 2, 178–9. On Ruggles, see Everett, *The Tory View*, 125–7. On Repton's commission, see Humphry Repton, Report on Spains Hall (1807), private collection. Edith Freeman, *A Family Story: The Ruggles of Spains Hall* (Sudbury, 1993), 74–5.
226 Hichberger, *Images of the Army*, 140–41; John Brewer, *The Pleasures of the Imagination: English Culture in the Eighteenth Century* (London, 1997), 525–8.
227 Repton, Red Book for Sheringham.
228 William Wordsworth, *Poetical Works* (Oxford, 1978), 545. On the spectre of vagrancy in London at this time, see Deborah Epstein Nord, 'The City as Theater: From Georgian to Victorian London', *Victorian Studies* (1988), 160–88.
229 I owe this point to John Macarthur's unpublished account of the view of Hare Street and to discussing it with him.
230 Humphry Repton to Sir Harry Fetherstonehaugh, 25 June 1815, Uppark Letters, private collection.
231 Repton, *Odd Whims and Miscellanies*, vol. 1, 21.
232 Humphry Repton to William Repton, 23 [April] 1816, Huntington Library, HM 40879.
233 Richard Gorer wonders if such roses as Repton depicts were actually available at this time. If they were, their blooms would have been very short lived, making the view more fragile still. 'The Puzzle of Repton's Roses', *Country Life* (11 March 1982): 654–6.
234 Humphry Repton to William Repton, 23 [April] 1816, Huntington Library, HM 40879.

CHAPTER 2

1 Humphry Repton, Red Book for Honing (1792), private collection; Memoir, Part two, autographed draft, British Library, Add. MS. 62112, 3.
2 Repton, *Fragments on the Theory and Practice of Landscape Gardening* (London, 1816), 195 (Works, 570); Red Book for Sheringham (1812), National Trust, on loan to the Royal Institute of British Architects, London.
3 On the county as a regional formation, see Alan Everitt, 'Country, County and Town: Patterns of Regional Evolution in England', *Transactions of the Royal Historical Society*, 29 (1979), 72–108; John Langton, 'The Industrial Revolution and the Regional Geography of England', *Transactions of the Institute of British Geographers*, 9 (1984), 131–44; Robin Butlin, 'Regions in England and Wales c.1600–1914', in R.A. Butlin and R.A. Dodgshon (eds), *A New Historical Geography of England and Wales*, second edition (London, 1978), 223–54. On Norfolk, see Tom Williamson, *The Origins of Norfolk* (Manchester, 1993).
4 Trevor Fawcett, 'Argonauts and Commercial Travellers: The Foreign Marketing of Norwich Stuffs in the Later Eighteenth Century', *Textile History*, 16 (1985), 151–81.
5 A.B., 'Biographical Notice', in Works, 5–6.
6 M.G. Buist, *At Spes non Fracta. Hope and Co 1770–1815: Merchant Bankers and Diplomats at Work* (The Hague, 1974), 11–12; A. Chuquet, ed. *Recollections of Baron de Frénilly* (1909), quoted in David Watkin, *Thomas Hope 1769–1831 and the Neo-Classical Idea* (London, 1968), 1.
7 Trevor Fawcett, 'Measuring the Provincial Enlightenment: The Case of Norwich', *Eighteenth-Century Life*, 8 (1982), 13–27; Trevor Fawcett, *Music in Eighteenth Century Norwich and Norfolk* (Norwich, 1979).
8 A.B., 'Biographical Notice', in Works, 8–9. Attending public concerts or playing in private recitals, music remained a defining feature of Repton's sensibility. On a visit to Harewood House in 1799 he joined in nightly music-making with William Wilberforce and the family and servants. Repton, Memoir, 92–3; The Red Book for Babworth has a scene with a flautist, probably Repton, accompanying Mrs Simpson 'celebrated for her fine voice and grace in singing'. Red Book for Babworth (1790), private collection. Anna Seward to William Hayley, 15 May 1793, *The Letters of Anna Seward Written between the Years 1784 and 1807*, ed. A. Constable (Edinburgh, 1811), vol. 1, 278. On music and domesticity, see Richard Leppert, *Music and Image: Domesticity, Ideology and Socio-Cultural Formation in Eighteenth-Century England* (Cambridge, 1988). See also Repton's comments on the role of music in Wilkie's painting *The Blind Fiddler*, enlivening 'the happy family and refining the subject of "low life"'. Humphry Repton to Samuel Whitbread, 10 May 1807, Bedford Record Office.

9 Fawcett, 'Argonauts and Commercial Travellers', 153, 164–5.
10 M.J. Armstrong (ed.), *History and Antiquities of the County of Norfolk*, vol. 3 (Norwich, 1787).
11 *The Beauties of England and Wales*, vol. 11, ed. J. Evans and J. Britton (London, 1810), 107. J. Sapwell, *A History of Aylsham* (Aylsham, 1960).
12 Armstrong, *History and Antiquities*, vol. 3, 24–5.
13 Humphry Repton, 'Law Wigs' (n.d.), Avery Architectural Library, Columbia University, New York.
14 Nathaniel Kent, *General View of the Agriculture of Norfolk* (London, 1796), 156; Arthur Young, *General View of the Agriculture of Norfolk* (London, 1804), 252.
15 Humphry Repton, Red Book for Warley (1795), Smethwick Public Library.
16 Armstrong, *History and Antiquities*, vol. 3, 269, 75. On Oxnead, see Anthea Taigel and Tom Williamson, 'Some Early Geometric Gardens in Norfolk', *Journal of Garden History*, 11 (1991), 82–3.
17 Tom Williamson and Anthea Taigel (eds), *Gardens in Norfolk* (Norwich, 1990), 41.
18 John Adey Repton, 'Oxnead Hall, Norfolk', *Gentleman's Magazine*, New Series 21 (1844), 21–45.
19 Repton, Memoir, 34, 116, 130. John Repton appears a more robust figure than his younger brother, sued for assault after trying to sort out a fight at an assembly at Aylsham and, to Humphry's concern, marrying a 'low woman', Bess. Humphry Repton, to William Repton, January 1814, Huntington Library, HM 40856.
20 R.W. Ketton-Cremer, *Felbrigg: The Story of a House* (Ipswich, 1962), 159–76.
21 Windham, *Diary*, quoted in Trevor Fawcett, 'John Crome and the Idea of Mousehold', *Norfolk Archaeology*, 38 (1982), 169–81 (171).
22 Pamela Horn, 'An Eighteenth-Century Land Agent: The Career of Nathaniel Kent (1737–1810)', *Agricultural History Review*, 30 (1982), 1–16.
23 Pamela Horn, *William Marshall (1745–1818) and the Georgian Countryside* (Sutton Courtenay, Abingdon, 1982), 16–19.
24 R.W. Ketton-Cremer, *A Norfolk Gallery* (London, 1948), 149–61.
25 Kent, *General View of Norfolk*, 13–14; William Marshall, *The Rural Economy of Norfolk* (London, 1787), 2–4.
26 Humphry Repton, *To Save All. To the Memory of the Late Nathaniel Kent Esq.* (n.d.), Avery Architectural Library; Humphry Repton, Red Book for Warley; Kent, *General View of Norfolk*, 56.
27 *Monthly Review*, January 1796, 91–100. For more on this, see Chapter three below.
28 Repton, Memoir, 2. Repton claimed that he himself invented the device of slide overlays.
29 Humphry Repton, *Observations on the Theory and Practice of Landscape Gardening* (London, 1803), 49–50, (Works, 173–4). After Marsham's death, Repton attempted (unsuccessfully) to edit his writings for publication, as, he said, Alexander Hunter had edited Evelyn, and Lord Sheffield Gibbon. Humphry Repton to Robert Marsham the Younger, 12 October 1801, Norfolk Record Office, Ketton-Cremer MSS 7/86.
30 A.B., 'Biographical Notice', in Works, 9.
31 Ibid., 11.
32 Ibid., 10. See also Repton's letter from Sustead to James Edward Smith, 23 January 1783, Scientific Correspondence of Sir James Edward Smith, vol. 25, no. 32, Linnean Society, London.
33 Humphry Repton to William Cobb, 27 April 1782; 25 January 1793, Norfolk Record Office, Ketton-Cremer MSS 7/85.
34 A.B., Biographical Notice, in Works, 10.
35 Humphry Repton, *Variety: A Collection of Essays* (London, 1787), 77–9.
36 Armstrong, *History and Antiquities*, vol. 3, 98. Hewett also exercised his influence further up the social hierarchy, for when his landlord left his younger sons poorly provided for, Hewett took them into the parsonage, sent them to train for holy orders and found a living for them, 'for he considers the descendants of his patron as his heirs'.
37 A.B., 'Biographical Notice', in Works, 10.
38 Armstrong, *History and Antiquities*, vol. 3, 109–10.
39 Repton, *Observations*, 148n (Works, 253n).
40 R.W. Ketton-Cremer, *Country Neighbourhood* (London, 1951), 164.
41 A.B., 'Biographical Notice', in Works, 10.
42 Humphry Repton to William Cobb, 22 March 1778; 25 July 1779; 13 May 1781, Norfolk Record Office, Ketton-Cremer MSS 7/85.
43 A.B., 'Biographical Notice', in Works, 10.
44 Armstrong, *History and Antiquities*, vol. 3, 28, 55.
45 Marshall, *The Rural Economy of Norfolk*, 366–7.
46 Horn, 'An Eighteenth-Century Land Agent', 1–3.
47 Kent, *General View of Norfolk*, 75, 46.
48 John Byng, *The Torrington Diaries*, ed. C. Bryn Andrews, vol. 3 (London, 1936), 12–13.
49 Kent, *General View of Norfolk*, 56.
50 John Phibbs argues, largely from field observation, that Repton was responsible for some of the landscaping at Felbrigg; 'A Reconsideration of Repton's Contribution to the Improvements at Felbrigg, Norfolk, 1778–84', *Garden History*, 16 (1988), 33–44.
51 A.B., 'Biographical Notice', in Works, 12–15.
52 *The Windham Papers*, ed. Earl of Roseberry (London, 1913), vol. 1, 34–57.
53 Humphry Repton to William Windham, 8 November 1790, British Library, Add. MS. 37917; Repton, *Odd Whims and Miscellanies* (London, 1804), vol. 1, vi–viii. Their mutual friend Edward Chamberlayne also suffered the anxieties of public office. Promoted to Secretary of the Treasury, an expressly political appointment, by the Whig administration, he found the pressure of preferment unbearable and threw himself from a window to his death (Henry Roseveare, *The Treasury, 1600–1870: The Foundations of Control* (London, 1973), 108–92).
54 A.B., 'Biographical Notice', in Works, 3.

55. Humphry Repton, Account Book, Norfolk Record Office; Humphry Repton to William Windham, 8 November 1790, British Library, Add. MS. 37917.
56. A.B., 'Biographical Notice', in Works, 13–14. On the mail-coach scheme see chapter one above.
57. Repton, Odd Whims and Miscellanies, vol. 2, 2; Dorothy Stroud, Humphry Repton (London, 1962), 131.
58. Fawcett, 'Measuring the Provincial Enlightenment', 19–20; Carter George, Patrick Goode and Kedrun Laurie, Humphry Repton: Landscape Gardener 1752–1818 (Norwich and London, 1982), 10.
59. Repton, 'The Friar's Tale', in Variety, 261–90. Reprinted in The Lady's Magazine (June, July and August 1792), vol. 23 (1792), 309–12, 349–51, 465–7. Republished with slight revisions and an illustration in Repton, Odd Whims and Miscellanies, vol. 1, 147–71.
60. Repton, Memoir, 1.
61. A.M.W. Stirling, Coke of Norfolk and His Friends (London, 1912), 233–4.
62. Repton, Account Book.
63. Horn, 'An Eighteenth-Century Land Agent', 4.
64. Repton, Account Book.
65. Humphry Repton to William Windham, 8 November 1790, British Library, Add. MS. 37917.
66. Jeremy Black, The British Abroad: The Grand Tour in the Eighteenth Century (Stroud, 1992), 19, 35–6.
67. Humphry Repton to Norton Nicholls, 26 August 1788, Bristol University Library, 180/1.
68. Repton, Memoir, 119.
69. Humphry Repton to Norton Nicholls, 26 August 1788, Bristol University Library, 180/1.
70. I.M. Manning, A History of Old Catton (Catton, 1981), 3.
71. Fawcett, 'Measuring the Provincial Enlightenment', 20; R.W. Liscombe, William Wilkins 1778–1839 (Cambridge, 1980), 16.
72. Sarah Bendall, Maps, Land and Society: A History, with a Carto-Bibliography of Cambridgeshire Estate Maps c.1600–1836 (Cambridge, 1992), 106–07.
73. Humphry Repton to Norton Nicholls, 26 August 1788, Bristol University Library, 180/1.
74. Carter et al., Humphry Repton, 99–100.
75. Tom Williamson and Anthea Taigel (eds), Gardens in Norfolk (Norwich, 1990), 42. See also Tom Williamson, The Archaeology of the Landscape Park: Garden Design in Norfolk 1680–1870 (Oxford, 1998), 275–6.
76. Repton, Observations, 143 (Works, 249).
77. R.A.C. Parker, Coke of Norfolk: A Financial and Agricultural Study 1707–1842 (Oxford, 1978), 83–133; Susanna Wade Martins, A Great Estate at Work: Holkham and Its Inhabitants in the Nineteenth Century (Cambridge, 1980); Williamson, The Archaeology of the Landscape Park, 245–7.
78. François de la Rouchefoucauld, 'A Frenchman's Year in Suffolk', ed. Norman Scarfe, Suffolk Records Society, 30 (1988), 194–200. There is an undated drawing by Repton in the Avery Architectural Library, Columbia University, inscribed 'Holkham, Norfolk: the lake and church as it appeared one evening from the statue gallery'; this was probably drawn on a visit from Sustead before he was commissioned by Coke.
79. Repton, Account Book; Humphry Repton, Red Book for Holkham Hall (1789). Collection, Lord Leicester, DL (MS. 772).
80. Repton, Red Book for Holkham Hall.
81. Humphry Repton, Red Book for Ferne[y] Hall (1789), Pierpont Morgan Library, New York. On the Ferney commission see Chapter three below.
82. Uvedale Price, Essays on the Picturesque (London, 1810), vol. 1, 67.
83. Ibid., 67. Repton, Memoir, 7.
84. Humphry Repton, Sketches and Hints on Landscape Gardening (London, 1795), 65 (Works, 103); Tom Wall, 'The Verdant Landscape: The Practice and Theory of Richard Payne Knight at Downton', in Stephen Daniels and Charles Watkins (eds), The Picturesque Landscape: Visions of Georgian Herefordshire (Nottingham, 1994), 49–61 (51–2). On Repton and Downton see Chapter three below.
85. Williamson, The Archaeology of the Landscape Park, 245–7.
86. Repton, Sketches and Hints, 29 (Works, 70), and Observations (Works, 166–7).
87. Tom Williamson, 'Parks in the 18th and 19th Centuries', in Peter Wade-Martins (ed.), An Historical Atlas of Norfolk (Norfolk, 1993), 110.
88. Repton, Memoir, 3.
89. Taigel and Williamson, 'Some Early Geometric Gardens in Norfolk', 16.
90. Repton, Memoir, 32.
91. Ibid., 24.
92. Repton, Odd Whims and Miscellanies, vol. 1, vi–vii.
93. Repton, Memoir, 9–11. On Repton and Portland, see Chapter four below.
94. Repton, Account Book; Carter et al., Humphry Repton, 158–9, 161–2.
95. Nigel Wright, The Gentry and their Houses in Norfolk and Suffolk from Circa 1550 to 1850, unpublished PhD thesis, University of East Anglia, 1990, 297–300.
96. C.B. Jewson, The Jacobin City: A Portrait of Norwich in Its Reaction to the French Revolution 1788–1802 (Glasgow and London, 1975), 144–5.
97. Harriet Martineau, Autobiography, 3 vols (London, 1877), vol. 1, 98.
98. Repton, Red Book for Honing.
99. Account book, Honing Hall, private collection. Wright, 'The Gentry', 300–02. Williamson, The Archaeology of the Landscape Park, 247–8. Sir Joane Soane was commissioned to submit a plan for altering the house in 1788, but little of this appears to have been implemented.
100. Repton, Sketches and Hints, 21n (Works 61n), and Observations, 186n (Works, 284n). The Red Books are not dated, but circumstantial evidence, such as the content and style and the date of land purchases, suggests 1792 (Carter et al., Humphry Repton, 158–9).
101. Humphry Repton, Red Book for Northrepps (n.d.), private collection.
102. Stroud, Humphry Repton, 66.

103 Humphry Repton, Red Book for Bracondale (n.d.), Norfolk Central Library.
104 Stroud, *Humphry Repton*, 66.
105 Evans and Britton, *The Beauties of England and Wales*, vol. 11, 197. Repton's illustration, of the riverside in early morning, echoes views he published of scenes around Purley to show the lighting effects of different positions of the sun. A morning walk to this vantage point at Bracondale would reveal a landscape of 'wood, water and distant country'; an evening walk 'houses, bridges, roads, boats, arable fields, and distant towns and villages'. Carter et al., *Humphry Repton*, 102. Repton, *Observations*, 28–9 (*Works*, 154–5). On the paradigm of the Thames Valley in river scenery, see Andrew Hemingway, *Landscape Imagery and Urban Culture in Early Nineteenth-Century Britain* (Cambridge, 1992), 257–67.
106 David Whitehead, 'John Nash and Humphry Repton: An Encounter in Herefordshire 1785–98', *Transactions of the Woolhope Naturalists Field Club*, 47 (1992), 210–36 (220–21); Liscombe, *William Wilkins*, 14.
107 Quoted in Jewson, *The Jacobin City*, 39.
108 Ketton-Cremer, *A Norfolk Gallery*, 160.
109 P.J. Corfield, *The Social and Economic History of Norwich 1650–1850: A Study of Urban Growth*, unpublished PhD thesis, University of London, 1976, 327–8; Fawcett, 'Argonauts and Commercial Travellers', 173–7.
110 Humphry Repton to William Repton, 10 January 1808, Huntington Library, HM 40848.
111 Repton, *Odd Whims and Miscellanies*, vol. 1; Liscombe, *William Wilkins*, 14.
112 *Windham Papers*, ed. Roseberry, vol. 2, 216–22.
113 Repton, *Odd Whims and Miscellanies*, vol. 2, 41n, 115n.
114 Edmund Bartell, *Hints for Picturesque Improvement in Ornamented Cottages and Their Scenery* (London, 1804), and *Cromer, Considered as a Watering Place; With Observations on the Picturesque Scenery in Its Neighbourhood* (1800; London, second edition 1806).
115 Hemingway, *Landscape Imagery and Urban Culture*, 262.
116 Humphry Repton, Red Book for Wood Hall (1806), private collection.
117 Ibid. On Josiah Boydell, see *Dictionary of National Biography* (Oxford, 1921–2), vol. 2, 1014–15.
118 Humphry and John Adey Repton, Plans for Barningham (1807), private collection; Repton, *Fragments*, 29–32 (*Works* 435–9); Thomas Mott to Humphry Repton, January 1807; Humphry Repton to John Adey Repton, 26 July 1807, Huntington Library; HM 40906, 40839.
119 William Windham to Humphry Repton, 16 August 1807, British Library, Add. MS. 37918.
120 Humphry Repton to William Repton, 10 January 1808, Huntington Library, HM 40848.
121 Humphry Repton to William Windham, 3 July 1808, British Library, Add. MS. 37919.
122 Humphry Repton to William Repton, 21 January 1811, Huntington Library, HM 40818.
123 Repton was commissioned at Stradsett near Downham Market in 1808 but replaced as consultant by Loudon. Williamson, *The Archaeology of the Landscape Park*, 281–2. Christobel Burroughs of Hoveton Hall commissioned Repton in 1809 and had not settled her bill six years later. Humphry Repton to William Repton, 3 October 1815, Huntington Library, HM 40877. Wright, 'The Gentry', 307.
124 Alison Yarrington, 'Nelson: The Citizen Hero: State and Public Patronage of Monumental Sculpture 1805–1818', *Art History*, 6 (1983), 315–29.
125 Humphry Repton to William Repton, 5 December 1808, Huntington Library, HM 40453.
126 William Repton to Humphry Repton, 29 December 1808, Huntington Library, HM 40854.
127 William Repton to William Windham, 5 March 1809, British Library, Add. MS. 37919; Dorothy Adey to William Repton, 21 April 1809, Huntington Library, HM 40887.
128 Humphry Repton to William Repton, 21 January 1809, Huntington Library, HM 40858.
129 Humphry Repton to William Repton, n.d., enclosed in a letter from Humphry Repton to Dorothy Adey, 11 December 1812, Huntington Library, HM 40837.
130 Susan Yaxley (ed.), *Sherringhamia: The Journal of Abbot Upcher 1813–16* (Stibbard, Norfolk, 1986), 3; Emma Pigott, *Memoir of the Honourable Mrs Upcher of Sheringham* (n.d.), private collection.
131 Repton, Red Book for Sheringham.
132 Armstrong, *History and Antiquities*, vol. 3, 101.
133 Samuel Pratt, *Gleanings in England*, 2 vols (London, 1801), vol. 1, 432, 431n.
134 Bartell, *Cromer*, 75–9; *Hints for Picturesque Improvement*, xi, 70–71, 94–5.
135 Pratt, *Gleanings in England*, 494–5. The Sheringham enclosure, awarded in 1811, and the occasion for Upcher's purchase, was one of several parliamentary enclosures on the ridge running along the coast. Sheringham Enclosure Award 1811, County Hall, Norwich, Legal Department.
136 *Comparative Account of the Population of Great Britain 1801–31* (London, 1831).
137 Rental of Sheringham Estate (1809), Norfolk Record Office, WKC 159/12.
138 A.J. Peacock, *Bread or Blood: A Study of the Agrarian Riots in East Anglia in 1816* (London, 1965), 11–48; A.D. Harvey, *Britain in the Early Nineteenth Century* (London, 1978), 286–95, 334–6.
139 Calculated from returns in Sheringham Overseers' Books, Sheringham Parish Church. For comparable figures, see Roy Taylor, 'The Development of the Old Poor Law in Norfolk', unpublished MA thesis, University of East Anglia, 1970, 156.
140 Humphry Repton to William Repton, 21 April 1812, Huntington Library, HM 40870.
141 Repton, Red Book for Sheringham.
142 Yaxley, *Sherringhamia*, 3.
143 Pigott, *Memoir*, 1–21.
144 Ibid., 36–7.
145 Repton, Red Book for Sheringham.
146 cf. William Marshall's comment that plantations 'accumu-

147 late in value, as money at interest upon interest', *Planting and Rural Ornament* (London, 1796), vol. 2, 113.
147 Pigott, *Memoir*, 45. The felling of oaks suggests that Repton may have advised on planting when living at Sustead.
148 Nigel Temple, 'Reptoniana', *Journal of Garden History*, 3 (1983), 55–7; Vicky Basford, *Historic Parks and Gardens of the Isle of Wight* (Newport, Isle of Wight, 1989), 49–56. *The Beauties of England and Wales*, vol. 6, ed. Edward Brayley and John Britton (London, 1805), 354.
149 George Repton to William Repton, 14 December 1814, Huntington Library, HM 40919.
150 Humphry Repton, 'On Deafness', enclosed in a letter from Humphry Repton to Mary Repton, 28 September 1811, Huntington Library, HM 40841.
151 Armstrong, *History and Antiquities*, vol. 3, 102.
152 On conflicts over game, see Michael J. Carter, *Peasants and Poachers: A Study of Rural Disorder in Norfolk* (Woodbridge, Suffolk, 1980), 2, 111–12.
153 Stephen Daniels, 'The Political Iconography of Woodland in Later Georgian England', in Denis Cosgrove and Stephen Daniels (eds), *The Iconography of Landscape* (Cambridge, 1988), 48. Cotman exhibited a picture of a harvest field at the 1810 exhibition of the Norwich Society of Artists. Sydney Kitson, *The Life of John Sell Cotman* (London, 1937), 131.
154 Pigott, *Memoir*, 69.
155 Nigel Everett, *The Tory View of Landscape* (New Haven and London, 1994), 136–45.
156 Ann Digby, *Pauper Palaces* (London, 1978); Keith Snell, *Annals of the Labouring Poor: Social Change and Agrarian England 1660–1900* (Cambridge, 1985), 117.
157 A. Campbell Errol, *A History of the Parishes of Sheringham and Beeston Regis* (Norwich, 1970), 85; Rental of Sheringham Estate (1809), Norfolk Record Office, WKC 159/12. On the Gilbert Act of 1787 and its consequences, see Digby, *Pauper Palaces*, 34; Felix Driver, *Power and Pauperism: The Workhouse System 1834–84* (Cambridge, 1993), 42–7.
158 Reports of the Poor Law Commissioners, XXIX, 1836, 147–9.
159 Repton, Red Book for Sheringham. It was shortly after his visit to Sheringham that Repton was asked to design a new workhouse at Crayford. Repton, *Fragments*, 227–31 (Works, 597–600). This is discussed in Chapter one above.
160 Barrell, *The Dark Side*, 149–56; Hemingway, *Landscape Art and Urban Culture*, 19–23.
161 Repton, *Fragments*, 232 (Works, 601). On Malthusian thought, see David Cannadine, 'Conspicuous Consumption by the Landed Classes 1790–1830', in Michael Turner (ed.), *Malthus and His Time* (Houndmills, Basingstoke, 1986), 96–111.
162 Pigott, *Memoir*, 37.
163 Repton, *Fragments*, 211 (Works, 586).
164 John Summerson, 'A Repton Portfolio', *Journal of the Royal Institute of British Architects* (25 February 1933), 313–24. There are correspondences between the unembellished building and one version of Repton's plans for the workhouse at Crayford, Kent, which were completed shortly after the first visit to Sheringham.
165 Nigel Wright points out that the final design is like one that Repton did for Hoveton Hall, Norfolk, in 1809. 'The Gentry', 310.
166 Yaxley, *Sherringhamia*, 4–5.
167 Humphry Repton to William Repton, 11 December 1812, Huntington Library, HM 40837.
168 Ibid.
169 Humphry Repton to William Repton, 15 December 1812, Huntington Library, no classmark, HM 40838?
170 Yaxley, *Sherringamia*, 5.
171 *Dictionary of National Biography*, vol. 24, 216.
172 Humphry Repton to William Repton, 22 May 1815, Huntington Library, HM 40876.
173 Yaxley, *Sherringhamia*, 8–9, 16.
174 Thomas Bedford had been employed by John Soane. He came to Sheringham from Carmarthen where he designed the gaol in 1811 and a villa near Llanderli. Howard Colvin, *A Biographical Dictionary of British Architects 1600–1840*, third edition (New Haven and London, 1995), 117.
175 Yaxley, *Sherringhamia*, 16–35.
176 Humphry Repton to James Edward Smith, 23 September 1814; 6 October 1816. *Scientific Correspondence of Sir James Edward Smith*, vol. 8, no. 168, Linnean Society, London.
177 Yaxley, *Sherringhamia*, 27.
178 Repton, *Fragments*, 195, 207 (Works, 570, 578).
179 Humphry Repton to Sir Harry Fetherstonehaugh, 1 May 1817, Uppark Letters, private collection.
180 *Excursions in the County of Norfolk*, 2 vols (London, 1818), vol. 1, 33; Andrew Moore, *John Sell Cotman 1782–1842* (Norwich, 1982), 67.
181 Charlotte Upcher returned to Sheringham eighteen years later when her eldest son married and moved into the mansion. She lived at the old farmhouse until her death in 1857. Yaxley, *Sherringhamia*, 37–9.
182 Humphry Repton to Sir Harry Fetherstonehaugh, 1 May 1817, Uppark Letters, private collection.
183 Quoted in *Aylsham Parish Magazine*, May 1936. My thanks to Ron Peabody for this reference.
184 Armstrong, *History and Antiquities*, vol. 3, 109.
185 *Gentleman's Magazine*, 88 (1818), 1, 648.
186 *Gentleman's Magazine*, 88 (1818), 2, 102.

CHAPTER 3

1 Humphry Repton, *Sketches and Hints on Landscape Gardening* (London, 1794), xv (Works, 30n).
2 Humphry Repton, Red Book for Hewell (1812), private collection.
3 Repton, *Sketches and Hints*, xiv (Works, 30).
4 John Byng, *The Torrington Diaries*, ed. C. Bryn Andrews, (London, 1936) vol. 3, 12–13. On the conservative reaction to Brown, see Nigel Everett, *The Tory View of Landscape* (New Haven and London, 1994).
5 Humphry Repton to Norton Nicholls, 6 November 1794, Bristol University Library; Humphry Repton, *A Letter to*

*Uvedale Price, Esq.* (London, 1794), 20; Kenneth Garlick and Angus Macintyre (eds), *The Diary of Joseph Farington*, vol. 1, July 1793–December 1794 (New Haven and London, 1978), 204 (entry for 23 June 1794).

6 The phrase 'the picturesque landscape' elides the characteristic expressions of Price and Knight, 'The Picturesque' and 'The Landscape', concealing differences that will become apparent in the course of this chapter. I have used it to signify their alliance against Repton and the landscape of their home county of Herefordshire. See Stephen Daniels and Charles Watkins (eds), *The Picturesque Landscape: Visions of Georgian Herefordshire* (Nottingham, 1994).

7 Michael Clarke and Nicholas Penny (eds), *The Arrogant Connoisseur: Richard Payne Knight 1751–1824* (Manchester, 1982); Andrew Ballantyne, *Architecture, Landscape and Liberty: Richard Payne Knight and the Picturesque* (Cambridge, 1997).

8 Repton, Memoir, Part two, autographed draft, British Library, Add. MS. 62112, 206. Repton and Soane were both commissioned at some sites, notably those of Pitt supporters. At Port Eliot, Cornwall, they produced rival architectural designs. On Repton's attempts to come to some agreement on this commission, see his letters to Soane of 13 September and 26 October 1804, Sir John Soane's Museum, London, uncatalogued.

9 Frank Donoghue, *The Fame Machine: Book Reviewing and Eighteenth-Century Literary Careers* (Stanford, 1996).

10 John Barrell, *The Dark Side of the Landscape: The Rural Poor in English Painting 1730–1840* (Cambridge, 1980), 173–4.

11 David Whitehead, 'Sense with Sensibility: Landscaping in Georgian Herefordshire', in Daniels and Watkins (eds), *The Picturesque Landscape*, 16–33.

12 Stephen Daniels and Charles Watkins, 'The Picturesque Landscape', in Daniels and Watkins, *The Picturesque Landscape*, 9–15.

13 Quoted in Dorothy Stroud, *Capability Brown* (London, 1975), 156.

14 Stephen Daniels, 'The Political Iconography of Woodland in Later Georgian England', in Denis Cosgrove and Stephen Daniels (eds), *The Iconography of Landscape* (Cambridge, 1988), 43–82 (62–7). Sidney K. Robinson, *Inquiry into the Picturesque* (Chicago, 1991); Tim Fulford, *Landscape, Liberty and Authority: Poetry, Criticism and Politics from Thomson to Wordsworth* (Cambridge, 1996), 116–56.

15 Stephen Daniels, Susanne Seymour and Charles Watkins, 'Border Country: The Politics of the Picturesque in the Middle Wye Valley', in Michael Rosenthal, Christiana Payne and Scott Wilcox (eds), *Prospects for the Nation: Recent Essays in British Landscape, 1750–1880* (New Haven and London, 1997), 157–82 (159–61).

16 Caroline Kirkham, 'Hafod: Paradise Lost', *Journal of Garden History*, 11 (1991), 207–16; Everett, *The Tory View*, 145–50; Charles Watkins, Stephen Daniels and Susanne Seymour, 'Uvedale Price's Marine Picturesque at Aberystwyth, 1790–1829', *The Picturesque*, no. 14 (1996), 1–11.

17 John Claudius Loudon, *A Treatise on Forming, Improving and Managing Country Residences* (London, 1806), vol. 2, 439.

18 Humphry Repton, Red Book for Sufton Court (1795), private collection.

19 Jay Appleton, 'Some Thoughts on the Geology of the Picturesque', *Journal of Garden History*, 6 (1986), 270–92 (284–6).

20 Clarke and Penny (eds), *The Arrogant Connoisseur*; David Whitehead, 'Belmont, Herefordshire: The Development of a Picturesque Estate 1788–1827, Part 2', *The Picturesque*, no. 12 (1995), 1–11 (10).

21 Tom Wall, 'The Verdant Landscape: The Practice and Theory of Richard Payne Knight at Downton Vale', in Daniels and Watkins, *The Picturesque Landscape*, 49–65; Ballantyne, *Architecture, Landscape and Liberty*, 240–80; David Morris, *Thomas Hearne and His Landscape* (London, 1989), 92–4.

22 *The Diary of The Right Hon. William Windham 1784–1810*, ed. Mrs Henry Baring (London, 1866), 126.

23 Humphry Repton, Red Book for Ferney Hall (1789), Pierpont Morgan Library, New York. The offending man is possibly Thomas Whitehead, a Bristol nurseryman who advertized in the Hereford Journal on 8 January 1784. My thanks to David Woodward for this information.

24 Richard Payne Knight, *The Landscape: A Didactic Poem*, second edition (London, 1795), 98.

25 Repton, *Sketches and Hints*, 65 (Works, 103).

26 Uvedale Price, *Essays on the Picturesque* (London, 1810), vol. 3, 90.

27 Knight, *The Landscape*, second edition, 98–9.

28 Repton, Memoir, 7–8.

29 Ibid., 7–8.

30 Knight, *The Landscape*, second edition, 103.

31 Ibid., 102, 99.

32 Repton, Memoir, 7.

33 Knight, *The Landscape*, second edition, 99.

34 Humphry Repton, Account Book, Norfolk Record Office; Knight, *The Landscape*, second edition, 99.

35 Price, *Essays*, vol. 1, iv–v.

36 Clarke and Penny (eds), *The Arrogant Connoisseur*, 56–64; Ballantyne, *Architecture, Landscape and Liberty*, 86–109.

37 Jay Appleton, 'Richard Payne Knight and "The Georgics"', *The Picturesque*, no. 5 (1993), 1–8.

38 Knight, *The Landscape*, first edition, 18, 64, 37, 29, 17, 14–15.

39 Wall, 'The Verdant Landscape'.

40 Ballantyne, *Architecture, Landscape and Liberty*, 190–239.

41 Knight, *The Landscape*, first edition, 73.

42 Daniels, 'The Political Iconography of Woodland', 62–7; On the cultural geography of Coalbrookdale, see Stephen Daniels, 'Loutherbourg's Chemical Theatre: *Coalbrookdale By Night*', in John Barrell (ed.), *Painting and the Politics of Culture* (Oxford, 1992), 195–230.

43 Knight, *The Landscape*, second edition, iv.
44 Repton, Memoir, 13.
45 Humphry Repton, Red Book for Hill Hall (1791), Essex Record Office, D/DU 640/1.
46 *Speeches in Parliament of the Right Honourable William Windham*, ed. T. Amyot (London, 1812), vol. 1, 156.
47 Humphry Repton, Red Book for Tatton Park (1792), National Trust, Tatton Park.
48 Knight, *The Landscape*, first edition, 11. In a footnote, Knight refers his readers to Repton's 'other expedients for shewing the extent of property', misquoting Repton's reference to emblazoning merestones [boundary markers] as 'placing the family arms upon neighbouring milestones' with its attendant 'difficulties [that] might arise among the trustees of the turnpikes'.
49 *The Diary of Joseph Farington*, vol. 1, 210 (entry for 4 July 1794).
50 Knight, *The Landscape*, first edition, 14.
51 Quoted in Frank J. Messman, *Richard Payne Knight: The Twilight of Virtuousity* (The Hague, 1974), 66.
52 Humphry Repton to Norton Nicholls, 6 November 1794, Bristol University Library.
53 *Monthly Review*, May 1794, 78–82.
54 Anna Seward, *The Letters of Anna Seward Written between the Years 1784 and 1807*, ed. A. Constable (Edinburgh, 1811), vol. 4, 10.
55 Quoted in Messman, *Richard Payne Knight*, 83. On conservative reductions of radical programmes to primitivist anarchy, see Gregory Claeys, *Thomas Paine, Social and Political Thought* (Boston, 1989), 139–64.
56 Repton, *Sketches and Hints*, 53–65 (Works, 95–102).
57 *The Diary of Joseph Farington*, vol. 2, 348 (entry for 1 June 1795).
58 Repton, *Sketches and Hints*, 51 (Works, 92n). My thanks to Richard Quaintance for alerting me to the pumicing. Norton Nicholls to Humphry Repton, 6 November 1794, Bristol University Library.
59 Ibid., 65 (Works, 102–3).
60 J. Butt to Richard Pole Carew, 16 June 1795, Antony House Muniments, CE/E/66/12.
61 Knight, *The Landscape*, second edition, 23n.
62 Ibid., 40–42.
63 Ibid., 104.
64 Quoted in Messman, *Richard Payne Knight*, 94.
65 Uvedale Price to Sir George Beaumont, 5 September 1797, Coleorton MSS, Pierpont Morgan Library, New York.
66 Knight, *The Landscape*, second edition, 92; Uvedale Price, 'Letter to H. Repton, Esq' in *Essays*, vol. 3, 178; Daniels, 'The Political Iconography of Woodland', 62–3; Everett, *The Tory View*, 103–6.
67 Ballantyne, *Architecture, Landscape and Liberty*, 79–85, 149–56.
68 Stephen Daniels and Charles Watkins, 'Picturesque Landscaping and Estate Management: Uvedale Price at Foxley, 1770–1829', *Rural History*, 2 (1991), 141–69.
69 Price, *Essays*, vol. 1, xviii.
70 Denis Lambin, 'Foxley: The Price's Estate in Herefordshire', *Journal of Garden History*, 7 (1987), 244–70; Beryl Hartley, 'Naturalism and Sketching: Robert Price at Foxley and on Tour', in Daniels and Watkins, *The Picturesque Landscape*, 34–9.
71 Price, *Essays*, vol. 1, 339–40.
72 Price, *Essays*, vol. 2, 125, 119.
73 Stephen Daniels and Charles Watkins, 'Picturesque Landscaping and Estate Management: Uvedale Price and Nathaniel Kent at Foxley', in Stephen Copley and Peter Garside (eds), *The Politics of the Picturesque* (Cambridge, 1994), 13–41.
74 Daniels and Watkins, 'Picturesque Landscaping', 1994; Watkins, Daniels and Seymour, 'Uvedale Price's Marine Picturesque at Aberystwyth'.
75 Ron Shoesmith, *Hereford: History and Guide* (Stroud, 1992), 70–82; David Whitehead, 'John Nash and Humphry Repton: An Encounter in Herefordshire 1785–98', *Transactions of the Woolhope Naturalists Field Club*, 47 (1992), 210–36 (210).
76 John Price, *An Historical Account of the City of Hereford* (Hereford, 1796), 74, 55.
77 Ibid., 183.
78 Ibid., 196–8.
79 This is especially trues of guides to river valleys. See Andrew Hemingway, *Landscape Imagery and Urban Culture in Early Nineteenth-Century Britain* (Cambridge, 1992), 216–91.
80 Price, 'Letter to H. Repton', *Essays*, vol. 3, 29.
81 Whitehead, 'John Nash and Humphry Repton', 219. Humphry Repton, Red Book for Garnons (1791), private collection.
82 Repton, Memoir, 200–02.
83 Humphry Repton to Norton Nicholls, 26 August 1788, Bristol University Library.
84 Repton, *Sketches and Hints*, 57 (Works, 97).
85 Humphry Repton, *Observations on the Theory and Practice of Landscape Gardening* (London, 1803), 122n (Works, 232n). Gérardin's essay was translated as *An Essay on Landscape; Or, On the Means of Improving and Embellishing the Country Round Our Habitations* (London, 1783).
86 John Geers Cotterell to William Wilkins, 2 February 1794; William Wilkins to John Geers Cotterell, 24 December 1794, Herefordshire Record Office, D52 5/7; 5/5.
87 Humphry Repton to John Geers Cotterell, 19 September 1793, Herefordshire Record Office, D52 6/4.
88 Humphry Repton, Red Book for Prestwood, Herefordshire Record Office; Whitehead, 'John Nash and Humphry Repton', 218.
89 David Whitehead, 'The Purchase and Building of Stoke Edith Park, Herefordshire 1670–1707', *Transactions of the Woolhope Naturalists Field Club*, 43 (1980), 181–202.
90 Humphry Repton, Red Book for Stoke Edith (1792), Herefordshire Record Office.
91 Repton, Red Book for Stoke Edith; William Wilkins, Designs for Lodges and Cottages at Stoke Edith, Herefordshire Record Office, B30/1.
92 Red Book for Stoke Edith.

93 John Edwards the Younger, 'An account of New Buildings, Roads and Alterations at Stoke Edith Oct 10 1792', Hereford Record Office, E 12/III/620.
94 Repton, *Observations*, 37n (Works, 224n).
95 Luke Booker, *The Hop-Garden* (Malvern, 1798), 13.
96 Quoted in Whitehead, 'John Nash and Humphry Repton', 226–7.
97 Price, *Hereford*, 196–7.
98 Whitehead, 'John Nash and Humphry Repton', 224–5.
99 Repton, Memoir, 85–6. Farington reported that the agreement was 2½ per cent for Repton out of 7 per cent on building costs, James Greig (ed.), *Farington's Diary*, vol. 1 (London, 1922), 251.
100 Humphry Repton to Edmund Burke, 9 January 1793, Sheffield City Archives, Fitzwilliam MSS 1/8785; Edmund Burke to Humphry Repton, 13 January 1793, *Correspondence of Edmund Burke*, ed. P.J. Marshall and John A. Woods (Cambridge, 1968), vol. 7, 330.
101 Repton, Memoir, 207.
102 Repton, *Letter to Uvedale Price*, 7 (Works, 105–06n).
103 Price, *Essays*, vol. 1, 1, 331, 33.
104 Ibid., vol. 1, 7, 11–12, vol. 2, 238.
105 Ibid., vol. 1, 338–9, 340, 13.
106 Ibid., vol. 1, 68, 114, 102, vol. 2, 242.
107 Ibid., vol. 1, 247–8, 23. In letters to friends Price frequently mentioned the virtues of hollowlanes (Uvedale Price to Lady Margaret Beaumont, 29 April 1803; 13 October 1803, Coleorton MSS, Pierpont Morgan Library, MA 1581 39, 60).
108 Price, *Essays*, vol. 1, 26–8, 30, 35.
109 Ibid., vol. 2, 55, vol. 1, 271, 166–7, 271, 165, 162.
110 Ibid., vol. 1, 293, 175–6.
111 *Correspondence of Edmund Burke*, vol. 7, 547–8.
112 Humphry Repton to Reginald Pole Carew, 14 July 1794, Antony House Muniments, CE/E/66.7. *The Diary of Joseph Farington*, vol. 2 (entry for 1 June 1795). Combe may have been willing to take on the job because he had fallen out with Price after being accused of stealing from Foxley during a visit twenty years before. Harlan W. Hamilton, *Doctor Syntax: A Silhouette of William Combe Esq* (London, 1969), 32–3.
113 Repton, *Letter to Uvedale Price*, 1–14 (Works, 104–08n).
114 Ibid., 7–8, 15, 17 (106n, 108n, 109n).
115 Price, *Essays*, vol. 3, 27, 33, 43, 137, 164, 128, 133, 47, 178–9. The lines at the end of the quotation are from William Mason's poem *The English Garden* (Book 1, line 548). Both Repton and Price appealed to the authority of Mason.
116 Humphry Repton to W. Robson, 24 December 1794, Newberry Library, Chicago.
117 Humphry Repton to Uvedale Price, 5 February 1795, Newberry Library.
118 Repton, *Sketches and Hints*, 70 (Works, 110–11). This is an astute manoeuvre, drawing professional landscaping into the literary world of Lichfield, notably the works of Thomas Mundy and of Thomas Gisborne, who was renowned for his sketches and poems of Needwood Forest and writings on the moral and scenic improvements to his residence there, and exiling Price from a vision to which in many ways he subscribed. On Gisborne and his influence, see Everett, *The Tory View*, 135–7. In a letter of 15 July 1789 to Repton, Anna Seward, the leading light of Lichfield, called Needwood 'our forest' but turned down Repton's invitation to accompany him on an excursion to Hainault Forest. Seward, *Letters*, vol. 1, 309.
119 Repton, *Sketches and Hints*, 70, 75, 82–4 (Works, 106, 111, 114–16).
120 Uvedale Price to Sir George Beaumont, 2 February 1795, Coleorton MSS. Pierpont Morgan Library.
121 William Marshall, *A Review of 'The Landscape' . . . and 'Essay on the Picturesque'* (London, 1795), 87, 185, 106.
122 Uvedale Price to Sir George Beaumont, 3 June 1795, Pierpont Morgan Library, Coleorton MSS.
123 'Extracts from Mr Burke's Table Talk at Crewe Hall', *Miscellanies of the Philobiblon Society*, vol. 7, no. 5 (1862–3), 43.
124 Anon. [John Matthews], *A Sketch from the Landscape* (London, 1794).
125 *The Diary of Joseph Farington*, vol. 3, 665 (entry for 24 September 1796).
126 David Whitehead, 'Belmont, Herefordshire. The Development of a Picturesque Estate 1788–1827 [Part 1]', *The Picturesque*, no. 11 (1995), 1–9.
127 David Whitehead, 'Belmont, Herefordshire: The Development of a Picturesque Estate 1788–1827 [Part 2]', *The Picturesque*, no. 12 (1995), 1–11.
128 Price, *Hereford*, 190–91.
129 Nigel Temple, *George Repton's Pavilion Notebook: A Catalogue Raisonné* (Aldershot, 1993), 135–43.
130 *The Diary of Joseph Farington*, vol. 1, 229.
131 Whitehead, 'Belmont', 8.
132 Anon. [Matthews], *A Sketch*, 28.
133 Knight, *The Landscape*, second edition, ix–xiii.
134 Price, *Essays*, vol. 3, 124–5.
135 Humphry Repton, Red Book for Sufton Court (1795), private collection.
136 Peter Goodchild, '"No Phantastical Utopia, But a Reall Place": John Evelyn, John Beale and Backbury Hill, Herefordshire', *Garden History*, 19 (1991), 105–27.
137 David Whitehead, 'Repton and the Picturesque Debate: The Text of the Sufton Red Book', *The Picturesque*, no. 1 (1992–3), 6–17.
138 Price, *Hereford*, 198. In July 1794 Repton continued his offensive against Price and Knight in North Wales at Rûg, an estate close to the well-travelled road from London to Holyhead. Richard Haslam, 'Rûg, Clwyd II', *Country Life* (13 October 1983), 986–9.
139 Repton, Memoir, 86.
140 Humphry Repton to Norton Nicholls, 13 February, 1796, Bristol University Library.
141 Boydell's to Humphry Repton, 11 July [1796]; Humphry Repton to Boydell's, 19 July 1796, letters tipped into Repton's copy of *Fragments*, private collection.
142 *Monthly Review* (January 1796), 97.
143 Humphry Repton to Norton Nicholls, 13 February 1796, Bristol University Library.

144 *The Times* (22 August 1795); *London Chronicle* (15–17 December 1795). My thanks to Mavis Batey for these references.
145 William Marshall, *Planting and Rural Ornament* (London, 1796), vol. 1, 113.
146 Humphry Repton, Red Book for Burley (1796), private collection.
147 Repton, *Observations*, 92–8 (Works, 207–12).
148 Humphry Repton to John Geers Cotterell, 20 July 1796, Herefordshire Record Office, D52 6/5.
149 Humphry Repton to Paul Methuen, 23 January 1798, Wiltshire Record Office, Corsham MSS, File 47, 6060.
150 National Trust, *Attingham Park* (London, 1994), 33. Knight's knowledge of the Classical culture of the southern Mediterranean was esteemed by the English *dilettanti* in Naples who gathered around the British envoy, Sir William Hamilton. Hamilton visited Knight at Downton in 1791 and sold him a bronze collection. The creator of a celebrated English-style garden overlooking the Bay of Naples, Hamilton was sympathetic to the attack on the Brown style in *The Landscape*, if dismayed at how Knight had brought in 'the politicks of the times' (Ian Jenkins and Kim Sloan, *Vases and Volcanoes: Sir William Hamilton and His Collection* (London, 1996), 288).
151 Barrie Trinder, *The Industrial Revolution in Shropshire* (London and Chichester, 1981), 85; P. Everson and P.A. Stamper, 'Berwick Maviston and Attingham Park', *Transactions of the Shropshire Archaeological Society*, 65 (1987), 64–70.
152 Humphry Repton, Red Book for Attingham (1798), National Trust, Attingham Park.
153 Cf. a passage in Price's *Essay*, vol. 1, 51, 55.
154 Repton, Red Book for Attingham.
155 Repton, *Memoir*, 1.
156 Lord Berwick's Account Book, Shropshire Record Office.
157 Seward, *Letters*, vol. 5, 74.
158 Repton, *Sketches and Hints*, v (Works, 24).
159 Repton, *Memoir*, 60, 207. It is uncertain whether this would have secured the post for Repton. Farington Reported that the king thought the Red Books he had seen 'rather coxcomical works'. *The Diary of Joseph Farington*, vol. 1, 163 (entry for 14 February 1794).
160 Uvedale Price to Sir George Beaumont, 2 February 1798, Pierpont Morgan Library, Coleorton MSS, MA 1581.
161 Uvedale Price to Sir George Beaumont, 17 February 1798, Pierpont Morgan Library, Coleorton MSS, MA 1581.
162 The duties were taken on by Lord Harcourt. Jane Roberts, *Royal Landscape: The Gardens and Parks of Windsor* (New Haven and London), 67, 70, 544, 127n.
163 Repton, *Memoir*, 207.
164 Ibid., 86.
165 Uvedale Price to Sir George Beaumont, March 1798, Pierpont Morgan Library, Coleorton MSS, MA 1581.
166 Uvedale Price, *Thoughts on the Defence of Property* (Hereford, 1797), 11, 28, 20, 19.
167 Uvedale Price to Lord Abercorn, 3 August 1798, British Library, Add. MSS.
168 John Wescomb Emmerton to Nicholas Wescomb, 27 March 1796, Nottingham Archive Office, DD 169/17. My thanks to Ben Cowell for this reference.
169 Repton, *Observations*, 107–8 (Works, 220).
170 Humphry Repton, Red Book for Stanage Park (1803), private collection.
171 Jonathan Williams, *The History of Radnorshire* (Tenby, 1859), 203–6.
172 Repton, Red Book for Stanage Park.
173 Ibid.
174 Gareth Williams, 'An Examination of Two Repton Red Books and their Historical, Social and Economic Contexts: Attingham Park and Longner Hall', unpublished MA thesis, University of Manchester, 1993.
175 Humphry Repton, Red Book for Longner (1804), private collection.
176 John Nash to Robert Burton, 31 July 1801, private collection.
177 Repton, Red Book for Longner.
178 Ibid.
179 Francis Leach (ed.), *The County Seats of Shropshire* (Shrewsbury, 1891), 195–200.
180 Humphry Repton, *An Enquiry into the Changes of Taste in Landscape Gardening*, (London, 1806), 70 (Works, 347n); Humphry Repton to Robert Burton, 29 April 1804, private collection.
181 Repton, *Fragments*, 187, 131 (Works, 563, 600).
182 Gareth Williams, 'Edward Haycock and the Picturesque: The Country House Practice of a Border Architect', unpublished BA thesis, 1992, Department of History of Art, University of Manchester.
183 Humphry Repton to Charles Rogers, 4 February 1810, private collection.
184 Humphry Repton, *Fragments on the Theory and Practice of Landscape Gardening* (London, 1816), 33–9 (Works, 440–45).
185 Repton, *Enquiry*, v (Works, 324).
186 Ibid., 116 (352).
187 Ibid., 118–22 (352–5).
188 Humphry Repton, Red Book for Endsleigh (1814), Woburn Abbey. When this extract was reprinted in *Fragments*, Turner's name and the site were omitted; Repton, *Fragments*, 217. Turner's picture was exhibited at the Royal Academy in 1811. Martin Butlin and Everlyn Joll, *The Paintings of J.M.W. Turner*, revised edition (New Haven and London, 1984), 82–3.
189 Humphry Repton, Red Book for Stoneleigh Abbey (1809), Leigh Collection, Shakespeare Birthplace Trust, Stratford-upon-Avon.
190 Mavis Batey, 'In Quest of Jane Austen's "Mr Repton"', *Garden History*, 5 (1977), 19–27 (27); Mavis Batey, *Jane Austen and the English Landscape* (London, 1996), 79–94.
191 Batey, 'In Quest of Jane Austen's "Mr Repton"', 27.
192 John Harris, 'Some Imperfect Ideas in the Genesis of the Loudonesque Flower Garden', in Elisabeth McDougall (ed.), *John Claudius Loudon and the Early Nineteenth Century in England* (Washington, DC, 1980), 47–57 (56).
193 Quoted in John Morley, *Regency Design 1790–1840* (London, 1993), 19.

194 Mark Laird, '*Corbeille, Parterre* and *Treillage*: The Case of Humphry Repton's Penchant for the French Style of Planting', *Journal of Garden History*, 16 (1996), 153–69.
195 Batey, 'In Quest of Jane Austen's "Mr Repton"', 27.
196 Humphry Repton, Red Book for Hewell Grange (1812), private collection. Copy in Worcestershire Record Office.
197 Repton, *Fragments*, 33 (Works, 440).
198 Ibid., 190–94 (567–70). This is discussed in detail in Chapter one above.
199 Repton, Memoir, 212.
200 Clarke and Penny, *The Arrogant Connoisseur*, 8–18; Ballantyne, *Architecture, Landscape and Liberty*, 281.
201 Humphry Repton, Plan for a Carriage Drive at Stoke Edith, Herefordshire Record Office, E12/IV/173/ B/2; Letters from Humphry Repton to John Geers Cotterell, 1797–1807, Herefordshire Record Office, D52 6/6–11.
202 Humphry Repton to William Repton, January [1809], Huntington Library, HM 408860.
203 Whitehead, 'Belmont', 9–10.
204 J. Mordaunt Crook, 'Metropolitan Improvement: John Nash and the Picturesque', in Celina Fox (ed.), *London – World City 1800–1840* (New Haven and London, 1992), 77–96 (78).
205 William Wordsworth to Samuel Rogers, 21 January 1825, in P.W. Clayden, *Rogers and His Contemporaries* (London, 1889), vol. 1, 405.
206 Price, *Essays*, vol. 1, xviii.
207 Uvedale Price to Sir George Beaumont, 12 September 1823, Pierpont Morgan Library, Coleorton MSS, MA 1581.
208 Uvedale Price to Lady Margaret Beaumont, 31 May 1803; 17 June 1803; 10 August 1820; 13 December 1820, Pierpont Morgan Library, Coleorton MSS, MA 1581. Sophieke Piebenga, 'William Sawrey Gilpin (1762–1843): Picturesque Improver', *Garden History*, 22 (1994), 175–96.
209 Jane Austen, *Mansfield Park* (1814; Oxford, 1980), 47, 49, 51. See Richard Quaintance, 'Humphry Repton, "any Mr Repton", and the "Improvement" Metonym in *Mansfield Park*', *Studies in Eighteenth-Century Culture*, 27 (1998), 365–84.
210 On details of career and influence, see McDougall, *John Claudius Loudon*; Melanie Louise Simo, *Loudon and the Landscape: From Country Seat to Metropolis 1783–1843* (New Haven and London, 1988).
211 John Claudius Loudon, 'A Treatise on the Improvements Proposed for Scone' (1803), private collection, facsimile in Scottish Record Office, Edinburgh.
212 John Claudius Loudon, 'Hints Respecting the Manner of Laying out the Grounds of the Public Squares in London, to the Utmost Picturesque Advantage', *Literary Journal*, 2 (1803), cols 739–42. For further discussion of this article in relation to Repton's plans for Russell Square, see Chapter four below.
213 John Claudius Loudon, *Observations on the Formation and Management of Useful and Ornamental Plantations, on the Theory and Practice of Landscape Gardening* (Edinburgh and London, 1804), 210.
214 Ibid., 214–15, 283–7.
215 Repton, *Observations*, 100n (Works, 214–15n).
216 Loudon, *A Treatise . . . Country Residences*, vol. 2, 439n, 658–9, 705–23, 355.
217 Repton, *Enquiry*, 60–64 (Works, 342–3).
218 John Claudius Loudon, *Observations on Laying Out Farms in the Scotch Style* (London, 1812), 72, 24.
219 Repton, *Observations*, 92–8 (Works, 207–12).
220 Humphry Repton, Red Book for Great Tew (1803), private collection.
221 Christopher Hussey, 'Great Tew, Oxfordshire, I and II', *Country Life* (22 and 29 July 1949), 254–7; Loudon, *Observations on Laying Out Farms*, 1–30; Simo, *Loudon and the Landscape*, 79–84.
222 General George F. Stratton, 'Origins and Progress of the Scotch System of Husbandry Introduced by Him in His Estates in Oxfordshire', in Sir John Sinclair, *An Account of the System of Husbandry Adopted in the More Improved Districts of Scotland* (Edinburgh, 1812), Appendix, 15–30.
223 Loudon, *Observations on Laying Out Farms*, 98; John Claudius Loudon, *An Encyclopaedia of Gardening* (London, 1822), 1076.
224 John Claudius Loudon, *Hints on the Formation of Gardens and Pleasure Grounds* (London, 1812).
225 Loudon, *Encyclopedia of Gardening*, 73, 1155.
226 *Gardener's Magazine*, 1 (1826), 116; Ibid., 12 (1836), 292–3.
227 Brent Elliott, *Victorian Gardens* (London, 1986), 21; *Gardener's Magazine*, 18 (1842), 590.
228 John Claudius Loudon, *The Suburban Gardener and Villa Companion* (London, 1838), 673–4.
229 Works, vii–viii.
230 *Gardener's Magazine*, 15 (1839), 466.
231 Works, 248n.

CHAPTER 4

1 Hugh Prince, *Parks in England* (Shalfleet I.o.W., 1967), 9; Dorothy Stroud, *Capability Brown* (London, 1975).
2 John Beckett, *The Aristocracy in England 1660–1914* (London, 1986), 303–5.
3 Humphry Repton, *Fragments on the Theory and Practice of Landscape Gardening* (London, 1816), 232 (Works, 601). This corresponds to principles of political economy set out at the same time by Thomas Malthus: David Cannadine, 'Conspicuous Consumption by the Landed Classes 1790–1830', in Michael Turner (ed.), *Malthus and His Time* (Houndmills, Basingstoke, 1986), 96–111.
4 Linda Colley, *Britons: Forging the Nation 1707–1837* (New Haven and London, 1992), 189.
5 Humphry Repton to Lord Sheffield, 22 December 1805, Pierpont Morgan Library, New York, MA 4138.
6 Humphry Repton, *An Enquiry into the Changes of Taste in Landscape Gardening* (London, 1806), 115–6 (Works, 352).
7 Humphry Repton, Memoir, Part two, autograph draft, British Library, Add. MS. 62112, 90–106.
8 Thomas Davis, 'Extracts from Mr Repton's Observations, July 1804', Longleat Archives, E6 B12. Repton later reported that 'almost all the objectionable trees have been removed by a spring blight . . . and the place has been greatly improved in consequence'. Repton, *Fragments*, 117n (Works, 508).

9. Humphry Repton to the Marquess of Bath, 22 December 1811; 'Mr Davis's Account, 36, 24 July 1804', Longleat Archives.
10. Capability Brown did not deal exclusively with 'Great Men', but the evidence of his encounters with women does not suggest a shared interest in arrangements of plants and flowers; in consultation with the bluestocking Elizabeth Montagu he discussed the employment of labour at Sandleford Priory, and in conversation with Hannah More at Hampton Court 'he compared his art to literary composition'. Stroud, *Capability Brown*, 195–6, 201.
11. Repton, *Fragments*, 124–8 (Works, 573–9).
12. Repton, Memoir, 158, 65–7, 118, 73.
13. Repton, *Fragments*, 8 (Works, 410).
14. Repton, Memoir, 169.
15. Ibid., 171.
16. Beckett, *The Aristocracy*, 196.
17. Repton, Memoir, 170–76, 208–10.
18. Humphry Repton to Sir Harry Fetherstonehaugh, 30 May 1815, Uppark Letters, private collection.
19. Humphry Repton to Sir Harry Fetherstonehaugh, November 1814, Uppark Letters, private collection.
20. Repton, Memoir, 96–7.
21. Ibid., 177. R. Stewart Brown, *Liverpool Ships in the Eighteenth Century* (Liverpool, 1932), 124. My thanks to Graeme J. Milne for helping to identify Walker's trading interests.
22. Repton published extracts from the (missing) Red Book in *Observations on the Theory and Practice of Landscape Gardening* (London, 1803), 176–82 (Works, 272–9).
23. Repton, Memoir, 177–92. On the kind of private masquerade put on by the Walkers, see David Watkin, *Thomas Hope 1769–1831 and the Neo-Classical Ideal* (London, 1968), 230–32.
24. John Brewer, *The Pleasures of the Imagination: English Culture in the Eighteenth Century* (London, 1997), 56–124.
25. Humphry Repton, *The Work of Twenty Years Brought to a Crisis in Twenty Days!* (Romford, 1814).
26. Humphry Repton to Sir Harry Fetherstonehaugh, 13 October 1813, Uppark Letters, private collection.
27. Repton, Memoir, 8.
28. Humphry Repton, *Sketches and Hints on Landscape Gardening* (London, 1794), x (Works, 26).
29. Humphry Repton to William Windham, 8 November 1790, British Library, Add. MS. 37917.
30. Humphry Repton, *Odd Whims and Miscellanies* (London, 1804), vol. 1, vi–viii.
31. Repton, Memoir, 8, 10–11, 16, 17, 9–10, 11.
32. A.B., 'Biographical Notice', in Works, 17.
33. A.S. Turbeville, *A History of Welbeck Abbey and Its Owners, vol. 2, 1755–1879* (London, 1934).
34. Susanne Seymour, *Eighteenth-Century Parkland 'Improvement' on the Dukeries Estates of North Nottinghamshire*, unpublished PhD thesis, University of Nottingham, 1988, 145–7.
35. Turbeville, *A History of Welbeck Abbey*, 51–2; *Survey of London*, vol. 32, pt 2 (London, 1963), 406.
36. Horace Walpole to Lady Ossary, 24 August 1777, in Horace Walpole, *Correspondence*, vol. 32, ed. W.S. Lewis (London, 1965), 374–5. My thanks to Susanne Seymour for this reference.
37. Seymour, 'Eighteenth-Century Parkland "Improvement"', 140–45.
38. Susanne Seymour, 'The Dukeries Estates: Improving Land and Landscape in the Later Eighteenth Century', *Transactions of the Thoroton Society*, 97 (1993), 117–28.
39. Hayman Rooke, *A Sketch of the Ancient and Present State of Sherwood Forest* (Nottingham, 1799), 19.
40. William Speechly to the third duke of Portland, 14 May 1771, Nottingham University Manuscripts Department, PWF 8443.
41. William Speechly, 'Account of Plantations upon the Estate of His Grace the Duke of Portland June 16 1775', in Robert Lowe, *General View of the Agriculture of the County of Nottingham* (London, 1798), 57–69.
42. John Byng, *The Torrington Diaries*, ed. C. Bryn Andrews (London, 1935), vol. 2, 15–16.
43. William Bray, *Sketch of a Tour into Derbyshire and Yorkshire*, second edition (London, 1785), 341; Hayman Rooke, *Description and Sketches of Some Remarkable Oaks in the Park at Welbeck* (London, 1790).
44. Robert Lowe, *General View*, 68.
45. William Speechly to the third duke of Portland, 25 January 1776; 17 February 1776, Nottingham University Manuscripts Department, PWF 8449a; PWD 8450a.
46. Rooke, *Some Remarkable Oaks*, 6; R. Thoroton, *The Antiquities of Nottinghamshire*, ed. J. Thorsby (Nottingham, 1796), 383.
47. Speechly, 'Account of Plantations', 61.
48. William Speechly to the third duke of Portland, 18 January 1769, Nottingham University Manuscripts Department, PWF 8433.
49. Turbeville, *A History of Welbeck Abbey*, 307–15.
50. Repton, Memoir, 9.
51. Repton, Account Book, private collection; Samuel contributed to William Angus, *The Seats of the Nobility and Gentry* (London, 1781).
52. Repton, Memoir, 10.
53. Ibid., 12. Portland's art collection was largely of Dutch and Flemish pictures, as well as the usual racing and hunting scenes. He displayed views of Welbeck by George Barrett at Burlington House. Inventory of pictures at Bulstrode, Nottingham University Manuscripts Department, PWH 2388–2390; Richard Goulding and C.K. Adams, *Catalogue of Pictures Belonging to His Grace the Duke of Portland* (London, 1936).
54. Repton, Memoir, 13.
55. Red Book for Welbeck (1790).
56. Thoroton, *Antiquities of Nottinghamshire*, 383; Bray, *Sketch of a Tour into Derbyshire*, 341.
57. Repton, Memoir, 16.
58. Humphry Repton, Red Book for Welbeck (1793), private collection.
59. Account of Repton's Improvements, 1790–1796,

Nottingham University Manuscripts Department, PWF 9851.
60 Repton, Account Book.
61 Repton, Memoir, 8.
62 Ibid., 10; Humphry Repton to Freke Evans, 1 March 1808, Freke Evans Correspondence, private collection. Photocopy in Northamptonshire Record Office.
63 Seymour, 'Eighteenth-Century Parkland "Improvement"', 182–5; Seymour, 'The Dukeries Estates', 121–3; J.H. Hodson et al., 'The Building and Alteration of the Second Thoresby House 1767–1804', *A Nottinghamshire Miscellany*, Thoroton Society Record Series, 21 (1962), 16–20.
64 Repton, Memoir, 161.
65 Anna Seward to Humphry Repton, 17 February 1790, *Letters of Anna Seward Written between the Years 1784 and 1807*, ed. A. Constable (Edinburgh, 1811), vol. 1, 372.
66 Humphry Repton, Red Book for Thoresby (1791), private collection, photographed copy in Nottingham University Manuscripts Department, 4P 21/1; Repton, *Observations*, 38 (Works, 162).
67 The crags feature as a backdrop to some of Stubbs's shooting scenes. Tate Gallery, *George Stubbs 1724–1806* (London, 1984), 102–10.
68 Bray, *Sketch of a Tour into Derbyshire*, 342.
69 Repton, Memoir, 162.
70 Ibid., 162.
71 Repton, *Observations*, 37n (Works, 162n). The engraving from the *Polite Repository* was reproduced in the Nottinghamshire volume of *The Beauties of England and Wales*, (London, 1812) vol. 12, part 1, opposite 368. The cascade's bubbling waters inspired some lines that Repton wrote on human vanity, *Odd Whims and Miscellanies*, vol. 2, 104.
72 Repton, Memoir, 163.
73 Repton, Red Book for Thoresby.
74 Hodson et al., 'Thoresby House'.
75 Repton, Memoir, 163.
76 Anna Seward to Humphry Repton, 4 June 1791, *Letters*, vol. 1, 62–5. On Seward's provincialism, see Brewer, *The Pleasures of the Imagination*, 573–614.
77 Repton, Memoir, 133–4; Repton, *Fragments*, 10–12 (Works, 418–21).
78 Repton, Red Book for Welbeck (1793).
79 Repton, *Sketches and Hints*, 37–8 (Works, 78–9).
80 Ibid., xiv (Works, 29). Repton was later critical of Speechly's replanting of Sherwood Forest. *Observations*, 48–9 (Works, 172).
81 Repton, *Sketches and Hints*, x (Works, 26).
82 Turbeville, *A History of Welbeck Abbey*, 316.
83 Repton, *Observations*, 165n (Works, 264n). The font was identified as Repton's design by Kedrun Laurie, as reported in *The Times*, 4 July 1985.
84 Turbeville, *A History of Welbeck Abbey*, 347–8.
85 Humphry Repton, Red Book for Welbeck (1803), private collection.
86 Peter Brandon, 'The Diffusion of Designed Landscapes in South-East England', in H.S.A. Fox and Robin Butlin (eds), *Change in the Countryside* (London, 1979), 165–86 (121); J.T. Coppock and Hugh C. Prince, *Greater London* (London, 1964), 337–43.
87 Bulstrode Estate Map, Buckinghamshire Record Office, D/RA/A 4A/1.
88 John Harris, 'Bulstrode', *Architectural Review*, 134 (1958), 319–20.
89 Stroud, *Capability Brown*, 212–13.
90 George Liscomb, *History and Antiquities of the County of Buckingham* (London, 1847), 507; James Joseph Sheahan, *History and Topography of Buckinghamshire* (London, 1862), 883.
91 Turbeville, *A History of Welbeck Abbey*, 18–25; David Elliston Allen, *The Naturalist in Britain* (London, 1976), 29–30; Roy Strong, *Royal Gardens* (London, 1992), 71–2.
92 Bulstrode Papers, Nottingham University Manuscripts Department, temporary folder 13/19.
93 Value of articles from Bulstrode to Burlington House, Nottingham University Manuscripts Department, Bulstrode Papers, uncatalogued. Bulstrode is not mentioned in the Board of Agriculture Reports on Buckinghamhire.
94 Turbeville, *A History of Welbeck Abbey*, 310.
95 A.W. Taylor, *The History of Beaconsfield* (Beaconsfield, 1983), 25, 33–6.
96 Richard W. Davis, *Political Change and Continuity 1760–1885: A Buckinghamshire Study* (Newton Abbot, 1972), 40; John Beckett, *The Rise and Fall of the Grenvilles: The Dukes of Buckingham and Chandos 1710–1921* (Manchester, 1994), 81–93.
97 Third duke of Portland to the marquis of Titchfield, 2 November 1795, Nottingham University Manuscripts Department, PWH 325/1; Turbeville, *A History of Welbeck Abbey*, 318–19.
98 Accounts of Buckinghamshire estates, Nottingham University Manuscripts Department, Bulstrode Papers, temporary folder 9/18; Harris, 'Bulstrode', 320.
99 Humphry Repton to James Edward Smith, 5 November 1800, *Scientific Correspondence of Sir James Edward Smith*, vol. 8, no. 160, Linnean Society, London; Repton, Memoir, 19–20; Roger Lonsdale, *Dr Charles Burney: A Literary Biography* (Oxford, 1965), 469.
100 *Gardener's Magazine*, 4 (1828), 116.
101 Quoted in Carol Colson, 'Repton's Involvement or Association with Kenwood', unpublished thesis submitted for Diploma in the Conservation of Historic Landscapes, Parks and Gardens at the Architectural Association, London (1988), 20.
102 *Gardener's Magazine*, 4 (1828), 116; David Jacques, *Georgian Gardens: The Reign of Nature* (London, 1983), 81, 112–13, 140.
103 Repton, *Observations*, 12 (Works, 140).
104 Repton, *Enquiry*, 58–9n (Works, 342n).
105 Repton, *Observations*, 12–13 (Works, 141).
106 Repton, Memoir, 14.
107 Repton, *Observations*, 12–13n (Works, 141n)
108 W.H. Ward and K.S. Block, *A History of the Manor and Parish of Iver* (London, 1933), 207–8, 228–30; *Reports on the Society for Bettering the Condition and Increasing the Comfort*

108 *of the Poor* (London, 1800), 371. On Bernard, see Everett, *The Tory View*, 136–44. William Speechly was a strong advocate of specialized field and forestry tasks for children. Speechly, 'Account of Plantations'; William Speechly, *Practical Hints on Domestic Economy* (London, 1820), 44–7.

109 Repton, *Observations*, 100 (Works, 213–14).

110 Humphry Repton to James Edward Smith, 5 November 1800, Scientific Correspondence of Sir James Edward Smith, vol. 8, no. 160.

111 Repton, *Observations*, 66–72 (Works, 186–92). This is the only written record of the commission. It does not echo Red Book conventions and one may not have been produced.

112 Repton, *Sketches and Hints*, xv (Works, 30n).

113 Repton, *Enquiry*, 9 (Works, 328).

114 Repton, *Observations*, 66 (Works, 187).

115 Richard Payne Knight, *The Landscape: A Didactic Poem* (London, 1794), 11.

116 Thomas Whately, *Observations on Modern Gardening* (London, 1770), 1.

117 Repton, *Observations*, 65 (Works, 186).

118 Repton, *Fragments*, 234 (Works, 602).

119 Repton, Memoir, 205.

120 According to a letter of 1814, it was fifty guineas a visit and a commission on architectural work. Humphry Repton to Sir Harry Featherstonehaugh, 2 March 1814, Uppark Letters, private collection.

121 Repton, Memoir, 74–6; 52–4.

122 David Spring, *The English Landed Estate in the Nineteenth Century: Its Administration* (Baltimore, 1963), 12–15. On William Adam, see *Dictionary of National Biography*, vol. 1 (Oxford, 1921–2), 90–91.

123 Beckett, *The Aristocracy*, 65, 72, 91; Dean Rapp, 'Social Mobility: The Whitbreads of Bedfordshire 1720–1815', *Economic History Review*, second series, 27 (1974), 382–3. Repton was commissioned by clients from three such families: Francis Pym at Hassells, Godfrey Thornton at neighbouring Moggerhanger, and William Page Turner at Battlesden. George Carter et al., *Humphry Repton: Landscape Gardener 1752–1818* (Norwich and London, 1982), 147. A letter from Repton to Whitbread with a critical discussion of Wilkie's painting *The Blind Fiddler* may have been an attempt to angle for a commission at Southill. Humphry Repton to Samuel Whitbread, 10 May 1807, Bedford Record Office, w1/2963.

124 Dorothy Stroud, *Henry Holland* (London, 1966), 105–11.

125 Quoted in Jacques, *Georgian Gardens*, 140.

126 *Dictionary of National Biography*, vol. 16 (Oxford, 1922–3), 695–6.

127 John Martin Robertson, 'Estate Buildings of the Fifth and Sixth Dukes of Bedford at Woburn 1787–1839', *Architectural Review*, 60 (1976), 276–81; Stephen Daniels, 'The Political Iconography of Woodland in Later Georgian England', in Denis Cosgrove and Stephen Daniels (eds), *The Iconography of Landscape* (Cambridge, 1988), 51.

128 Sarah Wilmot, *'The Business of Improvement': Agriculture and Scientific Culture in Britain c.1700–c.1870* (Norwich, 1990), 51–3.

129 Edmund Burke, *Works* (Oxford, 1907), vol. 6, 71, 72–3.

130 S. Dodd, *An Historical and Topographical Account of the Town of Woburn* (Woburn, 1818), 71.

131 *A Sketch of the Life of the Late John Duke of Bedford* (Woburn, 1839), 14; Thomas Batchelor, *General View of the Agriculture of the County of Bedford* (London, 1808), 215–16.

132 'Agriculture and the House of Russell', *Journal of the Royal Agricultural Society*, third series, 2 (1891), 123–45 (135–6); Delmelza Spargo, *This Land is Our Land: Aspects of Agriculture in English Art* (London, 1989), 54–5.

133 Paul Smith, *The Landed Estate as a Patron of Scientific Innovation: Horticulture and Agriculture at Woburn Abbey*, unpublished PhD thesis, Open University, 1983. Bedford ascribed his 'botanical enthusiasm' to the Revd Charles Abbot who had a living on the Woburn estate. Abbot's Linnean guide, *Flora Bedfordiensis*, was published in 1798. Georgiana Blakiston, *Woburn and the Russells* (London, 1980), 190.

134 Jan Golinski, *Science and Public Culture: Chemistry and Enlightenment in Britain 1760–1820* (Cambridge, 1992), 188–235; Iwan Morus, Simon Schaffer and Jim Secord, 'Scientific London', in Celina Fox (ed.), *London – World City 1800–1840* (New Haven and London, 1992), 129–42.

135 John Gascoigne, *Joseph Banks and the English Enlightenment: Useful Knowledge and Polite Culture* (Cambridge, 1994); David Philip Miller and Peter Hanns Reill (eds), *Visions of Empire: Voyages, Botany and Representations of Nature* (Cambridge, 1996).

136 Smith, 'The Landed Estate'.

137 *The Autobiography of Arthur Young*, ed. M. Bentham-Edwards (London, 1898), 396–7.

138 Humphry Repton, Red Book for Woburn Abbey (1805), Woburn Abbey.

139 Ibid.

140 'Report for his Grace the Duke of Bedford's perusal before he sees Mr Repton'; 'Proposals for Improving the Walks in the Pleasure Grounds'; Humphry Repton to the duke of Bedford, 1 September 1806, Salmon Papers, Bedford Record Office, Miscellaneous.

141 Repton, *Fragments*, 152n (Works, 539n); Stroud, *Henry Holland*, 109.

142 'Mr Holland on Improvements Proposed...in Mr Repton's Plan', Woburn Estate Papers, Bedford Record Office, R 3/2 114/521–2.

143 Stroud, *Capability Brown*, 66, 189; Repton, *Observations*, 167–9n (Works, 266–7n).

144 Alan Bewell, 'Jacobin Plants: Botany as Social Theory', *Wordsworth Circle*, 20 (1989), 132–9 (138).

145 Repton, Memoir, 25.

146 'Mr Repton's Plan', Salmon Papers, Woburn Estate Papers, Bedford Record Office, R3/2114/546–7.

147 'Accounts of Labour...under the Direction of Mr

148 William Adam, 'Notes of Report to the Duke', June 1806, Salmon Papers, Woburn Estate Papers, Bedford Record Office, R4/447–533.
149 William Adam, Memorandum on the Woburn Abbey Establishment, 4 April 1807, Salmon Papers, Woburn Estate Papers, Bedford Record Office, 461/2–3.
150 Repton, *Enquiry*, vi (Works, 324).
151 Ibid., vi, iii, 2, 115–16, 2, 65 (Works, 324, 323, 325, 340–52, 326, 345).
152 Repton, *Fragments*, 98n; 175–6 (Works, 493n, 557).
153 Repton, Memoir, 76–7. He also cultivated a friendship with William Adam, calling at his chambers in Lincoln's Inn and corresponding with him about his estate in Fife. Ibid., 52–4.
154 Humphry Repton to Mary Repton, 5 April 1809; Humphry Repton to William Repton, 4 April 1810, Huntington Library, HM 40842, 40866.
155 'Observations of the Supposed Effects of Ivy upon Trees', 17 April 1810, Linnean Society Miscellaneous Manuscripts, SP 948. Published as Humphry Repton, 'Observations on the Supposed Effects of Ivy upon Trees', *Transactions of the Linnean Society*, 11 (1815), 27–34. Humphry Repton to James Edward Smith, 19 June 1809, Scientific Correspondence of Sir James Edward Smith, Linnean Society, London. Much to his anxiety, Repton's paper took ten years to appear in the Society's *Transactions*, and then without the illustrations he provided. When it was eventually published, in 1815, Repton's career had collapsed. In a long letter to Smith, shot through with social and spiritual anxieties, Repton asked if he should ever be at a loss for a name,

> and could affix it to some plant of the Ivy tribe, or of any climbing genus which, like myself, want to be supported, I should rejoice to have my name recorded by your power of conferring immortality. My great predecessor *Adam* would never have been able to find names for a hundreth part of your vocabulary; but he lived in a garden with one friend and one enemy, who, like Buonaparte in our days, was the enemy of peace . . . Is it possible for you, who know so much more of the created evidences of the Deity, to feel satiety here, and a wish to enlarge your scene of observation? I have no doubt this will happen to all whose active minds lead them to wish for such enlargement; and then you and I shall meet, and compare our ideas on that and a great many other subjects.

Repton asked Smith if he could reprint his paper on ivy in *Fragments* but permission arrived after the book had gone to press. Repton also failed in his appeal to attach his name to ivy. Humphry Repton to James Edward Smith, 9 July 1815; 13 May 1816; 6 October 1816, Scientific Correspondence of Sir James Edward Smith, vol. 8, nos 169, 173, 174, Linnean Society, London.
156 Repton, *Fragments*, 13 (Works, 421–2).
157 Ibid., 14n (423n).
158 Repton, Red Book for Woburn, Supplement.
159 Rupert Gunnis, *Dictionary of British Sculptors 1660–1851* (London, 1953), 114; Stroud, *Henry Holland*, 115.
160 Repton, *Fragments*, 148 (Works, 536).
161 Blakiston, *Woburn and the Russells*, 181–2.
162 Repton, *Fragments*, 168 (Works, 551).
163 Smith, 'The Landed Estate', 143–72.
164 George Sinclair, *Hortus Gramineus Woburniensis* (London, 1816).
165 *Gardener's Magazine*, 1 (1826), 116.
166 James Forbes, *Hortus Woburniensis* (London, 1833), 245–92.
167 J.D. Parry, *A Guide to Woburn Abbey* (Woburn, 1831), 299–30.
168 Donald J. Olsen, *Town Planning in London: The Eighteenth and Nineteenth Centuries*, second edition (New Haven and London, 1982), 39–73.
169 Dan Cruikshank and Neil Burton, *Life in the Georgian City* (London, 1990), 201–02.
170 John Claudius Loudon, 'Hints Respecting the Manner of Laying out the Grounds of the Public Squares of London, to the Utmost Picturesque Advantage', *Literary Journal*, 2 (31 December 1803), cols 739–42; reprinted with commentary in Laurence Fricker, 'John Claudius Loudon: The Plane Truth?', in Peter Willis (ed.), *Furor Hortensis: Essays in the History of the English Landscape Garden in Memory of H.F. Clark* (Edinburgh, 1974), 76–88.
171 Olsen, *Town Planning*, 52.
172 E. Beresford Chancellor, *History of the Squares of London* (London, 1907), 183–201.
173 Repton, *Enquiry*, 60–64 (Works, 342–3).
174 Ibid., 60 (342).
175 Marie Busco, *Sir Richard Westmacott, Sculptor* (Cambridge, 1994), 88–9; Nicholas Penny, *Church Monuments in Romantic England* (New Haven, 1977), 186–8.
176 Repton, *Enquiry*, 62–3 (Works, 344).
177 Humphry Repton to William Adam, 3 March 1807. Copy in Earl Harwicke, private correspondence, Sir John Soane's Museum, London, XIII.9.10.
178 Bedford Estate Archives, Woburn Abbey, uncatalogued. The vista to Russell Square was kept open, and a statue by Westmacott of *Charles James Fox*, dressed like a Roman senator and clasping a Magna Carta, was erected in 1816 on the north side of Bloomsbury Square to face that of his old friend and ally. Busco, *Sir Richard Westmacott*, 72–3.
179 Nathaniel Kent to William Adam, 23 May 1802, Devon Record Office Bedford MSS, Miscellaneous Letters 117.
180 P.V. Denham, 'The Duke of Bedford's Tavistock Estate 1820–1838', *Transactions of the Devon Association for the Advancement of Science*, 110 (1978), 19–51; Robert Fraser, *General View of the Agriculture of the County of Devon* (London, 1794), 9–10; Charles Vancouver, *General View of the Agriculture of the County of Devon* (London, 1808), 34, 67; William Marshall, *The Rural Economy of the West of England* (London, 1796), 2, 294.
181 Frank Booker, *The Industrial Archaeology of the Tamar*

Valley (Newton Abbot, 1967), 103–18; Tristram Risdon, *The Chronological Description and Survey of the County of Devon* (London, 1811), i–xxxvi (xi).

182 Peter Hunt, 'John Swete and the Picturesque', in Steven Pugsley (ed.), *Devon Gardens: An Historical Survey* (Stroud, 1994), 59–75; Sam Smiles and Michael Pidgley, *The Perfection of England, Artist Visitors to Devon c.1750–1870* (Plymouth, 1995), 9–24; Sam Smiles, 'Turner in the West Country: From Topography to Idealisation', in J.C. Eade (ed.), *Projecting the Landscape* (Canberra, 1987), 36–53.

183 Humphry Repton to Reginald Pole Carew, 2 January 1793, Antony House Muniments, CE/E/66/3.

184 Humphry Repton, Red Book for Luscombe (1799), private collection.

185 Humphry Repton to William Repton, 4 April 1809, Huntington Library, HM 40859.

186 Humphry Repton, Red Book for Pentillie (1809), private collection. Reginald Pole Carew to Humphry Repton, 25 July 1809, Antony House Muniments, CE/E/66/22/1.

187 Anna Elizabeth Bray, *The Borders of the Tamar and the Tavy* (London, 1879), 432–40; Anna Elizabeth Bray, *Poetical Remains of the Late Edward Atkyns Bray* (London, 1859).

188 Commissioning letter, Woburn, 12 August 1809, Bedford Estate Office, Woburn Abbey; George Repton to Dorothy Adey, 20 August 1809, Huntington Library, HM 40915.

189 This was possibly the Hampshire architect of that name, but more probably it was the polymathic geologist who developed the Tavistock canal, managed the duke's mines and helped found a library in the town. Howard Colvin, *A Biographical Dictionary of British Architects 1600–1840*, third edition (New Haven and London, 1995), 814; Booker, *Industrial Archaeology*, 67, 103–7.

190 Humphry Repton to William Adam, 17 July 1814, Devon Record Office, Bedford MSS L1258 D 69. Carter et al., in *Humphry Repton*, 151, conclude that nothing was built.

191 Humphry Repton, 'The Cripple', 14 August 1815, Avery Architectural Library, Columbia University, New York.

192 Letter to Southey, 7 September 1832, in Anna Elizabeth Bray, *A Description of Devonshire* (London, 1836), vol. 1, 153.

193 Mavis Batey, *Regency Gardens* (Princes Risborough, 1995), 7–22.

194 Nigel Temple, *George Repton's Pavilion Notebook: A Catalogue Raisonné* (Aldershot, 1993).

195 Christopher Hussey, 'Endsleigh, Devon – II', *Country Life* (10 August 1961), 296–9 (298); Derek Linstrum, *Sir Jeffry Wyatville: Architect to the King* (Oxford, 1972), 93; Richard Stone, 'The Creation of Endsleigh: A Regency Masterpiece', in Pugsley, *Devon Gardens*, 76–90.

196 Stone, 'The Creation of Endsleigh', 80.

197 Humphry Repton to the duke of Bedford, 1 May 1814, Devon Record Office, Bedford MSS L1258 E 82.

198 Humphry Repton to the duke of Bedford, 5 May 1814, Devon Record Office, Bedford MSS L1258 E 82.

199 Humphry Repton to William Repton, 3 June 1814, Huntington Library, HM 40875.

200 Humphry Repton to William Adam, 11 August 1814, enclosed with 'Report Concerning Endsleigh Cottage', Devon Record Office, Bedford MSS L1258 DL 82.

201 Humphry Repton to William Adam, 22 November 1814, Devon Record Office, Bedford MSS L1258 E 82.

202 Humphry Repton to William Adam, 22 November 1814, Devon Record Office, Bedford MSS L1258 E 82.

203 Humphry Repton, 'Report Concerning Endsleigh Cottage', Devon Record Office, Bedford MSS L1258 DL 82.

204 Humphry Repton, Red Book for Endsleigh (1814), Woburn Abbey. The terrace gardens are relegated in the Red Book to a footnote to a sentence on the Hanging Gardens of Bablyon and a report of something similar 'still existing near Damascus'. The gardener Forrester was not convinced about the viability of these gardens (hence the original detailed explanation) and Repton may already have heard that they would not be built.

205 Blakiston, *Woburn and the Russells*, 175–85.

206 Vancouver, *General View of Devon*, 325–37.

207 Repton, Red Book for Endsleigh.

208 Humphry Repton to William Adam, 22 November 1814, Devon Record Office, Bedford MSS L1258 DL 82.

209 Humphry Repton to Sir Harry Fetherstonehaugh, 21 August 1815, Uppark Letters, private collection.

210 Humphry Repton to William Repton, 3 October 1815, Huntington Library.

211 Repton, *Fragments*, 213–26 (Works 586–97).

212 Stone, 'The Creation of Endsleigh', 88–90.

213 Endsleigh Accounts, Devon Record Office, Bedford MSS L1258 M/E/A/E 1811–16; E 21 1819–25.

214 Denham, 'The Duke of Bedford's Tavistock Estate', 22.

215 William Adam to the duke of Bedford, 15 February 1826, Devon Record Office, Bedford MSS, Miscellaneous Letters 117.

216 Humphry Repton to Norton Nicholls, 26 August 1788, Bristol University Library.

217 Repton, Memoir, 19. On royal domesticity, see Paul Langford, *A Polite and Commercial People: England 1727–1783* (Oxford, 1992), 581–2.

218 Repton, Memoir, 213.

219 Kenneth Garlick and Angus Macintyre (eds), *The Diary of Joseph Farington*, vol. 1, July 1793–December 1794 (New Haven and London, 1978), 163 (entry for 16 February 1794).

220 James Hakewill, *The History of Windsor and Its Neighbourhood* (London, 1813), 281.

221 Repton, Memoir, 214.

222 Ibid., 59.

223 I am grateful to Jane Roberts for clarifying the issue of the Deputy Rangership. See Jane Roberts, *Royal Landscape: The Gardens and Parks of Windsor* (New Haven and London, 1997), 67, 70, 544 n. 127.

224 Repton, Memoir, 218, 214.

225 Edmund Gilbert, *Brighton, Old Ocean's Bauble* (London, 1954), 90–120; Peter Brandon, *The Sussex Landscape* (London, 1974), 176–207; Sue Farrant, *Georgian Brighton 1740–1820*, University of Sussex Centre for Continuing Education, Occasional Papers 13 (1980).

226 Patrick Conner, 'Unexecuted Designs for the Royal Pavilion at Brighton', *Apollo*, 107 (1978), 192–9; Henry D. Roberts, *A History of the Royal Pavilion, Brighton* (London, 1939), 79–82; Sue Farrant, 'The Physical Development of the Royal Pavilion Estate and Its Influence on Brighton (East Sussex) 1785–1823', *Sussex Archaeological Collections*, 120 (1982), 171–84; John Dinkel, *The Royal Pavilion, Brighton* (London, 1983), 39.
227 Humphry Repton, Red Book for Brighton Pavilion (1806), Royal Library, Windsor.
228 Roberts, *A History of the Royal Pavilion*, 90; Stroud, *Henry Holland*, 89.
229 Humphry Repton, Designs for Carlton House, Royal Drawings, Windsor Castle, 17091a.
230 Strong, *Royal Gardens*, 82.
231 Repton, Memoir, 221.
232 Humphry Repton, Report on Montreal (1812), British Library, Microfilm of Exported MSS, RP 142; *Observations*, 100–03 (Works, 214–16).
233 Repton, Memoir, 219.
234 John Morley, *Regency Design 1790–1840* (London, 1993), 345–6.
235 Repton, Memoir, 222, 220–21.
236 Ibid., 222.
237 Ibid., 224–5, 226, 228. Before returning to Hare Street to prepare the Red Book, Repton called on a long-standing client in Sussex, Lord Sheffield, to try to organize planting at the Pavilion, reckoning that the county nobility would be honoured to help. Humphry Repton to Lord Sheffield, 22 December 1805, Pierpont Morgan Library, New York, MA 4138.
238 Repton, Memoir, 122–6. A design of *c*.1797 for a new façade for Holly Grove adjacent to Windsor Great Park is in a mixed Chinese–Indian style. See Roberts, *Royal Landscapes*, 300–01.
239 Christopher Hussey, *English Country Houses: Late Georgian 1800–1840* (London, 1958), 66–73.
240 James Malton, *Essay on British Cottage Architecture* (London, 1798), 9.
241 David Watkin, *Thomas Hope 1769–1831 and the Neo-Classical Ideal* (London, 1968), 233.
242 Ray Desmond, *The India Museum* (London, 1982), 1–31.
243 Francis Blagdon, *History of Ancient and Modern India* (London, 1805), 22. On scenery and triumphalism, see G.H.R. Tillotson, 'The Indian Picturesque: Images of India in British Landscape Painting, 1780–1880', in C.A. Bayly (ed.), *The Raj: India and the British 1600–1947* (London, 1990), 141–51.
244 Repton, Red Book for Brighton Pavilion.
245 Repton, *Enquiry*, 41 (Works, 340).
246 Conner, 'Unexecuted Designs'.
247 Repton, Red Book for Brighton Pavilion.
248 Repton, Memoir, 227–8.
249 Ibid., 231–2. Farrant, 'The Physical Development of the Royal Pavilion Estate', 179.
250 Royal Drawings, Royal Library, Windsor Castle, 17090, fol. 15.
251 Repton, Memoir, 233; Stroud, *Henry Holland*, 84.
252 Humphry Repton to Robert Gray, 22 May 1808, Royal Archives 31515, G.I.V. Accounts Box 7/30; 5 January 1808, Royal Archives, Unindexed Accounts. J. Stadler to Humphry Repton, 13 April 1808, Huntington Library, HM 40945.
253 Repton, *Sketches and Hints*, v–vii (Works, 24).
254 Humphry Repton, *Designs for the Pavillon at Brighton* (London, 1808), vii, x (Works, 369, 372). Repton had recently seen a machine for turning mouldings in Cambridge, invented by a student at Downing College, which he reckoned would turn out work cheaply. Humphry Repton to Freke Evans, 9 April 1808, Freke Evans (Latton) collection, private collection, photocopies in Northamptonshire Record Office.
255 Repton, *Designs for the Pavillon*, vii–viii, x (Works, 369–70, 373).
256 Farrant, 'The Royal Pavilion Estate'.
257 Humphry Repton to the Prince Regent, 13 December 1815, folded in the Red Book for Brighton Pavilion.
258 Repton, Memoir, 234.
259 Not even for the grounds of the East India College at Haileybury. R.G.C. Desmond, 'A Repton Garden at Haileybury', *Garden History*, 6 (1978), 16–19.
260 Repton, Memoir, 234.
261 J. Mordaunt Crook, 'Metropolitan Improvements: John Nash and the Picturesque', in Celina Fox (ed.), *London – World City 1800–1840* (New Haven and London, 1992), 77–96 (78).
262 Patrick Conner, *Oriental Architecture in the West* (London, 1979), 107–8; Batey, *Regency Gardens*, 67–8.
263 Repton, Memoir, 234.
264 Humphry Repton to Sir Harry Fetherstonehaugh, 9 June 1814, Uppark Letters, private collection. Once a favourite of the prince, Fetherstonehaugh was now exiled from his company.
265 Repton, *Fragments*, 232 (Works, 601).

CHAPTER 5

1 Humphry Repton, *Fragments on the Theory and Practice of Landscape Gardening* (London, 1816), 69 (Works, 469).
2 David Cannadine, *Lords and Landlords: The Aristocracy and the Towns 1774–1967* (Leicester, 1980); David Cannadine (ed.), *Patricians, Power and Politics in Nineteenth-Century Towns* (Leicester, 1982); T.R. Slater, 'Family, Society and the Ornamental Villa on the Fringes of English Country Towns', *Journal of Historical Geography*, 4 (1978), 129–44; T.M. Devine, 'Glasgow Colonial Merchants and Land, 1770–1815', in J.T. Ward and R.G. Wilson (eds), *Land and Industry: The Landed Estate and the Industrial Revolution* (Newton Abbot, 1971), 205–44.
3 The commissions for Tatton, the Royal Pavilion, Catton and Sufton are discussed above in Chapters one, four, two and three respectively.
4 Humphry Repton, Red Book for Mosely Hall (1792), Frances Loeb Library, Harvard University.
5 Caroline Arscott and Griselda Pollock with Janet Wolff,

'The Partial View: The Visual Representation of the Early Nineteenth-Century Industrial City', in Janet Wolff and John Seed (eds), *The Culture of Capital: Art, Power and the Nineteenth-Century Middle Class* (Manchester, 1988), 191–234.
6. Celina Fox (ed.), *London – World City 1800–1840* (New Haven and London, 1992).
7. Humphry Repton to Sir Harry Fetherstonehaugh, 21 January, 6 October 1813, Uppark Letters, private collection.
8. Repton, *Odd Whims and Miscellanies* (London, 1804), vol. 1, 5, 7.
9. Humphry Repton to Sir Harry Fetherstonehaugh, 28 October 1816, Uppark Letters, private collection.
10. Repton, *Fragments*, 9 (Works, 417).
11. Humphry Repton, *Observations on the Theory and Practice of Landscape Gardening*, (London, 1803), 165n (Works, 265n).
12. See Chapter four above.
13. J. Mordaunt Crook, 'Metropolitan Improvements: John Nash and the Picturesque', in Fox, *London – World City*, 76–96.
14. Humphry Repton, Memoir, Part two, autographed draft, British Library, Add. MS. 62112, 175–6, 208.
15. Humphry Repton, Red Book for Claybury (1791), Essex Record Office, D/DV 1113.
16. Repton, *Fragments*, 72–3 (Works, 471–2).
17. Humphry Repton, Red Book for Point Pleasant (1796), Mrs Paul Mellon, Oak Spring Garden Library, Upperville, VA.
18. Anna Seward to Humphry Repton, 15 July 1789, *The Letters of Anna Seward* (Edinburgh, 1811), vol. 1, 309.
19. Knight's residence was at Milton, near Cambridge. He contributed an essay to Repton's first collection of essays, *Variety*.
20. Arthur Young, *General View of the Agriculture of Essex* (London, 1813), 153.
21. Victoria County History, *A History of Essex*, vol. 6 (London, 1973), 274; vol. 5 (London, 1966), 290.
22. Humphry Repton, Red Book for Highams (1796), Vestry House Museum, Walthamstow, W72.2. Victoria County History, *Essex*, vol. 6, (London, 1973) 274.
23. Repton, Red Book for Claybury.
24. Repton, *Fragments*, 77–9 (Works, 475–6).
25. William Howitt, *The Northern Heights* (London, 1869).
26. Hugh C. Prince, 'North-West London 1814–1863', in J.T. Coppock and Hugh C. Prince, *Greater London* (London, 1964), 80–119 (80–94); John Middleton, *General View of the Agriculture of the County of Middlesex* (London, 1813), 27–47, 309–99, 623–7.
27. Julius Bryant, *Finest Prospects: Three Historic Houses: A Study in London Topography* (London, 1986), 11–16; F.M.L. Thompson, *Hampstead: The Building of a Borough 1650–1964* (London, 1974), 30.
28. Paul Lucas, 'A Collective Biography of Students and Barristers of Lincoln's Inn, 1680–1804: A Study in the "Aristocratic Resurgence" of the Eighteenth Century', *Journal of Modern History*, 46 (1974), 227–61.
29. Humphry Repton, Red Book for Brandsbury (1789), Dumbarton Oaks Library, Washington, DC. Facsimile in Stephen Daniels (ed.), *Humphry Repton: The Red Books for Brandsbury and Glemham Hall* (Washington, DC, 1994).
30. Victoria County History, *Hertford*, vol. 3 (London, 1912), 39, 41.
31. Repton, Memoir, 4–5.
32. Ibid., 5; Humphry Repton, *Sketches and Hints on Landscape Gardening* (London, 1795), 4 (Works, 42n); 'A Thousand Years of History', *Willesden Chronicle*, 1934.
33. Victoria County History, *Middlesex*, vol. 7 (London, 1982), 210.
34. Repton, Memoir, 5.
35. Repton, Red Book for Brandsbury; Middleton, *General View of the Agriculture of Middlesex*, 242.
36. Ibid.; Repton later revealed that the offending man was the architect employed to a alter the house. Repton, *Sketches and Hints*, 3 (Works, 40n).
37. Repton, Account Book; Repton, Memoir, 3, 6.
38. Repton, Account Book.
39. Repton usually produced schematic sketch maps based on existing surveys supplemented by a few observations. Occasionally, for prestigious commissions, a new map would be commissioned from a professional surveyor. See above, Introduction.
40. Repton, Memoir, 6.
41. Humphry Repton to Norton Nicholls, 15 April 1789, Bristol University Library.
42. Repton, Memoir, 5.
43. Red Book for Brandsbury.
44. Repton, Memoir, 6, 5.
45. Repton, *Sketches and Hints*, 4 (Works, 42n). For an admiring comment on the grounds, see Henry Hunter, *The History of London and Its Environs* (London, 1811), vol. 2, 89. Lady Salusbury's Hertfordshire seat at Offley was illustrated in *Peacock's Polite Repository* for 1795 so it is probable that Repton was commissioned there.
46. I am grateful to Carol Colson for letting me see her unpublished research on the landscape of Kenwood, some of which is published in Julius Bryant and Carol Colson, *The Landscape of Kenwood* (London, 1990). Christopher Ikin also kindly showed me a research paper of his on Kenwood, Fitzroy Farm and Evergreen Hill which helped me to reconstruct the particulars of Repton's commissions.
47. Julius Bryant, *The Iveagh Bequest, Kenwood* (London, 1990), 58–62.
48. Robert Oresko (ed.), *The Works in Architecture of Robert and James Adam* (London, 1975), 52.
49. Robert Robson, *The Attorney in Eighteenth-Century England* (Cambridge, 1959), 18n.
50. Bryant, *Kenwood*, 19–20; Bryant, *Finest Prospects*, 100–01.
51. Bryant, *Kenwood*, 64–5.
52. Jacob Simon, 'Humphry Repton at Kenwood', *Camden History Review*, 11 (1984), 4–11 (5–6).
53. Repton, Account Book; Alan Farmer, 'Colonel Fitzroy's Rustic Villa', *Camden History Review*, 10 (1982), 19–20.
54. Humphry Repton, Red Book for Kenwood (1793), private collection. Facsimile in Scottish Record Office, Edinburgh, RH2 8/113.

55 Simon, 'Humphry Repton at Kenwood', 6.
56 Bryant, *Kenwood*, 48–9.
57 Howitt, *The Northern Heights*, 88; Gillian Tindall, *The Fields Beneath* (London, 1980), 99.
58 Repton, Red Book for Kenwood.
59 Ibid.
60 Bryant, *Kenwood*, 52–3.
61 Repton, *Observations*, 212 (*Works*, 309).
62 Repton, Red Book for Kenwood.
63 *Forty Drawings of Roman Scenes by British Artists (1715–1830)* (London, 1911); David Solkin, *Richard Wilson: The Landscape of Reaction* (London, 1983), 187–8.
64 Quoted in John Fleming, *Robert Adam and His Circle in Edinburgh and Rome* (London, 1962), 145–6.
65 Simon, 'Humphry Repton at Kenwood', 6.
66 Humphry Repton to Lord Mansfield, 8 September 1793, Scone Archives, second series, bundle 278. My thanks to Carol Colson for sending me her transcription.
67 Bryant, *Kenwood*, 48; Howard Colvin, *A Biographical Dictionary of British Architects 1600–1840*, third edition (New Haven and London, 1995), 859–60.
68 Bryant, *Kenwood*, 50.
69 Repton, *Observations*, 201n (*Works*, 298n).
70 *Monthly Review*, July 1804, 225–359. Saunders is identified as the reviewer in *The Monthly Review Second Series 1790–1815: Indexes of Contributers and Reviewers* (Oxford, 1955).
71 Plan of Kenwood House, Offices and Adjoining Grounds, British Museum, Crace Collection. Reproduced in Julius Bryant and Carol Colson, *The Landscape of Kenwood* (London, 1990), 10–11.
72 John Claudius Loudon, *The Suburban Gardener and Villa Companion* (London, 1838), 665n.
73 Loudon, *The Suburban Gardener*, 671.
74 Pamela Horn, *William Marshall (1745–1818) and the Georgian Countryside* (Sutton Courtney, Abingdon, 1982), 27.
75 *Milne's Plan of the Cities of London and Westminster, Circumadjacent Towns and Parishes*, British Museum Map Library, K Top VI 95. On the map, see G.B.G. Bull, 'Thomas Milne's Land Utilization Map of the London Area in 1800', *Geographical Journal*, 122 (1956), 25–30. *The Beauties of England and Wales*, vol. 3, ed. F.W. Brayley and J. Britton (London, 1803), 179.
76 Bryant, *Finest Prospects*, 121–2.
77 J. Norris Brewer, *The Beauties of England and Wales*, vol. 10 (London, 1816), 176–8.
78 Loudon, *The Suburban Gardener*, 661.
79 Howitt, *The Northern Heights*, 56–7. Victoria County History, *Middlesex*, vol. 9, 68.
80 Ibid., 57–82.
81 Repton, *Memoir*, 44.
82 Humphry Repton, 'Law Whigs' (n.d.), Avery Architectural Library, Columbia University, New York.
83 For a small commission adjacent to Evergreen Hill, Golders Hill, for a Lincoln's Inn attorney John Coore, Repton received an engraved silver bread-basket. Repton, *Memoir*, 130.
84 Quoted in Howitt, *The Northern Heights*, 80.
85 Repton, *Memoir*, 47, 52.
86 The purchaser was Sir Nicholas Conyngham Tyndall, Chief Justice of the Commons Pleas. Victoria County History, *Middlesex*, vol. 9, 68; Victoria County History, *Sussex*, vol. 6, part 3 (London, 1987), 19–20.
87 Howitt, *The Northern Heights*, 80–81. Erskine subsequently makes fleeting appearances in Repton's papers, in 1812 in a letter from Repton's attorney son, William, concerning the mortgaging of Buchan Hill, and a client's wish to view it, and in a letter from Repton himself about travelling with Erskine from London to Sussex (William Repton to Lord Erskine, 4 December 1812; Humphry Repton to William Repton, 15 December 1812, Huntington Library, HM 40954).

Repton published an undated letter of advice to Erskine in *Fragments*. Erskine had wanted some shelter for his house 'without sacrificing my prospect'. Repton had recommended that he plant only beech, but Erskine wanted to add some silver firs, which Repton advised were out of character with the scene as saplings and would quickly obscure the view as they grew. The accompanying illustration is of a rural scene, 'a river quietly winding through a valley; a tower on the summit of a wooded promontory, and a cottage at the foot of a hill; a distant village spire, and more distant hills', but as the landscape 'is composed of those materials, which may rather be called tame and beautiful, than romantic or picturesque' to illustrate a point of principle, and as it scarcely recalls the thickly wooded Weald, the view is probably not from Buchan Hill. It is more likely to be a theoretical version of the view from Evergreen Hill, the grounds of Kenwood transformed in to a generalized image of rural England (Repton, *Fragments*, 55–9, (*Works*, 466–8)).
88 Humphry Repton to Reginald Pole Carew, 20 October 1795, Antony House Muniments, CE/E/66/13; Humphry Repton to G.J. Legh, 22 January 1797, Cornwall-Legh Papers, John Rylands Library, University of Manchester.
89 W.E. Minchinton, 'Bristol – Metropolis of the West in the Eighteenth Century', *Transactions of the Royal Historical Society*, fifth series, 4 (1954), 69–89.
90 Stewart Harding and David Lambert, *Parks and Gardens of Avon* (Bristol, 1994), 34–57.
91 Bryan Little, *The City and County of Bristol: A Study in Atlantic Civilization* (London, 1954), 178–9.
92 J. Shiercliff, *Bristol and Hotwells Guide* (Bristol, 1793), 13.
93 Patrick McGrath, *Bristol in the Eighteenth Century* (Newton Abbot, 1972), 194.
94 For the commission at Oldbury Court, see Harding and Lambert, *Parks and Gardens of Avon*, 62–3.
95 My thanks to Simon Bonvoisin of Nicholas Pearson Associates for letting me see 'Blaise Castle: Historic Landscape Survey and Management Plan' (1993). The section on Blaise in Nigel Temple, *John Nash and the Village Picturesque* (Gloucester, 1979), also provided me with important sources.
96 Hallen and Henbury Women's Institute, *A History of Henbury* (Bristol, 1993).
97 P.K. Stembridge, *Thomas Goldney's Garden* (Bristol, 1996);

98  Harding and Lambert, *Parks and Gardens of Avon*, 49–51; Temple, *John Nash*, 42–6.

99  John Scandrett Harford to Thomas Farr, 7 September 1789; Thomas Farr to John Scandrett Harford, 10 September 1789, Bristol Record Office, 28048 P41.

100  Quoted in Temple, *John Nash*, 37.

101  Ibid., 52–4; Alice Harford (ed.), *Annals of the Harford Family* (London, 1909), 56.

102  Harford, *Annals of the Harford Family*, 63; Humphry Repton, Red Book for Warley (1794), Smethwick Public Library.

103  Humphry Repton, Red Book for Blaise Castle (1796), Bristol Museum and Art Gallery.

104  Ibid.

105  Ibid.; Repton, *Observations*, 145 (*Works*, 251).

106  Repton, Red Book for Blaise Castle.

107  Repton, *Observations*, 161–2n (*Works*, 261n).

108  Hardy and Lambert, *Parks and Gardens of Avon*, 48.

109  Harford, *Annals of the Harford Family*, 56.

110  A.P. Woolrich, 'An American in Gloucestershire and Bristol: The Diary of Joshua Gilpin, 1796–7', *Transactions of the Bristol and Gloucester Archaeological Society*, 92 (1973), 169–89 (184–5).

111  James Edward Smith, *Tour to Hafod* (London, 1810), 5.

112  Harford, *Annals of the Harford Family*, 56.

113  Invoices, Corsham Court papers, box file 47, Wiltshire Record Office; Leslie Harcourt, *Mr Methuen's House*, (Weston-super-Mare, 1981), 73; Repton, Memoir, 85–6.

114  Temple, *John Nash*.

115  J. Storer and J. Brewer, *Delineations of Gloucestershire* (London, 1824), 108; J. Horner, *Nine Views of Blaise Hamlet* (n.p., 1825), Introduction.

116  Quoted in David Watkin, *The Life and Work of C.R. Cockerell* (London, 1974), 80–81.

117  Algernon Graves, *The Royal Academy of Arts: A Complete Dictionary of Contributors and their Work from its Foundation in 1769 to 1904*, 4 vols (Bath, 1970), vol. 3, 268; Repton, *Observations*, 184–6 (*Works*, 281–4).

118  Repton, *Observations*, 184–5, 185n, 196 (*Works*, 282–3, 283n, 284).

119  Andor Gomme, Michael Jenner and Bryan Little, *Bristol: An Architectural History* (London, 1979), 155–9; Walter Ison, *The Georgian Buildings of Bristol* (London, 1952), 25–45, 190–98.

120  John Latimer, *The Annals of Bristol in the Eighteenth Century* (Bristol, 1893), 495; George Parker, 'Tyndall's Park, Bristol, Fort Royal and the Fort House Therein', *Transactions of the Bristol and Gloucestershire Archaeological Society*, 51 (1929), 123–41.

121  Humphry Repton, Red Book for The Royal Fort (1801), Beineke Library, Yale University.

122  Perhaps in view of his client's military rank, Repton included an option of 'altering the house to make it what its name & situation denotes – The Fort might be restored to its original character as a Castle or Fortress'. Repton's drawing of the proposed scene shows a battlemented Gothic mansion. Set in an expanse of deer-stocked park, it projects a baronial authority.

123  Francis Greenacre and Sheena Stoddard, *The Bristol Landscape: The Watercolours of Samuel Jackson 1794–1869* (Bristol, 1987), 28.

124  John Collison, *The History and Antiquities of the County of Somerset* (Bath, 1791), vol. 2, 292–5; Anton Bantock, *The Later Smyths of Ashton Court, From Their Letters 1741–1802* (Bishopsworth, 1984), 174–95.

125  Repton, *Observations*, 200–02 (*Works*, 296–300).

126  Land Use Consultants, 'Ashton Court, Bristol' (1992), Bristol City Council, Leisure Services.

127  Humphry Repton to Sir Hugh Smyth, 11 October 1802, Bristol Record Office.

128  Humphry Repton to William Adam, 22 November 1814, Devon Record Office, Bedford MSS L1258 E82.

129  Humphry Repton to William Repton, 3 June 1814, Huntington Library, HM 40875.

130  C. Cave, *A History of Banking in Bristol* (Bristol, 1899), 73.

131  Robert Cooke, *West Country Houses* (London, 1957), 156.

132  Humphry Repton, Report for Leigh Court (1814), Bristol University Library.

133  Cave, *A History of Banking in Bristol*, 126.

134  Repton, Report for Leigh Court.

135  My thanks to John Phibbs for letting me look at his field research on Leigh Court presented at Debois Landscape Survey Group, 'Leigh Court, Avon Survey and Restoration Plan for Part of the Pleasure Grounds' (1993).

136  Repton, Report for Leigh Court.

137  Cooke, *West Country Houses*, 156.

138  Eric Adams, *Francis Danby: Varieties of Poetic Landscape*, (New Haven and London, 1973), 33.

139  Humphry Repton to William Repton, 4 April 1809, Huntington Library, HM 40861.

140  Edward Repton to William Repton, 27 December 1809, Huntington Library, HM 40911.

141  Repton, Memoir, 90–106; Memorandum of Improvements staked out by Repton, August 1800, Leeds City Archives, Harewood Building Box 1.

142  R.G. Wilson, *Gentlemen Merchants: The Merchant Community in Leeds 1700–1830* (Manchester, 1971), 169–70.

143  Ibid.

144  Trevor Fawcett, *The Rise of English Provincial Art* (Oxford, 1974), 168–70, 89; R.J. Morris, 'Middle-Class Culture 1700–1914', in Derek Fraser (ed.), *A History of Modern Leeds* (Manchester, 1980), 200–22 (209).

145  Maurice Beresford, 'East End, West End: The Face of Leeds during Urbanization', *Publications of the Thoresby Society*, 60–61 (1985–6), 364–79; Stephen Daniels, 'The Implications of Industry: Turner and Leeds', *Turner Studies*, 6 (1986), 10–17.

146  Bryan E. Coates, 'Park Landscapes of the East and West Ridings in the Time of Humphry Repton', *Yorkshire Archaeological Journal*, 41 (1965), 465–80 (476); A. Pemberton, 'Two Hundred Years of Banks in Leeds',

147 *Publications of the Thoresby Society*, 46 (1963), 54–86; Wilson, *Gentlemen Merchants*, 241.
147 Humphry Repton, Red Book for Oulton (1810), Leeds District Archives, DB 176.
148 Humphry Repton, Red Book for Armley (1810), Mrs Paul Mellon, Oak Spring Garden Library, Upperville, VA; Beresford, *East End, West End*, 274–5.
149 Dorothy Stroud, *Capability Brown* (London, 1975), 115–16.
150 Repton, Red Book for Oulton; on industrial history, see John Batty, *The History of Rothwell* (Rothwell, 1877); Albert Brown, *Rothwell in the 900 Years after Domesday* (Rothwell, 1987), 31, 50.
151 Repton, Red Book for Oulton.
152 Repton, *Fragments*, 74–6 (*Works*, 473–5). A map of 1816 indicates that Blayds carried out the improvements to the common much as Repton proposed, which suggests that he either spent the extra money to do so, or that there are details of alterations, say to the house, that do not show up. Henry Teal, *Plan of the Townships of Rothwell with Royds and Oulton with Woodesford* (1816), Leeds District Archives, Farrer & Co., no. 6.
153 W.B. Crump, 'The History of Gott's Mills', *Publications of the Thoresby Society*, 32 (1929), 254–71; H. Heaton, 'Benjamin Gott and the Industrial Revolution', *Economic History Review*, 3 (1931), 45–66; E.J. Connell and M. Ward, 'Industrial Development 1780–1914', in Derek Fraser (ed.), *A History of Modern Leeds* (Manchester, 1980), 142–76.
154 E.J. Connell, *Industrial Development in South Leeds 1790–1914*, unpublished PhD thesis, University of Leeds, 1975, 40–43, 371–3; 'Papers of Benjamin Gott', *Publications of the Thoresby Society*, 32 (1929), 231–3.
155 Heaton, 'Benjamin Gott'; Crump, 'Gott's Mills'.
156 Veronica Lovell, 'Benjamin Gott of Armley House, Leeds, 1762–1840: Patron of the Arts', *Publications of the Thoresby Society*, 59–61 (1985–6), 177–221 (188–90).
157 Benjamin Gott to Benjamin Gott the Younger, 7 April 1811, John Goodchild Loan MSS, Wakefield Central Library.
158 A. Aspinall (ed.), *Mrs Jordan and Her Family* (London, 1951), 130–32.
159 Elizabeth Gott to Benjamin Gott the Younger, 22–5 December 1809, John Goodchild Loan MSS, Wakefield Central Library, uncatalogued bundle of letters marked 'personal'.
160 Repton, Red Book for Armley.
161 Repton, *Observations*, 13n (*Works*, 14n).
162 Repton, *Fragments*, 207 (*Works*, 578).
163 Repton, Memoir, 199. On the building and destruction of the Mill, see A.W. Shrimpton, 'Samuel Wyatt and the Albion Mill', *Journal of the Society of Architectural Historians*, 14 (1971), 53–73.
164 Tim Warner, 'Combined Utility and Magnificence: Humphry Repton's Commission for Wingerworth Hall in Derbyshire', *Journal of Garden History*, 7 (1987), 271–301.
165 Repton, Red Book for Armley.
166 Fox, *London*, 291–2.
167 Benjamin Gott to Benjamin Gott the Younger, 9 June 1809, John Goodchild Loan MSS, Wakefield Central Library.
168 Repton, Red Book for Armley.
169 Elizabeth Gott's Diary, 13 and 16 January 1810, Brotherton Library, University of Leeds, Gott Papers 194 3/8.
170 T.D. Whitaker, *Loidis et Elmete* (Leeds, 1816), 100, 87.
171 J.P. Neale, *Views of the Seats of Noblemen and Gentlemen*, vol. 5 (London, 1822).
172 Lovell, 'Benjamin Gott', 186–8.
173 J. Mordaunt Crook, *The Greek Revival* (London, 1972), 31.
174 C.F. Schinkel, *Aus Schinkel's Nachlass* (Berlin, 1863), 86–9.
175 Lovell, 'Benjamin Gott', 215.
176 Sir Thomas Lawrence to Benjamin Gott, 10 October 1827, 20 December 1828, Brotherton Library, Gott Papers 194 2/34, 41.
177 R. Unwin, 'Leeds Becomes a Transport Centre', in Fraser, *A History of Modern Leeds*, 37.
178 J. Hanson, 'The Gott Family of Armley Leeds Part 1' (1926), Brotherton Library, Gott Papers 194 15/5/1.
179 *Comparative Account of the Population of Great Britain* (London, 1831), 324.
180 J.D. Marshall, 'Colonisation as a Factor in the Planting of Towns of North-West England', in H.J. Dyos (ed.), *The Study of Urban History* (London, 1968), 215–29; R. Dennis and S. Daniels, '"Community" and the Social Geography of Victorian Cities', *Urban History Yearbook* (1981), 7–23.
181 Daniels, 'The Implications of Industry'; Arscott et al., 'The Partial View'.
182 Victoria County History, *Essex*, vol. 6, 323–6; John Harris, 'The Artinatural Style', in Charles Hund (ed.), *The Rococo in England* (London, 1974), 9–20; Colin Shrimpton, *The Landed Society and the Farming Community of Essex in the Late Eighteenth and Early Nineteenth Centuries*, unpublished PhD thesis, University of Cambridge, 1965, 35–40; My thanks to the Debois Landscape Survey Group for letting me consult their 1990 Survey of Wanstead Park with its wealth of archival records and field evidence.
183 Shrimpton, 'The Landed Society', 36.
184 Victoria County History, *Essex*, vol. 6, 326.
185 Humphry Repton to William Repton, 24 April 1813, Huntington Library, HM 40892; Humphry Repton to William Tylney Long Pole Wellesey, 22 September 1813, Osborne Files, Beineke Library, Yale University.
186 Ibid.
187 Repton, *Fragments*, 129 (*Works*, 519).
188 Ibid., 133–4 (*Works*, 522–3).
189 *Gentleman's Magazine*, 831, pt 1 (March 1813), 279; Thomas Kitson Cromwell, *Excursions into the County of Essex* (London, 1819), vol. 2, 63.
190 Repton, *Fragments*, 134–6 (*Works*, 522–4).
191 Humphry Repton to William Repton, 3 October 1815, Huntington Library.
192 Repton, *Fragments*, 129 (*Works*, 519).
193 J. Doyley, Survey of Wanstead and Surrounding Parishes (1815–16), Essex Record Office, D/DCY P28:PH 2/30.
194 Shrimpton, 'The Landed Society', 38. Creditors seized the house in 1822, sold the contents and put it up for sale. Failing to find a buyer, the house was demolished for building stone in 1824. The park was let for grazing.

Wellesey lived on, in reduced circumstances, as lord of the manor, until 1856. The park was purchased by the Corporation of London in 1884 and managed for the public as part of Epping Forest. Areas were sold off in the early twentieth century for recreational development. The pattern of Repton's parterre is evident as an earthwork. Debois Landscape Survey Group, *Survey of Wanstead Park*.

195 Humphry Repton to William Repton, 31 March 1816, Huntington Library, HM 40878.
196 Humphry Repton to Sir Harry Fetherstonehaugh, 1 May 1817, Uppark Letters, private collection.
197 Ibid.
198 A.B., 'Biographical Notice of the Late Humphry Repton', in Works, 20.

# BIBLIOGRAPHY

## Manuscripts

### *Red Books, Reports and Drawings*

| Site | County | Date | Archive |
|---|---|---|---|
| Antony | Corn. | Dec. 1792 | Private collection; reprinted in Edward Malins (ed.) *The Red Books of Humphry Repton* London, 1976) |
| Armley | Yorks. | 1810 | Mrs Paul Mellon, Oak Spring Garden Library, Upperville, VA |
| Ashridge | Herts. | Mar. 1814 | Huntington Library, San Marino, CA |
| Aston Park | Chesh. | July 1793 | Mrs Paul Mellon, Upperville, VA |
| Attingham | Salop | Mar. 1798 | National Trust, Attingham |
| Babworth | Notts. | Apr. 1790 | Private collection |
| Barningham | Norfolk | 1807 | Private collection (drawings only) |
| Barton Seagrave | Northants | Apr. 1794 | The Holden Arboretum, Kirtland, OH |
| Bayham Abbey | Kent | Apr. 1800 | The Marquess Camden |
| Beausdesert | Staffs. | Jan. 1814 | Princeton University, Taylor Collection |
| Beeston Leosowes | Beds. | 1798 | Private collection |
| Betchworth | Surrey | Jan. 1800 | Private collection |
| Blaise Castle | Glos. | Feb. 1796 | Bristol Museum and Art Gallery |
| Bracondale | Norfolk | Undated (*c.*1792) | Norfolk Record Office |
| Brandsbury | Middx. | Mar. 1789 | Dumbarton Oaks Library, Washington, DC |
| Buckminster | Leics. | May 1793 | Private collection |
| Burley | Rutland | Apr. 1796 | Private collection |
| Carlton House | London | 1803 | Drawings, Royal Library, Windsor |
| Catchfrench | Corn. | Apr. 1793 | Private collection |
| Claybury | Essex | July 1791 | Essex Record Office |
| Cobham Hall | Kent | Dec. 1790 | Westwood Educational Trust |
| Compton | Sussex | Nov. 1803 | Chatsworth |
| Corridor House | Middx | 1806 | British Architectural Library (Drawings) |
| Courteenhall | Northants | Mar. 1793 | Private collection |
| Culford | Suffolk | May 1792 | Morton Arboretum, Lisle, IL |
| Dullingham | Camb. | Feb. 1802 | Private collection |
| Endsleigh | Devon | Sept.–Oct. 1814 | Woburn Abbey |

| | | | |
|---|---|---|---|
| Felbrigg | Norfolk | 1806 | Colman Collection, Norfolk Record Office (Drawing) |
| Finedon | Northants | May 1793 | Private collection |
| Ferne[y] Hall | Salop | Oct. 1789 | Pierpont Morgan Library, New York |
| Gaines Hall | Hunts. | June 1798 | Private collection |
| Garnons | Heref. | July 1791 | Private collection |
| Glemham Hall | Suffolk | Apr. 1791 | Dumbarton Oaks Library, Washington, DC |
| Glevering Hall | Suffolk | 1793 | Private collection |
| Great Tew | Oxon. | 1803 | Private collection |
| Gunton Hall | Norfolk | c. 1812 | National Trust, Blicking (Drawing) |
| Harewood | Yorks. | 1799 | Leeds District Archives (Report) |
| Hassells | Beds. | Dec. 1791 | F.L.Pym; typescript at Bedfordshire Record Office |
| Hatchlands | Surrey | 1800 | Pierpont Morgan Library, New York |
| Heathfield | Sussex | Apr. 1795 | East Sussex Record Office |
| Henham Hall | Suffolk | Apr. 1791 | Private collection |
| Hewell Grange | Worcs. | Jan. 1812 | Private collection; photographed copy in Gloucestershire Record Office |
| High Legh | Ches. | Oct. 1791 | Private collection |
| Higham Hill | Essex | Feb. 1794 | Vestry House Museum, Walthamstow |
| Hill Hall | Essex | Dec. 1791 | Essex Record Office |
| Holkham Hall | Norfolk | Oct. 1789 | Lord Leicester, Holkham Hall |
| Holme Park | Berks. | Dec. 1793 | Cambridge University Library |
| Honing Hall | Norfolk | May 1792 | Private collection |
| Hooton | Ches. | Oct. 1802 | Architectural Association Library, London |
| Hoveton House | Norfolk | Feb. 1807 | Private collection (Drawings) |
| Hoveton St Peter | Norfolk | 1809 | Norfolk Record Office (Drawings) |
| Kenwood | Middx. | May 1793 | Private collection; facsimile in Scottish Record Office, Edinburgh |
| Kippington | Kent | July 1808 | Royal Academy Library, London |
| Lamer | Herts. | Jan. 1792 | Mizbec Ltd |
| Langley | Kent | Dec. 1790 | British Architectural Library, Drawings Collection |
| Leigh Court | Som. | 1814 | Bristol University Library |
| Little Green | Sussex | Oct. 1793 | West Sussex Record Office |
| Livermere Park | Suffolk | Jan. 1790 | Private collection |
| Longleat | Wilts. | Feb. 1804 | Marquess of Bath, Longleat |
| Longner | Salop | Mar. 1804 | Private collection |
| Luscombe | Devon | June 1799 | Private collection |
| Magdalen College | Oxon. | Jan. 1801 | Magdalen College, Oxford |
| Milton Park | Northants | Sep. 1791 | Private collection |
| Mogenhanger | Beds. | Aug. 1792 | Private collection |
| Montreal | Kent | Jan. 1812 | Private collection; Microfilm of Exported Manuscripts, British Library |
| Moor Hall | Essex | May 1808 | Essex Record Office |
| Mosely Hall | Worcs. | Dec. 1792 | Harvard University, Frances Loeb Library, Cambridge, MA |
| Mulgrave Castle | Yorks. | Aug. 1793 | Private collection |
| Nacton | Suffolk | Feb. 1792 | Private collection |
| New Barnes | Herts. | Sept. 1802 | Private collection |
| New Park | Wilts. | May 1794 | Gloucestershire Record Office disbound (Drawings only) |
| Newton Park | Som. | May 1797 | Mrs Paul Mellon, Oak Spring Garden Library, Upperville, VA |
| Northrepps | Norfolk | undated (c.1792) | Private collection |
| Norton Hall | Northants | Mar. 1809 | Marquess of Bath, Longleat |
| Oulton Hall | Yorks. | Mar. 1810 | Leeds District Archives |
| Ouston | Yorks. | Feb. 1793 | Private collection; sold Christies, 20 April 1983 |
| Panshanger | Herts. | Feb. 1800 | Hertfordshire Record Office |
| Pentillie | Corn. | Feb. 1810 | Private collection |

| | | | |
|---|---|---|---|
| Plas Newydd | Anglesey | Jan. 1799 | National Library of Wales (Text only) |
| Point Pleasant | Surrey | Mar. 1796 | Mrs Paul Mellon, Oak Spring Garden Library, Upperville, VA |
| Port Eliot | Corn. | Feb. 1793 | Private collection |
| Prestwood | Staffs. | Jan. 1791 | Herefordshire Record Office |
| Purley | Berks. | Nov. 1793 | Private collection |
| Riffham Lodge | Essex | 1815 | Private collection |
| Rode Hall | Ches. | Dec. 1790 | Private collection |
| Rose Hill | Sussex | June 1806 | Bodleian Library, Oxford |
| Royal Pavilion, Brighton | Sussex | Feb. 1806 | Royal Library, Windsor |
| Rug Hall | Clwyd | Mar. 1795 | Private collection |
| Sarsden | Oxon. | Mar. 1796 | Private collection |
| Scarisbrick | Lancs. | Jan. 1803 | Sold at Phillips, 11 June 1981, lot 175 |
| Sezincote | Glos. | c.1803 | Royal Institute of British Architects, London (Drawing) |
| Shardeloes | Bucks. | Mar. 1794 | Private collection; photographed copy in Buckinghamshire Record Office |
| Shavington | Salop | Feb. 1793 | Private collection |
| Sheringham | Norfolk | July 1812 | National Trust, on loan to British Architectural Library, Drawings Collection |
| Shrubland | Suffolk | July 1789 | Private collection |
| Spains Hall | Essex | Oct. 1807 | Private collection |
| Stanage Park | Powys | Dec. 1803 | Private collection |
| Stansted Hall | Essex | Feb. 1790 | Essex Record Office |
| Stoke Edith | Heref | Oct. 1792 | Private collection; facsimile in Herefordshire Record Office |
| Stoke Park | Bucks. | June 1812 | Private collection |
| Stoneaston | Som. | Mar. 1793 | Private collection |
| Stonelands | Sussex | July 1806 | Yale University, New Haven |
| Stoneleigh Abbey | War. | May 1809 | Private collection; photocopy in Warwickshire Record Office. |
| Stubbers | Essex | 1796 | University of Essex (damaged, incomplete) |
| Sufton Court | Heref. | July 1795 | Private collection |
| Sundridge Park | Kent | June 1793 | Sundridge Park Management Centre |
| Sunning Hill | Berks. | Jan. 1790 | Sold Christies, 20 April 1983, lot 28 |
| Tavistock | Devon | Aug. 1809 | Bedford Archives, Woburn (Drawing) |
| Tatton Park | Ches. | Feb. 1792 | National Trust, Tatton Park |
| Tewin Water | Herts. | July 1799 | Hertfordshire Record Office |
| The [Royal] Fort | Glos. | Nov. 1801 | Beineke Library, Yale University, New Haven |
| Thoresby | Notts. | Oct. 1791 | Private collection; facsimile in Nottingham University Manuscripts Department |
| Tregothnan | Corn. | 1809 | Private collection |
| Trewarthenick | Corn. | Mar. 1793 | Cornwall Record Office |
| Uppark | Sussex | Oct./Nov. 1810 | Private collection |
| Valleyfield | Fife | c.1801 | Private collection |
| Wall Hall | Herts. | Apr. 1803 | Private collection; photographs at Hertfordshire Record Office |
| Warley | Worc. | Mar. 1795 | Smethwick Library |
| Warsley Park | Camb. | Aug. 1793 | Royal Horticultural Society Library |
| Welbeck | Notts. | Jan. 1790 | Private collection |
| | | May. 1793 | Private collection |
| | | Apr. 1803 | Private collection |
| Wentworth Woodhouse | Yorks. | Jan. 1791 | Private collection |
| Whitton | Middx. | Jan. 1796 | Sold Christies, 14 July 1982, lot 196 |
| Wimpole | Camb. | Oct. 1801 | National Trust, Wimpole |
| Wingerworth | Derbs. | Mar. 1810 | Private collection |

| | | | |
|---|---|---|---|
| Woburn Abbey | Beds. | Jan. 1805 | Woburn Abbey |
| Wood Hall | Norfolk | Feb. 1807 | Private collection |
| Wood Hill | Herts. | Apr. 1803 | Private collection |
| Woodford Hall | Essex | Aug. 1801 | Private collection; photocopy in Essex Record Office |

## Letters, Accounts, Estate Papers

Antony House, Torpoint, Cornwall. Letters between Humphry Repton and Reginald Pole Carew.

Avery Architectural Library, Columbia University, New York. Poems and sketches by Repton and his family.

Bedford Record Office. Woburn Estate Papers. Salmon Papers on improvements to Woburn Abbey.

Beineke Library, Yale University, New Haven. Osborne Files. Letter from Charles Burny to Repton, from Repton to William Tylney Long Pole Wellesey.

Bristol Record Office. Harford papers on improvements to Blaise Castle.

Bristol University Library. Letters from Repton to Norton Nicholls.

British Library, Department of Manuscripts. Draft of Humphry Repton's Memoir. Part Two. Add. MS. 62112; The Windham Papers. Letters from Humphry and William Repton to William Windham, 1783, 1790, 1807. Add. MSS 37873, 37917–19,

Brotherton Library, University of Leeds. Gott Papers.

Devon Record Office. Bedford MSS. Repton Papers; Dorothy Stroud Papers, courtesy of the Garden History Society.

Gloucestershire Record Office. Letters from Humphry Repton relating to Dyrham.

Herefordshire Record Office. Letters relating to Garnons; Account of alterations to Stoke Edith.

Huntington Library, San Marino, CA. Letters between Humphry Repton and other members of his family, principally his son William Repton. HM 40838–40960.

John Rylands Library, University of Manchester. Special Collections. Cornwall-Legh Papers. Letters on Improvements to High Legh.

Linnean Society, London. Scientific Correspondence of Sir James Edward Smith, vol. 8. Letters from Humphry Repton to Smith, 1783–1816.

Newberry Library, Chicago. Four letters between Humphry Repton and Uvedale Price, 1794–5.

Norfolk Record Office. Humphry Repton's Account Book, June 1788–December 1790. Ketton-Cremer MSS. Letters from Humphry Repton to Robert Marsham and to William Cobb, 1778–83.

Northamptonshire Record Office. Freke-Evans (Laxton Collection). Photocopies of letters between Humphry Repton and George Freke Evans relating to Laxton.

Nottingham University Manuscripts Department. Papers of third and fourth dukes of Portland. Account of Repton's Improvements at Welbeck; Inventory of Bulstrode; Letters between William Speechly and the third duke of Portland.

Pierpont Morgan Library, New York, Coleorton MSS. Letters between Uvedale Price and Sir George Beaumont.

Private Collections. Letters on improvements to Kenwood, Longner, Stanage Park and Uppark.

Public Record Office, London. The Will of Humphry Repton, PROB 11 1609.

Royal Library, Windsor. Letter on Improvements to Brighton Pavilion.

Shakespeare Birthplace Trust, Stratford-upon-Avon. Leigh Papers (Stoneleigh).

Sir John Soane's Museum, London. Letters between Humphry Repton and Sir John Soane (uncatalogued).

Staffordshire Record Office. Letters between Repton and J. Boughey on Aqualate 1812–13.

Wakefield Central Library. John Goodchild Loan MSS. Letters on improvements to Armley.

Wiltshire Record Office. Corsham Papers. Invoices and Letters 1797–1803.

## Published Sources

A.B. [John Adey Repton?], 'Biographical Notice of the Late Humphry Repton', in *The Landscape Gardening and Landscape Architecture of the Late Humphry Repton Esq.*, ed. John Claudius Loudon, London, 1840, 1–22.

Adams, Eric, *Francis Danby: Varieties of Poetic Landscape*, New Haven and London, 1973.

Amyot, T. (ed.), *Speeches in Parliament of the Right Honourable William Windham*, 3 vols, London, 1812.

Andrews, Malcolm, *The Search for the Picturesque: Landscape Aesthetics and Tourism in Britain, 1760–1800*, Stanford, 1989.

Angus, William, *The Seats of the Nobility and Gentry of Great Britain and Wales*, London, 1787.

Anon., 'Agriculture and the House of Russell', *Journal of the Royal Agricultural Society*, third series, 2, (1891), 123–45.

Anon., 'Papers of Benjamin Gott', *Publications of the Thoresby Society*, 32 (1929), 231–3.

Anon., Review of Humphry Repton, *Fragments on the Theory and Practice of Landscape Gardening, Quarterly Review*, January 1817, 416–30.

Anon., *A Sketch of the Life of the Late John Duke of Bedford*, Woburn, 1839.

Anon. [William Marshall], Review of Humphry Repton, *Sketches and Hints on the Theory and Practice of Landscape Gardening, Monthly Magazine*, January 1796, 1–10.

Anon. [John Matthews], *A Sketch from the Landscape*, London, 1794.

Anon. [George Saunders], Review of Humphry Repton, *Observations on the Theory and Practice of Landscape Gardening, Monthly Review*, July 1804, 225–40, 349–59.

Appleton, Jay, 'Some Thoughts on the Geology of the Picturesque', *Journal of Garden History*, 6 (1986), 270–92.

——, 'Richard Payne Knight and "The Georgics"', *The Picturesque*, 5 (1993), 1–8.

Armstrong, M.J. (ed.), *History and Antiquities of the County of Norfolk*, vol. 3, Norwich, 1787.

Arscott, Caroline, and Griselda Pollock, with Janet Wolff, 'The Partial View: The Visual Representation of the Early Nineteenth-Century Industrial City', in Janet Wolff and John Seed (eds), *The Culture of Capital: Art, Power and the Nineteenth-Century Middle Class*, Manchester, 1988, 191–234.

Austen, Jane, *Mansfield Park*, London, 1814.

Baetjer, Katherine (ed.), *Glorious Nature! British Landscape Painting 1750–1850*, New York, 1993.

Ballantyne, Andrew, *Architecture, Landscape and Liberty: Richard Payne Knight and the Picturesque*, Cambridge, 1977.

Bantock, Anton, *The Later Smyths of Ashton Court, from Their Letters 1741–1802*, Bishopsworth, 1984.

Baring, Mrs Henry (ed.), *The Diary of the Right Hon. William Windham 1784–1810*, London, 1866.

Barrell, John, *The Dark Side of the Landscape: The Rural Poor in English Painting 1730–1840*, Cambridge, 1980.

——, *The Idea of Landscape and the Sense of Place 1730–1840: An Approach to the Poetry of John Clare*, Cambridge, 1972.

Bartell, Edmund, *Hints for Picturesque Improvement in Ornamented Cottages and Their Scenery*, London, 1804.

Basford, Vicky, *Historic Parks and Gardens of the Isle of Wight*, Newport, Isle of Wight, 1989.

Batchelor, Thomas, *General View of the Agriculture of the County of Bedford*, London, 1808.

Batey, Mavis, 'In Quest of Jane Austen's "Mr. Repton"', *Garden History*, 5 (1977), 19–27.

——, *Jane Austen and the English Landscape*, London, 1996.

——, *Regency Gardens*, Princes Risborough, 1995.

Batty, John, *The History of Rothwell*, Rothwell, 1877.

Beckett, John, *The Aristocracy in England 1660–1914*, London, 1986.

——, *The Rise and Fall of the Grenvilles: The Dukes of Buckingham and Chandos 1710–1921*, Manchester, 1994.

Bentham-Edwards. M. (ed.), *The Autobiography of Arthur Young*, London, 1898.

Beresford, Maurice, 'East End, West End: The Face of Leeds during Urbanization', *Publications of the Thoroton Society*, 60–61 (1985–6).

Bermingham, Ann, *Landscape and Ideology: The English Rustic Tradition 1740–1860*, Berkeley, CA, 1986.

——, 'Reading Constable', in Simon Pugh (ed.), *Reading Landscape: Country–City–Capital*, Manchester, 1990, 97–120.

Bewell, Alan, 'Jacobin Plants: Botany as Social Theory', *Wordsworth Circle*, 20 (1989), 132–9.

Blagdon, Francis, *History of Ancient and Modern India*, London, 1805.

Blakiston, Georgiana, *Woburn and the Russells*, London, 1980.

Booker, Frank, *The Industrial Archaeology of the Tamar Valley*, Newton Abbot, 1967.

Booker, Luke, *The Hop Garden*, Malvern, 1798.

Brandon, Peter, 'The Diffusion of Designed Landscapes in South-East England', in H.S.A. Fox and R.A. Butlin (eds), *Change in the Countryside*, London, 1979, 165–87.

——, *The Sussex Landscape*, London, 1974.

Bray, Anna Elizabeth, *A Description of Devonshire*, 3 vols, London, 1836.

——, *Poetical Remains of the Late Edward Atkyns Bray*, London, 1859.

——, *The Borders of the Tamar and the Tavy*, London, 1879.

Brewer, John, *The Pleasures of the Imagination: English Culture in the Eighteenth Century*, London, 1997.

Bryant, Julius, *Finest Prospects: Three Historic Houses: A Study in London Topography*, London, 1986.

——, *The Iveagh Bequest, Kenwood*, London, 1990.

Bryant, Julius, and Carol Colson, *The Landscape of Kenwood*, London, 1990.

Bull, G.B.G., 'Thomas Milne's Land Utilization Map of the London Area in 1800', *Geographical Journal*, 122 (1956), 25–30.

Busco, Marie, *Sir Richard Westmacott, Sculptor*, Cambridge, 1994.

Butlin, Robin, 'Regions in England and Wales c.1600–1914', in R.A. Butlin and R.A. Dodgshon (eds), *A New Historical Geography of England and Wales*, second edition, London, 1978, 223–54.

Byng, John, *The Torrington Diaries*, ed. C. Bryn Andrews, 3 vols, London, 1936.

Cannadine, David, 'Conspicuous Consumption by the Landed Classes 1790–1830', in *Malthus and His Time*, Michael Turner (ed.), Houndmills, Basingstoke, 1986.

Cannadine, David, *Lords and Landlords: The Aristocracy and the Towns 1774–1967*, Leicester, 1980.
—— (ed.), *Patricians, Power and Politics in Nineteenth-Century Towns*, Leicester, 1982.
Carter, George, 'Humphry Repton at Hare Street, Essex', *Garden History*, 12 (1984), 120–31.
Carter, George, Patrick Goode and Kedrun Laurie, *Humphry Repton: Landscape Gardener 1752–1818*, Norwich and London, 1982.
Carter, Michael J., *Peasants and Poachers: A Study Of Rural Disorder in Norfolk*, Woodbridge, Suffolk, 1980.
*Cary's New Itinerary [of England and Wales]*, ninth edition, London, 1821.
Cave, C., *A History of Banking in Bristol*, Bristol, 1899.
Chancellor, E. Beresford, *History of the Squares of London*, London, 1907.
Chartres, John A., and Gerard Turnbull, 'Road Transport', in Derek Aldcroft and Michael J. Freeman (eds), *Transport in the Industrial Revolution*, Manchester, 1983, 64–99.
Claeys, Gregory, *Thomas Paine, Social and Political Thought*, Boston, 1989.
Clark, J.C.D., *English Society 1688–1832: Ideology, Social Structure and Political Practice During the Ancien Régime*, Cambridge, 1985.
Clarke, Michael, *The Tempting Prospect: A Social History of English Watercolour*, London, 1978.
Clarke, Michael, and Nicholas Penny (eds), *The Arrogant Connoisseur: Richard Payne Knight 1751–1824*, Manchester, 1982.
Clayden, P.W., *Rogers and His Contemporaries*, London, 1889.
Coates, Bryan E., 'Park Landscapes of the East and West Ridings in the Time of Humphry Repton', *Yorkshire Archaeological Journal*, 41 (1965), 465–80.
Coffin, David R., 'Repton's "Red Book" for Beaudesert', *Princeton University Library Chronicle*, 47 (1986), 121–46.
Colley, Linda, *Britons: Forging the Nation 1707–1837*, New Haven and London, 1992.
——, 'Whose Nation? Class and National Consciousness in Britain 1750–1830', *Past and Present*, 113 (1986), 97–117.
Collison, John, *The History and Antiquities of the County of Somerset*, 3 vols, Bath, 1791.
Colvin, Howard, *A Biographical Dictionary of British Architects 1600–1840*, third edition, New Haven and London, 1995.
Connell, E.J., *Industrial Development in South Leeds 1790–1914*, unpublished PhD thesis, University of Leeds, 1975.
Connell, E.J., and M. Ward, 'Industrial Development 1780–1914', in Derek Fraser (ed.), *A History of Modern Leeds*, Manchester, 1980, 142–76.
Conner, Patrick, *Oriental Architecture in the West*, London, 1979.
——, 'Unexecuted Designs for the Royal Pavilion at Brighton', *Apollo*, 107 (1978), 192–9.
Copeland, John, *Roads and Their Traffic*, New Abbot, 1968.
Copley, Stephen, and Peter Garside (eds), *The Politics of the Picturesque*, Cambridge, 1994.
Coppock, J.T., and Hugh C. Prince, *Greater London*, London, 1964.
Corfield, P.J., *The Social and Economic History of Norwich 1650–1850: A Study of Urban Growth*, unpublished PhD thesis, University of London, 1976.
Cosgrove, Denis and Stephen Daniels (eds), *The Iconography of Landscape*, Cambridge, 1988.
Cowell, Fiona, 'Richard Woods (?1716–93): A Preliminary Account, part I: "Woods, Surveyor at Chertsey in Surry and at London Stile"', *Garden History*, 14 (1986), 85–119; '. . . part II: "Mr Wood of Essex"', *Garden History*, 15 (1987), 19–54; '. . . part III: Influences, Style and Working Methods', *Garden History*, 15 (1987), 115–35.
Cromwell, Thomas Kitson, *Excursions into the County of Essex*, vol. 2, London, 1819.
Crook, J. Mordaunt, *The Greek Revival*, London, 1972.
——, 'Metropolitan Improvements: John Nash and the Picturesque', in Celina Fox (ed.), *London – World City 1800–1840*, New Haven and London, 1992, 77–96.
Cruikshank, Dan, and Neil Burton, *Life in the Georgian City*, London, 1990.
Crump, W.B., 'The History of Gott's Mills', *Publications of the Thoresby Society*, 32 (1929), 254–71.
Daniels, Stephen, 'Cankerous Blossom: Troubles in the Later Career of Humphry Repton Documented in the Repton Correspondence in the Huntington Library', *Journal of Garden History*, 6 (1986), 146–61.
——, *Fields of Vision: Landscape Imagery and National Identity in England and the United States*, Cambridge and Princeton, 1993.
——, 'Humphry Repton and the Morality of Landscape', in John C. Gold and Jacqueline Burgess (eds), *Valued Environments*, London, 1982, 124–44.
——, 'Humphry Repton at Sustead', *Garden History*, 11 (1983), 57–64.
——, 'Landscaping for a Manufacturer: Humphry Repton's Commission for Benjamin Gott at Armley in 1809–1810', *Journal of Historical Geography*, 7 (1981), 379–96.
——, 'Loutherbourg's Chemical Theatre: Coalbrookdale By Night', in John Barrell (ed.), *Painting and the Politics of Culture*, Oxford, 1992, 195–230.
——, 'Marxism, Culture and the Duplicity of Landscape', in Richard Peet and Nigel Thrift (eds), *New Models in Geography*, vol. 2, London, 1989, 196–220.
——, 'On the Road with Humphry Repton', *Journal of Garden History*, 16 (1996), 171–91.
——, 'Re-visioning Britain: Mapping and Landscape Painting 1750–1830', in Katherine Baetjer (ed.), *Glorious Nature!*

———, *British Landscape Painting 1750–1850*, New York, 1993, 61–72.

———, 'The Implications of Industry: Turner and Leeds', *Turner Studies*, 6 (1986), 10–17.

———, 'The Political Iconography of Woodland in Later Georgian England', in Denis Cosgrove and Stephen Daniels (eds), *The Iconography of Landscape*, Cambridge, 1988, 43–82.

———, 'The Red Books of Humphry Repton', Introduction to *Humphry Repton: The Red Books for Brandsbury and Glemham Hall*, Washington, DC, 1994.

Daniels, Stephen and Susanne Seymour, 'Landscape Design and the Idea of Improvement', in R.A. Dodgshon and R.A. Butlin (eds), *An Historical Geography of England and Wales*, second edition, London, 1990, 487–520.

Daniels, Stephen, Susanne Seymour and Charles Watkins, 'Border Country: The Politics of the Picturesque in the Middle Wye Valley', in Michael Rosenthal, Christiana Payne and Scott Wilcox (eds), *Prospects for the Nation: Recent Essays in British Landscape, 1750–1880*, New Haven and London, 1997, 157–82.

———, 'Estate and Empire: Sir George Cornewall's Management of Moccas and La Taste', *Journal of Historical Geography*, 24(1998), 313–51.

Daniels, Stephen, and Charles Watkins, 'Picturesque Landscaping and Estate Management. Uvedale Price and Nathaniel Kent at Foxley', in Stephen Copley and Peter Garside (eds), *The Politics of the Picturesque*, Cambridge, 1994, 13–41.

——— (eds), *The Picturesque Landscape: Visions of Georgian Herefordshire*, Nottingham, 1994.

———, Picturesque Landscaping and Estate Management: Uvedale Price at Foxley, 1770–1829', *Rural History*, 2 (1991), 141–69.

Daniell, Thomas, and William Daniell, *Oriental Scenery*, 6 parts, London, 1795–1808.

Davidoff, Leonore, and Catherine Hall, *Family Fortunes: Men and Women of the English Middle Class 1780–1850*, London, 1987.

Denham, P.V., 'The Duke of Bedford's Tavistock Estate, 1820–1838', *Transactions of the Devon Association for the Advancement of Science*, 110 (1978), 19–51.

Dennis, R., and S. Daniels, '"Community" and the Social Geography of Victorian Cities', *Urban History Yearbook* (1981), 7–23.

Desmond, Ray, *The India Museum*, London, 1982.

Desmond, R.G.C., 'A Repton Garden at Haileybury', *Garden History*, 6 (1978), 16–19.

Devine, T.M., 'Glasgow Colonial Merchants and Land, 1770–1815', in J.T. Ward and R.G. Wilson (eds), *Land and Industry: The Landed Estate and the Industrial Revolution*, Newton Abbot, 1971, 205–44.

Digby, Ann, *Pauper Palaces*, London, 1978.

Dinkel, John, *The Royal Pavilion, Brighton*, London, 1983.

Dodd, S., *An Historical and Topographical Account of the Town of Woburn*, Woburn, 1818.

Dodgshon, R.A., and R.A. Butlin (eds), *An Historical Geography of England and Wales*, second edition, London, 1990.

Donoghue, Frank, *The Fame Machine: Book Reviewing and Eighteenth-Century Literary Careers*, Stanford, 1996.

Earl of Roseberry (ed.), *The Windham Papers*, 2 vols, London, 1913.

Elliott, Brent, *Victorian Gardens*, London, 1986.

Errol, A. Campbell, *A History of the Parishes of Sheringham and Beeston Regis*, Norwich, 1970.

Evans, Robin, 'Figures, Doors and Passages', *Architectural Design*, 48 (1978), 267–78.

Everett, Nigel, *The Tory View of Landscape*, New Haven and London, 1994.

Everitt, Alan, 'Country, County and Town: Patterns of Regional Evolution in England', *Transactions of the Royal Historical Society*, 29 (1979), 79–108.

Everson, P., and P.A. Stamper, 'Berwick Maviston and Attingham Park', *Transactions of the Shropshire Archaeological Society*, 65 (1987), 64–70.

*Excursions in the County of Norfolk*, 2 vols, London, 1818.

Farington, Joseph, *The Diary of Joseph Farington*, vol. 1, *July 1793–December 1794*, ed. Kenneth Garlick and Angus Macintyre, New Haven and London, 1978.

———, *The Diary of Joseph Farington*, vol. 3, *September 1796–December 1798*, ed. Kenneth Garlick and Angus Macintyre, New Haven and London, 1979.

———, *The Diary of Joseph Farington*, vol. 9, July 1809–1810, ed. Katherine Cave, New Haven and London, 1982.

Farmer, Alan, 'Colonel Fitzroy's Rustic Villa', *Camden History Review*, 10 (1982), 19–20.

Farrant, Sue, *Georgian Brighton 1740–1820*, University of Sussex Centre for Continuing Education, Occasional Papers, 13 (1980).

———, 'The Development of Landscape Parks and Gardens in Eastern Sussex *c.*1700 to 1820 – A Guide and Gazetteer', *Garden History*, 17 (1989), 166–80.

———, 'The Physical Development of the Royal Pavilion Estate and its Influence on Brighton (East Sussex) 1785–1823', *Sussex Archaeological Collections*, 120 (1982), 171–84.

Fawcett, Trevor, 'Argonauts and Commercial Travellers: The Foreign Marketing of Norwich Stuffs in the Later Eighteenth Century', *Textile History*, 16 (1985), 151–82.

———, 'Measuring the Provincial Enlightenment: The Case of Norwich', *Eighteenth-Century Life*, 8 (1982), 13–27.

———, *Music in Eighteenth-Century Norwich and Norfolk*, Norwich, 1979.

———, *The Rise of English Provincial Art*, Oxford, 1974.

Fleming, John, *Robert Adam and His Circle in Edinburgh and Rome*, London, 1962.

Forbes, James, *Hortus Woburniensis*, London, 1833.

Fox, Celina (ed.), *London – World City 1800–1840*, New Haven and London, 1992.

Fraser, Derek (ed.), *A History of Modern Leeds*, Manchester, 1980.

Fraser, Robert, *General View of the Agriculture of the County of Devon*, London, 1794.

Freeman, Edith, *A Family Story: The Ruggles of Spains Hall*, Sudbury, 1993.

*Gardener's Magazine*, 18 (1842), 590.

Gascoigne, John, *Joseph Banks and the English Enlightenment: Useful Knowledge and Polite Culture*, Cambridge, 1994.

Gerardin, R.L., *An Essay on Landscape*, translated by Daniel Malthus, London, 1783.

Gilbert, Edmund, *Brighton, Old Ocean's Bauble*, London, 1954.

Gilpin, William, *Three Essays: On Picturesque Beauty; On Picturesque Travel; and Sketching Landscape, To Which Is Added a Poem On Landscape Painting*, London, 1794.

Girouard, Mark, *Life in the English Country House: A Social and Architectural History*, New Haven and London, 1978.

Golinski, Jan, *Science and Public Culture: Chemistry and Enlightenment in Britain 1769–1820*, Cambridge, 1992.

Gomme, Andor, Michael Jenner and Bryan Little, *Bristol: An Architectural History*, London, 1979.

Goodchild, Peter, *Humphry Repton: On the Spot at Mulgrave Castle*, n.p., n.d.

——, '"No Phantastical Utopia, But a Reall Place": John Evelyn, John Beale and Backbury Hill, Herefordshire', *Garden History*, 19 (1991), 105–27.

Gorer, Richard, 'The Puzzle of Repton's Roses', *Country Life*, 11 March 1982, 654–6.

Greenacre, Francis, and Sheena Stoddard, *The Bristol Landscape: The Watercolours of Samuel Jackson 1794–1869*, Bristol, 1987.

Gregory, Derek, 'The Fiction of Distance? Information Circulation and the Mails in Early Nineteenth-Century England', *Journal of Historical Geography*, 13 (1987), 130–54.

Gunnis, Rupert, *Dictionary of British Sculptors 1660-1851*, London, 1954.

Hakewill, James, *The History of Windsor and Its Neighbourhood*, London, 1813.

Hallen and Henbury Women's Institute, *A History of Henbury*, Bristol, 1993.

Hamilton, Harlan W., *Doctor Syntax: A Silhouette of William Combe Esq.*, London, 1969.

Harcourt, Leslie, *Mr Methuen's House*, Weston-super-Mare, 1981.

Harding, Stewart, and David Lambert, *Parks and Gardens of Avon*, Bristol, 1994.

Harford, Alice (ed.), *Annals of the Harford Family*, London, 1909.

Harris, John, 'Bulstrode', *Architectural Review*, 134 (1958), 319–20.

—— (ed.), *A Catalogue of British Drawings for Architecture, Decoration, Sculpture and Landscape Gardening 1550–1900*, New York, 1971.

——, 'The Artinatural Style', in Charles Hund (ed.), *The Rococo in England*, London, 1974, 9–20.

—— (ed.), *The Garden: A Celebration of a Thousand Years of British Gardening*, London, 1979.

Harvey, A.D., *Britain in the Early Nineteenth Century*, London, 1978.

Haslam, Richard, 'Rûg, Clwyd II', *Country Life*, 13 October 1983, 986–9.

Heaton, H., 'Benjamin Gott and the Industrial Revolution', *Economic History Review*, 3 (1931), 45–66.

Hemingway, Andrew, *Landscape Imagery and Urban Culture in Early Nineteenth-Century Britain*, Cambridge, 1992.

Hichberger, J.W.M., *Images of the Army: the Military in British Art 1815–1914*, Manchester, 1988.

Hodson, J.H. et al., 'The Building and Alteration of the Second Thoresby House 1767–1804', *A Nottinghamshire Miscellany*, Thoroton Society Record Series, 21 (1962), 16–20.

Horn, Pamela, 'An Eighteenth-Century Land Agent: The Career of Nathaniel Kent 1737–1810', *Agricultural History Review*, 30 (1982), 1–16.

——, *William Marshall (1745–1818) and the Georgian Countryside*, Sutton Courtenay, Abingdon, 1982.

Horner, J., *Nine Views of Blaise Hamlet*, 1825.

Hornor, Thomas, *Description of an Improved Method of Delineating Estates with a Sketch of the Progress of Landscape Gardening in England*, London, 1813.

Howitt, William, *The Northern Heights*, London, 1869.

Hunt, John Dixon (ed.), *Garden History: Issues, Approaches, Methods*, Washington, DC, 1980.

——, 'Sense and Sensibility in the Designs of Humphry Repton', *Studies in Burke and His Time*, 19 (1978), 3–28.

Hunter, Henry, *The History of London and Its Environs*, London, 1811.

Hussey, Christopher, *English Country Houses: Late Georgian 1800-1840*, London, 1958.

——, 'Endsleigh, Devon, II', *Country Life*, 10 August 1961, 296–9.

——, 'Great Tew, Oxfordshire, I', *Country Life*, 22 July 1949, 254–7.

——, *The Picturesque: Studies in a Point of View*, London, 1927.

Ison, Walter, *The Georgian Buildings of Bristol*, London, 1952.

Jacques, David, *Georgian Gardens: The Reign of Nature*, London, 1983.

Jewson, C.B., *The Jacobin City: A Portrait of Norwich in Its*

Joyce, Patrick, *Reaction to the French Revolution 1788–1802*, Glasgow and London, 1975.

Joyce, Patrick, *Democratic Subjects: The Self and the Social in Nineteenth-Century England*, Cambridge, 1994.

Kent, Nathaniel, *General View of the Agriculture of Norfolk*, London, 1796.

Ketton-Cremer, R.W., *A Norfolk Gallery*, London, 1948.

——, *Country Neighbourhood*, London, 1951.

——, *Felbrigg: The Story of a House*, Ipswich, 1962.

Kirkham, Caroline, 'Hafod: Paradise Lost', *Journal of Garden History*, 11 (1991), 207–16.

Knight, Richard Payne, *An Analytical Inquiry into the Principles of Taste*, London, 1805.

——, *The Landscape: A Didactic Poem*, London, 1794; second edition, London, 1795.

Kriz, Kay Diane, *The Idea of the English Landscape Painter: Genius as Alibi in the Early Nineteenth Century*, New Haven and London, 1997.

Laird, Mark, '*Corbeille*, *Parterre* and *Treillage*: The Case of Humphry Repton's Penchant for the French Style of Planting', *Journal of Garden History*, 16 (1996), 153–69.

Lambin, Denis, 'Foxley: The Price's Estate in Herefordshire', *Journal of Garden History*, 7 (1987), 244–70.

Langford, Paul, *A Polite and Commercial People: England 1727–1783*, Oxford, 1992.

Langton, John, 'The Industrial Revolution and the Regional Geography of England', *Transactions of the Institute of British Geographers*, 9 (1984), 131–44.

Latimer, John, *The Annals of Bristol in the Eighteenth Century*, Bristol, 1893.

Laugero, Greg, 'Infrastructures of Enlightenment: Roadmaking, the Public Sphere and the Emergence Of Literature', *Eighteenth Century Studies*, 29 (1995), 45–67.

Laurie, Kedrun, 'Humphry Repton 1752–1818: New Discoveries', *The Garden*, September 1983, 361–5.

Leach, Francis (ed.), *The County Seats of Shropshire*, Shrewsbury, 1891.

Linstrum, Derek, *Sir Jeffry Wyatville: Architect to the King*, London, 1972.

Liscombe, R.W., *William Wilkins 1778–1839*, Cambridge, 1980.

Little, Bryan, *The City and County of Bristol: A Study in Atlantic Civilization*, London, 1954.

Lonsdale, Roger, *Dr Charles Burney: A Literary Biography*, Oxford, 1965.

Loudon, John Claudius, *A Treatise on Forming, Improving and Managing Country Residences*, 2 vols, London, 1806.

——, *Encyclopaedia of Gardening*, 1822; revised 1824.

——, *Hints on the Formation of Gardens and Pleasure Grounds*, London, 1812.

——, 'Hints Respecting the Manner of Laying out the Grounds of the Public Squares in London, to the Utmost Picturesque Advantage', *Literary Journal*, 2 ([31 December] 1803), cols 739–42.

——, *Observations on Laying Out Farms in the Scotch Style*, London, 1812.

——, *Observations on the Formation and Management of Useful and Ornamental Plantations, on the Theory and Practice of Landscape Gardening*, Edinburgh and London, 1804.

——, *The Landscape Gardening and Landscape Architecture of the Late Humphry Repton Esq.*, London, 1840.

——, *The Suburban Gardener and Villa Companion*, London, 1838.

Lovell, Veronica, ' Benjamin Gott of Armley House, Leeds, 1762-1840: Patron of the Arts', *Publications of the Thoresby Society*, 59–61 (1985–6), 177–221.

Lowe, Robert, *General View of the Agriculture of the County of Nottingham*, London, 1798.

Lucas, Paul, 'A Collective Biography of Students and Barristers of Lincoln's Inn 1680–1804: A Study in the "Aristocratic Resurgence" of the Eighteenth Century', *Journal of Modern History*, 46 (1974), 227–61.

McDougall, Elizabeth (ed.), *John Claudius Loudon and the Early Nineteenth Century in England*, Washington, DC, 1980.

McGrath, Patrick, *Bristol in the Eighteenth Century*, Newton Abbot, 1972.

McKendrick, Neil, John Brewer and J.H. Plumb, *The Birth of Consumer Society*, London, 1982.

Malins, Edward, *The Red Books of Humphry Repton*, London, 1976.

Malton, James, *Essay on British Cottage Architecture*, London, 1798.

Manning, I.M., *A History of Old Catton*, Catton, 1981.

Marshall, J.D., 'Colonisation as a Factor in the Planting of Towns of North-West England', In H.J. Dyos (ed.), *The Study of Urban History*, London, 1968, 215–29.

Marshall, William, *A Review of 'The Landscape' and 'Essay on the Picturesque'*, London, 1795.

——, *Planting and Rural Ornament*, 2 vols, London, 1796.

——, *The Rural Economy of Norfolk*, London, 1787.

——, *The Rural Economy of the West of England*, London, 1796.

[Marshall, William], Review of Humphry Repton, *Sketches and Hints on Landscape Gardening*, *Monthly Review*, January 1796, 1–10.

Martins, Susanna Wade, *A Great Estate at Work: Holkham and Its Inhabitants in the Nineteenth Century*, Cambridge, 1980.

Mason, George, *An Essay on Design in Gardening*, second edition, London, 1795.

Mason, William, *The English Garden: A Poem in Four Books*, London, 1777.

[Matthews, John], *A Sketch from the Landscape*, London, 1794.

Meade-Fetherstonehaugh, M., and O. Warner, *Uppark and Its People*, London, 1964.

Messman, Frank J., *Richard Payne Knight: The Twilight of Virtuosity*, The Hague, 1974.

Middleton, John, *General View of the Agriculture of the County of Middlesex*, London, 1813.

Miller, David Philip, and Peter Hanns Reill (eds), *Visions of Empire: Voyages, Botany and Representations of Nature*, Cambridge, 1996.

Minchinton, W.E., 'Bristol – Metropolis of the West in the Eighteenth Century', *Transactions of the Royal Historical Society*, fifth series, 4 (1954), 69–89.

*Monthly Review*, July 1804, 225–359.

Morley, John, *Regency Design 1790–1840*, London, 1993.

Morris, David, *Thomas Hearne and His Landscape*, London, 1989.

Morris, R.J., 'Middle-Class Culture 1700–1914', in Derek Fraser (ed.), *A History of Modern Leeds*, Manchester, 1980, 200–22.

Morus, Iwan, Simon Schaffer and Jim Secord, 'Scientific London', in Celina Fox (ed.), *London – World City 1800–1840*, New Haven and London, 1992, 129–42.

Mowl, Tim, and Brian Earnshaw, *Trumpet at a Distant Gate: The Lodge as Prelude to the Country House*, London, 1985.

National Trust, *Attingham Park*, London, 1994.

Neale, J.P., *Views of the Seats of Noblemen and Gentlemen*, vol. 5, London, 1822.

Nord, Deborah Epstein, 'The City as Theater: From Georgian to Victorian London', *Victorian Studies* (1988), 160–88.

Ogborn, Miles, *Spaces of Modernity: London's Geographies, 1680–1780*, New York and London, 1998.

Olsen, Donald J., *Town Planning in London: The Eighteenth and Nineteenth Centuries*, second edition, New Haven and London, 1982.

Oresko, Robert (ed.), *The Works in Architecture of Robert and James Adam*, London, 1975.

Papworth, John Buonarotti, *Hints on Ornamental Gardening*, London, 1823.

——, *Rural Residences*, London, 1818.

Parker, George, 'Tyndall's Park, Bristol, Fort Royal and the Fort House Therein', *Transactions of the Bristol and Gloucestershire Archaeological Society*, 51 (1929), 123–41.

Parker, R.A.C., *Coke of Norfolk: A Financial and Agricultural Study 1707–1842*, Oxford, 1978.

Parry, J.D., *A Guide to Woburn Abbey*, Woburn, 1831.

Pawson, Eric, *Transport and Economy: The Turnpike Roads of Eighteenth-Century Britain*, London, 1977.

Peacock, A.J., *Bread or Blood: A Study of the Agrarian Riots in East Anglia in 1816*, London, 1965.

Pemberton, A., 'Two Hundred Years of Banks in Leeds', *Publications of the Thoresby Society*, 46 (1963), 54–86.

Penny, Nicholas, *Church Monuments in Romantic England*, New Haven, 1977.

Pevsner, Nikolaus, 'Humphry Repton: A Florilegium', *Architectural Review*, January 1948, 53–9.

Phibbs, John, 'A Reconsideration of Repton's Contribution to the Improvements at Felbrigg, Norfolk, 1778–84', *Garden History*, 16 (1988), 33–44.

Piebenga, Sophieke, 'William Sawrey Gilpin (1762–1843): Picturesque Improver', *Garden History*, 22 (1994), 175–96.

Pointon, Marcia, 'Aesthetic and Commodity: An Examination of the Verbal in Turner's Artistic Practice', in Simon Pugh (ed.), *Reading Landscape: Country–City–Capital*, Manchester, 1990, 81–96.

——, *Hanging the Head: Portraiture and Social Formation in Eighteenth-Century England*, New Haven and London, 1993.

Porter, Roy, *English Society in the Eighteenth Century*, London, 1982.

Price, John, *An Historical Account of the City of Hereford*, Hereford, 1796.

Price, Uvedale, *Essays on the Picturesque*, 3 vols, London, 1810.

——, *Thoughts on the Defence of Property*, Hereford, 1797.

Prince, C. Hugh, 'England circa 1800', in H.C. Darby (ed.), *A New Historical Geography of England after 1600*, Cambridge, 1976, 89–164.

——, 'Parkland in the Chilterns', *Geographical Review*, 49 (1959), 18–31.

——, *Parks in England*, Shalfleet Manor, Isle of Wight, 1967.

——, 'The Changing Landscape of Panshanger', *Transactions of the East Herts Archaeological Society*, 14 (1959), 42–58.

——, 'The Changing Rural Landscape 1750–1850', in G.E. Mingay (ed.), *The Agrarian History of England and Wales*, vol. 6, *1750–1850*, Cambridge, 1989, 7–83.

Pugsley, Steven (ed.), *Devon Gardens: An Historical Survey*, Stroud, 1994.

Pullan, Ann, 'Conversations on the Arts: Writing a Space for the Female Viewer in the *Repository of Arts* 1809–15', *Oxford Art Journal*, 15 (1992), 12–26.

Quaintance, Richard, 'Humphry Repton, "any Mr Repton", and the "Improvement" Metonym in *Mansfield Park*', *Studies in Eighteenth-Century Culture*, 27 (1998), 365–84.

Repton, Humphry, *An Enquiry into the Changes of Taste in Landscape Gardening*, London, 1806.

——, *Designs for the Pavillon at Brighton*, London, 1808.

——, *Fragments on the Theory and Practice of Landscape Gardening*, London, 1816.

——, *Humphry Repton: The Red Books for Brandsbury and Glemham*, ed. Stephen Daniels, Washington, DC, 1994.

——, *A Letter to Uvedale Price, Esq.*, London, 1794.

——, 'Observations on the Supposed Effects of Ivy upon Trees', *Transactions of the Linnean Society*, 11 (1815), 27–34.

——, *Observations on the Theory and Practice of Landscape Gardening*, London, 1803.

——, *Odd Whims and Miscellanies*, 2 vols, London, 1804.

——, *Sketches and Hints on Landscape Gardening*, London, 1795.

——, *The Bee: A Critique on the Exhibition at Somerset House*, London, 1788.

——, *The Bee; Or, a Companion to the Shakespeare Gallery*, London, 1789.

——, 'The Hundreds of North and South Erpingham', in M.J. Armstrong (ed.), *History and Antiquities of Norfolk*, vol. 3, Norwich, 1787.

——, *The Landscape Gardening and Landscape Architecture of the Late Humphry Repton*, ed. J.C. Loudon, London, 1840.

——, *The Work of Twenty Years Brought to a Crisis in Twenty Days!*, Romford, 1814.

——, *Variety: A Collection of Essays*, London, 1787.

Repton, John Adey, 'Oxnead Hall, Norfolk', *Gentleman's Magazine*, New Series 21 (1844), 21–44.

Risdon, Tristram, *The Chronological Description and Survey of the County of Devon*, London, 1811.

Ritvo, Harriet, *The Animal Estate: The English and Other Creatures in Victorian England*, Cambridge, MA, 1987.

Roberts, Henry D., *A History of the Royal Pavilion, Brighton*, London, 1939.

Robertson, John Martin, 'Estate Buildings of the Fifth and Sixth Dukes of Bedford at Woburn 1787–1839', *Architectural Review*, 60 (1976), 276–81.

Robinson, Sidney K., *Inquiry into the Picturesque*, Chicago, 1991.

Robson, Robert, *The Attorney in Eighteenth-Century England*, Cambridge, 1959.

Rooke, Hayman, *A Sketch of the Ancient and Present State of Sherwood Forest*, Nottingham, 1799.

——, *Description and Sketches of Some Remarkable Oaks in the Park at Welbeck*, London, 1790.

Ruggles, Thomas, *The History of the Poor*, 2 vols, London, 1793–4.

Rosenthal, Michael, *Constable: The Painter and His Landscape*, New Haven and London, 1983.

Rosenthal, Michael, Christiana Payne and Scott Wilcox (eds), *Prospects for the Nation: Recent Essays in British Landscape 1750–1880*, New Haven and London, 1997.

Sanecki, Kay, *Humphry Repton*, Princes Risborough, 1974.

[Saunders, George], Review of Humphry Repton, *Observations on the Theory and Practice of Landscape Gardening, Monthly Review*, July 1804, 225–40, 349–59.

Sapwell, J., *A History of Aylsham*, Aylsham, 1960.

Savage, Robert J.G., 'Natural History in the Goldney Garden Grotto, Bristol', *Garden History*, 17 (1989), 1–40.

Schinkel, C.F., *Aus Schinkel's Nachlass*, Berlin, 1863.

Searle, Arthur, and Colin Brazier, *A History of Hare Hall*, n.p., 1960.

Seward, Anna, *The Poetical Works of Anna Seward*, ed. Walter Scott, 3 vols, Edinburgh, 1810.

——, *The Letters of Anna Seward Written between the Years 1784 and 1807*, ed. A. Constable, 6 vols, Edinburgh, 1811.

Seymour, Susanne, 'The Dukeries Estates: Improving Land and Landscape in the Later Eighteenth Century', *Transactions of the Thoroton Society*, 97 (1993), 117–28

——, *Eighteenth-Century Parkland 'Improvement' on the Dukeries Estates of North Nottinghamshire*, unpublished PhD thesis, University of Nottingham, 1988.

Shiercliff, J., *Bristol and Hotwells Guide*, Bristol, 1793.

Shoesmith, Ron, *Hereford: History and Guide*, Stroud, 1992.

Shortland, Michael and Richard Yeo (eds), *Telling Lives in Science: Essays on Scientific Biography*, Cambridge, 1996.

Shrimpton, Colin, *The Landed Society and the Family Community of Essex in the Late Eighteenth and Early Nineteenth Centuries*, unpublished PhD thesis, University of Cambridge, 1965.

Simo, Melanie Louise, *Loudon and the Landscape: From Country Seat to Metropolis 1783–1843*, New Haven and London, 1988.

Simon, Jacob, 'Humphry Repton at Kenwood', *Camden History Review*, 11 (1984), 4–11.

Slater, T.R., 'Family, Society and the Ornamental Villa on the Fringes of English Country Towns', *Journal of Historical Geography*, 4 (1978), 129–44.

Smiles, Sam, 'Turner in the West Country: From Topography to Idealisation', in J.C. Eade (ed.), *Projecting the Landscape*, Canberra, 1987, 36–53.

Smiles, Sam, and Michael Pidgley, *The Perfection of England, Artist Visitors to Devon, c.1750–1870*, Plymouth, 1995.

Smith, James Edward, *Tour to Hafod*, London, 1810.

Smith, Paul, *The Landed Estate as a Patron of Scientific Innovation: Horticulture and Agriculture at Woburn Abbey*, unpublished PhD thesis, Open University, 1983.

Snell, Keith, *Annals of the Labouring Poor: Social Change in Agrarian England 1660–1900*, Cambridge, 1985.

Solkin, David, *Richard Wilson: The Landscape of Reaction*, London, 1983.

Spargo, Delmelza, *This Land is Our Land: Aspects of Agriculture in English Art*, London, 1989.

Sparkes, I.G., *Gidea Hall and Gidea Park*, Romford, 1966.

Spring, David, *The English Landed Estate in the Nineteenth Century: Its Administration*, Baltimore, 1963.

Stembridge, P.K., *Thomas Goldney's Garden*, Bristol, 1996.

Stirling, A.M.W., *Coke of Norfolk and His Friends*, London, 1912, 233–4.

Stone, Richard, 'The Creation of Endsleigh: A Regency Masterpiece', in Steven Pugsley (ed.), *Devon Gardens: An Historical Survey*, Stroud, 1994, 76–90.

Storer, J., and J. Brewer, *Delineations of Gloucestershire*, London, 1824.

Strong, Roy, *Royal Gardens*, London, 1992.

Stroud, Dorothy, *Capability Brown*, London, 1975.
——, *Henry Holland*, London, 1966.
——, *Humphry Repton*, London, 1962.
Stroud, George Sinclair, *Hortus Gramineus Woburniensis*, London, 1816.
Summerson, John, 'A Repton Portfolio', *Journal of the Royal Institute of British Architects*, 25 February 1933, 313–24.
——, *John Nash*, London, 1980.
Taigel, Anthea, and Tom Williamson, 'Some Early Geometric Gardens in Norfolk', *Journal of Garden History*, 11 (1991), 82–3.
Tait, A.A., *The Landscape Garden in Scotland 1735–1835*, Edinburgh, 1980.
Tate Gallery, *Landscape in Britain c.1750–1850*, London, 1973.
Temple, Nigel, *George Repton's Pavilion Notebook: A Catalogue Raisonné*, Aldershot, 1993.
——, 'Humphry Repton, Illustrator, and William Peacock's *Polite Repository* 1790–1811', *Garden History*, 13 (1985), 161–73.
——, *John Nash and the Village Picturesque*, Gloucester, 1979.
——, 'Reptoniana', *Journal of Garden History*, 3 (1983), 55–7.
*The Beauties of England and Wales*, vol. 3, ed. E.W. Brayley, and J. Britton, London, 1803.
*The Beauties of England and Wales*, vol. 5, ed. E.W. Brayley, and J. Britton, London, 1803.
*The Beauties of England and Wales*, vol. 6, ed. E.W. Brayley, and J. Britton, London, 1805.
*The Beauties of England and Wales*, vol. 11, ed. J. Evans and J. Britton, London, 1810.
Thompson, E.P., *Customs in Common*, London, 1993.
——, *Whigs and Hunters: The Origins of the Black Act*, London, 1975.
Thompson, F.M.L., *Hampstead: The Building of a Borough 1650–1964*, London, 1974.
Thoroton, R., *The Antiquities of Nottinghamshire*, ed. J. Throsby, Nottingham, 1796.
Thrift, Nigel, 'Inhuman Geographies: Landscapes of Speed, Light and Power', in Paul Cloke, Marcus Doel, David Matless, Martin Phillips and Nigel Thrift (eds), *Writing the Rural: Five Cultural Geographies*, London, 1994, 191–248.
Tillotson, G.H.R., 'The Indian Picturesque: Images of India in British Landscape Painting, 1780–1880', in C.A. Bayly (ed.), *The Raj: India and the British 1600–1947*, London, 1990, 141–51.
Trinder, Barrie, *The Industrial Revolution in Shropshire*, London and Chichester, 1981.
Turbeville, A.S., *A History of Welbeck Abbey and Its Owners*, vol. 2, 1755–1879, London, 1934.
Vancouver, Charles, *General View of the Agriculture of the County of Devon*, London, 1808.
Victoria County History: *Essex*, vol. 5, London, 1966; vol. 6, London, 1973.
Victoria County History: *Middlesex*, vol. 9, Oxford and London, 1989.
Victoria County History: *Sussex*, vol. 6, part 3, London, 1987.
Wallace, Anne D., *Walking, Literature and English Culture: the Origins and Uses of Peripatetic in the Nineteenth Century*, Oxford, 1994.
Warner, Tim, 'Combined Utility and Magnificence: Humphry Repton's Commission for Wingerworth Hall in Derbyshire', *Journal of Garden History*, 7 (1987), 271–301.
Watkin, David, *The Life and Work of C.R. Cockerell*, London, 1974.
——, *Thomas Hope 1769–1831 and the Neo-Classical Ideal*, London, 1968.
Watkins, Charles, Stephen Daniels and Susanne Seymour, 'Uvedale Price's Marine Picturesque at Aberystwyth, 1790–1829', *The Picturesque*, 14 (1996), 1–11.
Whately, Thomas, *Observations on Modern Gardening*, London, 1770.
Whitaker, T.D., *Loidis et Elmete*, Leeds, 1816.
Whitehead, David, 'Belmont, Herefordshire: The Development of a Picturesque Estate 1788–1827', *The Picturesque*, 11 (1995), 1–9; 12 (1995), 1–11.
——, 'John Nash and Humphry Repton: An Encounter in Herefordshire 1785–98', *Transactions of the Woolhope Naturalists Field Club*, 47 (1992), 210–36.
——, 'Repton and the Picturesque Debate: The Text of the Sufton Red Book', *The Picturesque*, 1 (1992–3), 6–17.
——, 'Sense with Sensibility: Landscaping in Georgian Herefordshire', in Stephen Daniels and Charles Watkins (eds), *The Picturesque Landscape: Visions of Georgian Herefordshire*, Nottingham, 1994, 16–33.
——, 'The Purchase and Building of Stoke Edith Park, Herefordshire 1670–1707', *Transactions of the Woolhope Naturalists Field Club*, 43 (1980), 181–202.
Williams, Gareth, 'An Examination of Two Repton Red Books and their Historical, Social and Economic Contexts: Attingham Park and Longner Hall', unpublished MA thesis, University of Manchester, 1993.
——, 'Edward Haycock and the Picturesque: The Country House Practice of a Border Architect', unpublished BA thesis, Department of History of Art, University of Manchester, 1992.
Williams, Robin, 'Rural Economy and the Antique in the English Landscape Garden', *Journal of Garden History*, 7 (1987), 73–96.
Williamson, Tom, 'Parks in the 18th and 19th Centuries', in Peter Wade-Martins (ed.), *An Historical Atlas of Norfolk*, Norfolk, 1993.
——, *Polite Landscapes: Gardens and Society in Eighteenth-Century England*, Stroud and Baltimore, 1995.
——, *The Archaeology of the Landscape Park: Garden Design in Norfolk 1680–1870*, Oxford, 1998.

——, 'The Landscape Park: Economics, Art and Ideology', *Journal of Garden History*, 13 (1993), 49–55.

——, *The Origins of Norfolk*, Manchester, 1993.

Williamson, Tom, and Anthea Taigel (eds), *Gardens in Norfolk*, Norwich, 1990.

Willis, Peter (ed.), *Furor Hortensis: Essays in the History of the English Landscape Garden in Memory of H.F. Clark*, Edinburgh, 1974.

Wilmot, Sarah, *The Business of Improvement: Agriculture and Scientific Culture in Britain c.1700–c.1870*, Norwich, 1990.

Wilson, R.G., *Gentlemen Merchants: The Merchant Community in Leeds 1700–1830*, Manchester, 1971.

Woolrich, A.P., 'An American in Gloucestershire and Bristol: The Diary of Joshua Gilpin, 1796–7', *Transactions of the Bristol and Gloucester Archaeological Society*, 92 (1973), 169–89.

Wright, Nigel, *The Gentry and their Houses in Norfolk and Suffolk from circa 1550 to 1850*, unpublished PhD thesis, University of East Anglia, 1990.

Yaxley, Susan (ed.), *Sherringhamia: The Journal of Abbot Upcher 1813–16*, Stibbard, Norfolk, 1986.

Young, Arthur, *General View of the Agriculture of Essex*, London, 1813.

——, *General View of the Agriculture of Norfolk*, London, 1804.

# Index

*Note:* a full list of the sites and clients of Humphry Repton's consultations is given in the Gazetteer, pp. 255–70.

Abbot, Charles, 90–91, 98, 194
Aberystwyth, 116, 135
Ackermann, Rudolph (see *Repository of Arts*)
approaches, 48–9, 98–9
architecture, 14–16, 164–5 (see also Gothic; Repton, John Adey; Nash, John; Wilkins, William; Wyatt, James; Wyattville, Jeffry)
Adam, Robert, 51, 219–223
  *View of the South Front of the Villa at Kenwood*, fig. 215
Adam, William, 177, 183, 186, 189
Adey, Dorothy, 67, 69
agriculture, 28, 54, 69–70, 72–6, 85–6, 89, 91–2, 97, 104, 106, 111, 123, 131, 145, 166, 189, 213
Armley, 245–50, *figs 238, 240, 242, 243, 244*
Armstrong, M.J.
  *History and Antiquities of the County of Norfolk*, 69, 91, 101
Appleton, Jay, 110
Ashridge, 46, 49, 50, 189, *figs 44, 50*
Ashton Court, 238–9, *fig. 234*
Aspley Wood,
  cottage at, 47, 179–80, *fig. 175*
Attingham, 131–4, *figs 133, 134*
Austen, Jane
  *Mansfield Park*, 25, 143, 286–7 n.24
  *Northanger Abbey*, 230
Aylsham, 67, 69–70, 101, 166, 186, *figs 69, 70, 105*

Babworth, 12–13, 55–6, *figs 8, 38*
Baconsthorpe Hall, *fig. 74*
Ballantyne, Andrew, 110, 111, 142
Banks, Joseph, 72, 178–9
Barningham, 90, 93, *fig. 94*
Barr, Thomas, 183
Barrell, John, viii, 28
Barrett, George
  Views of Welbeck, 301–02 n.53
Bartell, Edmund, 89, 92
Bath, 32, 35, 130, 239
Baty, Mavis, 140
Beaudesert, 49–50, *fig. 52*
Beaumont, Sir George, 114, 126, 134
Beckford, William, 38
Bedford, Sixth Duchess of, 173, 187
Bedford, Fifth Duke of, 181, *fig. 178*
Bedford, Sixth Duke of, 170–90
Bedford, Thomas, 100
Bedford House, 180
Bedfordshire, 170–71, *fig. 167*
Beeston St Lawrence, 84
beggars, 62–5
Belmont, 126, *fig. 126*
Benyon, Richard, 59–60
Berwick, Lord, 131
Biggleswade Fair, 4
Birmingham, 208
Black, Alexander, 61–2, 63
Blagdon, Francis
  *History of Ancient and Modern India*, 197

Blaise Castle, 48–9, 230–35, *figs 47, 48, 224, 227, 228, 229, 230*
Blaise Hamlet, 235, *fig. 231*
Blayds, John, 243–5
Bloomsbury, 180–83
Bonaparte, Napoleon, 20, 153
Booker, Luke
  *The Hop Garden*, 121
botany, 20–21
Boydell, John, 130
  The Shakespeare Gallery, 8–9, 13, 209
Boydell, Josiah, 90
Bracondale, 86–7, *fig. 90*
Brandsbury, 6, 214–19, *figs 6, 15, 211, 212, 213, 214*
Bray, Edward the Younger, 184
Brentry Hill, 235–6, *fig. 232*
Brewer, John, 21
Brighton, 192, 204, 207–08, *fig. 189*
Brighton Pavilion, 18, 192–205, *figs 24, 190, 191, 192, 194, 196, 198, 203, 204*
Bristol, 188, 228–242, *fig. 223*
Brown, Lancelot 'Capability', 79, 103, 104, 142, 149–50, 161, 167, 168, 175, 209, 212, 226, 252, 301 n.10
  as Repton's predecessor, 1, 16, 103, 149
  at Kenwood, 219
  at Stanmore, 215
  at Temple Newsam, 243
  followers of, 16, 104, 122
  style of, 47, 111, 112, 115, 124, 134, 166

Buchan Hill, 228
Bulstrode, 48, 166–70, *figs 163, 164, 165, 166*
Burke, Edmund, 123, 126, 166–7, 228
  *Letter to a Noble Lord*, 171
  on aesthetics, 4, 7, 111
  Repton's work commended by, 35, 51, 54, 122, 125
Burlington House, 154, 155, 157, 166
Burney, Charles, 167
Burney, Fanny, 88
Burton, Edward,
  tomb of, 138, *fig. 137*
Burton, Robert, 138
Buxton, 58
Byng, John, 76, 103, 205
Byron, Lord (see Hobhouse, John Cam)

Camden, Lord, 21, 129, 285 n.44
canals, 132, 247
Cannadine, David, 300 n.3
Carew, Reginald Pole, 35, 113
Carr, John, 158, 160, 161
*Cary's New Itinerary*, 30, *fig. 30*
Carter, George, viii, 284 n.1
Carlton House, 194, 203, 251, *fig. 193*
Cashiobury, 194
Catton, 79–80, 84, *figs 82, 83, 84*
Chamberlayne, Edward, 74
character, in portraiture and landscape gardening, 21–2
Chatsworth, 155, 161
Claude (Lorrain), 110, 122, 132, 146, 168
Claybury, 206, 212, *figs 17, 209*
Clerke, Lady Jennings, 191
Coape, John, 62
Cobbett, William
  on roads and society, 28, 30
Cobham, 47, 117, 151, 163
Cockerell, C.R., 235
Cockerell, Sir Charles, 194
Cockerell, Samuel Pepys, 194
Coke, Jane, 82
Coke, Thomas, 77–8, 80–84, 92, 171
Colchester, Lord, 150
Colley, Linda, 150
Colson, Carol, 307 n.46
Combe, William, 43, 123, 298 n.112
commons, 52–3, 76, 92
conduct, 27–30
Conner, Patrick, 197
Conway, *fig. 32*
Constable, Abram
  on beggars, 63
Constable, John
  paintings of Golding Constable's gardens, 290 n.192
  counties as cultural formations, 67–8, 105–08

Coryton, Charles, 184
Cotman, J.S.,
  *Sheringham Hall*, 100, *fig. 104*
cottages, 79–80, 83, 119, 187–8
Cotterell, John Geers, 36–7, 87, 117–19, 142
Coventry, Earl of, 210–11
Crabbe, George
  *The Borough*, 98
Cranstone, James, 117, 143
Craven Cottage, 194
Crayford, 57–8, 295 n.164
Creswell Crags, 161–2, *fig. 157*
Crewe, Frances Ann, 35, 126
Cubitt, Thomas, 85
Culford, 42

Danby, Francis, 242
  *Blaise Hamlet, fig. 231*
  *Landscape near Clifton, fig. 237*
Daniell, Thomas
  *Oriental Scenery*, 4, 17, 173, 194, *figs 195, 197, 199, 201*
Darnley, Lord, 117, 151, 163
Davey, Humphrey, 172
Davis, Thomas, 150
Downton (see Knight, Richard Payne)
Duberley, James, 13
Dublin, 32, 33, 76
Ducie, Lord, 36
Dughet, Gaspard ('Poussin'), 108, 122, 242
Dukeries, The, 155
Duncumb, Revd John, 105
  *Collections Towards the History and Antiquities of the County of Hereford, fig. 107*

Emes, William, 81, 220, 226
enclosure, 52–3, 76, 92, 127–8, 155
Endsleigh, 38, 41, 185–90, 239, *figs 179, 182, 183, 184, 185, 186*
English School
  *Edward Lord Russell, Son of Francis, Earl of Bedford, fig. 176*
English School of Painting, 8–9
Epping Forest, 212, *fig. 208*
Erskine, Thomas, 62, 227–8, 308 n.87
Essex, Lord, 151, 194
Evergreen Hill, 227–8, *fig. 222*
Eyam, 58

Faden, William
  *A Topographical Map of the County of Norfolk*, 84, 89, *figs 81, 85, 91, 95*
Farington, Joseph
  *Diary*, 37, 43, 114, 127
farming (see agriculture)
Farr, Thomas, 230
Felbrigg (see under Windham, William)
Ferney Hall, 49, 83, 109–10, *figs 112, 113*

Fetherstonehaugh, Sir Harry
  Humphry Repton's letters to, 28, 41, 62, 63, 101, 152, 153, 254
Fitzherbert, Mrs [Maria], 192, 202
Fitzroy Farm, 220, 222–3
Fitzwilliam, Earl, 35, 58
Foley, Edward, 19, 142
Fonthill, 38
Fort, The, 236–8, 309 n.122, *fig. 233*
Freke-Evans, George
  Repton's correspondence with, 38
French Revolution, 114, 128
Freeling, Francis, 33, 38
Frogmore, 191, *fig. 187*
Foxley (see under Price, Uvedale)

Gaines Hall, 13
Gainsborough, Thomas, 115
  *Beech Trees at Foxley, fig. 118*
game, 52–3, 96–7,
*Gardener's Magazine*, 145
Gardenesque, the, 143–7
Garnons, 117–19, 131, *figs 120, 121*
Garrard, George, 171, 180
  *Wobourn Sheepshearing, fig. 168*
*Gentleman's Magazine*, 101
geography, 2–3, 284 n.3
George III, 122, 134, 190–91
Georgic, the, 104, 110, 124, 128
Gérardin, Rene Louis
  *De la composition des Paysages* [*An Essay on Landscape*], 51, 79, 118
Gidea Hall, 59, *fig. 62*
Gilpin, William
  on picturesque scenery, 5, 46, 79, 80, 104, 143
Girtin, Thomas, 4
Glemham, *fig. 16*
Goldsmith, Oliver
  *The Deserted Village*, 55, 76, 103
Goode, Patrick, viii, 284 n.1
Goodenough, Samuel, 167
Gothic, 47, 73–4, 77, 88, 89–90, 98, 136, 138, 139, 165, 184, 194, 203, 232
Gott, Benjamin, 245–50
Gott, Elizabeth, 246, 249
graffitti, 61
Great Tew, 145
Grecian (style in architecture), 166, 203
Grimm, Samuel Hieronymus
  *The Cresswell Crags, fig. 157*
  *Blaise Castle, fig. 224*
Gurney, Bartlett, 85, 88

Hafod (see Johnes, Thomas)
Hainault Forest, 212
Hamilton, Sir William, 299 n.150
Hampstead, 180, 213, 217, 277–8
Hare Hall, 59–60, *fig. 63*

Hare Street, 18, 33, 35, 47, 58–65, 209, 254, *figs 61, 67*
Harewood House, 37, 58, 150, 152–3, *figs 56, 57*
Harewood, Lord, 152–3
Harford, John Scandrett, 231–5
Harman, John, 212
Hatch, James, 212
Hatchlands, 52
Hearne, Thomas, 111–12
  *An 'undressed' park; a park 'dressed in the modern style'*, fig. 115
  *Downton Castle viewed from the South Bank of the Teme*, fig. 110
  *The Overhanging Boulder with the Bow Bridge Beyond*, fig. 111
Hemingway, Andrew, 89
Hereford, 105, 108, 116, 142, 208
Hereford, Vale of, 116
Hereford, James, 128–9
*Hereford Journal*, 105, 121
Herefordshire, 104–30, 142, *figs 106, 109*
Hewell Grange, 140–41
High Legh, 51, 56, 235, *figs 52, 54*
Highams, 212
Hoare, Charles, 151, 184
Hobhouse, John Cam
  verses addressed to Lord Byron, 22
Hodges, William
  on Indian scenery, 17, 173, 197
Holland, Henry, 220
  at Brighton Pavilion, 192–7
  at Woburn Abbey, 171–4
  plan for Bloomsbury, 180
Holkham, 47, 80–84, 92, 97, *figs 85, 86, 87*
Holly Grove, 191
Holwood, 35, 113
Honing, 85–6, *fig. 88*
Hope, Zachary, 68–9
Hornor, Thomas, 25
  *Night, Daybreak*, from *Illustrations of the Vale of Neath*, fig. 28
horticulture, 172–5, 180, 197

Ibbetson, Julius Caesar, 226, 245
Ikin, Christopher, 307 n.46
Indian architecture and scenery, 17, 194, 197–205
industry, 55–6, 92, 107, 119, 132, 228, 242–50
Ireland (see Dublin)
Isle of Wight, 93–4
Irish labourers, 59
Ives, Jeremiah, 79–80, 84
ivy, 178–9

Jacobins, 88, 128
Jacobinism, 113
Johnes, Thomas
  Hafod, 106, 135, *fig. 108*

Jonson, Samuel, 113, 132, 210

Keck, Anthony, 128, 130
Kent, Nathaniel, 69, 72, 89, 97
  management at Felbrigg, 76
  survey of Foxley, 116
  survey of Tavistock, 183
Kent, William, 16, 81
Kentish Town, 223, 226
Kenwood, 52, 183, 219–26, *figs 215, 216, 217, 218, 220, 221*
Kerrison, Sir Roger, 91
Kidbrooke, 194
Knight, Richard Payne, 8, 16, 22, 43, 47, 83, 107–14, 128, 132, 139, 178, 252
  Downton, 83, 103, 106, 107–09, 116, 125, 135, 137, 144, *figs 110, 111*
  *An Analytical Inquiry into the Principles of Taste*, 139–40
  *The Landscape*, 14, 56, 97, 103, 110–14
  *The Progress of Civil Society*, 114
Knutsford, 55–6, 112, *fig. 59*

Lambert, David, 286 n.52, 309 n.94
Lapidge, Samuel, 167, 220
Lake District, 37
landscape
  as cultural representation, 2
landscape gardening, Repton's conception of, 1–25, 43–7, 85–8, 103–04, 123–4, 140, 164–6, 173–5, 181–2, 203–05, 216–17
law, 109, 214, 227–8
Laurie, Kedrun, viii, 255, 284 n.1, 302 n.83
Leeds, 242–50, *fig. 238*
Legh, George John, 36, 37
Legh, Revd Thomas, 140
Leigh Court, 239–42, *figs 235, 236*
Leigh Woods, 242
Lichfield, 20, 298 n.118
Linnean Society, 20, 178–9, 304 n.155
Longleat, 38, 150
Longner, 137–9, *figs 137, 138*
London, 28, 35, 123, 180–81, 208–28, 246, *fig. 206*
Loudon, John Claudius, 61
  on Humphry Repton, 4, 47–8, 144, 147
  on the Gardenesque, 143–7
Loughborough, Lord, 84–5
Louth, hermitage at, 194
Lowe, Elizabeth, 73
Luscombe, 184

Macarthur, John, 291 n.229
mail-coach system, 32–3, 38
Malthus, Daniel, 118
Malthus, Thomas
  on aristocratic consumption, 98
Mansfield, Lord Chief Justice, 219–20, 227
manufacturing (see industry)

maps, 11–12, 35, 168, 226–7
Marshall, William, 4, 25, 72, 113, 130
  at Kenwood, 226
  on Humphry Repton, 4, 25
  on Uvedale Price, 126
  *Planting and Rural Ornament*, 25, 130
  *Rural Economy of Norfolk*, 76
Marsham, Robert, 72, 77, 88
Martineau, Philip, 85
Martyn, Thomas
  *The Gardener's Dictionary*, 178
Mason, William, 113, 114, 122
  *The English Garden*, 12, 79, 218
Matlock, 124, *fig. 8*
Matthews, John, 126–8
  *A Sketch for the Landscape*, 126–8, *figs 127, 128*
McCaul, Peter, 290 n.204
Michel Grove, 153
Miles, John, 239–42
*Monthly Review*, 46, 116, 130, 226
Mosely Hall, 208, *fig. 205*
Mott, Thomas, 90
Mount Edgcumbe, 184
Mulgrave, Lord, 35
Mulgrave Castle, 36

Napoleon (see Bonaparte)
Napoleonic Wars, 18, 28, 42, 61, 89, 90, 106, 161, 203, 230, 245
Nash, John, 90, 138, 185, 204–05, 209
  partnership with Humphry Repton, 14, 36, 56–7, 121–2, 130, 131, 134–5, 142, 184, 211, 234, 235
  work with John Adey and George Stanley Repton, 93, 184
Neale, J.P.,
  *Armley House, Yorkshire*, fig. 245
Nelson, Admiral Horatio, 90, 91
Nelson Trust, the, 98
Newstead Abbey, 22
Nicholls, Norton, 79
  Humphry Repton's letters to, 84, 113, 190, 217
Norfolk, 37, 67–101, *figs 68, 80, 95*
Northcote, James
  *Memoirs of Sir Joshua Reynolds*, 20
Northern Society for the Encouragement of the Fine Arts, 245, 250
Northrepps, 86, *figs 5, 89*
Norwich, 30, 68, 79–80, 87, *fig. 81*
Nottinghamshire, 155
*nouveau riches*, 151–2, 207, 247, 251

Oldbury Court, 230, *figs 7, 9*
Osborne, *fig. 97*
Oulton, 243–5, *fig. 239*
Oxnead, 69, *fig. 73*

Palmer, John, 32–3

Palmer, Richard, 37, 287 n.60
Papworth, John Buonarotti, 286 n.55
　*Hints on Ornamental Gardening*, fig. 29
Paris, 114, 152
Paty, William, 231–2
Payne, William, 236
Peacock, Thomas Love
　*Headlong Hall*, 143
Peacock, William, 7
*Peacock's Polite Repository*, 7–8, 255, figs 7, 11
Pentillie, 184, 186, fig. 180
Phibbs, John, viii, 255, 289 n.136, 292 n.50
Phillips, John
　*Cider*, 119
Phipps, Samuel, 109–10
Picturesque, the, 29, 30, 60, 63, 83, 103–47, 150, 296 n.6
Pierrepont, Charles, 160–63
Pitt, William, 20, 39, 113, 134, 154, 191
planting (see trees)
Plymouth, 183, 187
Plymouth, Earl of, 211
Pocock, Nicholas,
　*View over Kingsweston to the Bristol Channel*, fig. 225
Point Pleasant, 211, fig. 207
*Polite Repository* (see *Peacock's Polite Repository*)
polite society, 7, 21–3, 27–8, 35, 67–8, 150, 205, 230
Porden, William, 192, 197, 202–03
Porter, Walsh, 194, 203
Portland, Second Duchess of, 155, 166
Portland, Third Duchess of, 160
Portland, Third Duke of, 35, 72, 84, 85, 111, 113, 134, 154–70, 191, 205, 228
portraiture, 21–2
postal system, 28, 32–3, 38
Pouncey, Benjamin,
　engraving after Thomas Hearne, 112, fig. 115
poverty, 51, 55–9, 62–3, 73, 92–3, 97–8, 168, 291 n.225
Prestwood, 119
Price, Robert, 115
Price, Uvedale, 37, 43, 47, 60, 103, 114, 178, 252, 298 n.112
　Foxley, 107, 115–17, 125, 126, figs 117, 118
　on butchers' shops in art, 63
　on the postal system, 28
　on Richard Payne Knight, 114
　on roads, 30
　on trellis, 54
　*Essay on the Picturesque*, 14, 22, 103, 116, 122–6, 127, 131–2
　*Essay on Artificial Water*, 134
　*Thoughts on the Defence of Property*, 135
Price, Uvedale Tomkins, 115

Prince, Hugh, viii
prospects, 124–5, 129–30
Prothero, Edward,
　his yellow house, 241, fig. 236
puns, 289 n.177
Purley, 294 n.105

Quaintance, Richard, 297 n.58
Quaker merchants, 228, 231, 234

Red Books, function and meaning, 1, 10–16, 46, 159–60, 164–5, 173–4, 186
Reindeer Tavern, 212
Rennie, John, 189, 250
*Repository of Arts*, 29, 286 n.55
Repton, George Stanley, 93, 185, 194, 235
Repton, Humphry
　charges, 37–8
　clientele, 1, 36–7, 154, 207
　collaboration with James Wyatt, 14, 37, 52, 57
　collaboration with William Wilkins, 14, 37, 84, 86, 118–19, 164, 218
　death and burial, 22, 101, 249
　drawing, 3–4, 13, 39, 56–7
　domesticity, 38–9, 41–2, 48–9, 58–63, 73–4, 151
　illness and injury, 19–20, 39–43, 49, 64–5, 100–01
　money, 18, 25, 37–8, 52, 69, 134, 159–60, 215
　morality, 22, 52–3, 67–76, 153
　music, 12–13
　partnership with John Nash, 36, 56–7, 121–2, 130, 131, 134–5, 142, 184, 211, 234, 235
　partnership with John Adey Repton, 4, 14, 36, 84, 136–7, 179–80, 194
　Picturesque controversy, the, 83–4, 97, 103–147, 150, 191, 178
　political campaigning, 76–9
　residence: Bath, 32–3, 35; Dublin, 32–3; Hare Street, 58–66, 209; Norwich, 30, 68–70; Sustead, 70–76
　sense of self, 1–25
　women, relations with, 22, 38–9, 82–3, 150–51, 202
WORKS
**Drawings and illustrations (not from Red Books):**
　*A Common Improved in Yorkshire* [Oulton], fig. 239
　*A Ferry Boat of Novel Construction*, fig. 45
　*A General View of Influence Operating on the Elections for the County of Norwich*, fig. 80
　*A Plan Explained*, fig. 146
　*A View of Life*, fig. 42
　*An Inquiry into the Changes in Architecture*, fig. 23
　*Arrangement Proposed for the Gardens at Ashridge*, fig. 51
　*Ashton-Court*, fig. 234
　*Aylsham: A Celebration of the Festival of the Peace, 15 July 1814*, fig. 70
　*Aylsham Market Place*, fig. 69
　*Baconsthorpe Hall*, fig. 74
　*Barningham, Norfolk*, fig. 94
　*Belmont, Herefordshire*, fig. 126
　*Bulstrode in Buckinghamshire*, fig. 164
　*Catton, Norfolk*, fig. 82
　*Catton Park*, fig. 83
　*Catton Park with Norwich in the Distance*, fig. 84
　*Conway – Drawn in 1783 on My Way from Ireland*, fig. 32
　*Corsham House*, fig. 21
　*Design for a Conduit Proposed at Ashridge*, fig. 44
　*Design for a goldfish bowl and birdcage*, fig. 66
　*Diagram of Reflections*, fig. 22
　*Design for the Frontispiece for the Views in Wales*, fig. 31
　'Docks and thistles', fig. 116
　*Endsleigh Cottage*, fig. 182
　*Entrance Arch, Harewood*, fig. 56
　*Entrance to Blaise Castle*, fig. 227
　*Epping Forest with Mr Knight Cutting our Joint Names*, fig. 208
　*Farm and Park*, fig. 132
　*Felbrigg Hall, Norfolk*, fig. 78
　*Felbrigg, the Seat of William Windham Esq. FRS.*, fig. 71
　*Flower Garden at Bulstrode*, fig. 165
　*Frontispiece to Memoir*, fig. 1
　*General View of Sheringham Bower*, fig. 49
　*Gidea Hall in Essex*, fig. 62
　*Hare Hall, Essex*, fig. 63
　*Improvements*, fig. 55
　*Lady Jane and Lord Blazon*, fig. 4
　*Luxury of Gardens*, fig. 50
　*Map of Bulstrode*, fig. 166
　*Map of Sustead*, fig. 77
　*North Front* [of Brighton Pavilion] *towards the Parade*, fig. 191
　*Old Longner House and the Tomb of Edward Burton Esq.*, fig. 137
　*Oxnead Hall, Norfolk*, fig. 73
　*Pantomime from Memory*, fig. 3
　*Proof Impressions of Plates Engraved*, fig. 11
　*Rivenhall Place*, fig. 20
　*Scene at Attingham*, fig. 133
　*Scene at Oldbury Court, Glocestershire* [sic.], fig. 9
　*Scene at Osborne, in the Isle of Wight*, fig. 97

315

*Scene on the Tamer [sic.] above Pentille [sic.]*, fig. *180*
*Scene on the Wye near Goodrich Castle*, fig. *141*
*St John's in the Isle of Wight*, fig. *10*
*Sunshine after Rain*, fig. *25*
*Sustead Old Hall*, fig. *75*
*The Banks of the Frome*, fig. *7*
*The Cottage at Aspley Wood*, fig. *175*
*The Cascade at Thoresby*, fig. *158*
*The Cottage of H. Repton, Esq.*, fig. *64*
*The Entrance to Lord Chancellor Erskine's Garden at Hampstead*, fig. *222*
*The Entrance of Somerhill, Kent – Seat of W. Woodgate Esq.*, fig. *37*
*Flower Garden, Valley-Field*, fig. *143*
*The Friar's Tale*, fig. *79*
*The Interior View of Tavistock Abbey*, fig. *181*
*The Lady and the Looking Glass*, fig. *65*
*The Norwich Mail: Sketch for a Transparency*, fig. *34*
*The Pump Room, Bath, in the Year 1784, with the Characters of that Day*, fig. *33*
*The Thornery at Woburn Abbey*, fig. *174*
*The Villages of Beeston and Runton from Sheringham Heath*, fig. *96*
*The High Tor at Matlock*, fig. *8*
*The Wier in Herefordshire*, fig. *142*
*The Work House*, fig. *60*
*Tailpiece to Memoir*, fig. *27*
*The Hand on the Tiller Steers the Nation from the Arts of War to the Arts of Peace*, fig. *26*
*Trade card*, fig. *13*
*View from my Cottage*, fig. *67*
*View from the House at Tatton*, fig. *114*
*View from the Portico of a Villa* [Wanstead House], fig. *248*
*View from the Proposed Private Apartment* [of Brighton Pavilion], fig. *192*
*View from the Terrace at Kenwood*, fig. *220*
*View from the Fort near Bristol*, fig. *233*
*View of Her Majesty's Lodge at Frogmore, near Bristol*, fig. *187*
*View of the Lake and some of the Oaks at Welbeck*, fig. *43*
*Villa at Brentry Hill, near Bristol*, fig. *232*
*West-Front of the Pavillon*, fig. *24*
*William Windham Delivering the Norwich Petition*, fig. *72*

**Published writings:**
*An Enquiry into the Changes of Taste in Landscape Gardening*, 16–17, 139, 177–8
*A Letter to Uvedale Price Esq.*, 37, 123–5
*Designs for the Pavillon at Brighton*, 17, 203–04
*Fragments on the Theory and Practice of Landscape Gardening*, 17–19, 47, 52–3, 205, 207, 243–4
'Observations on the Supposed Effects of Ivy upon Trees', 178–9
*Observations on the Theory and Practice of Landscape Gardening*, 3, 14–15, 46–7, 135, 235
*Odd Whims, or Two at a Time*, 35, 58, 77, 89
'The Friar's Tale', 77
*Sketches and Hints on Landscape Gardening*, 13–14, 37, 43, 103, 111, 113, 130, 154, 191
*The Bee; Or, a Companion to the Shakespeare Gallery*, 8–9
*The Landscape Gardening and Landscape Architecture of the late Humphry Repton Esq.* (ed. J.C. Loudon), 147
*Variety: A Collection of Essays*, 34–5
*The Work of Twenty Years Brought to a Crisis in Twenty Days!*, 153

**Red Books and Reports:**
Armley, 245–50, figs *240, 242, 243, 244*; Attingham, 131–4, figs *133, 134*; Babworth, 12–13, 55–6, figs *8, 38*; Beaudesert, 49–50, fig. *52*; Blaise Castle, 48–9, 230–35, figs *47, 48, 224, 227, 228, 229, 239*; Bracondale, 86–7, fig. *90*; Brandsbury, 214–19, figs *5, 6, 15, 211, 212, 213, 214*; Brentry Hill, 235–6; Brighton Pavilion, 192–205, figs *194, 196, 198*; Bulstrode, 166–70; Carlton House, 194, 203, fig. *193*; Claybury, 206, 212, figs *17, 209*; Endsleigh, 185–90, figs *183, 184, 185*; Ferney Hall, 109–10, figs *112, 113*; The Fort, 236–8; Gaines Hall, 13, fig. *19*; Garnons, 117–19, figs *120, 121*; Great Tew, 145; Harewood House, 152–3; Hatchlands, 53; Hewell Grange, 140–41; High Legh, 51, 56, figs *52, 54*; Highams, 212; Holwood, 35, 113; Kenwood, 219–226, figs *216, 217, 218*; Leigh Court, 239–42, figs *235, 236*; Longner, 137–9, fig. *138*; Mosely Hall, 208, fig. *205*; Northrepps, 86, figs *5, 89*; Pentillie, 184; Prestwood, 119; Reindeer Tavern, 212; Russell Square, 181–3; Sheringham, 51, 67, 90–101, figs *53, 99, 100, 101, 102, 103*; Streatham, 211; Sufton Court, 128–30, figs *129, 130, 131*; Tatton Park, 55–6, 111–12, fig. *59*; Tewin Water, 52; Thoresby, 160–63, figs *46, 156, 158*; Uppark, 41, 101, fig. *41*; Valleyfield, 46–7; Wanstead, 250–54; Welbeck Abbey, 154–66, figs *151, 152, 153, 154, 155, 159, 160, 161, 162*; Wingerworth, 247, fig. *241*; Woburn Abbey, 170–80, figs *14, 170, 171, 172, 173*

**Unpublished writings:**
Letters, 20–21, 28
Memoir, 21–22, 151–2, 154, 161, 214, 227–8

Repton, Humphry, the Younger, 39, 194
Repton, John (brother), 69, 77, 292 n.19
Repton, John (father), 30, 68
Repton, John Adey, 4, 14, 36, 37, 39, 47, 69, 84, 89, 94, 136–7, 166, 179–80, 194, 236
'great work of gothic architecture', 88
Repton, Mary (*née* Clarke), 38–9, 69
Repton, Mary Dorothy, 4, 39
*Floral Arrangement*, fig. *38*
*Penshurst*, fig. *39*
Repton, William, 21, 61, 67, 91–2, 98–9, 254
Reynolds, Joshua, 8, 20, 35, 152, 197
roads, 27–65, 94, 119, 132
Rivenhall Place, figs *15, 145*
Rocque, John
*Plan of Wanstead*, fig. *247*
Rogers, Charles, 135
Rome, 225, fig. *219*
Rooke, Hayman, 155
*Descriptive Sketches of Some Remarkable Oaks in the Park at Welbeck*, fig. *149*
roses, 63, 101, 175
Rowlandson, Thomas, 32
Rug, 298 n.138
Russell Square, 144, 181–3, fig. *178*
Ruggles, Thomas, 291 n.225
Ruisdael, Jacob van, 110, 123, 132

Salmon, Robert, 171, 177–8
Salte, William, 210, 288 n.100
Salusbury, Lady, 214–19
Samuel, George, 4, 157
Sandby, Thomas, 191
Saunders, George, 225–6
Schalch, J.J.
*Foxley*, fig. *117*
Scotland, 46–7
Scott, Walter,
on Humphry Repton's use of overlays, 4
Seward, Anna, 13, 20, 113, 134, 161, 163, 212, 227
Shakespeare Gallery, 8–9
Shardeloes, 48, 51
Sheffield, Lord, 306 n.237
Shelley, Samuel, 22
*Humphry Repton*, fig. *2*

Shepherd, Thomas,
　*Russell Square and the Statue of the Duke of Bedford*, fig. *178*
Sheringham, 51, 67, 90–101, figs *49, 53, 98, 99, 100, 101, 102, 103, 104*
Sherwood Forest, 155
Siddons, Sarah, 33
Sidmouth, Lord, 254
Siluria, 106
Simpson, Mrs, 12–13, 55, 291 n.8
Sinclair, George, 180
Smirke, Robert
　design for Armley House, 249–50
Smith, James Edward, 20, 69, 72, 168, 172, 178–9, 234, 304 n.155
Smith, John Warwick
　*Cascade above the Mossy Seat* [at Hafod], fig. *108*
Smyth, Sir Hugh, 238–9
Soane, Sir John, 104, 296 n.8
Somerhill, 37, figs *12, 37*
Speechly, William, 155–7, 158, 165, 303 n.108
St. John, the Hon. Frederick, 211
St John's, fig. *10*
St Paul's cathedral, 209, 218, 254
Stadler, J.C., 13, 43, 203
Stillingfleet, Benjamin,
　at Foxley, 115
Stoke Edith, 52, 117, 119–21, figs *122, 123, 124, 125*
Stoneleigh Abbey, 49, 140, fig. *140*
Stormont, Lord, 107, 220
Stratton Strawless, 72, 88
Streatham, 211
Stroud, Dorothy, 284 n.1
Stuttgart, 254
Sublime, the, 123, 225
Suffolk, 85
Sufton Court, 117, 128–30, 208, figs *129, 130, 131*
surveying, 11–12, 35, 216–17
Sustead, 33, 69, 70–75, figs *75, 76, 77*
Sussex, 192, 306 n.237, fig. *188*

Taigell, Anthea, 69, 80, 84
Tamar, River, 183, 187, 179, fig. *180*
Tatton Park, 55–6, 111–12, 130, 207, figs *59, 114*
Tavistock, 183–5, fig. *181*

taxation, 18, 24, 37, 62, 134
Taylor, John (surveyor), 184
Taylor, John (banker), 208
Teme, River, 134
Temple, Nigel, 235, 255
Temple Newsam, 243
Tewin Water, 52
Thames Valley, 211–12, 213–14
theatre, 58, 227–8
Thoresby, 48, 160–63, figs *46, 156, 158*
Tichfield, Marquess of, 166
Torrington, Viscount (see Byng, John)
Tories, 149, 154
tourism, 29–30, 42, 124–5, 183, 202
trees
　planting, 91–2, 156
　symbolism, 52–3, 94–6, 129, 161, 214–15
Turner, J.M.W.
　demotic imagery, 250
　naturalism, 10, 140
　*Leeds*, fig. *246*
　*Somer-Hill*, fig. *12*
Tyndall, Thomas, 238

United Friars, College of, 77
Upcher, Abbot, 91–101
Upcher, Charlotte, 92, 101, 295 n.181
Uppark, 41, 101, 254, fig. *41, 147*
Uxbridge, Lord, 21, 51, 65

Valleyfield, 46–7, 143, 145, 194, fig. *143*

Wales, 32, 105–06, 115, 136–7
Walker, Richard, 152–3
Wall, Tom, 110
Wallinger, John, 59–60
Walpole, Horace, 86, 105, 114, 122, 155
Wanstead, 250–54, figs *247, 248*
war (see Napoleonic Wars)
water, management of, 133–4, 161–2, 302 n.71
Watkins, Charles, 286 n.56
Watteau, Jean Antoine, 140
Welbeck Abbey, 170–80, figs *43, 148, 149, 150, 151, 152, 153, 154, 155, 159, 160, 161, 162*
Wellesley, William Tylney Long Pole, 251–4
Weltje, Louis, 192

Wentworth Woodhouse, 35
Westmacott, Richard
　*The Fifth Duke of Bedford*, 181
　*Charles James Fox*, 304 n.178
Westminster Bridge, 209
Whately, Thomas
　*Observations on Modern Gardening*, 46, 149, 168
Whigs, 35, 70, 77–8, 105, 109, 124, 126, 149, 154–5, 170
Whitaker, T.D.
　on Leeds, 249
Whitbread, Samuel, 171, 303 n.123
Whitehead, David, 126, 296 n.23
Wier, The, fig. *42*
Wilberforce, William, 56, 152, 291 n.8
Wilkie, David,
　*The Blind Fiddler*, 292 n.8, 303 n.123
Wilkins, William, Senior, 14, 37, 79–80, 84, 86–8, 118–19, 164, 218, 225
　*Designs for the Village at Stoke*, figs *124, 125*
Williamson, Tom, viii, 69, 80, 84
Wilson, Richard
　*Rome from the Ponte Molle*, fig. *219*
Windham, William, 36, 88, 90, 97, 101, 109, 111, 116, 119–20, 134, 191, fig. *72*
　Felbrigg, 70, 72, 75–6, 90, 116, figs *71, 78*
　in Dublin with Repton, 32, 76–9
　letter from Humphry Repton, 85
　open letter supporting Repton, 125–6
　politics in Norfolk, 70–72
Windsor Castle, 191
Wingerworth, 247, fig. *241*
Woburn Abbey, 38, 170–80, figs *169, 170, 171, 172, 173, 174*
Wood Hall, 89–90, figs *91, 92*
Woods, Richard, 59
Wordsworth, William
　on beggars, 63, 65
　on Uvedale Price, 142–3
workhouses, 57–8, 97–8, fig. *57*
women, 38–9, 82–3, 202, 301 n.10, 150–51
Wurttemberg, King of, 254
Wyatt, James, 14, 37, 52, 57, 117–18, 126, 203
Wyatt, Samuel, 81, 82, 246
Wyatville, Jeffrey, 172, 185–9
Wye Valley, 116–18, 123–4, figs *119, 141*